Learn iOS App Development

James Bucanek

Learn iOS App Development

Copyright © 2013 by James Bucanek

This work is subject to copyright. All rights are reserved by the Publisher, whether the whole or part of the material is concerned, specifically the rights of translation, reprinting, reuse of illustrations, recitation, broadcasting, reproduction on microfilms or in any other physical way, and transmission or information storage and retrieval, electronic adaptation, computer software, or by similar or dissimilar methodology now known or hereafter developed. Exempted from this legal reservation are brief excerpts in connection with reviews or scholarly analysis or material supplied specifically for the purpose of being entered and executed on a computer system, for exclusive use by the purchaser of the work. Duplication of this publication or parts thereof is permitted only under the provisions of the Copyright Law of the Publisher's location, in its current version, and permission for use must always be obtained from Springer. Permissions for use may be obtained through RightsLink at the Copyright Clearance Center. Violations are liable to prosecution under the respective Copyright Law.

ISBN-13 (pbk): 978-1-4302-5062-3

ISBN-13 (electronic): 978-1-4302-5063-0

Trademarked names, logos, and images may appear in this book. Rather than use a trademark symbol with every occurrence of a trademarked name, logo, or image we use the names, logos, and images only in an editorial fashion and to the benefit of the trademark owner, with no intention of infringement of the trademark.

The use in this publication of trade names, trademarks, service marks, and similar terms, even if they are not identified as such, is not to be taken as an expression of opinion as to whether or not they are subject to proprietary rights.

While the advice and information in this book are believed to be true and accurate at the date of publication, neither the authors nor the editors nor the publisher can accept any legal responsibility for any errors or omissions that may be made. The publisher makes no warranty, express or implied, with respect to the material contained herein.

> President and Publisher: Paul Manning
> Lead Editor: Steve Anglin
> Developmental Editor: Tom Welsh
> Technical Reviewer: Charles Cruz
> Editorial Board: Steve Anglin, Mark Beckner, Ewan Buckingham, Gary Cornell, Louise Corrigan, Morgan Ertel, Jonathan Gennick, Jonathan Hassell, Robert Hutchinson, Michelle Lowman, James Markham, Matthew Moodie, Jeff Olson, Jeffrey Pepper, Douglas Pundick, Ben Renow-Clarke, Dominic Shakeshaft, Gwenan Spearing, Matt Wade, Tom Welsh
> Coordinating Editor: Katie Sullivan
> Copy Editor: Lori Cavanaugh
> Compositor: SPi Global
> Indexer: SPi Global
> Artist: SPi Global
> Cover Designer: Anna Ishchenko

Distributed to the book trade worldwide by Springer Science+Business Media New York, 233 Spring Street, 6th Floor, New York, NY 10013. Phone 1-800-SPRINGER, fax (201) 348-4505, e-mail orders-ny@springer-sbm.com, or visit www.springeronline.com. Apress Media, LLC is a California LLC and the sole member (owner) is Springer Science + Business Media Finance Inc (SSBM Finance Inc). SSBM Finance Inc is a Delaware corporation.

For information on translations, please e-mail rights@apress.com, or visit www.apress.com.

Apress and friends of ED books may be purchased in bulk for academic, corporate, or promotional use. eBook versions and licenses are also available for most titles. For more information, reference our Special Bulk Sales–eBook Licensing web page at www.apress.com/bulk-sales.

Any source code or other supplementary materials referenced by the author in this text is available to readers at www.apress.com. For detailed information about how to locate your book's source code, go to www.apress.com/source-code/.

To Deborah and Doug, best friends forever

Contents at a Glance

About the Author xxv
About the Technical Reviewer xxvii
Acknowledgments xxix
Introduction xxxi

■Chapter 1: Got Tools? 1
■Chapter 2: Boom! App 17
■Chapter 3: Spin a Web 57
■Chapter 4: Coming Events 97
■Chapter 5: Table Manners 137
■Chapter 6: Object Lesson 177
■Chapter 7: Smile! 189
■Chapter 8: Model Citizen 217
■Chapter 9: Sweet, Sweet Music 255
■Chapter 10: Got Views? 291
■Chapter 11: Draw Me a Picture 321
■Chapter 12: There and Back Again 367
■Chapter 13: Networking, the Social Kind 411

- Chapter 14: Networking, The Nerdy Kind 429
- Chapter 15: If You Build It 485
- Chapter 16: Apps with Attitude 507
- Chapter 17: Where Are You? 529
- Chapter 18: Remember Me? 551
- Chapter 19: Doc, You Meant Storage 581
- Chapter 20: Being Objective 617
- Chapter 21: The Elephant in the Room 653
- Chapter 22: Êtes-vous Polyglotte? 671
- Chapter 23: Faster, Faster 691
- Chapter 24: Twice As Nice 713

Index 735

Contents

About the Author xxv
About the Technical Reviewer xxvii
Acknowledgments xxix
Introduction xxxi

■Chapter 1: Got Tools? 1
   Requirements 1
   Installing Xcode 2
   What is Xcode? 3
   Becoming an iOS Developer 4
   Getting the Projects 5
   Launching Xcode the First Time 5
   Welcome To Xcode 9
      Navigation Area 10
      Editor Area 11
      Utility Area 12
      Debug Area 14
      Toolbar 14
   Running Your First App 14
   Summary 16

Chapter 2: Boom! App 17
Design 17
Creating the Project...18
Setting Project Properties 20
Building an Interface 21
Adding Objects 23
Deleting and Connecting Objects 24
Adding Views to a View..27
Editing Object Properties 30
Adding Resources..31
Customizing Buttons..33
Using Storyboards 34
Adding New Screens 35
Creating a Segue 40
Setting Navigation Titles 41
Testing Your Interface...42
Finishing Your App..43
Debugging Your App...45
Adding Constraints 46
Testing Your App 54
Summary..55

Chapter 3: Spin a Web 57
Design 58
Creating the Project...58
Building a Web Browser 59
Coding a Web Browser 63
Adding Outlets to SUViewController 64
Connecting Custom Outlets 64
Adding Actions to SUViewController 66

Setting Action Connections	69
Testing the Web Browser	71
Debugging the Web View	72

Adding URL Shortening ... 73
Designing the URL Shortening Code	76
Becoming a Web View Delegate	77
Shortening an URL	81

Final Touches ... 89
Cleaning Up the Interface	90
Creating the iPad Version	93

Summary ... 96

Chapter 4: Coming Events ... 97

Run Loop ... 98
Event Queue ... 98
Event Delivery ... 100
Direct Delivery	100
Hit Testing	100
The First Responder	102

Event Handling ... 103
The Responder Chain ... 104
High- vs. Low-Level Events ... 107
Eight Ball ... 107
Design	108
Create the Project	108
Create the Interface	109
Writing the Code	114
Handling Shake Events	116
Testing Your EightBall App	117
Finishing Touches	120

Testing on a Physical iOS Device ... 121
Other Uses for The Responder Chain ... 123

Touchy	124
Design	125
Creating the Project	125
Creating a Custom View	126
Handling Touch Events	128
Drawing Your View	131
Adding Custom Objects in Interface Builder	132
Testing Touchy	133
Advanced Event Handling	134
Summary	135

Chapter 5: Table Manners ... 137

Table Views	137
Plain Tables	138
Grouped Tables	138
Cell Styles	139
Cell Accessories	141
Custom Cells	142
How Table Views Work	142
Table Cells and Rubber Stamps	143
MyStuff	144
Design	144
Creating The Project	145
Creating Your Data Model	146
Creating a Data Source	149
Implementing Your Rubber Stamp	152
Table Cell Caching	153
Where's the Data?	156
Testing MyStuff	156
Adding the Detail View	157
Creating the Detail View	157
Configuring the Detail View	159

Editing 163
Inserting and Removing Items 164
Enabling Table Editing 166
Editing Details 168
Observing Changes to MyWhatsit 170

Modal vs. Modeless Editing 174

Little Touches 174

Advanced Table View Topics 174

Summary 175

Chapter 6: Object Lesson 177

Two Houses, Both Alike in Dignity 177

Romeo Meets Juliet 179

Classes and Cookies 179

Classes and Objects and Methods, Oh My! 180

Inheritance 182
Abstract and Concrete Classes 183
Overriding Methods 183

Design Patterns and Principles 184
Encapsulation 184
Singularity of Purpose 185
Stability 185
Open Closed 185
Delegation 186
Other Patterns 187

Summary 188

Chapter 7: Smile! 189

Design 190

Extending Your Design 190
Revising the Data Model 191
Adding an Image View 193

Updating the View Controller 196
　　Connecting a Choose Image Action 197

Taking Pictures 201
　　You Can't Always Get What You Want.. 202
　　Presenting the Image Picker 203
　　Importing the Image 205
　　Cropping and Resizing... 206
　　Winding Up 208
　　Testing the Camera... 209

Building the iPad Interface 210
　　Adding a Popover 212

Sticky Keyboards...213

Advanced Camera Techniques 216

Summary...216

Chapter 8: Model Citizen 217

The Model-View-Controller Design Pattern..217
　　Data Model Objects 218
　　View Objects... 219
　　Controller Objects 219
　　MVC Communications... 220

Color Model 221
　　Creating Your Data Model 223
　　Creating View Objects... 224
　　Writing Your Controller... 227
　　Wiring Your Interface 228

Having Multiple Views 231

Consolidating Updates...235

Complex View Objects 239
　　Replacing UIView with CMColorView.. 239
　　Connecting the View to Your Data Model 240
　　Drawing CMColorView 240

Being a K-V Observer 244
Key Value Observing 244
Observing Key Value Changes 244
Creating KVO Dependencies 246

Multi-Vector Data Model Changes 248
Handling Touch Events 248
Binding The Sliders 250
Final Touches 251

Cheating 251

Summary 252

Chapter 9: Sweet, Sweet Music 255

Making Your Own iPod 256
Design 256
Adding a Music Picker 257
Using a Music Player 260
Adding Playback Control 262
Receiving Music Player Notifications 264
Adding Media Metadata 266
Observing the Playing Item 269

Make Some Noise 271
Living in a Larger World 272
Configuring Your Audio Session 273
Playing Audio Files 275
Creating AVAudioPlayer objects 277
Adding the Sound Buttons 280
Activating Your Audio Session 283

Interruptions and Detours 284
Dealing with Interruptions 285
Adding Your Interruption Handlers 285
Dealing with Audio Route Changes 287

Other Audio Topics 288

Summary 289

Chapter 10: Got Views? 291

Learning by Example 291
Buttons 294
    The Responder and View Classes 295
    The Control Class 296
    Button Types 296
    Control States 299
    Button Code 300
Switches and Sliders 300
Page Control 302
Steppers 303
Segmented Controls 304
Progress Indicators 305
Text Views 307
    Labels 307
    Text Fields 308
    Text Editing Behavior 310
    Text Views 311
Pickers 312
    Date Picker 313
    Anything Picker 314
Image Views 315
Grouped Tables 316
The View You Never See 317
Summary 320

Chapter 11: Draw Me a Picture 321

Creating a Custom View Class 321
    View Coordinates 322
    When Views Are Drawn 325
    Drawing a View 326

Shapely 329
Creating Views Programmatically 330
The -drawRect: Method 332
More Shapes, More Colors 340

Transforms 345
Applying a Translate Transform 346
Applying a Scale Transform 349

Animation: It's Not Just for Manga 351
Using Core Animation 352
Adding Animation to Shapely 352
OpenGL 354

The Order of Things 355

Images and Bitmaps 359
Creating Images from Bitmaps 360
Creating Bitmaps From Drawings 362

Advanced Graphics 363
Text 363
Shadows, Gradients, and Patterns 364
Blend Modes 364
The Context Stack 364

Summary 365

Chapter 12: There and Back Again 367

Measure Twice, Cut Once 367
What is Navigation? 368
View Controller Roles 368

Designing Wonderland 369
Weighing Your Navigation Options 369
Wonderland Navigation 371

Creating Wonderland 372
Adding Wonderland's Resources 374
Configuring a Tab Bar Item 375

The First Content View Controller	376
Presenting a Modal View Controller	378
Dismissing a View Controller	381
Creating a Navigable Table View	383
Breathing Data Into Your Table View	386
Pushing the Detail View Controller	393
Creating a Page View Controller	395
Adding the Page View Controllers	396
Designing a Prototype Page	397
Coding the One Page View	400
The Paginator	402
Coding the Page View Data Source	405
Initializing a Page View Controller	407
Using Pop-Over Controllers	409
Advanced Navigation	409
Summary	410
Chapter 13: Networking, the Social Kind	**411**
Color My (Social) World	411
Having Something to Share	412
Presenting the Activity View Controller	413
Sharing More	416
Extracting Code	416
Providing More Items to Share	419
Excluding Activities	420
The Curse of the Lowest Common Denominator	421
Providing Activity Specific Data	422
Promises, Promises	424
Big Data	425
Sharing with Specific Services	425
Other Social Network Interactions	426
Summary	427

Chapter 14: Networking, The Nerdy Kind 429

SunTouch 430
- Creating SunTouch 431
- Designing the Initial Screens 431

Creating the Single Player Version 434
- Loading STGameViewController 435
- How SunTouch Works 436
- Customizing Core Animations 437
- Playing the Game 438

Plugging into Game Center 440
- Configuring a Game Center–aware app 440
- Enabling Game Center 442
- Creating an App in the iTunes Store 444
- Configuring Game Center 446
- Adding GameKit to Your App 448
- Obtaining the Local Player 449
- Adding a Game Center Button 450
- Recording Leaderboard Scores 452
- Creating a Test Player 453

Peer-To-Peer Networking 454
- Turning SunTouch Into a Two-Player Game 455
- Matchmaking 461
- Exchanging Data with Another Device 465

Advanced Networking 479
One Last Detail 480
Summary 482

Chapter 15: If You Build It 485

How Interface Builder Files Work 486
- Compiling Interface Builder Files 486
- Loading a Scene 486
- Loading an .xib File 488

Placeholder Objects and the File's Owner 489
Creating Objects 490
Editing Attributes 493
Connections 493
Sending Action Messages 496

Taking Control of Interface Builder Files 496
Declaring Placeholders 497
Designing SYShapeView 498
Connecting the Gesture Recognizers 499
Build Your Shape Factory 501
Loading an Interface Builder File 504
Replacing Code 505

Summary 506

Chapter 16: Apps with Attitude 507

Leveler 508
Creating Leveler 508

Getting Motion Data 514
Creating CMMotionManager 515
Starting and Stopping Updates 516
Push Me, Pull You 516
Timing is Everything 517
Herky-Jerky 519

Getting Other Kinds of Motion Data 524
Gyroscope Data 524
Magnetometer Data 525
Device Motion and Attitude 525
Measuring Change 527

Summary 528

Chapter 17: Where Are You? 529

Creating Pigeon 529

Collecting Location Data 531

Using a Map View 533
Decorating Your Map 537
Adding an Annotation 537
Map Coordinates.. 539
Adding a Little Bounce... 540
Pointing the Way..542
Location Monitoring 545
Approximate Location and Non-GPS Devices 546
Monitoring Regions.. 546
Reducing Location Change Messages 547
Movement and Heading.. 547
Geocoding 547
Getting Directions 548
Summary..548

Chapter 18: Remember Me? 551
Property Lists 551
Serializing Property Lists..552
User Defaults...552
Making Pigeon Remember 553
Minimizing Updates and Code 554
Defining Your Keys... 554
Writing Values to User Defaults 555
Getting Values from User Defaults 555
Testing User Defaults... 556
Registering Default Values 557
Turning Objects into Property List Objects 559
Preserving and Restoring savedLocation 560
Persistent Views..563
Fading Into the Background 564
Preserving View Controllers... 565

Assigning Restoration Identifiers 566
Customizing Restoration 568
Deeper Restoration 569

Pigeons in the Cloud 569
Storing Values in the Cloud 570
Cloud Watching 571
Enabling iCloud 573
Testing the Cloud 574

Bundle Up Your Settings 575
Creating a Settings Bundle 575
Using Your Settings Bundle Values 578
Testing Your Settings Bundle 579

Summary 580

Chapter 19: Doc, You Meant Storage 581

Document Overview 581

Where, Oh Where, Do My Documents Go? 582

MyStuff on Documents 583

Supplying Your Document's Data 585
Wrapping Up Your Data 587
Using Wrappers 587
Incremental Document Updates 588
Constructing Your Wrappers 588
Interpreting Your Wrappers 589

Archiving Objects 591
Adopting NSCoding 591
Archiving and Unarchiving Objects 593
The Archiving Serialization Smackdown 593
Serialization, Meet Archiving 594

Document, Your Data Model 595

Tracking Changes 598

Testing Your Document 600

Setting Breakpoints 600
Stepping Through Code and Examining Variables 601

Storing Image Files 608

Odds and Ends 615
iCloud Storage 615
Archive Versioning 615

Summary 616

Chapter 20: Being Objective 617

Objective-C is C 618

Objective-C Classes 619
Implementing Your Class 620
Creating and Destroying Objects 621
Class Clusters 622
Referring to Objects 622
Can I See Your id? 623

Method Names 624
Method Name Construction 625
The +initialize Method 626

Properties 627
Instance Variables 627
Using Getters and Setters 627
Declared Properties 628
Automatic Properties 630
The Anatomy of a Property 631
Keeping Your Promises 633

Introspection 634
Class 634
Method 635
Protocol 635

Protocols 636
Adopting Protocols 636
Referring to Conforming Objects 637

Categories ... 638
Single Responsibility ... 639
Module Organization ... 639
Private Methods ... 640
Extensions ... 640
nil is Your Friend ... 641
The Unbearable Lightness of nil ... 641
The Virtues of Being Positive ... 641
When nil Is Bad ... 642
Copying Objects ... 642
Adopting NSCopying ... 643
Inheriting NSCopying ... 644
Copying Something Special ... 644
Copying an Object ... 645
Mutable Copies ... 645
Attributed Strings ... 645
Collections ... 648
Collection Classes ... 648
Enumeration ... 649
Fast Object Enumeration ... 649
Collection Enumeration ... 650
Shortcuts ... 650
Summary ... 651

Chapter 21: The Elephant in the Room ... 653
Memory Management ... 654
Your Grandfather's Memory Management ... 655
Garbage Collection ... 656
Reference Counting ... 657
Manual Reference Counting ... 659
Jumping into the Pool ... 660
Quick Summary ... 662

Breaking the Cycle	663
Scared Straight	665

Automatic Reference Counting ... 665

Enabling ARC	666
Strong and Weak References	667
What ARC Doesn't Do	668

Summary ... 669

Chapter 22: Êtes-vous Polyglotte? ... 671

The Localization Process ... 671

Language Bundles ... 672

Programmatic Localization	673

Localize Now! ... 674

Internationalizing Your App ... 680

Internationalizing String Constants	680
Using the genstrings Tool	681
Localizing Your Strings File	683
Testing Your String Localization	684

Localizing Interfaces Using Localizable Strings ... 685

Localizing Settings.bundle ... 685

Other Code Considerations ... 688

Localizing Your App's Name ... 689

Summary ... 690

Chapter 23: Faster, Faster ... 691

Performance Optimization ... 692

Fixing a Slow Tap ... 693

Launching Instruments	694

Finding the Hot Spots ... 696

The Hubris of Experience	699
Picking the Low Hanging Fruit	700
Deferring Notifications	700
Once More into The Breach	701

Precious Memory 702
Breaking MyStuff 703
Measuring Memory 704
Memory Instruments 706
Heed the Warnings 708
Stress Test, Round #2 710
Summary 712

Chapter 24: Twice As Nice 713
Concurrent Programming 714
Threads 715
Synchronization 715
Running Multiple Threads 716
Creating an Operation Queue 717
Adding an Operation 718
Measuring the Effects 718
Execution Order 720
Thread Safety 721
Don't Talk About Thread Safety 722
Not Sharing Is Caring 722
Promise Me You'll Never Change 723
The Atomic Age 723
Concurrency Roundup 729
The Thread-Safe Landscape 729
Sending Messages To Main 729
Lock Objects 730
Deadlocks 731
Spin Locks 733
Further Reading 734
Summary 734

Index 735

About the Author

James Bucanek has spent the past 30 years programming and developing microprocessor systems. He has experience with a broad range of computer hardware and software, from embedded consumer products to industrial robotics. His development projects include the first local area network for the Apple II, distributed air conditioning control systems, a piano teaching system, digital oscilloscopes, silicon wafer deposition furnaces, and collaborative writing tools for K-12 education.

James holds a Java Developer Certification from Sun Microsystems and was awarded a patent for optimizing local area networks. James is currently focused on OS X and iOS software development, where he can combine his deep knowledge of UNIX and object-oriented languages with his passion for elegant design. James holds an Associate's degree in classical ballet from the Royal Academy of Dance, and can occasionally be found teaching at Adams Ballet Academy.

About the Technical Reviewer

Charles Cruz is a mobile application developer for the iOS, Android, and Windows Phone platforms. He graduated from Stanford University with B.S. and M.S. degrees in engineering. He lives in Southern California and runs a photography business with his wife (www.facebook.com/BellaLenteStudios). When not doing technical things, he plays lead guitar in an original metal band (www.taintedsociety.com).

Charles can be reached at codingandpicking@gmail.com and @CodingNPicking on Twitter.

Acknowledgments

Clay Andres started this ball rolling by introducing me to Apress. Steve Anglin is largely responsible for deciding what Apress prints, and I was genuinely flattered when he asked me to write this book. Tom Welsh, my editor, kept a watchful eye on every paragraph, keeping the message clear and comprehensible. Tom was great to work with and immeasurably improved the quality of this book. Charles Cruz checked every line of code and symbol to ensure complete accuracy. Any technical errors are ultimately my responsibility, but there are significantly fewer thanks to Charles. Lori Cavanaugh dotted my i's, crossed my t's, and corrected my (egregious) spelling. If you find this book easy to read, you have Lori's blue pencil to thank.

The entire project was stewarded by a phalanx of coordinating editors. Anamika Panchoo, Katie Sullivan, and Christine Ricketts juggled schedules, liaised between editors, tracked production, and herded everyone towards a common goal. To all the folks at Apress, thank you, thank you, thank you!

Finally, I want to shout a "thank you" to Apple's Xcode development team for creating the most advanced mobile app development tool in the world. iOS development would be nearly impossible without it.

Introduction

I'm standing on a street corner in San Francisco, a city I visit far too infrequently. In my hand I hold an electronic device. The device is receiving status updates about the city's public transportation system in real-time. It is telling me that the F-line rail will arrive at the Market & 5th Street station in 7 minutes. It displays a map of the city and, by timing radio waves it receives from outer space, triangulates and displays my exact location on that map. A magnetometer determines which direction I'm holding the device and uses that information to indicate the direction I should walk to meet the rail car in time to board it. My friends call me, wondering when I will arrive. A tiny video camera and microphone share my image and voice with them as I walk. I'm meeting them at a gallery opening. It's an exhibition of new artwork, by artists from all over the world, created entirely using devices similar to the one I hold in my hand. When I arrive, I use my device to create an interactive virtual reality of the gathering, share my experiences with friends and family back home, exchange contact information with people I meet, and look up restaurant suggestions for where we might eat later.

This is a true story. A couple of decades ago, it would have been science fiction.

We live in a time in which personal electronics are literally changing how we work, travel, communicate, and experience the world. A day doesn't go by without someone discovering another novel use for them. And while I'm sure you enjoy benefiting from this new technology, you're reading this book because you want to participate in this revolution. You want to create apps.

You've come to the right place.

Who is This Book For?

This book is for anyone who wants to learn the basic tools and techniques for creating exciting, dynamic, applications for Apple products that run the iOS operating system. As of this writing, that includes the iPad, iPhone, and iPod Touch.

This book assumes you are new to developing iOS apps and that you have limited programming experience. If you've been learning Objective-C, that's perfect. If you know C, Java, C#, or C++ you shouldn't have too much trouble following along, and there's an Objective-C primer chapter that you'll want to read. If you are completely new to programming computers, I suggest getting a basic

Objective-C programming book—say, Objective-C for Absolute Beginners, by Gary Bennett, Mitchell Fisher, and Brad Lees—and read that first, or in parallel. All iOS app development is done using the Objective-C language.

This book will explain the fundamentals of how iOS apps are designed, built, and deployed. You'll pick up some good design habits, get some core programming skills, and learn your way around the development tools used to create apps.

This book is not an in-depth treatise on any one technology. It's designed to stimulate your imagination by giving you a head start in building apps that use a variety of device capabilities, such as finding your location on a map, using the accelerometer, taking pictures with the built-in camera, communicating in real-time with other devices, participating in social networks, and storing information in the cloud. From there, you can leap beyond these examples to create the next great iOS app!

Old School vs. Too Cool for School

I'm an Old School programmer. I learned programming from the bit up (literally). The first program I wrote was on a 4-bit micro-controller using toggle switches to input the machine instructions. So I pretty much knew everything there was to know about machine code before I started to program in "high-level" languages like BASIC and C. I knew C backwards and forwards before I dipped my toe into C++, and I was an expert in C++ before I wrote my first graphical user interface (GUI) application for the (revolutionary) Macintosh computer.

While I value this accumulated knowledge, and much of it is still useful, I realize that a "ground up" approach isn't necessary to develop great apps for iOS today. Many of the advances in software development over the past few decades have been in insulating the developer—that's you—from the nitty-gritty details of CPU instructions, hardware interfaces, and software design. This frees you to concentrate on harnessing these technologies to turn your idea into reality, rather than spending all of your time worrying about register allocations and memory management.

So the exciting news is that you can jump right in and create full-featured iOS apps with only a minimal knowledge of computer programming or the underlying technologies that make them possible. And that's what this book is going to do in the first couple of chapters—show you how to create an iOS app without any traditional programming whatsoever.

That's not to say you don't need these skills in order to master iOS development. On the contrary; the more skilled you are in programming, the more proficient you're going to be. What's changed is that these skills aren't the prerequisites that they once were. Now, you can learn them in parallel while you explore new avenues of iOS development.

How to Use this Book

This book embraces an "explore as go" approach. Some chapters will walk you through the process of creating an iOS app that uses the camera or plays music. These chapters may gloss over many of the finer details. In between, you'll find chapters on basic software development skills. There are chapters on good software design, memory management, and the Objective C programming language.

So instead of the "traditional" order of first learning all of the basic skills and then building apps using those skills, this book starts out building apps, and then explores the details of how that happened.

You can read the chapters in any order, skipping or returning to chapters, as you need. If you really want to know more about objects in an earlier chapter, jump ahead and read the chapter on objects. If you've already learned about Objective-C memory management, skip that chapter when you get to it. Treat this book as a collection of skills to learn, not a series of lessons that have to be taken in order.

Here's a preview of the chapters ahead:

- **Got Tools?** shows you how to download and install the Xcode development tools. You'll need those.
- **Boom! App** will walk you through the core steps in creating an iOS app—no programming needed.
- **Spin a Web** creates an app that leverages the power of iOS's built-in web browser.
- **Coming Events** discusses how events (touches, gestures, movement) get from the device into your app, and how you use them to make your app respond to the user.
- **Table Manners** shows you how data gets displayed in an app, and how it gets edited.
- **Object Lesson** dishes the straight dope on objects and object oriented programming.
- **Smile!** shows you how to integrate the camera and photo library into your app.
- **Model Citizen** explains the magic incantation that software engineers call "Model-View-Controller."
- **Sweet, Sweet Music** will jazz up your mix by showing you how to add music and iTunes to your apps.
- **Got Tools?** takes you on a brief survey of the tools (views, controls, and objects) available in the Cocoa Touch framework. So when you need a tool, you'll know how to find it.
- **Draw Me a Picture** will show you how to create custom views, unlocking the power to draw just about anything in an iOS app.
- **There and Back Again** lays out the basics of app navigation: how your users get from one screen to another, and back again.
- **Networking, the Social Kind** will get your app plugged into Facebook, Twitter, email, and more.
- **Networking, the Nerdy Kind** demonstrates real-time communications between multiple iOS devices using Game Kit.
- **If You Build It...** explains some of the magic behind Interface Builder.

- **Apps With Attitude** shakes up your apps with the accelerometer and compass.
- **Where Are You?** will draw you a map—literally.
- **Remember Me?** shows you how user preferences are set and saved, and how to share them with other iOS devices using iCloud.
- **Doc, You Meant Storage** explains how app documents are stored, exchanged, and synchronized.
- **Being Objective** is a crash course in the Objective C programming language.
- **The Elephant in the Room** explores the technology, techniques, and traps of memory management.
- **Êtes-vous polyglotte?** will show you how to create apps that speak multiple languages.
- **Faster, Faster!** will explain the basics of performance analysis and optimization, so your apps will run like bunnies.
- **Twice as Nice** will up your game with multi-tasking, showing your how your app can do two, or three, or four things at the same time.

Chapter 1

Got Tools?

If you want to build something, you are probably going to need some tools: hammer, nails, laser, crane, and one of those IKEA hex wrenches. Building iOS apps requires a collection of tools called *Xcode*.

This chapter will show you how to get and install Xcode, and give you a brief tour of it, so you'll know your way around. If you've already installed and used Xcode, check the Requirements section to make sure you have everything you need, but you can probably skip most of this chapter.

Requirements

In this book, you will create apps that run on iOS version 7. Creating an app for iOS 7 requires Xcode version 5. Xcode 5 requires OS X version 10.8 (a.k.a. Mountain Lion), which requires an Intel-based Mac. Did you get all of that? Here's your complete checklist:

- Intel-based Mac
- OS X 10.8 (or later)
- A few gigabytes of free disk space
- An Internet connection
- At least one iOS device (iPad Touch, iPhone, or iPad) running iOS 7.0 (or later)

Make sure you have an Intel-based Mac computer with OS X 10.8 (Mountain Lion), or later, installed, enough disk space, and an Internet connection. You can do all of your initial app development right on your Mac, but at some point you'll want to run your apps on a real iOS device (iPhone, iPod Touch, or iPad), and for that you'll need one.

> **Note** As a general rule, later versions are better. The examples in this book were developed for iOS 7.0, built using Xcode 5.0, running on OS X 10.8.5 (Mountain Lion). By the time you read this there will probably be a newer version of all of these, and that's OK.

Installing Xcode

Apple has made installing Xcode as easy as possible. On your Mac, launch the App Store application and search for Xcode, as shown in Figure 1-1.

Figure 1-1. Xcode in the App Store

Click the install button to start downloading Xcode. This will take a while (see Figure 1-2). You can monitor its progress from the Purchases tab of the App Store. Be patient. Xcode is huge and, even with a fast Internet connection, it will take some time to download.

Figure 1-2. Downloading Xcode

While Xcode is downloading, let's talk about it and some related topics.

What is Xcode?

So what is this huge application you're downloading?

Xcode is an *Integrated Development Environment* (IDE). Modern software development requires a dizzying number of different programs. To build and test an iOS app you're going to need editors, compilers, linkers, syntax checkers, cryptographic signers, resource compilers, debuggers, simulators, performance analyzers, and more. But you don't have to worry about that; Xcode orchestrates all of those individual tools for you. All you have to do is use the Xcode interface to design your app, and Xcode will decide what tools need to be run, and when. In other words, Xcode puts the "I" in IDE.

As well as including all of the tools you'll need, Xcode can host a number of *Software Development Kits* (SDKs). An SDK is a collection of files that supply Xcode with what it needs to build an app for a particular operating system, like iOS 7. Xcode downloads with an SDK to build iOS apps and an SDK to build OS X apps, for the most recent versions of each. You can download additional SDKs as needed.

An SDK will consist of one or more *frameworks*. A framework tells Xcode exactly how your application can use an iOS service. This is called an *Application Programming Interface* (API). While it's possible to write code in your app to do just about anything, much of what it will be doing is making requests to iOS to do things that have already been written for you: display an alert, look up a word in the dictionary, take a picture, play a song, and so on. Most of this book will be showing you how to request those built-in services.

> **Note** A framework is a bundle of files in a folder, much like the app bundles you'll be creating in this book. Instead of containing an app, however, a framework contains the files your app needs to use a particular segment of the operating system. For example, all of the functions, constants, classes, and resources needed to draw things on the screen are in the Core Graphics framework. The AVFoundation framework contains classes that let you record and playback audio. Want to know where you are? You'll need the functions in the CoreLocation framework. There are scores of these individual frameworks.

Wow, that's a lot of acronyms! Let's review them:

- IDE: Integrated Development Environment. Xcode is an IDE.
- SDK: Software Development Kit. The supporting files that let you build an app for a particular operating system, like iOS 7.
- API: Application Programming Interface. A published set of functions, classes, and definitions that describe how your app can use a particular service.

You don't need to memorize these. It's just good to know what they mean when you hear them, or talk to other programmers.

Becoming an iOS Developer

The fact that you're reading this book makes you an iOS developer—at least in spirit. To become an official iOS developer, you need to join Apple's iOS Developer program.

You must be an iOS Developer if you want to do any of the following:

- Sell, or give away, your apps through Apple's App Store.
- Gain access to Apple's Developer Forums and other resources.
- Give your apps to people directly (outside of the App Store).
- Develop apps that use Game Kit, in-app purchases, push notifications, or similar technologies.
- Test your apps on a real iOS device.

The first reason is the one that prompts most developers to join the program, and is probably the reason you'll join. You don't, however, have to join to build, test, and run your apps in Xcode's simulator. If you never plan to distribute your apps through the App Store, or run your app on an iOS device, you may never need to become an iOS Developer. You can get through most of this book without joining.

Another reason for joining is to gain access to the iOS Developer's community and support programs. Apple's online forums contain a treasure trove of information. If you run into a problem and can't find the answer, there's a good chance someone else has already bumped into the same problem. A quick search of the Developer Forums will probably reveal an answer. If not, post your question and someone might have an answer for you.

Even if you don't plan to sell or give away your masterpiece on the App Store, there are a couple of other reasons to join. If you want to install your app on a device, Apple requires that you become a registered developer. Apple will then generate special files that will permit your app to be installed on an iOS device.

As a registered developer, Apple will also allow you to install your apps on someone else's device directly (i.e., not through the App Store). This is called *ad-hoc distribution*. There are limits on the number of people you can do this for, but it is possible.

Finally, some technologies require your app to communicate with Apple's servers. Before this is allowed, you must register yourself and your app with Apple, even just to test them. For example, if you plan to use Game Kit in your app—and this book includes a Game Kit example—you'll need to be an iOS Developer.

Bookmark this URL: `http://developer.apple.com/`

As I write this book, the cost of becoming an iOS Developer is $99(US). It's an annual subscription, so there's no point in joining until you need to. Follow that link to find more information about Apple's developer programs.

So is there anything at developer.apple.com that's free? There's quite a lot, actually. You can search through all of Apple's published documentation, download example projects, read technology guides, technical notes, and more—none of which require you to be an iOS Developer. Some activities require you to log in with your AppleID (your iTunes or iCloud account will work), or you can create a new AppleID.

Paid registration also gives you the opportunity to buy tickets to the World Wide Developers Conference (WWDC) held by Apple each year. It's a huge gathering, and it's just for Apple developers.

Getting the Projects

Now would be a good time to download the project files for this book. There are numerous projects used throughout this book. Many can be recreated by following the steps in each chapter, and I encourage you to do that whenever possible so you'll get a feel for building your apps from scratch. There are, however, a number of projects that don't explain every detail, and some projects include binary resources (image and sound files) that can't be reproduced in print.

Go to this book's page at `http://www.apress.com` (you can search for it by name, ISBN, or the author's name). Below the book's description, you'll see some folder tabs, one of which is labeled Source Code/Downloads. Click that tab. Now find the link that downloads the projects for this book. Click that link and a file named `Learn iOS Development Projects.zip` will download to your hard drive.

Locate the file `Learn iOS Development Projects.zip` in your Downloads folder (or wherever your browser saved it). Double-click the file to extract its contents, leaving you with a folder named `Learn iOS Development Projects`. Move the folder wherever you like.

Launching Xcode the First Time

After the Xcode application downloads, you will find it in your Applications folder. Open the Xcode application, by double-clicking it, using Launchpad, or however you like to launch apps. I recommend adding Xcode to your Dock for easy access.

Xcode will present a licensing agreement (see Figure 1-3), which you are encouraged to at least skim over, but must agree to before proceeding.

Figure 1-3. License Agreement

Once you've gotten through all of the preliminaries, you'll see Xcode's startup window, as shown in Figure 1-4.

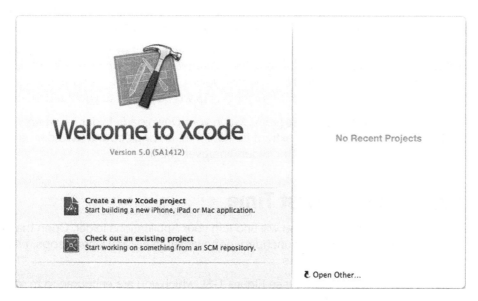

Figure 1-4. Xcode's Startup Window

The startup window has several self-explanatory buttons to help you get started. It also lists the projects you've recently opened.

The interesting parts of Xcode don't reveal themselves unless you have a project open, so start by creating a new project. Click on the **Create a new Xcode project** button in the startup window (or choose **File ➤ New ➤ Project…** from the menu). The first thing Xcode will want to know is what kind of project you want to create, as shown in Figure 1-5.

Figure 1-5. Project Template Browser

The template browser lets you select a project template. Each template creates a new project pre-configured to build something specific (application, library, plug-in, and so on) for a particular platform (iOS or OS X). While it's possible to manually configure any project to produce whatever you want, it's both technical and tedious; save yourself a lot of work and try to choose a template that's as close to the final "shape" of your app as you can.

In this book, you'll only be creating iOS apps, so choose the Application category under the iOS section—but feel free to check out some of the other sections. As you can see, Xcode is useful for much more than just iOS development.

With the Application section selected, click the Single View Application template, and then click on the Next button. In the next screen, Xcode wants some details about your new project, as shown in Figure 1-6. What options you see here will vary depending on what template you chose.

Figure 1-6. New project options

For this little demonstration, give your new project a name in the Product Name field. It can be anything you want—I used `MyFirstApp` for this example—but I recommend you keep the name simple. The Organization Name is optional, but I suggest you fill in your name (or the company you're working for, if you're going to be developing apps for them).

The Company Identifier and Product Name, together, create a *Bundle Identifier* that uniquely identifies your app. The Company Identifier is a reverse domain name, which you (or your company) should own. It isn't important right now, as you'll only be building this app for yourself, so use any domain name you like. When you build apps that you plan to distribute through the App Store, these values will have to be legitimate.

The rest of the options don't matter for this demonstration, so click the **Next** button. The last thing Xcode will ask is where to store your new project (see Figure 1-7). Every project creates a *project folder*, named after your project. All of the documents used to create your app will be stored in that project folder. You can put your project folder anywhere (even on the Desktop). In this example, I'm creating a new `iOS Development` folder so that I can keep all of my project folders together.

Figure 1-7. Creating a new project

Welcome To Xcode

With all of the details about your new project answered, click the Create button. Xcode will create your project and open it in a *workspace window*. An exploded view of a workspace window is shown in Figure 1-8. This is where the magic happens, and where you'll be spending most of your time in this book.

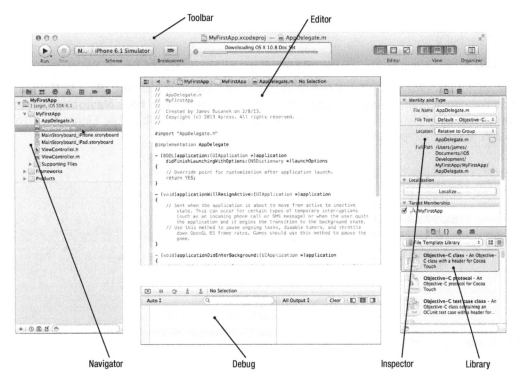

Figure 1-8. Xcode workspace window

A workspace window has five main parts:

- Navigator area (left)
- Editor area (center)
- Utility area (right)
- Debug area (bottom)
- Toolbar (top)

You can selectively hide everything except the editor area, so you may not see all of these parts. Let's take a brief tour of each one, so you'll know your way around.

Navigation Area

The navigators live on the left side of your workspace window. There are eight navigators:

Project

Symbol

Find

Issue

Test

Debug

Breakpoint

Log

Switch navigators by clicking on the icons at the top of the pane, or from the **View ➤ Navigator** submenu. You can hide the navigators using the **View ➤ Navigator ➤ Hide Navigator** command (Command+0) or by clicking the left side of the **View** button in the toolbar (see Figure 1-9). This will give you a little extra screen space for the editor.

Figure 1-9. Navigator view controls

The project navigator (see Figure 1-8) is your home base, and the one you'll use the most. Every source file that's part of your project is organized in the project navigator, and it's how you select a file to edit.

> **Note** A *source file* is any original document used in the creation of your app. Most projects have multiple source files. The term is used to distinguish them from *intermediate files* (transient files created during construction) and *product files* (the files of your finished app). Your product files appear in a special `Products` folder, at the bottom of the project navigator.

The symbol navigator keeps a running list of the symbols you've defined in your project. The search navigator will find text in multiple files. The issues, debug, breakpoint, and log navigators come into play when you're ready to build and test your app.

Editor Area

The editor area is where you create your app—literally. Select a source file in the project navigator, and it will appear in the editor area. What the editor looks like will depend on what kind of file it is.

> **Note** Not all files are editable in Xcode. For example, image and sound files can't be edited in Xcode, but Xcode will display a preview of them in the editor area.

What you'll be editing the most are program source files, which you edit like any text file (see Figure 1-8), and Interface Builder files, which appear as graphs of objects (see Figure 1-11) that you connect and configure.

The editor area has three modes:

- Standard editor
- Assistant editor
- Version editor

The standard editor edits the selected file. The assistant editor splits the editor area and (typically) loads a *counterpart* file on the right side. For example, when editing an Objective-C source file, as shown in Figure 1-10, the assistant automatically loads its counterpart file—the header file that contains the definitions for that file—on the right. When editing Interface Builder files, it may display the Objective-C source file for the object that's being edited, and so on.

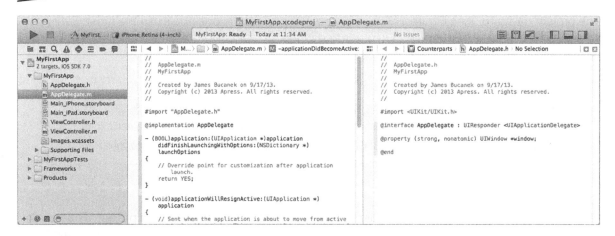

Figure 1-10. *The assistant editor*

> **Tip** The assistant editor is very flexible and can be used to edit almost any second file you choose. If the assistant editor stops automatically loading counterpart files in the right pane, choose **Counterparts** from the ribbon above the right-hand pane to restore that functionality.

The version editor is used to compare a source file with an earlier version. Xcode supports several version control systems. You can "check-in" or take a "snapshot" of your project, and later compare what you've written against an earlier version of the same file. We won't get into version control in this book. If you're interested, read the section *Save and Revert Changes to Projects* in the Xcode Users Guide.

To change editor modes, click the Editor control in the toolbar or use the commands in the View menu. You can't hide the editor area.

Utility Area

On the right side of your workspace window is the utility area. As the name suggests, it hosts a variety of useful tools, as shown in Figure 1-11.

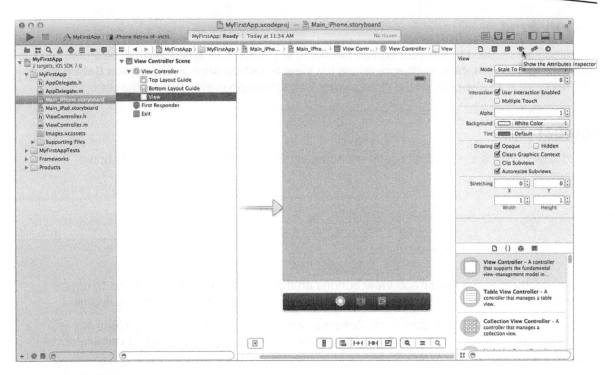

Figure 1-11. Editing an Interface Builder file

At the top of the utilities area are the *inspectors*. These will change depending on what kind of file is being edited, and what you have selected. As with the navigators, you can switch between different inspectors by clicking on the icons at the top of the pane, or from the **View ➤ Utilities** submenu (see Figure 1-12). You can hide the utility area using the **View ➤ Utilities ➤ Hide Utilities** command, or by clicking on the right side of the **View** control in the toolbar (see Figure 1-12).

Figure 1-12. Utility view controls

At the bottom of the utility area is the library. Here you'll find ready-made objects, resources, and code snippets that you can drag into your project.

Debug Area

The debug area is used to test your app and work out any kinks. It usually doesn't appear until you run your app. To make it appear, or disappear, use the **View ➤ Debug Area ➤ Show/Hide Debug Area** command. You can also click on the close drawer icon in the upper-left corner of the debug pane.

Toolbar

The toolbar contains a number of useful shortcuts and some status information, as shown in Figure 1-13.

Figure 1-13. Workspace window toolbar

You've already seen the **Editor** and **View** buttons on the right. On the left are buttons to run (test) and stop your app. You will use these buttons to start and stop your app during development.

Next to the **Run** and **Stop** buttons is the **Scheme** control. This multi-part pop-up menu lets you select how your project will be built (called a *scheme*) and your app's destination (a simulator, an actual device, the App Store, and so on).

In the middle of the toolbar is your project's status. It will display what activities are currently happening, or have recently finished, such as building, indexing, and so on. If you've just installed Xcode, it is probably downloading additional documentation in the background, and the status will indicate that.

You can hide the toolbar, if you want, using the **View ➤ Show/Hide Toolbar** command. All of the buttons and controls in the toolbar are just shortcuts to menu commands, so it's possible to live without it. This book, however, will assume that it's visible.

If you're interested in learning more about the workspace window, the navigators, editor, and inspectors, you will find all of that (and more) in the *Xcode Overview*, under the Help menu.

Running Your First App

With your workspace window open, click on the **Scheme** control and choose one of the **iPhone** choices from the submenu, as shown in Figure 1-14. This tells Xcode where you want this app to run when you click the Run button.

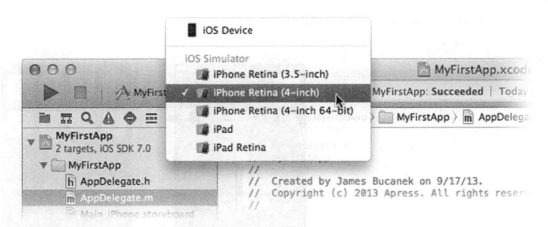

Figure 1-14. Choosing the scheme and target

Click the **Run** button. OK, there's probably one more formality to attend to. Before you can test an application, Xcode needs to be granted some special privileges. The first time you try to run an app, Xcode will ask if this is OK (see Figure 1-15). Click **Enable** and supply your account name and password.

Figure 1-15. Enabling developer mode

Once you're past the preliminaries, Xcode will assemble your app from all of the parts in your project—a process known as a *build*—and then run your app using its built-in iPhone simulator, as shown on the left in Figure 1-16.

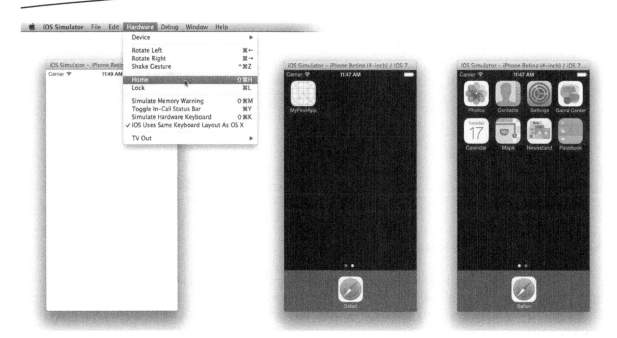

Figure 1-16. The iPhone simulator

The simulator is just what it sounds like. It's a program that pretends—as closely as possible—to be a real iPhone, iPad, or iPod Touch. The simulator lets you do much of your iOS app testing right on your Mac, without ever having to load your app into a real iOS device. It also allows you to test your app on different kinds of devices, so you don't have to go buy one of each.

Congratulations, you just created, built, and ran an iOS app on a (simulated) iPhone! This works because Xcode project templates always create a runnable project; what's missing is the functionality that makes your app do something wonderful. That's what the rest of this book is about.

While you're here, feel free to play around with the iPhone simulator. Although the app you created doesn't have any functionality—beyond that of a lame "flashlight" app—you'll notice that you can simulate pressing the home button using the **Hardware ➤ Home** command and return to the springboard (the middle and right in Figure 1-16). There you'll find your app, the Settings app, Game Center, and more, just as if this were a real iPhone. Sorry, it won't make telephone calls.

When you're finished, switch back to the workspace window and click on the Stop button in the toolbar.

Summary

You now have all of the tools you need to develop and run iOS apps. You've learned a little about how Xcode is organized, and how to run your app in the simulator.

The next step is to add some content to your app.

Chapter 2

Boom! App

In this chapter you're going to create an iOS app that does something. Not much—these are early days—but enough to call it useful. In the process, you will:

- Use Xcode's Interface Builder to design your app
- Add objects to your app
- Connect objects together
- Customize your objects to provide content
- Add resource files to your project
- Use storyboards to create segues
- Control the layout of visual elements using constraints

Amazingly, you're going to create this app without writing a single line of computer code. This is not typical, but it will demonstrate the flexibility of Xcode.

The app you're going to create presents some interesting facts about women surrealists of the twentieth century. Let's get started.

Design

Before firing up Xcode and typing furiously, you need to have a plan. This is the design phase of app development. Over the lifetime of your app, you may revise your design several times as you improve it, but before you begin you need a basic idea of what your app will look like and how you want it to work.

Your design may be written out formally, sketched on a napkin, or just be in your head. It doesn't matter, as long as you have one. You need to, at the very least, be able to answer some basic questions. What kinds of devices will your app run on (iPhone/iPod, iPad, or both)? Will your app run in portrait mode, sideways, or both? What will the user see? How will the user navigate? How will they interact with it?

A rough sketch of this app is shown in Figure 2-1. The app is very simple, so it doesn't require much in the way of initial design. The surrealist app will have an opening screen containing portraits of famous women surrealists. Tapping one will transition to a second screen showing a representative painting and a scrollable text field with information about the artist's life. You've decided this is going to run only on an iPhone or iPod Touch, and only in Portrait orientation. This will simplify your design and development.

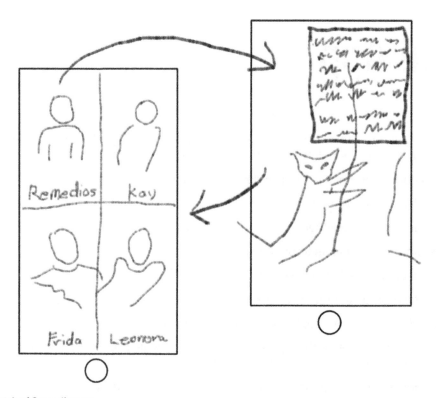

Figure 2-1. Sketch of Surrealist app

Creating the Project

The first step is to create your project. Click the **New Project** button on the startup window or choose the **New ▶ New Project…** command. Review the available templates, as shown in Figure 2-2.

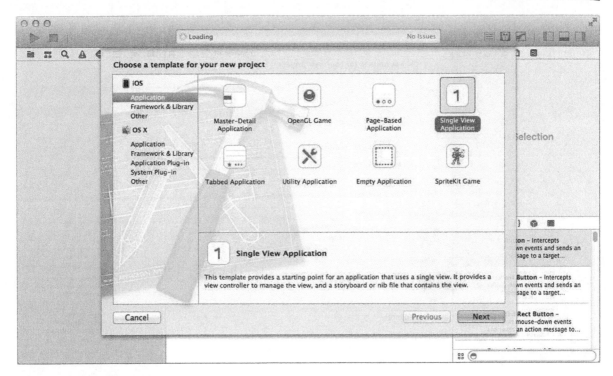

Figure 2-2. iOS project templates

Your design gives you a basic idea of how your app will work, which should suggest which Xcode project template to start with. Your app's design isn't a perfect fit with any of these, so choose the Single View Application template—it's the simplest template that already has a view. Click on the **Next** button.

The next step is to fill in the details about your project (see Figure 2-3). Name the project Surrealists and fill in your organization name and identifier. Consistent with your design choices, change the Devices option from Universal to iPhone, as shown in Figure 2-3.

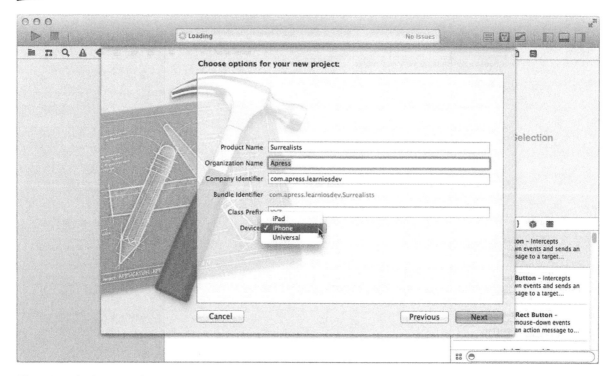

Figure 2-3. Setting the project details

> **Note** Developing for the iPhone is the same as developing for the iPod Touch (unless your app uses features only available on the iPhone). From here on, I'll only mention the iPhone, but please remember that this also includes the iPod Touch.

There's also a `Class Prefix` setting. This option sets a very short string that will be used to consistently name all new classes you add to your project. It's traditionally two capital letters, but it could be anything. You'll want to avoid the two character prefixes already used by iOS, particularly NS and UI. Leave it blank for this project—you won't be creating any classes.

Click the **Next** button. Pick a location on your hard drive to save the new project and click **Create**.

Setting Project Properties

You now have an empty Xcode project; it's time to start customizing it. Begin with the project settings by clicking on the project name (Surrealists) in the project navigator, as shown in the upper left of Figure 2-4. The editor area will display all of the settings for this project. Choose the `Surrealist` target from the pop-up menu, in the upper-left corner of the editor (see Figure 2-4), and then choose the `General` tab in the middle.

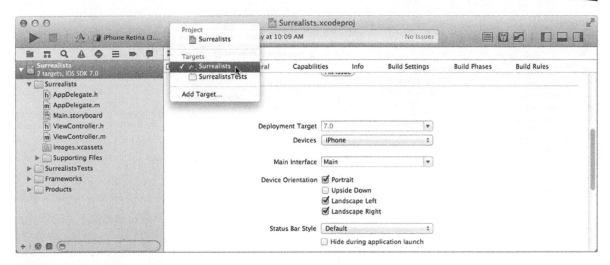

Figure 2-4. Target Settings

Scroll down the target settings until you find the Deployment Info section. Uncheck the Landscape Left and Landscape Right boxes in Device Orientation, so that only the Portrait orientation is checked.

To review, you've created an iPhone-only app project that runs exclusively in portrait orientation. You're now ready to design your interface.

Building an Interface

Click the Main.storyboard file in the project navigator. Xcode's Interface Builder editor appears in the edit area, as shown in Figure 2-5.

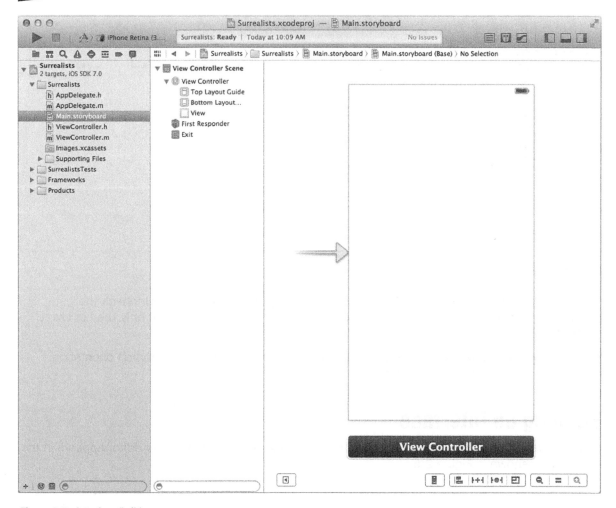

Figure 2-5. Interface Builder

Interface Builder is the secret sauce in Apple's app kitchen. In a nutshell, it's a tool that adds, configures, and interconnects objects within your app—without writing any code. You can define most of the visual elements of your app in Interface Builder. Interface Builder edits storyboard, xib, and (legacy) nib files.

> **Note** Modern Interface Builder files have extensions of xib or storyboard. Legacy Interface Builder files have a nib (pronounced "nib") extension, and you'll still hear programmers refer to all of them generically as "nib" files. The nib acronym stands for **N**ext **I**nterface **B**uilder, because the roots of Xcode, Interface Builder, and the Cocoa Touch framework stretch all the way back to Steve Job's "other" company, NeXT. Later in this book, you'll see a lot of class names that begin with "NS," which an abbreviation for **N**e**XTS**tep, the name of NeXT's operating system.

Interface Builder displays the objects in the file in two views. On the left (see Figure 2-5) are the objects organized into a hierarchical list, called the *outline*. Some objects can contain other objects, just as folders can contain other folders, and the outline reflects this. Use the disclosure triangles to reveal contained objects.

The view on the right is called the *canvas*. Here you'll find the visual objects in your Interface Builder file. Only visual objects (like buttons, labels, images, and so on) appear in the canvas. Objects that don't have a visual aspect will only be listed the outline. If an object appears in both, it doesn't matter which one you work with—they're the same object.

> **Note** If you've been learning an Object-Oriented programming language, then you know what an "object" is. If you don't know what an "object" is, don't panic. For now, just think of objects as Lego® bricks; a discrete bundle that performs a specific task in your app, and can be connected to others to make something bigger. Feel free to skip ahead to Chapter 6 if you want to learn about objects right now.

Adding Objects

You get new objects from the library. Choose the **View ➤ Utilities ➤ Show Object Library** command. This will simultaneously make the utility area on the right visible and switch to the object library (the little cube), as shown in Figure 2-6.

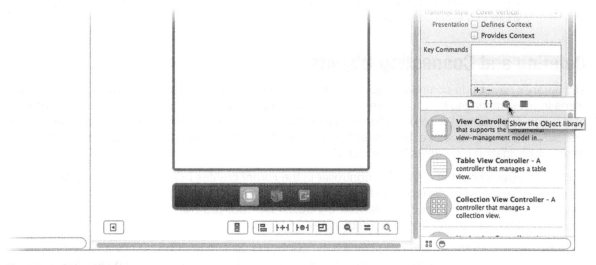

Figure 2-6. Object Library

To add an object to your app, drag it from the library and drop it into the Interface Builder editor. Your app needs a navigation controller object, so scroll down the list of objects until you find the `Navigation Controller`. You can simplify your search by entering a keyword into the search field at the bottom of the library pane (see Figure 2-7).

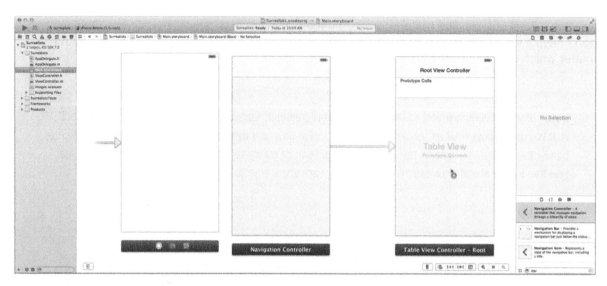

Figure 2-7. Adding a Navigation Controller

Drag the navigation controller object from the library into the canvas, as shown in Figure 2-7, and drop it anywhere in the blank space. You just added an object—several, actually—to your app.

Deleting and Connecting Objects

The library's navigation controller object is really a cluster of objects. A navigation controller, as the name implies, manages how a user moves between multiple screens, each screen being controlled by a single view controller object. The navigation controller is connected to the view controller of the first screen that will appear, called its *root view controller*. Don't worry about the details; you'll learn all about navigation controllers in Chapter 12.

For your convenience, the navigation controller in the library creates both a navigation controller object and the root view controller that it starts with. This root view controller happens to be a table view controller. You don't need a table view controller. Instead, you want this navigation controller to use the no-frills view controller you already have.

Start by discarding the superfluous table view controller. Select just the table view controller that's connected to the navigation controller, as shown in Figure 2-8. Press the **Delete** key, or choose **Edit ➤ Delete**.

CHAPTER 2: Boom! App   25

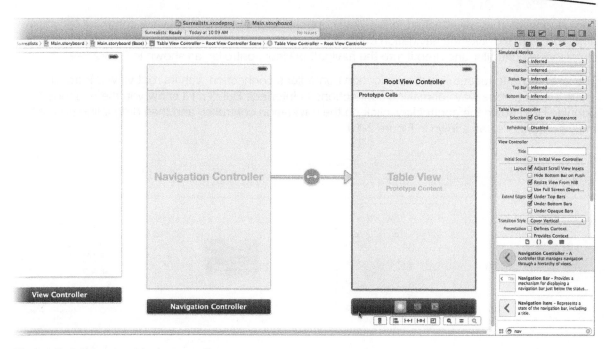

Figure 2-8. *Deleting the table view controller*

Now you need to connect your new navigation controller to the plain-vanilla view controller your project came with. Drag the view controller and position it to the right of the navigation controller (see Figure 2-9).

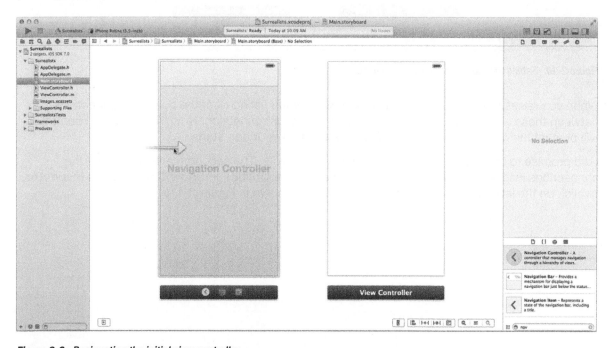

Figure 2-9. *Designating the initial view controller*

The unconnected arrow attached to the view controller indicates the initial view controller for your app. You want to make the navigation controller the first controller, so drag the arrow away from the simple view controller and drop it into the navigation view controller, as shown in Figure 2-9.

The last step is to reestablish the navigation controller's connection with its root view controller. There are numerous ways of making connections in Interface Builder. I'll show you the two most popular. Hold down the control key, click on the navigation controller, and then drag a line from it to the view controller, as shown in Figure 2-10.

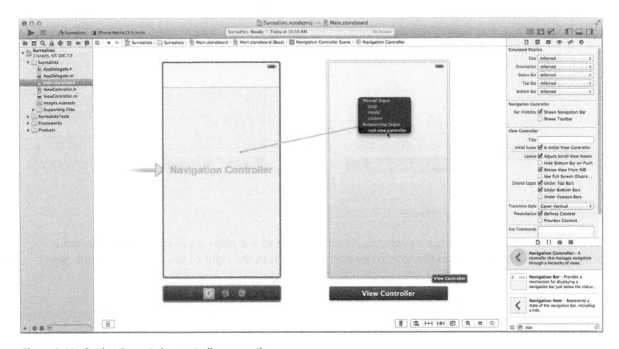

Figure 2-10. Setting the root view controller connection

When you release the mouse, a pop-up menu will appear listing all of the possible connections between these two objects. Click the root view controller connection. Now the navigation controller will present this view controller as the first screen when your app starts.

I did promise to teach you two ways of connecting objects. The second method is to use the connections inspector in the utility area. Choose **View ➤ Utilities ➤ Show Connections Inspector**, or click on the little arrow icon in the utilities pane, as shown in Figure 2-11.

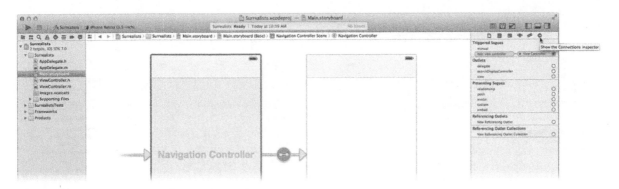

Figure 2-11. Using the connections inspector

To use the inspector, first choose an object. In this case, choose the navigation controller. The connections inspector will show all of the connections for that object. Find the connection labeled `root view controller`. To the right of each connection is a little circle. To set a connection, click and drag that circle to the object you want it connected to—in this case, the view controller. To clear (or "break") a connection, click the small "x" in the connection field.

So far, you've created a new project. The project template included a simple view controller. You added a new navigation controller object (along with an unneeded table view controller, which you discarded) to your app. You designated the navigation controller as the one that takes control of your app when it starts, and you connected that controller to the empty view controller. Now it's time to put something in that empty view.

Adding Views to a View

Now we get to the fun part of this project: creating your app's content. Start by adding four buttons, which you'll customize, to your opening screen. To do that, you need to work in your initial screen's view object.

The view controller object is not a single object, it's a bag of objects. I said earlier that some object may contain other objects; view controllers and views are two such objects. Start by selecting the view object. There are two ways of doing this in Interface Builder. You can find the object in the outline on the left (see Figure 2-12), and select it. The other is to "drill down" to the object you want. Click in the center of the view controller object (in the middle of Figure 2-12). This will select the view controller object. Click again and you'll select the view object contained in that object. If that view contained another object, clicking again would select it, and so on.

CHAPTER 2: Boom! App

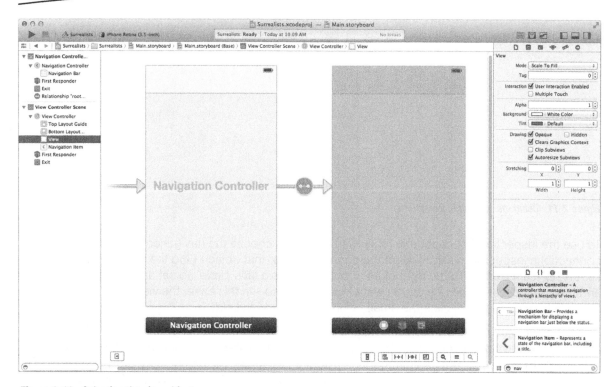

Figure 2-12. Selecting the view object

Now that you know how to find and select an embedded view object, it's time to add some new view objects to it. In the object library, find the Button object—type "button" in the search field to make this easier. Grab a Button object and drag it into the view object, as shown in Figure 2-13.

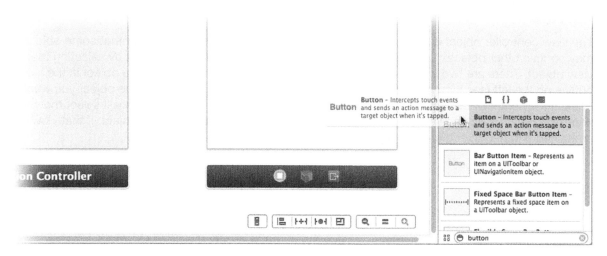

Figure 2-13. Adding a button object

> **Note** The view objects that a view contains are called its *subviews*. The view that a view is contained in is called its *superview*.

Repeat this three more times, so you have four button objects inside the view, approximately like those shown in Figure 2-14. Now you want to resize these buttons so they fill the entire screen. To help you lay them out evenly, add some guides. Click inside the superview so that none of the button objects are selected and choose Editor ➤ Add Vertical Guide. By default, a new guide is created in the middle of the view, which is exactly what you want.

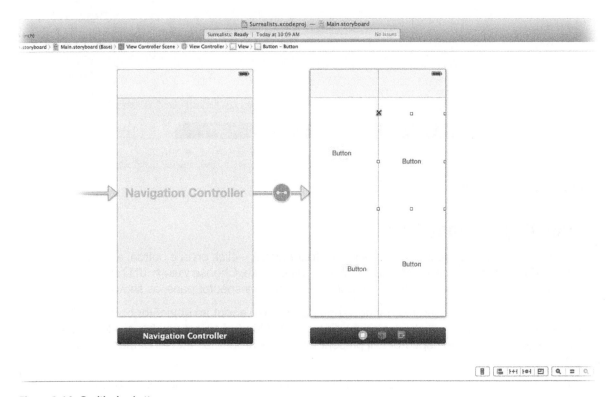

Figure 2-14. Positioning buttons

Using the guides, position and resize each button so it fills one quarter of the view. Start by dragging the button to the lower left corner of a quadrant. The view will "snap" to the nearest layout guide. Grab the opposite resizing handle and drag it out to fill the quadrant, as shown in Figure 2-14. It doesn't have to be perfect at this stage; you'll neaten this up later in the chapter.

When you're all done, you'll have four buttons that fill the screen (see Figure 2-15).

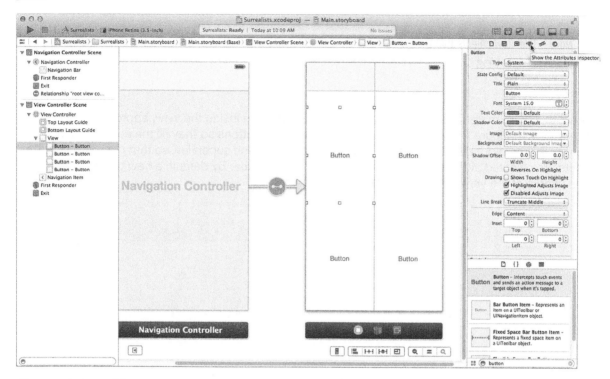

Figure 2-15. Customizing button objects

Editing Object Properties

Now it's time to customize your buttons. Select all four buttons—click on one button, and then while holding down the shift key, click once on each of the other three. Choose View ➤ Utilities ➤ Show Attributes Inspector, or click on the small control icon in the inspector pane, as shown in Figure 2-15.

The attributes inspector is used to change various properties about an object (or objects). The properties in the inspector will change depending on what kind of object you have selected. If you select multiple objects, the inspector will present just those properties that all of those objects have in common.

With the four buttons selected, make the following changes using the attributes inspector:

- Change Type to Custom
- Click the up arrow next to the font attribute until it reads System Bold 18.0
- Click the Text Color drop-down arrow and choose white
- Find the Control group and select the bottom vertical alignment icon

When you're all done, your view should look like the one in Figure 2-16. The next step is to add an image and a label to each one, individually. To do that, you're going to need to add some resources to your project.

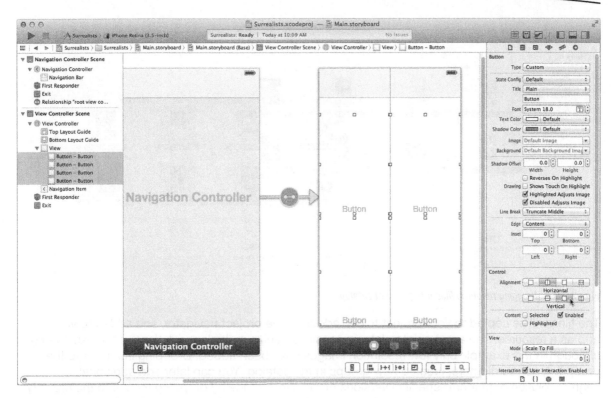

Figure 2-16. Customized buttons

Adding Resources

Everything that your app needs to run must be part of the app that you build. If your app needs an image, that image must be included in its *resources*. Image files, Interface Builder files, sound files, and anything else that's not computer code, are collectively referred to as resources.

You can add virtually any file as a resource to your app. Resource files are copied into your app's *bundle* when it is built and are available to your app when it runs.

Xcode has a special way of organizing commonly used resources, like images, into a single resource called an *asset catalog*. To add new images to an asset catalog, select the catalog in the project navigator, as shown in Figure 2-17. Locate the resource files you want to add in the Finder. Find the Learn iOS Development Projects folder you downloaded in Chapter 1. Inside the Ch 2 folder you'll find the Surrealists (Resources) folder, which contains eight image files. With the files and your workspace window visible, drag the image files into the group list (left side) of the asset catalog, as shown in Figure 2-17.

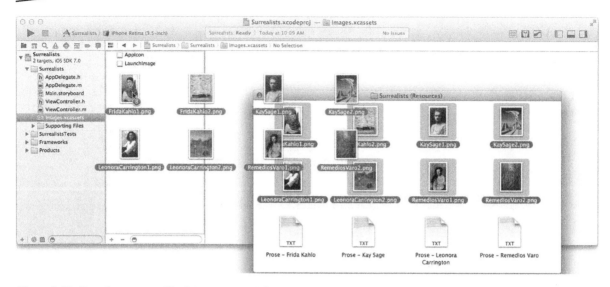

Figure 2-17. Dragging resource files into an asset catalog

The files will be copied to your project folder, added to the project navigator, and added to your app as a resource. The asset catalog lets you easily organize multiple resolutions of the same image, although in this example only low resolution images have been added. Dropping images into the group list, as you did here, created new groups in the catalog. You can later add additional (high-resolution or platform-specific) versions of the same image by dropping them into the preview pain of a group, shown on the right in Figure 2-18. Xcode can't edit these files, but the preview pane (see Figure 2-18) let's you review thumbnails of them.

Figure 2-18. Previewing image files

Customizing Buttons

With the necessary resource files added, it's time to customize your buttons. Select the Main.storyboard file again and select the upper-left button. Reveal the attributes inspector (**View ➤ Utilities ➤ Show Attributes Inspector**) and change the title property to Remedios Varo and the background property to RemediosVaro1, as shown in Figure 2-19.

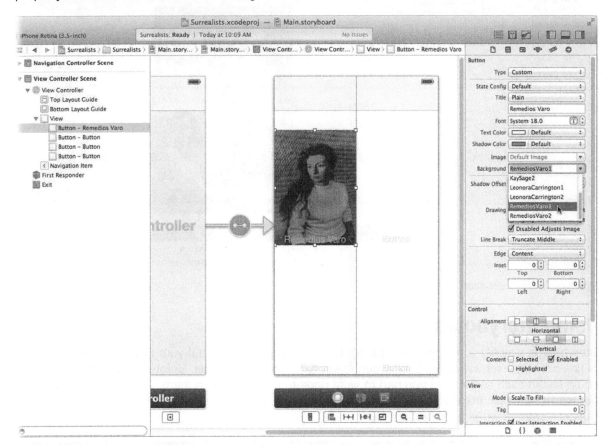

Figure 2-19. Customizing the first button

The background property is the resource name of the image you want the button to use for its background. You can type it in, but Xcode recognizes common image types and includes the image resources you just added to the drop-down list. Just select the filename from that list.

Customize the remaining three buttons (working clockwise), setting their title and background image as follows:

- Kay Sage, KaySage1
- Leonora Carrington, LeonoraCarrington1
- Frida Kahlo, FridaKahlo1

As a finishing touch, select Kay Sage's button and change the text color to black (so it's easier to read). When you're all done, your interface should look like Figure 2-20.

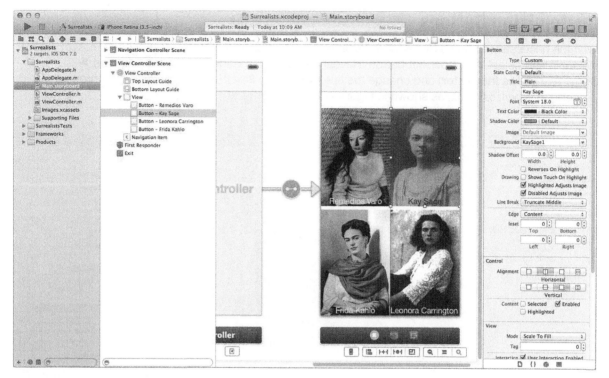

Figure 2-20. Finished buttons

Using Storyboards

Storyboards simplify your app development by allowing you to plan out your app's screens, and define how the user will navigate between them, all in Interface Builder. Before storyboards, you could layout each screen, but you had to write code to move between them. It wasn't a lot of code, nor was it complex, but it was a chore. With storyboards, you can do most of that work in Interface Builder—without writing any code at all.

FRICTIONLESS DEVELOPMENT

Repetitive code is a drag on development. The time you spend writing the same code, over and over again, is time you don't have to develop cool new features. What you want is a *frictionless* development environment, where the simple tasks are taken care of for you, leaving you time to work on the stuff that makes your app special.

Apple works very hard on making iOS and Xcode as frictionless as possible. Every release adds new classes and development tools to make developing high-quality apps easier. For example, before the introduction of gesture recognizers, writing code to detect multi-touch gestures (like a pinch or a three-fingered swipe) was a complicated task, often requiring a page or more of code. Today—as you might have guessed already—your app can detect these gestures simply by dropping a gesture recognizer object into your design and connecting it to an action.

Let's use storyboards to define the remaining screens of your app, and how the user will navigate between them.

Adding New Screens

Before you can create a transition between two screens, called a *segue* (pronounced "seg-way"), you must first create another screen (called a *scene* in storyboard-speak). Return to the object library and drag in a new view controller object into your `Mainstoryboard` file, as shown in Figure 2-21.

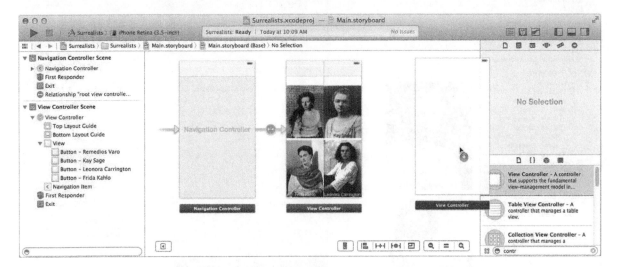

Figure 2-21. Adding a new view controller

In Figure 2-21, I've zoomed out (using the magnifying controls in the bottom right corner of the editor pane) so I can see the entire storyboard. To edit the contents of a view, however, Interface Builder needs to be zoomed in on that view. There are a couple of ways to accomplish this:

- Double-click in the canvas to zoom out/in.
- Click the zoom toggle (=) or magnifying glass (+) in the lower-right of the canvas and scroll to center the view.

Locate the `Image View` object in the library. Drag one into the empty view, as shown in Figure 2-22.

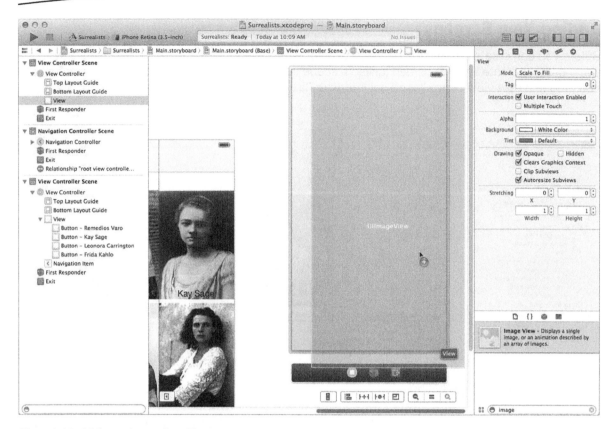

Figure 2-22. Adding an image view object

If the image view object didn't snap to fill the whole view, drag it around until it does. With the new image view object still selected, switch to the attributes inspector. Change the Image property to `RemediosVaro2`, and change the image mode to `Aspect Fill`, as shown in Figure 2-23.

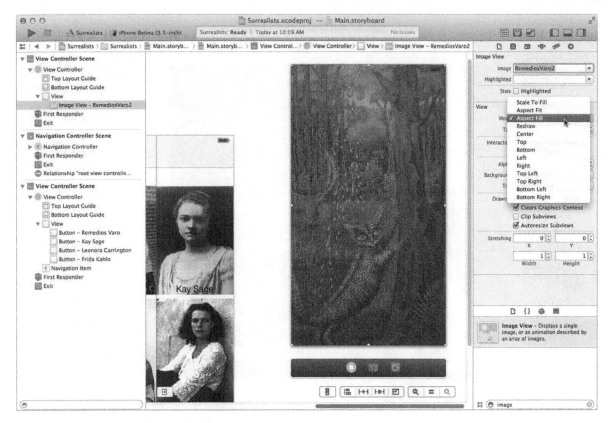

Figure 2-23. Customizing the background image view

Now add a scrolling text field to this screen. Locate the Text View (not the Text Field!) object in the library. Drag a new text view into the window and position it, using the automatic user interface guides, in the upper-right corner of the screen, as shown in Figure 2-24.

CHAPTER 2: Boom! App

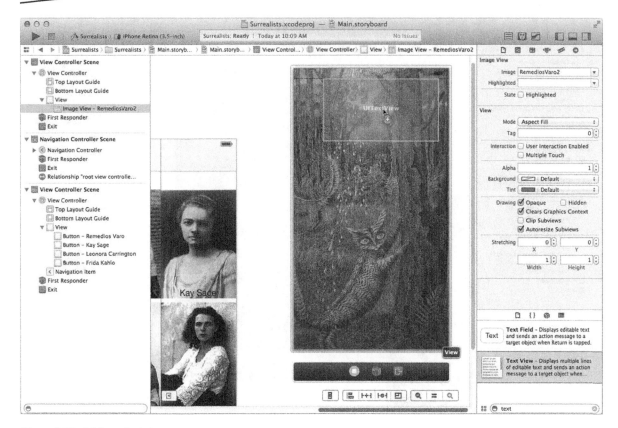

Figure 2-24. Adding a text view

With the text view selected, use the attributes inspector to change the following properties:

- Set text color to white
- Reduce the font size to 12.0
- Uncheck the editable option
- Further down, uncheck Shows Horizontal Scrollers
- Click on the background color, in the color picker use the grey slider to choose 50% grey with a 33% alpha or opacity (see Figure 2-25)

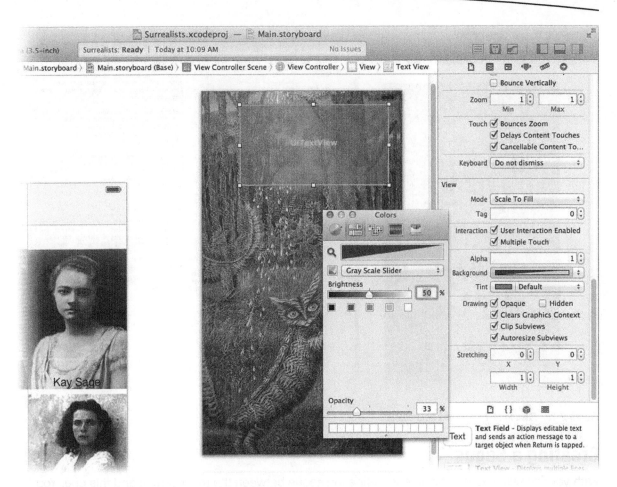

Figure 2-25. *Setting a semi-transparent background color*

The text for this object can be found in the `Surrealists (Resources)` folder where you found the image files. You won't add these files to your project, however. Instead, open the file named `Prose - Remedios Varo`, copy the text, switch back to Xcode, and paste it into the text property of the attributes inspector, as shown in Figure 2-26.

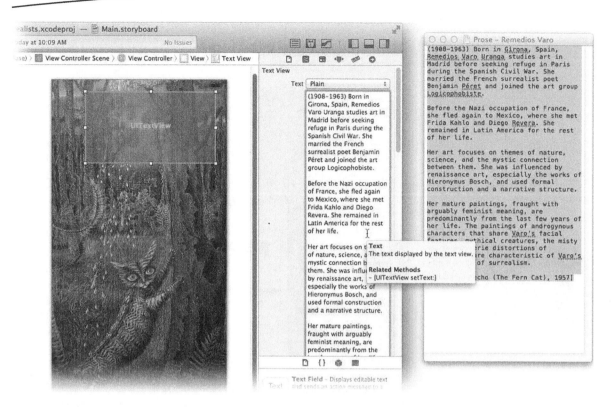

Figure 2-26. Pasting text into a text field object

Creating a Segue

With your screen finished, it's time to define the segue between the main screen and this one. You want this screen to appear when the user taps on the Remedios Varo button. To create this segue, hold down the control key, click on the Remedios Varo button, drag the connection to this new view controller, and release the mouse, as shown in Figure 2-27.

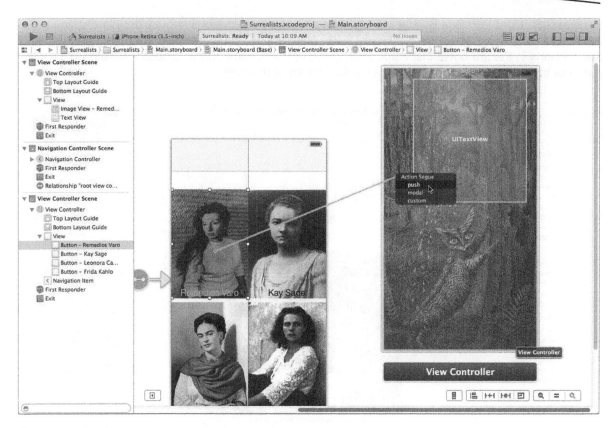

Figure 2-27. Creating a segue

When you release the mouse button, a pop-up menu will appear with the possible segue types. Choose push (see Figure 2-27). When your user taps the Remedios Varo button, your app will perform a "push" transition (sliding the new screen into view) and present the new view.

Setting Navigation Titles

The initial view controller is, itself, under the control of the navigation controller object you created at the beginning. The job of the navigation controller is to present a series of views underneath a *navigation bar*. The navigation bar—which you've seen a hundred times—displays the title of the screen you're looking at, and optionally has a back button to return you to the screen you came from. The navigation controller handles all of the details.

When you added a push segue to the second screen, the second screen fell under the control of the navigation controller too. A push segue—which only works in conjunction with navigation controllers, by the way—replaces one view with another, and makes the original view the target of the back button in the new view.

So that this is meaningful to your user, you'll want to set the titles for each screen. This will make the navigation bar intelligible.

Select the navigation bar in the initial view controller and have the attributes inspector handy. Change the title of the navigation bar to Woman Surrealists, and set the back button property to

Surrealists. Most Interface Builder objects with a title can be edited simply by double-clicking on the title in the canvas, and shown in Figure 2-28. Alternatively, you can select the object and edit its title property in the attributes inspector. Setting the optional back button property will assign a more succinct title to the back button on screens that return to this one.

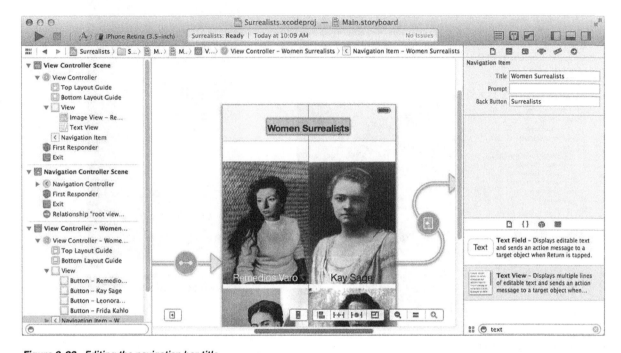

Figure 2-28. Editing the navigation bar title

Finally, select the navigation bar in the second screen you created and change its title to Remedios Varo. You might want to adjust the size or position of the text field so the navigation bar doesn't obscure it.

Testing Your Interface

You have now built enough of your app to see it in action! Make sure the run target is set to one of the iPhone simulators, as shown in Figure 2-29.

Figure 2-29. Selecting the run target

Click the Run button. Xcode will build your app and start it running in the simulator. If, for some unexpected reason, there are problems building your app, messages describing those problems can be found in the issue navigator (View ➤ Navigator ➤ Show Issue Navigator).

Your app will appear in the iPhone simulator, and should look like the one on the left in Figure 2-30.

 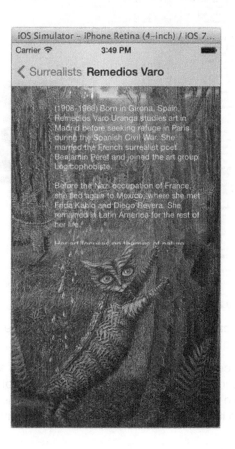

Figure 2-30. The first test of your app

Tap the button in the upper-left, and the second screen slides smoothly into view. (Don't worry if the placement of the buttons isn't ideal—you'll fix that shortly.) Scroll the text by dragging it with your mouse (remember that the mouse is your simulated finger). Tap the back button to return to the initial screen. Your app has all of the standard behavior of an iOS app: a touch interface, title bars, animation, navigation, and everything works exactly as you expect it to.

Finishing Your App

Return to the Xcode workspace window and click the Stop button in the toolbar to stop your app. Finish your app by repeating (most of) the steps in the section "Adding New Screens." Start by adding three more view controllers, as shown in Figure 2-31.

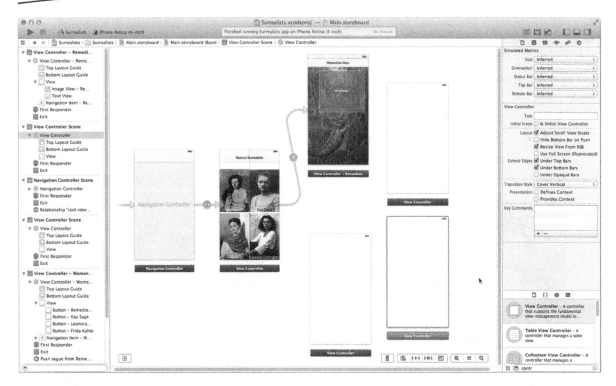

Figure 2-31. Adding the remaining view controllers

Into each new view controller, add an image view object and set its image resource name to one of the following (working clockwise): KaySage2, LeonoraCarrington2, and FridaKahlo2.

You could repeat all of the steps for adding and customizing a new text view for each of the three new images, or you could save yourself a lot of work by copying the work you've already done. While holding down the Option key, drag the UITextView object from the Remedios Varo scene and drop it into the Kay Sage scene, as shown in Figure 2-32. This gesture duplicates an object.

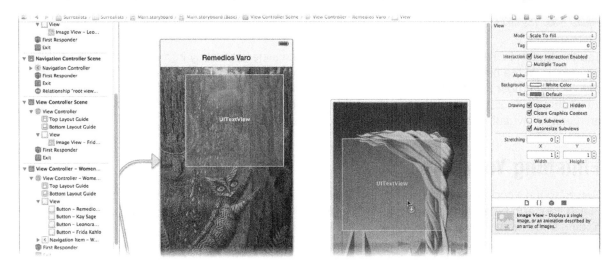

Figure 2-32. Replicating a text view object

Duplicating an object in Interface Builder creates a new object with all of the properties of the original. The only thing left to do is position it in the view and change its text. You'll find the text for the other three screens in the Surrealists (Resources) folder. When you get to the text view for Frida Kahlo, change the text color to black, so it's easier to read.

The last step is to create a push segue from each button to the appropriate view and set the title of its navigation bar. When you're done, you'll have a storyboard that looks like Figure 2-33.

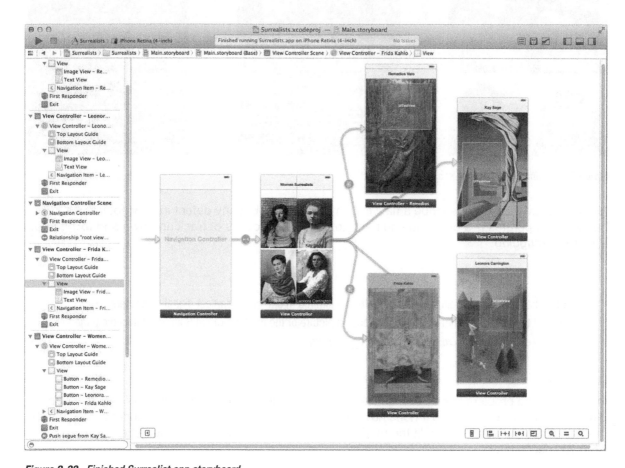

Figure 2-33. Finished Surrealist app storyboard

Debugging Your App

Run your new app. Tap a button to show the details for that artist. Browse the text and use the navigation bar to return to the initial screen. Return to Xcode. Stop the app and change the simulator to iPhone Retina (3.5–inch), and run it again. Does something seem out of sorts?

The buttons on the initial screen have odd gaps, and get cut off on the 3.5-inch iPhone. In other scenes, images and text views are also clipped, as shown in Figure 2-34. This is a problem. Programmers call it a bug.

 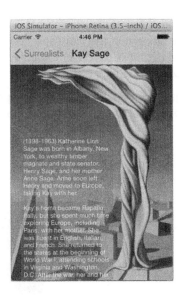 

Figure 2-34. Initial test of Surrealist app

"Bug" is usually used to describe a flaw in computer code, but any defect in how your app behaves or operates is a bug, and you need to fix it. The process of tracking down and fixing bugs is called *debugging*.

> **Note** The term "bug" originated from a moth that expired in one of the earliest digital computers, causing it to malfunction. I'm not kidding. There's a picture of the moth on Grace Hopper's Wikipedia page (http://en.wikipedia.org/wiki/Grace_hopper).

In this case, the problem has to do with how the buttons are resized, or repositioned, for different devices. Various models of the iPhone have different screen dimensions and resolutions. iOS adjusts the size of your screen views to fit the model that it's running on, which may alter the layout from what you see in Interface Builder.

Adding Constraints

When a view changes size, a feature called *auto-layout* repositions its subviews. Those subviews are repositioned based on a set of *constraints*. A constraint is simply a rule about an object. Here are some examples of constraints:

- the height of the object must be at least 40 pixels
- the bottom edge of the object should be 20 pixels from the bottom edge of its superview
- the object should be centered horizontally

There are often several such constraints for a single view. iOS evaluates all of the constraints to determine how each view should be adjusted so that all of the constraints are satisfied.

You can define individual constraints in Interface Builder or ask Xcode to generate some or all of them for you. Xcode creates constraints based on how you've positioned your view and its relationship with nearby views. Usually, Xcode's guess is exactly what you want. If it's not, you can define them yourself.

Your Surrealist app needs constraints so that the text and images in the four artist scenes resize properly on different devices; and you want the four buttons in the initial scene to evenly fill the screen. Start with the former, as those are the easiest.

Return to Xcode and the Main.storyboard file. Select the Kay Sage scene by clicking on the view controller object dock immediately below the scene, as shown in Figure 2-35. In the bottom right corner of the editor pane, click on the **Resolve Auto Layout Issues** button (the one with the dot in the middle), and choose the **Reset to Suggested Constraints in View Controller** item, also shown in Figure 2-35.

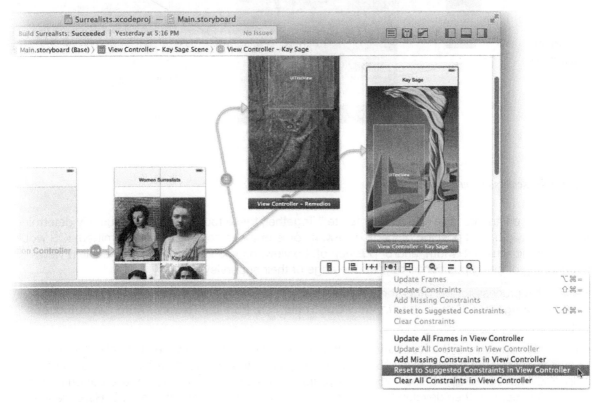

Figure 2-35. Using the suggested constraints

Xcode analyses the layout of your views in the scene and adds its recommended constraints to each one. Select the text view, and Interface Builder shows you the constraints now attached to that view, as shown in Figure 2-36. Xcode has added vertical and horizontal constraints that keep the text view positioned a pleasing distance from the top, left, and bottom edges of its superview, and a width constraint that determines its width. Click on a constraint to view, or edit, its properties in the attributes inspector, shown on the right in Figure 2-36.

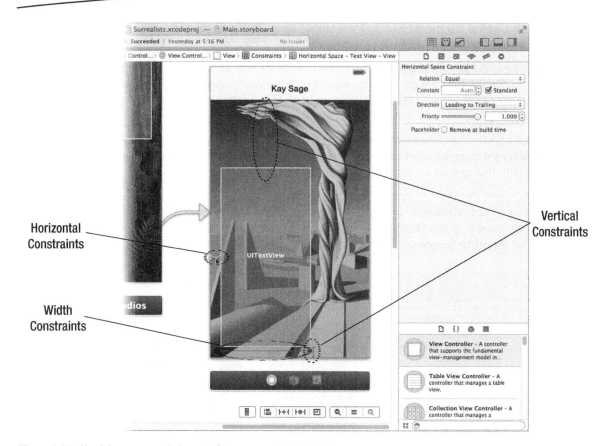

Figure 2-36. Xcode's recommended constraints

This set of constraints is said to be "complete." Together, these four rules unambiguously determine the height, width, and position of the text view. If some of these constraints were omitted, iOS would use the original height, width, and/or position of the view. As you've seen, this can result in views overlapping or being positioned beyond the edge of their superview.

Repeat this process for the other three scenes: select the scene's view controller and choose the **Reset to Suggested Constraints in View Controller** item from the **Resolve Auto Layout Issues** button.

The position and size of the four buttons in the initial scene are not, however, typical of the size or placement of button objects in iOS. Xcode's suggested constraints, therefore, won't be much help. You'll have to design these constraints yourself. Consider how you want these buttons sized and positioned, and then develop the simplest set of rules that describe that to iOS. Here are the constraints that I came up with:

> The top edges of the upper two buttons should be at the bottom edge of the navigation bar.
>
> The bottom edges of the lower two buttons should be at the bottom edge of the superview.

The left edges of the left two buttons should be at the left edge of the superview.

The right edges of the right two buttons should be at the right edge of the superview.

The buttons on the left should touch the buttons on the right.

The upper buttons should touch the lower buttons.

All of the buttons should be the same height and width.

> **Note** There are many ways to describe the same position for a view with constraints, none of which is wrong. For example, you can add both a leading edge and a trailing edge constraint for a view. This will define the horizontal position *and* width of the view. Alternatively, you could add a trailing edge constraint and a "center horizontally" constraint. Those also define the horizontal position and width of the view. Use the constraints that make sense to you.

That set of rules will position and size the four buttons so they completely fill the screen, creating four equal-sized quadrants. You add these constraints to Xcode just as they are described here. Start with the first constraint. Either hold down the Control key and click, or right-click, the Remedios Varo button and drag up to the navigation bar area. Release the mouse button and choose **Top Space to Top Layout Guide**, as shown in Figure 2-37.

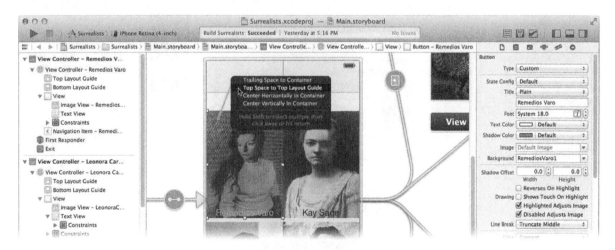

Figure 2-37. Adding a vertical constraint to a button

You've now created a constraint that tells iOS to position the top edge of the Remedios Varo button some distance from the bottom edge of the navigation bar. But you don't want it to be "some distance," you want it to touch the navigation bar. Click on the constraint to select it, as shown in Figure 2-38, and use the attributes inspector to set the constraint's value to 0. The constraint now says there should be no distance between the top edge of the button view and the bottom of the navigation bar.

Figure 2-38. Editing the properties of a constraint

Repeat this with the Kay Sage button. You've now established the first set of constraints. The next set is created just like the first. Control+click/right-click on the Frida Kahlo button, drag down, and choose the **Bottom Space To Bottom Layout** item from the menu, as shown in the middle of Figure 2-39. This sets the space between the bottom edge of the view and the bottom edge of its superview.

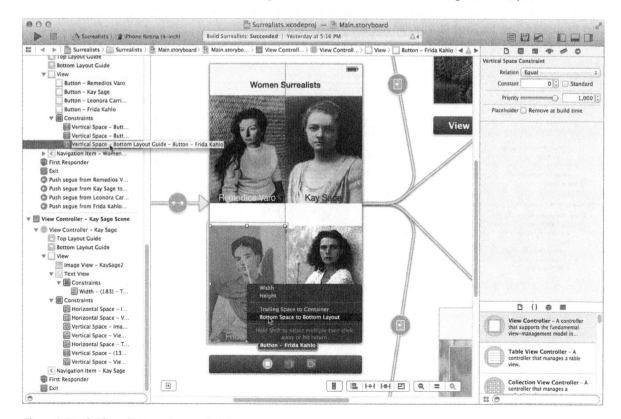

Figure 2-39. Setting a bottom edge constraint

Repeat with the Leonora Carrington button. Zero-width constraints are difficult to select, but you can select it in the object outline, as shown on the left in Figure 2-39. These buttons were already positioned at the bottom of the superview, so the constraint's value is already 0 (as shown on the right in Figure 2-39).

Continue adding constraints until you've defined them all:

1. With the two left buttons: control+click/right-click on the button, drag left, and choose **Leading Space to Container**.

2. With the two right buttons: control+click/right-click on the button, drag right, and choose **Trailing Space to Container**.

3. With the two left buttons: control+click/right-click on the button, drag to the button on its right, and choose **Horizontal Spacing**. Make sure the constraint's value is 0, meaning the right edge of the left view should touch the left edge of the right view.

4. With the two upper buttons: control+click/right-click on the button, drag down to the button below it, and choose **Horizontal Spacing**. There's probably a gap between the two buttons, so select the constraint and set its value to 0 in the attributes inspector.

5. Again with the two upper buttons: control+click/right-click on the button, drag down to the button below it, and choose **Equal Height**. This constraint says that the height of the upper button should be the same as the lower button.

> **Tip** You can also add just the constraints you want and let Xcode fill in the remaining ones using the **Add Missing Constraints** commands in the **Resolve Auto Layout Issues** menu. If you add enough constraints so that Xcode can guess the rest, this will save you time.

The constraints for the buttons on the initial screen are now complete. The only solution to the set of constraints you just created must position the four buttons so they are all the same size and fill the screen. The current size and position of the buttons do not, however, agree with those constraints and Xcode indicates this with adjustment warnings (those little orange numbers), as shown in Figure 2-40.

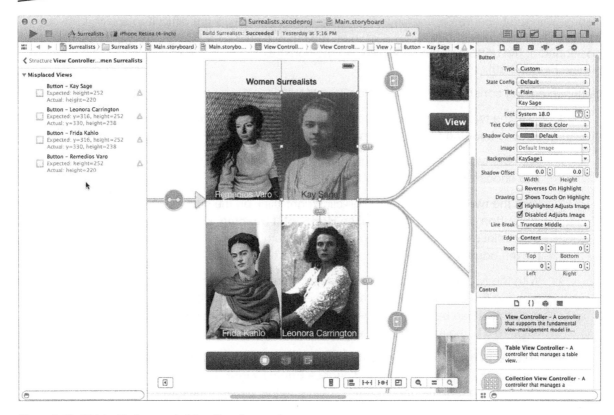

Figure 2-40. Finished button constraints with resize warnings

The warnings are telling you that iOS will resize or move the view by the displayed amount when your app runs. You can ignore the warnings if you like. But if you want your Interface Builder layout to look more like what your interface will be when it runs, adjust the position of your views so they agree with their constraints.

Xcode will do that for you. You can click on the warning arrow next to the view controller group in the outline. It will slide over to reveal the warnings for the views in that controller (shown on the left in Figure 2-40). From here, you can review and resolve each issue individually. Alternatively, choose the **Update All Frames in View Controller** item from the **Resolve Auto Layout Issues** button, as shown on the lower-right in Figure 2-41. Xcode adjusts the size and position of your views so the layout in Interface Builder agrees with the constraints.

CHAPTER 2: Boom! App   53

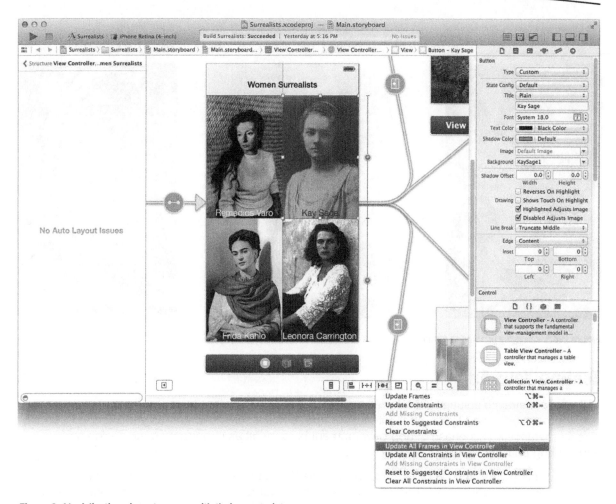

Figure 2-41. Adjusting views to agree with their constraints

Note If you have missing or conflicting constraints, these will also appear (in red) in the object outline.

Run your app, as shown in Figure 2-42. Compare these screens with those in Figure 2-34.

Figure 2-42. Correctly positioned buttons

Testing Your App

Will your constraints solution work for all devices? That's an excellent question. As part of your app development, you need to thoroughly test your app to make sure it works—as you intended—under all circumstances. This phase of app development is every bit as important as the design and engineering phases.

Start by testing your app on different devices. The iOS Simulator can simulate all available device form factors. Choose different hardware, as shown in Figure 2-43, to test how your app runs in other configurations. Some testing has to be done on real hardware, and you'll explore that in later chapters.

Figure 2-43. Testing different hardware configurations

This is a pretty simple app, but there are still a number of things you'll want to test before pronouncing it finished:

- See that the layout of all screens looks pleasing on different devices
- Make sure each button segues to the correct screen
- Test that the text is correct and can be scrolled
- Check all of the titles

Does everything check out? Then your first iOS app is a success!

Summary

Give yourself a round of applause; you've covered a lot of ground in this chapter. You've learned your way around Xcode, added resources to a project, and used Interface Builder to create, configure, and connect the objects of your interface. And, you did that all without writing a single line of computer code.

The point of this chapter wasn't to avoid writing Objective-C code. We are, after all, computer programmers. If we're not writing code, what are we getting paid for? The point was to illustrate how much functionality you can add, and how much tedious detail you can avoid, using Interface Builder and iOS objects.

Are your coding fingers itchy? In the next chapter you'll write a more traditional app—one with code.

Chapter 3

Spin a Web

Warm up your coding fingers. This chapter will introduce you to some of the core skills of iOS app development, along with a healthy dose of Objective-C code. The app you'll create in this chapter, and the steps you'll take, are very typical of the way iOS apps are built. From that perspective, this will be your first "real" iOS app.

You've already learned to use Interface Builder to add library objects to your app, customize them, and connect them together. In this chapter you will also:

- Customize an Objective-C class
- Add outlets and actions to your custom class using Objective-C
- Connect those outlets to objects using Interface Builder
- Connect objects to your custom actions using Interface Builder
- Alter the behavior of a library object by connecting it to a delegate

The app you're going to build is an URL shortening app. This app relies on one of the many URL shortening services available. These take an URL of any length and generate a much shorter URL, which is far more convenient to read, recite over the phone, and use in a Tweet. An URL shortening service works by remembering the original URL. When anyone in the world attempts to load the web page at the short URL, the service returns a *redirect* response, directing the browser to the original URL.

To make this app, you'll learn how to embed a web browser in it—a trick that has many applications. It will also show you how to programmatically send and receive an HTTP request from your app, a useful tool for creating apps that use Internet services.

> **Note** To computer programmers, the word "programmatically" means "by writing computer code." It means you accomplished something by writing instructions in a computer language, such as Objective-C, as opposed to any other way. For example, Interface Builder will let you connect two objects by dragging a line between those objects. You can write Objective-C code to connect those same two objects. If you used the latter method, you could say that you "set the connection programmatically."

Design

This app needs some basic elements. The user will need a field to type in, and edit, an URL. It would be nice to have a built-in web browser so they can see the page at that URL and tap links to go to other URLs. It needs a button to convert the long URL into a short one, and some place to display the shortened URL.

That's not a particularly complicated design, and everything should easily fit on one screen, like the sketch in Figure 3-1. Let's toss in one extra feature: a button to copy the shortened URL to the iOS clipboard. Now the user has an easy way to paste the shortened URL into another app.

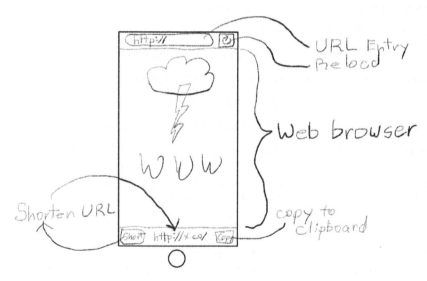

Figure 3-1. Sketch of Shorty app

Your app will run on all iOS devices, and work in both portrait and landscape orientation. Now that you have a basic design, it's time to launch Xcode and get started.

Creating the Project

As with any app, start by creating a new project in Xcode. This is a one-screen app, so the obvious choice is the `Single View Application` template.

Fill in the project details, as shown in Figure 3-2. Name the project Shorty, set the Class Prefix to SU (for "Short URL"), and set the Devices to Universal.

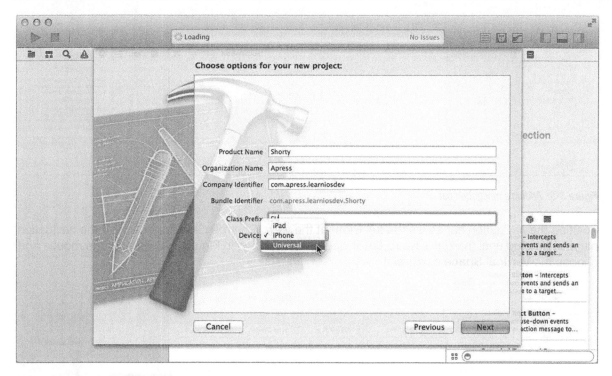

Figure 3-2. Shorty project details

Click the **Next** button. Choose a location to save your new project, and click **Save**.

Building a Web Browser

Start by building the web browser portion of your app. This will consist of a text field, where the user enters the URL they want to visit/convert, and a web view that will display that page. Let's also throw in a refresh button, to reload that page at the current URL.

Select the Main_iPhone.storyboard file in the navigator. Start by developing your app for the iPhone. You'll create the iPad version later in the chapter.

In the object library, find the Navigation Bar object and drag it into the view, towards the top, as shown in Figure 3-3. Navigation bar objects are normally created by navigation controllers to display a title, a back button, and so on. You saw this in the Surrealist app. Here, however, you're going to use one on its own.

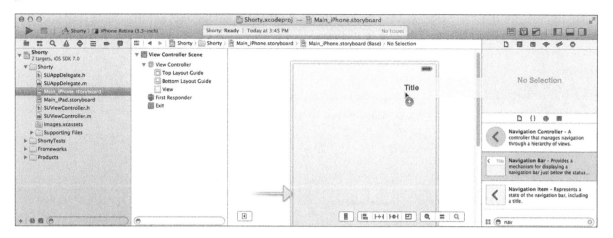

Figure 3-3. Adding a navigation bar

Position the navigation bar so it's the full width of the view. Control+click/right-click on the navigation bar and drag up until the Top Layout Guide appears, as shown in Figure 3-4. Release the mouse and choose the **Vertical Space** constraint.

Figure 3-4. Adding a vertical constraint to the navigation bar

Just as you did in the previous chapter, select the constraint and set its value to 0, as shown in Figure 3-5. This tells iOS to position the navigation bar at the recommended position at the top of the screen, just below the system's status bar.

Figure 3-5. Constraining the toolbar to the top layout guide

Find the Web View object in the library, and drag one into the lower portion of the screen. Move and resize the web view so it exactly fills the rest of the view, from the navigation bar to the bottom of the screen, as shown in Figure 3-6.

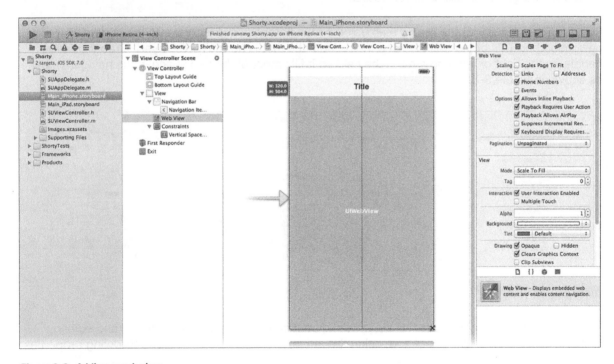

Figure 3-6. Adding a web view

Select the view controller (by clicking on either the object dock below the view or the View Controller object in the outline) and choose **Add Missing Constraints in View Controller** from the **Resolve Auto Layout Issues** button. Interface Builder uses the one constraint you established and fills in any additional constraints needed to establish this layout for all devices.

Find the Bar Button Item in the library and drag one into the right side of the navigation bar. Bar button items are button objects specifically designed to be placed in a navigation bar or toolbar. Once there, select it. Switch to the attributes inspector and change the Identifier of the new button to Refresh (see Figure 3-7). The icon of the button will change to a circular arrow.

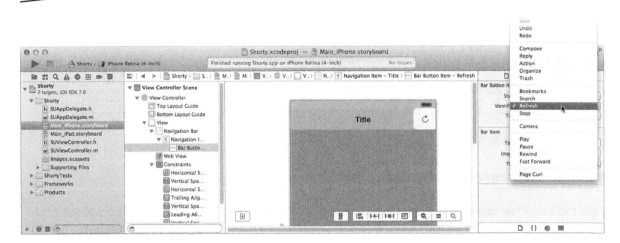

Figure 3-7. Making a refresh button in the navigation bar

Find the Text Field (not the Text View!) object in the library, and drag one into the middle of the navigation bar. This object will displace the default title that is normally displayed. Grab the resize handle on the right or left, and stretch the field so it fills most of the free space in the navigation bar, as shown in Figure 3-8.

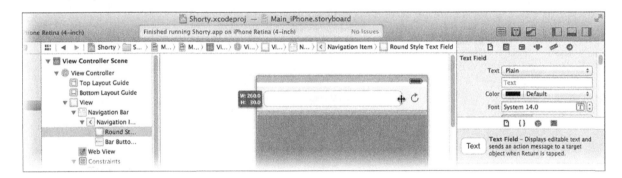

Figure 3-8. Resizing the URL field

The user will type their URL into this field. Configure it so it is optimized for entering and editing URLs. Select the text field object and, using the attributes inspector, change the following properties:

- Set text to http://
- Set Placeholder to http://
- Change Clear Button to Appears while editing
- Change Correction to No
- Change Keyboard to URL
- Change Return Key to Go

These settings set the initial content of the field to http:// (so the user doesn't have to type that), and if they clear the field, a ghostly http:// will prompt them to enter a web URL. Turning spelling correction off is appropriate (URLs are not a spoken language). When the keyboard appears, it will be optimized for URL entry, and the return key of the keyboard will display the word "Go," indicating that the URL will load when they tap it.

You've created, and laid out, all of the visual elements of your web browser. Now you need to write a little code to connect those pieces and make them work together.

Coding a Web Browser

Select the SUViewController.h file in the project navigator (see Figure 3-9). The SUViewController.h and SUViewController.m files, together, define the SUViewController class. This is a custom class, which you created—well, technically, it was created on your behalf by the project template, but you can take credit for it. I won't tell anyone. The job of your SUViewController object is to add functionality to, and manage the interactions of, the view objects it's connected to. Your app only has one view, so you only need one view controller.

Figure 3-9. Adding properties to SUViewController.h

Different objects have different roles to play in your app. These roles are explained in Chapter 8. When you add code to your app, you need to decide what class to add it to. This app is very simple; you'll add all of your customizations to the SUViewController class.

> **Tip** Are the terms *class* and *object* confusing? Read the first part of Chapter 6 for an explanation.

The SUViewController class is a subclass of the UIViewController class, which is defined by the Cocoa Touch framework. This means that your SUViewController class inherits all of the features and behavior of a UIViewController—which is a lot, UIViewController is quite sophisticated. If you did nothing else, your SUViewController objects would behave exactly like any other UIViewController object.

The fun is in editing SUViewController.h and SUViewController.m to add new features, or change the behavior it inherited.

Adding Outlets to SUViewController

Start by adding two new properties to SUViewController. A *property* defines a value associated with an object. In its simplest form, it merely creates a new variable that the object will remember. Add these properties to SUViewController.h:

```
@property (weak,nonatomic) IBOutlet UITextField *urlField;
@property (weak,nonatomic) IBOutlet UIWebView *webView;
```

When you're done, your class definition should look like the one in Figure 3-9. So, what does all this mean? Let's examine these declarations in detail:

- @property is the keyword that tells the Objective-C compiler this is a property declaration.
- (weak,nonatomic) are optional *property attributes*. These change certain characteristics of the property. weak means this property does not hang on to the object it's connected to (see Chapter 21). nonatomic makes accessing this property more efficient by relaxing certain rules with respect to multi-tasking (see Chapter 24).
- IBOutlet is a very important keyword that makes this property appear as an outlet in Interface Builder.
- UITextField*/UIWebView* is the *type* of the property. In this case, it's the class of the object this property stores. The asterisk means this property is a reference to an object, not the object itself. In Objective-C, you can only store references to objects.
- urlField/webBrowser is the *name* of the property.

By adding these properties to SUViewController, you enable an SUViewController object to be directly connected to one text field object (via its urlField property) and one web view object (via its webBrowser property).

You've defined the potential for being connected to two other objects, but you haven't connected them. For that, you'll use Interface Builder.

Connecting Custom Outlets

Click on the Main_iPhone.storyboard file in the project navigator. Find, and select, the View Controller object in the outline or in the dock below the view, both shown in Figure 3-10.

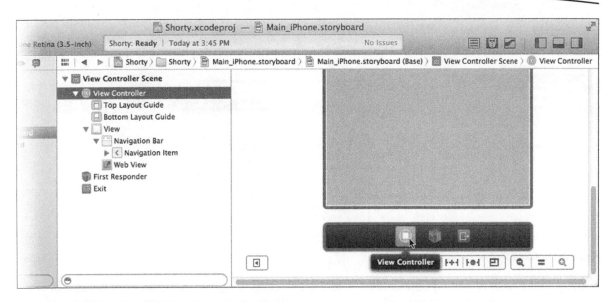

Figure 3-10. Selecting the View Controller object for a scene

In most cases, a screen in iOS starts out as just a single view controller object. When it's time for that view to appear on the screen, the view controller loads its view objects from an Interface Builder file—either a scene in a `.storyboard` file or from an `.xib` file. In this app, your `SUViewController` object will load the `SUViewController` scene in the `Main_iPhone.storyboard` file, creating all the objects and connections therein. Connections between objects and the view controller will be made between the new objects and the existing controller object. Once the scene file is loaded, the connected properties of the controller now refer to the objects created by the Interface Builder file.

> **Note** Don't worry if you don't get this concept right away. Interface Builder is very elegant and simple, but it takes most people a while to fully grasp how it works. Check out Chapter 15 for an in-depth explanation of how Interface Builder works its magic.

You've created the objects, and now you're going to connect them together. Show the connections inspector. In it, you'll see the `urlField` and `webView` properties you just added to `SUViewController.h`. These appear in Interface Builder because you included the `IBOutlet` keyword in your `@property` declaration.

Drag the connection circle to the right of the `urlField` and connect it to the text field object in the navigation bar, as shown in Figure 3-11. Now, when the `SUViewController` scene is loaded, the `urlField` property of your `SUViewController` object will refer (point) to the text field object in your interface. Pretty cool, huh?

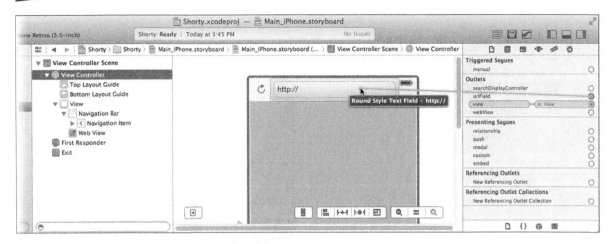

Figure 3-11. *Connecting an owner object outlet*

Another handy way of setting connections is to control+drag or right-click+drag from the object with the connection to the object you want it connected to. Holding down the control key, click the View Controller object and connect it to the web view object, as shown in Figure 3-12.

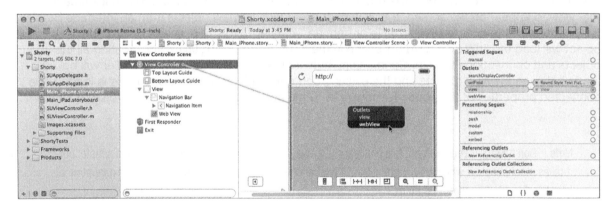

Figure 3-12. *Connecting the web view outlet*

When you release the mouse button, a pop-up menu will appear asking you to choose which outlet to set. Choose webView.

Adding Actions to SUViewController

So why did you do all of this (creating outlet properties and connecting them in Interface Builder)? Your controller object needs to get the value of the URL typed by the user and communicate that to the web view object, so the web view knows what URL to load. Your SUViewController is acting as a liaison or manager, getting data from one object (the text field) and assigning tasks to another (the web view). Do you see now why it's called a controller?

It's a simple task, but there has to be some code that will make it happen. Select the SUViewController.m file in the project navigator and switch to the assistant editor view, as shown in Figure 3-13.

Figure 3-13. Assistant view of SUViewControler.m and SUViewController.h

The assistant editor view shows both sides of your SUViewController class. On the left is its @implementation (in the .m file), and on the right is its @interface (in the .h file). A class's interface describes what an object does. Its implementation defines how it does it.

> **Tip** If the right side of the assistant editor isn't showing the SUViewController.h file, choose *Counterparts* from the navigation menu just above the editing pane, as shown in Figure 3-13.

The code you write to accomplish things goes in the .m (implementation) file, where you give each task a method name. In the .h (interface) file you then declare the names of those methods and properties that other objects need to use your object. This is how objects encapsulate, or hide, the details of what they do. This makes them simpler to use, just as a complicated device (like an iPod) hides the details of how it works behind an easy-to-use interface. The entire iOS is written this way. In fact, the Cocoa Touch software development kit (SDK) is mostly the .h files that Apple wrote to make iOS work. Apple gives you the .h files, so you know how to use any object in iOS, while the .m files—the part with the actual code—stays locked away in Cupertino.

In the SUViewController.m file, you see that two methods (-viewDidLoad and -didReceiveMemoryWarning) already exist. Between those and the @end statement, add this new method:

```
- (IBAction)loadLocation:(id)sender
{
    NSString *urlText = self.urlField.text;

    if (![urlText hasPrefix:@"http:"] && ![urlText hasPrefix:@"https:"]) {
        if (![urlText hasPrefix:@"//"])
```

```
            urlText = [@"//" stringByAppendingString:urlText];
        urlText = [@"http:" stringByAppendingString:urlText];
    }

    NSURL *url = [NSURL URLWithString:urlText];

    [self.webView loadRequest:[NSURLRequest requestWithURL:url]];
}
```

This method does one simple task: load the web page at the URL entered by the user. This will require three basic steps:

1. Get the string of characters the user typed into the text field
2. Convert that string of characters into an URL object
3. Request that the web view object load the page at that URL

Here's the breakdown of this code.

```
NSString *urlText = self.urlField.text;
```

The first line declares a new string object variable, named urlText, and assigns it the value of the text property of the urlField property of this object. The self keyword refers to this object (SUViewController). The urlField property is the one you just added to this class. Your urlField refers to a UITextField object, and a UITextField object has a text property that contains the characters currently in the field—either ones the user typed or those you put there programmatically. (See, I used the word "programmatically" again.)

> **Tip** To see the documentation for any class or constant, hold down the option key and single-click (quick view) or double-click (full documentation) on its name. To see the properties and methods of the UITextField class, hold down the option key and double-click the word UITextField in the .h file.

Part one of your task is already accomplished; you've retrieved the text of the URL using the urlField property you defined and connected. The next few lines might look a little strange.

```
if (![urlText hasPrefix:@"http:"] && ![urlText hasPrefix:@"https:"]) {
    if (![urlText hasPrefix:@"//"])
        urlText = [@"//" stringByAppendingString:urlText];
    urlText = [@"http:" stringByAppendingString:urlText];
}
```

If you're comfortable with Objective-C, take a close look at this code. It isn't critical to your app; you could leave it out, and your app would still work. It does, however, perform a kindness for your users. It checks to see if the string the user typed in starts with http:// or https://, the standard protocols for a web page. If these standard URL elements are missing, this code inserts one automatically.

Computers tend to be literal, but you want your app to be forgiving and friendly. The above code allows the user the type in just www.apple.com (for example), instead of the correct http://www.apple.com, and the page will still load. Does that make sense? Let's move on.

Object-oriented programming is all about encapsulating the complexity of things in objects. While a string object can represent the characters of an URL, it's still just a string (an array of characters). Most methods that work with URLs expect an URL object. In Cocoa Touch, the class of URL objects is NSURL. How do you turn the NSString object you got from the text field into an NSURL object you can use with the web view? I thought you'd never ask.

```
NSURL *url = [NSURL URLWithString:urlText];
```

This line of code asks the NSURL class to create a new URL object from a string object. The string object you pass to the +URLWithString method is the urlText reference you got in the first line. A reference to the new URL object is returned and stored in the new url variable. As you can see, it's pretty easy to convert a string object into an URL object, and there are methods that convert the other way too, which you'll use later in this chapter.

With the second step accomplished, the last thing left to do is display the web page at that URL in the web view. That's accomplished with the last line in your method:

```
[self.webView loadRequest:[NSURLRequest requestWithURL:url]];
```

self.webView is the webView property you created earlier, and it's connected to the web view object on the screen. You send that object a -loadRequest: message to load the page. It turns out, however, that a web view needs an URL request (NSURLRequest) object, not just a simple URL object. An URL request represents not just an URL, but also describes how that URL should be transmitted over the network. For your purposes, a plain-vanilla HTTP GET request is all you need, and the expression [NSURLRequest requestWithURL:url] asks the NSURLRequest class to create you a simple URL request from the given URL, which you pass on to -loadRequest:. The rest of the work is done by the web view.

Setting Action Connections

Let's review what you've accomplished so far. You have:

- created a text field object where the user can type in an URL
- created a web view object that will display the web page at that URL
- added two outlets (properties) to your SUViewController class
- connected the text field and web view object to those properties
- wrote a -loadLocation: method that takes the URL in the text view and loads it in the web view

What's missing? The question is "how does the -loadLocation: method get invoked?" That's a really important question and, at the moment, the answer is "never." The next, and final, step is to connect the -loadLocation: method to something so it runs and loads the web page.

Start by declaring the -loadLocation: method in SUViewController's interface. Add the following line, just before the @end statement, to your SUViewController.h file:

- (IBAction)loadLocation:(id)sender;

When you're done, your files should look like those in Figure 3-14. This declaration tells the rest of the world—well, the other objects in your app—that SUViewController has a method that will load a web page. The IBAction keyword tells Interface Builder that this is a method that can be connected to an object, just as the IBOutlet keyword told Interface Builder that the property was a connectable outlet. A method that can be connected to objects (like buttons and text fields) in your interface is called an *action*.

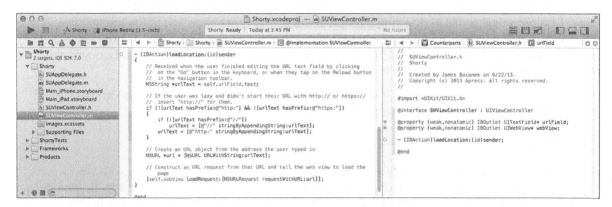

Figure 3-14. Finished -loadLocation: action

Click on the Main_iPhone.storyboard file again. Select the text field object and switch to the connections inspector. Scroll down until you find Did End On Exit in the Sent Events section. Drag the connection circle to the View Controller object and release the mouse, as shown in Figure 3-15. A pop-up menu will ask you what action you want this event connected to; choose -loadLocation: (which is currently the only action).

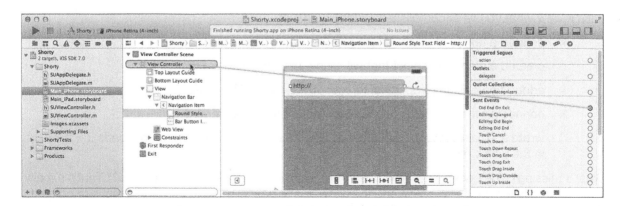

Figure 3-15. Setting the Did End On Exit action connection

You also want the web page loaded when the user taps the refresh button, so connect the refresh button to the same action. The refresh button is simpler than the text field, and only sends one kind of event ("I was tapped"). Use an Interface Builder shortcut to connect it. Hold down the control key, click on the refresh button, and drag the connection to the View Controller object. Release the mouse button and select the -loadLocation: action, as shown in Figure 3-16.

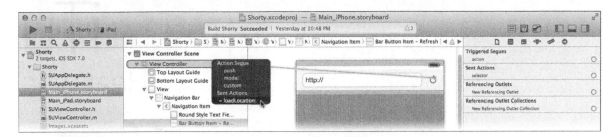

Figure 3-16. Setting the action for the refresh button

Testing the Web Browser

Are you excited? You should be. You just wrote a web browser app for iOS! Make sure the build destination is set to an iPhone Simulator (see Figure 3-17) and click on the **Run** button.

Figure 3-17. Setting iPhone Simulator destination

Your app will build and launch in the iPhone simulator, as shown on the left in Figure 3-18. Tap the text field and an URL-optimized keyboard appears. Tap out an URL (I'm using www.apple.com for this example), and tap the Go button. The keyboard retracts and Apple's home page appears in the web view. That's pretty darn nifty.

Figure 3-18. Testing Your Web Browser

So how does it work? The text field object fires a variety of events, depending on what's happening to it. You connected the `Did End On Exit` event to your `-loadLocation:` action. This event is sent when the user "ends" editing, by tapping the action button in the keyboard (Go). When you ran the app and tapped Go, the text field triggered its `Did End On Exit` event, which sent your `SUViewController` object a `-loadLocation:` message. Your method got the URL the user typed in and told the web view to load it. Voila! The web page appears.

> **Note** The iOS simulator uses your computer's Internet connection to emulate the device's Wi-Fi or cellular data connection. If you're working through this chapter on a desert island, your app might not work.

Debugging the Web View

What you've developed so far is pretty impressive. Go ahead, try any web page, I'll wait. There are only two things about it that bother me. First, when you tap a link in the page the URL in the text field doesn't change. Secondly, the web pages are crazy big.

The second problem is easy to fix. Quit the simulator, or switch back to Xcode and click the Stop button in the toolbar. Select the web view object in Interface Builder and switch to the attributes inspector, as shown in Figure 3-19. Find and check the `Scale Page to Fit` option. Now, when the web view loads a page, it will zoom the page so you can see the whole thing.

Figure 3-19. Setting Scale Page to Fit property

The first problem is a little trickier to solve, and requires some more code. We'll address that one as you add the rest of the functionality to your app.

Adding URL Shortening

You now have an app that lets you enter an URL and browse that URL in a web browser. The next step, and the whole purpose of this app, is to convert the long URL of that page into a short one.

To accomplish that, you'll create and layout new visual objects in Interface Builder, create outlets and actions in your controller class, and connect those outlets and actions to the visual object, just as you did in the first part of this chapter. If you haven't guessed by now, this is the fundamental app development workflow: design an interface, write code, and connect the two.

Start by fleshing out the rest of the interface. Edit Main_iPhone.storyboard, select the web view object, grab its bottom resizing handle, and drag it up to make room for some new view objects at the bottom of the screen, as shown in Figure 3-20. Select the vertical constraint beneath the view (also shown in Figure 3-17) and delete it. You no longer want the bottom edge of the web view to be at the bottom edge of the superview; you now want it to snuggle up to the toolbar view, which you'll add in a moment.

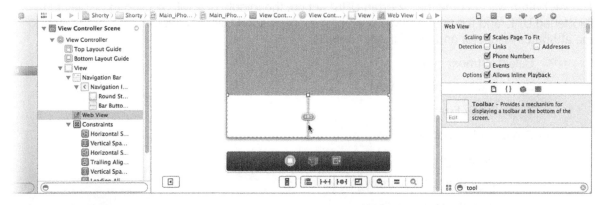

Figure 3-20. Making room for new views

In the library, find the `Toolbar` object (not a `Navigation Bar` object, they look similar) and drag it into the view, as shown in Figure 3-21. Position it so it fits snugly at the bottom of the view.

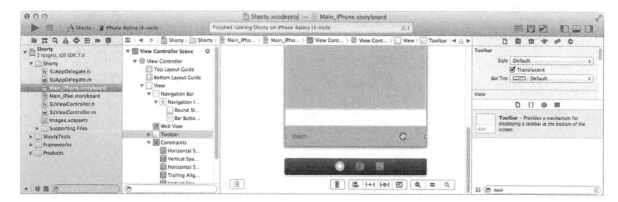

Figure 3-21. Adding a toolbar

Find the `Bar Button Item` in the library and add toolbar button objects to the toolbar, as shown in Figure 3-22, until you have three buttons.

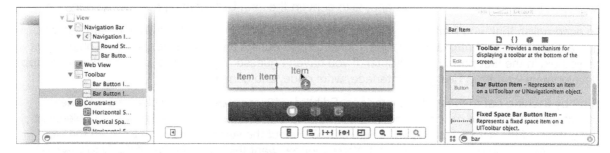

Figure 3-22. Adding additional button objects to the toolbar

You're going to customize the look of the three buttons to prepare them for their roles in your app. The left button will become the "shorten URL" action, the middle one will be used to display the shortened URL, and the right one will become the "copy short URL to clipboard" action. Switch to the attributes inspector and make these changes:

- Select leftmost button
    - change identifier to `Play`
    - uncheck Enabled
- Select middle button
    - set style to `Plain`
    - change title to "Tap arrow to shorten"
    - change tint to `Black Color`

- Select the rightmost button
  - change title to "Copy"
  - uncheck Enabled

Now select and resize the web view, so it touches the new toolbar. Finish the layout by choosing **Add Missing Constraints in View Controller** from the **Resolve Auto Layout Issues** button. The final layout should look like Figure 3-23.

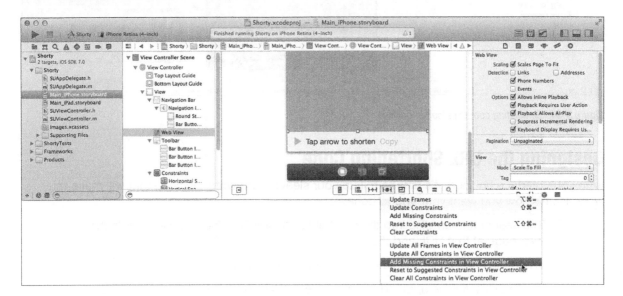

Figure 3-23. Finished interface

Just like before, you'll need to add three outlets to the SUViewController class so your object has access to these three buttons. Select the SUViewController.h file in the project navigator, and add these three declarations:

```
@property (weak,nonatomic) IBOutlet UIBarButtonItem *shortenButton;
@property (weak,nonatomic) IBOutlet UIBarButtonItem *shortLabel;
@property (weak,nonatomic) IBOutlet UIBarButtonItem *clipboardButton;
```

Select the Main_iPhone.storyboard Interface Builder file, select the View Controller object, and switch to the connections inspector. The three new outlets will appear in the inspector. Connect the shortenButton outlet to the left button, the shortLabel outlet to the middle button, and the clipboardButton to the right button, as shown in Figure 3-24.

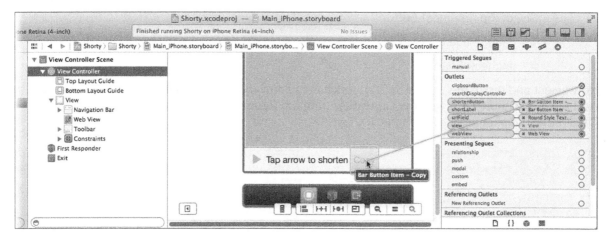

Figure 3-24. Connecting outlets to toolbar buttons

Designing the URL Shortening Code

With your interface finished, it's time to roll up your sleeves and write the code that will make this work. Here's how you want your app to behave:

- The user enters an URL into the text field and taps Go. The web view loads the web page at that URL and displays it.
- When the page is successfully loaded, two things happen:
  - The URL field is updated to reflect the actual URL loaded.
  - The "shorten URL" button is enabled, allowing the user to tap on it.
- When the user taps the "shorten URL" button, a request is sent to the URL shortening service.
- When the URL shortening service sends its response, two things happen:
  - The shortened URL is displayed in the toolbar.
  - The "copy to clipboard" button is enabled, allowing the user to tap on it.
- When the user taps on the "copy to clipboard" button, the short URL is copied to the iOS clipboard.

You can already see how most of this is going to work. The "shorten URL" and "copy to clipboard" button objects will be connected to actions that perform those functions. The outlets you just created will allow your code to alter their state, such as enabling the buttons when they're ready.

The pieces in between these steps are a little more mysterious. The "When the page is successfully loaded" makes sense, but how does your app learn when the web page has loaded, or if it was successful? The same it true with the "when the URL shortening service sends its response." When does that happen? The answer to these questions is found in multitasking and delegates.

"Multi-what" you ask? *Multitasking* is doing more than one thing at a time. Usually, the code you write does one thing at a time, and doesn't perform the next thing until the first is finished. There are, however, techniques that enable your app to trigger a block of code that will execute in parallel, so that both blocks of code are running, more or less, concurrently. This is explained in more detail in Chapter 24. You've already done this in your app, probably without realizing it:

```
[self.webView loadRequest:[NSURLRequest requestWithURL:url]];
```

The -loadRequest: message you sent the web view object didn't load the URL; it simply *starts the process* of loading the URL. The call to this method returns immediately and your code continues on, doing other things. This is called an *asynchronous* method. One of those things you want to keep doing is responding to user touches—something that's covered in Chapter 4. This is important, because it keeps your app responsive.

Meanwhile, code that's part of the UIWebView class started running on its own, quietly sending requests to a web server, collecting and interpreting the responses, and ultimately displaying the rendered page in the web view. This is often referred to as a *background thread*, or *background task*, because it does its work silently, and independently, of your main app (called the *foreground thread*).

Becoming a Web View Delegate

All of this multitasking theory is great to know, but it still doesn't answer the question of how your app learns when a web page has, or has not, loaded. There are several ways tasks can communicate with one another. One of those ways is to use a *delegate*. A delegate is an object that agrees to undertake certain decisions or tasks for another object, or would like to be notified when certain events occur. It's this last aspect of delegates that you'll use in this app.

The web view class has a delegate outlet. You connect that to the object that's going to be its delegate. Delegates are a popular programming pattern in iOS. If you poke around the Cocoa Touch library, you'll see that a lot of classes have a delegate outlet. Chapter 6 covers delegates in some detail.

Becoming a delegate is a three-step process:

1. In your custom class, adopt the delegate's protocol.
2. Implement the appropriate protocol methods.
3. Connect the delegate outlet of the object to your delegate object.

A *protocol* is a contract, or promise, that your class will implement specific methods. This lets other objects know that your object has agreed to accept certain responsibilities. A protocol can declare two kinds of methods: *required* and *optional*. All required methods must be included in your class's implementation. If you leave any out, you've broken the contract, and your project won't compile.

It's up to you to decide which optional methods you implement. If you implement an optional method, your object will receive that message. If you don't, it won't. It's that simple. Most delegate methods are optional.

> **Tip** A few older classes rely on what is called an *informal protocol*. It really isn't a protocol at all, but a documented set of methods that your delegate is expected to implement. The documentation for the class will explain which you should use. All of the steps for using an informal protocol are the same, except that there's no formal protocol name to add to your class.

The first step is to decide what object will act as the delegate and adopt the appropriate protocol. Select your SUViewController.h file. Change the line that declares the class so it reads:

@interface SUViewController : UIViewController **<UIWebViewDelegate>**

The change is adding the <UIWebViewDelegate> to the end of the class declaration, between less than and greater than symbols, sometimes referred to as "angled brackets." Adding this to your class definition means that your class agrees to handle messages listed in the UIWebViewDelegate protocol, and is prepared to be connected to a UIWebView's delegate outlet.

Looking up the UIWebViewDelegate protocol, you find that it lists four methods, all of which are optional:

```
- (BOOL)webView:(UIWebView *)webView
    shouldStartLoadWithRequest:(NSURLRequest *)request
    navigationType:(UIWebViewNavigationType)navigationType;
- (void)webViewDidStartLoad:(UIWebView *)webView;
- (void)webViewDidFinishLoad:(UIWebView *)webView;
- (void)webView:(UIWebView *)webView didFailLoadWithError:(NSError *)error;
```

The first method, -webView:shouldStartLoadingWithRequest:navigationType:, is sent to the delegate whenever the user taps on a link. It allows your delegate to decide if that link should be taken. You could, for example, create a web browser that kept the user on a particular site, like a school calendar. Your delegate could block any link that took the user to another site, or maybe just warn them that they were leaving. This app doesn't need to do anything like that, so just ignore this method. By not implementing this method, the web view will let the user tap, and follow, any link they want.

The next three methods are the ones you're interested in. -webViewDidStartLoad: is sent to your delegate when a web page begins to load. -webViewDidFinishLoad: is sent when it's finished. And finally, -webView:didFailLoadWithError: is sent if the page could not be loaded for some reason.

You want to implement all three of these methods. Get started with the first one. Select your SUViewController.m (the implementation) file, and find a place to add this method:

```
- (void)webViewDidStartLoad:(UIWebView *)webView
{
    self.shortenButton.enabled = NO;
}
```

When a web page begins to load, this method will disable (by setting the enabled property to NO), the button that shortens an URL. You do this simply so the short URL button can't be triggered between pages, and also we're not sure if the page can be loaded successfully yet. You'd like to limit the URL shortening to URLs you know are good.

Below that method, add this one:

```
- (void)webViewDidFinishLoad:(UIWebView *)webView
{
    self.shortenButton.enabled = YES;
    self.urlField.text = webView.request.URL.absoluteString;
}
```

This method is invoked after the web page is finished loading. The first line uses the shortenButton outlet you created earlier to enable the "shorten URL" button. So as soon as the web page loads, the button to convert it to a short URL becomes active.

The second line fixes up an issue I brought up earlier in the "Debugging" section. You want the URL in the text field at the top of the screen to reflect the page the user is looking at in the web view. This code keeps the two in sync. After a web page loads, this line digs into the webView object to find the URL that was actually loaded. The request property (an NSURLRequest) contains an URL property (an NSURL), which has a property named absoluteString. This property returns a plain string object (NSString) that describes the complete URL. In short, it turns an URL into a string, the reverse of what you did in -loadLocation:. The only thing left to do is to assign it to the text property of the urlField object, and the new URL appears in the text field.

The last method is received only if the web page couldn't be loaded. It is, ironically, the most complicated method because we want to take the time to tell the user why the page wasn't loaded—instead of just making them guess. Here's the code:

```
- (void)webView:(UIWebView *)webView didFailLoadWithError:(NSError *)error
{
    NSString *message = [NSString stringWithFormat:
                         @"A problem occurred trying to load this page: %@",
                         error.localizedDescription];
    UIAlertView *alert = [[UIAlertView alloc] initWithTitle:@"Could not load URL"
                                                    message:message
                                                   delegate:nil
                                          cancelButtonTitle:@"That's Sad"
                                          otherButtonTitles:nil];
    [alert show];
}
```

The first statement creates a message that says "A problem occurred…" and includes a description of the problem from the error object the web view sent along with this message. The next two statements create an alert view—a pop-up dialog—presenting the message to the user.

You've now done everything you need to make your SUViewController object a web view delegate, but it isn't a delegate yet. The last step is to connect the web view to it. Select the Main_iPhone.storyboard file. Holding down the control key, drag from the web view object and connect it to the View Controller. When you release the mouse button, choose the delegate outlet, as shown in Figure 3-25.

CHAPTER 3: Spin a Web

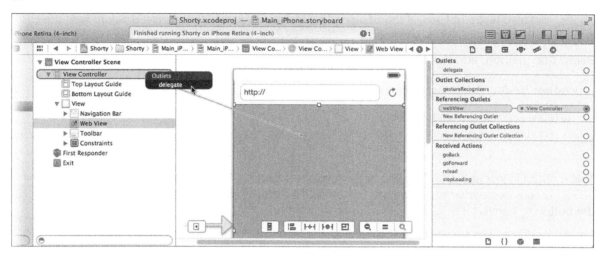

Figure 3-25. Connecting the web view delegate

Now your `SUViewController` object is the delegate for the web view. As the web view does its thing, your delegate receives messages on its progress. You can see this working in the simulator. Run your app, go to an URL (the example in Figure 3-26 uses `http://developer.apple.com`), and now follow a link or two in the web view. As each page loads, the URL in the text field is updated.

Figure 3-26. URL field following links

> **Tip** Also try loading an URL or two that can't be loaded by entering an invalid domain name or non-existing path, as shown in Figure 3-26. It's important to test how your app handles failure too.

Shortening an URL

You've finally arrived at the moment of truth: writing the code to shorten the URL. But first, let's review what has happened so far:

- The user has entered an URL and loaded it into a web view.
- When the web view loaded, it sent your `SUViewController` object a `-webViewDidFinishLoad:` message, where your code enabled the "shorten URL" button.

What you want to happen next is for the user to tap the "shorten URL" button and have the long URL be magically converted into a short one. That sounds like an action. Select your `SUViewController.m` file again and add this new method:

```
- (IBAction)shortenURL:
(id)sender
{
    NSString *urlToShorten = self.webView.request.URL.absoluteString;
    NSString *urlString = [NSString ↪
 stringWithFormat:@"http://api.x.co/Squeeze.svc/text/%@?url=%@",
                           kGoDaddyAccountKey,
                           [urlToShorten ↪
 stringByAddingPercentEscapesUsingEncoding:NSUTF8StringEncoding]];

    shortURLData = [NSMutableData new];

    NSURLRequest *request = [NSURLRequest requestWithURL:[NSURL ↪
URLWithString:urlString]];
    shortenURLConnection = [NSURLConnection connectionWithRequest:request
                                                         delegate:self];

    self.shortenButton.enabled = NO;
}
```

In `SUViewController.h`, also add this line (just before the `@end` statement):

```
- (IBAction)shortenURL:(id)sender;
```

This line declares the `-shortURL:` method to be an action and lets Interface Builder know that it can connect objects to it.

The `-shortenURL:` method sends a request to the X.co URL shortening service. iOS includes a number of classes that make complicated things—like sending and receiving an HTTP request to a web server—relatively easy to write.

> **X.CO URL SHORTENING SERVICE**
>
> I chose to use the X.co URL shortening service in this project for several reasons. First, the service is free. Second, it has a well-documented and straightforward API (Application Program Interface) that can be used by performing a simple HTTP request. Finally, it has some debugging and management features. The service lets you log in and see what URLs your app has shortened, which is useful while you're trying to debug it.
>
> The X.co service is provided by GoDaddy. To use X.co, go to the X.co web page and either create a free account or log in with your existing GoDaddy account (if you're already a customer). In your X.co account settings, you'll find an account key—a 32-character hexadecimal string—that uniquely identifies you to the X.co service. This key must be included in your requests. Once you have your key, add the following line to the beginning of your SUViewController.m file (just before the @implementation statement), replacing the dummy number between the quotes with your account key:
>
> `#define kGoDaddyAccountKey @"0123456789abcdef0123456789abcdef"`
>
> There are other URL shortening services out there, and you could easily adapt this app to use almost any of them. Some services, such as bitly, even offer an iOS SDK that you can download and include in your project!

The X.co services will accept an HTTP GET request that includes the URL to be shortened, and replies with a shortened URL. It's that simple. A GET request is particularly easy to construct, because all of the needed information is in the URL.

Writing -shortenURL:

Begin by constructing the URL. You'll need three pieces of information:

- The service request URL
- Your GoDaddy account key
- The long URL to shorten

The first piece of information is documented at the X.co web site. To convert a long URL into a short one, and have the service return the shortened URL as plain text, submit an URL with this format:

`http://api.x.co/Squeeze.svc/text/`**`<YourAccountKey>`**`?url=`**`<LongURL>`**

To construct this URL, you'll need the values for the two placeholders, <YourAccountKey> and <LongURL>. Get your account key from GoDaddy and use it to define the kGoDaddyAccountKey preprocessor macro (see the X.co URL Shortening Service sidebar).

The last bit of information you need is the URL to shorten. Start with that, just as you did in -webViewDidFinishLoad: method, and assign it to the urlToShorten variable:

`NSString *urlToShorten = self.webView.request.URL.absoluteString;`

The second line of code is the most complicated statement in your app. It constructs the entire URL using NSString's +stringWithFormat: method. The first parameter is the format string, or template, for the finished string object. The two %@ sequences in the format are replaced with the values of the next two parameters. The first is the kGoDaddyAccountKey constant you defined earlier, and the second is the URL you want shortened, currently residing in the urlToShorten variable.

Notice that the urlToShorten value isn't used directly. Instead, it is sent the -stringByAddingPercentEscapesUsingEncoding: message. This message replaces any characters that have special meaning in an URL with a character sequence that won't be confused for something important. The sidebar "URL String Encoding" explains why this is done and how it works.

URL STRING ENCODING

Computers, and thus computer programmers, deal with strings a lot. A string is a sequence of characters. Often, some characters in a string have special meaning. An URL can be represented as a string. Special characters separate the various parts of the URL. Here's a generic URL with the special characters in bold:

scheme**://**some.domain.net**/**path**?**param1**=**value1**&**param2**=**value2**#**anchor

The colon, forward slash, question mark, ampersand, equals, and pound sign (hash) characters all have special meaning in an URL: they're used to identify the various parts of the URL. All of the characters following the question mark are the query string portion of the URL. The ampersand character separates multiple name/value pairs. The fragment ID follows the pound sign character, and so on.

So how do you write an URL that has a question mark character in the path, or an ampersand character in one of the query string values? You can't write the following, it won't make any sense:

http://server.net/what?artcl?param=red&white

This is the problem you're faced with when sending an URL to the X.co service. The query string of your URL contains another URL—it's full of special characters, all of which have to be ignored. What you need is a way to write a character that normally has special meaning, without its special meaning. What you need is an escape sequence.

An *escape sequence* is a special sequence of characters used to represent a single character so it's treated like any other character, instead of something special. (Read that again until it makes sense.) URLs use the percent character (%) followed by two hexadecimal digits. When an URL sees a percent character followed by two hex digits, as in %63, it treats it as a single character, determined by the value of the two digits. Converting characters into escape sequences to preserve their values is call *encoding* a string.

The sequence %63 represents a single question mark character (?) and %38 means a single ampersand character (&). Now you can encode that pesky URL, and it will make sense to the recipient:

http://server.net/what**%63**artcl?param=red**%38**white

The -stringByAddingPercentEscapesUsingEncoding: method converts any characters that might be confusing to an URL and replaces them with escape sequences that mean the same character, but without any special meaning. Now you have a string you can safely append to the query portion of the URL without confusing anyone.

```
shortURLData = [NSMutableData new];
```

The third line of code might seem like a bit of a mystery. It sets an instance variable named shortURLData to a new, empty, NSMutableData object. Don't worry about it now. It will make sense soon.

The next line of code is very similar to what you used earlier to load a web page:

```
NSURLRequest *request = [NSURLRequest requestWithURL: 
  [NSURL URLWithString:urlString]];
```

Just like the web view, the NSURLConnection class (the class that will send the URL for us) needs an NSURLRequest. The NSURLRequest needs an NSURL. Working backwards, this line creates an NSURL from the URL string you just constructed, and uses that to create a new NSURLRequest object, saving the final results in the request variable.

The next statement is what does (almost) all of the work:

```
shortenURLConnection = [NSURLConnection connectionWithRequest:request
                                                     delegate:self];
```

NSURLConnection's +connectionWithRequest: creates a new NSURLConnection object and immediately starts the process of sending the requested URL. Just like the web view's -loadRequest: method, this is an asynchronous message—it simply starts a background task and returns immediately. And just like the web view, you supply a delegate object to receive messages about its progress, as they occur.

Unlike a web view, however, the delegate for an NSURLConnection is passed (programmatically) when you make the request. That's what the delegate:self part of the message does; it tells NSURLConnection to use this object (self) as the delegate.

What's that you say? You haven't made the SUViewController class an URL connection delegate? You're absolutely right, and that's not your only problem. Xcode is also complaining that the variables shortURLData and shortenURLConnection don't exist either, as shown in Figure 3-27. Start by fixing the missing variables.

Figure 3-27. Compiler errors in -shortenURL:

Adding Private Instance Variables

The missing variables needed to be added to your `SUViewController` class. When receiving the information from a remote service, a couple of pieces of information must be maintained while that happens. These are the `NSURLConnection` object, that's doing the work, and an `NSMutableData` object, that will collect the data sent back from the web server.

These variables, however, are not for public consumption; they don't need to be accessed by other objects, or connected in Interface Builder. Simply put, these are *private* variables. You create private variables by declaring them in the private interface of the `SUViewController`. Scroll to the beginning of the `SUViewController.m` file and find the `@interface SUViewController ()` section. Change it so it looks like this (new code in bold):

```
@interface SUViewController ()
{
    NSURLConnection *shortenURLConnection;
    NSMutableData *shortURLData;
}
@end
```

As soon as you add this, the warnings you saw in -shortenURL: will go away.

> **Tip** Another way of creating private variables is to add them to your public `@interface` `SUViewController` section in `SUViewController.h`, but precede them with a `@private` directive. Read all about `@private` and private interfaces in Chapter 20.

Becoming an NSURLConnection Delegate

You can now follow the same steps you took to make `SUViewController` a delegate of the web view, to turn it into an `NSURLConnection` delegate as well. There's no practical limit on how many objects your object can be a delegate for.

Step one is to adopt the protocols the make your class a delegate. `NSURLController` declares a couple of different delegate protocols, and you're free to adopt the ones that make sense to your app. In this case, you want to adopt the `NSURLConnectionDelegate` and `NSURLConnectionDataDelegate` protocols. Do this by adding those protocol names to your `SUViewController` class, in your `SUViewController.h` file, like this:

```
@interface SUViewController : UIViewController <UIWebViewDelegate,
                              NSURLConnectionDelegate,
                              NSURLConnectionDataDelegate>
```

The `NSURLConnectionDelegate` defines methods that get sent to your delegate when key events occur. There are a slew of messages that deal with how your app responds to authenticated content (files on the web server that are protected by an account name and password). None of that applies to this app. The only message you're interested in is -connection:didFailWithError:. That message is sent if the request fails for some reason. Open your SUViewController.m file and add this new method:

```
- (void)connection:(NSURLConnection *)connection 
  didFailWithError:(NSError *)error
{
    self.shortLabel.title = @"failed";
    self.clipboardButton.enabled = NO;
    self.shortenButton.enabled = YES;
}
```

It's unlikely that an URL shortening request would fail. The only likely cause would be that your iPhone has temporarily lost its Internet connection. Nevertheless, you want your app to behave itself, and do something intelligent, under all circumstances. This method handles a failure by doing three things:

- Sets the short URL label to "failed", indicating that something went wrong
- Disables the "copy to clipboard" button, because there's nothing to copy
- Turns the "shorten URL" button back on, so the user can try again

With the unlikely stuff taken care of, let's get to what should happen when you send a request. The NSURLConnectionDataDelegate protocol methods are primarily concerned with how your app gets the data returned from the server. It, too, defines a bunch of other methods you're not interested in. The two you are interested in are -connection:didReceiveData: and -connectionDidFinishLoading:. Start by adding this -connection:didReceiveData: method to your implementation:

```
- (void)connection:(NSURLConnection *)connection didReceiveData:(NSData *)data
{
    [shortURLData appendData:data];
}
```

The X.co service returns the shortened URL in the body of the HTTP response, as a simple string of ASCII characters. Your delegate object will receive a -connection:didReceiveData: message every time new body data has been received from the server. In this app, that's probably only going to be once, since the amount of data you're requesting is so small. If your app requested a lot of data (like an entire web page), this message would be sent multiple times.

The only thing this method does it take that data that was received (in the data parameter), and adds it to the buffer of data you're maintaining in shortURLData. Remember the shortURLData = [NSMutableData new]; statement back in -shortenURL:? That statement set up an empty buffer (NSMutableData) before the request was started. As you receive the answer to that request, it accumulates in your shortURLData variable. Does that all make sense? Let's move on to the final method.

The last method should be self-explanatory by now. The -connectionDidFinishLoading: message is sent when the transaction is complete: you've sent the URL request, received all of the data, and the whole thing was a success. Add this method to your implementation:

```
- (void)connectionDidFinishLoading:(NSURLConnection *)connection
{
    NSString *shortURLString = [[NSString alloc] initWithData:shortURLData
                                                     encoding:NSUTF8StringEncoding];
    self.shortLabel.title = shortURLString;
    self.clipboardButton.enabled = YES;
}
```

The first statement turns the ASCII bytes you received in -connection:didReceiveData: and turns them into a string object. String objects use Unicode character values, so turning a string of *bytes* into a string of *characters* requires a little conversion.

> **Tip** If you need to convert NSString objects to or from other forms, such as C strings or byte arrays, it would help to learn a little about Unicode characters. There's a great article for beginners, titled "The Absolute Minimum Every Software Developer Absolutely, Positively Must Know About Unicode and Character Sets (No Excuses!)" by Joel Spolsky at http://joelonsoftware.com/articles/Unicode.html.

The second line sets the title of the shortLabel toolbar button to the short URL you just received (and converted). This makes the short URL appear at the bottom of the screen.

The last step is to turn on the "copy to clipboard" button. Now that your app has a valid short URL, it has something to copy.

Testing The Service

You're almost ready to test your app, there's just one tiny detail to attend to first. You've written the code that sends the request to the X.co service, you've set up delegate methods to collect the data that comes back, and you've written code to deal with any problems. The only thing left to do is connect the "shorten URL" button in the interface to your -shortenURL: action, so all that happens when you tap the button.

Select the Main_iPhone.storyboard file. Holding down the control key, click on the "shorten URL" button and connect its action to the File's Owner. Release the mouse button and choose the -shortenURL: method, as shown in Figure 3-28.

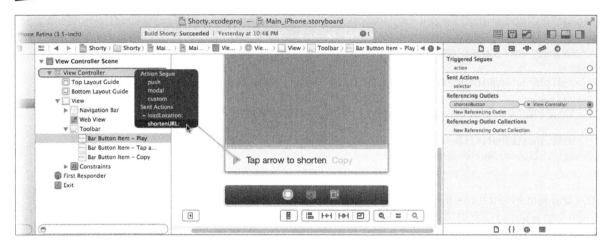

Figure 3-28. Connecting the "shorten URL" button

Run your app and enter an URL. In the example shown in Figure 3-25, I've entered http://www.apple.com. When the page loads, the "shorten URL" button becomes active. Tap on it and, within a second or two, a short URL to this page appears in the toolbar (on the right in Figure 3-29).

Figure 3-29. The Shorty app in action

This calls for a celebration! You've created a remarkably sophisticated app by leveraging the power of existing iOS classes, judiciously connecting the right objects together, and writing action and delegate methods to handle the details.

Final Touches

You're still not quite done. You've yet to write the action that copies the short URL to the system clipboard. Fortunately, that's not difficult to code either. In your SUViewController.m file, add this method:

```
- (IBAction)clipboardURL:(id)sender
{
    NSString *shortURLString = self.shortLabel.title;
    NSURL *shortURL = [NSURL URLWithString:shortURLString];
    [[UIPasteboard generalPasteboard] setURL:shortURL];
}
```

The first line gets the text of the URL from the shortLabel button that was set by -connectionDidFinishLoading:. The second line turns the text of the short URL into an URL object, just as you did in the -loadLocation: method you wrote at the beginning of the chapter. Finally, the [UIPasteboard generalPasteboard] method returns the system-wide pasteboard for "general" data—what most people think of as the clipboard. You send that pasteboard object the -setURL: message, passing it the URL object you just created. And almost as if by magic, the short URL is now on the clipboard.

In your SUViewController.h file, add this line:

```
- (IBAction)clipboardURL:(id)sender;
```

Now you can use Interface Builder to connect the "copy to clipboard" button to the -clipboardURL: method. Do this the same way you connected the "shorten URL" button (refer to Figure 3-24).

With everything hooked up, run your app again. You should get in the habit of running your app as you write it, testing each new feature and function as it is developed. In the simulator, go to an URL, and generate a shortened one, as shown on the left in Figure 3-30. Once you have a shortened URL, tap the Copy button.

Figure 3-30. Testing the clipboard

Tap in the text field again, and clear the field. Hold down your mouse (simulated finger) until the Paste pop-up button appears (middle in Figure 3-30). Tap the paste button, and the shortened URL will be pasted into the field, as shown on the right in Figure 3-30. This would also work with any other app that allows you to paste text.

As a final test, tap the Go button. The shortened URL will be sent to the x.co server, the server will redirect your browser back to the original URL, and the web page you started at will reappear in the browser, along with the original URL in the text field.

Cleaning Up the Interface

You app is fully functional, but there are still a few quirks in the interface. With the simulator still running, choose the Hardware ➤ Rotate Left command. This simulates turning the device 90° counter-clockwise, as shown in Figure 3-31. Most of it still looks OK, but the buttons in the bottom toolbar get squished over to the left, which looks cheesy.

Figure 3-31. Testing device rotation

Quit the simulator, change the project destination in the toolbar to iPad Simulator, and run your app again, this time on a simulated iPad (on the right in Figure 3-31). This is terrible! The iPad version doesn't show any interface at all!

That's because you haven't created one. All of your interface objects were created and connected in the Main_iPhone.storyboard file. As you are undoubtedly realizing, that's the Interface Builder file that gets loaded when your app runs on your iPhone. The Main_iPad.storyboard file is still empty. You'll take care of both of these problems in short order.

> **Note** There are some standard file suffixes (~ipad, ~iphone, and @2x) that the iOS resource loader (NSBundle) recognizes. You can use these to create multiple variants of any resource file, optimized for a specific platform (~ipad/~iphone) or for a retina display (@2x). This, however, is not what's happening with Main_iPhone.storyboard and Main_iPad.storyboard. The storyboard that loads when your app starts is determined by settings in your project. Select the project in the navigator, choose the app target, and switch to the General tab. In the Deployment Info section you'll find the name of the storyboard that an iPhone or iPad will load when your app starts. They can be any storyboard file you choose; they can even be the same storyboard file.

Start by fixing the layout of the toolbar. Quit the simulator, or click the stop button in Xcode. Select the Main_iPhone.storyboard file. In the library, find the Flexible Space Bar Button Item. This object, with a ridiculously long name, acts as a "spring" that fills the available space in a toolbar so the button objects on either side get pushed to the edge of the screen.

Drag one flexible space item object and drop it between the "shorten URL" button and the short URL field. Drop a second between the URL field and the "copy the clipboard" button, as shown in Figure 3-32.

Figure 3-32. Adding flexible space bar button items

With two flexible items, the "springs" share the empty space, causing the label in the middle to be centered, and the copy button to shift all the way to the right. It's not obvious in portrait orientation, but if you rotate the device to landscape it works perfectly. Switch back to the iPhone simulator, run your app (see Figure 3-33), and rotate the device to the left (or right). Now the toolbar looks much nicer (on the right in Figure 3-33).

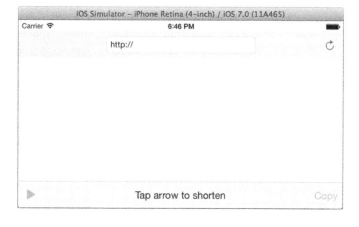

Figure 3-33. Testing iPhone rotation

Creating the iPad Version

The very last step will be to create the iPad version of your app. You might be groaning, thinking that you have to start over from the beginning. Don't worry; you're surprisingly close to being finished. First, a lot of the work in this app was the code, which you've already written. Second, just as you did in the Surrealist app, you can copy and paste objects you've already created.

Select the `Main_iPhone.storyboard` file. Using the outline, select all of the top-level objects in the view and copy them, as shown in Figure 3-34.

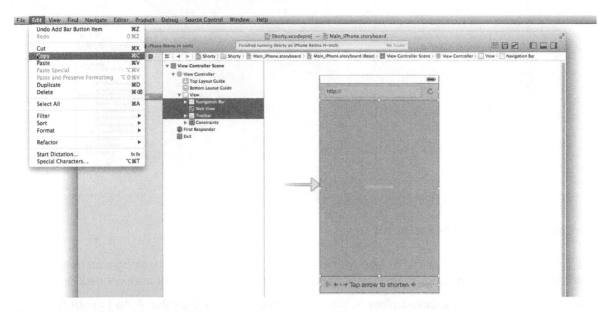

Figure 3-34. Copying the iPhone interface

Select the `Main_iPad.storyboard` file. Select the view object in the outline, and paste all of the objects you just copied, as shown in Figure 3-35.

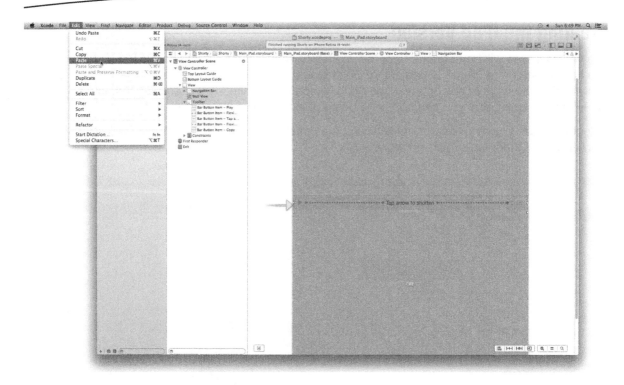

Figure 3-35. Pasting object into the iPad interface

The clipboard duplicates all of the objects you created for the iPhone version, along with their attributes. What it doesn't copy is their positions, most constraints, or any of their connections.

Start by choosing **Clear All Constraints in View Controller** from the **Resolve Auto Layout Issues** button. Exactly as you did for the iPhone interface (refer to Figure 3-4), add a **Vertical Spacing** constraint from the toolbar and the Top Layout Guide and set the constraint's value to 0. Arrange the remaining objects in the iPad interface so they look like the iPhone's. Everything will be bigger than the iPhone version, including a wider text field in the navigation bar. When done, choose the **Add Missing Constraints** item in the **Resolve Auto Layout Issues** button.

Using the connections inspector, or by control+dragging, establish the same connections you did for the iPhone. This will include:

- Connect each of the File's Owner outlets to the correct interface object
    - urlField to the text field
    - webView to the web view
    - shortenButton to the "shorten URL" (left) button in toolbar
    - shortLabel to the plain (middle) button in the toolbar
    - clipboardButton to the "copy to clipboard" (right) button in the toolbar

CHAPTER 3: Spin a Web   95

- Connect the sent events of the text field and each button to their respective action:
    - text field's Did End On Exit event to `-loadLocation`:
    - refresh button to `-loadLocation`:
    - "shorten URL" (left) button to `-shortenURL`:
    - "copy to clipboard" (right) button to `-clipboardURL`:
- Don't forget to set the web view's delegate outlet

> **Tip** When making connections in Interface Builder using the control+drag shortcut, direction matters. To connect an outlet, drag *from* the object with the outlet *to* the object you want it connected to. To connect an action, drag *from* the object that sends the event *to* the object where the action is defined.

When you're done, you'll have a finished iPad app too. Switch to the iPad simulator and test it out, as shown in Figure 3-36.

Figure 3-36. Testing iPad version

Summary

This was a really important chapter, and you made it through with flying colors. You learned a lot about the fundamentals of iOS app development and Xcode's workflow. You will use these skills in practically every app you develop.

You learned how to whip up a web browser, something that can be used in a lot of ways, not just displaying web pages. For example, you can create static web content by adding `.html` resource files to your app, and have a web view load those files. The web view class will also let you interact with its content using JavaScript, opening all kinds of possibilities.

Learning to create, and connect, outlets is a crucial iOS skill. As you've discovered, an iOS app is a web of objects, and outlets are the threads that connect that web together.

Most importantly, you learned how to write action methods and create delegates. These two patterns appear repeatedly throughout iOS.

In the next chapter, I'll explain how events turn a finger touch into an action.

Chapter 4

Coming Events

Now that you've seen an iOS app in action, you might be wondering what keeps your app "alive," so to speak. In the Shorty app, you created action methods that were called when the user tapped on a button or the Go key on the keyboard. You created delegate objects that received messages when certain milestones were reached, like when a web page had problems loading or the URL shortening service responded. You never wrote any code to see if the user had touched something or checked to see if the web page had finished loading. In other words, you didn't go out and get this information; your app waited for this information to come to it.

iOS apps are *event-driven* applications. An event-driven application doesn't (and shouldn't!) spin in a loop checking to see if something has happened. Event-driven applications set up the conditions they want to respond to (a user's touch, a change in the device's orientation, the completion of a network transaction). The app then sits quietly, doing nothing, until one of those things happen. All of those things are collectively referred to as *events*, and are what this chapter is all about.

In this chapter you're going to learn about:

- Events
- Run loops
- Event delivery
- Event handling
- The first responder and the responder chain
- Running your app on a real iOS device

I'll start with some basic theory about how events get from the device's hardware into your application. You'll learn about the different kinds of events and how they navigate the objects in your app. Finally, you'll create two apps: one that handles high-level events, and one that handles low-level events.

Run Loop

iOS apps sit perfectly still, waiting for something to happen. This is a very important feature of app design, because it keeps your app efficient; the code in your app only runs when there's something important to do.

This, seemingly innocuous, arrangement is critical to keeping your user's happy. Running computer code requires electricity, and electricity in mobile devices is a precious commodity. Keeping your code from running at unnecessary times allows iOS to conserve power. It does this by turning off, or minimizing, the amount of power the CPU and other hardware accessories use when they are not needed. This power management happens hundreds of times a second, but it's crucial to the battery life of mobile devices, and users love mobile devices with long battery life.

The code in your app is at the receiving end of two mechanisms: a run loop and an event queue. The run loop is what executes code in your app when something happens, and stops your app from running when there's nothing to do. The event queue is a data structure containing the list of events waiting to be processed. As long as there are events in the queue, the run loop sends them—one at a time—to your app. As soon as all of the events have been processed, and the event queue is empty, your app stops executing code.

Conceptually, your app's run loop looks like this:

```
while ( true ) {
    UIEvent *event = [iOS waitForNextEvent];
    [yourApp processEvent:event];
}
```

The magic is in the -waitForNextEvent message (which doesn't exist, I made it up). If there's an event waiting to be processed, that event is removed from the queue and returned. The run loop passes it to your app for processing. If there's no event, the function simply doesn't return; your app is suspended until there's something to do. Now let's look at what those events are and where they come from.

Event Queue

Events waiting to be processed are added to a FIFO (first in, first out) buffer called the *event queue*. There are different kinds of events, and events come from different sources, as shown in Figure 4-1.

CHAPTER 4: Coming Events 99

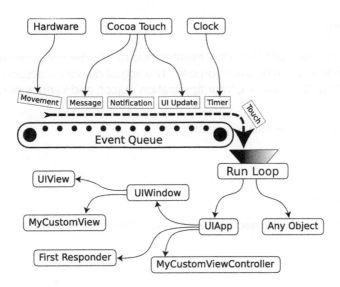

Figure 4-1. The Event Queue

Let's follow one event through your app. When you touch your finger to the surface of an iOS device, here's what happens:

1. Hardware in the screen detects the location of the touch.
2. This information is used to create a touch event object, which records the position of the touch, what time it occurred, and other information.
3. The touch event object is placed in the event queue of your app.
4. The run loop pulls the touch event object from the queue and passes it to your application object.
5. Your application object uses the geometry of the active views in your app to determine which view your finger "touched."
6. An event message, containing the touch event, is sent to that view object.
7. The view object decides what the touch event means and what it will do. It might highlight a button or send an action message.

When you touched the "shorten URL" button in the Shorty app from Chapter 3, that's how the physical act of touching the screen turned into the `-shortenURL:` message your view controller received.

Different event types take different paths. The next few sections will describe the different delivery methods, along with the types of events that each deliver.

Event Delivery

Event delivery is how an event gets from the event queue to an object in your app. Different types of events take different paths, befitting their purpose. The actual delivery mechanism is a combination of logic in the Cocoa Touch framework, your application object, and various methods defined by your app objects.

Broadly speaking, there are three delivery methods:

- Direct delivery
- Hit testing
- First responder

The next few sections will describe each of these three methods, and the events that get delivered that way.

Direct Delivery

Direct delivery is the simplest form of event delivery. A number of event types target specific objects. These events know which object(s) will receive them, so there's not much to know about how these events are delivered, beyond the fact that they're dispatched by the run loop.

For example, an Objective-C message can be placed in the event queue. When that event is pulled from the queue, the message is sent to its target object. That's how the web view told your Shorty app when the web page had loaded. When the network communications code (running in its own thread) determined the page had finished loading, it pushed a -webViewDidFinishLoad: message onto the main thread's event queue. As your main thread pulled events from its event queue, one of those events sent that message to your web view delegate object, telling it that the page had loaded.

> **Note** That isn't exactly how asynchronous delegate messages are delivered. But from an app developer's perspective—which is you—it's conceptually accurate; the details aren't important.

Other events that are sent to specific objects, or groups of objects, are notifications, timer events, and user interface updates. All of these events know, either directly or indirectly, which objects they will be sent to. As an app developer, all you need to know is that when those events work their way to the end of the event queue, the run loop will send an Objective-C message to one or more objects.

Hit Testing

Hit testing delivers events based on the geometry of your user interface, and it applies only to touch events. When a touch event occurs, the UIWindow and UIView objects work together to determine which view object corresponds to the location of the touch. Messages are then sent to that view object, which interprets those events however it chooses; it may flip a switch, scroll a shopping list, or blow up a spaceship. Let's take a quick look at how hit testing works.

When a touch event is pulled from the event queue, it contains the absolute hardware coordinates where the touch occurred, as shown on the left in Figure 4-2. This example will use a stylized representation of the Shorty app from the previous chapter.

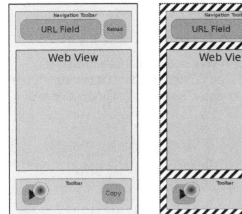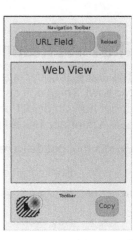

Figure 4-2. Hit testing a touch event

Your `UIApplication` object uses the event coordinates to determine the `UIWindow` object that's responsible for that portion of the screen. That `UIWindow` object receives a `-sendEvent:` message containing the touch event object to process.

The `UIWindow` object then performs *hit testing*. Starting at the top of its view hierarchy, it sends a `-hitTest:withEvent:` message to its top-level view object, as shown in the second panel of Figure 4-2.

The top-level view first determines if the event is within its bounds. It is, so it starts to look for any subviews that contain the touch coordinate. The top-level view contains three subviews: the navigation toolbar at the top, the web view in the middle, and the toolbar at the bottom. The touch is within the bounds of the toolbar, so it passes on the `-hitTest:withEvent:` message to the toolbar.

The toolbar repeats the process, looking for a subview that contains the location, as shown in the third frame of Figure 4-2. The toolbar object discovers that touch occurs inside the leftmost bar button item bounds. The bar button item is returned as the "hit" object, which causes `UIWindow` to begin sending it low-level touch event messages.

Being a "button," the bar button item object examines the events to determine if the user tapped the button (as opposed to swiping it or some other irrelevant gesture). If they did, the button sends its action message, in this case `-shortenURL:`, to the object its connected to.

> **Tip** Hit testing is highly customizable, should you ever need to. By overriding the `-pointInside:withEvent:` and `-hitTest:withEvent:` methods of your view objects, you can literally rewrite the rules that determine how touch events find the view object they will be sent to. See the *Event Handling Guide for iOS*, which can be found in Xcode's Documentation and API Guide, for the details.

The First Responder

The *first responder* is a view, view controller, or window object in your active interface (a visible window). Think of it as the *designated receiver* for events that aren't determined by hit testing. I'll talk about how an object becomes the first responder later in this chapter. For now, just know that every active interface has a first responder.

Events that get delivered to the first responder are:

- Shake motion events
- Remote control events
- Key events

The shake motion event tells your app that the user is shaking their device (moving it rapidly back and forth). This information comes from the accelerometer hardware.

So-called remote control events are generated when the user presses any of the multi-media controls, which include:

- Play
- Pause
- Stop
- Skip to Next Track
- Skip to Previous Track
- Fast Forward
- Fast Backward

These are called "remote" events because they could originate from external accessories, such as the play/pause button on the cord of many headphones. In reality, they most often come from the play/pause buttons you see on the screen.

Key events come from tapping on the virtual keyboard, or from a hardware keyboard connected via Bluetooth.

To review, direct delivery sends event objects or Objective-C messages directly to their target object(s). Touch events use hit testing to determine which view object will receive them, and all other events are sent to the first responder. Now it's time to handle those events.

Event Handling

You've arrived at the second half of your event processing journey: event handling. In simple terms, an object *handles* or *responds* to an event if it contains code to interpret that event and decide what it wants to do about it.

I'll get the direct delivery events out of the way first. An object receiving a direct delivery event *must* have a method to process that event, message, or notification. This is not optional. If the object doesn't implement the message sent it, your application will malfunction and could crash. That's all you need to know about directly delivered events.

> **Caution** When requesting timer, message, or notification events, make sure the object receiving them has the correct method(s) implemented.

Other event types are much more forgiving. Much like optional delegate methods, if your object implements the methods for handling an event, it will receive those events. If it isn't interested in handling that type of event, you simply omit those methods from its implementation and iOS will go looking for another object that wants to handle them.

To handle touch events, for example, you add the following methods to your class' implementation:

- (void)touchesBegan:(NSSet *)touches withEvent:(UIEvent *)event
- (void)touchesMoved:(NSSet *)touches withEvent:(UIEvent *)event
- (void)touchesEnded:(NSSet *)touches withEvent:(UIEvent *)event
- (void)touchesCancelled:(NSSet *)touches withEvent:(UIEvent *)event

If hit testing determines that your object should receive touch events, it will receive a -touchesBegan:withEvent: message when the hardware detects a physical touch in your view, a -touchesMoved:withEvent: whenever the position changes (a dragging gesture), and a -touchesEnded:withEvent: message when contact with the screen is removed. As the user taps and drags their fingers across the screen, your object may receive many of these messages, often in rapid succession.

> **Note** The -touchesCancelled:withEvent: message is the oddball of the group. This message is sent to your object if something interrupts the sequence of touch events, such as your app changing to another screen in the middle of a tap gesture. You only need to handle the cancel event if an incomplete sequence of touch events (such as receiving a "began" but no "ended" message) would confuse your object.

If you omit all of these methods from your class, your object will not handle any touch events.

All of the methods for handling events are inherited from the UIResponder class, and each type of event has one or more methods that you must implement if you want to handle that event. The UIResponder class documentation has a complete list of event handling methods.

So what happens if the hit test or first responder object ignores the event? That's a good question, and the answer is found in the responder chain.

The Responder Chain

The *responder chain* is a string of objects that represent the "focus" of your user interface. What I mean by "focus" is those objects controlling the currently visible interface, and those view objects that are most relevant to what the user is doing. Does that sound all vague and confusing? A picture and an explanation of how iOS creates and uses the responder chain will make things clear.

The responder chain starts with the *initial responder* (see Figure 4-3). When delivering motion, key, and remote events, the first responder is the initial responder object. For touch events, the initial responder is the view object determined by hit testing.

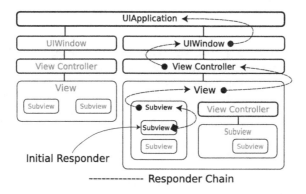

Figure 4-3. First responder chain

> **Note** All objects in the responder chain are subclasses of UIResponder. So, technically, the responder chain consists of UIResponder objects. UIApplication, UIWindow, UIView, and UIViewController are all subclasses of UIResponder. By extension, the initial responder (first responder or hit test result) is always a UIResponder object.

iOS begins by trying to deliver that event to the initial responder. "Trying" is the key word here. If the object has methods that handle that event, it does so. If not, iOS moves onto the next object in the chain until it either finds an object that wants to process the event or it gives up and throws the event away.

Figure 4-3 shows the conceptual organization of view objects in an app with two screens. The second screen is currently being shown to the user. It consists of a view controller object, a number of subviews, some nested inside of other subviews, and even a sub-view controller. In this example, a sub-sub-view has been designated the initial responder, which would be appropriate after a hit test determined that the user touched that view.

iOS will try to deliver the touch event to the initial responder (the sub-sub-view). If that object doesn't handle touch events, iOS sees if that view has a view controller object (it doesn't) and tries to send the event to its controller. If neither the view nor its controller handle touch events, iOS finds the view that contains that view (its superview), and repeats the entire process until it runs out of views and view controllers to try.

After all of the view and view controller objects have been given a chance to handle the event, delivery moves on to the window object for that screen, and finally to the single application object.

What makes the responder chain so elegant is its dynamic nature and ordered processing of events. The responder chain is created automatically, so your object doesn't have to do anything to be a part of the responder chain, except to make sure that either it, or a subsidiary view, is the initial responder. Your object will receive event messages while that portion of your interface is active, and won't receive events when it's not.

The other aspect is the specific-to-general nature of responder chain event handling. The chain always starts at the view that's most relevant to the user: the button they touched, an active text input field, or a row in a list. That object always receives the events first. If the event has specific meaning to those views, it's processed accordingly. At the same time, your view controller or UIApplication object could also respond to those events, but if one of the subviews handles it first, those objects won't receive it.

If the user moves to another screen, as shown in Figure 4-4, and presses the "pause" button on their headphones, a new responder chain is established. This chain starts at the first responder, which in this case is a view controller. The chain doesn't include any view objects at all, because the top-level view controller object is the first responder.

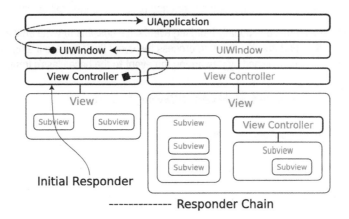

Figure 4-4. Second responder chain

If the view controller handles the "pause" event, then it does so. The view controllers in other interfaces never see the event. By implementing different "pause" event handling code in the various controllers, your app's response to a "pause" event will be different, depending on which screen is active.

Your application object could also handle the "pause" event. If none of the view controllers handled the "pause" event, then all "pause" events would trickle down to the application object. This would be the arrangement you'd use if you wanted all "pause" events to be handled the same way, regardless of what screen the user was looking at.

Finally, you can mix these solutions. A "pause" event handler in the application could handle the event in a generic way, and then specific view controllers could intercept the event if pressing the "pause" button has special meaning in that screen.

> **Tip** It's rare to create a custom subclass of UIApplication, and even rarer to subclass UIWindow. In a typical app, all of your event handling code will be in your custom view and view controller objects.

CONDITIONALLY HANDLING EVENTS

In practical terms, you implement an event handling method (such as -touchesBegan:withEvent:) to handle that event type, or you omit an implementation to ignore it. In reality, it's a little more nuanced.

Events are handled by receiving specific Objective-C messages (like -touchesBegan:withEvent:). Your object inherits these methods from the UIResponder base class. So every UIResponder object has a -touchesBegan:withEvent: method and will receive the touch event object via this message. So, how does the object ignore the event?

The secret is in UIResponder's implementation of these messages. The inherited base class implementation for all event handling messages simply passes the event up the responder chain. So a more precise description is this: To handle events, you override UIResponder's event handler method and process the event. To ignore it, you let the event go to UIResponder's method, which ignores the event and passes it to the next object in the responder chain.

Which brings up an interesting feature: conditionally handling events. It's possible to write an event handler that decides if it wants to handle an event. It can arbitrarily choose to process the event itself or pass it along to the next object in the responder chain. Passing it on is accomplished by forwarding the event to the base class's implementation, like this:

```
- (void)touchesBegan:(NSSet *)touches withEvent:(UIEvent *)event
{
    if ( [self iWantToHandleTheseTouches:touches] )
        // handle event
        [self doSomethingWithTheseTouches:touches];
    else
        // ignore event and pass it up the responder chain
        [super touchesBegan:touches withEvent:event];
}
```

Using this technique, your object can dynamically decide which events it wants to handle and which events it will pass along to other objects in the responder chain.

Now that you know how events are delivered and handled, you're ready to build an app that uses events directly. To do that, you'll need to consider what kind of events you want to handle and why.

High- vs. Low-Level Events

Programmers are perpetually labeling things as high level or low level. Objects in your app form a kind of pyramid. A few complex objects at the top are constructed from more primitive objects in the middle, which are themselves constructed from even more primitive objects. The complex objects on top are called the "high-level" objects (UIApplication, UIWebView). The simple objects at the bottom are called the "low-level" objects (NSNumber, NSString). Similarly, programmers will talk about high- and low-level frameworks, interfaces, communications paths, and so on.

Events, too, come in different levels. Low-level events are the nitty-gritty, moment-by-moment, details that are happening right now. The touch events are examples of low-level events. Another example is the instantaneous force vector values that you can request from the accelerometer and gyroscope hardware.

At the other end of the scale are high-level events, like the shake motion event. Another example is the UIGestureRecognizer objects that interpret complex touch event patterns and turn those into a single high-level event, like "pinched" or "swiped."

When you design your app, you must decide what level of events you want to process. In the next app, you're going to use the shake motion event to trigger actions in your app.

To do that, you could request and handle the low-level accelerometer events. You would have to create variables to track the force vectors for each of the three movement axes (X, Y, and Z). When you detected that the device was accelerating in a particular direction, you would record that direction and start a timer. If the direction of travel reversed, within a reasonable angle of trajectory and within a short period of time, and then reversed two or three more times, you could conclude that the user was shaking the device.

Or, you could let iOS do all of those calculations for you and simply handle the shake motion events generated by the Cocoa Touch framework. When the user starts to shake their device, your first responder receives a -motionBegan:withEvent: message. When the user stops shaking it, your object receives a -motionEnded:withEvent: message. It's that simple.

That doesn't mean you'll never need low-level events. If you were writing a game app where your user directed a star-nosed mole through the soil of a magical garden by tilting the device from side-to-side, then interpreting the low-level accelerometer events would be the correct solution. You'll use the low-level accelerometer events in Chapter 16.

Decide what information you need from events, and then handle the highest-level events that give you that information. Now you're ready to start designing your app.

Eight Ball

The app you'll create mimics the famous Magic Eight Ball toy from the 1950s (http://en.wikipedia.org/wiki/Magic_Eight_Ball). The app works by displaying an eerily prescient message whenever you shake your iOS device. Start by sketching out a quick design for your app.

Design

The design for this app is the simplest so far: a screen containing a message is displayed in the center of a "ball," as shown in Figure 4-5. When you shake the device, the current message disappears. When you stop shaking it, a new message appears.

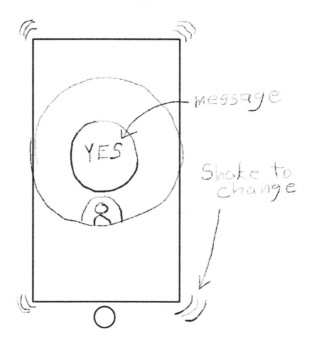

Figure 4-5. *EightBall app design*

Create the Project

Launch Xcode and choose **File ➤ New Project**. Select the Single View iOS app template. In the next sheet, name the app `EightBall`, set the class prefix to `EB`, and choose `iPhone` for the device, as shown in Figure 4-6.

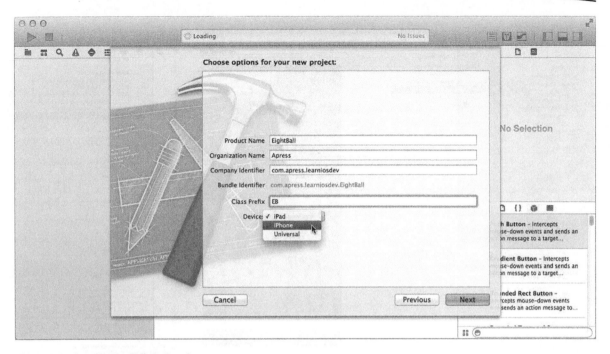

Figure 4-6. Creating the EightBall project

Choose a location to save the new project and create it. In the project navigator, select the project, select the EightBall target from the pop-up menu (if needed), select the General tab, and then turn off the two landscape orientations in the supported interface orientation section, so only the portrait orientation is enabled.

Create the Interface

Select the `Main.storyboard` Interface Builder file and select the single view object. Using the attributes inspector set the background color to `Black`, as shown in Figure 4-7.

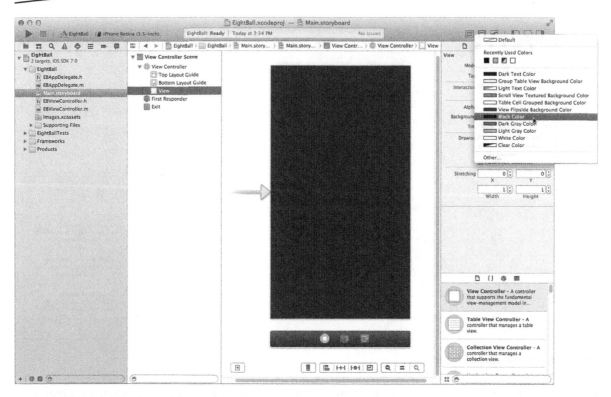

Figure 4-7. Setting main view background color

From the library, drag a new image view object into the interface. Using the size inspector to set the height and width to 320 pixels. Drag the image object so it snaps to the vertical and horizontal centering guides, as shown in Figure 4-8.

CHAPTER 4: Coming Events   111

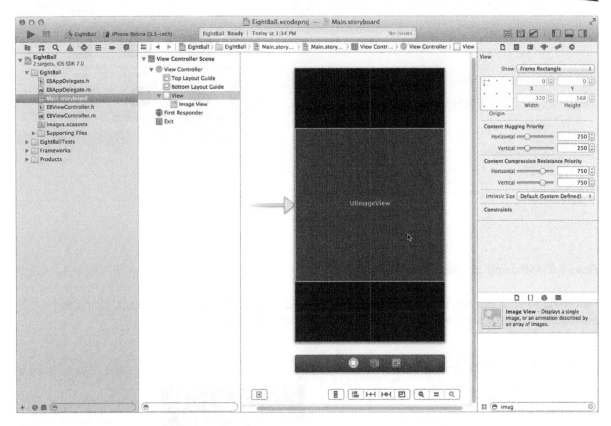

Figure 4-8. Centering the image view

Set the first constraint by control+clicking/right-clicking in the image view and dragging down a little. Release the mouse and choose the **Height** constraint. This will fix the height of the image view. From the **Resolve Auto Layout Issues** control, choose the **Add Missing Constraints in View Controller**. Xcode will add sufficient constraints to make them complete. Because the view was centered in the screen, Xcode will add constraints to keep it centered.

Just as you did in Chapter 2, you're going to add some resource image files to your project. In the project navigator, select the Images.xcassets assets catalog. In the Finder, locate the Learn iOS Development Projects folder you downloaded in Chapter 1. Inside the Ch 4 folder you'll find the EightBall (Resources) folder, which contains five image files. Select the files eight-ball.png and eight-ball@2x.png. With these files and your workspace window visible, drag the two image files into the assets catalog, as shown in Figure 4-9.

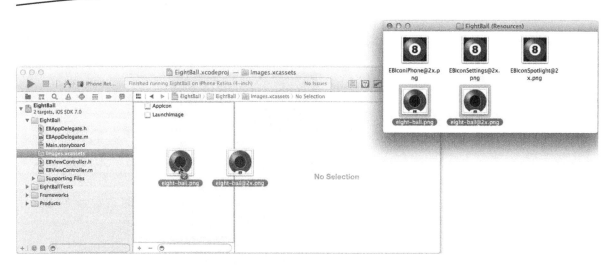

Figure 4-9. Adding eight-ball images to the asset catalog

Returning to your project, select Main.storyboard, and select the image view object. Using the attributes inspector set the image property to eight-ball, as shown in Figure 4-10.

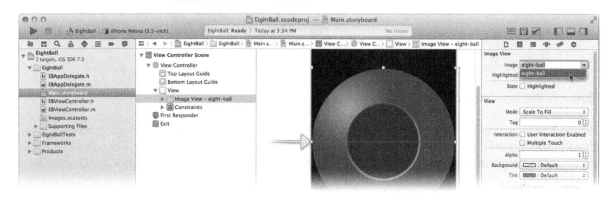

Figure 4-10. Setting the image

Now you need to add a text view to display the magic message. From the object library, drag in a new text view (not a text field) object, placing it over the "window" in the middle of the eight ball Use the size inspector to set the width of the text view to 160 pixels and the height to 112. Center the text view using the centering guides, as shown in Figure 4-11.

CHAPTER 4: Coming Events 113

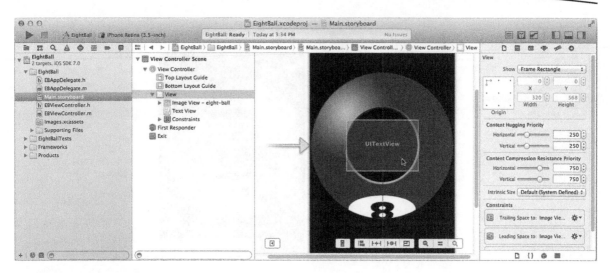

Figure 4-11. Centering text view

Using the control+click/right-click gesture again, add the following constraints:

> Drag up (or down), inside the text view, release, and choose a **Height** constraint.
>
> Drag right (or left), inside the text view, release, and choose a **Width** constraint.
>
> Drag from text view up (or down) to the image view. Choose the **Center Y** constraint.
>
> Drag right (or left), from the text view to the image view. Choose the **Center X** constraint.

The text view now has a fixed size and will always be centered over the image view.

Select the text view. Using the attributes inspector set the following properties:

> Set text to SHAKE FOR ANSWER, on three lines (see Figure 4-12). Hold down the Option key when pressing the Return key to insert a literal "return" character into the text property field.
>
> Make the text view color white.
>
> Click the up arrow in the font property until it reads System 24.0.
>
> Choose the centered (middle) alignment.
>
> Uncheck the Editable behavior property.
>
> Further down, find the background property and set it to default (no background).

Your interface design is finished, and should look like the one in Figure 4-12. Now it's time to move on to the code.

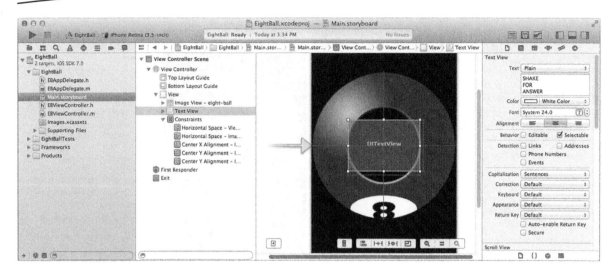

Figure 4-12. Finished EightBall interface

Writing the Code

Your EBViewController object will need a connection to the text view object. Select your EBViewController.h file and add the following property:

```
@property (weak,nonatomic) IBOutlet UITextView *answerView;
```

Now it's time to write the code that displays the messages. Switch to your implementation file (EBViewController.m). Just above the @implementation line, add this code:

```
static NSString* gAnswers[] = {
    @"\rYES",
    @"\rNO",
    @"\rMAYBE",
    @"I\rDON'T\rKNOW",
    @"TRY\rAGAIN\rSOON",
    @"READ\rTHE\rMANUAL"
};
#define kNumberOfAnswers (sizeof(gAnswers)/sizeof(NSString*))

@interface EBViewController ()
- (void)fadeFortune;
- (void)newFortune;
@end
```

The first statement creates a static array of NSString string objects. Each object is one possible answer to appear in the eight ball. The \r characters are called an escape sequence. They consist of a backslash (left leaning slash) character followed by a code that tells the compiler to replace the sequence with a special character. In this case, the \r is replaced with a literal "carriage return" character—something you can't type into your source without starting a new line.

The #define creates a constant, kNumberOfAnswers, that evaluates to the number of string objects in the gAnswers array. It does this by dividing the overall size of the array (sizeof(gAnswers)) by the size of a single element in the array (sizeof(NSString*)). You do this so that you don't have to keep track of how many strings are in the gAnswers array. If you want to add more answers, just add new elements to the array. The kNumberOfAnswers macro will change to reflect however many there are.

The @interface EBViewController () statement declares the two methods used to update the message display: -fadeFortune and -newFortune. They are declared here, instead of in EBViewController.h, because these are private methods—not for use by objects other than EBViewController.

Create the two methods you just promised by adding the following code to your implementation (that is, between the @implementation and @end statements):

```
- (void)fadeFortune
{
    [UIView animateWithDuration:0.75 animations:^{
        self.answerView.alpha = 0.0;
    }];
}

- (void)newFortune
{
    self.answerView.text = gAnswers[arc4random_uniform(kNumberOfAnswers)];
    
    [UIView animateWithDuration:2.0 animations:^{
        self.answerView.alpha = 1.0;
    }];
}
```

The -fadeFortune method uses iOS animation to change the alpha property of the answerView text view object to 0. The alpha property of a view is how opaque the view appears. A value of 1 is completely opaque, 0.5 makes it 50% transparent, and a value of 0 makes it completely invisible. -fadeFortune makes the text view object fade away to nothing, over a period of ¾ of a second.

> **Note** Animation is covered in more detail in Chapter 11.

The -newFortune method is where all the fun is. The first statement does three things:

1. The arc4random_uniform() function is called to pick a random number between 0 and a number less than kNumberOfAnswers. So if kNumberOfAnswers is 6, the function will return a random number between 0 and 5 (inclusive).

2. The random number is used as an index into the gAnswers array to pick one of the constant NSString objects.

3. The random answer is used to set the text property of the text view object. Once set, the text view object will display that text in your interface.

Finally, iOS animation is used again to change the alpha property slowly back to 1, going from invisible to opaque over a period of 2 seconds, causing the new message to gradually appear.

There's one minor detail remaining: connecting the `answerView` outlet to the text view object in the interface. Switch to the `Main.storyboard` Interface Builder file. Select the view controller object, and use the connections inspector to connect the `answerView` outlet, as shown in Figure 4-13.

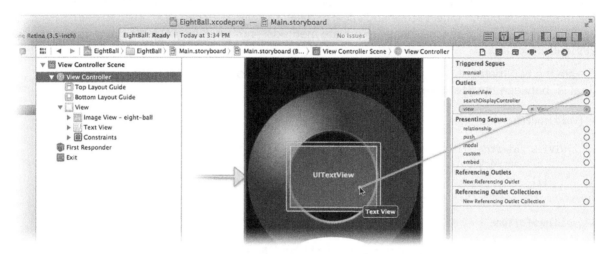

Figure 4-13. Connecting the answerView outlet

Handling Shake Events

Your app now has everything it needs to work, except the event handling that will make it happen. In the Xcode documentation (**Help ➤ Documentation and API Reference**), take a look at the documentation for UIResponder. In it, you'll find documentation for three methods:

```
- (void)motionBegan:(UIEventSubtype)motion withEvent:(UIEvent *)event
- (void)motionEnded:(UIEventSubtype)motion withEvent:(UIEvent *)event
- (void)motionCancelled:(UIEventSubtype)motion withEvent:(UIEvent *)event
```

Each message is sent during a different phase of a motion event. Motion events are very simple—remember these are "high-level" events. Motion events begin and they end. If the motion is interrupted, or never finishes, your object receives a motion canceled message.

To handle motion events in your view controller, add these three event handler methods to your `EBViewController` implementation:

```
- (void)motionBegan:(UIEventSubtype)motion withEvent:(UIEvent *)event
{
    if (motion==UIEventSubtypeMotionShake)
        [self fadeFortune];
}
```

```
- (void)motionEnded:(UIEventSubtype)motion withEvent:(UIEvent *)event
{
    if (motion==UIEventSubtypeMotionShake)
        [self newFortune];
}

- (void)motionCancelled:(UIEventSubtype)motion withEvent:(UIEvent *)event
{
    if (motion==UIEventSubtypeMotionShake)
        [self newFortune];
}
```

Each method begins by examining the motion parameter to see if the motion event received describes the one you're interested in (the shake motion). If not, you ignore the event. This is important. Future versions of iOS may add new motion events; your object should only pay attention to the ones it's designed to work with.

The -motionBegan:withEvent: handler sends a -fadeFortune message. When the user starts to shake the device, the current message fades away.

The -motionEnded:withEvent: handler sends the -newFortune message. When the shaking stops, a new fortune appears.

Finally, the -motionCancelled:withEvent: handler makes sure a message is visible if the motion was interrupted or interpreted to be some other gesture.

Testing Your EightBall App

Make sure you have an iPhone Simulator selected in the scheme and run your app. It will appear in the simulator, as shown in Figure 4-14.

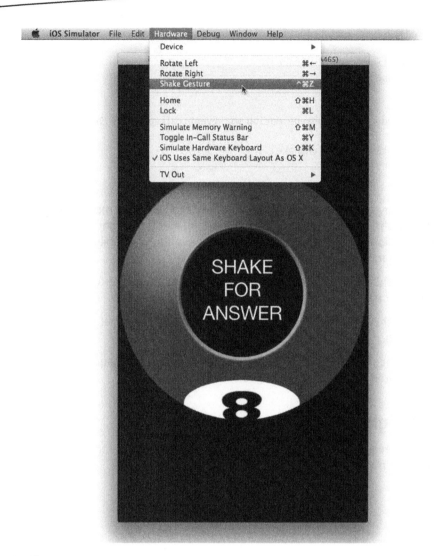

Figure 4-14. Testing EightBall

Choose the **Hardware ➤ Shake Gesture** command in the simulator. This command simulates the user shaking their device, which will cause shake motion events to be sent to your app.

Congratulations, you've successfully created a shake-motion event handler! Each time you shake your simulated device a new message appears, as shown in Figure 4-15.

Figure 4-15. The working EightBall app

FIRST RESPONDER AND THE RESPONDER CHAIN

Technically, it isn't necessary that your view controller be the first responder. What's required is that your view controller be *in the responder chain*. If any view, or subview, in your interface is the first responder, your view controller will be in the responder chain and will receive motion events—unless one of those other views intercepts and handles the event first.

By default, your view controller isn't the first responder and can't become the first responder. An object that wants to be a first responder must return YES when sent the -canBecomeFirstResponder message. The base class implementation of UIResponder returns NO. Therefore, any subclass of UIResponder is ineligible to be the first responder unless it overrides its -canBecomeFirstResponder method.

After making your object eligible to be the first responder, the next step is to explicitly request to be the first responder. This is often done in your -viewDidAppear: method, using code like this:

```
[self becomeFirstResponder];
```

Specific Cocoa Touch classes—most notably the text view and text field classes—are designed to be first responders, and they return YES when sent -canBecomeFirstResponder. These objects establish themselves as the first responder when touched or activated. As the first responder, they handle keyboard events, copy and paste requests, and so on.

At this point you might be wondering why your view controller is getting motion events, if it's not the first responder and it's not in the responder chain? You can thank iOS 7 for that. Recent changes in iOS deliver motion events to the active view controller if there is no first responder or the window is the first responder. If you want your app to work with earlier versions of iOS too, you'd need to make sure your view controller can become the first responder (by overriding -canBecomeFirstResponder), and then request that it is ([self becomeFirstResponder]) when the view loads.

Here's an experiment that demonstrates the responder chain in action. In The `Main.storyboard` file, select the `UITextView` and use the attributes inspector to check the `Editable` behavior. Run the app, tap and hold the text field, and when the keyboard pops up edit the fortune text. Now choose the simulator's **Hardware ➤ Shake Gesture** command. What happens? The text in the field changes, just as you programmed it to.

Return to the `EBViewController.m` file and comment out all three of your motion event handling methods. Do this by selecting the text of all three methods and choose **Editor ➤ Structure ➤ Comment Selection** (Command+/). Now run your app again, select the text, change it, and shake the simulator. What happens? This time you see an "Undo" dialog, asking if you want to undo the changes you made to the text.

Motion events are initially sent to the first responder (the text field), eventually pass through the view controller, and ultimately land in the `UIApplication` object. The `UIApplication` object interprets a shake event to mean "undo typing". By intercepting the motion events in your view controller, you overrode the default behavior supplied by the `UIApplication` object.

Put your app back the way it was by returning to `EBViewController.m` and choosing **Edit ➤ Undo**. Do the same to `Main.storyboard`.

Finishing Touches

Put a little spit and polish on your app with a nice icon. Well, at least with the icon you'll find in the `EightBall (Resources)` folder. In your project navigator, select the `images.xcassets` file, and then select the `AppIcon` group. With the `EightBall (Resources)` folder visible, drag the three icon images files into the `AppIcon` preview area, as shown in Figure 4-16. Xcode will automatically assign the appropriate image file to each icon resource, based on its size.

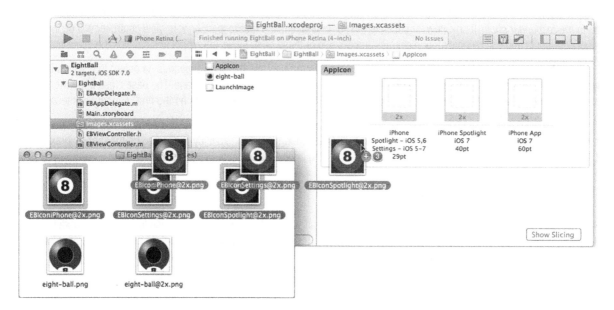

Figure 4-16. Importing app icons

> **Note** iOS 7 introduced a different set of icon sizes than those used in previous versions of iOS. If you intend your app to run on earlier versions of iOS, consult the "App Icon" section of the *iOS Human Interface Guidelines* for a complete list of the required icon resources, and their sizes.

With that detail taken care of, let's shake things up—literally—by running your app on a real iOS device.

Testing on a Physical iOS Device

You can test a lot of your app using Xcode's iPhone and iPad simulator, but there are few things the simulator can't emulate. Two of those things are multiple (more than two) touches and real accelerometer events. To test that, you need a real iOS device, with real accelerometer hardware, that you can touch with real fingers.

The first step is to connect Xcode to your iOS Developer account. Choose **Xcode ➤ Preferences…** and switch to the Accounts tab. Choose **Add Apple ID…** from the + button at the bottom of the window, as shown in Figure 4-17.

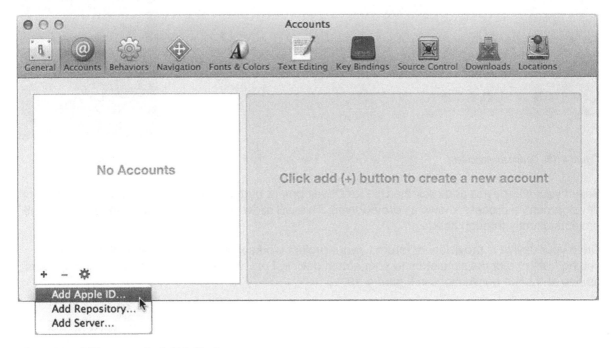

Figure 4-17. Adding a new Apple ID to Xcode

Supply your Apple ID and password, and then click the **Add** button. If you're not a member of the iOS Developer Program yet, there's a convenient **Join Program…** button that will take you to Apple's website.

> **Note** Before you can run your app on a device, you must first become a member of the iOS Developer Program. See http://developer.apple.com/programs/ios to learn how to become a member. Once you are a member, Xcode will use your Apple ID to download and install the necessary security certificates required to provision a device.

Plug an iPhone, iPad, or iPod Touch in to your computer's USB port. Open the Xcode organizer window (**Window ➤ Organizer**). In the toolbar, switch to the devices tab. The iOS device you plugged in will appear on the left, as shown in Figure 4-18. If a "trust" dialog appears on your device, as shown on the right in Figure 4-18, you'll need to grant Xcode access to your device.

Figure 4-18. Device management

Select your iOS device and click the Use for Development button. Xcode will prepare your device for development, a process known as *provisioning*. This will allow you to build, install, and run most iOS projects directly through Xcode.

Once your device is provisioned, return to your project workspace window. Change the scheme setting from one of the simulators to your actual device. I provisioned an iPhone, so iPhone appears as one of the run destinations in Figure 4-19.

Figure 4-19. Selecting an iOS device to test

Run the EightBall app again. This time, your app will be built, copied onto your iOS device, and the app will start running there. Pretty neat, isn't it?

The amazing thing is that Xcode is still in control—so don't unplug your USB connection just yet! You can set breakpoints, freeze your app, examine variables, and generally do anything you could do in the simulator.

With EightBall app running, shake your device and see what happens. When you're done, click the Stop button in the Xcode toolbar. You'll notice that your EightBall app is now installed on your device. You're free to unplug your USB connection and take it with you; it is, after all, your app.

Other Uses for The Responder Chain

While the responder chain concept is still fresh in your mind, I want to mention a couple of other uses for the responder chain, before you move on to low-level events. The responder chain isn't used solely to handle events. It also plays an important role in actions, editing, and other services.

In earlier projects, you connected the actions of buttons and text fields to specific objects. Connecting an action in Interface Builder sets two pieces of information:

- The object that will receive the action (`SUViewController`)
- The action message to send (`-shortenURL:`)

It's also possible to send an action to the responder chain, rather than a specific object. In Interface Builder you do this by connecting the action to the First Responder placeholder object, as shown in Figure 4-20.

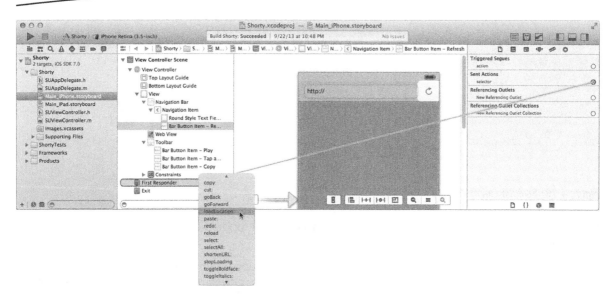

Figure 4-20. Connecting an action to the responder chain

When the button's action is sent, it goes initially to the first responder object—whatever that object is. For actions, iOS tests to see if the object implements the expected message (-loadLocation:, in this example). If it does, the object receives that message. If not, iOS starts working its way through the responder chain until it finds an object that does.

This is particularly useful in more complex apps where the recipient of the action message is outside the scope of the Interface Builder file. You can only make connections between objects in the same scene. If you need a button to send an action to another view controller, or the application object itself, you can't make that connection in Interface Builder. But you can connect your button to the first responder. As long as the intended recipient is in the responder chain when the button fires its action, your object will receive it.

Editing also depends heavily on the responder chain. When you begin editing text in iOS, like the URL field in the Shorty app, that object becomes the first responder. When the user types on the keyboard—virtual or otherwise—those key events are sent to the first responder. You can have several text fields in the same screen, but only one is the first responder. All key events, copy and paste commands, and so on, go to the active text field.

Touchy

You've learned a lot about the so-called high-level events, the initial responder, and the responder chain. Now it's time to dig into low-level event handling, and you're going to start with the most commonly used low-level events: touch events.

The Touchy app is a demonstration app. It does nothing more than show you where you're touching the screen. It's useful both to see this in action and to explore some of the subtleties of touch event handling. You'll also learn a new, and really important, Interface Builder skill: creating custom objects in your interface.

Design

The Touchy app also has a super-simple interface, as depicted in Figure 4-21. Touchy will display the location, or locations, where you're touching your view object. So the app isn't too boring, you'll jazz it up a little with some extra graphics, but that's not the focus of this outing.

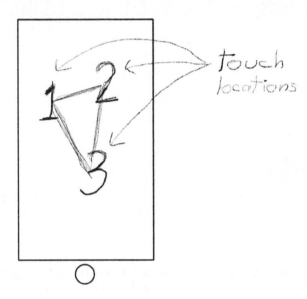

Figure 4-21. Sketch of Touchy app

The app will work by intercepting the touch events using a custom view object. Your custom view object will extract the coordinates of each active touch point and use that to draw their positions.

Creating the Project

As you've done several times already, start by creating a new Xcode project based on the Single View iOS application template. Name the project Touchy, set the class prefix to TY, and choose Universal for the device, as shown in Figure 4-22.

126   CHAPTER 4: Coming Events

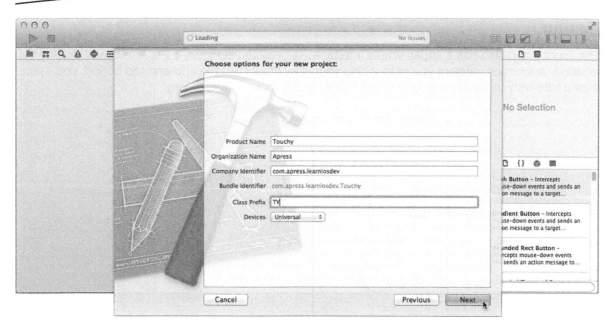

Figure 4-22. Creating the Touchy project

Choose a location to save the new project and create it. In the project navigator, select the project, select the EightBall target, select the summary tab, and then turn off the two landscape orientations in the supported interface orientation section, so only the portrait orientation is enabled.

Creating a Custom View

You're going to depart from the development pattern you've used in previous apps. Instead of adding your code to the TYTouchViewController class, you're going to create a new custom subclass of UIView. "Why" is explained in Chapter 11. "How" will be explained right now.

Select the Touchy group (not the project) in the project navigator. From the File menu, or by right/control+clicking on the Touchy group, choose the New File... command, as shown in Figure 4-23.

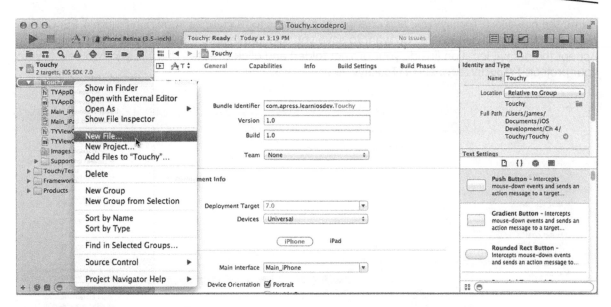

Figure 4-23. Creating a new source file

Much like the project template assistant, Xcode provides templates for creating individual files too. You're going to create a new Objective-C class, so choose the `Objective-C Class` template in the iOS Cocoa Touch group, as shown in Figure 4-24.

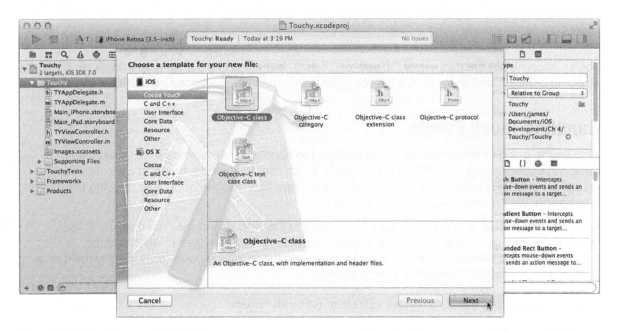

Figure 4-24. Choosing a new file template

Name the new file TYTouchyView, and change its subclass to UIView, as shown in Figure 4-25. Click **Next** and Xcode will ask where you want to save your file. Make sure the Touchy target is checked. Accept the default location (inside your project folder) and click **Create**. This will add two new files to your project: TYTouchView.h and TYTouchyView.m.

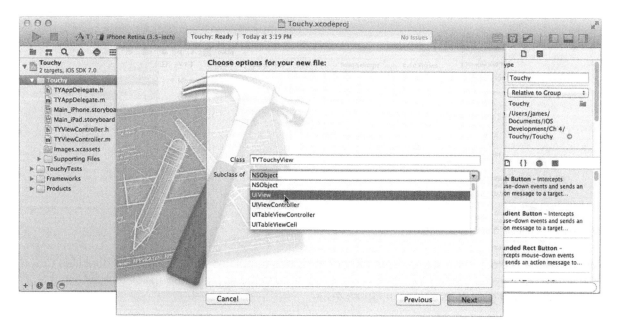

Figure 4-25. Naming your new Objective-C class

You've successfully created a new Objective-C class! Your class is a subclass of UIView, so it inherits all of the behavior and features of a UIView object, and can be used anywhere a UIView object can.

Handling Touch Events

Now you're going to customize your UIView object to handle touch events. Remember that the base class UIResponder and UIView don't handle touch events. Instead, they just pass them up the responder chain. By implementing your own touch event handling methods, you're going to change that so your view responds directly to touches.

As you already know, touch events will be delivered to the view object they occurred in. If you didn't know that, go back and read the section "Hit Testing." All you have to do is add the appropriate event handling methods to your class. Add the following code to your TYTouchyView.m implementation file, just before the @end statement:

```
- (void)touchesBegan:(NSSet *)touches withEvent:(UIEvent *)event
{
    [self updateTouches:event.allTouches];
}
```

```
- (void)touchesMoved:(NSSet *)touches withEvent:(UIEvent *)event
{
    [self updateTouches:event.allTouches];
}

- (void)touchesEnded:(NSSet *)touches withEvent:(UIEvent *)event
{
    [self updateTouches:event.allTouches];
}

- (void)touchesCancelled:(NSSet *)touches withEvent:(UIEvent *)event
{
    [self updateTouches:event.allTouches];
}
```

> **Note** Xcode will be showing some errors in your source code. Ignore them for now; you'll fix that when you add the `-updateTouches:` method.

Each touch event message includes two objects. An `NSSet` object, containing the touch objects of interest, and a `UIEvent` object that summarizes the event that caused the message to be sent.

In a typical app, your method would be interested in the `touches` set. This set, or unordered collection, of objects contains one `UITouch` object for every touch relevant to the event. Each `UITouch` object describes one touch position: its coordinates, its phase, the time it occurred, its tap count, and so on.

For a "began" event, the touches set will contain the `UITouch` objects for the touches that just began. For a "moved" event, it will only contain those touch points that moved. For an "ended" event, it will contain only those touch objects that were removed from the screen. This is very convenient, from a programming perspective, because most view objects are only interested in the `UITouch` objects that are relevant to that event.

The Touchy app, however, is a little different. Touchy wants to track all of the active touches, all of the time. You're not actually interested in what just happened. Instead you want "the big picture": the list of all touch points currently in contact with the screen. For that, move over to the event object.

The `UIEvent` object's main purpose is to describe the single event that just occurred; or, more precisely, the single event that was just pulled from the event queue. But `UIEvent` has some other interesting information that it carries around. One of those is the `allTouches` property that contains the current state of all touch points on the device, regardless of what view they are associated with.

So now I can explain what all of your event handling methods are doing. They are waiting for any change to the touch state of the device. They ignore the specific change, and dig into the event object to find the state of all active touch objects, which it passes to your `-updateTouches:` method. This method will record the position of all active touches and use that information to draw those positions on the screen.

So, I guess you need write that method! Immediately above the touch event handler methods you just added in TYTouchyView.m, add this method to your implementation:

```
- (void)updateTouches:(NSSet*)set
{
    NSMutableArray *array = [NSMutableArray array];
    for ( UITouch *touch in set )
        {
        switch (touch.phase) {
            case UITouchPhaseBegan:
            case UITouchPhaseMoved:
            case UITouchPhaseStationary:
                [array addObject:[NSValue valueWithCGPoint: ↵
                                    [touch locationInView:self]]];
                break;
            default:
                break;
            }
        }
    touchPoints = array;
    [self setNeedsDisplay];
}
```

You'll also want to declare that method in a private interface before the @implementation statement, and you'll also need to define a variable to store the active touch points:

```
@interface TYTouchyView ()
{
    NSArray* touchPoints;
}
- (void)updateTouches:(NSSet*)set;
@end
```

Now, back to the -updateTouches: method. It starts by creating an empty array object. This is where you'll store the information you're interested in. -updateTouches: then loops through each of the UITouch objects in the set and examines its *phase*. The phase of a touch is its current state: "began," "moved," "stationary," "ended," or "canceled." Touchy is only interested in the states that represent a finger that is still touching the glass ("began," "moved," and "stationary"). The switch statement matches these three states, obtains the coordinates of the touch relative to this view object, and converts that into an NSValue object (suitable for adding to a collection). The NSValue object is then added to the collection.

When all of the active touch coordinates have been gathered, the new collection is saved in your object's private touchPoints variable. Finally, your view object sends itself a -setNeedsDisplay message. This message tells your view object that it needs to redraw itself.

Drawing Your View

So far, you haven't written code to draw anything. You've just intercepted the touch events sent to your view and extracted the information you want about the device's touch state. In iOS, you don't draw things when they happen. You make note of when something needs to be drawn, and wait for iOS to tell your object when to draw it. Drawing is initiated by the user interface update events I mentioned at the beginning of this chapter.

How drawing works is described in Chapter 11, so I won't go into any of those details now. Just know that when iOS wants your view to draw itself, your object will receive a -drawRect: message. Add this -drawRect: message to your implementation:

```
- (void)drawRect:(CGRect)rect
{
    CGContextRef context = UIGraphicsGetCurrentContext();
    [[UIColor blackColor] set];
    CGContextFillRect(context,rect);

    UIBezierPath *path = nil;
    if (touchPoints.count>1)
        {
        path = [UIBezierPath bezierPath];
        NSValue* firstLocation = nil;
        for ( NSValue *location in touchPoints )
            {
            if (firstLocation==nil)
                {
                firstLocation = location;
                [path moveToPoint:location.CGPointValue];
                }
            else
                {
                [path addLineToPoint:location.CGPointValue];
                }
            }
        if (touchPoints.count>2)
            [path addLineToPoint:firstLocation.CGPointValue];

        [[UIColor lightGrayColor] set];
        path.lineWidth = 6;
        path.lineCapStyle = kCGLineCapRound;
        path.lineJoinStyle = kCGLineJoinRound;
        [path stroke];
        }
    unsigned int touchNumber = 1;
    NSDictionary* fontAttrs = @{
        NSFontAttributeName: [UIFont boldSystemFontOfSize:180],
        NSForegroundColorAttributeName: [UIColor yellowColor]
        };
```

```
        for ( NSValue *location in touchPoints )
        {
        NSString *text = [NSString stringWithFormat:@"%u",touchNumber++];
        CGSize size = [text sizeWithAttributes:fontAttrs];
        CGPoint touchPoint = location.CGPointValue;
        CGPoint textCorner = CGPointMake(touchPoint.x-size.width/2,
                                        touchPoint.y-size.height/2);
        [text drawAtPoint:textCorner withAttributes:fontAttrs];
        }
}
```

Wow, that's a lot of new code. Again, the details aren't important, but feel free to study this code to get a feel for what it's doing. I'll merely summarize what it does.

The first part fills the entire view with the color black.

The middle section is a big loop that creates a Bezier path, named after the French engineer Pierre Bézier. A Bezier path can represent practically any line, polygon, curve, ellipsis, or any arbitrary combination of those things. Basically, if it's a shape, a Bezier path can draw it. You'll learn all about Bezier paths in chapter 11. Here, it's used to draw light grey lines between the touch points. It's pure eye candy, and this part of the -drawRect: method could be left out and the app would still work just fine.

The last part is the interesting bit. It loops through the touch coordinates and draws a big "1," "2," or "3" centered underneath each finger that's touching the screen, in yellow.

Now you have custom view class that collects touch events, tracks them, and draws them on the screen. The last piece of this puzzle is how to get your custom object into your interface.

Adding Custom Objects in Interface Builder

Select your Main_iPhone.storyboard Interface Builder file and select the one and only view object in the view controller scene. Switch to the identity inspector. The identity inspector shows you the class of the object selected. In this case, it's the plain-vanilla UIView object created by the project template.

Here's the cool trick: You can use the identity inspector to change the class of the object to any subclass of UIView that you've created. Change the class of this view object from UIView to TYTouchyView, as shown in Figure 4-26. You can do this either by using the pull-down menu or by just typing in the name of the class.

Figure 4-26. Changing the class of an Interface Builder object

Now instead of creating a `UIView` object as the root view, your app will create a `TYTouchyView` object, complete with all of the methods, properties, outlets, and actions you defined. You can do this to any existing object in your interface. If you want to create a new custom object, find the base class object in the library (`NSObject`, `UIView`, etc.), add that object, and then change its class to your custom one.

There are still a few properties of your new `TYTouchyView` object that need to be customized for it to work correctly. With your `TYTouchyView` object still selected, switch to the attributes inspector and check the `Multiple Touch` option under Interaction. By default, view objects don't receive multi-touch events. In other words, the `-touchSomePhase:withEvent:` message will never contain more than one `UITouch` object, even if multiple touches exist. To allow your view to receive all of the touches, you must turn on the multiple touch option.

Select the `Main_iPad.storyboard` Interface Builder file and make the same changes you just made to `Main_iPhone.storyboard`. Now your app is ready to test.

> **Note** If you want to, give Touchy an icon too. Open the `Touchy (Resources)` folder, locate the five `TYIcon....png` files, and drag them into the `AppIcon` group of the `Images.xcassets` asset catalog, just as you did for the EightBall app.

Testing Touchy

Set your scheme to the iPhone or iPad simulator and run your project. The interface is completely—and ominously—black, as shown on the left in Figure 4-27.

Figure 4-27. Running Touchy in the simulator

Click on the interface and the number "1" appears, as shown in the middle of Figure 4-27. Try dragging it around. Touchy is tracking all changes to the touch interface, updating it, and then drawing a number under the exact location of each touch.

Hold down the option key and click again. Two positions appear, as shown on the right in Figure 4-27. The simulator will let you test simple two finger gestures when you hold down the option key. With just the option key, you can test pinch and zoom gestures. Hold down both the option and shift keys to test two-finger swipes.

But that's as far as the simulator will go. To test any other combination of touch events, you have to run your app on a real iOS device. Back in Xcode, stop your app, change the scheme to iOS Device (iPhone, iPad, or iPod Touch—whatever you have plugged in). Run your app again.

Now try out Touchy on your iOS device. Try touching two, three, four, or even five fingers. Try moving them around, picking one up, and putting it down again. It's surprisingly entertaining.

Advanced Event Handling

There are a couple of advanced event handling topics I'd like to mention, along with some good advice. I'll start with the advice.

Keep your event handling timely. As you now know, your app is "kept alive" by your main thread's run loop. That run loop delivers everything to your app: touch events, notifications, user interface updates, and so much more. Every event, action, and message that your app handles must execute and return before the next event can be processed. That means if any code you write takes too long, your app will appear to have died. And if code you write takes a really, really, long time to finish, your app *will* die—iOS will terminate your app because it's stopped responding to events.

I'm sure you've had an app "lock up" on you; the display is frozen, it doesn't respond to touches, or shaking, or anything. This is what happens when an app's run loop is off doing something other than processing events. It's not pleasant. Most iOS features that can take a long time to complete have asynchronous methods (like the ones you used in Shorty) so those time-consuming tasks won't tie up your main thread. Use these asynchronous methods, pay attention to how long your program takes to do things, and be prepared to reorganize your app to avoid "locking up" your run loop. I'll demonstrate all of these techniques in later chapters.

Secondly, handling multiple touch events can be tricky, even confusing. iOS does its best to untangle the complexity of touch events and present them to your object in a rational, and digestible, form. iOS provides five features that will make your touch event handling simpler:

- Gesture recognizers
- Filtering out touch events for other views
- Prohibiting multi-touch events
- Providing exclusive touch event handling
- Suspending touch events

Gesture recognizers are special objects and intercept touch events on behalf of a view object. Each recognizer detects a specific touch gesture, from a simple tap to a complex multi-finger swipe. If it detects the gesture it's programmed to recognize, it sends an action—exactly like the button objects you've used in earlier projects. All you need to do is connect that action to an object in Interface Builder and you're done. This feature alone has saved iOS developers tens of thousands of lines of touch event handling code. I'll show you how to use gesture recognizer objects in later chapters.

As I described earlier, the touch event methods (like -eventBegan:withEvent:) only include the relevant touch objects—those touches that originated in your view object—in the touches parameter. Your code doesn't have to worry about other touches in other views that might be happening at the same time. In Touchy, this was actually a disadvantage, and you had to dig up the global set of touch objects from the UIEvent object. But normally, you only pay attention to the touches in your view.

You've also seen how iOS will prohibit multi-touch events using UIView's multipleTouchEnabled property. If this property is NO, iOS will only send your view object events associated with the first touch—even if the user is actually touching your view with more than one finger. For the Touchy app to get events about all of the touches, you had to set this property to YES. Set this property to NO if your view only interprets single touch events and you won't have to write any code that worries about more than one touch at a time.

If you don't want iOS to be sending touch events to two view objects simultaneously, you can set UIView's exclusiveTouch property to YES. If set, iOS will block touch events from being sent to any other views once a touch sequence has begun in yours (and vice versa).

Finally, if your app needs to, you can temporary suspend all touch events from being sent to a specific view or even your entire app. If you want to make an individual view "deaf" to touch events, set its userInteractionEnabled property to NO. You can also send your application object the -beginIgnoreingInteractionEvents message, and all touch events for you app will be silenced. Turn them back on again by sending -endIgnoringInteractionEvents. This is useful for preventing touch events from interfering with something else that's going on (say, a short animation), but don't leave them turned off for very long.

Summary

By now you have a pretty firm grasp on how messages and events get into your app and how they are handled. You know about the event queue and the run loop. You know that events in the queue are dispatched to the objects in your app. You know that some of them go directly to your objects, touch events use hit testing, and the rest get sent to the first responder.

You've learned a lot about the responder chain. The responder chain performs a number of important tasks in iOS, beyond delivering events.

You know how to configure an object to handle, or ignore, specific types of events. You've written two apps, one that handled high-level events, and a second that tracked low-level touch events.

Possibly even more astounding, you built and ran your app on a real iOS device! Feel free to run any other projects on your device too. Creating your very own iOS app that you can carry around with you is a very impressive feat!

In the next chapter, you're going to learn a little about data models and how complex sets of data get turned into scrolling lists on the screen.

EXERCISES

According to the instructions that come with the Magic Eight Ball, you should not shake the ball; it causes bubbles to form in the liquid. Of course, this never stopped my brother and I from shaking the daylights out of it. Instead, you were supposed to place the ball, "8" up, on a table, ask a question, gently turn it over, and read the answer.

For extra credit, rewrite the EightBall app so it uses the device orientation events, instead of shake motion events, to make the message disappear and appear. A device's orientation will be one of portrait, landscape left, landscape right, upside down, face up, or face down.

Changes in device orientation are delivered via notifications. You haven't used notifications yet, but think of them as just another kind of event (at least in this context). Unlike events, your object must explicitly request the notifications it wants to receive. Whenever the device changes orientation, such as when the user turns their iPhone over, your object will receive a notification message.

All of the code you need to request and handle device orientation change notifications is shown in the *Event Handling Guide for iOS*, under the section "Getting the Current Device Orientation with UIDevice." In Xcode, choose **Help ➤ Documentation and API Guide**, and search for "Event Handling Guide".

Change EightBall so it requests device orientation notifications instead of handling shake motion events. When your app receives an orientation change notification, examine the current orientation of the current UIDevice object. If the orientation property is UIDeviceOrientationFaceUp, make a new message appear. If it's anything else, make the message disappear. Now you have a more "authentic" Magic Eight Ball simulator! You can find my solution to this exercise in the EightBall E1 folder.

Chapter 5

Table Manners

Tables are a powerful and flexible iOS interface element. So flexible that—in many applications—table views *are* the interface. In this chapter you're going to learn about table views and pick up some class organization and inter-object communication skills in the process. By the end of this chapter you'll know about:

- Table views
- Table cells
- Cell caching
- Table editing
- Notifications

The app you'll create in this chapter will depend a lot more on Objective-C code than Interface Builder. This is typical of table view interfaces because the table view classes already provide much of the look of your table, so there's not much for you to design. (That doesn't mean you *can't* design your own, and I'll discuss that too.) First, you need to know what a table view looks like.

Table Views

A *table view* is a `UITableView` object that presents, draws, manages, and scrolls a single vertical list of rows. Each *row* is one element in the table. Rows can all be alike (homogeneous) or can be substantially different (heterogeneous) from one another. A table can appear as a continuous list of rows or it may organize rows into groups.

If you've used an iPhone, iPad, or iPod for more than a few minutes, you've seen table views in action. In fact, there are probably more than a few iOS app interfaces that you didn't realize are table views. By the time you're done with this section, you'll be able to spot them from a mile away.

The overall appearance of a table is set by the *table style* you choose when the table view is created. Its contents can be further refined by the style and layout of the individual rows. I'll start by describing the overall table styles.

Plain Tables

The plain table style (UITableViewStylePlain) is the one you're most likely to recognize as a table view or list. The view on the left of Figure 5-1 shows a snapshot of my Settings app. The list of regions is a plain style table view. Each row shows one region. The arrow on the right (called an accessory view) indicates that tapping that row will navigate to another list.

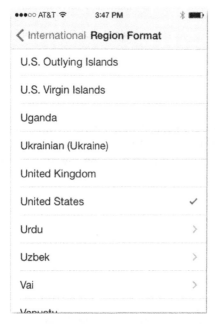 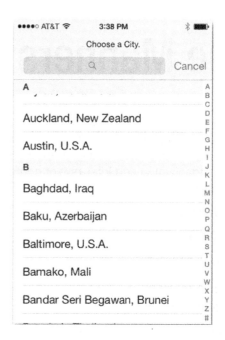

Figure 5-1. Plain table styles

On the right of Figure 5-1 is a plain style table with an index, a common embellishment for long lists. An index adds section labels that group similar items, and provides a quick way of jumping to a particular group in the list, using the index on the right.

Another, somewhat obscure, plain table style is the selection list style (not shown). It looks just like a plain style table with section titles, but has no index. It's used to choose one or more options from a (potentially long) list of options.

Grouped Tables

The grouped table style (UITableViewStyleGrouped) is the other table style. This style clumps sets of rows together into groups. Each group has an optional header and an optional footer, allowing you to surround the group with a title, description, or even explanatory text. Examples of grouped tables are shown in Figure 5-2.

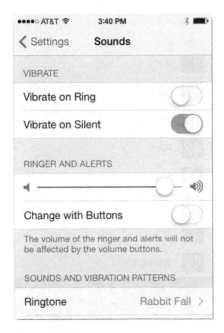 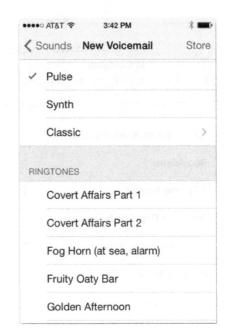

Figure 5-2. Grouped table style

The iPhone's Settings app (see Figure 5-2) is built almost exclusively from table views. The title above each group is a *group header*. The text below is a *group footer*. The individual setting controls are each one row of the table. It almost doesn't look like a table at all, but it uses the same UITableView object that Figure 5-1 does. Grouped lists do not have indexes.

The style you choose for the list sets the overall tone of your table. You then have a lot of choices when it comes to how each individual row looks.

Cell Styles

A *table view cell* object controls the appearance and content of each row. iOS comes with several styles of table cells:

- Default
- Subtitle
- Value1
- Value2

The default style (UITableViewCellStyleDefault) is the basic one, as shown in Figure 5-3.

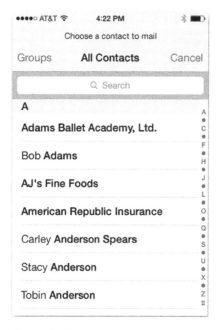 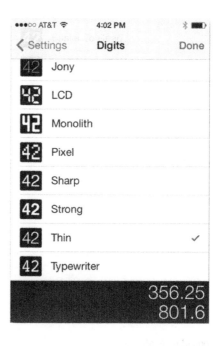

Figure 5-3. Default cell style

The default style has a bold title. It may optionally include a small image, which appears on the left. The arrow, checkmark, or control on the right is called an accessory view, and I'll talk about those shortly.

The second major cell style is the subtitle style (`UITableViewCellStyleSubtitle`), shown in Figure 5-4. Almost identical to the default style, it also shows a deemphasized line of text below each title. The subtitle text is also optional. If you leave out the subtitle it will look like the default style.

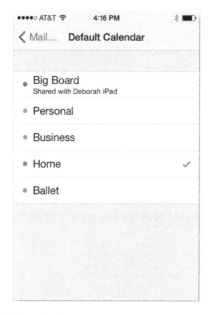 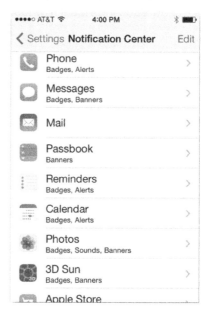

Figure 5-4. Subtitle cell style

The last two styles are the value1 and value2 styles (`UITableViewCellStyleValue1` and `UITableViewCellStyleValue2`), as shown in Figure 5-5. The value1 style (on the left in Figure 5-5) is typically used to display a series of values or settings; the title of the cell describes the value and the field on the right shows the current value.

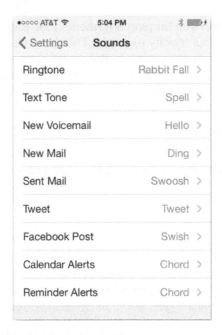 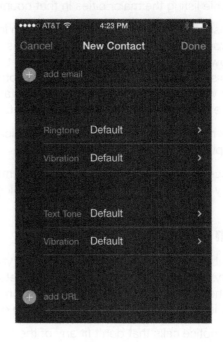

Figure 5-5. Value1 and value2 cell styles

The alternate style, value2, puts more emphasis on the value and less on its title, as shown on the right of Figure 5-5. You'll see this style of cell used in the Contacts app. Neither value1 nor value2 cell styles allow an image.

Cell Accessories

On the right of all standard cell styles is the optional *accessory view*. iOS provides three standard accessory views, as shown in Figure 5-6.

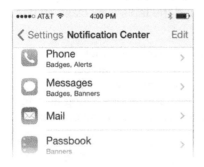 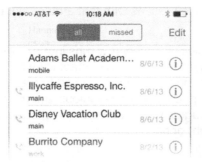 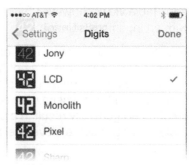

Figure 5-6. Standard accessory views

The standard accessory views are (from left to right in Figure 5-6) the disclosure indicator, detail disclosure button, and checkmark. The first two are used to indicate that tapping the row or the button will disclose—navigate to—another screen or view that displays details about that row. Nested lists are often organized this way. For example, in a table of countries each row navigates to another table listing the major cities in that country.

The disclosure indicator is not a control. It's an indication that tapping anywhere in the row will navigate you to some additional information, as in the country/city example. The detail disclosure button, however, is a regular button. You must tap the accessory view button to navigate to the details. This frees the row itself to have some other purpose. The Phone app's recent calls table works this way (see the middle of Figure 5-6); tapping a row places a call to that person, while tapping the detail disclosure button navigates to their contact information.

The check mark is just that, and is used to indicate when a row has been selected or marked, for whatever purpose.

A cell's accessory view can also be set to a control view of your choosing (such as a toggle switch). This is very common in tables that display settings (see Figure 5-2).

Custom Cells

The two table view styles, four cell styles, and various accessory views provide a remarkable amount of flexibility. If you peruse just the Contacts, Settings, and Music apps from Apple, it's almost stunning the number of interfaces (dozens, by my count) that are just different combinations of the built-in table and cell styles, with judicious use of optional images, subtitles, and accessory views.

You'll also notice cells that don't fit any of the styles I've described. There's a wildcard in the table cell deck: you can design your own cell. A `UITableCell` object is a subclass of `UIView`. So, in theory, a table cell can contain *any* view objects you want, even custom ones you've designed yourself using Objective-C and Interface Builder. So don't fret if the standard styles don't exactly fit your needs, you can always create your own.

Now that you have an idea of what's possible, it's time to take a closer look at how tables work.

How Table Views Work

Up to this point, every visual element in your apps has been a view object. In other words, there's been a one-to-one relationship between what you see on your device and a `UIView` object in your app. Table views, however, have a few issues with that arrangement, and the table view class comes with an ingenious solution.

A table view that creates a cell object for every row runs into a number of problems when the number of rows is large. It's not hard to imagine a contact list with several hundred names, or a music list with several *thousand* songs. If a table view had to create a cell object for every single song, it would overwhelm your app, consume a ridiculous amount of memory, require a long time to create, and generally result in a sluggish and cumbersome interface. To avoid all of these problems, table views use some clever sleight of hand.

Table Cells and Rubber Stamps

If you've ever filed papers with the county clerk, or shopped in a supermarket in the days before UPC barcodes, you're familiar with the idea of a rubber stamp that can be altered to stamp a particular date or price, using a dial or movable segments. It would be ludicrous if your county clerk had to have a different rubber stamp for every date. Similarly, table views don't create cell objects for every row. They create one cell object—or at least a very small number—and reuse that cell object to draw each row in the table, kind of like a rubber stamp.

Figure 5-7 shows the concept of reusing a cell object. In this figure, there are only three (principal) view objects: a UITableView object, a UITableViewCell object, and a data source object. The table view reuses the one cell object to draw each row.

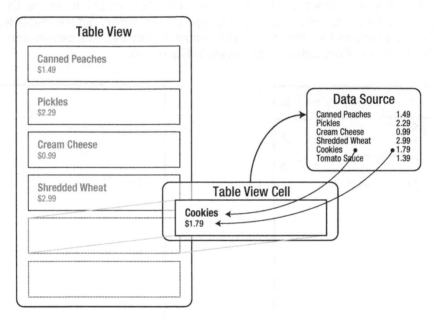

Figure 5-7. Reusable cell object

The table view does this using a delegate object, just like the delegate object you used in the Shorty app. When you create a table view object you must provide it with a *data source* object. Your data source object implements specific delegate methods that the table view object will send when it wants a cell object configured to draw a particular row.

Continuing with the rubber stamp analogy, pretend you have a table view that wants to print a list of products and their prices. It starts by handing your (data source) object the rubber stamp (cell object) and saying, "Please configure this stamp for the first product in the list." Your object then sets the properties of the stamp (product name and price) and hands the configured stamp back to the table view. The table view uses the stamp to print the first row. It then turns around and repeats this process for the second row, and so on, until all of the rows have been printed.

Using this technique, a table view can draw tables that are thousands of rows tall using only a few objects. It's fast, flexible, and wickedly efficient.

MyStuff

You're going to create a personal inventory app named MyStuff. It's a relatively simple app that manages a list of items you own, recording the name of each item and where you keep it (living room, kitchen, and so on).

Design

This app's design is slightly more involved than the last two. It's complicated, a little, by the differences between the iPhone and iPad. Apple's Mail app looks substantially different on the iPhone versus the iPad. That's because the iPhone only has enough screen space to comfortably display one thing at a time—either the list of messages or the content of a message. On the iPad there's plenty of room for both. The underlying app logic is very similar, but the visual design is quite different. You'll have to account for this in both your visual design and, to a certain extent, in your logic design. Start with the iPhone design, as shown in Figure 5-8.

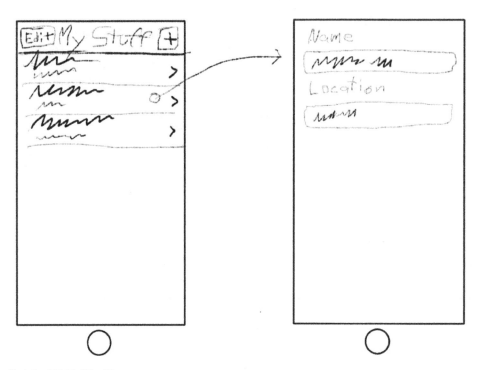

Figure 5-8. Sketch of MyStuff for iPhone

The iPhone design is simple, and typical of how table views work. The main screen is a list of your items, listing their description and location. Tapping an item navigates to a second screen where you can edit those values.

The iPad design is less structured. In landscape orientation, the list of items will appear on the left, as shown in Figure 5-9. Tapping an item makes the details of that item appear on the right, where they can be changed. In portrait orientation (not shown) the item detail consumes the screen while the list of items becomes a pop-up that the user accesses via a button in the upper-left corner of the screen.

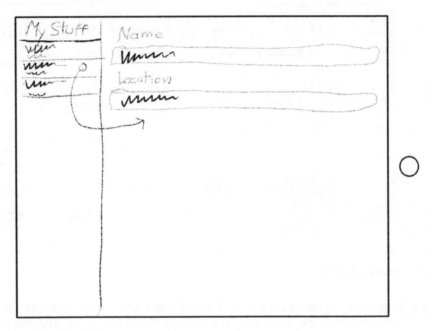

Figure 5-9. Sketch of MyStuff for iPad

If this interface looks familiar, it's the same one used by Apple's Mail app. This is not a trivial interface to program, but you're in luck; Xcode has an app template that includes all of the code needed to make this design work. You just have to fill in the details, which is exactly what you're going to do next.

Creating The Project

As with all apps, begin by creating a new project in Xcode. This time, choose the Master Detail iOS application template, as shown in Figure 5-10.

Figure 5-10. Creating a Master Detail app

The Master Detail template is so named because it's what computer developers call this kind of interface. The list is your *master* view, displaying a summary of all of the data. The master view segues to a secondary *detail* view that might show more specifics about that item or provide tools for editing it.

Name the project `MyStuff`, give it a class prefix of `MS`, and make sure `Use Core Data` is turned off. Set the devices option to `Universal`. Click **Next** and save your new project folder somewhere.

The first thing you'll notice is that there's a lot of code in this project already. The Master Detail template includes all of the code needed to display a list of items, navigate to a detail interface, create new items, delete items, and handle orientation changes. The content of its table is simple `NSDate` objects. Your job is to replace those placeholder objects with something of substance.

> **Tip** You'd do well to spend some time looking over the code included by the project template. It does "all the right things" when it comes to navigation, orientation changes, presenting pop-up views, and so on. You'll read more about navigation in Chapter 12.

Creating Your Data Model

You know that you want to display a list of "things"—the individual items that you own. And you know that each thing is going to need at least two properties, a name property and a location property, both strings. So what object is going to represent each thing? That's a very important question, because this mysterious object (or objects) is what's called your *data model*. Your data model comprises the objects that represent whatever concept your table view is displaying.

> **Note** The theory and practice behind data models is described in Chapter 8.

Clearly the Cocoa Touch framework doesn't include such an object, so you'll have to create one! In the project navigator, select the `MyStuff` folder (not the project) towards the top of the navigator. From either the **File** menu, or by right/control+clicking on the folder, choose the **New File**… command.

In the template assistant, select the iOS Cocoa Touch group, and then choose the Objective-C Class template. Click **Next**. Name the class `MyWhatsit` and make it a subclass of `NSObject`, as shown in Figure 5-11.

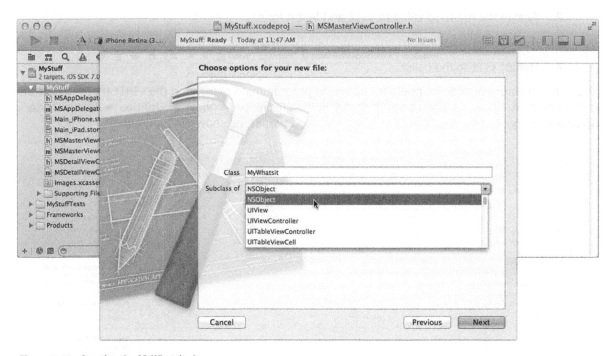

Figure 5-11. Creating the MyWhatsit class

Click **Next**, accept the default location (the `MyStuff` project folder), and click Create. Now you have a new class of objects in your app named `MyWhatsit`. Select the `MyWhatsit.h` interface file in the navigator. It's pretty bleak. This is the class of objects that will represent each item that you own. Each one will need a name and a location property. Define those now by adding the following to its interface:

```
@property (strong,nonatomic) NSString *name;
@property (strong,nonatomic) NSString *location;
```

Congratulations, you now have a data model. You'll also want to create your `MyWhatsit` objects with something other than nothing for a name and location, so define an "init" method that creates an object and sets both properties in a single statement. (This isn't a requirement, but it will make some of your code easier to write.) Start by adding this method declaration to your interface file:

```
- (id)initWithName:(NSString*)name location:(NSString*)location;
```

Switch to your implementation of MyWhatsit (MyWhatsit.m). Initialization (or just "init") methods are object constructor methods. They exist to correctly instantiate a new instance of that class. Every class inherits the plain vanilla -init method, but many classes define more elaborate initialization methods, and you're free to create your own.

All init methods follow a well-defined pattern, or contract. Every -init method must:

1. Start by sending the appropriate -init message to its superclass.
2. Assign the returned value to self and test it for nil.
3. If self is not nil, initialize any class-specific properties.
4. Return self to the caller.

Xcode has a library of code snippets for common programming tasks, and the -init method pattern is no exception. Show the code snippet library in the utilities pane (**View ▶ Utilities ▶ Show Code Snippit Library**). Locate the Objective-C init Method snippet, as shown in Figure 5-12.

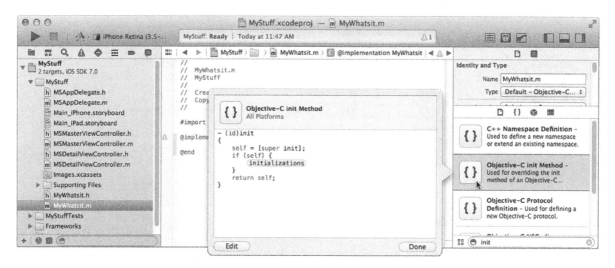

Figure 5-12. Objective-C init method snippet

Drag the snippet into the @implementation section of your MyWhatsit.m file. Replace the generic -(id)init declaration with yours:

```
- (id)initWithName:(NSString*)name location:(NSString*)location
```

Hold down the Control key and press the / (forward slash) key. This editor shortcut jumps to the placeholder in the -init method template. Code snippets often contain placeholders that you need to replace with your code. This navigation command lets you jump right to them. Replace the placeholder with:

```
self.name = name;
self.location = location;
```

When you're finished, your implementation should look like the one in Figure 5-13.

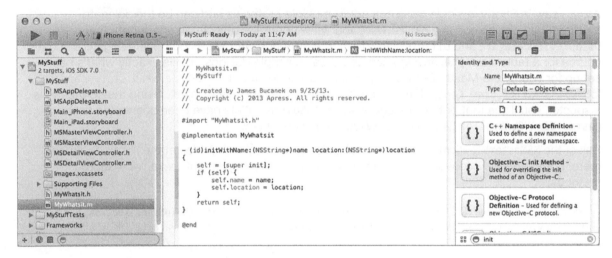

Figure 5-13. Complete MyWhatsit implementation

Now that you have a data model, your next task is to teach the table view class how to use it.

Creating a Data Source

A table view object (UITableView) has *two* delegate properties. Its delegate property works just like the delegates you used in earlier chapters. The table view delegate is optional. If you choose to use one, it must be connected to an object that adopts the UITableViewDelegate protocol.

The table view's other delegate is its *data source* object. For a table view to work, you must set its dataSource property to an object that adopts the UITableViewDataSource protocol. This delegate is not optional—without it, your table won't display anything.

The data source's job is to provide the table view with all of the information it needs to arrange and display the contents of the table. At a minimum, your data source must:

- Report the number of rows in the table
- Configure the table view cell (rubber stamp) object for each row

A data source can also provide lots of optional information to the table view. Your data source for this app won't need to implement any of these, but here are the kinds of things you can customize:

- Organize rows into groups
- Display section titles

- Provide an index (for indexed lists)
- Provide custom header and footer views for grouped tables
- Control which rows are selectable
- Control which rows are editable
- Control which rows are movable

As you saw in Shorty, a single class can adopt multiple protocols and can be the delegate for more than one object. In a similar vein, your view controller object can adopt both the `UITableViewDelegate` and `UITableViewDataSource` protocols and act as both the delegate and data source for a table view. This arrangement is typical in simple designs, and is exactly what's been set up for you by the Master Details project template. Click the `Main_iPhone/iPad.storyboard` file, locate the `Master View Controller` scene, and select the table view object. Using the connections inspector, you'll see that both its delegate and dataSource outlets have been connected to the `Master View Controller` (your `MSMasterViewController` object).

Select the `MSMasterViewController.m` implementation file and take a look at the methods defined there. For a table view to work, your data source object must implement these two required methods:

```
- (NSInteger)tableView:(UITableView *)tableView numberOfRowsInSection:(NSInteger)section;
- (UITableViewCell *)tableView:(UITableView *)tableView cellForRowAtIndexPath:(NSIndexPath *)indexPath;
```

The first message is sent to your data source object whenever the table view wants to know how many rows are in a particular section of your table. Remember, some tables can be grouped into sections, with each section having a different number of rows. For a simple table (like yours) there's only one section (0), so just return the total number of rows.

You're going to store your `MyWhatsit` objects in an array. One has already been defined in `MSMasterViewController`, but let's rename it. At the top of the `MSMasterViewController.m` file, find the `@interface` section, select the _objects instance variable, right/control+click on it, and choose **Refactor ➤ Rename...** from the pop-up menu, as shown in Figure 5-14.

Figure 5-14. Renaming a variable

Xcode's refactoring system makes changing names, promoting and demoting methods, splitting classes, and so on relatively painless. In the rename dialog, change the name from _objects to things and click the Preview button. Xcode will find every reference to that variable and present a dialog showing your source before and after the proposed changes, as shown in Figure 5-15. Click the Save button. (Xcode may ask to take a snapshot of your project; go ahead, it's a good idea.)

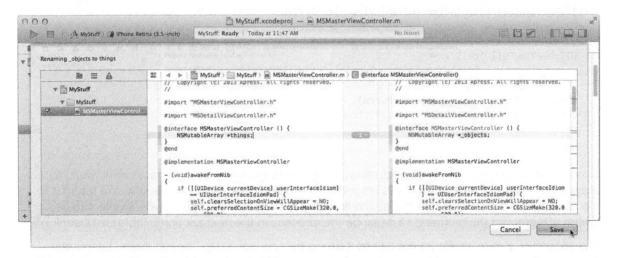

Figure 5-15. Previewing a variable name change

So why did I have you change the name of _objects? There are two reasons. The first is that code is easier to understand if the names you choose for variables have specific meanings. The variable _objects was just a little too generic for my tastes. Secondly, you shouldn't create variable names that begin with an underscore. I know you didn't name it, but it bothers me nonetheless.

> **Tip** Apple reserves all symbol names that begin with a single underscore. The Objective-C compiler reserves all symbol names that begin with two underscores. To avoid name conflicts, don't start your variable, class, or preprocessor names with a single or double underscore. The Master Detail template can get away with this because the template was developed by Apple (not you).

Now it's time to visit those two required data source methods.

Implementing Your Rubber Stamp

Find the -tableView:numberOfRowsInSection: method. Here's what it looks like:

```
- (NSInteger)tableView:(UITableView *)tableView numberOfRowsInSection:(NSInteger)section
{
    return things.count;
}
```

There's nothing to change here. The method already does exactly what you need it to do: return the number of rows (MyWhatsit objects) in your table.

Move on to the -tableView:cellForRowAtIndexPath: method. The code currently looks like this:

```
- (UITableViewCell *)tableView:(UITableView *)tableView
         cellForRowAtIndexPath:(NSIndexPath *)indexPath
{
    UITableViewCell *cell = ↪
                    [tableView dequeueReusableCellWithIdentifier:@"Cell"
                                                    forIndexPath:indexPath];
    NSDate *object = things[indexPath.row];
    cell.textLabel.text = [object description];
    return cell;
}
```

This is your rubber stamp. Your object receives this message every time the table view wants to draw a row. Your job is to prepare a UITableViewCell object that will draw that row and return it to the sender. This happens in two steps. The first step is to get the UITableViewCell object to use. Ignore that step for the moment; I'll describe this process in the next section ("Table Cell Caching").

The second step is to configure the cell so it draws the row correctly. The last three statements are where that happens. Right now, it expects to get an NSDate object from the array and set the label of the cell to its description. This is the code you need to replace. But first, your

`MSMasterViewController.m` file needs to know about your `MyWhatsit` object. At the top of the file, just below the other #import statements, add this line:

```
#import "MyWhatsit.h"
```

Now go back to your `-tableView:cellForRowAtIndexPath:` method and replace the last three statements in the method with:

```
MyWhatsit *thing = things[indexPath.row];
cell.textLabel.text = thing.name;
cell.detailTextLabel.text = thing.location;
return cell;
```

Now your rubber stamp gets the `MyWhatsit` object for the row to be drawn (from the `indexPath` object) and stores it in the `thing` variable. It then uses the `name` and `location` properties to set the `textLabel` (title) and `detailTextLabel` (subtitle) of the cell.

> **Note** Table views use `NSIndexPath` objects to identify rows in a table. The `NSIndexPath` objects used by `UITableView` have a `section` and `row` property that unambiguously identifies each row. Since your table only has one section, you can ignore the `section` property; it will always be 0.

The cell you return will be used to draw the row. That was the easy part. Now take one step back and look at the first part of that method again.

Table Cell Caching

In the rubber stamp analogy, I said that the table view "gives you a rubber stamp and asks you to configure it." I lied—at least a little. The table view doesn't give you the cell object to use because it doesn't know what kind of cell object you need. Instead, a cell object is created by either the storyboard or code you write, and the table view hangs onto it so you can reuse it again next time. This is called the *table cell cache*.

There are three ways of using the table cell cache:

- Let your storyboard create the cell objects
- Lazily create cell objects programmatically, as needed
- Ignore the cache entirely

In this app, you'll take the first approach. The Master Detail project template has already defined a single table cell object, with the unimaginative identifier `"Cell"`. Select the `Main_iPhone.storyboard` file and select the table view object in the `Master View Controller` scene, as shown in Figure 5-16.

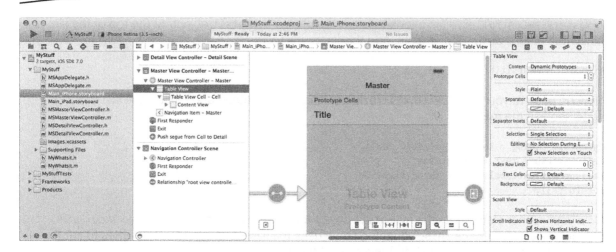

Figure 5-16. Table view with prototype table cell

At the top of the table view you'll see a `Prototype Cells` region. This is where Interface Builder lets you design the cell objects that your table view will use. The `Prototype Cells` count (shown in the attributes inspector on the right of Figure 5-16) declares how many different cell objects your table needs. You only need one.

Click on the one and only prototype cell template, as shown in Figure 5-17. Now you're editing a single table cell object. Notice that the `Identifier` property is set to `Cell`; this identifies the cell in the cache and must exactly match the identifier you pass in the `-dequeueReusableCellWithIdentifier:forIndexPath:` message.

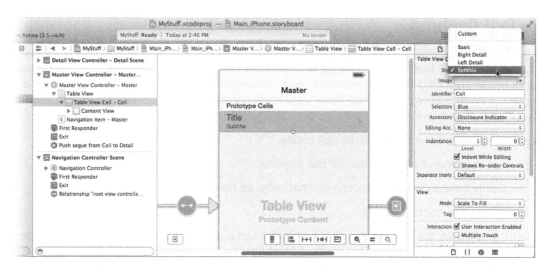

Figure 5-17. Editing a table cell prototype

Your table will display the name of the object and its location. The standard cell type that fits that description is the subtitle style (UITableViewCellStyleSubtitle). Change the cell's style to Subtitle, as shown in the upper-right of Figure 5-17.

Your table view design is complete. You've defined a single cell object, with an identifier of "Cell", that uses the subtitle table cell style.

CELL OBJECT IDENTIFIERS AND REUSE

The table view cell cache makes it easy for your -tableView:cellForRowAtIndexPath: method to efficiently reuse table cell view objects, and there are a variety of different ways to use it.

At one extreme, you don't have to use the cache at all. Your -tableView:cellForRowAtIndexPath: method could return a new cell object every time it's called. This would be appropriate for a tiny number of rows, where each row was completely different—the kind of interface you see in the Settings app, for example.

An alternative, and the more traditional, way of using the table cell cache is to programmatically create your table cell view objects, as needed. This is also called *lazy* object creation. You do this by checking to see if the cell object you need is already in the cache and create one only if it isn't. The code to do that looks like this:

```
id cellIdent = @"LazyCell"; // choose appropriate cell here
UITableViewCell *cell;
cell = [tableView dequeueReusableCellWithIdentifier:cellIdent];
if (cell==nil)
    {
    cell = [[UITableViewCell alloc] initWithStyle:UITableViewCellStyleSubtitle
                                                    reuseIdentifier:cellIdent];
    // one-time cell view configuration goes here
    cell.accessoryType = UITableViewCellAccessoryDisclosureIndicator;
    }
```

This code asks the table cell cache if a cell with that identifier has already been added. If not, the message will return nil, indicating there's no such object in the cache. Your code responds by creating a new cell object, assigning it the same cell identifier. When you return this cell object to the table view, it will automatically add it to its cache. Next time, that cell view object will be in the cache.

A third alternative is to register a cell view class or Interface Builder file with the table using the -registerClass:для CellReuseIdentifier: or -registerNib:forCellReuseIdentifier: messages. After you do that, requests for a cell with that identifier that's not in the cache will automatically create one for you. (This is, essentially, what happens when you design prototype cells using the storyboard.)

Using cell identifiers, you can also maintain a small stable of different cell objects. In your MyStuff app, you might one day decide to have a different row design for Star Wars memorabilia and another row design for stuff you got from your grandmother. You would assign each cell object its own identifier (@"Cell", @"Star Wars", @"Me Ma"). The table view cell cache would then keep all three cell objects, returning the appropriate one when you send it the

-dequeueReusableCellWithIdentifier: message. To do this using a storyboard, set the Prototype Cells count to 3 and assign a unique identifier to each prototype cell.

You are free to mix and match any of these techniques. A single table could have some cell view objects that are defined in the storyboard, others registered to be created by class name, and your code could lazily create the rest.

While you're here, change the name in the navigation bar from Master to My Stuff. Do this by double-clicking on the "Master" title in navigation bar above the table view (see Figure 5-17). You've now implemented all of the code needed to display your MyWhatsit objects in a table view. There's only one thing missing...

Where's the Data?

You can run your app right now, but it won't display anything. That's because you don't have any MyWhatsit objects to display. To make things worse, you haven't written any of the code to create or edit objects yet, so if you tried to create one your app will just crash.

My solution in these situations is to cheat; programmatically create a few test objects so the interface has something to display. Find the -awakeFromNib method in MSMasterViewController.m. This message is sent to any object created by an Interface Builder file. It gives you an opportunity to do any additional setup that couldn't be accomplished in Interface Builder.

The last statement in that method will be [super awakeFromNib]. Immediately before that, add this code (in bold):

```
things = [@[
            [[MyWhatsit alloc] initWithName:@"Gort"
                                  location:@"den"],
            [[MyWhatsit alloc] initWithName:@"Disappearing TARDIS mug"
                                  location:@"kitchen"],
            [[MyWhatsit alloc] initWithName:@"Robot USB drive"
                                  location:@"office"],
            [[MyWhatsit alloc] initWithName:@"Sad Robot USB hub"
                                  location:@"office"],
            [[MyWhatsit alloc] initWithName:@"Solar Powered Bunny"
                                  location:@"office"]
            ] mutableCopy];
[super awakeFromNib];
```

This code creates five new MyWhatsit objects and assembles them into an array object. A mutable version of that array is then assigned to the things property variable. Now when your controller is first created, it will have a set of MyWhatsit objects to show.

Testing MyStuff

Set your scheme to one of the iPhone Simulators and run your app. Your table view of MyWhatsit objects appear, as shown on the left in Figure 5-18.

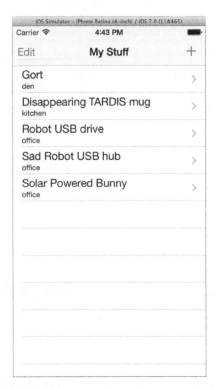 

Figure 5-18. Working table view

That's pretty cool! You've created your own data model object and implemented everything required to display your custom set of objects in a table view, using a cell format of your choosing.

But it's clear that this app isn't finished yet. If you tap one of the rows, you get a new screen (on the right in Figure 5-18) that doesn't make a lot of sense, and certainly isn't part of your design.

The next step is to design your details view. After that, you'll implement the code needed to edit the list and individual items.

Adding the Detail View

Now you're at the second half of the Master Detail design. Your detail view is controlled by the `MSDetailViewController` object. `MSDetailViewController` is a plain old `UIViewController` that load the view objects in the `Detail View Controller` scene. You need to create label and text field objects to display and edit your `MyWhatsit` properties. You'll need to create Interface Builder outlets in `MSDetailViewController` to connect with those text fields, and you'll need to connect them to their objects in Interface Builder. This should be familiar territory by now, so let's get started.

Creating the Detail View

Start with the iPhone interface. Select the `Main_iPhone.storyboard` file and then select the Detail View Controller object, as shown in Figure 5-19. Select and delete the label object in the view. You don't need it.

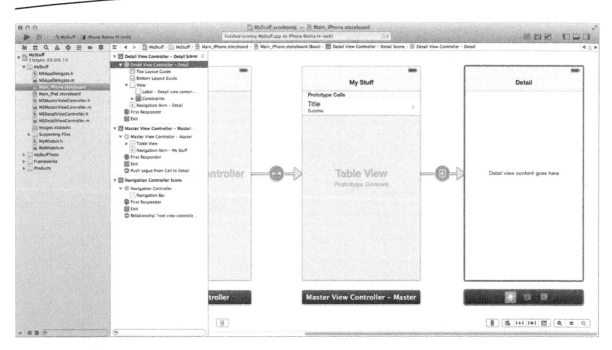

Figure 5-19. Template detail view

In the object library, locate the label object and add two of them to your view. Find the text field object and add two of those. Set the text of one label to Name and the other to Location. Arrange and resize them so your interface looks like the one in Figure 5-20. Choose the **Editor ➤ Resolve Auto Layout Issues ➤ Reset to Suggested Constraints in Detail View Controller** command.

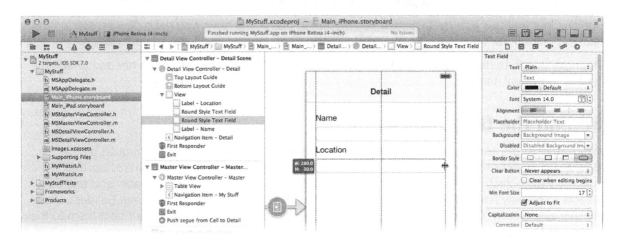

Figure 5-20. Finished detail view

Switch to the `MSDetailViewController.h` interface file. Underneath the `#import` statement, add another (so the compiler knows about your `MyWhatsit` class):

```
#import "MyWhatsit.h"
```

Change the type of the `detailItem` property so it's specifically a `MyWhatsit` object:

```
@property (strong,nonatomic) MyWhatsit *detailItem;
```

Delete the existing `detailDescriptionLabel` property and replace it with two new outlet properties:

```
@property (weak,nonatomic) IBOutlet UITextField *nameField;
@property (weak,nonatomic) IBOutlet UITextField *locationField;
```

Switch back to the `Main_iPhone.storyboard` file. Select the Detail View Controller object and use the connections inspector to connect the two new outlets (`nameField` and `locationField`) to the appropriate text field objects in the interface, as shown in Figure 5-21.

Figure 5-21. Connecting the text field outlets

Configuring the Detail View

You might be asking how the values of a `MyWhatsit` object are going to get into the two `UITextField` objects you just created. That's an excellent question. It's going to happen when the user taps on a row in the table view. Most of the code to get from that tap to your detail view has already been written for you (as part of the Master Detail Xcode template), but it's important to understand how it all works. Let's walk through the process of tapping on a row.

On the iPhone, tapping a row triggers a "push" seque that slides the detail view onto the screen. This push seque—the arrow connecting the master view to the detail view, shown in Figure 5-19—was pre-defined as part of the Master Detail project template. You can create your own seques by control/right-dragging from a prototype cell to the scene you want that cell to navigate to.

Just before a seque occurs, your view controller receives a `-prepareForSeque:sender:` message. Find that method in your `MSMasterViewController.m` file now. All seques from this view to another view send the same message. By examining the `seque.identifier` property, you can determine which seque is occurring—assuming you assigned each seque a unique identifier. In this case, you're interested in the `"showDetail"` seque.

The next step is to prepare the new view to be displayed. The existing code gets the object to edit from the `things` array. Unfortunately, this is template code that thinks there are `NSDate` objects in the array. Change it so it's a `MyWhatsit` object, like this (modified code in bold):

MyWhatsit *object = things[indexPath.row];

The rest of the code doesn't require any modification. It takes the `MyWhatsit` object and uses it to set the `detailItem` of the destination view controller, which you know to be the `MSDetailViewController`. Since you already changed the type of the `detailItem` to `MyWhatsit`, the two object types agree and the compiler warning disappears.

In the case of the iPad, the code path is a little different. There is no seque on the iPad because both the master list and the detail view are visible simultaneously. Click on the `Main_iPad.storyboard` file and notice that the cell prototype has no seque or disclosure accessory. Instead, your master view controller will intercept the user tapping on a cell in the list and update the detail view (which is already visible).

Whenever your user taps on a cell, the table view's delegate object receives a `-tableView:did SelectRowAtIndexPath:` message. Find this method in your `MSMasterViewController.m` file. The existing code first determines if this is an iPad or not. If it is, it performs the exact same task that `-prepareForSeque:sender:` does. It's also just as wrong. Make the same edit that you did in `-prepareForSeque:sender:`, changing the `NSDate` to `MyWhatsit`.

> **Note** The `-tableView:didSelectRowAtIndexPath:` message is sent to the table view's delegate object, not its data source object. In fact, this is the only table view delegate method your `MSMasterViewController` class implements. If you didn't need this message, you wouldn't need a table view delegate object at all.

Following the chain of events, find the `-setDetailItem:` method in the `MSDetailViewController.m` implementation file. This is the message the `MSDetailViewController` receives when you assign a value to the `detailItem` property (that is, when `self.detailViewController.detailItem = object` executes).

> **Tip** Hold down the Command key and click on a symbol to jump to its definition in the project. For example, in the expression `self.detailViewController.detailItem`, hold down the Command key and click on the symbol `detailItem`. Xcode will jump immediately to the `-setDetailItem:` method.

The -setDetailItem: method sets its internal _detailItem variable with the new object to display. It then sends itself a -configureView message. This is the message you're looking for (even if you didn't know it yet). The rest of the -setDetailItem: message handles the case where the item was chosen from a pop-over list on the iPad interface.

The -configureView message is received whenever your detail view controller needs to prepare itself to display a new MyWhatsit object. This is the method you need to rewrite so your MyWhatsit property values will appear in your interface. Edit -configureView so it looks like this:

```
- (void)configureView
{
    if (self.detailItem!=nil)
        {
        self.nameField.text = self.detailItem.name;
        self.locationField.text = self.detailItem.location;
        }
}
```

This new method checks to see if a detailItem object has been set. If it has, it uses the nameField and locationField connections to set the contents of its two text fields to the values of the name and location properties of the MyWhatsit object.

This completes the (iPhone) detail view! When the user taps a row, the delegate gets the MyWhatsit object for that row, passes it to your MSDetailViewController, which sends itself -configureView to make those values appear in the view. The MSDetailViewController then becomes the active view and viola, your detail appears, as shown on the right in Figure 5-22.

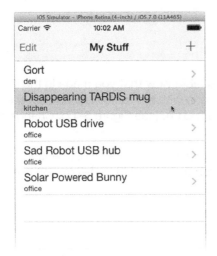

Figure 5-22. Working detail view

The only thing left to do is flesh out the iPad detail view. Like in previous projects, most of the work has already been done. In your `Main_iPhone.storyboard` file, copy the four view objects you just added; drag out a rectangle to select the two label and two text fields, and choose **Edit ➤ Copy**. Now switch to your `Main_iPad.storyboard` file. Delete the existing label object, click once in the blank view so Xcode knows where to paste your objects, and choose **Edit ➤ Paste**. Reposition and resize them so they fit the iPad interface, as shown in Figure 5-23. Choose **Reset to Suggested Constraints in Detail View Controller** from the **Resolve Auto Layout Issues** button. Select the Detail View Controller and use the connections inspector to connect the `nameField` and `locationField` outlets.

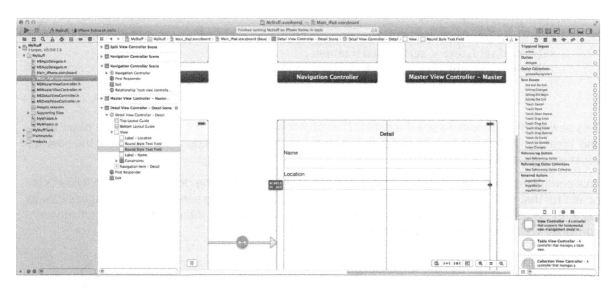

Figure 5-23. Finished iPad detail view

You'll also need to make the same changes in the iPad's table view that you made in the iPhone's table view. Find the `Master View Controller` scene (the one with the table view). Select the prototype table cell view object and change its style to `Subtitle` (see Figure 5-17). Change the navigation title from "Master" to "My Stuff".

Now run your project in an iPad simulator. The iPad interface is considerably different. In portrait mode, you see the detail view instead of the table view (on the left in Figure 5-24). You get to the table view via the Master button (in the middle of Figure 5-24).

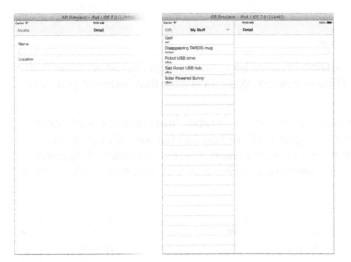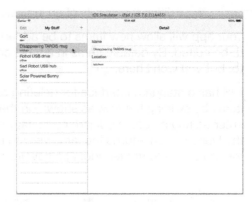

Figure 5-24. MyStuff running on an iPad

If you turn the iPad on its side (choose Hardware ➤ Rotate Left in the simulator), you get a split view with your table view on the left and your detail view on the right (on the right of Figure 5-24).

> **Tip** If you want the Master button to be labeled My Stuff (consistent with the navigation bar title), locate the split view controller delegate methods in `MSDetailViewController.m` and change the `title` of the `barButtonItem` to `"My Stuff"` (i.e., `barButtonItem.title = @"My Stuff"`). The template code assigns the title using a localization macro, which I explain in chapter 22. You can ignore it for now.

You may notice that you can edit the text fields, but they don't change anything. The last part of your app development will be to set up editing of your `MyWhatsit` objects, allow the user to create new ones, change them, and delete ones they don't want.

Editing

I'm not going to lie to you; editing is hard. That's not to say you can't tackle it, and you're going to add editing to MyStuff. But don't fret, you already have a huge head start. The table view and collection classes do most of the heavy lifting, and most of the code you need to write to support table editing has already been included in your app, thanks to the Master Detail project template. There's still code you need to write, but mostly you need to understand what's already been written and how the pieces fit together.

Editing tables can be reduced to a few basic tasks:

- Creating and inserting a new item into the table
- Removing an item from the table

- Reorganizing items in a table
- Editing the details of an individual item

Your app will allow new items to be added, existing items to be removed, and the details of an item to be edited. By default, items in a table can't be reordered. You can enable that feature if you need to, but you won't here.

iOS has a standard interface for deleting and reordering items in a table. You can individually delete items by swiping the row, as shown on the left in Figure 5-25, or you can tap the Edit button and enter editing mode. In editing mode, tapping the minus button next to a row will delete it. Tapping the Done button returns the table view to regular viewing. iOS also provides a standard "plus" button for you to use to trigger adding a new item.

Figure 5-25. Table editing interface

These interfaces are part of the table view classes. The only work you need to do is to set up the interface objects to trigger these actions. You'll start by providing the code to add new objects, then I'll describe the set up that enables editing of your table, and finally you'll write the code to edit the properties of a single MyWhatsit object.

Inserting and Removing Items

Inserting a new item into your list is a two-step process:

1. Create the new object and add it to your collection.
2. Inform that table view that you added a new object, and where.

The Master Detail template includes an action method, `-insertNewObject:`, that does this. The template code, however, doesn't know about your data model so you'll need to make some small adjustments to create the correct kind of object.

In the `MSMasterViewController.m` implementation file, find the `-insertNewObject:` method. The template code looks something like this:

```
- (void)insertNewObject:(id)sender
{
    if (!things)
        things = [[NSMutableArray alloc] init];
    [things insertObject:[NSDate date] atIndex:0];
    NSIndexPath *indexPath = [NSIndexPath indexPathForRow:0 inSection:0];
    [self.tableView insertRowsAtIndexPaths:@[indexPath]
                          withRowAnimation:UITableViewRowAnimationAutomatic];
}
```

The first two lines lazily create your `NSMutableArray` collection. This handles the case where this is the first object being added to your collection; prior to this point, you might not have a collection array.

> **Note** In your app, as it stands now, this code will never get executed because you explicitly created an array collection full of test data during controller initialization. In later versions of your app you'll take that code out, so it's a good idea to leave this code here.

The next line satisfies the first step of adding a new item to the table. It creates a new object and adds it at the beginning of the collection (by inserting it at index 0). The only problem is, it's the wrong kind of object. Replace that line of code with the following:

```
static unsigned int itemNumber = 1;
NSString *newItemName = [NSString stringWithFormat:@"My Item %u",itemNumber++];
MyWhatsit *newItem = [[MyWhatsit alloc] initWithName:newItemName location:nil];
[things insertObject:newItem atIndex:0];
```

Your code generates a unique name for the new item (starting with "My Item 1"), uses that name to create a new `MyWhatsit` object, and inserts that new object into the collection.

> **Tip** If you want your new items to appear at the end of the list, instead of the beginning, insert that new object at the end of the array (using `-addObject:`) and then tell the table view it was added at the end (using `[NSIndexPath indexPathForRow:things.count-1 inSection:0]`).

The rest of the code remains the same. You're still inserting your object at the beginning of the collection, so the code that tells the table view that doesn't need to change.

Now, you may be wondering when, and how, the -insertNewObject: message gets sent. After all, you don't send it anywhere and it's not an object created in any of the Interface Builder files. The answer to that question can be found in the next section.

Enabling Table Editing

To allow any row in your table to be deleted (via the standard iOS editing features, that is) your data source object must tell the table view that it's allowed. If you don't, iOS won't permit that row to be deleted. Your data source does this via its optional -tableView:canEditRowAtIndexPath: method. The Master Detail template provided one for you:

```
- (BOOL)tableView:(UITableView *)tableView canEditRowAtIndexPath:(NSIndexPath *)indexPath
{
    return YES;
}
```

The method provided by the template allows all rows in your table to be editable. By default, "editable" means it can be deleted. If you don't want a row to be editable, return NO.

> **Note** Technically, the -tableView:canEditRowAtIndexPath: message only determines if a row *could* be edited. If it is, then the table view delegate object gets to determine if or how via its optional -tableView:editingStyleForRowAtIndexPath: method. The default edit style, which you're using here, allows the row to be deleted (UITableViewCellEditingStyleDelete).

If -tableView:canEditRowAtIndexPath: returns YES for a row, iOS allows the swipe gesture to delete the row. If you also want to enable "editing mode" for the entire list (where minus signs appear in each row), you hook that up in the navigation bar, provided by the UITableViewController (which your MSMasterViewController inherits). iOS provides all the needed button objects, and most of the behavior, that you need. All you have to do is turn them on. In your MSMasterViewController implementation, find the -viewDidLoad method. The beginning of the method should look like this:

```
- (void)viewDidLoad
{
    [super viewDidLoad];
    self.navigationItem.leftBarButtonItem = self.editButtonItem;
    UIBarButtonItem *addButton = [[UIBarButtonItem alloc]
                    initWithBarButtonSystemItem:UIBarButtonSystemItemAdd
                                         target:self
                                         action:@selector(insertNewObject:)];
    self.navigationItem.rightBarButtonItem = addButton;
```

The first line calls the superclass's -viewDidLoad: method, so the superclass can do whatever it needs to do when the view objects load.

The next line creates the **Edit** button you see on the left side of the navigation bar (see Figure 5-23). It sets the left-hand button to the view controller's editButtonItem. The editButtonItem property is a preconfigured UIBarButtonItem object that's already set up to start and stop the edit action for its table.

The button to create and insert a new item requires a little more set up, but not much. The next line creates a new UIBarButtonItem. It will have the standard iOS "+" symbol (UIBarButtonSystemItemAdd). When the user taps it, it will send an -insertNewObject: message to this object (self). The last line adds the new toolbar button to the right-hand side of the navigation bar.

That's it! This is the code that adds the **Edit** and + buttons to your table's navigation bar. The **Edit** button takes care of itself, and you configured the + button to send your controller object the -insertNewObject: message when it's tapped. In the previous section, you rewrote -insertNewObject: to insert the correct kind of object.

It's time to try it out. Set your scheme back to the iPhone Simulator and run your app. Try swiping a row, or using the **Edit** button. Add some new items by tapping the + button. Your efforts should look like those in Figure 5-23.

There's one last detail that you should be aware of. When adding a new object, your code created the object, added it to your data model, and then told the table view what you'd done. When deleting a row, the table view is deciding what row(s) to delete. So how does the actual MyWhatsit object get removed from the things array? That happens in this data source delegate method, which was already written for you:

```
- (void)tableView:(UITableView *)tableView
commitEditingStyle:(UITableViewCellEditingStyle)editingStyle
forRowAtIndexPath:(NSIndexPath *)indexPath
{
    if (editingStyle == UITableViewCellEditingStyleDelete) {
        [things removeObjectAtIndex:indexPath.row];
        [tableView deleteRowsAtIndexPaths:@[indexPath]
                        withRowAnimation:UITableViewRowAnimationFade];
    } else if (editingStyle == UITableViewCellEditingStyleInsert) {
        // ... insert item here ...
    }
}
```

When a user edits a table and decides to delete (or insert) a row, that request is communicated to your data source object by sending it this message. Your data source object must examine the editingStyle parameter to determine what's happening—a row is being deleted, for example—and take appropriate action. The action to take when a row is deleted is to remove the corresponding MyWhatsit object from the array and let the table view know what you did.

That's all of the code needed to edit your table. Now it's time to put the last big piece of the puzzle into place: editing the details of a single item.

Editing Details

To edit the details of an item, you're going to need to:

1. Create a view where the user can see all of the details.
2. Set the values of that view with the properties of the selected item in the table.
3. Record changes to those values.
4. Update the table with the new information.

The good news is that you've already done half of this work. You already modified the MSDetailViewController to display the name and location properties of a MyWhatsit object, and you added code to fill in the text fields with the property values of the selected item (-configureView). Now you just have to add some code to do the next two steps, and your app is nearly done.

Start with the iPhone interface—because the iPad interface is going to work a little differently. Create an action that will respond to changes made to the name and location text fields. Start by adding a method prototype to MSDetailViewController.h:

```
- (IBAction)changedDetail:(id)sender;
```

In the MSDetailViewController.m implementation file, add the actual method:

```
- (IBAction)changedDetail:(id)sender
{
    if (sender==self.nameField)
        self.detailItem.name = self.nameField.text;
    else if (sender==self.locationField)
        self.detailItem.location = self.locationField.text;
}
```

This action method will be received when either the name or location text field is edited. It's not obvious which of the fields caused the message to be sent, so the code compares the sender parameter (the object that caused the action message to be sent) against your two text field connections. If one is a match, you know which text field sent the message and can update the appropriate MyWhatsit property with the new value.

Connect the Did End Editing message of the two text fields to this action in Interface Builder. Select the Main_iPhone.storyboard file. Select the name property text field. Using the connections inspector, connect its Editing Did End event to the -changedDetail: action of the Detail View Controller (your MSDetailViewController), as shown in Figure 5-26. Repeat with the location text field.

CHAPTER 5: Table Manners 169

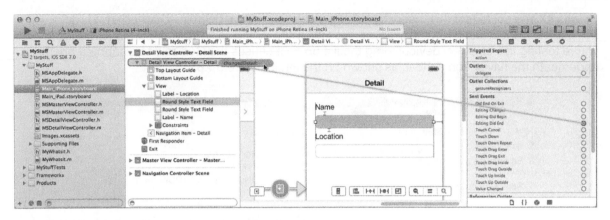

Figure 5-26. Connecting Editing Did End to -changedDetail: action

Now when you edit one of the text fields in the detail view, it will change the property values of the original object, updating your data model. Give it a try.

Make sure your scheme is still set to an iPhone simulator and run your app. Your items appear in the list, shown on the left in Figure 5-27.

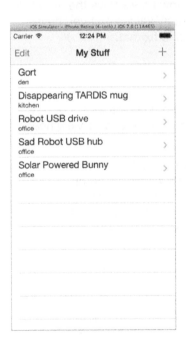  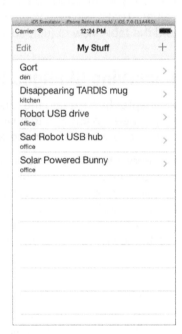

Figure 5-27. Testing detail editing

Tapping the Gort item shows you its details. Edit the details of the first row. In the example in Figure 5-27, I'm changing its name to "Gort statue" and its location to "living room." Clicking the My Stuff button in the navigation bar returns you to the list. But wait! The Gort `MyWhatsit` object wasn't updated.

Or was it? You could test this theory by setting a debugger breakpoint in -changedDetail: to see if it was sent (it was). No, the problem is a little more insidious. With your cursor (or finger, if you're testing this on a real device), drag the list up so it causes the Gort row to disappear briefly underneath the navigation toolbar, as shown on the left in Figure 5-28.

Figure 5-28. *Redrawing the first row*

Release your mouse/finger and the list snaps back. Notice that the first row now shows the updated values. That's because your -changedDetail: method changed the property values, but you never told the table view object, so it didn't know to redraw that row. You need to fix that.

Observing Changes to MyWhatsit

In Chapter 8 I'll explain the rationale behind data model and view object communications. For now, all you need to know is that when the properties of a MyWhatsit object change, the table view needs to know about it so it can redraw that row.

In theory, this is an easy problem to solve: when the MyWhatsit property is updated, a message needs to be sent to the table view to redraw the table, just like you did when you added or removed an object. In practice, it's a little trickier. The problem is that neither the MyWhatsit object nor MSDetailViewController have a direct connection to the table view object of the MSMasterViewController view. While there's nothing stopping you from adding one and connecting it in Interface Builder or programmatically, in this case there's a cleaner solution.

> **Note** In a good model-view-controller design, it would be completely inappropriate for a data model object (like MyWhatsit) to have a direct connection to a view object (like a table view). So this isn't just a clever solution, it's actually good software design.

There's a software design pattern called the *observer pattern*. It works like this:

1. Any object interested in knowing when something happens registers as an observer.
2. When something happens, the object responsible posts a notification.
3. The iOS notification center distributes that notification to all interested observers.

The real beauty of this arrangement is that neither the observers nor the objects posting notifications have to know anything about each other. You'll use notifications to communicate changes in MyWhatsit objects to the MSMasterViewController. The first step is to design a notification and have MyWhatsit post it at the appropriate time.

Posting Notifications

In your MyWhatsit.h interface file, add this method prototype:

```
- (void)postDidChangeNotification;
```

Towards the top of the file, add this constant definition:

```
#define kWhatsitDidChangeNotification    @"MyWhatsitDidChange"
```

Switch to your MyWhatsit.m implementation file, and add the method:

```
- (void)postDidChangeNotification
{
    [[NSNotificationCenter defaultCenter] ↩
                    postNotificationName:kWhatsitDidChangeNotification
                                  object:self];
}
```

When received, this method will post a notification named kWhatsitDidChangeNotification. The object of the notification is itself. The name of the notification can be anything you want, you just want to make sure it's unique so it isn't confused with a notification used by another object.

Back in your -changedDetail: method (MSDetailViewController.m), add one additional line to the end of the method:

```
[self.detailItem postDidChangeNotification];
```

Now whenever you edit the details of your MyWhatsit object, it will post a notification that it changed. Any object interested in that fact will receive that notification. The very last step is to make MSMasterViewController observe this notification.

Observing Notifications

The basic pattern for observing notifications is:

1. Create a method to receive notification messages.
2. Become an observer for the specific notification(s) your object is interested in.
3. Process any notifications received.
4. Stop observing notifications when you don't need them anymore, or before your object is destroyed.

The first step is simple enough. In your `MSMasterViewController.m` implementation file, add a `-whatsitDidChangeNotification:` method. Start by adding a method prototype at the end of the `@interface MSMasterViewController ()` section:

```
- (void)whatsitDidChangeNotification:(NSNotification*)notification;
```

Then, towards the bottom of the `@implementation` section, add the actual method:

```
- (void)whatsitDidChangeNotification:(NSNotification*)notification
{
    NSUInteger index = [things indexOfObject:notification.object];
    if (index!=NSNotFound)
        {
        NSIndexPath *path = [NSIndexPath indexPathForItem:index inSection:0];
        [self.tableView reloadRowsAtIndexPaths:@[path]
                        withRowAnimation:UITableViewRowAnimationNone];
        }
}
```

All notification messages follow the same pattern: `-(void)`*myNotification*`:(NSNotification*)`*theNotification*. You can name your method whatever you want, but it must expect a single `NSNotification` object as its only parameter.

The `notification` parameter has all of the details about the notification. Often you don't care, particularly if your object only wants to know that the notification happened and not exactly why. In this case, you're interested in the `object` property of the notification. Every notification has a `name` and an `object` it's associated with—often it's the `object` that caused the notification.

The first line of your method looks for the notification's object in your `things` collection. If the object is a `MyWhatsit` object in your collection, the `-indexOfObject:` method will return its index in the collection. If not, it will return the constant `NSNotFound`.

If the object is in your table (`index!=NSNotFound`), then the next two lines of code create an `NSIndexPath` to the location of that object in your table and then tells the table view to reload (redisplay) that row, sans animation.

The end result is that whenever the detail view changes a `MyWhatsit` object, this method will cause the corresponding row of your table to redraw, showing that change. Now you just have to register `MSMasterViewController` with the notification center so it will receive this message.

Locate the -awakeFromNib method. Right after the code you added to create the test array of things, add this statement:

```
[[NSNotificationCenter defaultCenter]
             addObserver:self
                selector:@selector(whatsitDidChangeNotification:)
                    name:kWhatsitDidChangeNotification
                  object:nil];
```

This message tells the notification center to register this object (self) to receive the given message (-whatsitDidChangeNotification:) whenever a notification with the name kWhatsitDidChangeNotification is posted for any object (nil).

NOTIFICATION MATCHING

Registering to be a notification observer is very flexible. By passing the nil constant for either the name or object parameters in -addObserver:selector:name:object:, you can request to receive notifications with a given name, for a specific object, or both. The following table shows the effect of the name and object parameters when becoming an observer.

Notification observer matching

name:	object:	Notifications received
@"Name"	object	Receive only notifications named @"Name" for the object object
@"Name"	nil	Receive all notifications named @"Name" for any object
nil	object	Receive every notification for the object object
nil	nil	Receive every notification (not recommended)

In this situation, you want to be notified when any MyWhatsit object is edited. Your code then looks at the specific object to determine if it's interesting. In other situations, you'll want to receive notifications only when a specific object sends a specific notification, ignoring similar notifications from unrelated objects.

Just as important as registering to receive notifications, is to unregister when your object should no longer receive them. For this app, there's no point at which the notifications are irrelevant, but you still must make sure that your object is no longer an observer before it's destroyed. Leaving a destroyed object registered to receive notifications is a notorious cause of app crashes in iOS. So make absolutely sure your object is removed from the notification center before it ceases to exist.

It's really easy to ensure this, so you don't have any excuses for not doing it. Just above your -awakeFromNib method, add this method:

```
- (void)dealloc
{
    [[NSNotificationCenter defaultCenter] removeObserver:self];
}
```

The `-dealloc` message is sent to your object just before it is destroyed. In it, you should clean up any "loose ends" that wouldn't be taken care of automatically. This statement tells the notification center that this object is no longer an observer for any notification. You don't even have to remember what notifications or objects you'd previously ask to observe; this message will undo them all.

Run your app in an iPhone simulator again. Edit an item and return back to the list. This time your changes appear in the list!

Modal vs. Modeless Editing

You're in the home stretch. In fact, you're so close to the finish line that you can almost touch it. There's only one vexing detail to fix: the iPad interface.

The iPhone interface uses, what software developers call, a *model interface*: when you tap a row to edit an item, you're transported to a screen where you can edit its details (editing mode), and then you exit that screen and return to the list (browsing mode).

The iPad interface doesn't work like that. Particularly in landscape orientation, you can jump between the master list and the detail view at will. This means you can start editing a title or location and then switch immediately to another item in the list. This is called a *modeless interface*.

While this makes for a fluid user experience, it's a disaster for your app. If you go to the Main_iPad.storyboard file and connect the `Editing Did End` events of the name and location text fields to the `-changedDetail:` message, as you did in the iPhone interface, you can see that it doesn't work.

Go ahead; give it a try. I'll wait.

It's because the editing of the text field never gets a chance to "end" before you can change to another `MyWhatsit` object in the list. Fortunately, there's an easy out. Instead of connecting the `Editing Did End` events to `-changedDetail:`, connect the `Editing Changed` events instead. This event is a "lower level" event that's sent whenever the user makes *any* change in the text field. Now the rows in the table view will update as the user edits the details.

Little Touches

Polish your app by giving it an icon, just as you did for the EightBall app in the previous chapter. Locate the `Learn iOS Development Projects` folder you downloaded in Chapter 1. Inside the `Ch 5` folder you'll find the `MyStuff (Icons)` folder. Select the `images.xcassets` item in the navigator, and then select the `AppIcon` image group. Drag all of the image files from the `MyStuff (Icons)` folder and drop them into the group. Xcode will sort them out.

Your app is finished, but I'd like to take a moment to direct you to other table-related topics.

Advanced Table View Topics

You can now see that table views are used for a lot more than just listing contacts and song titles. The table view classes are powerful and flexible, but that means they are—at times—complicated and confusing. The good news is that they are extensively documented and there are lots of sample projects, which you can download from Apple, that demonstrate various table view techniques.

The place to start is the *Table View Programming Guide for iOS*. Choose **Help ➤ Documentation and API Reference**, in the search field enter Table View Programming, and click on the **Table View Programming Guide for iOS** in the auto-completion list, as shown in Figure 5-29.

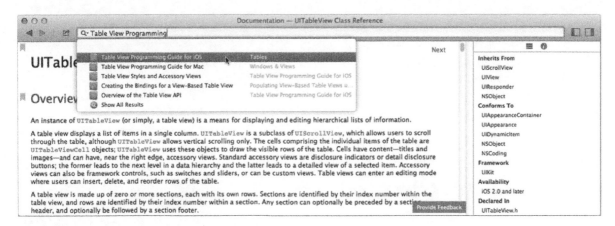

Figure 5-29. Locating the Table View Programming Guide

This guide will explain every major feature of table views and how to use them. It's not a short read, but if you want to know how to do something specific—like create an indexed list—this is where you should start.

Most major iOS classes have links in their documentation that will take you to a guide explaining how to use it, and related classes. In the overview section for the UITableView class, for example, there are several links to table-specific programming guides.

Summary

Give yourself a big "high five!" You've taken another huge step in iOS app development. You've learned how table views works and how to use cell objects. You know what messages your app receives when a user taps on a row, how to handle editing of rows, and how to create new rows. You created a data model and you learned how to post and observe notifications between unconnected objects.

This app still falls short in a few categories. The details of a particular item could be, well, more detailed. But probably the most annoying issue is that your app doesn't remember anything. If you restart your app, any changes you made are lost. So for an app that's supposed to keep track of your stuff, it doesn't do a very good job.

Don't worry; we'll attack those shortcomings in future chapters. Before you get there, take a well-deserved rest from app development and take a brief stroll through the theory of object-oriented programming.

Chapter 6

Object Lesson

I'd like to take a break from app development for a chapter. Good iOS development requires conceptual and design skills that go beyond just knowing how to write for loops or connect a button to an outlet. Software engineers call these design patterns and design principles. To appreciate these philosophies, I'll start with the foundation for it all: the object.

"Hey!" you say, "I've been using objects, what's to understand?" You'd be surprised at the number of programmers who can't describe exactly what an "object" is. If you haven't had any questions about the terms used in this book so far (class, object, instance, method, message, and so on), and you're already familiar with design patterns and principles, feel free to skip or skim this chapter. If you have questions, keep reading.

In this chapter I will

- Give a brief history of objects and object-oriented programming
- Explain exactly what a class, object, and instance are
- Describe inheritance and encapsulation
- Explain delegation and a few other design patterns
- Touch on a few key design principles

To appreciate objects, it helps to know what came before them and why they're such a big deal.

Two Houses, Both Alike in Dignity

There are two basic types of information rattling around inside a computer. *Data* is the binary values that represent values and quantities, such as your name, a URL, or the airspeed velocity of an unladen swallow. *Code* is the binary values that represent instructions that tell the computer to do things like draw your name on the screen, load a URL, or choose a favorite color.

It's easy to see this division in computer languages. The syntax of a programming language, like Objective-C, is largely divided between statements that define, retrieve, and store values and statements that change values, make decisions, and invoke other methods. Think of them as the nouns and verbs of the computer's language.

Like the Montagues and the Capulets,[1] these two aspects of programming stayed separate for a long time. As computers got bigger and faster, and computer programs got longer and more complicated, a number of problems began to develop.

Programmers encountered more solutions where multiple pieces of information needed to be kept together. A person doesn't just have a name; they also have a height, an age, a tax identification number, and so on. To keep these related facts together, they started combining multiple values into a single block of memory called a *structure*. In the C programming language, a structure looks like this:

```
struct Person {
    char name[kLongestName];
    bool female;
    float birthdate;
    float height;
    int taxNumber;
};
```

These structures became so handy that programmers started to use them as if the whole thing was a single value. They would pass a Person to a function, or store a Person in a file. They would write functions that operated solely on a Person structure (as opposed to a single value, like a date), writing a function that determined if it was that person's birthday, like IsBirthdayToday(struct Person *person).

Programmers also started to encounter situations where there were lots of structures that resembled one another. A Player structure has all the same properties that a Person structure does, except that it had more variables for things like the player's total score. They quickly figured out that they could create structures from structures, like this:

```
struct Player {
    struct Person person;
    int gamesPlayed;
    int totalScore;
};
```

What got programmers really excited was that they could now reuse the functions they wrote for the Person structure for the Player structure! They even gave this idea a name: *subtype polymorphism*. You'll get extra credit if you work that into a conversation at your next party.

Things should have been swell, but they weren't. The number of structures and functions grew at a dizzying pace. Projects would have thousands and thousands of individual functions and nearly as many different structures. Some functions would work with Person structures, most wouldn't.

---

[1]The Montagues and the Capulets were the two alienated families in the play Romeo and Juliet. I mention this in case your reading list is skewed towards Jules Verne and not William Shakespeare.

The problem was that data structures and functions were still in separate families; they didn't mix. Trying to figure out what functions should be used with what structures became unmanageable. Programs didn't work. Large software projects were failing. Something needed to happen—and it did.

Romeo Meets Juliet

In the late 1960s something magical happened: structures and functions got together, and the object was born. An *object* is the fusion of property values (the data structure) and the methods that act on those values (the functions) into a single entity that owns both. It seems so simple, but it was a dramatic turning point in the evolution of computer languages.

Before objects, programmers spent their days writing and calling functions (also called procedures), passing them the correct data structures. Computer languages that work this way are called *procedural* languages. When the concept of an object was introduced it turned the way programmers wrote and thought about programs inside out. Now the center of the programmer's world is the object; you take an object and invoke its methods. These new computer languages are called *object-oriented* languages.

Objects also created programs that felt "alive." A data structure is an inert collection of values, and a function is an abstract sequence of instructions, but an object is both; it's an entity that has both characteristics and can do things when told. In this sense, objects are much more analogous to the kinds of things you deal with in the real world.

Now that you know what an object is, I'm going to give you a short course in how objects are defined and created, and what that looks like in Objective-C. Chapter 20 describes this in much more detail.

Classes and Cookies

An object is the tangible embodiment of a *class*. An object's class defines what properties that object can have and what actions it can perform. Objects are the things you actually work with. Think of it this way: Classes are the cookie cutters. Objects are the cookies. See Figure 6-1.

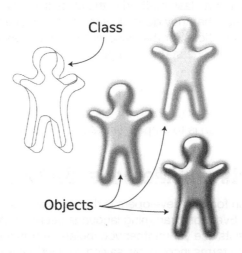

Figure 6-1. Classes and objects

In Objective-C, a class is defined using an @interface directive:

```
@interface MyClass
// Class definition goes here
@end
```

A class doesn't do much by itself. A class is simply the "shape" used to create new objects. When you create an object, you do so by specifying the class of object you want to create and then telling the class to create one. In Objective-C that code looks like this:

```
MyClass *object = [[MyClass alloc] init];
```

The result of that expression is a new *instance of a class*, which is synonymous with *an object*. The object includes its own storage (data structure) where all of its individual property values are kept. Each object has its own storage; changing the value of one object won't change the value of any other object in the system.

Each object is also associated with a number of methods (functions) that act only on that class of objects. The class defines those methods and every object of that class is endowed with those actions. In Objective-C the code for methods appears in the @implementation section of that class:

```
@implementation MyClass
// Methods go here
@end
```

Methods that do their thing on a particular object (instance) of a class are called *instance methods*. Instance methods always execute in the context of a single object. When the code in an instance method refers to a property value, or the special self variable, it's referring to the property of the specific object it was invoked for. In Objective-C, instance methods start with a hyphen (dash):

```
- (void)doSomething;
```

There are also special *class methods*. A class method is defined by a class but can't be invoked on any specific object. The context of a class method is the class itself. Class methods are very similar to old-style functions in the sense that they don't do something to a particular object. Instead, they usually perform utilitarian functions for the class, like creating new objects or changing global settings. In Objective-C, class methods start with a plus sign:

```
+ (id)makeSomething;
```

The +alloc method is a class method. It's sent to the class to create (allocate) a new object. The -init method is an instance method. Its job is to prepare (initialize) that single object so it can be used.

Classes and Objects and Methods, Oh My!

A continual source of confusion for new developers is the profusion, and confusion, of terms used in object-oriented programming. Every programming language seems to pick a slightly different set of terms to use. Computer scientists use yet another vocabulary. Terms are often mixed up and even seasoned programmers will use terms incorrectly, saying "object" when they really mean "class."

Table 6-1 will help you navigate the world of object-oriented programming terms. It lists common Objective-C programming terms, their meaning, and some synonyms that you'll encounter. I'll explain most in more detail, later in this chapter.

Table 6-1. Common Objective-C terms

Term	Meaning	Similar terms
class	The definition of a class of objects. It defines what property values those objects can store and what methods they implement.	interface, type, definition, prototype
object	An instance of a class.	class instance, instance
property	A value stored in an object.	instance variable, attribute
method	A function that executes in the context of a single object.	instance method, function, procedure, business logic
class method	A function that executes outside the context of any particular object.	class function, static function
override	Supplanting the implementation of an inherited method with a different one.	
message	A value that chooses a particular method to execute.	selector
send	Using a message to invoke an object's method.	invoke a method, call a function
sender	The object that is sending a message to another object.	caller
receive	Being sent a message.	
receiver	The object performing the method. The context of the running method.	self
responds	Having a method that executes when sent a particular message.	implements
client code	The code outside of the class that is using the public interface of that class or its objects.	user, client
abstract class	A class, property, or method that is defined or declared, but has no useful functionality. Used to define a concept that subclasses will implement in a meaningful way.	abstraction layer, placeholder, stub
concrete class	A class, property, or method that does something and is usable.	

By now you should have a solid understanding of the relationship between a class, its objects, and its properties and methods. Objective-C puts a little spin on all of this with the concept of a *message*. In most other object-oriented languages, a method is simply "called" or "invoked." This is the equivalent of calling an old-style procedural function and passing it the data structure of the object it should work on.

Objective-C works a little differently than most other object-oriented languages. Invoking a method involves a constant numeric value called a *selector*. Every Objective-C method in the entire system (such as -init or -setObject:forKey:) has a unique selector. This selector is used to choose which of the object's methods (if any) it will execute. This process is normally invisible to you, but it gives rise to the language of Objective-C, where programmers speak of "sending a message to an object," "receiving a message," or asking "does an object respond to this message?" One side effect: the terms "message" and "method" are often used interchangeably.

Inheritance

Earlier I mentioned that programmers found many situations where a class or structure that they needed was very similar, possibly with only minor additions, to another object or structure that already existed. Furthermore, the methods they'd written for the existing object/structure were all applicable to the new one. This idea is called *inheritance*, and is a cornerstone of object-oriented languages.

The idea is that classes can be organized into a tree, with the more general classes at the top, working down to more specific classes at the bottom. This arrangement might look like something in Figure 6-2.

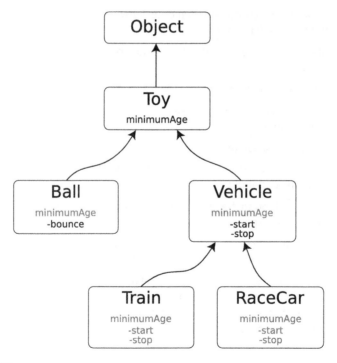

Figure 6-2. A class hierarchy

In Figure 6-2, the generic Object is the base class of all other objects. In Objective-C the base class is NSObject. A subclass of Object is Toy. Toy defines a set of properties and methods common to all Toy objects. The subclasses of Toy are Ball and Vehicle. Subclasses of Vehicle are Train and RaceCar.

The Toy class defines a `minimumAge` property that describes the youngest age the toy is appropriate for. All subclasses of Toy inherit this property. Therefore, a `Ball`, `Vehicle`, `Train`, and `RaceCar` all have a `minimumAge` property.

Similarly, classes inherit methods too. The `Vehicle` class defines two methods: `-start` and `-stop`. All subclasses of `Vehicle` inherit these two methods, so you can send a `-start` message to a `Train` and a `-stop` message to a `RaceCar`. The `-bounce` message can only be sent to a `Ball`.

This is what computer scientists call subtype polymorphism. It means that if you have an object, parameter, or variable of a specific type (say, `Vehicle`), you can use or substitute any object that's a subclass of `Vehicle`. You can pass a method that has a `Vehicle` parameter a `Train` or a `RaceCar` object, and the method will act on the more complex object just as effectively. A variable that refers to a `Toy` can store a `Toy`, a `Ball`, or a `Train`. A variable that refers to a `Vehicle`, however, cannot be set to a `Ball`, because a `Ball` is not a subclass of `Vehicle`.

You've already seen this in the apps you've written. `NSResponder` is the base class for all objects that respond to events. `UIView` is a subclass of `NSResponder`, so all view objects respond to events. The `UIButton` is a subclass of `UIView`, so it can appear in a view and it responds to events. A `UIButton` object can be used in any situation that expects a `UIButton` object, a `UIView` object, or an `NSResponder` object.

Abstract and Concrete Classes

Programmers refer to the `Toy` and `Vehicle` classes as *abstract classes*. These classes don't define usable objects; they define the properties and methods common to all subclasses. You'll never find an instance of a `Toy` or `Vehicle` object in your program. The objects you'll find in your program are `Ball` and `Train` objects, which inherit common properties and methods from the `Toy` and `Vehicle` classes. The classes of usable objects are called *concrete classes*.

Overriding Methods

Starting a train is a lot different than starting a car. A class can supply its own code for a specific method, replacing the implementation it inherited. This is called *overriding* a method.

As an example, all subclasses of `NSObject` inherit a `-description` method. This returns an `NSString` describing the object. Of course, the version of `-description` supplied by `NSObject` is generic and can't know about the specifics of any subclass. As a programmer, you can override `-description` in `Ball` to describe what kind of ball it is, and override `-description` in `Train` to describe what kind of train it is.

Sometimes a class—particularly abstract classes—will define a method that doesn't do anything at all; it's just a placeholder for subclasses to override. The `Vehicle` class methods `-start` and `-stop` don't do anything. It's up to the specific subclass to decide what it means to start and stop.

For example, the `UIViewController` class defines the method `-viewWillAppear:`. This method doesn't do anything. It's just a placeholder method that gets called just before the controller's view appears on the screen. If *your* view controller subclass needs to do something before your view appears, your class would override `-viewWillAppear:` and perform whatever it is you need it to do.

If your class's method also needs to invoke the method defined by its superclass, Objective-C has a special syntax for that. The `super` keyword means the same thing as `self`, but messages sent to `super` go to the methods defined by the superclass (ignoring the method defined in this class), as if that method had not been overridden:

```
[super viewWillAppear:animated];
```

This is a common pattern for extending (rather than replacing) the behavior of a method. The overriding method calls the original method and then performs any additional tasks.

Design Patterns and Principles

With the newfound power of objects and inheritance, programmers discovered that they could build computer programs that were orders of magnitude more complex than what they had achieved in the past. They also discovered that if they designed their classes poorly, the result was a tangled mess, worse than the old way of writing programs. They began to ponder the question "what makes a good class?"

A huge amount of thought, theory, and experimentation has gone into trying to define what makes a good class and the best way to use objects in a program. This has resulted in a variety of concepts and philosophies, collectively known as design patterns and design principles. *Design patterns* are reusable solutions to common problems—a kind of programming best practices. *Design principles* are guidelines and insights into what makes a good design. There are dozens of these patterns and principles, and you could spend years studying them. I'll touch on a few of the more important ones.

Encapsulation

An object should hide, or *encapsulate*, its superfluous details from clients—the other classes that use and interact with that class. A well-designed class is kind of like a food truck. The outside of the truck is its interface; it consists of a menu and a window. Using the food truck is simple: you choose what you want, place your order, and receive your food through the window. What happens inside the truck is considerably more complicated. There are stoves, electricity, refrigerators, storage, inventory, recipes, cleaning procedures, and so on. But all of those details are encapsulated inside the truck.

Similarly, a good class hides the details of what it does behind the simple interface defined in its `@interface` section. Properties and methods that the clients of that object needs should be declared there. Everything else should be "hidden" in the `@implementation` or in private `@interface` sections.

This isn't just for simplicity, although that's a big benefit. The more details a class exposes to its clients, the more entangled it becomes with the code that uses it. Computer engineers call this a *dependency*. The fewer dependencies, the easier it is to change the inner workings of a class without disrupting how that class is used. For example, the food truck can switch from using frozen French fries to slicing fresh potatoes and cooking them. That change would improve the quality of its French fries, but it wouldn't require it to modify its menu or alter how customers place their order.

Singularity of Purpose

The best classes are those that have a single purpose. A well-designed class should represent exactly one thing or concept, encapsulate all of the information about that one thing, and nothing else. A method of a class should perform one task. Software engineers call this the *single responsibility principle*.

A button object that starts a timer has limited functionality. Sure, if you need a button that starts a timer, it would work great. But if you need a button that resets a score, or a button that turns a page, it would be useless. On the other hand, a UIButton object is infinitely useful because it does only one thing: It presents a button the user can tap. When a user taps it, it sends a message to another object. That other object could start a timer, reset a score, or turn a page.

Great objects are like Lego™ blocks. Create objects that do simple, self-contained, tasks and connect them to other objects to solve problems. Don't create objects that solve whole problems. I'll discuss this more in Chapter 8.

Stability

A ball should be useable all of the time. If you picked a ball you would expect it to bounce. It would be strange to find a ball that wouldn't bounce until you first turned it over twice, or had to paint it a color.

Strive to make your objects functional regardless of how they were created or what properties have been set. In the Ball example, the -bounce method should work whether the `minimumAge` property has been set or not. Software engineers call these *pre-conditions*, and you should keep them to a minimum.

Open Closed

There are two corollaries to the single responsibility principle. The first is the so-called "open closed" principle: classes should be *open* to extension and *closed* to change. This is a strange one to grasp, but it basically means that a class is well designed if it can be reused to solve other problems by extending the existing class or methods, rather than changing them.

Programmers abhor change, but it's the one constant in software development. The more things you have to change in an app, the more chance that it's going to affect some other part of your project adversely. Software engineers call this *coupling*. It's a polite way of saying that by changing one thing, you'll create a bug somewhere else. The open closed principle tries to avoid changing things by designing your classes and methods so you don't have to change them in the future. This takes practice.

Using the toy classes again, both the `Train` and `RaceCar` might be electric. You might be tempted to add properties and methods that relate to electric propulsion (`voltage`, `-switchOn`, and so on) to the `Vehicle` class. The problem is what happens when you want to define a wind-up `RaceCar`. You'll have to change `Vehicle`, and that's going to affect every `Train` and `RaceCar` object in your app.

Thinking ahead, you could have added another layer of classes between `Vehicle` and its subclasses, such as `ElectricVehicle` and `WindUpVehicle`. This would let you create a subclass of `WindUpVehicle` without changing the subclasses of `ElectricVehicle`. Now you're extending your design, not changing it. You're also thinking beyond the code you write today, to the code you might want to write tomorrow.

Delegation

Another lesson of the single responsibility principle is to avoid mixing in knowledge or logic that's beyond the scope of your object. A ball has a -bounce method. To know how high the ball will bounce, the method must know what kind of surface the ball is bouncing against. Since this calculation has to be made in the -bounce method, it's tempting to include that logic in the Ball class. You might do this by adding a -howHigh method that calculates the height of a bounce.

That design decision, unfortunately, leads you down a crazy path. Since the bounce calculation varies depending on the environment, the only way to modify the calculation is to override the -howHigh method in subclasses. This forces you to create subclasses like BallOnWood, BallOnConcrete, BallOnCarpet, and so on. If you then want to create different kinds of balls, like a basketball and a beach ball, you end up subclassing all of those subclasses (BeachBallOnWood, BasketBallOnWood, BeachBallOnCarpet, and on and on). Your classes are spiraling out of control, as shown in Figure 6-3.

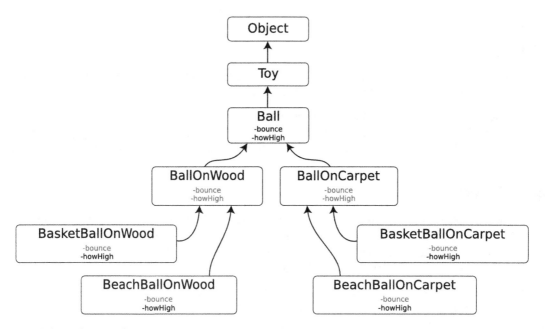

Figure 6-3. Subclassing "solution"

A design pattern that avoids this mess is the delegate pattern. As you've seen, the delegate pattern is used extensively in the Cocoa Touch framework. The *delegate pattern* defers—delegates—key decisions to another object, so that logic doesn't distract from the single purpose of the class.

Using the delegate pattern, you would create a surface property for the ball. The surface property would connect to an object that implements a -bounceHeightForBall: method. When the ball wants to know how high it should bounce, it sends its surface delegate a -bounceHeightForBall: message, passing itself as the ball in question. The Surface object would perform the calculation and return the answer. Subclasses of Surface (ConcreteSurface, WoodSurface, CarpetSurface, GrassSurface) would override -bounceHeightForBall: to adjust its behavior, as shown in Figure 6-4.

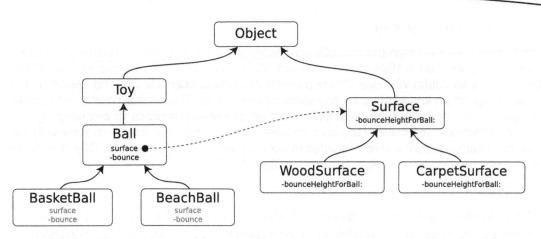

Figure 6-4. Delegate solution

Now you have a simple, and flexible, class hierarchy. The abstract `Ball` class has `BasketBall` and `BeachBall` subclasses. Any of which can be connected to any of the `Surface` subclasses (`ConcreteSurface`, `WoodSurface`, `CarpetSurface`, `GrassSurface`) to provide the correct physics. This arrangement also preserves the open closed principle: you can *extend* `Ball` or `Surface` to create new balls or new surfaces, without *changing* any of the existing classes.

Other Patterns

There are many, many other design patterns and principles. I don't expect you to memorize them—just be aware of them. With an awareness of design patterns, you'll begin to notice them as you see how classes in the Cocoa Touch framework and elsewhere are designed; iOS is a very well-designed system.

Here are other common patterns you'll encounter:

- Singleton pattern: a class that maintains a single instance of an object for use by the entire program. The `[UIApplication sharedApplication]` is a singleton.

- Factory pattern and class clusters: a method that creates objects for you (instead of you creating and configuring them yourself). Often, your code won't know what object, or even what class of objects, needs to be created. A factory method handles (encapsulates) those details for you. The `+[NSURL URLWithString:]` method is a factory method. The class of NSURL object returned will be different, depending on what kind of URL the string describes.

- Decorator pattern: dress up an object using another object. A UIBarButtonItem is not, ironically, a button object. It's a decorator that may present a button, a special control item, or even change the positioning of controls in a toolbar.

- Lazy initialization pattern: waiting until you need an object (or its properties) before creating it. Lazy initialization makes some things more efficient and reduces pre-conditions. `UITableView` lazily creates table cell objects; it waits until the moment it needs to draw a row before asking the data source delegate to provide a cell for that row.

There are, of course, many others.

The first major book of design patterns (*Design Patterns: Elements of Reusable Object-Oriented Software*) was published in 1994 by the so-called "Gang of Four": Erich Gamma, Richard Helm, Ralph Johnson, and John Vlissides. Those patterns are still applicable today, and design patterns have become a "must know" topic for any serious programmer. The original book is not specific to any particular computer language; you could apply these principles to any language, even non-object-oriented ones. Many authors have since reapplied, and refined, these patterns to specific languages. So if you're interested in learning these skills primarily for Objective-C, for example, look for a book on design patterns for Objective-C.

> **Note** An interesting offshoot of design patterns has been the emergence of *anti-patterns*: programming pitfalls that developers repeatedly fall into. Many anti-patterns have entertaining names like "God object" (an object that does too much) and "Lasagna code" (a software design with too many layers).
> See `http://en.wikipedia.org/wiki/Anti-patterns` for their history and other examples.

Summary

That was a lot of theory, but it's important to learn these basic concepts. Understanding design pattern and principles will help you become a better software designer, and you'll also appreciate the design of the iOS classes. Observe how iOS and other experienced developers solve problems, identify the principles they used, and then try to emulate that in your own development.

Theory is fun, but do you know what's even more fun? Cameras!

Chapter 7

Smile!

Pictures and video are a big part of mobile apps. This is made possible by the amazing array of audio/video hardware built into most iOS devices. Your apps can take advantage of this hardware—and it's not that difficult. Apple has made it exceptionally easy to present an interface where your user can take a picture, or choose an existing picture from their photo library, and use that image in your app.

In this chapter you're going to add pictures to MyStuff. You're going to allow a user to choose, or take, a picture for each item they own, and display that image in both the detail view and master list. In doing that, you'll learn how to:

- Create a camera or image picker controller and display it
- Retrieve the image the user took or chose
- Use Core Graphics to crop and resize the image
- Save the image to the user's camera roll
- Show images in the rows of a table view

Along the way, you'll learn a few other useful skills:

- Add a tap gesture recognizer to a view object
- Present a view controller in a popover
- Dismiss the keyboard

This chapter will extend the MyStuff app you wrote in Chapter 5 ("Table Manners"). You can continue working on the version you wrote in Chapter 5 or locate the finished version in the `Ch 7` folder of the `Learn iOS Developer Projects` folder. If you're adding to the project in Chapter 5—which I highly recommend—you will need the resource file in the `Ch 7 ➤ MyStuff (Resources)` folder.

Design

Expanding your MyStuff app won't be difficult. You've already created the master/detail interface and you have table views and editing working for both the iPhone and iPad interfaces. All of the hard work is done; you just need to embellish it a little. In the detail view you'll add a UIImageView object to display an image of the item, and in the table view you'll add icons to show a smaller version in the list, as shown in Figure 7-1.

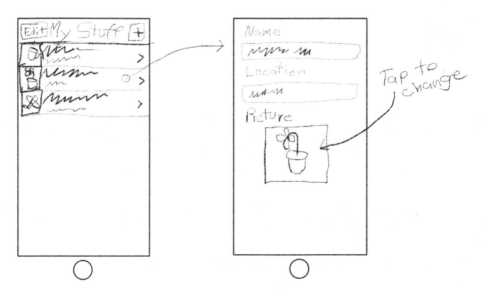

Figure 7-1. Updated MyStuff design

When the user taps the image in the detail view, your app will present either a camera interface or an image picker interface. The camera interface will allow them to take a picture with the device's built-in camera. The image picker interface lets the user choose an existing image from their photo library. The new image will appear in both the detail view and the master list. Let's get started!

Extending Your Design

To extend your design, you'll need to make small alterations to a number of existing classes and interface files. Whether you realize it or not, your MyStuff app uses a model-view-controller design pattern. I describe the model-view-controller design in the next chapter, but for now just know that some of the objects in your app are "data model" objects, some are "view" objects, and others are "controller" objects. Adding pictures to MyStuff will require:

1. Extending your data model to include image objects
2. Adding view objects to display those images
3. Expanding your controller objects to take a picture and update the data model

Revising the Data Model

The first step is to extend your data model. Locate your MyWhatsit.h interface file and add two new properties:

```
@property (strong,nonatomic) UIImage *image;
@property (readonly,nonatomic) UIImage *viewImage;
```

The first property adds a UIImage object reference to each MyWhatsit object. Now every MyWhatsit object has an image. Gee, that was easy!

The second property requires a little more explanation. In all of the view objects (both the details view and in the table view) you want to display the image of the item. If there is no image, however, you want to display a placeholder image—an image that says, "there's no image." The viewImage property will contain either the item's image or a placeholder image if there isn't one. It's a readonly property, which means that clients of this object can't change it; in other words, the statement myWhatsit.viewImage = newImage is not allowed.

VIEWIMAGE IS BAD

Adding the viewImage property to the MyWhatsit class is actually poor software design. The problem is that the MyWhatsit class is a data model class and the viewImage property is in the domain of the view classes. In plain English, it solves a problem displaying the image, not in storing the image. You're adding view-specific functionality to a data model object, which is something you should avoid.

In a well-organized model-view-controller (MVC) design, the domain of each class should be pure: the data model classes should only have data model related properties and functions—nothing else. The problem here is that it's so darned convenient to add a viewImage property to the MyWhatsit class: it encapsulates the logic of providing a "display image" for the item, which simplifies our code elsewhere. Code that encapsulates logic and makes the object easier to use can't be bad, right?

It isn't bad. It's actually good, but is there a way to avoid the architectural "flaw" of adding viewImage directly to the MyWhatsit class? The solution is to use a category. A category is an unusual feature of Objective-C that solves thorny domain issues like this, without making your objects more difficult to use. Using a category you can still add a viewImage property to your MyWhatsit objects, but do it in a different module—a view module, separate from your MyWhatsit class. You get the benefits of adding a viewImage property to MyWhatsit, while keeping your data model code separate from your view code. I explain categories in Chapter 20.

At runtime (when your app runs) your MyWhatsit object still has a viewImage property, just as if you'd added it directly to your MyWhatsit class. So what does it matter? Not much, and for a small project like this the ramifications are negligible, which is why I didn't have you create a category for viewImage. Sometimes pragmatism trumps a fanatic adherence to design patterns. Just know that in a much more complex project, defining viewImage in MyWhatsit could become an obstacle and the solution would be to move it into a category.

The viewImage property isn't a traditional property. It's what programmers refer to as a *synthetic property*; it's a value determined by some logic, rather than simply returning the value of an instance variable. To make it work, you need to add that logic. Click on the MyWhatsit.m implementation file and add the following method:

```
- (UIImage*)viewImage
{
    if (self.image!=nil)
        return self.image;
    return [UIImage imageNamed:@"camera"];
}
```

This method provides the value for the viewImage property. Whenever client code requests the viewImage property (detailItem.viewImage), this method will be invoked and the value it returns will be the value of viewImage. This is commonly referred to as the property's getter method.

> **Note** Every @property you define in a class automatically creates a *getter* method—a method that "gets" the property's value—with the same name, as in -viewImage. If the property can be modified (it's not a readonly property), then a second *setter* method is also generated, with the name prefixed by "set," as in -setViewImage:. You're free to replace the compiler's default implementations of either the getter or the setting method if you want to do something special whenever clients get or change the property.

If the MyWhatsit object has a value for its image property, viewImage returns that same object. If not (self.image==nil), then it returns the image in the camera.png resource file. For this to work, you need to add that placeholder image file to your project. Find the camera.png file in the MyStuff (Resources) folder and drag it into the group list of your Images.xcassets asset catalog, as shown in Figure 7-2.

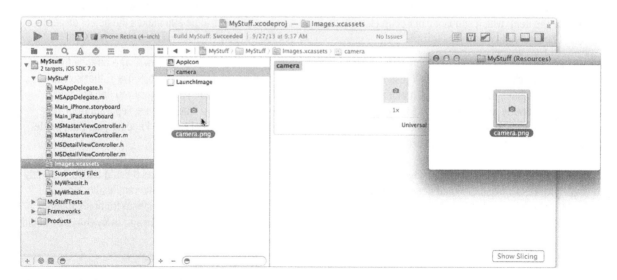

Figure 7-2. *Adding camera.png resource*

MyWhatsit is finished, so it's time to add the new view objects to your interface.

Adding an Image View

The next step is to add the view objects to your detail interface. This should feel like familiar territory by now:

- Add an `imageView` outlet to your `MSDetailViewController` class
- Add label and image view objects to your `MSDetailViewController` interface file
- Connect the `imageView` outlet to the image view object

Start in your `MSDetailViewController.h` interface file. Add the following property:

`@property (weak,nonatomic) IBOutlet UIImageView *imageView;`

Start with the iPhone interface by selecting the `Main_iPhone.storyboard` file. From the object library, add a new label object. Position it below the location text field, and resize it so it's the width of the text field above it, as shown in Figure 7-3. Change the label's title to "Picture."

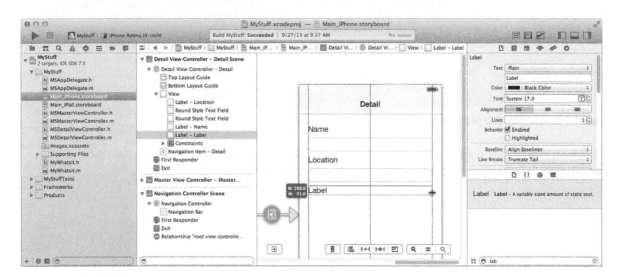

Figure 7-3. Adding the picture label

Add an image view object and drop it anywhere in the lower portion of the interface. Select it. Using the size inspector set its width and height to 128, as shown in Figure 7-4.

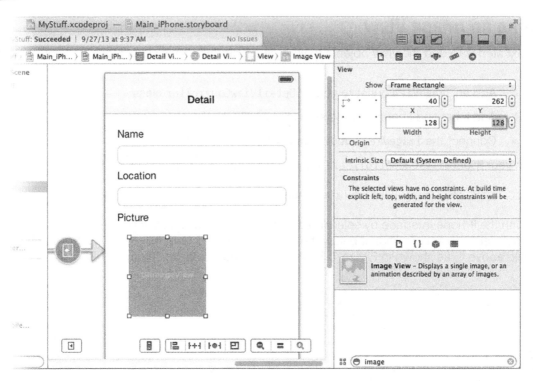

Figure 7-4. Fixing the size of the image view

Now you can drag the image into position. Place it so that it is centered in the display, the recommended distance below the label object, as shown in Figure 7-5.

CHAPTER 7: Smile! 195

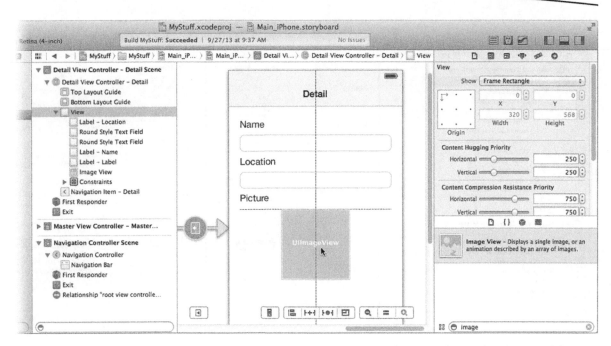

Figure 7-5. Positioning the image view

The guides will indicate when the image object is centered and a comfortable distance from the label object. (You made the label object the width of the display so the image object would "bump" against it, acquiring the recommended spacing.) Now turn these suggested positions into constraints:

1. Control-click/right-click in the image view, drag down a little, release, and choose **Height** from the constraint menu. This will fix the height of the image view object.

2. Repeat for the width, dragging horizontally and choosing Width.

3. Select the image view and the label object (the ones you just added). Do this by selecting one, holding down the Shift key, and selecting the other. Alternatively, you can drag out a selection rectangle that touches both objects. With the two selected, choose **Add Missing Constraints** from the **Resolve Auto Layout Issues** button.

The last step is to select the Detail View Controller. Switch to the connections inspector and locate the imageView outlet you added to the controller. Connect it to the image view object, as shown in Figure 7-6.

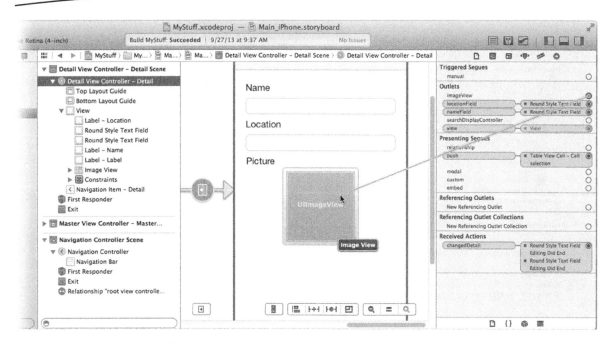

Figure 7-6. Connecting the imageView outlet

With the view objects in place, it's time to add the code to make your item images appear.

Updating the View Controller

You need to modify the code in the master view controller to add the image to the table cell, and in the detail view controller to make the image appear in the new image view. Start with MSMasterViewController.m. Locate the following code in -tableView:cellForRowAtIndexPath: and add the one bold line:

```
cell.textLabel.text = thing.name;
cell.detailTextLabel.text = thing.location;
cell.imageView.image = thing.viewImage;
return cell;
```

The new line sets the image for the cell (cell.imageView.image) to the viewImage of the row's MyWhatsit object. Remember that the view image will be either the item's actual image or a placeholder. The act of setting the cell's image view will alter the cell's layout so the image appears on the left. (Refer to the "Cell Style" section in Chapter 5.)

You're all done with MSMasterViewController. Click on MSDetailViewController.m and locate the -configureView method. Find the following code and add the one bold line:

```
self.nameField.text = self.detailItem.name;
self.locationField.text = self.detailItem.location;
self.imageView.image = self.detailItem.viewImage;
```

This new line sets the image of the UIImageView object (connected to the imageView outlet) to the image of the MyWhatsit object being edited.

From a data model and view standpoint, everything is ready to go, so give it a try. Set the scheme to the iPhone simulator and run the project. You'll see the placeholder images appear in the table and the detail view, as shown in Figure 7-7.

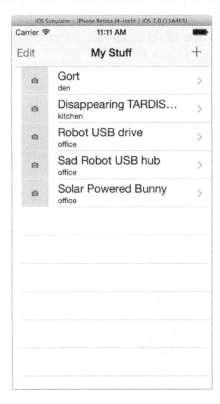 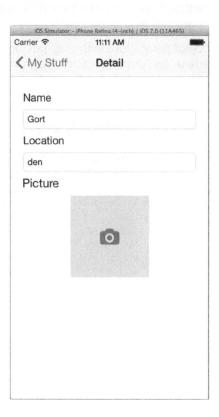

Figure 7-7. Placeholder images

So far everything is working great—there's just no way to change the picture. To accomplish that, you'll need to create an action.

Connecting a Choose Image Action

You want the camera, or photo library picker, interface to appear when the user taps on the image in the detail view. That's simple enough to hook up: create an action method and connect the image view to it. Start by defining a new action in MSDetailViewController.h (you don't need to write it yet, just declare it):

- (IBAction)choosePicture:(id)sender;

Now switch back to the Main_iPhone.storyboard interface, select the image view object, and connect its action outlet to the -choosePicture: action in the Detail View Controller.

Uh oh, we seem to have a problem. The image view object isn't a button, or any other kind of control view; it doesn't send an action message. In fact, by default, it ignores all touch events (its User Interaction Enabled property is NO). So how do you get the image view object to send an action to your view controller?

There are a couple of ways. One solution would be to subclass UIImageView and override its touch event methods, as was described in Chapter 4 ("Coming Events"). But there's a much simpler way: attach a gesture recognizer object to the view.

In the object library, locate the tap gesture recognizer. Drag a new tap gesture recognizer object into the interface and drop it into the image view object, as shown in Figure 7-8.

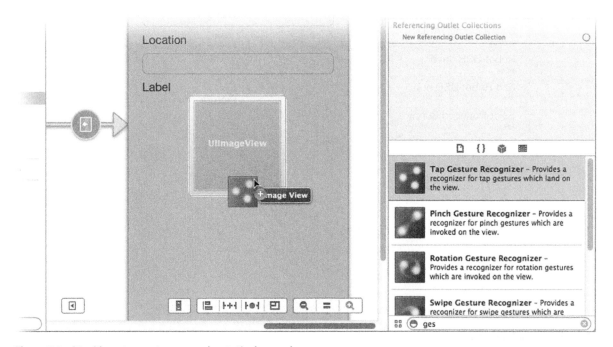

Figure 7-8. Attaching a tap gesture recognizer to the image view

When you drop a gesture recognizer into a view object, Interface Builder creates a new gesture recognizer object and connects the view object to it. This is a one-to-many relationship: a view can be connected to multiple gesture recognizers, but a recognizer only works on a single view object. To see the relationship, select the view object and use the connections inspector to see its recognizers, as shown in upper-right of Figure 7-9. Hover your cursor over the connection and Interface Builder will highlight the object it's connected to, shown at the bottom of Figure 7-9.

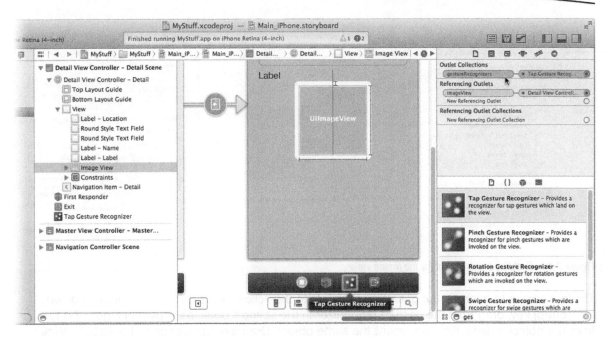

Figure 7-9. Examining the gesture recognizer connection of the image view object

> **Tip** You can also see the inverse connections in the connections inspector. Select an object. Towards the bottom of the inspector you'll find the *referencing outlet collections* section. This section shows the connections from other objects *to* the object you're inspecting.

By default, a new tap gesture recognizer is configured to recognize single finger tap events, which is exactly what you want. You do, however, need to change the attributes of the image view object. Even though you have it connected to a gesture recognizer, the view object is still set to ignore touch events, so it will never receive any events to recognize. Rectify this by selecting the image view object and use the attributes inspector to check the User Interaction Enabled property, as shown in Figure 7-10.

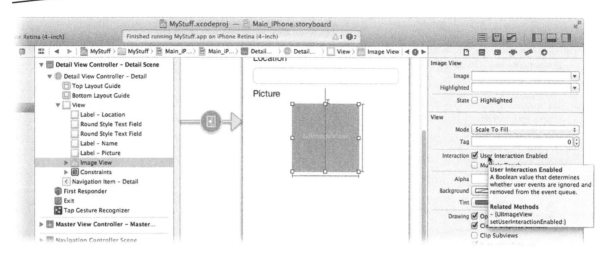

Figure 7-10. Enabling touch events for the image view

The last step is to connect the gesture recognizer to the -choosePicture: action. Holding down the control key, drag from the gesture recognizer in the scene's dock, as shown in Figure 7-11, or from the object outline. Both represent the same object. Drag the connection to the Detail View Controller and connect it to the -choosePicture: action, also shown in Figure 7-11.

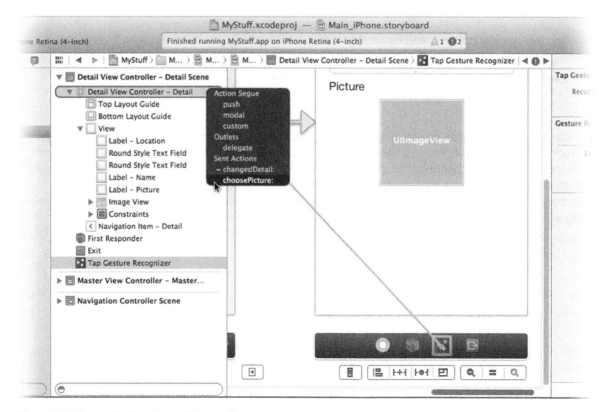

Figure 7-11. Connecting the -choosePicture: action

A -choosePicture: message will now be sent to the detail view controller when the user taps on the image. Now you have to implement the -choosePicture: method, which brings you to the fun part: letting the user take a picture.

Taking Pictures

The UIImagePickerController class provides simple, self-contained, interfaces for taking a picture, recording a movie, or choosing an existing image from the user's photo library. The image picker controller does all of the hard work. For the most part, all your app has to do is create a UIImagePickerController object and present it as you would any other view controller. The delegate of the controller will receive messages that contain the image the user picked, the photo they took, or the movie they recorded.

That's not to say the image picker controller can do everything. There are a number of decisions and considerations that your app must make before, and after, the image picker has done its thing. This will be the bulk of the logic in your app, and I'll explain these decisions as you work through the code. Start by adding this -choosePicture: method to your MSDetailViewController.m implementation:

```
- (IBAction)choosePicture:(id)sender
{
    if (self.detailItem==nil)
        return;

    BOOL hasPhotoLibrary = [UIImagePickerController isSourceTypeAvailable:UIImagePickerControllerSourceTypePhotoLibrary];
    BOOL hasCamera = [UIImagePickerController isSourceTypeAvailable:UIImagePickerControllerSourceTypeCamera];
    if (!hasPhotoLibrary && !hasCamera)
        return;

    if (hasPhotoLibrary && hasCamera)
        {
        UIActionSheet *actionSheet = [[UIActionSheet alloc]
                    initWithTitle:nil
                        delegate:self
                cancelButtonTitle:@"Cancel"
           destructiveButtonTitle:nil
                otherButtonTitles:@"Take a Picture",@"Choose a Photo",nil];
        [actionSheet showInView:self.view];
        return;
        }
    [self presentImagePickerUsingCamera:hasCamera];
}
```

The first decision is easy: this action only does something if the detail view is currently editing a MyWhatsit object. If not (self.detailItem==nil), then return and do nothing. This can happen in the iPad interface when the detail view is visible, but the user has yet to select an item to edit.

You Can't Always Get What You Want

The rest of the code deals with deciding what image picker interfaces are available to your app. This is the intersection of what your user wants to do and what your app can do. The `UIImagePickerController` has the *potential* to present a still camera, video camera, combination still and video camera, photo library picker, or camera roll (saved) photo picker. That doesn't, however, mean it can do all of those things. Different iOS devices have different hardware. Some have a camera, some don't, some have two. Some cameras are capable of taking movies, while others aren't. Even on devices that have cameras and photo libraries, security or restrictions may prohibit your app from using those resources.

The first step to using the image picker is to decide what you want to do, and then find out what you can do. For this app, you want to present either a still camera interface or present a picker interface to choose an existing image from the photo library. Use the `UIImagePickerController` method `-isSourceTypeAvailable:` to find out if you can do either of those. You pass the message a constant indicating the kind of interface you'd like to present, and the method tells you if that interface can be used.

The next two lines of code save the result of asking if the photo library picker interface can be used in `hasPhotoLibrary` variable. The `hasCamera` variable will remember if the live camera interface is available.

> **Note** There's a third interface, `UIImagePickerControllerSourceTypeSavedPhotosAlbum`. This presents the same interface as the photo library picker, but only allows the user to choose images in their camera roll—called the "Saved Photos" album on devices that don't have a camera.

The next line of code considers the situation where neither interface is available. In that situation, there's nothing to present and the action returns without doing anything.

> **Tip** In the real world, it would be a good idea to put up an alert message telling the user that there are no available image sources, rather than just ignoring their tap—but I'll leave that as an exercise you can explore on your own.

The next block of code considers the more likely situation where both the camera and the photo library picker are available. So which interface do you present? That's a question for the user to answer, so ask them.

A `UIActionSheet` is a pop-up controller that presents a series of buttons and asks the user to pick one. You create the object with a (optional) title, a delegate, and the titles of the buttons you want to appear. In this app, you ask the user if they want to "Take a Picture" or "Choose a Photo." You then send `-showInView:` to present those choices to the user. Its delegate object will receive a message when the user taps one, so this method returns and waits for that to happen.

The last line of code handles the situation where there is only one interface available (either the camera or the photo library picker is available, but not both). In this situation there's no point in asking the user, just start the one interface they can use. But before you get to that, add the code to respond to the action sheet.

A `UIActionSheet` delegate must adopt the `UIActionSheetDelegate` protocol. Add that to the `MSDetailViewController` class definition in `MSDetailViewController.h`:

```
@interface MSDetailViewController : UIViewController <UISplitViewControllerDelegate,
                                                      UIActionSheetDelegate>
```

Back in `MSDetailViewController.m`, add the only `UIActionSheetDelegate` method you're interested in:

```
- (void)actionSheet:(UIActionSheet *)actionSheet
 clickedButtonAtIndex:(NSInteger)buttonIndex
{
    switch (buttonIndex) {
        case 0: // camera button
        case 1: // photo button
            [self presentImagePickerUsingCamera:(buttonIndex==0)];
            break;
    }
}
```

When the user chooses one of the action sheet buttons, your delegate receives an `-actionSheet:clickedButtonAtIndex:` message. The `buttonIndex` parameter tells you which button the user tapped. Use that to decide which interface to present.

To review, you've queried the `UIImagePickerController` to determine which interfaces, in the subset of interfaces you'd like to present, are available. If none, do nothing. If only one is available, present that interface immediately. If more than one is available, ask the user which one they would like to use, wait for their answer, and present that. The next big task is to present the interface.

Presenting the Image Picker

Now add a `-presentImagePickerUsingCamera:` method to your class. Start by adding its method prototype to the private `@interface MSDetailViewController ()` section at the top of the `MSDetailViewController.m` file:

```
@interface MSDetailViewController ()
@property (strong, nonatomic) UIPopoverController *masterPopoverController;
- (void)configureView;
- (void)presentImagePickerUsingCamera:(BOOL)useCamera;
@end
```

Now add the `-presentImagePickerUsingCamera:` method to its `@implementation`:

```
- (void)presentImagePickerUsingCamera:(BOOL)useCamera
{
    UIImagePickerController *cameraUI = [UIImagePickerController new];
```

```
        cameraUI.sourceType = ( useCamera ? UIImagePickerControllerSourceTypeCamera
                                          : UIImagePickerControllerSourceTypePhotoLibrary );
        cameraUI.mediaTypes = @[(NSString*)kUTTypeImage];
        cameraUI.delegate = self;
        [self presentViewController:cameraUI animated:YES completion:nil];
}
```

This method starts by creating a new `UIImagePickerController` object.

The `sourceType` property determines which interface the image picker will present. It should only be set to values that returned YES when sent to `-isSourceTypeAvailable:`. In this code, it's set to either `UIImagePickerControllerSourceTypeCamera` or `UIImagePickerControllerSourceTypePhotoLibrary`, which you've already determined is available.

The `mediaTypes` property is an array of data types that your app is prepared to accept. Your choices are kUTTypeImage, kUTTypeMovie, or both. This property modifies the interface (camera or picker) so that only those image types are allowed. Setting only kUTTypeImage when presenting the camera interface limits the controls so the user can only take still images. If you included both types (kUTTypeImage and kUTTypeMovie), then the camera interface would allow the user to switch between still and movie capture as they please (assuming their device was capable of video capture).

There's also one little problem with this code: the constants for kUTTypeImage and kUTTypeMovie aren't defined by the standard Cocoa Touch framework. To pull these constants into this module, add this import statement at the very top of your source file:

```
#import <MobileCoreServices/UTCoreTypes.h>
```

> **Note** There are a number of other `UIImagePickerController` properties that you could set before you start the interface. For example, set its `allowsEditing` property to NO if you do not want the user to have the ability to crop (zoom) pictures or trim movies.

The last two lines of `-presentImagePickerUsingCamera:` set your controller as the delegate for the picker and start its interface. The controller slides into view and waits for the user to take a picture, pick an image, or cancel the operation. When one of those happens, your controller receives the appropriate delegate message. But to be the image picker delegate, your controller must adopt both the `UIImagePickerControllerDelegate` and `UINavigationControllerDelegate` protocols. Add those to your `MSDetailViewController` class declaration now:

```
@interface MSDetailViewController : UIViewController <UISplitViewControllerDelegate,
                                            UIImagePickerControllerDelegate,
                                            UINavigationControllerDelegate,
                                            UIActionSheetDelegate>
```

> **Note** Your `MSDetailViewController` isn't interested in, and doesn't implement, any of the `UINavigationControllerDelegate` messages. It adopts the protocol simply to avoid the compiler warning that results if it doesn't.

With the picker up and running, you're now ready to deal with the image the user takes or picks.

Importing the Image

Ultimately, the user will take or choose a picture. This results in a `-imagePickerController:didFinishPickingMediaWithInfo:` message sent to your controller. This is the method where you'll take the image the user took/selected and add it to the `MyWhatsit` object. All of the information about what the user did is contained in a dictionary, passed to your method via the `info` parameter. Add this method to your MSDetailViewController.m file. The method starts out simply enough:

```
- (void)imagePickerController:(UIImagePickerController *)picker
didFinishPickingMediaWithInfo:(NSDictionary *)info
{
    NSString *mediaType = info[UIImagePickerControllerMediaType];
    if ([mediaType isEqualToString:(NSString*)kUTTypeImage])
        {
        UIImage *whatsitImage = info[UIImagePickerControllerEditedImage];
        if (whatsitImage==nil)
            whatsitImage = info[UIImagePickerControllerOriginalImage];
```

The first task is to get the media type of the data being returned by the image picker. You specified only one type (kUTTypeImage), so that's the only thing the picker should return, but it's a good idea to check anyway. Once you're sure you're getting back a still image from the picker, the next step is to obtain the image object.

There are, potentially, two possible images: the original one and the edited one. If the user cropped, or performed any other in-camera editing, the one you want is the edited version. Start by requesting that one (`UIImagePickerControllerEditedImage`) from the info dictionary. If that value is `nil`, then the original (`UIImagePickerControllerOriginalImage`) is the only image being returned.

The next couple of lines consider the case where the user has taken a picture. When users take a picture, especially using the standard iOS camera interface, they expect their photo to appear in their camera roll. This isn't a requirement, and another app might act differently, but here you meet the user's expectations by adding the picture they just took to their camera roll.

```
if (picker.sourceType==UIImagePickerControllerSourceTypeCamera)
    UIImageWriteToSavedPhotosAlbum(whatsitImage,nil,nil,nil);
```

You don't want to do this if the user picked an existing image from their photo library, which is why you first test to see if the interface was `UIImagePickerControllerSourceTypeCamera`.

> **Tip** Many apps allow users to save an image to their camera roll. You can do this at any time using the `UIImageWriteToSavedPhotosAlbum()` function. This function isn't limited to being used in conjunction with the image picker interface.

Cropping and Resizing

Now that you have the image, what do you do with it? You could just set the `MyWhatsit` image property to the returned image object and return. While that would work, it's a bit crude. First, modern iOS devices have high-resolution cameras that produce big images, consuming several megabytes of memory for each one. It won't take too many such pictures before your app will run out of memory and crash. Also, the images are rectangular, and both the details interface and the table view would look better using square images.

To solve both of these problems, you'll want to scale down and crop the user's image. Start by cropping the image with this code, which is the next part of your `-imagePickerController:didFinishPickingMediaWithInfo:` method:

```
CGImageRef coreGraphicsImage = whatsitImage.CGImage;
CGFloat height = CGImageGetHeight(coreGraphicsImage);
CGFloat width = CGImageGetWidth(coreGraphicsImage);
CGRect crop;
if (height>width)
    {
    crop.size.height = crop.size.width = width;
    crop.origin.x = 0;
    crop.origin.y = floorf((height-width)/2);
    }
else
    {
    crop.size.height = crop.size.width = height;
    crop.origin.y = 0;
    crop.origin.x = floorf((width-height)/2);
    }
CGImageRef croppedImage = CGImageCreateWithImageInRect(coreGraphicsImage,crop);
```

The first step is to get a Core Graphics image reference from the `UIImage` object. `UIImage` is a convenient and simple to use object that handles all kinds of convoluted image storage, conversion, and drawing details for you. It does not, however, let you manipulate or modify the image in any significant way. To do that, you need to "step down" into the lower-level Core Graphics frameworks, where the real image manipulation and drawing functions reside. A `CGImageRef` is a reference (think of it like an object reference) that contains primitive image data.

The next step is to get the height and width (in pixels) of the image. That's accomplished by calling the functions `CGImageGetHeight()` and `CGImageGetWidth()`.

C VS. OBJECTIVE-C PROGRAMMING

Many of the methods of Cocoa Touch objects are actually written in C, not Objective-C. C is the procedural language that the object-oriented Objective-C language is built on top of. In Chapter 6 I spoke of writing programs entirely by defining structures and passing those structures to functions. This is exactly how you program using C and the framework of C functions called Core Foundation.

While C is not an object-oriented language, you can still write object-oriented programs; it's just more work. In Core Foundation, a class is called a *type* and an object is a *reference*. Instead of sending messages to the object, you call a function and pass it a reference (typically as the first parameter). In other words, instead of writing myImage.height to the get height of an image, you write CGImageGetHeight(myImageRef).

While most Core Foundation types will only work with Core Foundation functions, a few fundamental types are interchangeable with Objective-C objects. These include NSString/CFStringRef, NSNumber/CFNumberRef, NSArray/CFArrayRef, NSDictionary/CFDictionaryRef, NSURL/CFURLRef, and others. Any function or Objective-C method that expects one will accept the other as-is. This is called the *toll-free bridge*, and you've already used it in this app. The kUTTypeImage string is really a CFStringRef, not an NSString object. But since the two are interchangeable, it was possible to pass the Core Foundation kUTTypeImage string value in the parameter that expected an NSString object.

The if block decides if the image is horizontal (width>height) or vertical (height>width). Based on this, it sets up a CGRect that describes a square in the middle of the image. If horizontal, it makes the rectangle the height of the image and insets the left and right edges. If vertical, the rectangle is the width of the image, and the top and bottom are trimmed.

The function after the if/else block does all of the work. The CGImageCreateWithImageInRect() function takes an existing Core Graphics image, picks out just the pixels in the rectangle, and copies them to a new Core Graphics image. The end result is a square Core Graphics image with just the middle section of the original image.

The next step is to turn the CGImageRef back into a UIImage object, so it can be stored in the MyWhatsit object. At the same time, you're going to scale it down so it's not so big.

```
whatsitImage = [UIImage imageWithCGImage:croppedImage
                                   scale:MAX(crop.size.height/512,1.0)
                             orientation:whatsitImage.imageOrientation];
```

The UIImage class method -imageWithCGImage:scale:orientation: creates a new UIImage object from an existing CGImageRef. At the same time, it can scale the image and change its orientation. The scale calculates a ratio between the size of the original image and a 512-pixel one. This scales down the (probably) larger image size from the device's camera down to a 512x512 pixel image, which is a manageable size. The MAX() macro is used to keep the ratio from dropping below 1.0 (1:1); this prevents an image that's already smaller than 512 pixels from being made larger.

> **Note** UIImage has an `orientation` property. Core Graphic images do not. Images taken with the camera are all in landscape format. When you take a vertical (portrait) picture, you get a UIImage with a landscape image and an `orientation` that tells UIImage to draw the image vertically. When you started working with the CGImageRef, that orientation information was lost. If you step through the program with the Xcode debugger, you'll see that the code crops a landscape image (width>height), even if you took a portrait photo. So to make the photo draw the way it was taken, you have to supply the original orientation when creating the new UIImage.

The very last detail is to release the Core Graphics image reference created by the `CGImageCreateWithImageInRect()` function. This is memory management, and something that Objective-C usually takes care of for you. When using the Core Foundation functions, however, you're responsible for doing this yourself. See Chapter 21 for more details.

```
CGImageRelease(croppedImage);
```

Winding Up

All of the hard part is over. The only thing left for this method to do is store the cropped and resized image in the MyWhatsit object and dismiss the image picker controller:

```
    _detailItem.image = whatsitImage;
    self.imageView.image = whatsitImage;
    [_detailItem postDidChangeNotification];
    }

    [self dismissImagePicker];
}
```

The first line stores the new image in the new image property of the MyWhatsit object. The second updates the image view in the detail view, so it reflects the same change. Finally, you must remember to post a change notification so the master list knows to redraw this item's row with the new image.

I've encapsulated the image picker dismissal code in a separate function. There are two places where the image picker needs to be dismissed: here, after a successful new image has been imported, and if the user taps the "cancel" button, indicating that they don't want to change the image after all. When the latter happens your controller will receive a `-imagePickerControllerDidCancel:` message. Handle that by adding the appropriate delegate method:

```
- (void)imagePickerControllerDidCancel:(UIImagePickerController *)picker
{
    [self dismissImagePicker];
}
```

This method does nothing but dismiss the controller, making no change to your `MyWhatsit` object. The last piece of this puzzle is the method to dismiss the controller:

```
- (void)dismissImagePicker
{
    [self dismissViewControllerAnimated:YES completion:nil];
}
```

You'll also want to add a prototype for the `-dismissImagePicker` method in the private `@interface MSDetailViewController ()` section at the beginning of the file.

Testing the Camera

You're ready to test out your image picker interface—for real. The simulator, unfortunately, does not emulate the camera hardware nor does it come with any images in its photo library. To test this app, you'll need to run it on a real iOS device. Since you've only built the iPhone interface, you'll need an iPhone, iPod Touch, or something similar. If not, you'll just have to read along until we get to the iPad interface.

Plug in your iPhone and set the project's scheme to iPhone. Run it. Your app's interface should look like that in Figure 7-12.

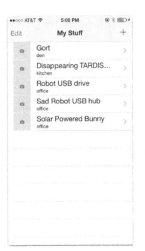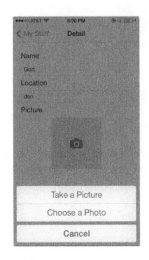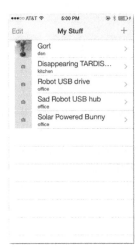

Figure 7-12. Testing the iPhone Interface

Tap an item, tap the placeholder image in the detail view, tap "Take a Picture", and take a picture. The cropped image should appear in the detail view, and again back in the master table, as shown in Figure 7-12.

Congratulations, you've added picture taking to your app! You're not quite done yet, but enjoy the moment and have fun with the camera.

Building the iPad Interface

The iPad interface is almost identical to the iPhone interface. Follow the steps back in the sections "Adding an Image View" and "Connecting a Choose Image Action" to add the view objects and the tap gesture recognizer, and connect them all to the appropriate outlets and actions. (Don't forget to set the User Interaction Enabled property of the image view.) The only changes I suggest are to position the iPad image view on the left—it's too far away from the label when centered—and change the size of the image view to 256x256, instead of 128x128. Your finished iPad interface should look like the one in Figure 7-13.

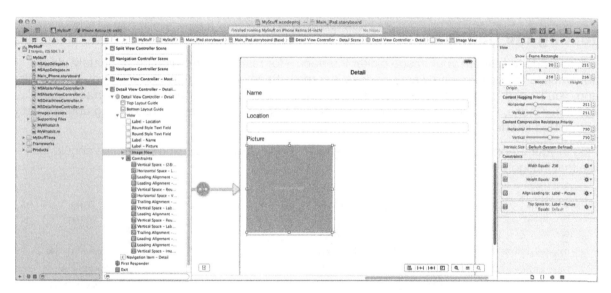

Figure 7-13. Finished iPad interface

Run the iPad version in the iPad simulator or on your iPad. If your iPad has a camera, that will work just fine. Picking an image from your photo library presents a ridiculously large interface that only works in portrait orientation, as shown in Figure 7-14.

Figure 7-14. iPad photo library picker

This, clearly, isn't the ideal iPad interface. Consulting the documentation for `UIImagePickerController`, you'll find this statement:

> On iPad, the correct way to present an image picker depends on its source type, ... if you specify a source type of UIImagePickerControllerSourceTypePhotoLibrary or UIImagePickerControllerSourceTypeSavedPhotosAlbum, you must present the image picker using a popover controller ...

So while the full-screen camera interface works just fine on the iPad—and is the recommended interface—the photo library picker should be presented as a popover.

> **Caution** While it's *recommended* that you present the photo library picker in a popover in iOS 7, in earlier versions of iOS it's *required*. Fail to do so and your app will crash.

Presenting a view controller inside a popover is accomplished using a `UIPopoverController` object. To use it, you must:

- create a popover controller for the view controller you want to display
- use the popover controller to present the interface
- dismiss the popover controller when finished

Adding a Popover

The first thing you'll need is an instance variable where you can save a reference to the popover controller object. You'll need to maintain a reference to the popover controller until you're done with it. Add these three lines of bold code to the private @interface MSDetailViewController () section at the beginning of the MSDetailViewController.m implementation file:

```
@interface MSDetailViewController ()
{
    UIPopoverController *imagePopoverController;
}
@property (strong, nonatomic) UIPopoverController *masterPopoverController;
- (void)configureView;
- (void)presentImagePickerUsingCamera:(BOOL)useCamera;
- (void)dismissImagePicker;
@end
```

In the -presentImagePickerUsingCamera: method, replace the last line of code ([self presentViewController:cameraUI animated:YES completion:nil]) with this logic:

```
if (useCamera || UIDevice.currentDevice.userInterfaceIdiom==UIUserInterfaceIdiomPhone)
    {
    [self presentViewController:cameraUI animated:YES completion:nil];
    }
else
    {
    imagePopoverController = [[UIPopoverController alloc] initWithContentViewController:cameraUI];
    [imagePopoverController presentPopoverFromRect:self.imageView.frame
                                    inView:self.view
                     permittedArrowDirections:UIPopoverArrowDirectionAny
                                    animated:YES];
    }
```

The new code first checks to see if the user wants to see the camera interface or if they're running on an iPhone. If either of these is true, present the cameraUI view controller as a full-screen interface, just as before.

If both of those conditions are false, then the user wants to pick an image from their photo library on an iPad. The else block creates and new UIPopoverController for the cameraUI view controller, and saves it in your new instance variable. It then uses the popover controller to present the picker interface. The FromRect: and inView: parameters anchor the popover to the image view.

Now find your -dismissImagePicker method and replace its code with the following:

```
if (imagePopoverController!=nil)
        {
        [imagePopoverController dismissPopoverAnimated:YES];
        imagePopoverController = nil;
        }
    else
```

```
{
[self dismissViewControllerAnimated:YES completion:nil];
}
```

The new code determines how `-presentImagePickerUsingCamera:` presented the picker interface—by examining the `imagePopoverController` variable—and dismissing the image picker in the same fashion it was presented.

There's one tiny bit of housekeeping to do. At the very beginning of the `-presentImagePickerUsingCamera:` method, add this line:

```
imagePopoverController = nil;
```

The reason this needs to be done is that the `imagePopoverController` variable is used as a flag to indicate which technique was used to present the image picker. If the user chooses an image, or cancels, your delegate method is called, which ultimately results in the popover being dismissed and `imagePopoverController` being set to nil again.

The user can, however, also dismiss the iPad image picker by tapping outside of the popover. You could catch this by implementing a popover delegate and writing a `-popoverControllerDidDismissPopover:` method—but that seems like a lot of work. It's easier to just reset the variable before presenting the next interface, destroying any stray popover controller that might have been left over.

Your iPad photo library picker interface is now ready to use on the iPad, as shown in Figure 7-15.

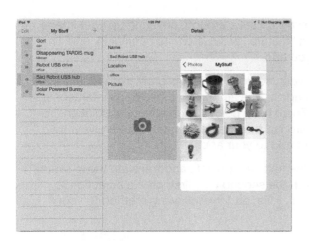

Figure 7-15. iPad popover photo picker

Sticky Keyboards

One quirk of your app, if you haven't noticed, is the sticky keyboard. No, I'm not talking about the kind you get from eating chocolate while programming. I'm talking about the virtual keyboard in iOS. Figure 7-16 shows the virtual keyboard that appears when you tap inside a text field.

CHAPTER 7: Smile!

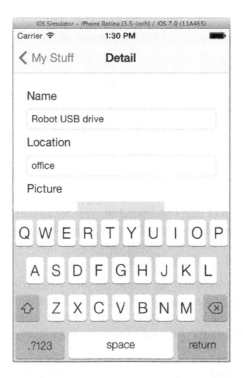

Figure 7-16. iOS's virtual keyboard

The problem is that, once summoned, it won't go away. It hangs around, covering up your image view, and generally being annoying. This has been a "feature" of iOS from its beginning, and it's something you must deal with if it's a problem for you app.

Now I'm sure you've noticed that many other apps you use don't have this problem. Tapping outside of a text field makes the keyboard go away again. The authors of those apps intercept taps outside of the text field and dismiss the keyboard. There have been a wide variety of solutions to this problem, and you'll find many of them floating around the Internet. I'm going to show you a particularly simple one that will only take a minute to add to your app.

The "trick" is to catch touch events outside any of the text field objects and translate those events into an action that will retract the keyboard. Start with the second part first: create an action to retract the keyboard. In your `MSDetailViewController.m` file, add the following method to your implementation:

```
- (IBAction)dismissKeyboard:(id)sender
{
    [self.view endEditing:NO];
}
```

This simple method sends the `-endEditing:` message to the root view of your interface. The `-endEditing:` method is ready-built to solve this problem; it searches through the view's subviews looking for an editable object that's currently being edited. If it finds one, it asks the object to resign its first responder status, ending the editing session, and retracting the keyboard.

> **Tip** The single value passed to the -endEditing: message is the force parameter. If YES, it forces the view to end editing, even if it doesn't want to. Passing NO lets the view decide, and might not end the editing session. I elected to be polite and let the view decide.

Now add a prototype for this method to your public @interface in MSDEtailViewController.h file, so Interface Builder can see it:

- (IBAction)dismissKeyboard:(id)sender;

Now you're going to add another tap gesture recognizer. In the Main_iPhone.storyboard file, find the tap gesture recognizer in the object library. Drag one into your interface and drop it into the root view object, either by dropping it into the empty space in the interface or directly into the root view object in the outline, as shown in Figure 7-17.

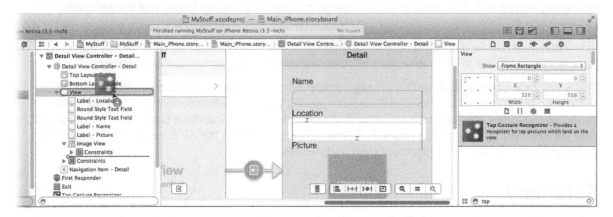

Figure 7-17. Adding a tap gesture recognizer to the root view

Control/right+click on the new gesture recognizer, drag it to the Detail View Controller, and connect it to the new -dismissKeyboard: action. (If you can't figure out which gesture recognizer object belongs to the root view, use the connections inspector (see Figure 7-9) in the section "Connecting a Choose Image Action.") Now any tap that occurs outside a specific subview will pass those touch events to the root view, dismissing the keyboard. If you're not sure why that happens, review the section "Hit Testing" in Chapter 4.

Give it a try. Run the iPhone interface, tap inside a text field, and then tap outside the text field. You should see the keyboard appear and then disappear.

Now add a tap gesture recognizer to the root view of the iPad interface (Main_iPad.storyboard) and connect it to the same action.

To be thorough, find the point in the `-choosePicture:` method where the app intends to present an interface, and add this one bold line of code:

```
[self dismissKeyboard:self];
if (hasPhotoLibrary && hasCamera)
    {
```

This will cause the keyboard to retract when the user taps on the image view to change it. Remember that in hit testing, it's the most specific view object that gets the touch events. Since the image view object receives touch events, those events won't make their way to the root view.

Advanced Camera Techniques

I'm sure you're excited to add camera and photo library features to your app. If your goal, however, is to create the next Hipstamatic or Instagram, the `UIImagePickerController` isn't what you want; you want the low-level camera controls. You'll find that kind of control in the `AVCaptureDevice` class. That object represents a single image capture device (a.k.a. a camera), and gives you excruciatingly precise control over every aspect of it, from turning on the flash to controlling the white balance of the exposure.

This is part of the much larger `AV Foundation` framework, which also encompasses video capture, video playback, audio recording, and audio playback. You'll explore some parts of this framework later in this book. Some of its features are object-oriented, while others are C functions.

The advantage of using a class like `UIImagePickerController` is that so many of the picture-taking details are taken care of for you. But it also constrains your app's functionality and design. The lower-level classes and functions open up a world of design and interface possibilities, but require that you deal with those details yourself. To learn more, start with the *AV Foundation Programming* guide you'll find in Xcode's Documentation and API reference.

Summary

Adding picture taking to your MyStuff app spiffed it up considerably and made it much more exciting to use. You also learned a little about presenting view controllers and manipulating images. You now know how to export an image to the user's camera roll, add tap gesture recognizers to an existing view, link to additional frameworks, and get that pesky keyboard out of the way. You're also getting comfortable with outlets, connections, and delegates; in other words, you're turning into an iOS developer!

Throughout the past few chapters, I've constantly referred to "view," "controller," and "data model" objects. The next chapter is going to take another short recess from development to explain what that means and explore an important design pattern.

EXERCISES

If there's no camera or photo library, it would be nice to tell the user that, rather than just ignoring them. In the Shorty app, you put up an alert when a web page couldn't be loaded for some reason. Use the same technique to present a dialog if neither the camera nor photo library picker interfaces are available.

Also consider how to test this code. In the devices you're likely to own, and in the simulator, one of those interfaces is always going to be available. A modified MyStuff project, with comments, can be found in the `MyStuff E1` project folder for this chapter.

Chapter 8

Model Citizen

This chapter is all about the model-view-controller design pattern. Design patterns, which I talked about in Chapter 6, are reusable solutions to common programming problems. The model-view-controller (MVC) design pattern is, arguably, the most important and wide-ranging design pattern used today. In this chapter you'll learn:

- What the model-view-controller design pattern is
- What makes a good data model
- What makes a good view object
- What makes a good controller object
- How MVC objects communicate with each other
- When you can cheat

You might be thinking that all of this MVC stuff is a bunch of esoteric computer science theory that won't really help you write your Death Star Laser Cannon Control app. On the contrary, learning (even a little) about the MVC design pattern will not only make your Death Star Laser Cannon Control app more reliable, it will actually make it easier to write and maintain. Good MVC design might require a little more thought and consideration up front, but you save a whole lot of work in the end—and your app is likely to have fewer bugs.

So feel free to skip this chapter, but when you press the "Destroy Alderaan" button on your app and nothing happens . . . you'll have to answer to Lord Vader, not me.

The Model-View-Controller Design Pattern

In Chapter 6 I talked about the single responsibility principle, encapsulation, and the "open closed" principle. All of these can be distilled into a simple concept:

An object should do one thing, and do it well.

To do anything useful, your app must store data, display that data in an interface, and allow the user to interact with it. The model-view-controller design pattern organizes what your app must do (store, display, and interact) into objects that do just one thing (data objects, view objects, and controller objects), and describes how those objects work together. Let's start with the simplest of the three: data model objects.

Data Model Objects

Your data model consists of the objects that store your app's information. Data model objects should:

- Represent the data in your app
- Encapsulate the storage of that data
- Avoid assumptions about how the data is displayed or changed

The data of your app is whatever values, information, or concepts your app uses. In your MyStuff app, your data model was simply the names, locations, and images of the things you own. A chess app would have a slightly more complex data model; there would be an object that represented the chess board, objects for each player, objects for each piece, objects that recorded the moves, and so on. An astronomical catalog app might require dozens of classes and hundreds of thousands of objects to keep track of the visible stars.

The first job of your data model classes is to represent the data for your app, while hiding (encapsulating) how that data is stored. It should present the rest of your app with a simple interface so the other classes can get the information they need, without needing to know exactly how that data is represented or stored.

Even for "simple" apps, like MyStuff, encapsulation is important for the future of your app. For example, the image property of MyWhatsit stored a UIImage object with the picture of that item. Simple, right? But images can take up a lot of memory, and if your app is going to inventory hundreds, instead of dozens, of items, your app can't keep all of those images in memory—it will run out of memory and crash.

You could address this problem by changing your data model so images that you're not currently displaying—after all, you can't display them all at once—are written to flash memory as individual image files. The next time an object requests the image property of a MyWhatsit object, your data model can determine if it has that image in memory or whether it needs to retrieve it from flash storage.

The key concept is that all of these decisions are encapsulated in your data model. The other classes that use your MyWhatsit object just request the image property; they don't know how, or where, that information is stored, and they shouldn't care. Review the food truck analogy in the "Encapsulation" section of Chapter 6, if that isn't clear.

The other really important aspect of the data model is what it is *not*. The data model is at the bottom of the MVC design and it shouldn't contain any properties or logic that are not directly related to your app's data or how that data is maintained.

Specifically, it shouldn't know anything about, or make any assumptions about, the view or controller objects it works with. It shouldn't contain references to view objects, have methods that present the data in the user interface, or directly handle user actions. In this respect, the data model is the purest of the three MVC roles; it's all about the data, and nothing else.

View Objects

View objects sit in the middle of the MVC design. A good view object:

- Presents some aspect of the data model to the user
- Understands the data it displays, and how to display it, but nothing more
- May interpret user interface events and send actions to controller objects

A view object's primary purpose is to display the value(s) in your data model. View objects must, by necessity, understand at least some aspects of your data model, but know nothing about controller objects.

How much does a view object know about the data model? That depends on the complexity of what's being displayed. In general, it should know just enough to do its job, and no more. A view that displays a string only needs to know the string value to display. A view that draws an animated picture of the night sky needs a lot of information: the list of visible stars, their magnitude and color, the coordinates of the observer, the current time, the azimuth, elevation, the angle of view, and so on. To find examples, you have to look no further than the Cocoa Touch framework, which is full of view objects that display everything from the simplest string (UILabel) to entire documents (UIWebView).

It's common for view objects, especially complex ones, to maintain a reference to the data model objects they display. Such a view object not only understands how to display the data, but also knows what data to display.

View objects may also interpret user interface events (like a "swipe" or a "pinch" gesture) and translate those into action messages (-nextPage: or -zoomOut:), which it sends to a controller object. A view object should not act on those actions; it should simply pass them to a controller.

> **Note** View objects that interpret events and send action messages are called *controls*—not to be confused with controllers. Most control views (text field, button, slider, toggle switch, and so on) are subclasses of UIControl.

Controller Objects

Controllers are at the top of the MVC design and are the "business end" of your app. Controller objects are supervisors that oversee, and often coordinate, the data model and view objects. Controller objects:

- Understand, and often create, the data model objects
- Configure, and often create, the view objects
- Perform the actions received from view objects
- Make changes to the data model
- Coordinate communications between the data model and view objects
- May take responsibility for keeping the view objects updated

It's almost easier to explain what a controller is not, than what it is. It is not your data model; a controller object does not store, manage, or convert your app's data.[1] It is not a view object; it does not draw the interface or interpret low-level events. It is, essentially, everything else.

Controllers can be involved in the initialization of your data model and view objects, often creating the data model objects and loading your view objects from an Interface Builder file.

Controller objects contain all of the business logic of your app. They perform the commands initiated by the user, respond to high-level events, and instigate changes to the data model. In complex apps, there are often multiple controller objects, each responsible for a particular feature or interface.

Your controller objects are also either the recipient or source of most of the messages within your app. How they are involved depends on your design, which brings us to the topic of inter-object communications.

MVC Communications

In its simplest form, the communications between MVC objects forms a loop (see Figure 8-1):

- Data model objects notify view objects of changes
- View objects send actions to controller objects
- Controller objects modify the data model

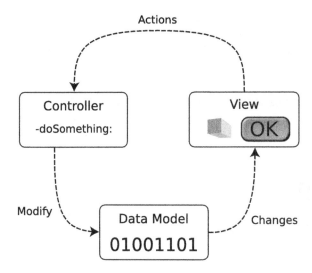

Figure 8-1. Simple MVC communications

In this arrangement, the data model is responsible for notifying any observers of changes. The view objects are responsible for observing and displaying those changes and sending actions to the controller objects. The controller objects perform the actions, often making changes to the data model, and the whole cycle starts again.

---

[1] There's an exception to this rule that I'll describe toward the end of this chapter.

Counter-intuitively, this simplified arrangement only happens in fairly sophisticated apps. Most of the time, the data model is not set up to post notification and the view objects don't observe changes directly. Instead, the controller object steps in and takes responsibility for notifying the view objects when the data model changes, as shown in Figure 8-2.

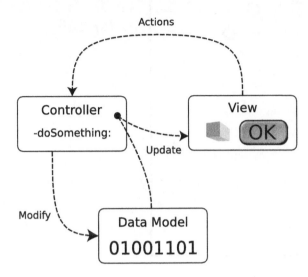

Figure 8-2. Typical MVC communications

Now that you have the basics of the MVC design pattern, let's put together another iOS app. Instead of focusing on a particular iOS technology, like the motion events or the camera, I want you to pay attention to the roles of your objects, their design, and how they change as your app evolves.

Color Model

You're going to develop a new app called ColorModel. It's an app that lets you choose a color using the hue-saturation-brightness color model. Its initial design is simple, as shown in Figure 8-3. The interface consists of three sliders, one for each of the HSB values, and a view where the chosen color appears.

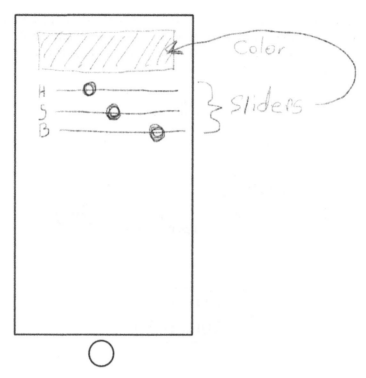

Figure 8-3. Initial design of ColorModel

> **Note** A color model, or color space, is a mathematical representation of a visible color. There are several common models, suited to different applications. Computer displays and televisions use the red-green-blue (RGB) model, artists like to use the hue-saturation-brightness (HSL) model, while printers use the cyan-magenta-yellow-black (CMYK) model. See http://en.wikipedia.org/wiki/Color_model.

Start by launching Xcode. Create and configure a new project:

- Use the Single View Application template
- Name the project ColorModel
- Set the class prefix to CM
- Set devices to iPhone
- Create the project
- In the General tab of the ColorModel target, uncheck the Landscape Left and Landscape Right orientations, so only Portrait orientation is checked

Creating Your Data Model

The first step (after design) of almost any app is to develop your data model. The data model in this app is remarkably simple; it's a single object that maintains the values for hue, saturation, and brightness. It also translates those values into a color object suitable for display and other uses. Start by adding a new Objective-C source file to your project. Select the ColorModel group (the folder, not the project) in the project navigator and choose the **File ➤ New ➤ File…** command (or right/control+click on the group and choose **New File…**). From the iOS category, select the Objective-C class template, name it CMColor, and make it a subclass of NSObject. You will now have an empty data model class, as shown in Figure 8-4.

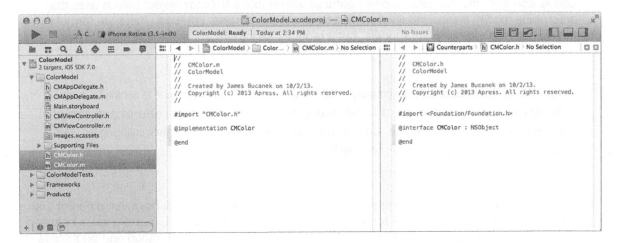

Figure 8-4. Empty CMColor class

Create your data model's public interface by adding the following properties to the @interface section of the CMColor.h file:

```
@property (nonatomic) float hue;
@property (nonatomic) float saturation;
@property (nonatomic) float brightness;
@property (readonly,nonatomic) UIColor *color;
```

The first three properties are floating point values, one each for the color's hue, saturation, and brightness. The hue is in degrees and can range between 0° and 360°. The other two are expressed as a percentage and can range between 0% and 100%.

The last property is readonly—which just means clients of this object can't change it. It contains a UIColor object that represents the color of the current hue/saturation/brightness triplet. The color property is a synthetic property: a value calculated from the values of the other three properties. Implement this by replacing the default getter method with your own in `CMColor.m`:

```
- (UIColor*)color
{
    return [UIColor colorWithHue:self.hue/360
                      saturation:self.saturation/100
                      brightness:self.brightness/100
                           alpha:1];
}
```

The conversion from the hue-saturation-brightness values into a `UIColor` object (which uses the red-green-blue model) is thoughtfully provided by the `UIColor` class. I'm glad. There are formulas for converting between various color models, but it requires a lot more math than I want to explain.

> **Note** It's possible to make the color property settable too: you'd just need to add code to update the hue, saturation, and brightness values to match. Data models should be consistent; if the `color` property always represents the color of the current hue, `saturation`, and `brightness` properties, then changing the color should also change the hue, saturation, and brightness so they still agree.

The values that `UIColor` uses to express hue, saturation, and brightness are, however, different than the one you choose—OK, I choose—for the data model. In your data model, hue is a value between 0 and 360. `UIColor` expects a value between 0 and 1. Likewise, `UIColor` saturation and brightness values are also between 0 and 1. To convert between our model and the one used by `UIColor`, you must scale the values by dividing them by their range. This is the kind of detail that data models encapsulate (hide) from the rest of your app.

With your data model complete, it's time to move on to the view objects.

Creating View Objects

Select your `Main.storyboard` Interface Builder file. In the objects library, find the plain View object and drag one into your interface. Resize and position it so it occupies the top of the display, inset from the left, top, and right using the positioning guides. Using either the resizing handles or the size inspector, set its height to 80 pixels, as shown in Figure 8-5. This will be the view where the user's chosen color appears.

CHAPTER 8: Model Citizen   225

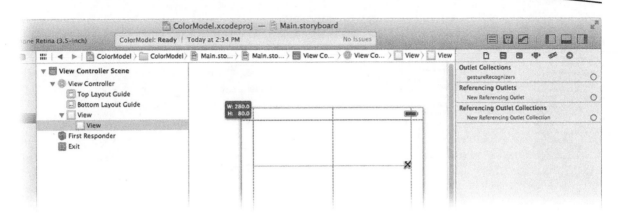

Figure 8-5. Adding a simple view object

Control/Right-click on the new view object, drag down, release, and choose the Height constraint to fix the height of the view at 80 pixels.

Find the Label object in the library and drag one into your interface. Position it immediately below the lower-left corner of the view object. Set its title to H. Locate the Slider object in the library and drag one into your interface, positioning it just below the color view and immediately to the right of the label you just added, as shown in Figure 8-6.

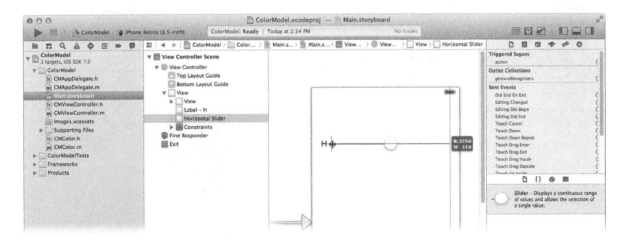

Figure 8-6. Adding the first label and slider

Select the slider and grab the right-center resizing handle. Resize it so its right edge is aligned with the view. You need two more label/slider pairs, so let's quickly duplicate the ones you just created. Select both the label and slider views (by holding down the shift key, or by dragging out a selection rectangle that selects both). Now press the option key. While holding down the option key, click and drag the pair down. The option key turns the drag into a copy operation. Position the pair immediately below the first two, as shown in Figure 8-7, and release the mouse.

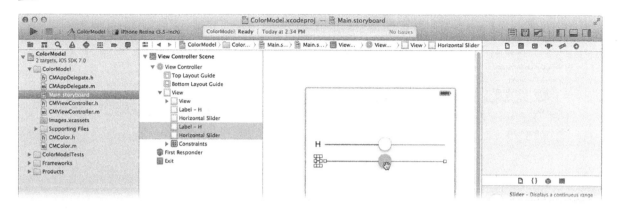

Figure 8-7. Duplicating the label and slider

Repeat the copy again so you have three labels and three slider controls. Control/Right-click on the top slider, drag down to the middle slider, release, and choose Equal Widths from the constraints menu. Repeat, dragging to the bottom slider, as shown in Figure 8-8. This adds constraints to keep the three slider controls the same width.

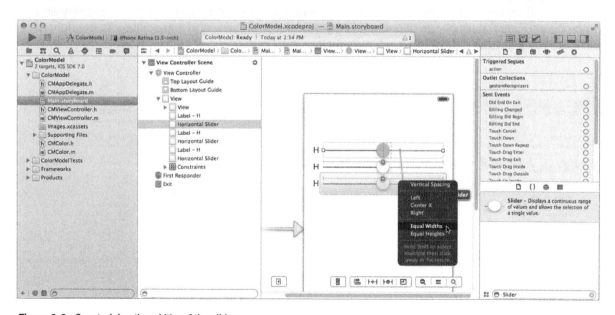

Figure 8-8. Constraining the widths of the sliders

Retitle the second and third labels to S and B. You now have all of the view objects you need. Flesh out the constraints by choosing **Add Missing Constraints in View Controller** from the **Resolve Auto Layout Issues** control.

In your data mode, the hue value ranges from 0° to 360° and saturation and brightness range from 0% to 100%. Change the value range of the three sliders to match. Select the top (hue) slider and use the attributes inspector to change its Maximum value from 1 to 360, as shown in Figure 8-9. Change the maximum value of the other two sliders to 100.

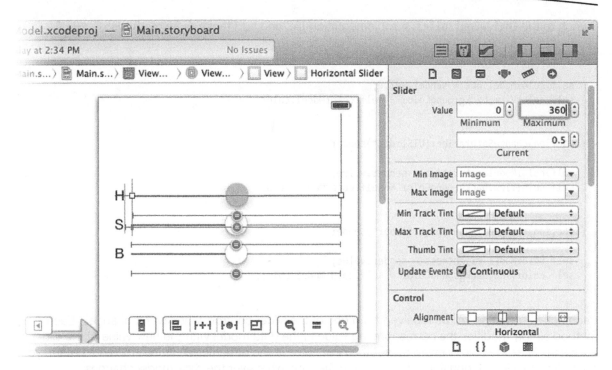

Figure 8-9. Establishing value range of slider control

Writing Your Controller

The Xcode project template already provides you with a controller class; you just need to fill it out. Select your CMViewController.h interface file. Your controller will need a reference to your data model object, along with outlets and actions to connect with your interface. Start by adding an #import statement above the @interface directive so your controller knows about your CMColor class:

#import "CMColor.h"

Inside the @interface, add two properties:

@property (strong,nonatomic) CMColor *colorModel;
@property (weak,nonatomic) IBOutlet UIView *colorView;

The first is your controller's connection with your data model. The second is an outlet that you'll connect to your color view. This will let your controller update the color displayed in the view.

Finally, your controller will need three actions, one for each slider control, that will adjust one value in the data model:

- (IBAction)changeHue:(UISlider*)sender;
- (IBAction)changeSaturation:(UISlider*)sender;
- (IBAction)changeBrightness:(UISlider*)sender;

Switch to the `CMViewController.m` implementation file, and add these three methods:

```
- (IBAction)changeHue:(UISlider*)sender
{
    self.colorModel.hue = sender.value;
    self.colorView.backgroundColor = self.colorModel.color;
}

- (IBAction)changeSaturation:(UISlider*)sender
{
    self.colorModel.saturation = sender.value;
    self.colorView.backgroundColor = self.colorModel.color;
}

- (IBAction)changeBrightness:(UISlider*)sender
{
    self.colorModel.brightness = sender.value;
    self.colorView.backgroundColor = self.colorModel.color;
}
```

Each action message will be received from one of the slider controls whenever it changes. Each method simply modifies the corresponding value in the data model with the new value of the slider. It then updates the color view to reflect the new `color` in the data model. In this implementation, your controller is taking responsibility for updating the view whenever the data model changes (see Figure 8-2).

The last detail is to create the data model when the controller is loaded. Find the `-viewDidLoad` method and add the one bold line:

```
- (void)viewDidLoad
{
    [super viewDidLoad];
    self.colorModel = [CMColor new];
}
```

Wiring Your Interface

The last step is to connect your controller's outlets and actions to the view objects. Select the `Main.storyboard` Interface Builder file again. Select the View Controller object and use the connections inspector to connect your controller's `colorView` outlet to the `UIView` object, as shown in Figure 8-10.

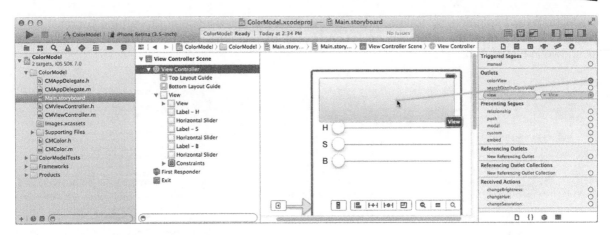

Figure 8-10. Connecting the colorView outlet

Now connect the actions of the three sliders to the controller's -changeHue:, -changeSaturation:, and -changeBrightness: methods. Select the top slider. Using the connections inspector, connect the Value Changed event to the controller's -changedHue: action. Repeat, connecting the middle slider to the -changeSaturation: method, and the bottom slider to the -changeBrightness: method, as shown in Figure 8-11.

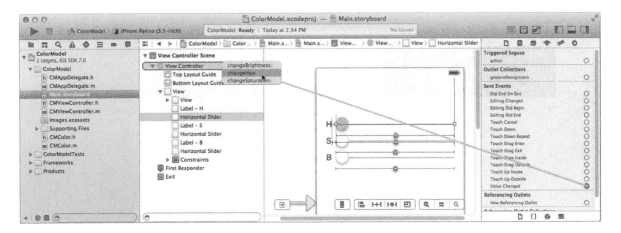

Figure 8-11. Connecting slider actions

> **Tip** You could have made these connections by right/control+clicking on a slider and dragging to the controller. This works because the Value Changed event is the default event for control objects when connecting an action message.

There's one last, cosmetic, detail to attend to. The values for the hue, saturation, and brightness in the data model all initialize to 0.0 (black). The default color in the color view is not black, and the initial positions of the sliders are all 0.5. So that your view objects are consistent with your data model from the beginning, select the sliders and use the attributes inspector to set the Current property to 0.0. Select the color view object and set its background attribute to Black Color, as shown in Figure 8-12.

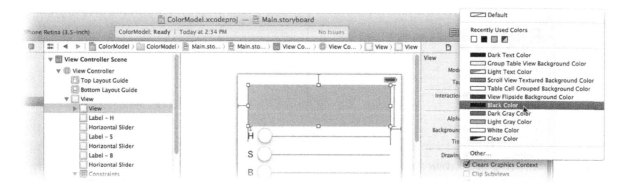

Figure 8-12. Finished ColorModel interface

Run your app in the iPhone simulator. It appears with the color black and all three sliders set to their minimum values. Change the values of the sliders to explore different combinations of hue, saturation, and brightness, as shown on the right in Figure 8-13.

 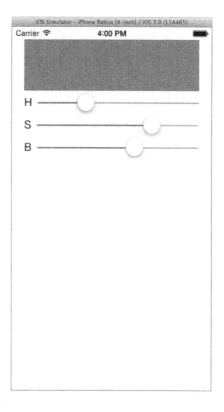

Figure 8-13. First ColorModel app

Having Multiple Views

One reason the MVC design pattern separates the data model from the view objects is to avoid a one-to-one relationship between the two. With MVC you can create a one-to-many, or even a many-to-many, relationship between your data model and view objects. Exploit this by creating more view objects that display the same data model and in different ways.

Start by selecting your `Main.storyboard` Interface Builder file. Using the right resizing handle, make the width of the three sliders considerably shorter. You want to temporarily create some room to add new view objects to their right, as shown in Figure 8-14.

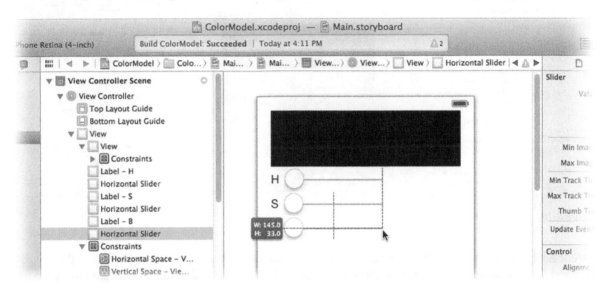

Figure 8-14. Making room for new view objects

Find the label object in the library and add three new labels, to the right of each slider and aligned with the right edge of the color view, as shown in Figure 8-15.

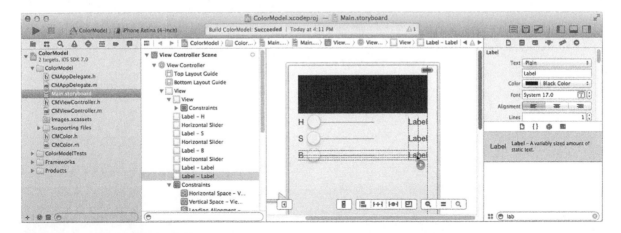

Figure 8-15. Adding HSB value labels

Each label will display the textual value of one property. Edit the text property of the three labels, either using the attributes inspector or by double-clicking on the label object. Change the top label to 360° (press shift+option+8 to get the degrees symbol), and the other two to 100%, as shown in Figure 8-16. If the labels shift position after editing, drag them so their right edges are once again aligned with the right edge of the color view.

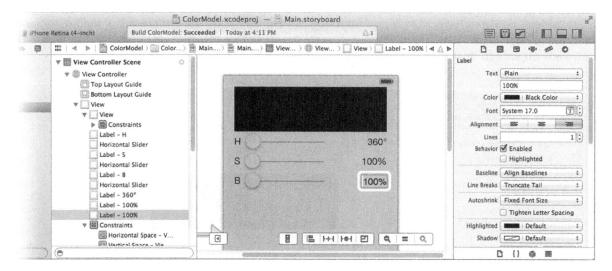

Figure 8-16. Setting placeholder values

Select all three labels. Using the attributes inspector, change their `Alignment` property to right justified (the rightmost of the three alignment buttons). This will keep the values neatly lined up.

Select the top slider. Select the right-edge constraint, created by Xcode, just to the right of the slider, as shown in Figure 8-17. Using the attributes inspector, set its value to -60. This changes the constraint so the right edge of the top slider is now inset from the right edge of the color view by 60 pixels, leaving room for the labels you just added.

CHAPTER 8: Model Citizen 233

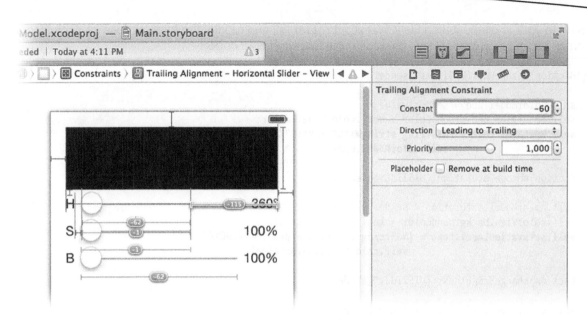

Figure 8-17. Adjusting slider constraint

If you want to see the effects of this change, select all three sliders and choose **Update Frames** from the **Resolve Auto Layout Issues** control. To finish the layout, choose **Add Missing Constraints in View Controller** from the **Resolve Auto Layout Issues** control.

You'll need outlets to use these three views, so add these to your CMViewController.h interface file:

```
@property (weak,nonatomic) IBOutlet UILabel *hueLabel;
@property (weak,nonatomic) IBOutlet UILabel *saturationLabel;
@property (weak,nonatomic) IBOutlet UILabel *brightnessLabel;
```

Connect these three outlets in Interface Builder. Switch back to the Main.storyboard file, select the View Controller, and use the connections inspector to connect the outlets to their respective UILabel objects, as shown in Figure 8-18.

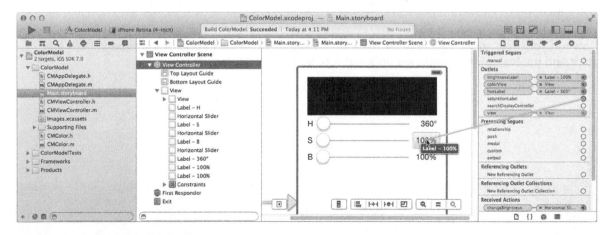

Figure 8-18. Connecting the label outlets

Switch to your implementation file (CMViewController.m), and modify the three actions so each also updates its respective label view, by adding the following bold code:

```
- (IBAction)changeHue:(UISlider*)sender
{
    self.colorModel.hue = sender.value;
    self.colorView.backgroundColor = self.colorModel.color;
    self.hueLabel.text = [NSString stringWithFormat:@"%.0f\u00b0",
                            self.colorModel.hue];
}
- (IBAction)changeSaturation:(UISlider*)sender
{
    self.colorModel.saturation = sender.value;
    self.colorView.backgroundColor = self.colorModel.color;
    self.saturationLabel.text = [NSString stringWithFormat:@"%.0f%%",
                            self.colorModel.saturation];
}
- (IBAction)changeBrightness:(UISlider*)sender
{
    self.colorModel.brightness = sender.value;
    self.colorView.backgroundColor = self.colorModel.color;
    self.brightnessLabel.text = [NSString stringWithFormat:@"%.0f%%",
                            self.colorModel.brightness];
}
```

These three new statements change the text in the label fields to display the textual value of each property. The %.0f format specifier rounds the data model's floating point value to the nearest integer. Literally, it means "format (%) the floating point value (f), so there are zero (.0) digits to the right of its radix point."

> **Note** The escape sequence \u00b0 is the degrees character (shift+option+8). The %% escape sequence means a single % character. Format string specifiers begin with % (such as %u or %02x). To include a single percent character in a format string you use %%.

Now run your app again. This time, whenever you adjust the value of one of the sliders, both the color and the textual HSB value are updated too, as shown in Figure 8-19.

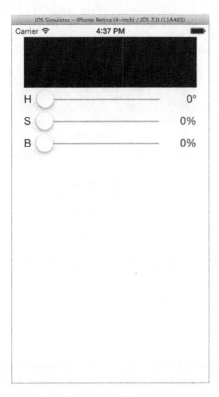 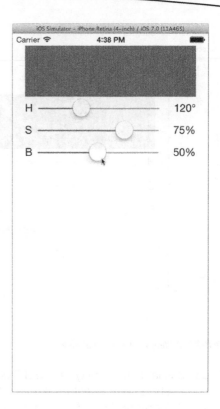

Figure 8-19. ColorModel with HSB values

Consolidating Updates

Now your data model appears, in different forms, in four different views. But why stop there? In the CMViewController.xib file, add two more labels. Set the text of one to #000000 and the other to Web:. Position them as shown in Figure 8-20, and set the alignment property of the one on the right to right justified. Choose **Add Missing Constraints in View Controller** from the **Resolve Auto Layout Issues** control.

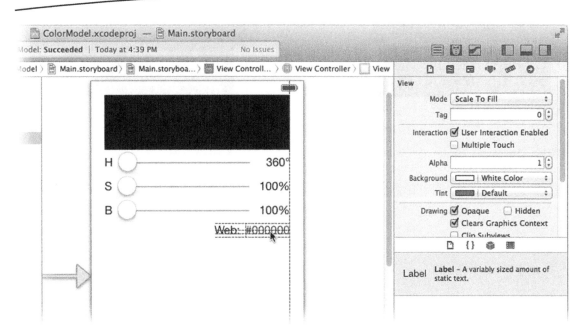

Figure 8-20. Adding web-safe color view

You'll use this label to display the "web" color selected. This is the RGB value of the chosen color, as an HTML short color constant. You should be able to do the next two steps in your sleep: Add the following outlet property to CMViewController.h:

@property (weak,nonatomic) IBOutlet UILabel *webLabel;

Switch back to Main.storyboard and connect the webLabel outlet to the #000000 label object, as shown in Figure 8-21.

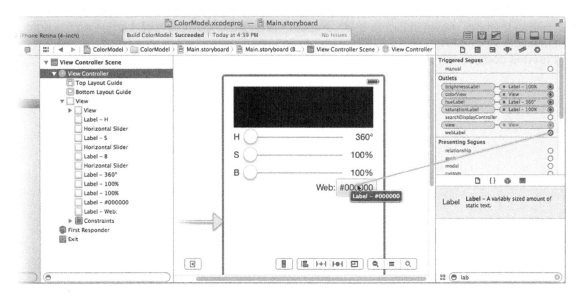

Figure 8-21. Connecting webLabel outlet

Now switch to the `CMViewController.m` implementation file and consider what needs to change. Here's the code to set the `webLabel` view to display the hex value of the color:

```
CGFloat red, green, blue, alpha;
[self.colorModel.color getRed:&red green:&green blue:&blue alpha:&alpha];
self.webLabel.text = [NSString stringWithFormat:@"#%02lx%02lx%02lx",
                      lroundf(red*0xff),
                      lroundf(green*0xff),
                      lroundf(blue*0xff)];
```

This code extracts the individual red, green, and blue values from the `UIColor` object. It then uses those values (in the range of 0.0 to 1.0) to create a string of six hexadecimal digits, two for each color, in the range of 00 to ff, rounding to the closest integer.

While that's not a lot of code, it is a lot of code to repeat three times, because each action method (-changeHue:, -changeSaturation:, -changeBrightness:) must also update the new web value view.

There's an old programming adage that says:

> *If you're repeating yourself, refactor.*

It means that if you find yourself writing the same code, again and again, it's probably a good time to reorganize and consolidate your code. It's a truism that the more code you write, the more chance you have of introducing a bug. A common goal of software engineers is to minimize the amount of code they write. Not just because we're lazy (at least, many of us are), but because it results in more succinct solutions.

Consolidate the updates to your various view objects into a single method named -updateColor. Start by adding a prototype for the new method at the beginning of the `CMViewController.m` file:

```
@interface CMViewController ()
- (void)updateColor;
@end
```

Replace the individual updates in each action with a single message to update all of the view objects:

```
- (IBAction)changeHue:(UISlider*)sender
{
    self.colorModel.hue = sender.value;
    [self updateColor];
}

- (IBAction)changeSaturation:(UISlider*)sender
{
    self.colorModel.saturation = sender.value;
    [self updateColor];
}

- (IBAction)changeBrightness:(UISlider*)sender
{
    self.colorModel.brightness = sender.value;
    [self updateColor];
}
```

Finally, write the -updateColor method:

```
- (void)updateColor
{
    self.colorView.backgroundColor = self.colorModel.color;
    self.hueLabel.text = [NSString stringWithFormat:@"%.0f\u00b0",
                          self.colorModel.hue];
    self.saturationLabel.text = [NSString stringWithFormat:@"%.0f%%",
                                 self.colorModel.saturation];
    self.brightnessLabel.text = [NSString stringWithFormat:@"%.0f%%",
                                 self.colorModel.brightness];
    CGFloat red, green, blue, alpha;
    [self.colorModel.color getRed:&red green:&green blue:&blue alpha:&alpha];
    self.webLabel.text = [NSString stringWithFormat:@"#%02lx%02lx%02lx",
                          lroundf(red*255),
                          lroundf(green*255),
                          lroundf(blue*255)];
}
```

The first line updates the background color of the color view object, a task that had been repeated in each of the three actions. The next three statements update the three HSB label views, and the block of code at the end calculates the hexadecimal RGB value and updates `webLabel`.

Run your app again, as shown in Figure 8-22. Each change to the data model updates five different view objects, and your controller code is arguably simpler and easier to maintain than it was before. You can easily add new actions that update the data model; all you have to do is send -updateColor before returning. Similarly, new view objects could be added and you'd only have to add an outlet and modify -updateColor.

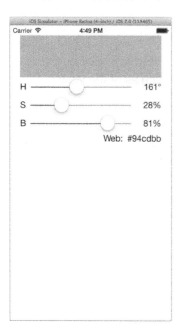
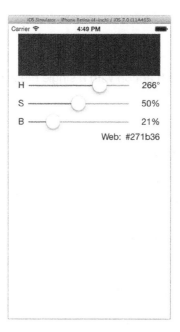
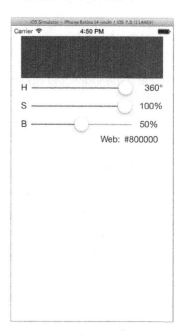

Figure 8-22. ColorModel with web value

Complex View Objects

So far, the view objects you've used in ColorModel display relatively trivial (NSString or UIColor) values. Sometimes view objects display much more complex data types. It's not uncommon for complex view objects to maintain a reference to the data model. This gives them direct access to all of the information they need.

To make ColorModel a little more interesting, you're going to replace the simple UIView object with a custom view object that displays a hue/saturation color chart, in addition to identifying the exact color selected by the hue, saturation, and brightness sliders. Revising your design, your new app should look like the one in Figure 8-23.

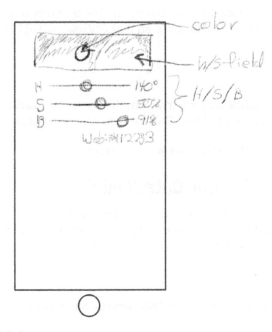

Figure 8-23. Updated ColorModel design

Replacing UIView with CMColorView

Your new design will replace the UIView object in your current design with your own custom CMColorView object. Start by adding a new Objective-C class to your project. Select the ColorModel group (folder) in the project navigator and choose the **File ➤ New ➤ File...** command (or right/control+click on the group and choose New **File...**). Select the Objective-C class template, name it CMColorView, make it a subclass of UIView, and add it to your project.

Upgrade the plain view in your interface from a UIImage object to your new CMColorView object. In Main.storyboard, select the UIImage view object. Use the identity inspector to change the class of the object from UIView to CMColorView, as shown in Figure 8-24.

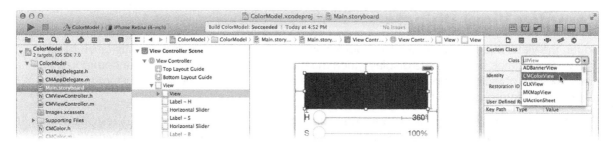

Figure 8-24. Changing the UIView into a CMColorView

In your CMViewController.h interface file, find the colorView property that refers to this object. Add an #include statement toward the top of the file so that CMViewController knows about CMColorView objects:

#import "CMColorView.h"

Now change the type of the colorView property from UIView to CMColorView (modified code shown in bold). Now your controller is connected to a CMColorView object instead:

@property (weak,nonatomic) IBOutlet **CMColorView** *colorView;

Connecting the View to Your Data Model

Unlike the view objects you've used so far, your CMColorView object will both understand and refer to your CMColor data model. So that it understands CMColor, add this #include statement near the top of your new CMColorView.h interface file:

#include "CMColor.h"

Now add a property to the @interface so that CMColorView has a connection to the CMColor object:

@property (strong,nonatomic) CMColor *colorModel;

> **Note** The colorModel property is not an Interface Builder outlet (IBOutlet), because you'll be setting this property programmatically rather than in Interface Builder. That's not to say that it couldn't be an outlet, it just doesn't need to be for this project.

Drawing CMColorView

Now switch to your CMColorView.m implementation file. You're going to add a -drawRect: method that draws a 2D hue/saturation color chart at the current brightness level. At the position within the color chart that represents current hue/saturation, the view draws a circle filled with that color.

It's a fair amount of code, and it's not the focus of this chapter, so I'll gloss over the details. The code you need to add to CMColorView.m is in Listings 8-1 and 8-2. If you're writing this app as you work through this chapter, I applaud you. I will, however, suggest that you save yourself a lot of typing and copy the code for the -dealloc and -drawRect: methods from the CMColorView.m file that you'll find in the Learn iOS Development Projects ➤ Ch 8 ➤ ColorModel-4 ➤ ColorModel folder.

Listing 8-1. CMColorView.m private @interface

```
#define kCircleRadius 40.0f
@interface CMColorView ()
{
    CGImageRef hsImageRef;
    float brightness;
}
@end
```

Listing 8-2. CMColorView.m -dealloc and -drawRect: methods

```
- (void)dealloc
{
    if (hsImageRef!=NULL)
        CGImageRelease(hsImageRef);
}

- (void)drawRect:(CGRect)rect
{
    CGRect bounds = self.bounds;
    CGContextRef context = UIGraphicsGetCurrentContext();

    if (hsImageRef!=NULL &&
        ( brightness!=_colorModel.brightness ||
          bounds.size.width!=CGImageGetWidth(hsImageRef) ||
          bounds.size.height!=CGImageGetHeight(hsImageRef) ) )
        {
        CGImageRelease(hsImageRef);
        hsImageRef = NULL;
        }

    if (hsImageRef==NULL)
        {
        brightness = _colorModel.brightness;
        NSUInteger width = bounds.size.width;
        NSUInteger height = bounds.size.height;
        typedef struct {
            uint8_t red;
            uint8_t green;
            uint8_t blue;
            uint8_t alpha;
        } Pixel;
        NSMutableData *bitmapData =
            [NSMutableData dataWithLength:sizeof(Pixel)*width*height];
```

```objc
        for ( NSUInteger y=0; y<height; y++ )
            {
            for ( NSUInteger x=0; x<width; x++ )
                {
                UIColor *color = [UIColor colorWithHue:(float)x/(float)width
                                    saturation:1.0f-(float)y/(float)height
                                    brightness:brightness/100
                                    alpha:1];
                float red,green,blue,alpha;
                [color getRed:&red green:&green blue:&blue alpha:&alpha];
                Pixel *pixel = ((Pixel*)bitmapData.bytes)+x+y*width;
                pixel->red = red*255;
                pixel->green = green*255;
                pixel->blue = blue*255;
                pixel->alpha = 255;
                }
            }
        
        CGColorSpaceRef colorSpace = CGColorSpaceCreateDeviceRGB();
        CGDataProviderRef provider = CGDataProviderCreateWithCFData( ↵
                                        (__bridge CFDataRef)bitmapData);
        hsImageRef = CGImageCreate(width,height,8,32,width*4,
                                    colorSpace,kCGBitmapByteOrderDefault,
                                    provider,NULL,false,
                                    kCGRenderingIntentDefault);
        CGColorSpaceRelease(colorSpace);
        CGDataProviderRelease(provider);
        }
    
    CGContextDrawImage(context,bounds,hsImageRef);
    CGRect circleRect = CGRectMake( ↵
        bounds.origin.x+bounds.size.width*_colorModel.hue/360-kCircleRadius/2,
        bounds.origin.y+bounds.size.height*_colorModel.saturation/100-kCircleRadius/2,
        kCircleRadius,
        kCircleRadius);
    UIBezierPath *circle = [UIBezierPath bezierPathWithOvalInRect:circleRect];
    [_colorModel.color setFill];
    [circle fill];
    circle.lineWidth = 3;
    [[UIColor blackColor] setStroke];
    [circle stroke];
}
```

In a nutshell, the `CMColorView` draws a two-dimensional graph of the possible hue/saturation combinations at the current brightness level. (When iOS devices come out with 3D displays, you can revise this code to draw a 3D image instead!) I'll refer back to this code in Chapter 11, where I explain various drawing techniques.

The point of interest (for this chapter) is that the `CMColorValue` has a direct reference to the `CMColor` data model object, so your controller doesn't have to explicitly update it with a new color value anymore. All your controller needs to do is tell the `CMColorView` object when it needs to redraw; the `CMColorView` will use the data model directly to obtain whatever information it needed to draw itself.

> **Note** When you create an instance variable by declaring a @property, such as colorModel, Objective-C generates a pair of getter and setter methods (-colorModel and -setColorModel:) that you can send or access via the property syntax (viewObject.colorModel). It also creates an instance variable with the same name beginning with an underscore (_colorModel). Code within your CMColorView class can access this instance variable directly (_colorModel = nil). This is slightly faster and more efficient than using the property syntax (self.colorModel).

For this to happen, your controller needs to establish this connection when it creates the data model and view objects. In your CMViewController.m file, find the -viewDidLoad method and add this one bold line:

```
- (void)viewDidLoad
{
    [super viewDidLoad];
    self.colorModel = [CMColor new];
    self.colorView.colorModel = self.colorModel;
}
```

When the view objects are created (when the Interface Builder file loads), the controller creates the data model object and connects it to the colorView object.

Now replace the code that you used to set the color to draw (via colorView's backgroundColor property) with code that simply tells the colorView object that it needs to redraw itself, shown in bold:

```
- (void)updateColor
{
    [self.colorView setNeedsDisplay];
}
```

Run your new app and try it out. This is a dramatically more interesting interface, as shown in Figure 8-25.

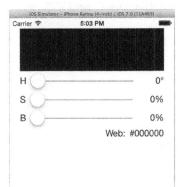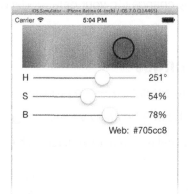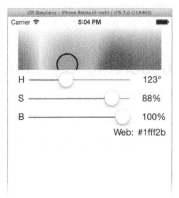

Figure 8-25. ColorModel with CMColorView

This version of your app represents the next level of MVC sophistication. Instead of spoon-feeding simple values to your view objects, you now have a view object that understands your data model and obtains the values it needs directly. But the controller still has to remember to refresh all of the views whenever it changes the data model. Let's take a different approach, and have the data model tell the controller when it changes.

Being a K-V Observer

Way back in the "MVC Communications" section, I described a simple arrangement where the data model sent notifications to view objects (see Figure 8-1) letting them know when they need to update their display. You've already done this in your MyStuff app. You added a -postDidChangeNotification method to your MyWhatsit class. That method notified any interested parties that an item in your data model had changed. Your table view observed those notifications and redrew itself as needed.

Using NSNotificationCenter to communicate data model changes to views is a *perfect* example of MVC communications. Save that in your bag of "iOS solutions I know." I won't repeat that solution here. Instead, I'm going to show you an even more sophisticated method of observing changes in your data model.

Key Value Observing

I told you that design patterns run deep in iOS and Objective-C. You're about to find out just how deep. MVC communications is based, in part, on the observer pattern. The *observer pattern* is a design pattern in which one object (the observer) receives a message when some event in another object (the subject) occurs. In MVC, the data model (the subject) notifies view or controller objects (the observers) whenever it changes. This relieves the controller from having to remember to update the view objects ([self updateColor]) whenever it changes the data model. Now it, or any other object, can just change the data model at will; any changes will send notifications to the observers.

In MyStuff you accomplished this using NSNotifcation objects. In ColorModel you're going to use some Objective-C magic called *Key Value Observing* (KVO for short). KVO is a technology that notifies an observer whenever the property of an object is set. The amazing thing about KVO is that you (usually) don't have to make any changes to your data model objects; Objective-C and iOS do all of the work for you.

Observing Key Value Changes

Observing property changes in an object is a two-step process:

1. Become an observer for the property (key value).
2. Implement an -observeValueForKeyPath:ofObject:change:context: method.

The first step is simple enough. In your CMViewController.m implementation file, find the
-viewDidLoad method and add the following code at the end:

```
[_colorModel addObserver:self forKeyPath:@"hue" options:0 context:NULL];
[_colorModel addObserver:self forKeyPath:@"saturation" options:0 context:NULL];
[_colorModel addObserver:self forKeyPath:@"brightness" options:0 context:NULL];
[_colorModel addObserver:self forKeyPath:@"color" options:0 context:NULL];
```

Each statement registers your CMViewController object (self) to observe changes to a specific property (the key path) of the receiving object (_colorModel).

Thereafter, every time one of the observed properties of _colorModel changes, your controller will receive an -observeValueForKeyPath:ofObject:change:context: message. The keyPath parameter describes the property that changed on the object parameter. Use these parameters to determine what changed and take the appropriate action.

Your new -observeValueForKeyPath:ofObject:change:context: method will replace your old -updateColor method, because it serves the same purpose. Replace -updateColor with the code in Listing 8-3. The code in bold shows what's new.

Listing 8-3. -observeValueForKeyPath

```
- (void)observeValueForKeyPath:(NSString *)keyPath
                      ofObject:(id)object
                        change:(NSDictionary *)change
                       context:(void *)context
{
    if ([keyPath isEqualToString:@"hue"])
        {
        self.hueLabel.text = [NSString stringWithFormat:@"%.0f\u00b0",
                            self.colorModel.hue];
        }
    else if ([keyPath isEqualToString:@"saturation"])
        {
        self.saturationLabel.text = [NSString stringWithFormat:@"%.0f%%",
                            self.colorModel.saturation];
        }
    else if ([keyPath isEqualToString:@"brightness"])
        {
        self.brightnessLabel.text = [NSString stringWithFormat:@"%.0f%%",
                            self.colorModel.brightness];
        }
    else if ([keyPath isEqualToString:@"color"])
        {
        [self.colorView setNeedsDisplay];
        CGFloat red, green, blue, alpha;
        [self.colorModel.color getRed:&red green:&green blue:&blue alpha:&alpha];
        self.webLabel.text = [NSString stringWithFormat:@"#%02lx%02lx%02lx",
                            lroundf(red*255),
                            lroundf(green*255),
                            lroundf(blue*255)];
        }
}
```

The code is simple and straightforward. It checks to see if the keyPath parameter matches one of the property names that you expect to change. Each if block updates the view objects affected by changes to that property.

You can now remove all of the references to -updateColor. Delete the method prototype in the private @interface section, and remove all of the [self updateColor]; statements in the action methods. Now your -changeHue: method looks like this:

```
- (IBAction)changeHue:(UISlider*)sender
{
    self.colorModel.hue = sender.value;
}
```

None of your methods that change the properties of your data model have to remember to update the view, because the data model object will notify your controller automatically whenever that happens. Run your app and try it out, as shown in Figure 8-26.

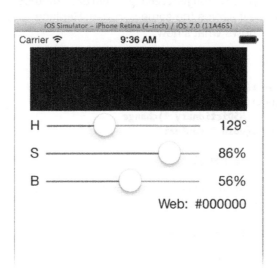

Figure 8-26. Defective KVO

Some parts of it work, but clearly something is wrong. Let's think about the problem for a moment.

Creating KVO Dependencies

Your controller is receiving changes for the hue, saturation, and brightness properties, because the three label objects are getting updated. The colorView and webLabel objects, however, never change. Your controller is not receiving change notifications for the "color" property.

That's because nothing ever changes the color property. (It's not even allowed to change, because it's a readonly property.) The problem is that color is a synthesized property value: code, that you wrote, makes up the color value based on the values of hue, saturation, and brightness. Objective-C and iOS don't know that. All they know is that no one ever sets the color property (colorModel.color = newColor), so it never sends any notifications.

There are two, straightforward, ways to address this. The first would be to add code to your controller so that it updates the `color`-related views whenever it receives notifications that any of the other three (`hue`, `saturation`, or `brightness`) changed. That's a perfectly acceptable solution, but there's an alternative.

You can teach the KVO system about a property (the *derived key*) that is affected by changes to other properties (its *dependent keys*). Open your `CMColor.m` data model implementation file and add this special class method:

```
+ (NSSet*)keyPathsForValuesAffectingColor
{
    return [NSSet setWithObjects:@"hue",@"saturation",@"brightness",nil];
}
```

Now run your app again and see the difference (see Figure 8-27) that one method makes.

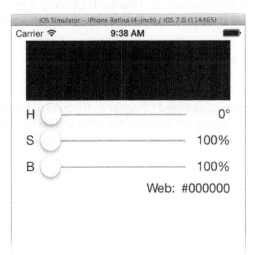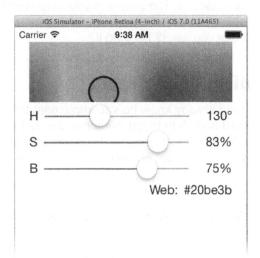

Figure 8-27. Working KVO updates

So what's happening? The special class method +keyPathsForValuesAffectingColor tell the KVO system that there are three properties (key paths) that affect the value of the color property: "hue", "saturation", and "brightness". Now, whenever the KVO mechanism sees one of the first three properties change, it knows that `color` changed too and it sends a second notification for the "color" key path.

> **Tip** KVO is very flexible, and there are several ways to describe dependent keys. You can also write code that determines exactly what property change notifications are sent, when, and what information those notifications include. For a much more in-depth explanation, check out the *Key-Value Observing Programming Guide* that you'll find in Xcode's Documentation and API Reference.

I'm sure you're thinking this is pretty cool, but you might also be thinking that it's not that much less work than the `-updateColor` method you wrote in the previous section. And you're right; it's not. But that's also because all of your data model changes come from one source (the slider controls), and there's a relatively small number of places where your data model is altered. If that situation changes, however, it becomes a whole new ballgame.

Multi-Vector Data Model Changes

As your app matures, it's likely to get more complex, and changes to your data model can occur in more places. The beauty of KVO is that the change notifications happen in the same place the changes occur—in the data model.

It was OK to call `-changeColor` when the only places that changed the color were the three slider actions. But what if you added a fourth control view object that also changed them—or five, or nine?

Here's an example. The sliders in your app are nice, but they're sooooo Twentieth Century. We live in the age of the touch interface. Wouldn't it be nicer to just touch the hue/saturation graph and point to the color you want? Let's do it.

Handling Touch Events

You should already know how to implement this—unless you skipped Chapter 4. If you did, go back and read it now. Add touch event handler methods to your custom `CMColorView` class. The handlers will use the coordinates within the color chart to choose a new hue and saturation. Since you know what you're doing, get started by adding three touch event handlers to `CMColorView.m`:

```
- (void)touchesBegan:(NSSet *)touches withEvent:(UIEvent *)event
{
    [self changeHSToPoint:[(UITouch*)[touches anyObject] locationInView:self]];
}

- (void)touchesMoved:(NSSet *)touches withEvent:(UIEvent *)event
{
    [self changeHSToPoint:[(UITouch*)[touches anyObject] locationInView:self]];
}

- (void)touchesEnded:(NSSet *)touches withEvent:(UIEvent *)event
{
    [self changeHSToPoint:[(UITouch*)[touches anyObject] locationInView:self]];
}
```

These three handlers catch all touch began, moved, and ended events, extract the one touch object, gets the position of that touch in this view's coordinates (using `-locationInView:`), and passes those coordinates to the `-changeHSToPoint:` method.

> **Note** Remember that, by default, a view object's `multipleTouchEnabled` property is NO, which means that its touch event handler methods will never see more than one touch object in `touches`, even if your user is touching the view with more than one finger.

Now add the `-changeHSToPoint:` method. Start by adding a method prototype to the private `@interface` section near the top of the `CMColorView.m` file:

```
- (void)changeHSToPoint:(CGPoint)point;
```

Finally, add the body of the method at the end of the `@implementation`:

```
- (void)changeHSToPoint:(CGPoint)point
{
    CGRect bounds = self.bounds;
    if (CGRectContainsPoint(bounds,point))
        {
        _colorModel.hue = (point.x-bounds.origin.x)/bounds.size.width*360;
        _colorModel.saturation = (point.y-bounds.origin.y)/bounds.size.height*100;
        }
}
```

Your `-changeHSToPoint:` method takes the touch point and works backwards to determine the hue and saturation values represented at the position. It then changes the `hue` and `saturation` properties of the data model directly.

Notice that it didn't send an action message to the controller. It could have—that would be a perfectly reasonable implementation too. But since you have KVO, you don't need to. Any object can make changes to the data model directly, and all the observers will receive the necessary notifications.

Try it out. Run your app. Move the brightness slider off of 0%, and then use the mouse to drag around inside the color chart. The hue and saturation change as you drag your (simulated) finger around, as shown in Figure 8-28.

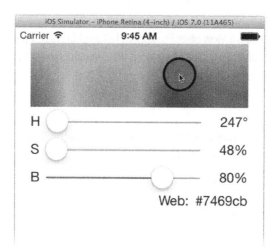

Figure 8-28. Turning CMColorView into a control

Binding The Sliders

The only thing that doesn't work is the hue and saturation sliders don't move when you touch the color view. That's because they're still acting only as inputs. Up until this point, the only way the hue and saturation could have changed was to move the slider. Now that there are other pathways to changing these properties, you need to keep the sliders in synchronization with the data model too.

You'll need a connection to the three sliders, so add that to your CMViewController.h file:

```
@property (weak,nonatomic) IBOutlet UISlider *hueSlider;
@property (weak,nonatomic) IBOutlet UISlider *saturationSlider;
@property (weak,nonatomic) IBOutlet UISlider *brightnessSlider;
```

Switch to the Main.storyboard Interface Builder file and connect these new outlets from your View Controller object to the three UISlider controls.

Find the -observeValueForKeyPath:ofObject:change:context: method in CMViewController.m and insert these three lines of bold code:

```
if ([keyPath isEqualToString:@"hue"])
    {
    self.hueLabel.text = [NSString stringWithFormat:@"%.0f\u00b0",
                                          self.colorModel.hue];
    self.hueSlider.value = _colorModel.hue;
    }
else if ([keyPath isEqualToString:@"saturation"])
    {
    self.saturationLabel.text = [NSString stringWithFormat:@"%.0f%%",
                                          self.colorModel.saturation];
    self.saturationSlider.value = _colorModel.saturation;
    }
```

```
else if ([keyPath isEqualToString:@"brightness"])
        {
        self.brightnessLabel.text = [NSString stringWithFormat:@"%.0f%%",
                                                    self.colorModel.brightness];
        self.brightnessSlider.value = _colorModel.brightness;
        }
```

Now when the hue value changes, the hue slider will be changed to match, even if the change came from the hue slider.

> **Caution** Moving a slider won't cause an infinite loop of messages: the slider sends an action to the controller, which changes the data model, which updates the slider, which sends an action to the controller, and so on. That's because slider controls only send action messages when the user drags them around, not when their value is set programmatically. Not all views, however, are so clever, and it's possible to create infinite MVC message loops. The way to solve that is to only send actions or notifications when the value actually changes.

The color view and the sliders now update whenever the data model changes, and the color view can directly change the data model. Software engineers would say that these views are *bound* to properties of the data model. A *binding* is a direct, two-way, linkage between a data model and a view.

Final Touches

You can now also easily fix an annoying bug in your app. The display values for the hue, saturation, and brightness are wrong (360°, 100%, and 100%) when the app starts. The values in the data model are 0°, 0%, and 0%. At the very end of -viewDidLoad, add this code:

```
_colorModel.hue = 60;
_colorModel.saturation = 50;
_colorModel.brightness = 100;
```

Since this code executes after your controller starts observing changes to your data model, these statements will not only initialize your data model to a color that's not black, but will also update all relevant views to match. Try it!

There's also some icon resources in the Learn iOS Development Projects ➤ Ch 8 ➤ ColorModel (Icons) folder. Add them to the AppIcon group of the Images.xcassets item, just as you did for earlier projects.

Cheating

The model-view-controller design pattern will improve the quality of your code, make your apps simpler to write and maintain, and give you an attractive, healthy, glow. Do not, however, fall under its spell and become its slave.

While the use of design patterns gives you an edge in your quest to become a master iOS developer, I caution against using them just for the sake of using them. Pragmatic programmers call this *over engineering*. Sometimes the simple solutions are the best. Take this example:

```
@interface MyScoreController : NSObject
@property NSUInteger score;
@property (weak,nonatomic) IBOutlet UILabel *scoreView;
- (IBAction)incrementScore:(id)sender;
@end

@implementation MyScoreController
- (IBAction)incrementScore:(id)sender
{
    _score += 1;
    self.scoreView.text = [NSString stringWithFormat:@"%lu",(unsigned long int)_score];
}
@end
```

So what's wrong with this controller? MVC purists will point out that there's no data model object. The controller is also acting as the data model, storing and manipulating the score property. This violates the MVC design pattern as well as the single responsibility principle.

Do you want my opinion? There's nothing wrong with this solution; it's just one #@$%&* integer! There's nothing to be gained in creating a new class just to hold one number, and you'll waste a whole lot of time doing it.

If, someday, maybe, your data model grew to three integers, a string, and a localization object, then sure: refactor your app, pull the integer out of your controller, and move it to a real data model object. But until that day arrives, don't worry about it.

There's a programming discipline called *agile development* that values finished, working, software over plans and pristine design. In these situations, my advice is to use the simplest solution that does the job. Be aware when you're taking shortcuts in your MVC design, and have a plan to fix it when (and if) that becomes a problem, but don't lash yourself to a design philosophy. Design patterns should make your development easier, not harder.

Summary

To summarize: MVC is good.

Is all of this computer science study making you want to take a break and listen to your favorite tunes? Well then, the next chapter is for you.

> **EXERCISE**
>
> While your ColorModel app came very close to the idealized MVC communications, it still relied on the controller to observe the changes and forward update events the view objects. Given the work you've done so far, how difficult would it be to make the color view observe data model changes directly?
>
> It wouldn't be that hard, and that's your exercise for this chapter: Modify `CMViewController` and `CMColorView` so that `CMColorView` is the direct observer of "color" changes in the `CMColor` object.
>
> This is a common pattern in fairly extensive apps that have complex data models and lots of custom view objects. The advantage is that each view object takes on the responsibility of observing the data model changes specific to that view, relieving your controller objects from this burden.
>
> You'll find my solution to this exercise in the `Learn iOS Development Projects` ➤ `Ch 8` ➤ `ColorModel E1` folder.

Chapter 9

Sweet, Sweet Music

Choosing and playing music from your iPod library is a great way to add some toe-tapping fun to your app. You can also add your own music and audio effects to actions and games. Both are relatively easy to do, and I'll get to those straight away. But don't stop reading this chapter at that point. Sound in iOS apps exists in a larger world of competing audio sources, real-world events, and an ever-changing configuration of hardware. Making audio work nicely in this demanding, and sometimes complex, environment is the real test of your iOS development skills. This chapter covers:

- Choosing tracks from the iPod music library
- Playing music in the iPod music library
- Obtaining the details (title, artist, album, artwork) of a track
- Playing sound files
- Configuring the behavior of audio in your app
- Mixing music with other sounds
- Responding to interruptions
- Responding to hardware changes

Along the way, you'll learn some timesaving Xcode tricks and a way of using view objects without an outlet connection. Are you ready to make some noise?

> **Note** The app in this chapter requires a provisioned iOS device to run it. An app that accesses the iPod music library won't run in the simulator; the simulator does not include the required iPod frameworks. If you attempt to run this app in the simulator, it will simply crash.

Making Your Own iPod

The two most common sources for pre-recorded sounds in an iOS app are audio resource files and audio files in the user's iPod library. The app you'll develop in this chapter plays both—at the same time! It's a dubbing app that lets you play a track from your iPod's music library and then spontaneously add your own percussive instrument sounds. So if you've ever felt that Delibes' Flower Duet (Lakmé, Act 1) would sound so much better with a tambourine, this is the app you've been waiting for.

Design

Your app design is a simple, one screen, affair that I've named DrumDub. At the bottom are controls for choosing a track from your music library and for pausing and resuming playback. At the top you'll find information about the track that's playing. In the middle are buttons to add percussive sounds, all shown in Figure 9-1.

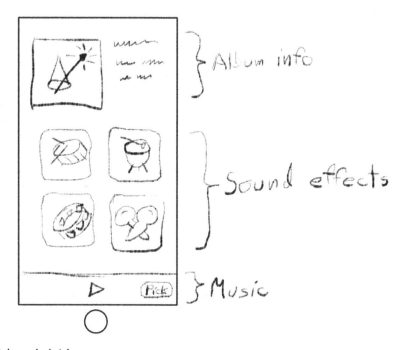

Figure 9-1. DrumDub rough sketch

You'll start by building the iPod music playback. Later you'll add the album artwork, and finally mix in the percussion sounds. As always, start by creating a new Xcode project:

1. Use the Single View Application Xcode template
2. Name the project DrumDub
3. Set the class prefix to DD

4. Set the device to iPhone (see note)
5. Save the project
6. In the project's supported interface orientations, turn off landscape left and right

> **Note** Because this app requires an iOS device to run, you'll need an iPhone or iPad to test it. If you only have an iPad, consider stretching your developer legs a little and setting the supported devices to iPad instead. As you work through this chapter, adjust the iPhone interface layout to fit the iPad. The logic and code will remain the same.

Adding a Music Picker

The first step is to create an interface so the user can choose a song, or songs, from their iPod music library. After Chapter 7 (where you used the photo library picker), you shouldn't be surprised to learn that iOS provides a ready-made music picker interface. All you have to do is configure it and present it to the user.

You'll present the music picker interface when the user taps the "Song" button in the interface. For that you'll need an action. Start by declaring this action in the @interface section of your DDViewController.h file:

```
- (IBAction)selectTrack:(id)sender;
```

The MPMediaPickerController class provides the music picker interface. Your -selectTrack: method will create a new MPMediaPickerController, configure it, and present it to the user. Just like the photo library picker, your app finds out what the user picked via delegate methods. While you're still editing DDViewController.h, make your DDViewController an MPMediaPickerControllerDelegate:

```
@interface DDViewController : UIViewController <MPMediaPickerControllerDelegate>
```

You'll notice that Xcode is now flagging this line with a compiler error. That's because the media picker and player header files are not part of the standard UIKit frameworks. Import the definition of MPMediaPickerControllerDelegate (along with all of the other music player and picker symbols) by adding the following #import statement immediately after your other #import statements:

```
#import <MediaPlayer/MediaPlayer.h>
```

Switch to the Main.storyboard Interface Builder file. In the object library, find the Toolbar object. Drag a toolbar into your interface, positioning it at the bottom of the view. The toolbar already includes a bar button item. Select it and change its title property to Song. Connect its sent action (control/right-drag) to the View Controller's -selectTrack: action, as shown in Figure 9-2.

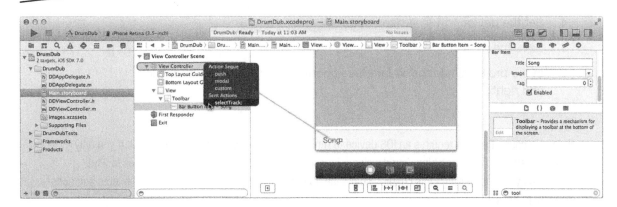

Figure 9-2. Adding the toolbar and "Song" button

Now you're ready to write your -selectTrack: action. Switch to the DDViewController.m file and add this code to your @implementation section:

```
- (IBAction)selectTrack:(id)sender
{
    MPMediaPickerController *picker = [[MPMediaPickerController alloc] 
                                    initWithMediaTypes:MPMediaTypeAnyAudio];
    picker.delegate = self;
    picker.allowsPickingMultipleItems = NO;
    picker.prompt = @"Choose a song";
    [self presentViewController:picker animated:YES completion:nil];
}
```

This code creates a new MPMediaPickerController object that will let the user choose any audio type. The media picker is rather flexible, and can be set up to present various types of audio and/or video content on the device. The categories for audio content are:

- Music (MPMediaTypeMusic)
- Podcasts (MPMusicTypePodcast)
- Audiobooks (MPMediaTypeAudioBook)
- iTunes U (MPMediaTypeITunesU)

By combining these binary values together, you can configure your media picker to present any combination of those categories you desire. The constant MPMediaTypeAnyAudio includes all categories, allowing the user to choose any audio item in their library. A similar set of flags allows video content.

> **Tip** Some integer parameters, like the `mediaTypes` parameter in `-initWithMediaTypes:`, are interpreted, not as a single integer value, but as a collection of bits or flags. Each individual `MPMediaType` constant is a power of 2—a single 1 bit in the integer. You can combine them by adding, or logically ORing, the values together to form arbitrary combinations, such as (`MPMediaTypeMusic|MPMediaTypeAudioBook`). The resulting value would choose any music track or audiobook, but would not let the user pick podcasts or iTunes U content. The convenient `MPMediaTypeAnyAudio` constant is just all-possible audio flags OR'd together.

You then make your `DDViewController` object the picker's delegate. Next, the option to allow picking multiple tracks at once is disabled. The user will only be able to choose one song at a time. Set a prompt, or title, so the user knows what you're asking them to do.

Finally, the controller is presented, allowing it to take over the interface and choose a song. This is enough code to see it working, so give it a try. Set the project's scheme to your iOS device and click the Run button, as shown in Figure 9-3. The toolbar appears, you can tap the "Song" button to bring up the music picker, browse your audio library, and choose a song.

Figure 9-3. Testing the audio picker

QUERYING THE IPOD MUSIC LIBRARY

You don't have to use the media picker to choose items from the user's iPod library. It's just the most convenient method.

It's possible to create your own interface, or not have an interface at all. The iPod framework provides classes that allow your app to explore and search the user's media collection as if it was a database. (Come to think of it, it is a database, so that description is literally true.)

You do this by creating a query object that defines what you're searching for. This can be as simple as "all R&B songs" or more nuanced, such as "all tracks longer than 2 minutes, belonging to the 'dance' genre, with a BPM tag between 110 and 120." The result is a list of media items matching that description, which you can present any way you like (*cough*—table—*cough*).

You can read more about this in the *iPod Library Access Programming Guide* that you will find in Xcode's Documentation and API Reference. Read the section "Getting Media Items Programmatically" to get started.

Using a Music Player

What happens next is, well, nothing happens next. When the user picks a track, or taps the Cancel button, your delegate receives one of these messages:

-mediaPicker:didPickMediaItems:
-mediaPickerDidCancel:

Nothing happened, because you haven't written either. Start by writing -mediaPicker:didPickMediaItems:. This method will retrieve the audio track the user picked and start it playing using an MPMusicPlayerController object.

First, define a private instance variable and a readonly property so you can keep a reference to, and easily request, your music player object. Add the following bold code to the private @interface section at the beginning of the DDViewController.m file:

```
@interface DDViewController ()
{
    MPMusicPlayerController *music; // (store for @property musicPlayer)
}
@property (readonly,nonatomic) MPMusicPlayerController *musicPlayer;
@end
```

Now you're ready to implement the first delegate method:

```
- (void)mediaPicker:(MPMediaPickerController*)mediaPicker
   didPickMediaItems:(MPMediaItemCollection*)mediaItemCollection
{
    if (mediaItemCollection.count!=0)
        {
        [self.musicPlayer setQueueWithItemCollection:mediaItemCollection];
        [self.musicPlayer play];
        }
    [self dismissViewControllerAnimated:YES completion:nil];
}
```

The `mediaItemCollection` parameter contains the list of tracks the user picked. Remember that the picker can be used to choose multiple items at once. Since you set the `allowsPickingMultipleItems` property to NO, your picker will always return a single item.

We double check to see that at least one track was chosen (just to be sure) and then use the collection to set the music player's playback queue. The *playback queue* is a list of tracks to play and works just like a playlist. In this case, it's a playlist of one. The next statement starts the music playing. It's that simple.

> **Note** While the music player's playback queue works just like a playlist, it isn't an iPod playlist. It won't appear in the iPod interface as a playlist, and iOS won't save it for you. If you want this functionality in your app, you can do it yourself. Using what you learned in Chapter 5, present the items in the media collection as a table, allowing the user to reorder, delete, or add new items (using the media picker again) as they like. Send the music player a `-setQueueWithItemCollection:` message again with the updated collection.

So what's the problem with this code? The problem is there is no `musicPlayer` object yet! Write a property getter method for `musicPlayer` that lazily creates the object:

```
- (MPMusicPlayerController*)musicPlayer
{
    if (music==nil)
        {
        music = [MPMusicPlayerController applicationMusicPlayer];
        music.shuffleMode = NO;
        music.repeatMode = NO;
        }
    return music;
}
```

> **Tip** This method follows two well-used design patterns: singleton and lazy initialization. The method implements the getter method for the `musicPlayer` property; any code that requests that property (`self.musicPlayer`) invokes this method. The method checks to see if an `MPMusicPlayerController` object—stored in `music`—has already been created. If not, it creates one, configures it, and saves it in the `music` instance variable. This only happens once. All subsequent calls to `-musicPlayer` see that the `music` variable is already set, and immediately returns the (single) object.

You obtain the `MPMusicPlayerController` object using the `+applicationMusicPlayer` class method. This creates an application music player (see the "Application and iPod Music Players" sidebar). The music player inherits the current iPod playback settings for things like shuffle and repeat modes. You don't want any of that, so you turn them off.

> **APPLICATION AND IPOD MUSIC PLAYERS**
>
> Your app has access to two different music player objects. The *application music player* belongs to your app. Its current playlist and settings exist only in your app, and it stops playing when your app stops.
>
> You can also request the *iPod music player* object, using `[MPMusicPlayerController iPodMusicPlayer]`. The iPod music player object is a direct connection to the iPod player in the device. It reflects the current state of music playing in the iPod app. Any changes you make (like pausing playback or altering shuffle mode) change the iPod app. Music playback continues after your app stops.
>
> There's only one quirk. The iPod music player object won't report information about media that's being streamed, say via home sharing. But other than that, the iPod music player object is a transparent extension of the built-in iPod app, and allows your app to participate in, and integrate with, the user's current music activity.
>
> Only one music player can be playing at a time. If your app starts an application music player, it takes over the music playback service, causing the built-in iPod player to stop. Likewise, if your application music player is playing and the user starts the iPod player, your music player is stopped.

Now toss in a delegate method to handle the case where the user declines to choose a track:

```
- (void)mediaPickerDidCancel:(MPMediaPickerController*)mediaPicker
{
    [self dismissViewControllerAnimated:YES completion:nil];
}
```

Your basic playback code is now complete. Run your app, choose a track, and enjoy the music.

The `MPMusicPlayerController` object is self-contained. It takes care of all of the standard iPod behavior for you. It will, for example, automatically fade out if interrupted by an alarm or incoming call, or stop playback when the user unplugs their headphones. I'll talk a lot more about these events later in this chapter.

That's not to say you can't influence the music player. In fact, you have a remarkable amount of control over it. You can start and stop the player, adjust the volume, skip forwards or backwards in the playlist, set shuffle and repeat modes, change the playback rate, and more. The player will also tell you a lot about what it's doing and playing. Using these properties and methods, you could create your own, full-featured, music player.

For this app, you don't need a full-featured music player. But it would be nice to at least know what's playing and be able to pause it. Get ready to add that next.

Adding Playback Control

Start by adding some buttons to pause and play the current song. These buttons will need actions, so add these two method declarations to your `DDViewController.h` file:

```
- (IBAction)play:(id)sender;
- (IBAction)pause:(id)sender;
```

You'll also need to update the state of the play and pause buttons, so add some connections for that:

```
@property (weak,nonatomic) IBOutlet UIBarButtonItem *playButton;
@property (weak,nonatomic) IBOutlet UIBarButtonItem *pauseButton;
```

Switch to your `Main.storyboard` file and add the following objects to the toolbar, inserting them to the left of the "Song" button, in order, as shown in Figure 9-4:

1. A Flexible Space Bar Button Item
2. A Bar Button Item, changing its style to Plain, its identifier to Play, and unchecking enabled
3. A Bar Button Item, changing its style to Plain, its identifier to Pause, and unchecking enabled
4. A Flexible Space Bar Button Item

Figure 9-4. Adding controls to the toolbar

Finally, set all of the connections. Right/control+click on the play button and connect its action to the `-play:` action (in the `View Controller`), and the pause button to the `-pause:` action. Select the `View Controller` object and use the connections inspector to connect the `playButton` outlet to the play button, and the `pauseButton` outlet to the pause button.

With the interface objects created and connected, consider for a moment how these buttons should work. You want:

- the play button to be active (tappable) when the music player is not currently playing
- the play button's action to start the music playing
- the pause button to be active when the music player is playing
- the pause button's action to pause the music player

The button's actions will start and stop the music player. You'll need to update the enabled state of the buttons whenever the player starts or stops playing. The first part is pretty simple. In DDViewController.m, add the implementation for the -play: and -pause: actions:

```
- (IBAction)play:(id)sender
{
    [self.musicPlayer play];
}

- (IBAction)pause:(id)sender
{
    [self.musicPlayer pause];
}
```

The second half is updating the button states (enabling or disabling them) at the appropriate times.

Receiving Music Player Notifications

The music player runs in a background thread. Normally, it plays tracks in its playlist until it runs out and stops. It can also pause in response to external events: the user presses the pause button on their headphone cable or they unplug the iPod from a dock. How do you think your app will learn about these events?

If you said, "by receiving a delegate message or notification," give yourself a big round of applause! Reading the documentation for the MPMusicPlayerController class, you discover that the music player will *optionally* send notifications whenever important changes occur, which happen to include when it starts or stops playing. To be notified of those events, you'll need to register your controller object to receive them. As you remember from Chapter 5, to receive notifications you must:

- Create a notification method
- Register with the notification center to become an observer for the notification

Start by adding this notification method to your DDViewController.m implementation:

```
- (void)playbackStateDidChangeNotification:(NSNotification*)notification
{
    BOOL playing = (music.playbackState==MPMoviePlaybackStatePlaying);
    _playButton.enabled = !playing;
    _pauseButton.enabled = playing;
}
```

Also add a method prototype to the private @interface section at the beginning of the source file:

```
- (void)playbackStateDidChangeNotification:(NSNotification*)notification;
```

Your notification handler examines the current playbackState of your music player. The player's playback state will be one of stopped, playing, paused, interrupted, seeking forward, or seeking backwards. In this implementation, the only likely states are playing, stopped, interrupted, and paused.

Note The -playbackStateDidChangeNotification: method used the instance variable (music) instead of the property value getter (self.musicPlayer). Accessing the former, instead of the latter, avoids lazily creating a music player object if one didn't exist—only to find that the newly created player wasn't playing. That would be a waste of time and code. In this particular app, it's impossible for music to be nil because the notification message is only received when the music player changes state, and for that to happen the music player object must have already been created.

If the player is playing, the pause button is enabled and the play button is disabled. If it's not playing, the opposite occurs. This presents the play button as an option whenever the player is not playing, and the pause button when it is.

Your controller won't receive these notifications until two additional steps are taken. First, you must register to receive these notifications. In the -musicPlayer getter method, add this new code immediately after the player object is created and configured (at the end of the if { ... } block):

```
NSNotificationCenter *notificationCenter = [NSNotificationCenter defaultCenter];
[notificationCenter addObserver:self
                    selector:@selector(playbackStateDidChangeNotification:)
                        name:MPMusicPlayerControllerPlaybackStateDidChangeNotification
                      object:music];
```

The second step is to enable the music player's notifications. MPMusicPlayerController does not, by default, send these notifications. You must explicitly request that it does. Immediately after the above code, add one more line:

```
[music beginGeneratingPlaybackNotifications];
```

Your playback controls are now finished. Run your app and see that they work, as shown in Figure 9-5.

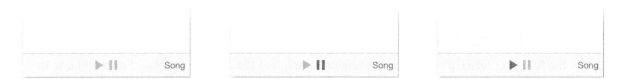

Figure 9-5. Working playback controls

Both buttons start out disabled. When you choose a track to play, the pause button becomes active (the middle of Figure 9-5). If you pause the song, or let it finish playing, the play button becomes active (on the right in Figure 9-5).

> **MVC AT WORK**
>
> You're watching the model-view-controller design pattern at work—again. In this scenario, your music player (despite the fact the it's called a "music controller") is your data model. It contains the state of the music playback. Whenever that state changes, your controller receives a notification and updates the relevant views—in this case, the play and pause buttons.
>
> You didn't write any code to update the play or pause button when you start or stop the player. Those requests are just sent to the music player. If one of those requests results in a state change, the music player posts the appropriate notifications, and the affected views are updated.

While functional, your app lacks a certain je ne sais quoi. Oh, who are we kidding? This interface is as dull as dishwater! Let's spruce it up a bit.

Adding Media Metadata

A colorful aspect of the music player object is its `nowPlayingItem` property. This property returns an object containing metadata about the song that's playing. The object works like a dictionary, revealing all kinds of interesting tidbits about the current song. This includes information like its title, the artist, the track number, the musical genre, any album artwork, and much more.

> **Note** *Metadata* is "data about data." A file, like a document, contains data. The name of that file, when it was created, and so on, is its metadata—it's data that describes the data in the file. A waveform stored in a song file is data. The name of the song, the artist, its genre, and so on, is all metadata.

For your app, you'll add an image view to display the album's cover and text fields to show the song's title, the album it came from, and the artist. Start by adding new interface objects to `Main.storyboard`.

Creating a Metadata View

Select the `Main.storyboard` file. Using the object library, find the `Image View` object and add one to the interface. Using the size inspector, set both its width and height to 140 pixels, and position it (using the guides) in the upper-left corner of the view, as shown in Figure 9-6.

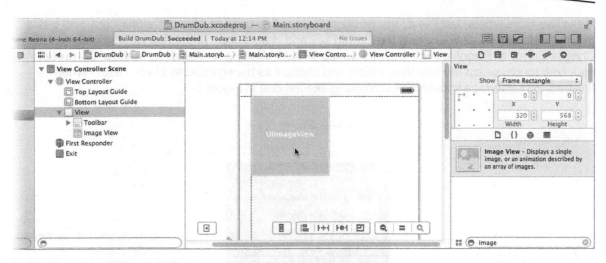

Figure 9-6. Positioning the album view

With the view object selected, choose **Editor ➤ Pin ➤ Width**. Select the view again and choose **Editor ➤ Pin ➤ Height**. This adds constraints that will prevent the view from being resized. These commands are an alternative to control/right-dragging in the view. Finish the layout by choosing **Editor ➤ Resolve Auto Layout Issues ➤ Add Missing Constraints in View Controller**.

Add a label object, just to the right of the image view (see Figure 9-7). Resize its width so the label fills the display, as shown in Figure 9-7. Using the attributes inspector, change its color to White Color and reduce its font size to System 12.0.

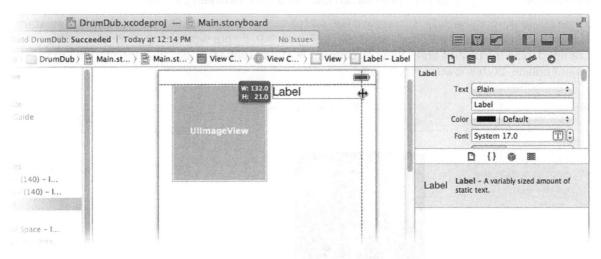

Figure 9-7. Adding a metadata label

Make two more labels, just like it, and position them below the first. You can either copy and paste the first label object, or hold down the Option key and drag a copy of the first label to make another. Choose **Editor ➤ Resolve Auto Layout Issues ➤ Add Missing Constraints in View Controller**. As a final touch, select the root view object and change its background to `Black Color`. When finished, your interface should look something like the one in Figure 9-8.

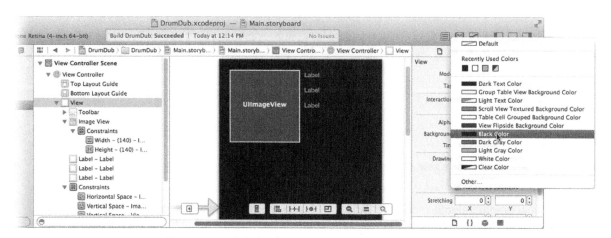

Figure 9-8. Finished metadata interface

You know what's coming next. I'm going to ask you to switch to `DDViewController.h`, add some outlet properties, and then switch back to `Main.storyboard` to connect them.

Well, I'm not. Sure, you're going to create and connect some outlets, but I'm going to show you a nifty Xcode trick so you don't have to switch back and forth between the files.

While still looking at the `Main.storyboard` file, switch to the assistant editor view (**View ➤ Assistant Editor ➤ Show Assistant Editor**), as shown in Figure 9-9. If your workspace window is a little cramped, hide the utilities area (**View ➤ Utilities ➤ Hide Utilities**) or collapse the storyboard's object outline, both shown in Figure 9-9.

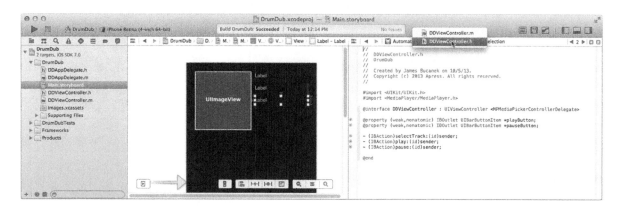

Figure 9-9. Viewing Main.storyboard in the assistant editor

When viewing an Interface Builder file, Xcode's assistant editor conveniently places the interface file of the scene in the right-hand pane. (If it doesn't, choose the `DDViewController.h` file from the navigation menu, immediately above the right-hand pane, as shown in figure 9-9.) Those little circles next to the property and action declarations work just like the ones in the connections inspector. If you're not excited already, you should be. It means you can declare an outlet or action, and then connect it to an interface object, without switching between files. How cool is that?

Add these four new outlets to `DDViewController.h` (now on the right-hand side of the editing area):

```
@property (weak,nonatomic) IBOutlet UIImageView *albumView;
@property (weak,nonatomic) IBOutlet UILabel *songLabel;
@property (weak,nonatomic) IBOutlet UILabel *albumLabel;
@property (weak,nonatomic) IBOutlet UILabel *artistLabel;
```

Now drag the connections that appear to the left of those declarations and connect them directly to the interface objects, as shown in Figure 9-10.

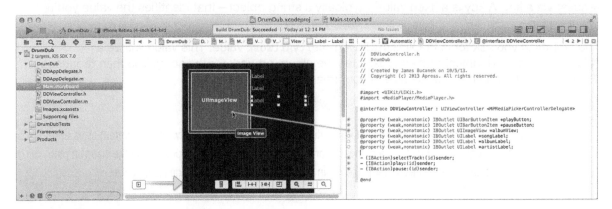

Figure 9-10. Connecting outlets directly from the interface file

You created the outlet properties, and connected them to the interface object, using a single window. Switch back to the standard editor (**View ➤ Standard Editor ➤ Show Standard Editor**) and select the `DDViewController.m` file. It's time to write the code to update these new interface objects.

Observing the Playing Item

The music player object also sends notifications when the item being played changes. This occurs when a new song starts playing, or one finishes playing. The notification is different than the one your controller is currently observing, so you'll need to create another notification handler and register to observe the additional notification. Start by adding a prototype for your new function to the private `@interface DDViewController ()` section at the beginning of the `DDViewController.m` file:

```
- (void)playingItemDidChangeNotification:(NSNotification*)notification;
```

Near the -playbackStateDidChangeNotification: method, add your new notification handler:

```
- (void)playingItemDidChangeNotification:(NSNotification*)notification
{
    MPMediaItem *nowPlaying = music.nowPlayingItem;
    MPMediaItemArtwork *artwork = [nowPlaying valueForProperty:MPMediaItemPropertyArtwork];
    UIImage *albumImage = [artwork imageWithSize:_albumView.bounds.size];
    if (albumImage==nil)
        albumImage = [UIImage imageNamed:@"noartwork"];
    _albumView.image = albumImage;
    _songLabel.text = [nowPlaying valueForProperty:MPMediaItemPropertyTitle];
    _albumLabel.text = [nowPlaying valueForProperty:MPMediaItemPropertyAlbumTitle];
    _artistLabel.text = [nowPlaying valueForProperty:MPMediaItemPropertyArtist];
}
```

The method gets the nowPlayingItem property object. Rather than have a bunch of fixed properties (like typical objects), the MPMediaItem object contains a variable number of property values that you request via a key. A key is a fixed value—typically a string object—that identifies the value you're interested in.

The first thing you ask for is the MPMediaItemPropertyArtwork value. This value will be a MPMediaItemArtwork object that encapsulates the album artwork for the song. You then request a UIImage object, optimized for the size of your image view.

> **Tip** MPMediaItemArtwork objects may store multiple versions of the item's artwork, at different sizes and resolutions. When requesting a UIImage of the artwork, specify a size as close as possible to the size you plan on displaying the image, so the media item object can return the best possible image for that size.

The thing to remember about media metadata is that there are no guarantees. Any song in the iPod library might have values for title, artist, and artwork. Or, it might not have any of those values. Or, it might have a title and artist, but no artwork, or artwork and no title. The bottom line is, be prepared for the case where something you ask for isn't available.

In this app, you test to see if MPMediaItemArtwork declined to return a displayable image (albumImage==nil). In that case, replace the image with a resource image named "noartwork."

For that statement to work, you'll need to add the noartwork.png and noartwork@2x.png files to your project. Select the Images.xcassets item in the navigator. Find the Learn iOS Development Projects ➤ Ch 9 ➤ DrumDub (Resources) folder and drag the noartwork.png and noartwork@2x.png files into the asset catalog.

The last three statements repeat this process, obtaining the title, album title, and artist name for the item. In this code you don't have to worry about missing values. If an item doesn't have an album name—for example, requesting MPMediaItemPropertyAlbumTitle—the media item will return a nil value. It just so happens that setting a UILabel's text property to nil blanks the view—which is exactly what you want to happen if there's no album name.

The last step is observing the item changed notifications. Find the `-musicPlayer` property getter method. Find the code that observes the playback state changes, and insert this new statement:

```
[notificationCenter addObserver:self
         selector:@selector(playingItemDidChangeNotification:)
             name:MPMusicPlayerControllerNowPlayingItemDidChangeNotification
           object:music];
```

Now whenever a new song starts playing, your controller will receive a "playing item did change" notification and display that information to the user. Give it a try.

Run your app, select a song, and start it playing. The song information and artwork display, as shown in Figure 9-11. If you let the song play to its end, the information disappears again.

Figure 9-11. Album artwork and song metadata

The only thing I don't like about this interface is that the artwork view and the three label views are filled with the placeholder information when the app launches. Fix that in the `Main.storyboard` file by clearing the text property of the three metadata labels, and setting the image view's initial image to `noartwork.png`.

Make Some Noise

So far, you've essentially created a (minimal) iPod app. That's an impressive feat, but it isn't the only way to add sound to your app. You may want to add sound effects to actions, or play music files that you've bundled. Maybe you want to play live audio streams from a network data source. Those are all easy to do, even easier than playing songs from the iPod library—which was pretty easy.

I'll get the easy part out of the way first. To play and control almost any kind of audio data your app has access to:

1. Create an `AVAudioPlayer` object.

2. Initialize the player with the source of the audio data, typically a URL to a resource file.

3. Send it a `-play` message

And just like the `MPMusicPlayerController`, the `AVAudioPlayer` object takes care of all of the details, including notifying your delegate when it's done.

So you might be thinking that it won't take more than a dozen lines of code and some buttons to finish this app. Sadly, you would be mistaken.

Living in a Larger World

What makes playing audio in this app complicated is not the code to play your sounds. The complication lies in the nature of iOS devices, and the environment they exist in.

Consider an iPhone. It's a telephone and videophone; audio is used to indicate incoming calls and play the audio stream from the caller. It's a music player; you can play your favorite music or audiobook, or stream Internet radio, even while using other apps. It's an alarm clock; timers can remind you of things to do any time of the day or night. It's a game console; games are full of sounds, sound effects, and ambient music. It's a pager; messages, notifications, and alerts can occur for countless reasons, interrupting your work (or play) at a moment's notice. It's also a video player, TV, answering machine, GPS navigator, movie editor, Dictaphone, and digital assistant.

All of these audio sources share a *single* output. To do that effectively—creating a pleasant experience for the user—all of these competing audio sources have to cooperate. Game sounds and music playback have to stop when a telephone call arrives. Background music needs to temporarily lower its volume, if the user is expected to hear a reminder or recorded message. iOS refers to these as *interruptions*.

Adding to this complexity, iOS devices have many different ways of producing sound. There's the built-in speakers, the head phone jack, wireless Bluetooth devices, AirPlay, and the dock connecter. iOS calls these *audio routes*. Audio can be directed to any one of these, and switched to a different one at any time (called a *route change*). Audio playback must be aware of this and your app may need to react to those changes. For example, Apple recommends that unplugging the headphones should cause music playback to pause, but game sound effects should continue playing.

And just to add one more dash of complication, most iOS devices have a ring/silence switch. Audio that's intended as an alert, alarm, embellishment, or sound effect should play only when the ring switch is in its normal position. More deliberate audio, like movies and audiobooks, should play normally, even when the silence switch is engaged.

Taken together, your app needs to

- Decide the intent and purpose of each source of audio in your app

- Declare this purpose, so iOS can adjust its behavior to accommodate your audio

- Observe interruptions and audio route changes, and take appropriate action

The good news is that not every audio-endowed app you write has to do all of these things. In fact, if you *only* use the iPod music player or *only* play incidental sounds using AVAudioPlayer objects, you probably don't have to do anything at all. Both of these classes will "do the right thing."

For an app like DrumDub, however, that wants to manage its own music playback while mixing in additional sound effects, all of these steps need to be taken. So before you start adding sound effects to your app, lay some of the groundwork.

Configuring Your Audio Session

You communicate your intent—describe the kinds of sounds your app will make and how those will affect other audio sources—to iOS through an *audio session*. Every iOS app gets a generic audio session, pre-configured with a basic set of behaviors. That's why, if you only play music through a music player controller, you don't have to do anything special; the default audio session is just fine.

DrumDub needs to both playback and mix audio. This is unusual, so it will need to reconfigure its audio session. Apps that only play audio can typically configure their audio session once and leave it.

> **Note** Apps that record audio, or record and playback audio, are more complicated. They must repeatedly reconfigure their audio session as they switch between recording, playback, and processing.

In your `DDAppDelegate.m` file, you'll find the implementation for your app's delegate object. One of the messages sent to your app's delegate is the `-application:didFinishLaunchingWithOptions:` message. As the name implies, it's sent immediately after your app has loaded, initialized, and is about to start running. It's the perfect place to put code that needs to run just once, and run before anything else gets underway. Add the following code (in bold) to the beginning of that method:

```
- (BOOL)application:(UIApplication *)application
   didFinishLaunchingWithOptions:(NSDictionary *)launchOptions
{
    AVAudioSession *audioSession = [AVAudioSession sharedInstance];
    [audioSession setCategory:AVAudioSessionCategoryPlayback
               withOptions:AVAudioSessionCategoryOptionMixWithOthers
                     error:NULL];
```

> **Note** This code will be flagged as an error by the compiler. You'll fix that shortly.

An audio session has a category and a set of options. There are seven different categories to choose from, as listed in Table 9-1.

Table 9-1. Audio session categories

Session Categories	App description
AVAudioSessionCategoryAmbient	Plays "background" audio or non-essential sound effects. The app will work just fine without them. App audio mixes with other audio (the iPod) playing at the same time. The ring/silence switch silences the app's audio.
AVAudioSessionCategorySoloAmbient	Plays non-essential audio that does not mix with other audio; other audio sources are silenced when the app plays. The ring/silence switch silences the app's audio.
AVAudioSessionCategoryPlayback	Plays music or other essential sounds. In other words, audio is the principle purpose of the app and it wouldn't work without it. The ring/silence switch does not silence its audio.
AVAudioSessionCategoryRecord	Records audio.
AVAudioSessionCategoryPlayAndRecord	Plays and records audio.
AVAudioSessionCategoryAudioProcessing	Performs audio processing (using the hardware audio codecs), while neither playing nor recording.
AVAudioSessionCategoryMultiRoute	Needs to output audio to multiple routes simultaneously. A slideshow app might play music through a dock connector, while simultaneously sending audio prompts through the headphones.

The default category is AVAudioSessionCategorySoloAmbient. For DrumDub, you've decided that audio is its raison d'être—its reason to exist. Use the -setCategory:withOptions:error: message to change its category to AVAudioSessionCategoryPlayback. Now your app's audio won't be silenced by the ring/silence switch.

You can also fine-tune the category with a number of category-specific options. The only option for the playback category is AVAudioSessionCategoryOptionMixWithOthers. If set, this option allows audio played with your AVAudioPlayer objects to "mix" with other audio playing at the same time. This is exactly what you want for DrumDub. Without this option, playing a sound would stop other audio sources.

All of these symbols are defined in the AVFoundation framework, so you'll need to #import the AVFoundation.h header to get them. Add this statement above all the other #import statements in DDAppDelegate.m:

```
#import <AVFoundation/AVFoundation.h>
```

See, that wasn't too hard. In fact, there was a lot more explanation than code. With your audio session correctly configured, you can now add (mix in) sound effects with your music.

Playing Audio Files

You're finally at the heart of your app's design: playing sounds. You're going to have four buttons, each playing a different sound. To implement this, you will need:

- Four button objects
- Four images
- Four `AVAudioPlayer` objects
- Four sampled sound files
- And an action method to play a sound

It will be easier to build the interface once you have added the resources and defined the action method, so start there. Find your Learn iOS Development Projects ➤ Ch 9 ➤ DrumDub (Resources) folder and locate the 12 files in this table:

Sound Sample	Button Image	Retina Display Image
snare.m4v	snare.png	snare@2x.png
bass.m4v	bass.png	bass@2x.png
tambourine.m4v	tambourine.png	tambourine@2x.png
maraca.m4v	maraca.png	maraca@2x.png

Begin by adding the button image files. Select the Images.xcassets asset catalog item. In it, you'll see the noartwork resource you added earlier. Drag the eight instrument image files (two each of snare, bass, tambourine, and maraca) into the asset catalog's group list, as shown in Figure 9-12.

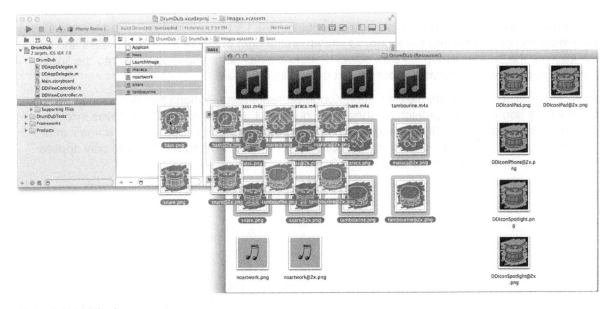

Figure 9-12. Adding image resources

While you're here, select the AppIcon group of the asset catalog and drag the appropriate app icon image files into it, as you've done for earlier projects. If you're building the iPhone version of this project, that would be the DDIconIPhone@2x, DDIconSpotlight, and DDIconSpotlight@2x files. If you're building an iPad version, add the DDIconIPad, DDIconIPad@2x, DDIconSpotlight, and DDIconSpotlight@2x files.

The four sound files (bass.m4a, maraca.m4a, snare.m4a, and tambourine.m4a) will also become resource files, but they're not the kind of resources managed by an asset catalog. You can add any kind of file you want directly to a project, and have that file included as a resource in your app's bundle.

For the sake of neatness, begin by creating a new group for these resource files. Control+click/right-click on the DrumDub group (not the project) in the navigator and choose the **New Group** command, as shown on the left in Figure 9-13.

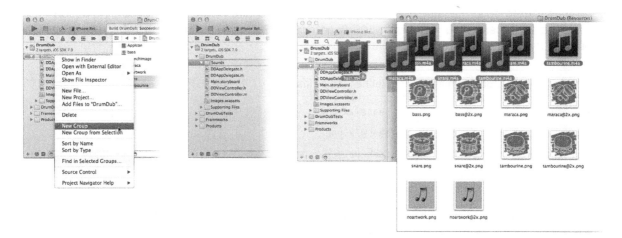

Figure 9-13. Adding non-image resources

Name the group Sounds, as shown in the middle of Figure 9-13. Locate the four sound sample files in the Finder and drag them into the group, as shown on the right of Figure 9-13. If you miss and add the items to the DrumDub group instead, select them in the navigator and drag them into the Sounds group. You can always reorganize your project items as you please.

After dropping your items into the navigator, Xcode presents some options that determine how the items will be added to your project, as shown in Figure 9-14. Make sure the **Copy items into destination group's folder (if needed)** option is checked. This option copies the new items into your app's project folder. The second option (**Create groups for any added folders**) only applies when adding folders full of resource files.

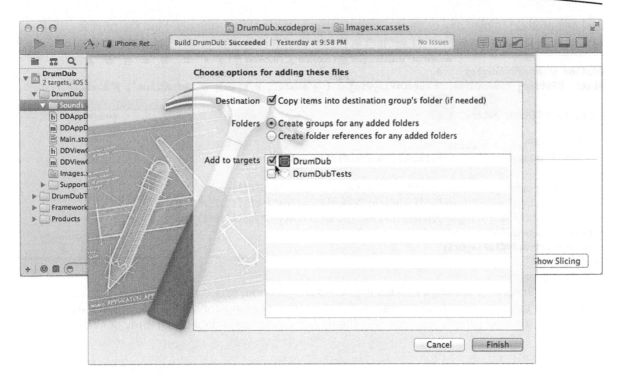

Figure 9-14. Add project file options

> **Caution** If you fail to check the **Copy items into destination group's folder (if needed)** option, Xcode will add only a *reference* to the original item, which is still outside your project's folder. This works fine, until you rename one of the original files, move your project, or copy it to another system—then your project suddenly stops building. Save yourself some grief and keep all of your project's resources inside your project folder.

Finally, make sure the DrumDub target is checked, as shown in Figure 9-14. This option makes these items *members* of the DrumDub app target, which means they'll be included as resource files in your finished app. (If you forget to check this, you can later change the target membership of any item using the file inspector.) Click Finish and Xcode will copy the sound sample files into your project folder, add them to the project navigator, and include them in the DrumDub app target. These files are now ready to be used in your app.

Creating AVAudioPlayer objects

You'll play the sound sample files using AVAudioPlayer objects. You'll need four. Rather than creating four AVAudioPlayer variables and writing four play actions, create one array to hold all of the objects and one method to play any of them. Start with the AVAudioPlayer objects. Find the private @interface DDViewController () section in DDViewController.m, and add the code in bold:

```
#define kNumberOfPlayers    4
static NSString *SoundName[kNumberOfPlayers] = { @"snare", @"bass", @"tambourine", @"maraca" };

@interface DDViewController ()
{
    MPMusicPlayerController *music;
    AVAudioPlayer           *players[kNumberOfPlayers];
}
@property (readonly,nonatomic) MPMusicPlayerController *musicPlayer;
- (void)playingItemDidChangeNotification:(NSNotification*)notification;
- (void)playbackStateDidChangeNotification:(NSNotification*)notification;
- (void)createAudioPlayers;
- (void)destroyAudioPlayers;
@end
```

The kNumberOfPlayers constant defines the number of sounds, sound player objects, and sound buttons that this app uses. Also defined is a static array of string constant objects. Each element is the name of a sound sample resource file. The players instance variable is an array of AVAudioPlayer objects.

> **Tip** It's a good practice to define almost any constant as a symbol (like kNumberOfPlayers), for two reasons. First, it makes your code more descriptive. The expression (6*2) is much more mysterious than (kDiceSides*kNumberOfDice). See the "Magic Numbers" anti-pattern at http://en.wikipedia.org/wiki/Magic_number_(programming). It also defines a single point in your code where that value can be changed. If the next version of DrumDub has six sound buttons, all of the various for loops and array sizes can be updated by changing a single statement.

The methods -createAudioPlayers and -destroyAudioPlayers create and destroy all four audio player objects at once. Add them to the end of your @implementation section:

```
- (void)createAudioPlayers
{
    for ( NSUInteger i=0; i<kNumberOfPlayers; i++)
        {
        NSURL *soundURL = [[NSBundle mainBundle] URLForResource:SoundName[i]
                                                  withExtension:@"m4a"];
        players[i] = [[AVAudioPlayer alloc] initWithContentsOfURL:soundURL
                                                  error:NULL];
        players[i].delegate = self;
        [players[i] prepareToPlay];
        }
}
```

```
- (void)destroyAudioPlayers
{
    for ( NSUInteger i=0; i<kNumberOfPlayers; i++)
        players[i] = nil;
}
```

-createAudioPlayers loops through the array of sound name constants (SoundName[i]) and uses that to create a URL that refers to the m4a sound resource file that you added earlier. This URL is used to create and initialize a new AVAudioPlayer object that will play that sound file.

Your controller object is set to be the sound player's delegate (you'll use that later). Finally, some optimization is applied. The -prepareToPlay message is sent to the sound player. This preps the player object so that it is immediately ready to play its sound.

> **Note** Normally, player objects prepare themselves lazily, waiting until you request them to play before actually reading the sound sample data file, allocating their buffers, configuring hardware codecs, and so on. All of this takes time. When your user taps a sound button, they don't want to wait for the sound to play; they want it to play immediately. The -prepareToPlay message eliminates that initial delay.

The -destroyAudioPlayers method is self-explanatory, and you don't need it yet. It will come into "play" later.

Next up are the buttons to play these sounds and the action method to make that happen. Get the action declaration, and a few odds and ends, out of the way first. Switch to your DDViewController.h file. Underneath the #import statements, add a new one:

`#import <AVFoundation/AVFoundation.h>`

This imports the definitions for the AVAudioPlayer and related classes. Next, make your controller an AVAudioPlayerDelegate:

`@interface DDViewController : UIViewController <MPMediaPickerControllerDelegate,`
                                                    AVAudioPlayerDelegate>

Add a new action method to the @interface:

`- (IBAction)bang:(id)sender;`

Now you're ready to design the interface.

Adding the Sound Buttons

Return to your Main.storyboard Interface Builder file. Drag in a new UIButton object. Select it and do the following (see Figure 9-15):

- Use the size inspector to set both its width and height to 100 pixels.
- Use the attributes inspector to:
  - Set its type property to Custom.
  - Clear its title text property (deleting "Button").
  - Set its image property to snare.
  - Scroll down to its tag property and change it from 0 to 1.
- Choose **Editor ➤ Pin ➤ Width**.
- Select the button again and choose **Editor ➤ Pin ➤ Height**.
- Use the connections inspector to connect its Touch Down event to the new -bang: action of the View Controller object.

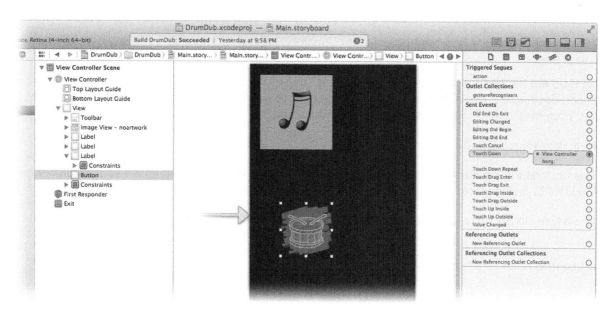

Figure 9-15. Creating the first bang button

There are a couple of noteworthy aspects to this button's configuration. First, you've connected the Touch Down event, instead of the more common Touch Up Inside event. That's because you want to receive the -bang: action message the *instant* the user touches the button. Normally, buttons don't send their action message until the user touches them and releases again, with their finger still inside the button. Thus, the action name "Touch Up Inside."

Secondly, you didn't create an outlet to connect to this button. You're going to identify, and access, the object via its `tag` property. All `UIView` objects have an integer `tag` property. It exists solely for your use in identifying views; iOS doesn't use it for anything else. You're going to use the `tag` to determine which sound to play, and later to obtain the `UIButton` object in the interface.

Duplicate the new button three times, to create four buttons in all. You can do this either using the clipboard, or by holding down the Option key and dragging out new copies of the button. Arrange them in a group, as shown in Figure 9-16, and then center that group in the interface. Choose **Editor ➤ Resolve Auto Layout Issues ➤ Add Missing Constraints in View Controller**.

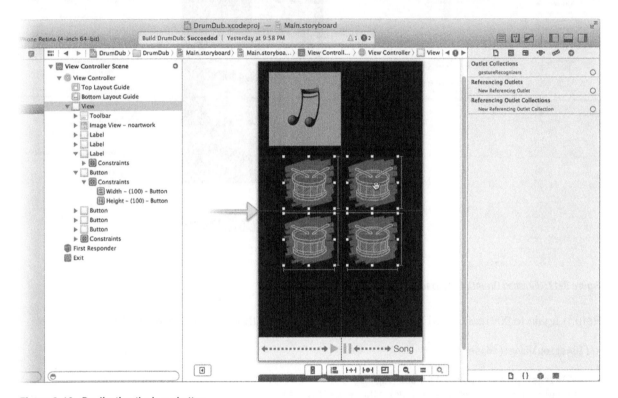

Figure 9-16. Duplicating the bang button

All of the buttons have the same type, image, tag, constraints, and action connection. Use the attributes inspector to change the image and tag properties of the other three, starting with the upper-right button and working clockwise, using the following table:

Button	Image	Tag
Upper-right	`bass`	2
Lower-right	`maraca`	4
Lower-left	`tambourine`	3

The finished interface should look like the one in Figure 9-17.

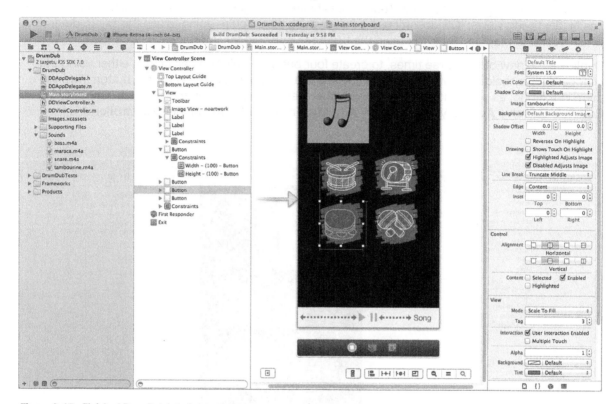

Figure 9-17. Finished DrumDub interface

Return again to `DDViewController.m` and add the `-bang:` method to your implementation:

```
- (IBAction)bang:(id)sender
{
    NSInteger playerIndex = [sender tag]-1;
    if (playerIndex>=0 && playerIndex<kNumberOfPlayers)
        {
        AVAudioPlayer *player = players[playerIndex];
        [player pause];
        player.currentTime = 0;
        [player play];
        }
}
```

All four buttons send the same action. You determine which button sent the message using its `tag` property. Your four buttons have `tag` values between 1 and 4, which you will use as an index (0 through 3) to obtain that button's `AVAudioPlayer` object.

Once you have the button's `AVAudioPlayer`, you first send it a `-pause` message. This will suspend playback of the sound if it's currently playing. If not, it does nothing.

Then the `currentTime` property is set to 0. This property is the player's logical "play head," indicating the position (in seconds) where the player is currently playing, or will begin playing. Setting it to 0 "rewinds" the sound so it plays from the beginning.

Finally, the `-play` message starts the sound playing. The `-play` message is asynchronous; it starts a background task to play and manage the sound, and then returns immediately.

There are just two more details to take care of before your sounds will play.

Activating Your Audio Session

It's not strictly required, but the documentation for the `AVAudioSession` class recommends that your app activate the audio session when it starts, and again whenever your audio session is interrupted. You'll take this opportunity to prepare the audio player objects at the same time. Add an `-activateAudioSession` method to your `DDViewController.m` implementation. Start by adding a prototype to the private `@interface` section at the top:

```
- (void)activateAudioSession;
```

Find the –viewDidLoad method and send the controller this message when it first loads (the new line in bold):

```
- (void)viewDidLoad
{
    [super viewDidLoad];
    [self activateAudioSession];
}
```

And add the method to the @implementation:

```
- (void)activateAudioSession
{
    BOOL active = [[AVAudioSession sharedInstance] setActive:YES error:NULL];
    if (active && players[0]==nil)
        [self createAudioPlayers];
    if (!active)
        [self destroyAudioPlayers];
    for ( NSUInteger i=0; i<kNumberOfPlayers; i++)
        [(UIButton*)[self.view viewWithTag:i+1] setEnabled:active];
}
```

The first line obtains your app's audio session object (the same one you configured back in `-application:didFinishLaunchingWithOptions:`). You send it a `-setActive:error:` message to activate, or reactivate, the audio session.

The `-setActive:error:` message returns YES if the audio session is now active. There are a few obscure situations where this will fail (returning NO), and your app should deal with that situation gracefully.

In this app, you look to see if the session was activated and send `-createAudioPlayers` to prepare the `AVAudioPlayer` objects for playback. If the session couldn't be activated (which means your app can't use any audio), then you destroy any `AVAudioPlayer` objects you previously created and disable all of the sound effect buttons in the interface.

Since you don't have an outlet connected to those buttons, you'll get them using their `tag`. The `-viewWithTag:` message searches the hierarchy of a view object and returns the first subview object matching that tag. Your bang buttons are the only views with tag values of 1, 2, 3, and 4. The loop obtains each button view and enables, or disables, it.

> **Tip** Tags are a convenient way to manage a group of view objects, without requiring you to create an outlet for each one.

The functional portion of your app is now finished. By functional, I mean that you can run your app, play music, and annoy anyone else in the room with cheesy percussion noises, as shown in Figure 9-18.

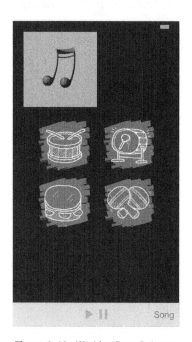

Figure 9-18. Working DrumDub app

Interruptions and Detours

In the "Living in a Larger World" section, I described the multitude of events and situations that conspire to complicate your app's use of audio. Most people hate interruptions or being forced to take a detour, and I suspect app developers are no different. But dealing with these events gracefully is the hallmark of a finely crafted iOS app. First up are interruptions.

Dealing with Interruptions

An *Interruption* occurs when another app or service needs to activate its audio session. The most common sources of interruptions are incoming phone calls and alerts (triggered by alarms, messages, notification, and reminders).

Most of the work of handling interruptions is done for you. When your app's audio session is interrupted, iOS fades out your audio and deactivates your session. The usurping session then takes over and begins playing the user's ring tone or alert sound. Your app, audio, and music player delegates then receive "begin interruption" messages.

Your app should do whatever is appropriate to respond to the interruption. Often, this isn't much. You might update the interface to indicate that you're no longer playing music. Mostly, your app should just make a note of what it was doing so it can resume when the interruption ends.

Interruptions can be short: a few seconds, for alarms. Or they can be very (very) long: an hour or more, if you accept that incoming phone call from chatty aunt May. Don't make any assumptions on how long the interruption will last, just wait for iOS to notify your app when it's over.

When the interruption is over, your app will receive "end interruption" messages. This is where the work begins. First, your app should explicitly reactivate its audio session. This isn't a strict requirement, but it's recommended. It gives your app a chance to catch the (very rare) situation where your audio session can't be reactivated.

Then you need to resume playback, reload audio objects, update your interface, or whatever else your app needs to do so it is once again running, exactly as it was before the interruption occurred. In DrumDub, there's surprisingly little work to do, as most of the default music and audio player behavior is exactly what you want. Nevertheless, there's still some rudimentary interruption handling you need to add.

Adding Your Interruption Handlers

Interruption messages can be received in a number of different ways. Your app only needs to observe those it wants and are convenient; there's no need to observe them all. Begin and end interruption messages are sent to:

- The audio session delegate (AVAudioSessionDelegate)
- All audio player delegates (AVAudioPlayerDelegate)
- Any observer of music player state change notifications (MPMusicPlayerControllerPlaybackStateDidChangeNotification)

Decide how you want your app to respond to interruptions, and then implement the handlers that conveniently let you do that. When something interrupts DrumDub, you want to:

- Pause the playback of the music.
- Stop any percussion sound that's playing (so it doesn't resume when the interruption is over).

When the interruption ends, you want DrumDub to:

- Reactivate the audio session and check for problems.
- Resume playback of the music.

Pausing and resuming the music player requires no code. The `MPMusicPlayerController` class does this automatically in response to interruptions. You don't even need to add any code to update your interface. When the music player is interrupted, its `playbackState` changes to `MPMusicPlaybackStateInterrupted` and your controller receives a `-playbackStateDidChangeNotification:` message, which updates your play and pause buttons. When the interruption ends, the music player resumes playing and sends another state change notification.

So DrumDub's only non-standard behavior is to silence any playing percussion sounds when an interruption arrives. That's so the "tail end" of the sound bite doesn't start playing again when the interruption is over. Handle that by adding this audio player delegate method to `DDViewController.m`:

```
- (void)audioPlayerBeginInterruption:(AVAudioPlayer *)player
{
    [player pause];
}
```

Your controller object is already the delegate for all four of the audio players. Your controller can receive this message up to four times (once for each player).

> **Note** `AVAudioPlayer` delegate objects also receive an `-audioPlayerDidFinishPlaying: successfully:` message when the player is finished playing a sound, and an `-audioPlayerEndInterruption:withOptions:` message when an interruption ends. DrumDub doesn't need either of these messages, but your next app might.

The last task on the list is to reactivate the audio session when the interruption is over. To do that, make your `DDViewController` object the audio session's delegate and handle the `-endInterruption` delegate message. Start by modifying the class declaration in `DDViewController.h`:

```
@interface DDViewController : UIViewController <MPMediaPickerControllerDelegate,
                                                AVAudioSessionDelegate,
                                                AVAudioPlayerDelegate>
```

Back in `DDViewController.m`, locate the `-viewDidLoad` method and set the session's delegate property:

```
- (void)viewDidLoad
{
    [super viewDidLoad];
    [[AVAudioSession sharedInstance] setDelegate:self];
    [self activateAudioSession];
}
```

Finally, implement an -endInterruption method so your controller will receive this message from the audio session:

```
- (void)endInterruption
{
    [self activateAudioSession];
}
```

You already wrote the code to (re)activate the audio session and update your interface. All -endInterruption has to do is perform that again.

With the tricky business of interruptions taken care of, it's time to deal with detours (route changes).

Dealing with Audio Route Changes

An audio route is the path that data takes to get to the eardrum of the listener. Your iPhone might be paired to the speakers in your car. When you get out of your car, your iPhone switches to its built-in speakers. When you plug in some headphones, it stops playing through its speaker and begins playing through your headphones. Each of these events is an audio route change.

You deal with audio route changes exactly the way you deal with interruptions: decide what your app should do in each situation, and then write handlers to observe those events and implement your policies. From DrumDub, you want to implement Apple's recommended behavior of stopping music playback when the user unplugs their headphones, or disconnects from external speakers. If these were sound effects in a game, or something similar, it would be appropriate to let them continue playing. But DrumDub's music will stop playing when the headphones are unplugged, so the instrument sounds should stop too.

Audio route notifications are posted by the AVAudioSession object, all you have to do is observe them. Begin by defining an audio route change notification handler, adding its prototype to the private @interface DDViewController () section in DDViewController.m:

```
- (void)audioRouteChangedNotification:(NSNotification*)notification;
```

Next, request that your DDViewController object receive audio route change notifications. At the end of the -viewDidLoad method, add this code:

```
[[NSNotificationCenter defaultCenter] addObserver:self
                  selector:@selector(audioRouteChangedNotification:)
                      name:AVAudioSessionRouteChangeNotification
                    object:nil];
```

Now add the method to your @implementation section:

```
- (void)audioRouteChangedNotification:(NSNotification*)notification
{
    NSNumber *changeReason = ↩
            notification.userInfo[AVAudioSessionRouteChangeReasonKey];
    if ([changeReason integerValue]== ↩
            AVAudioSessionRouteChangeReasonOldDeviceUnavailable)
        {
        for ( NSUInteger i=0; i<kNumberOfPlayers; i++)
            [players[i] pause];
        }
}
```

The method begins by examining the reason for the audio route change. It gets this information from the notification's userInfo dictionary. If the value of the AVAudioSessionRouteChangeReasonKey is AVAudioSessionRouteChangeReasonOldDeviceUnavailable, it indicates that a previously active audio route is no longer available. This happens when headphones are unplugged, the device is removed from a dock connector, a wireless speaker system is disconnected, and so on. If that's the case, it stops playback of all four audio players.

That wraps up this app! Go ahead and run it again to make sure everything is working. You'll want to test your interruption and audio route change logic by doing things like:

- Setting an alarm to interrupt playback
- Calling your iPhone from another phone
- Plugging and unplugging headphones

Testing your app under as many situations as you can devise is an important part of app development.

Other Audio Topics

This chapter didn't even begin to approach the subjects of audio recording or signal processing. To get started with these, and similar topics, start with the *Multimedia Programming Guide*. It provides an overview and roadmap for playing, recording, and manipulating both audio and video in iOS.

If you need to perform advanced or low-level audio tasks (such as analyzing or encoding audio), refer to the *Core Audio Overview*. All of these documents can be found in Xcode's Documentation and API Reference.

Here's something else to look at: if you need to present audio or video in a view, want your app to play music in the background (that is, when your app is not running), or need to handle remote events, take a look at the AVPlayer and AVPlayerLayer classes. The first is a near-universal media player for both audio and video, similar to MPMusicPlayerController and AVAudioPlayer. It's a little more complicated, but also more capable. It will work in conjunction with an AVPlayerLayer object to present visual content (movie) in a view, so you can create your own YouTube-style video player.

Summary

Sound adds a rich dimension to your app. You've learned how to play and control audio from the iPod library as well as resource files bundled in your app. You understand the importance of configuring your audio session, and intelligently handing interruptions and audio route changes. "Playing nice" with other audio sources creates the kind of experience that users enjoy, and will want to use again and again.

But is there more to iOS interfaces than labels, buttons, and image views? Join me in the next chapter to find out.

EXERCISE

Blend DrumDub further into the iOS experience by using the iPod music player, instead of an application music player. This will require a couple of subtle changes:

- Obtain the +iPodMusicPlayer object, instead of the +applicationMusicPlayer object.
- Create and initialize the music player as soon as the view loads, rather than doing it lazily when the user chooses a song.
- Don't arbitrarily change the player's settings (like the shuffle or repeat modes). Remember that you're changing the user's iPod settings; most people won't like your app fiddling with their iPod.

When you're done, DrumDub will be "plugged in" to the user's iPod app. If their iPod music is playing when they launch DrumDub, the song will appear the moment your app launches. If the user starts a song playing and quits DrumDub, the music plays on.

You'll find my solution to this exercise in the Learn iOS Development Projects ➤ Ch 9 ➤ DrumDub E1 folder.

Chapter 10

Got Views?

You now have a lot of experience adding view objects to your design, arranging them, connecting them to outlets and actions, and customizing them. You've created iOS apps using buttons, labels, image views, a few text fields, and the odd toolbar. While you probably haven't been yearning for other kinds of view objects, there are more available. The Cocoa Touch framework provides all kinds of switches, toggles, sliders, specialty buttons, pickers, indicators, do-dads, and gizmos you can use to build your apps. And if that isn't enough, many of those objects can be customized in ways you haven't explored yet. In this chapter you'll learn about:

- Downloading sample projects
- Button views
- Switches, sliders, and steppers
- Indicators
- Labels, text fields, and text views
- Pickers
- Grouped table views
- Scroll views

Anyone who's spent time building Lego figures, Erector Set constructions, or experimental aircraft will know one thing: your ability to imagine what's possible is directly linked to your knowledge about what parts you have to work with. To that end, I invite you on a guided tour of iOS view objects.

Learning by Example

Software development is a lot like cooking. It's one thing to read recipes, talk about the process, and enjoy the results. It's another thing to actually do it. One of the best ways to learn how to cook is to watch someone who knows what they're doing, and emulate them.

Apple provides many example projects—fully written, ready to run apps—that demonstrate the use of various technologies in iOS. All you have to do is download one, build it, run it, and then mine it for all of its secrets. These example projects are a great way to get started using, or at least understanding how to use, many of the frameworks and features in iOS.

Not only does Apple provide these example projects free of charge, they've made it ridiculously simple to download them. Xcode will search for, download, and open sample code projects with the click of a button. Start in Xcode's documentation organizer (**Help ➤ Documentation and API Reference**) window, as shown in Figure 10-1.

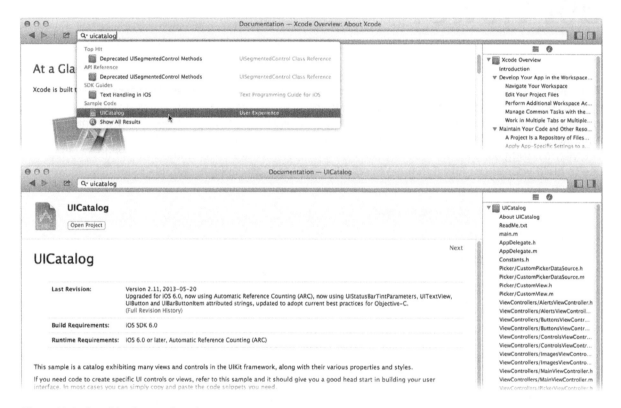

Figure 10-1. Searching for sample code

Search for the UICatalog project, as shown in Figure 10-1. It will appear under the Sample Code category. Click on it and the project's documentation page appears. At the top is an **Open Project** button. Click it. Xcode downloads the project's ZIP file, un-archives it, and opens the project in a new workspace window, as shown in Figure 10-2. How easy was that?

CHAPTER 10: Got Views?   293

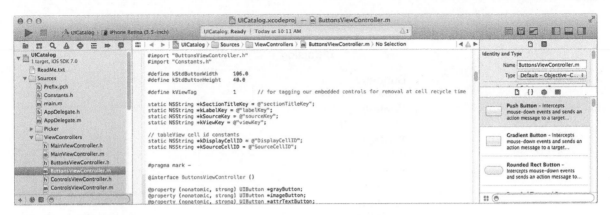

Figure 10-2. UICatalog project

> **Note** Sample projects are not part of the Xcode installation package and require an Internet connection to download.

You'll find that the documentation for many classes contains links to sample projects, making it easy to download code that shows you those classes in action.

> **Tip** While Apple's so-called "walled garden" keeps most iOS app projects within the developer community—after all, you have to be a developer to build and run apps on your iOS device—that hasn't stopped the open-source community. There is a wide variety of open-source iOS projects out there, available to developers (like you) and to brave individuals who have "jailbroken" their device. A quick Internet search will turn up open-source apps, as well as frameworks and code libraries you can use in your own projects.

The UICatalog project is extra special. It's an iPhone app that demonstrates every major view object supplied by iOS. So not only is it a handy visual reference to the kinds of view objects iOS supplies, but you can see exactly how these objects are created and used in an app.

Run the UICatalog app in an iPhone simulator (or on your own device, if you like). First in the list is buttons, as shown in Figure 10-3, and that's a great place to start.

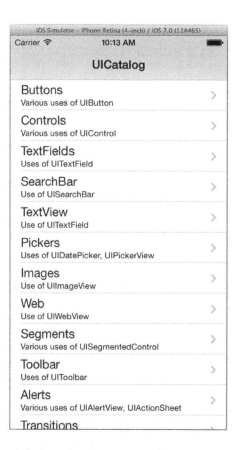

Figure 10-3. UICatalog app

Buttons

A button is a very straightforward view object; it acts like a physical button. The UIButton class draws a button and observes touch events to determine how the user is interacting with it. It translates what the user is doing into action events, such as "user touched inside the button," "user moved their finger outside the button," "user moved back inside the button," and "user released their finger while still inside the button." That's pretty much all it does.

I know what you're thinking. Well, maybe I don't. But I hope you're thinking, "but a button does more than that! It sends action messages to another object, it remembers its state, it can be disabled, and it can have gesture recognizers attached to it. That's a lot!"

It is a lot, but the UIButton class doesn't do any of those things. UIButton is at the end of a chain of classes, each of which is responsible for one set of closely related behaviors. Software engineers say that each class performs a *role*. The role of a UIButton object is to act like a button. Other classes do all of that other stuff. So that you can get a clearer picture of what's going on, I think it's time for you to dissect a UIButton. This will not only help you understand how UIButton was built, but how all control views are constructed.

> **Note** No `UIButton` objects were harmed in the making of this book.

The Responder and View Classes

A `UIButton` is a subclass of `UIControl`, which is a subclass of `UIView`, which is a subclass of `UIResponder`. Each class adds one layer of functionality that, taken together, makes a button.

The `UIResponder` class defines all of the event-related functions of the objects, most notably the methods that handle touch events. You learned all about `UIResponder` in Chapter 4, and you created a custom `UIView` object that overrode the touch event handling methods with your own, so I won't repeat any of that here.

The next layer that `UIButton` inherits is `UIView`. `UIView` is a big, complicated class. It has dozens of properties and over a hundred methods. It's huge because it's responsible for every aspect of how every visible object in the iOS universe gets displayed on a screen. It handles the geometry of the view, its coordinate systems, transformations (like rotation, scaling, and skewing), animation, how the view gets repositioned when the screen size changes, and hit testing. It's also responsible for drawing itself, drawing its subviews, deciding when those views need to be redrawn, and more.

One, seemingly unrelated, property of `UIView` is its `gestureRecognizers` property. The `UIView` class doesn't do anything with gesture recognizers directly. But a `UIView` defines a visible region of the display, and any visible region can have a gesture recognizer attached to it, so that property exists in `UIView`.

HOW GESTURE RECOGNIZERS GET EVENTS

Gesture recognizers are fed events by the `UIWindow` object during touch event delivery. In Chapter 4, I explained that hit testing is used to determine the view that will receive the touch events. That description oversimplified the process somewhat.

Starting with iOS 3.2, the `UIWindow` first looks at the initial (hit test) view to see if it has any gesture recognizer objects attached to it. If it does, the touch events are first sent to those gesture recognizer objects, instead of being delivered directly to the view object. If the gesture recognizers aren't interested, then the event eventually makes its way to the view object.

If you need to, there are a variety of ways to alter this behavior, but it's a tad complicated. For all of the details, read the "Gesture Recognizers" chapter of the *Event Handling Guide for iOS*, that you'll find in Xcode's Documentation and API Reference.

So everything that's visual about the button is defined in the `UIView` class. Now move on to the next layer, the `UIControl` class.

The Control Class

UIControl is the abstract class that defines the properties common to all control objects. This includes buttons, sliders, switches, steppers, and so on. A control object:

- Sends action messages to target objects
- Can be enabled or disabled
- Can be selected
- Can be highlighted
- Establishes how content is aligned

The first item in the above list is the most important. The UIControl class defines the mechanism for delivering action messages to recipients, typically controller objects. Every UIControl object maintains a table of events that trigger actions, the object that will receive that action, and the action message it will send. When you're editing an Interface Builder file and you connect an event to an action method in another object, you're adding one entry to that object's event dispatch table.

> **Note** Remember from Chapter 4 that an event can be associated with an action message which is sent to the first responder. You do this by specifying the message to send and using nil as the target object for that message.

The other properties (enabled, selected, and highlighted) are general indicators of the control's appearance and behavior. Subclasses of UIControl determine exactly what those properties mean, if anything.

The enabled property is the most consistent. A control object interacts with the user when enabled, and ignores touch events when disabled (control.enabled=NO). Most control classes indicate that they are disabled by dimming, or graying, their image to show the user the control is inert.

The highlighted property is used to indicate that the user is currently touching the control. Many controls "light up" when touched, and this property reflects that.

The selected property is for controls that can be turned "on" or "off," such as the UISwitch class. Controls that don't, such as buttons, ignore this property.

The UIControl class also introduces the concept of an alignment (vertical and horizontal) through the contentVerticalAlignment and contentHorizontalAlignment properties. Most control objects have some sort of title or image and use these properties to position that in the view.

Button Types

You've now worked your way back to the UIButton class. It's this class that implements the button-specific behavior of a control+view+responder object. The UIButton class supplies a handful of pre-defined button looks, along with a plethora of customizations so you can make it look just about any way you want.

The most important property of a button is its type. A button can be one of these types:

- Rounded Rectangle
- Custom
- A "disclose detail" arrow
- An "info" button (light or dark)
- An "add contact" plus symbol

All of these button types, except custom, are shown in the UICatalog app, as shown in Figure 10-4. The important thing to remember is that a button's type is determined when it is created. Unlike all of its other properties, it cannot be changed afterwards. A rounded rectangle button is a rounded rectangle button for life.

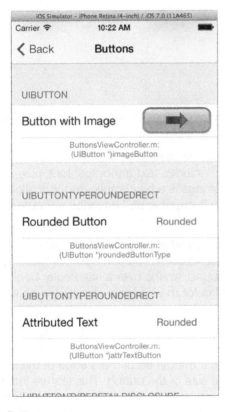

Figure 10-4. Buttons

The rounded rectangle button is the workhorse of iOS. It's the standard, default, button style used throughout the iOS interface. You'll also notice that there's nothing "rounded" about a Rounded Button (middle-left of Figure 10-4). iOS 7 introduced a new, streamlined, UI design that echews the skeuomorphic button design of earlier versions. The class and constant names, however, have not changed. Choose the "rounded" button when you want to present the standard button design for the version of iOS your users are running.

The custom button style is a blank canvas. iOS (all versions) adds nothing to the look of a custom button, allowing you complete control over its appearance. You used the custom button style for the Surrealists app in Chapter 2.

You can dramatically alter a button's basic look by adjusting its color, text, text style, or even supply your own images for the button's title and background.

> **Note** The UICatalog project had not been fully updated for the new UI design in iOS 7 when this book was written. I fully expect that it will be revised, so the controls in your app may appear differently from what you see here.

The premier properties that adjust your button's look are:

- Tint color
- Title text (plain or attributed) and color
- Foreground image
- Background image or color

The `tintColor` property sets the highlight and accent color of rounded rectangle buttons. The standard color is blue. Other button types ignore this property.

The button's title can be a simple string value (which you've used in your projects so far), or it can be attributed string. An *attributed string* is a string that includes text attributes: font, size, italics, bold, subscript offset, and so on. Creating attributed strings is a bit complicated, but allows you to create buttons with whatever font and style the system is capable of. I describe attributed strings in Chapter 20.

You can also use an image instead of text for your button's label by setting the image property. Similarly, the background can be set to an image or a solid color. You can also mix these in any combination you want: text title over an image background, image over a solid color background, image with no background (by setting the background color to `UIColor`'s `clearColor` object), and so on.

The buttons with the rounded rectangle look (in the upper-left of Figure 10-4) are supplying their own background image, `whiteButton.png` in this case. Images used for a button's background can utilize the cap insets (`capInsets`) property to define a margin around the edge of the image that is not scaled when the image is stretched to fit the size of the button. This feature lets you design a single graphic image that will fill any button size, without distorting its edges. Compare the `whiteButton.png` resource image in Xcode with how it appears in the button when the app runs.

> **Tip** Although I'm going to teach the primary ways you can customize the look of your buttons, sliders, and so on, I encourage you think before you do. Don't change the look of a button just because you can. Users know what a button does because it looks like a button. Changing it—just to be different—makes your app that much harder to use. I consider customizing the look of controls only when their standard look clashes, esthetically, with the rest of the design.

The remaining button types (detail disclosure, info, add contact, and so on) are predefined buttons with few options for customization. Use these types where your app provides those exact features, and your users will understand exactly what they mean.

Control States

When creating and configuring the button's title, image, background image, and background color, you must consider the various states the button (control) can be in. The UIControl's enabled, highlighted, and selected properties combine to form a single state value (UIControlState) for that control. The state will always be one of: normal, highlighted, disabled, or selected.

When the button is displaying normally, its state is UIControlStateNormal. When the user is touching it, its state changes to UIControlStateHighlighted. When it's disabled, its state becomes UIControlStateDisabled.

When you set a button's title, image, background, or color you do so for a particular state. This allows you to set one button image for when the button is enabled and alternate button image(s) for when it's disabled, highlighted, or selected. You see this reflected in the methods that set these properties:

- (void)setTitle:(NSString *)title forState:(UIControlState)state
- (void)setTitleColor:(UIColor *)color forState:(UIControlState)state
- (void)setImage:(UIImage *)image forState:(UIControlState)state
- (void)setBackgroundImage:(UIImage *)image forState:(UIControlState)state

You don't have to set values for every state. At a minimum, you should set the value for the normal (UIControlStateNormal) state. If that's all you set, that value will be used for all other states. If you then want it to have a different title, image, background, or color for one of the other states, set that too.

There are lots of other, subtler, properties for fine-tuning your button's look and feel. You can, for example, control the shadow thrown by the title text or change the position (inset) of the title, image, and background image. Read through the documentation for UIButton for all of the available properties.

The last four button types—disclosure arrow, info (light), info (dark), and add contact—are convenience types for well-defined user interface buttons. There is almost nothing about the look or behavior of these buttons that you can customize.

Button Code

You now know enough about button properties to take a peek at the button construction code in UICatalog. Up to now, you've created button objects using Interface Builder—which is fine, there's nothing wrong with that. But you can also create any iOS object programmatically, as you've done with other objects like arrays and images.

The UICatalog app creates most of its objects programmatically, and it even provides hints as to where that happens so you can go find the code. In Figure 10-4, the text underneath the button says "ButtonsViewController.m: (UIButton*)roundedButtonType." Switch back to Xcode and find the ButtonsViewController.m file. Click on it and locate the -roundedButtonType method. It should look something like this:

```
- (UIButton *)roundedButtonType
{
    if (roundedButtonType == nil)
    {
        roundedButtonType = [[UIButton buttonWithType:UIButtonTypeRoundedRect] retain];
        roundedButtonType.frame = CGRectMake(182.0, 5.0,
                                             kStdButtonWidth, kStdButtonHeight);
        [roundedButtonType setTitle:@"Rounded" forState:UIControlStateNormal];
        roundedButtonType.backgroundColor = [UIColor clearColor];
        [roundedButtonType addTarget:self action:@selector(action:)
                    forControlEvents:UIControlEventTouchUpInside];
        roundedButtonType.tag = kViewTag;
    }
    return roundedButtonType;
}
```

This method lazily creates the button that appears in the UICatalog app as "Rounded Button." If you want to try out different rounded rectangle button properties to see what they look like, fiddle with this code and run the app again.

Switches and Sliders

Next up on the tour are switches and sliders. Both are input devices. Unlike buttons, switches and sliders retain a value. A switch is just that, as shown in Figure 10-5. It presents a sliding button that can change between "on" and "off" values by either tapping or swiping it with your finger. You see these everywhere in iOS, as shown on the right in Figure 10-5.

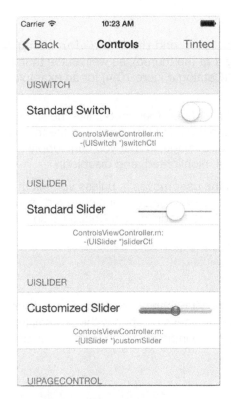

Figure 10-5. Switches, sliders, and the Settings app

A `UISwitch` object has a single Boolean value property named, appropriately enough, `on`. Getting that property will tell you which position the switch is in. Setting the property changes it. You can request that `UISwitch` perform a little animation eye-candy, when you change its value programmatically, by sending it the `-setOn:animated:` message, passing `YES` for the animated parameter.

A number of properties let you customize your switch's appearance:

- `tintColor`, `onTintColor`, and `thumbTintColor`: the first two set the colors used when the switch is off and on. The `thumbTintColor` makes the "thumb" of the switch (the circle you drag) a different color than `tintColor`.
- `onImage` and `offImage`: normally a switch displays either (localized) "On" or "Off" text titles next to the thumb. You can replace these with images of your choosing. There are important size restrictions, so read the documentation.

Like most controls with a value, a switch sends a "value changed" event (`UIControlEventValueChanged`) whenever the user changes it. Connect this event to your controller to receive an action message when the switch is flipped.

Sliders, also shown in Figure 10-5, are another input control that lets the user choose a value by dragging a slider to a position within a predetermined range. While a switch's value is Boolean, a slider's value property is a floating-point value that represents a continuous range of numbers.

The slider's value property is constrained to the range set by the `minimumValue` and `maximumValue` properties. These default to 0 and 1, respectively. Unless you change those, value will be a fractional number between 0 and 1 (inclusive).

The key visual customization properties are:

- `minimumTrackTintColor`, `maximumTrackTintColor`, and `thumbTintColor`: changes the colors of the tracks (to the left and right of the thumb), as well as the thumb itself. See the Customized Slider in the UICatalog (Figure 10-4) for an example, and the code that does it.
- `minimumValueImage`, `maximumValueImage`, `thumbImage` (per `state`): like the slider, you can change the image used to draw the tracks of the slider, and the thumb itself. The thumb image works like `UIButton`'s image, in that you can supply different images for different states (normal, highlighted, and disabled).

A slider sends a single "value changed" event when the user moves it, unless you set the `continuous` property to YES. If you set `continuous`, the control fires a barrage of "value changed" messages as the user drags the slider. You used this setting in the ColorModel app in Chapter 8 so color changes happened "live" as you dragged around a slider.

Page Control

A page control (`UIPageControl`) object, shown in Figure 10-6, can be thought of as a discrete slider control. As its name implies, it's intended to indicate the user's position within a small (up to 20) number of pages or items. Apple's Weather app uses it to indicate which location the user is currently viewing, shown on the right in Figure 10-6.

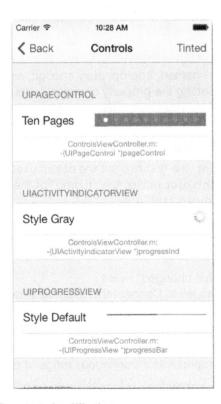 

Figure 10-6. *Page control and Weather app*

UIPageControl's integer `currentPage` property is its value, and its `numberOfPages` property determines the former's range and the number of dots that appear. Its appearance can be slightly modified with these properties:

- `pageIndicatorTintColor`: sets the color for the page indicator
- `hidesForSinglePage`: if set to YES, the control doesn't draw anything if there's only one page (`numberOfPages<=1`).

Tapping a page control object to the right or left of the current page either decrements or increments the `currentPage` property (moving forwards or backwards one page) and sends a "value changed" event.

Steppers

A stepper (`UIStepper`) has the face of `UIButton` and the heart of `UIPageControl`, as shown in Figure 10-7. It displays two buttons, side by side. Use a stepper when your user needs to increase or decrease something—"something" is up to you, the stepper doesn't display a value—one step at a time.

Figure 10-7. Stepper

Like a slider, the stepper's `minimumValue` and `maximumValue` properties set the range for its `value` property. The `stepValue` property determines what "one step" means. As an example, Table 10-1 would be the property values you'd set for a stepper with 11 possible values, between 1.0 and 6.0.

Table 10-1. Property values for a stepper with 11 possible values (1.0 to 6.0, inclusive)

Property	Value
minimumValue	1.0
maximumValue	6.0
stepValue	0.5

A stepper's visual appearance can be customized using increment, decrement, and background images, which you set the same way you do for a button. There's also a `UIButton`-ish `tintColor` property.

A stepper sends a "value changed" action every time the user taps the increment or decrement button. There are three properties that alter this behavior:

- continuous: the continuous property works just like is does for the slider.
- autorepeat: setting autorepeat to YES allows the user to continuously change the value (one step at a time) by holding down one of the buttons.
- wraps: this property lets the value "wrap" around the range. Using the example in Table 10-1, tapping + when the value was already a 6.0 would change the value back to 1.0. When wraps is YES, the buttons do not disable when the value is at the beginning or end of the range.

Segmented Controls

Closely related to steppers is the UISegmentedControl class. A segmented control displays multiple segments. Each segment acts as a button for a choice, as shown in Figure 10-8. Use a segmented control when you want the user to pick between a small number of mutually exclusive choices.

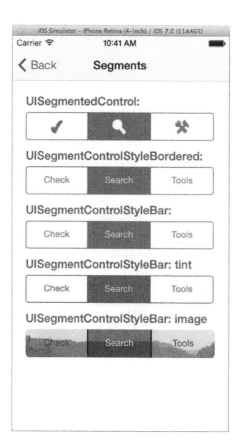

Figure 10-8. Segmented controls

Segmented controls come in four flavors: plain, bordered, bar, and bezeled. The UICatalog app demonstrates the first three. The bar and bezeled styles can be tinted by setting the `tintColor` property, also demonstrated in UICatalog.

To use a segmented control, first tell it how may segments there are by setting the `numberOfSegments` property. You can then set the label of each segment to either a string title or an image using one of these methods:

```
- (void)setTitle:(NSString *)title forSegmentAtIndex:(NSUInteger)segment
- (void)setImage:(UIImage *)image forSegmentAtIndex:(NSUInteger)segment
```

Alternatively, you can choose to insert (or remove) segments one at a time. Using these methods, you have the option of having the view animate the change, sliding and resizing the other segments to make room:

```
- (void)insertSegmentWithTitle:(NSString *)title atIndex:(NSUInteger)segment animated:(BOOL)animated
- (void)insertSegmentWithImage:(UIImage *)image atIndex:(NSUInteger)segment animated:(BOOL)animated
```

A segmented control sends a "value changed" event (`UIControlEventValueChanged`) when the user changes it. Its `selectedSegmentIndex` property tells you which segment is selected, or can be used to change that. The special value `UISegmentedControlNoSegment` means no segment is selected.

Normally, the buttons in a segment are "sticky"—they stay down to indicate which segment is selected. If you set the `momentary` property to YES, buttons don't stay down and the `selectedSegmentIndex` goes back to `UISegmentedControlNoSegment` when the user removes their finger.

Progress Indicators

iOS provides two progress indicators, `UIActivityIndicatorView` and `UIProgressView`, that provide your users feedback during time-consuming activities, or to display relative quantities (such as the amount of storage used), as shown in Figure 10-9. Use these to let your user know that your app is hard at work; they should remain calm and stay in their seats, with their seatbelts securely fastened.

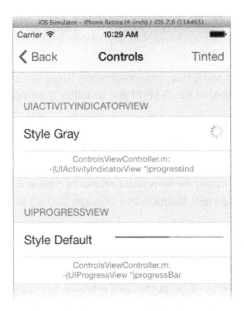

Figure 10-9. Activity and progress indicator

The `UIActivityIndicatorView` is often called a "spinner" or "gear." Use it when space is limited or the duration of the activity is indeterminate or unknown. There are three spinner styles to choose from: small grey (`UIActivityIndicatorViewStyleGray`), small white (`UIActivityIndicatorViewStyleWhite`), and large white (`UIActivityIndicatorViewStyleWhiteLarge`).

Using a spinner is easy. Send it a `-startAnimating` message to start it spinning, and `-stopAnimating` to stop it again. Its `hidesWhenStopped` and `color` properties are self-explanatory.

The second indicator is the progress bar (`UIProgressView`). It presents a progress indicator, familiar to anyone who's had days of their life siphoned away waiting on computers to finish something. The view has two looks:

- `UIProgressViewStyleDefault`: the regular style progress bar
- `UIProgressViewStyleBar`: a style designed to be used in a toolbar

You control the view by periodically setting its `progress` property to a value between 0 (empty) and 1 (full). Setting the `progress` property makes the indicator jump to that position. By sending `-setProgress:animated:` you can ask the indicator to smoothly animate to the new setting, which is less jarring for big changes.

Use the `trackImage` or `trackTintColor` properties to customize the look of the unfinished segment of the view, and the `progressImage` and `progressTintColor` properties to adjust the finished segment. The UICatalog app has a **Tint** button in the toolbar that demonstrates what happens when `progressTintColor` and `trackTintColor` are set to blue.

Text Views

Text views come in three flavors: labels, text fields, and text views. The *label* is the simplest. It's used to place a single string of text in your interface, often next to another field or view to explain its purpose, which is where it gets its name. A *text field* is a general-purpose input field, providing full-featured editing for a single line of text. A *text view* can display, and edit, multiple lines of text. Let's start with the simple one.

Labels

You see labels everywhere in iOS (see practically any figure in this book), and you've used them numerous times in your own projects. Use a UILabel object wherever you simply want to display some text, for whatever purpose. Use label object as labels by setting their text in Interface Builder and forgetting about them—no connection required. If you connect the label to an outlet, your controller can update the text, as you did in the ColorModel app.

Labels have a select number of properties that let you alter how the text string is displayed, as listed in Table 10-2.

Table 10-2. Label display properties

Property	Description
numberOfLines	The maximum number of lines the label will display, normally 1. Set it to 0 to display as many lines as are needed.
font	The text's font (face, size, and style)
textColor	The color used to draw the text
textAlignment	One of left, center, right, justified, or natural. Natural employs the native alignment of the font.
attributedText	Draws an attributed string, instead of the simple text property. Use this to display text with a mixture of different fonts, sizes, styles, and colors. The text attributes in the string override the other text style properties (font, textColor, shadowOffset, and so on).
lineBreakMode	Determines how an overly long string is made to fit in the available space of the view.
adjustsFontSizeToFitWidth	An alternative to shortening the string, it makes the text smaller so the whole string will fit.
adjustLetterSpacingToFitWidth	A third option to get a string to fit within the given space.

If you plan on displaying a variable amount of text, pay attention to the properties that control what happens when the string is too big to fit in the view. First are the `numberOfLines` and `lineBreakMode` properties. The line break mode controls how the string is broken up across multiple lines. The choices for multiple line labels (`numberOfLines!=1`) are to break text at the nearest character (`NSLineBreakByCharWrapping`) or at the nearest word (`NSLineBreakByWordWrapping`).

For single line labels (`numberOfLines==1`), text that won't fit in the view is either unceremoniously cut off (`NSLineBreakByClipping`), or a portion of the beginning (`NSLineBreakByTruncatingHead`), middle (`NSLineBreakByTruncatingMiddle`), or end (`NSLineBreakByTruncatingTail`) of the string is replaced by an ellipsis (...) character.

The alternate method of getting text to fit is to set the `adjustsFontSizeToFitWidth` or `adjustLetterSpacingToFitWidth` properties to YES. These options cause either the spacing between words, or the size of the font—you can also set both—to be reduced in an attempt to make the string fit in the available space. The spacing between words will never be reduced to nothing and its size will never be shrunk below the `minimumScaleFactor` property. If the text still won't fit, the `lineBreakMode` is applied.

> **Caution** Do not set `adjustsFontSizeToFitWidth` or `adjustsLetterSpacingToFitWidth` for a multi-line (`numberOfLines!=1`) label, or in conjunction with a multi-line line break mode (char or word wrapping). Doing so is a programming error and the behavior of the view will be unpredictable.

Text Fields

Use a text field (`UITextField`) when you want the user to enter or edit one line of text. The Shorty app used a text field to get an URL from the user.

The UICatalog app demonstrates four text fields, as shown in Figure 10-10. Consistent with the complexity of editing almost any kind of text, you have a broad range of choices when it comes to the view's appearance and behavior.

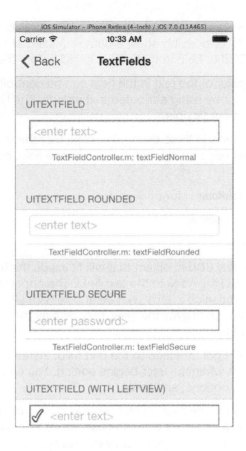

Figure 10-10. Text fields

Let's start with the appearance of the field. There are four basic style to choose from, controlled by the borderStyle property:

- UITextBorderStyleBezel: surrounds the field with a chiseled border, giving the illusion of the field being inset.
- UITextBorderStyleRoundedRect: draws a simple rounded rectangle around the field.
- UITextBorderStyleLine: draws a thin grey rectangle around the field
- UITextBorderStyleNone: does not draw a border

The UICatalog app only demonstrates the bezel and rounded rectangle style, but the other two aren't hard to imagine. You can provide a more dramatic look by setting the background property to your own UIImage. The background property overrides the borderStyle property. In other words, you can't supply a background image for a chiseled border; if you want that look, your image will need to include a chiseled border.

The `placeholder` property shows a string (in light grey) when the field is empty. Use this to prompt the user (like "Your Name Here"), or possibly show a default value. Set the `clearsOnBeginEditing` to YES if you want the text in the field to be automatically cleared before the user begins typing.

The font face, size, style, and color of the text in the field can be controlled either by setting the `font` and `textColor` properties, or by using attributed text strings. The latter is considerably more complicated and considerably more flexible.

You can also insert accessory views in three different places. Use these to add additional controls or indicators, such a button that pops up a set of options for the field, or a progress indicator. The accessory view properties are:

- `leftView` and `leftViewMode`
- `rightView` and `rightViewMode`
- `inputAccessoryView`

The left and right views can be any `UIView` object that will fit inside the text field. The UICatalog app demonstrates this by adding a `UIImageView` to the text field. The appearance of both right and left views are controlled by their companion `rightViewMode` and `leftViewMode` properties. Each can be set to never display the view, always display the view, only display the view when editing, or only display the view when not editing.

The input accessory view doesn't get attached to the text field. Instead, it gets attached to the top of the virtual keyboard that appears when the user begins editing. You can use an input accessory view to add special controls, presets, options, and so on.

Text fields send a variety of events. The most useful are the "editing did end on exit" event (`UIControlEventEditingDidEndOnExit`), sent when the user stops editing a field, and the "value changed" event (`UIControlEventValueChanged`), sent whenever the text in the field is modified. You connected actions to both of these events in the MyStuff app. To receive even more editing-related messages, and exert some control over editing, create a delegate object for the text field (`UITextFieldDelegate`). The delegate receives messages when editing begins and ends, and it can also control if editing is allowed to begin, editing is allowed to end, or a specific change is allowed to be made.

Text Editing Behavior

There are a dizzying number of properties that affect how text in a field is edited. If you look in the documentation for `UITextField`, you won't find any of them. That's because they are defined in the `UITextInput` and `UITextInputTraits` protocols, which `UITextField` and `UITextView` both adopt. The number of properties and options are almost overwhelming, so I've listed the highlights in Table 10-3.

Table 10-3. Important text editing properties

Property	Description
autocapitalizationType	Controls the auto-capitalization mode: off or capitalize sentences, words, or characters
autocorrectionType	Turns auto-correction on or off
spellCheckingType	Turns spell checking, suggestions, and dictionary lookup on or off
keyboardType	Chooses the virtual keyboard to use (normal, URL, just numbers, telephone dial, email address, Twitter, and so on)
returnKeyType	If the keyboard has a "go" key, this property determines how it's labeled: Go, Google, Join, Next, Route, Search, Send, Yahoo!, Done, or Emergency Call.
secureEntry	Hides the characters as the user types them to discourage onlookers from seeing the contents. Set this option for sensitive information, like passwords.

Text Views

Text views (UITextView) objects are the synthesis of labels and text fields. It's not a subclass of either, but it essentially inherits the capabilities of both, and adds a few extra features of its own. Whether a text view can be edited or not is controlled by its editable property.

With editable set to NO, a text view act much like a multi-line label. It displays multiple lines of text in a variety of fonts, sizes, and styles, with control over line breaks. To this it adds some additional talents: scrolling, selection, and data detectors.

Unlike a label, if the text won't fit in the vertical space of view, the user can scroll the text in the view to see the rest of it. You used this feature in the Surrealist app.

The user can select text in a text view (by touching and holding on the text). The selected text can be copied to the clipboard or used to look up words in the dictionary. In addition, you can enable data detectors. *Data detectors* are a technology that recognizes the purpose of certain text (such as a telephone number or someone's email address). The user can then tap the text to do something useful (place a phone call, address a new email message, and so on).

With the editable property set to YES, the text view becomes a (miniature) word processor. The user can type, select, cut, copy, and paste to their heart's content. All of the editing features and options described in the "Text Fields" section apply to text views. About the only thing missing are the borders; text views do not draw a border.

A text view is also capable of editing styled (attributed) text, but you'll have to supply the additional user interface elements that allow the user to choose a font face, size, style, color, and so on. The text view will handle the mechanics of applying those styles to what the user is typing, but your controller will have to tell the text view what those styles are.

Use a text view, instead of a label or text field, when:

- The user needs to edit multi-line text
- There's more text than will fit in the view and you want it to scroll
- You want the user to have the ability to select and copy text or look up definitions
- You want to use data detectors

Pickers

In iOS a "picker" is a user interface that lets the user choose something from a predetermined set. You used the image picker in your MyStuff to choose a picture from the photo library, and a media picker to choose a song from the iTunes library in DrumDub. These are both big interfaces that take over the entire user experience.

iOS also supplies a couple of smaller picker view objects. There's the specialty `UIDatePicker`, for choosing dates and times, and the customizable `UIPickerView`, for anything else. Both present a view containing a number of vertical "wheels" that the user spins to choose the value or item they want, as shown in Figure 10-11.

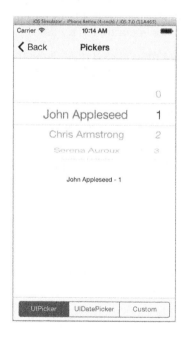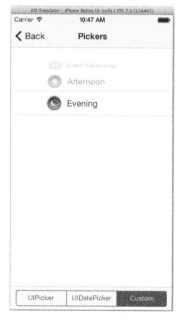

Figure 10-11. Picker views

Date Picker

Use the date picker when you want the user to choose a date, time, or duration. The date picker has four different interfaces, controlled by its datePickerMode property. This can be set to one of the four values listed in Table 10-4. The four different modes are shown in Figure 10-12.

Table 10-4. Date picker modes

Mode	Description
UIDatePickerModeTime	Choose a time of day
UIDatePickerModeDate	Choose a calendar date
UIDatePickerModeDateAndTime	Choose a date and time
UIDatePickerModeCountDownTimer	Choose a duration (hours and minutes)

Figure 10-12. Date picker modes

The picker's date property reports the value the user has selected. Setting it changes the date/time in the view. If you want to set the date and have the "wheels" spin to their new positions, send -setDate:animated:. The time portion of the date property is 0:00 when using the date-only interface. Similarly, the calendar day of the date property is meaningless when using the time-only or duration interface.

If you want to limit the range of values the user can choose from, set the minimumDate and/or maximumDate properties. For example, to force the user to choose a day in the future, set the minimumDate to tomorrow.

You can also reduce the granularity of time choices with the minuteInterval property. When set to 1, the user can choose any time or duration in one-minute increments (2:30, 2:31, 2:32, and so on). Setting minuteInterval to 5 narrows the user's choices to 5-minute intervals (2:30, 2:35, 2:40, 2:45, and so on).

> **Caution** The value of `minuteInterval` must divide evenly into 60 and can't be more than 30.

If you plan on using date picker, and your interface leaves the picker visible while time progresses, Apple recommends updating the picker in real time. For example, if your interface uses a duration picker and a start button, pressing the start button will probably cause some timer in your app to begin counting down. During that time, your app should periodically update the picker so it slowly (once a minute) changes as the time counts down to zero.

Anything Picker

What if you don't need to pick a date or a time? What if you need to pick an ice cream flavor, a model of car, or an arch nemesis? The `UIPicker` object is the catchall picker view. It looks and functions just like the date picker, except that you define the wheels and the content of each (see Figure 10-11).

A `UIPicker` uses a delegate and data source arrangement that's eerily similar to a table view (Chapter 5). A `UIPicker` needs a delegate object (`UIPickerDelegate`) and a data source object (`UIPickerDataSource`). The picker's data source determines the number of wheels (called *components*) and the number of choices (called *rows*) on each wheel. The delegate object provides the label for each choice. At a minimum, you must implement these `UIPickerDataSource` methods:

```
- (NSInteger)numberOfComponentsInPickerView:(UIPickerView *)pickerView
- (NSInteger)pickerView:(UIPickerView *)pickerView numberOfRowsInComponent:(NSInteger)component
```

And *one* of these `UIPickerDelegate` methods:

```
- (NSString *)pickerView:(UIPickerView *)pickerView titleForRow:(NSInteger)row
forComponent:(NSInteger)component
- (NSAttributedString *)pickerView:(UIPickerView *)pickerView attributedTitleForRow:(NSInteger)row
forComponent:(NSInteger)component
- (UIView *)pickerView:(UIPickerView *)pickerView viewForRow:(NSInteger)row
forComponent:(NSInteger)component reusingView:(UIView *)view
```

> **Tip** Most often, a single object is both the delegate and the data source for a picker, so the division of methods between the two protocols doesn't matter.

The first data source method tells your picker how many wheels it has. The second method is then received once for each wheel; it returns the number of rows in that wheel.

Finally (much like the table view data source) a delegate method returns the label for each row in each wheel. You have three choices for which method you implement, depending on how sophisticated you want to be with the content of each row:

- Implement `-pickerView:titleForRow:forComponent:` to show plain text labels. Your method returns a simple string value for each row. This is the most common. See the middle of Figure 10-11.

- Implement `-pickerView:attributedTitleForRow:forComponent:` to display labels containing special fonts or styles. Your method returns an attributed string for each row. UICatalog doesn't include an attributed string example, but it just means that label could have a mixture of fonts, sizes, and styles.

- Implement `-pickerView:viewForRow:forComponent:reusingView:` to display anything you want in a row. Your method returns a UIView object, which is then used to draw that row. See the right of Figure 10-11.

The last method is the most like the table view's use of cell objects. For a picker, you can supply a different UIView objects for each row or reuse a single UIView object over and over again. There's no row cell object cache, as in the table view. Instead, the last UIView returned is passed back to your delegate the next time `-pickerView:viewForRow:forComponent:reusingView:` is sent. If you're reusing a single UIView object, alter that view and return it again. If not (or the view parameter is nil), return a new view object.

If you want to control the width of each wheel or the height of the rows in a wheel, implement the optional `-pickerView:widthForComponent:` or `-pickerView:rowHeightForComponent:` methods, respectively.

Look at the code that implements the simple picker view in the UICatalog app (in the middle of Figure 10-11). You'll find it in the `PickerViewController.m` file. The code that implements the picker using custom view objects (on the right in Figure 10-11) can be found in the `CustomPickerDataSource.m` file. The view object used as the rubber stamp for each row is defined in `CustomView.m`.

UIPickerView objects are not control objects; they are not subclasses of UIControl and they don't send action messages. Instead, the picker's delegate receives a `-pickerView:didSelectRow:inComponent:` message when the user changes one of the wheels.

Image Views

You've already used enough image views to know your way around them. There are, however, a couple of properties that I'd like to mention. The first is the contentMode. This property controls how the image (which may not be the same size as the view) gets arranged. The choices are listed in Table 10-5.

Table 10-5. View content mode

Mode	Description
UIViewContentModeScaleToFill	Stretches or squeezes the image to exactly fill the view. It may distort the image if the aspect ratio of the view is not the same as the image.
UIViewContentModeScaleAspectFit	Scales the image, without distorting it, so it just fits inside the view. Some parts of the view many not contain any image (think letterboxing).
UIViewContentModeScaleAspectFill	Scales the image, without distorting it, so it completely fills the view. Some parts of the image may get clipped.
UIViewContentModeCenter	Centers the image without scaling it.
UIViewContentModeTop, UIViewContentModeBottom, UIViewContentModeLeft, or UIViewContentModeRight	The middle of one edge of the image is aligned with the corresponding edge of the view. The image is not scaled. The image may not fill, or be clipped, in the other three directions.
UIViewContentModeTopLeft, UIViewContentModeTopRight, UIViewContentModeBottomLeft, or UIViewContentModeBottomRight	One corner of the image is aligned with the same corner of the view. The image is not scaled. The image may not fill the entire view, or will be clipped if it overfills it.

> **Note** The contentMode property is actually defined in the UIView class, but it's particularly germane to UIImageView.

UIImageView also has a quirky talent: it can show a sequence of images either quickly (like a flipbook or a really short movie), or slowly (like a slideshow). Put the images you want to display into an array (NSArray) and use that array to set the animationImages property. Set the animationDuration and, optionally, the animationRepeatCount to control the speed of each frame and how many times the entire sequence plays. (Set animationRepeatCount to 0 to play forever.)

Once set up, send the view -startAnimation to begin the show and -stopAnimation to stop it again. Code that demonstrates this is in the ImagesViewController.m file of the UICatalog project.

Grouped Tables

Chapter 5 mentioned that you can create grouped table views, like those used in the Settings app. I didn't, however, actually show you how to do that. You already have all of the basics, but if you want a concrete example, look no further than the UICatalog project. Most of the sample views (buttons, controls, text fields, and segments) are presented in a group table view. Each group is a single example.

Start with the sample buttons. Its view controller is the ButtonsViewController class, which is subclass of UITableViewController. A table view controller is a UIViewController designed specifically to manage a table view. A UITableViewController is both a UITableViewDelegate and a `UITableViewDataSource`. Find these delegate methods, which define the table contents, and see how they work:

- (NSInteger)numberOfSectionsInTableView:(UITableView *)tableView
- (NSString *)tableView:(UITableView *)tableView titleForHeaderInSection:(NSInteger)section
- (NSInteger)tableView:(UITableView *)tableView numberOfRowsInSection:(NSInteger)section
- (UITableViewCell *)tableView:(UITableView *)tableView cellForRowAtIndexPath:(NSIndexPath *)indexPath

The View You Never See

That wraps up most of the important view objects in iOS. I'll talk about toolbars a little in Chapter 12 and a lot more about `UIView` in Chapter 11. But I want to mention a very special view—one that's used a lot, but you never see.

It's the `UIScollView` class. A scroll view adds the dynamics of scrolling to your interface. You never see the scroll view; you see its effects. A scroll view works by presenting a larger view inside a smaller view. The effect is like having a window into that larger view. When you drag inside the window, you are "sliding" the view behind it around so you can see different portions of it, as illustrated in Figure 10-13.

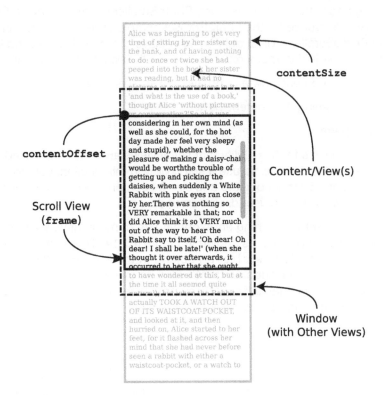

Figure 10-13. Conceptual arrangement a scroll view

It's easiest to think about a scroll view as being two views in one. For most view objects, the size of its content (called its *bounds*) and the size it occupies in your interface (called its *frame*) are the same. So a view, say a button, that's 30 by 100 pixels will occupy a region of 30 by 100 pixels in your interface.

A scroll view breaks this relationship. A scroll view has a special contentSize property that's divorced from its frame size. It's frame becomes the "window" that appears in your interface. The contentSize defines the logical size of the view, only a portion of which is visible through the window.

The contentOffset property determines exactly what portion is visible. This property is the point in the content area that appears at the upper-left corner of the frame—the portion visible to the user. contentOffset is initially 0,0. This places the upper-left corner of the content at the upper-left corner of the frame. As the contentOffset moves down, the content appears to scroll up, keeping the contentOffset point at the upper-left corner of the frame.

Table views, web views, and text views all provide scrolling and are all subclasses of UIScrollView. You can subclass UIScrollView yourself to create a custom view that supports scrolling, or you can use a UIScrollView object on its own by simply populating its content view with whatever subviews you like. You can even have a scroll view inside another scroll view; it's weird but there are notes in the *Scroll View Programming Guide for iOS* on how to do it.

A great place to get started with scroll views is the PhotoScroller example project. Search Xcode's Documentation and API Reference for the PhotoScroller sample code project and click on the **Open Project** button. The PhotoScroller project defines a subclass of UIScrollView used to display, pan, and zoom an image. This project demonstrates two of scroll view's three major talents:

- Scrolling a larger content view around inside a smaller view
- Pinching and zooming the content view
- Scrolling by "page"

The first is its basic function. It's for this ability that scroll views are most often used, which includes table views, web views, and text views. To use a scroll view in this fashion, you don't have to subclass it or use a delegate. Simply populate and size its content view with the views you want to display, and the scroll view will let the user drag it around.

The scroll view's second talent is pinching and zooming its content view, so it not only scrolls it, but magnifies and shrinks it as well, as shown in Figure 10-14. This feature requires the use of a scroll view delegate (UIScrollViewDelegate) object. In the PhotoScroll project, the custom ImageScrollView is a UIScrollView subclass that's also its own delegate—an arrangement that's perfectly legitimate, if a little unusual. UIScrollView processes the touch events and handles the most of the panning and zooming details for you.

 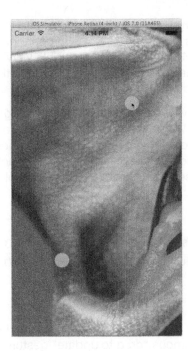 

Figure 10-14. PhotoScroller app

You can also cause the view to scroll programmatically by setting its `contentOffset` property to any point in the content view you want. If you want to make the view animate its journey to the new position, send it the `-setContentOffset:animate:` message.

SCROLL VIEWS AND THE KEYBOARD

Scroll views can contain text fields—usually indirectly, by placing a text field in a table view, which you now know is a scroll view. When the keyboard appears, it can cover up the very text field the user wants to edit. The solution is to cause the scroll view to scroll up so the text field is visible above the keyboard.

To do that, your controller will need to observe keyboard notifications (such as `UIKeyboardDidShowNotification`). These notifications contain the coordinates of the virtual keyboard on the screen. You use this information to determine if the keyboard is covering your text field. If it is, send the scroll view a `-setContentOffset:animate:` message that will cause the text field to scroll to a position above the virtual keyboard.

The mechanics of this is described in the *Text, Web, and Editing Programming Guide for iOS*, which you'll find in Xcode's documentation. Look for the aptly named section "Moving Content That Is Located Under the Keyboard" in the "Managing the Keyboard" chapter.

The PhotoScroller project also demonstrates an advanced technique called *tiling*. In the beginning of Chapter 5, I explained that an iOS device doesn't have enough memory or CPU power to create thousands of individual row objects for a table. Instead, it draws just the portion of the table that is visible to the user, as the user scrolls through the list.

The contents of an exceptionally large content view may fall into the same category. The PhotoScroller project demonstrates how to dynamically prepare only those view objects that are currently visible through the scroll view's "window." The table view—which, as you remember, is based on UIScrollView—already does this for you, only preparing the view objects for those rows that are visible in the table.

A much less common use of scroll views is to view content in "pages." This is enabled by setting the pagingEnabled property to YES. When you do that, the scroll view forces the content view (technically, its contentOffset property) to move in discrete distances, exact multiples of its frame size. Conceptually, it divides your content view into a grid (the exact size of the window) and any scrolling eventually settles on one segment. There's a PageControl sample project that demonstrates this feature.

> **Note** The PhotoScroller project let's you swipe between images, but it's not using UIScrollView's paging feature. Instead, it uses a UIPageViewController. You'll use UIPageViewController to create a similar interface in Chapter 12.

Advanced use of scroll views is not for the faint of heart. This can be really complex stuff, but it's the stuff of really cool apps. The now famous "drag to update" gesture that has become the mainstay of iOS apps is all done with scroll views and scroll view delegates. If you need this feature in a table view, most of the work is already done for you: create a UIRefreshControl object and connect it to the table view controller's refreshControl property. Now the user can drag down to update the table. To dive into the power of scroll views, start with the *Scroll View Programming Guide for iOS*.

Summary

Your command of the "language" of iOS is growing. You started out with the syntax and grammar of iOS, learning to create objects, connect them, and send messages. In this chapter you've expanded your vocabulary, acquiring an impressive number of view and control objects you can add and customize. You also saw how grouped tables are made, and got a glimpse of the magic behind scrolling. In the process, you learned how to download sample code and unlock its secrets.

You can go a long way using pre-made view and control objects. But there are limits, and at some point you're going to want a view that no one has created yet. Creating your own views is the next step of your journey, and the next chapter in this book.

Chapter 11

Draw Me a Picture

You have arrived at a critical point in your mastery of iOS development. You have a good deal of experience adding existing view objects to your app. You've had them display your data, connected them to your custom controller logic, and customized their look and feel. But you've still been limited to the view classes that Apple has written for you. There's no substitute for creating your very own view object—an object that will draw things no one else has imagined.

OK, that's not entirely true. You have created custom view objects, but in both cases I neglected to explain how they worked. Instead, there was a little note attached that read "Ignore the view behind the curtain; all will be explained in Chapter 11." Welcome to Chapter 11! In this chapter you will learn (more) about:

- Creating view subclasses
- View geometry
- How, and when, views are drawn
- Core Graphics
- Bézier paths
- Animation
- Gesture Recognizers
- Bitmaps and images

This chapter is going to get a little technical, but I think you're ready.

Creating a Custom View Class

You create a custom view by subclassing either `UIView` or `UIControl`, depending on whether your intent is to create a display object or something that acts like a control, like a new kind of switch. In this chapter you'll only be subclassing `UIView`.

Caution Do not subclass concrete view classes, such as `UIButton` or `UISwitch`, in an attempt to "fiddle" with how they function. This is a recipe for disaster. Their internal workings are not public and often change from one iOS release to the next, meaning your class might stop working in the near future. View classes designed to be subclassed, like `UIControl`, are clearly documented, usually by including a section in their documentation titled "Subclassing Notes."

To create your own view class, you need to understand three things:

- The view coordinate system
- User interface update events
- How to draw in a Core Graphics context

Let's start at the top—literally.

View Coordinates

The device's screen, windows, and views all have a graphics *coordinate system*. The coordinate system establishes the position and size of everything you see on the device: the screen, windows, views, images, and shapes. Every view object has its own coordinate system. The origin of a coordinate system is at its upper-left corner and has the coordinates (0,0), as shown in Figure 11-1.

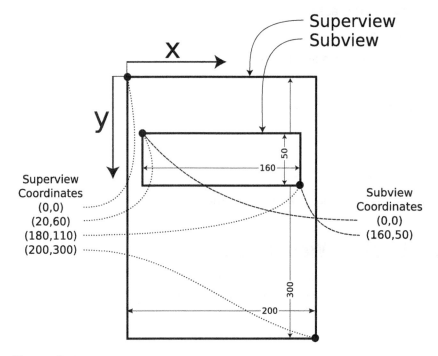

Figure 11-1. *Graphics coordinate system*

X coordinates increase to the right and Y coordinates increase downward. The Y-axis is upside-down from the Cartesian coordinate system you learned in school, or maybe from reading geometry books in your spare time. For computer programs, this arrangement is more convenient; most content "flows" from the upper-left corner, so it's usually simpler to perform calculations from the upper-left corner than the lower-left corner.

> **Note** If you've done any OS X programming, you'll notice a lot of similarities between iOS and OS X view objects. iOS, however, has no flipped coordinates—they're always flipped, from an OS X perspective.

There are four key variable types used to describe coordinates, positions, sizes, and areas in iOS, all listed in Table 11-1.

Table 11-1. Coordinate value types

Type	Description
CGFloat	The fundamental scalar value. CGFloat is floating point type used to express a single coordinate or distance.
CGPoint	A pair of CGFloat values that specify a point (x,y) in a coordinate system.
CGSize	A pair of CGFloat values that describe the dimensions (width,height) of something.
CGRect	The combination of a point (CGPoint) and a size (CGSize) that, together, describe a rectangular area.

Frame and Bounds

View objects have two rectangle (CGRect) properties: bounds and frame. The bounds property describes the coordinate system of the object. All of the view's graphic content, which includes any subviews, uses this coordinate system. The really important thing to understand is that all drawing of a view's content is performed by that view, and it's done using the view's coordinate system—often referred to as its *local coordinates*.

Moving the view around (in its superview) does not change the view's coordinate system. All of the graphics within the view remain the same, relative to the origin (upper-left corner) of that view object. In Figure 11-1, the subview is 160 pixels wide by 50 pixels high. Its bounds rectangle is, therefore, ((0,0),(160,50)); it has an origin (x,y) of (0,0) and a size (width,height) of (160,50). When the subview draws itself, it draws within the confines of that rectangle.

The frame property describes the view in the coordinates of its superview. In other words, the frame is the location of a subview in another view—often called its *superview coordinates*. In Figure 11-1, the origin of the subview is (20,60). The size of the view is (160,50), so its frame is ((20,60),(160,50)). If the view were moved down 10 pixels, its frame would become ((20,70),(160,50)). Everything drawn by the view would move down 10 pixels, but it wouldn't change the bounds of the view or the relative coordinates of what's drawn inside the view.

The size of the bounds and frame are linked. Changing the size of the frame changes the size of its bounds, and vice versa. If the frame of the subview in Figure 11-1 was made 60 pixels narrower, its frame would become ((20,60),(100,50)). This change would alter its bounds so it was now ((0,0),(100,50)). Similarly, if the bounds were changed from ((0,0),(160,50)) to ((0,0),(100,40)), the frame would automatically change to ((20,60),(100,40)).

> **Note** There are a few exceptions to the "size of the frame always equals the size of the bounds" rule. You've already met one of those exceptions: the scroll view. The size of a scroll view's content (bounds) is controlled by its contentSize property that is independent of its frame size, the portion that appears on the screen. Other exceptions occur when transforms are applied, which I'll talk about later.

UIView also provides a synthetic center property. This property returns the center point of the view's frame rectangle. Technically, center is always equal to (CGRectGetMidX(frame),CGRectGetMidY(frame)). If you change the center property, the view's frame will be moved so it is centered over that point. The center property makes it easy to both move and center subviews, without resizing them.

Converting Between Coordinate Systems

It will probably take you a while—it took me a long time—to wrap your head around the different coordinate systems and learn when to use bounds, when to use frame, and when to translate between them. Here are the quick-and-dirty rules to remember:

- The bounds are a view's *inner coordinates*: the coordinates of everything inside that view.
- The frame is a view's *outer coordinates*: the position of that view in its superview.

Should you need them, there are a number of methods that translate between the coordinate systems of views. The four most common are the UIView methods listed in Table 11-2. As an example, let's say you have the coordinates of the lower-right corner of the subview in Figure 11-1 in its local coordinates, (160,50). If you want to know the coordinate of that same point in the superview's coordinate system, send the message [superview convertPoint:CGPointMake(160,50) fromView:subview]. That statement will return the point (180,110), the same point, but in the superview's coordinate system.

Table 11-2. Coordinate translation methods in UIView

UIView method	Description
-convertPoint:toView:	Converts a point in the receiver's local coordinate system to the same point in the local coordinates of another view.
-convertPoint:fromView:	Converts a point in another view's coordinates into the receiver's local coordinate system.
-convertRect:toView:	Converts a rectangle in the receiver's local coordinate system to the same rectangle in the local coordinates of another view.
-convertRect:fromView:	Converts a point in another view's coordinates into the receiver's local coordinate system.

Also, all of the event-related classes that deliver coordinates report them in the coordinate system of a specific view. For example, the UITouch class doesn't have a location property. Instead, it has a -locationInView: method that translates the touch point into the local coordinates of the view you're working with.

When Views Are Drawn

In Chapter 4, you learned that iOS apps are event-driven programs. Refreshing the user interface (programmer speak for drawing stuff on the screen) is also triggered by the event loop. When a view has something to draw, it doesn't just draw it. Instead, it remembers what it wants to draw and then it requests a draw event message. When your app's event loop decides that it's time to update the display, it sends user interface update messages to all the views that need to be redrawn. A view's drawing lifecycle, therefore, repeats this pattern:

1. Change the data to draw.
2. Send your view object a -setNeedsDisplay message. This marks the view as needing to be redrawn.
3. When the event loop is ready to update the display, your view will receive a -drawRect: message.

You rarely need to send another view a -setNeedsDisplay message. Most views send themselves that message whenever they change in a way that would require them to redraw themselves. For example, when you set the text property of a UILabel object, the label object sends itself -setNeedsDisplay so the new label will appear. Similarly, a view automatically receives -setNeedsDisplay if it's changed in a way that would require it to redraw itself, such as adding it to a new superview.

That doesn't mean that every change to a view will trigger another -drawRect: message. When a view draws itself, the resulting image is saved, or cached, by iOS—like taking a snapshot. Changes that don't affect that image, such as moving the view around the screen (without resizing it), won't result in another -drawRect: message; iOS simply reuses the snapshot of the view it already has.

> **Note** The rect parameter passed to your -drawRect: method is the portion of your view that needs to be redrawn. Most of the time, it's the same as bounds, which means you need to redraw everything. In rare cases, it can be a smaller portion. Most -drawRect: methods don't pay much attention to it and simply draw their entire view. It never hurts to draw more than what's required, just don't draw less than what's needed. If your drawing code is really complicated and time consuming, you might try to save time by only updating the area in the rect parameter.

So now you know when and why views draw themselves, now you just need to know how.

Drawing a View

When your view object receives a `-drawRect:` message, it must draw itself. In simple terms, iOS prepares a "canvas" which your view object must then "paint." The resulting masterpiece is then used by iOS to represent your view on the screen—until it needs to be drawn again.

Your "canvas" is a *Core Graphics Context*, also called your *current context*, or just *context* for short. It isn't an object, per say. It's a drawing environment, which is prepared before your object receives the `-drawRect:` message. While your `-drawRect:` method is executing, your code can use any of the Core Graphics drawing routines to "paint" into the prepared context. The context is valid until your `-drawRect:` method returns, and then it goes away.

> **Caution** Your view's Core Graphics context only exists when your `-drawRect:` method is invoked by iOS. Because of this, you should never send your view a `-drawRect:` message and you should never use any of the Core Graphics drawing functions outside of your `-drawRect:` method. (The exception is "off-screen" drawing, which I'll describe towards the end of this chapter.)

For most of the object-oriented drawing methods, the current context is implied. That is, you perform some painting (`[myShape fill]`) and the `-fill` method draws into the current context. If you use any of the C drawing functions, you'll need to get the current context reference and pass that as the call's first parameter, like this:

```
CGContextRef currentContextRef = UIGraphicsGetCurrentContext();
CGContextSetAlpha(currentContextRef,0.5f);
```

A lot of the details of drawing are implied by the state of the current context. The graphics context *state* is all of the settings and properties that will be used for drawing in that context. This includes things like the color used to fill shapes, the color of lines, the width of lines, the blend mode, and so on.

Rather than specify all of these variables for every action, like drawing a line, you set up the state for each of the individual properties first. Let's say you want to draw a shape (myShape), filling it with the red color and drawing the outline of the shape with the color black:

```
[redColor setFill];
[blackColor setStroke];
[myShape fill];
[myShape stroke];
```

The `-fill` message uses the context's current fill color, and `-stroke` uses the current stroke color. This arrangement makes it very efficient to draw multiple shapes or effects using the same, or similar, parameters.

Now the only question remaining is what tools you have to draw with. Your fundamental painting tools are:

- Simple fill and stroke
- Bézier path (fill and stroke)
- Images

That doesn't sound like a lot, but taken together, they are remarkably flexible. Let's start with the simplest, the fill functions.

Fill and Stroke Functions

The Core Graphics framework includes a handful of functions that fill a region of the context with a color. The two principal functions are `CGContextFillRect` and `CGContextFillEllipseInRect`. The former fills a rectangle with the current fill color. The latter fills an oval that just fits inside the given rectangle (which will be a circle if the rectangle is a square).

`CGContextFillRect` is often used to fill in the background of the entire view before drawing its details. It's not uncommon for a `-drawRect:` method to begin something like this:

```
- (void)drawRect:(CGRect)rect
{
    CGContextRef context = UIGraphicsGetCurrentContext();
    [self.backgroundColor setFill];
    CGContextFillRect(context,rect);
```

This code starts by getting the current graphics context (which you'll need for the `CGContextFillRect` call). It then obtains the background color for this view (`self.backgroundColor`) and makes that color the current fill color. It then fills the view with that color. Everything drawn after that will draw over a background painted with `backgroundColor`.

> **Tip** Drawing in a Core Graphics context works much like painting on a real canvas. Whenever you draw something, you're drawing over what's been drawn before. So, just like a painting, you typically start by covering the entire surface with a neutral color—artists call this a *ground*. You then paint with different colors and shapes on top of that, until you've painted everything.

The functions `CGContextStrokeRect` and `CGContextStrokeEllipseInRect` perform a similar function, but instead of filling the area inside the rectangle or oval, it draws a line over the outline of the rectangle or oval, using the current line color, line width, and line joint style. *Stroke* is the term used to describe the act of drawing a line.

Bézier Paths

You'll notice that there are hardly any Core Graphics functions for drawing really simple things, like lines. Or what about the rounded rectangles you see everywhere in iOS, or triangles, or any other shape, for that matter? Instead of giving you a bazillion different functions for drawing every shape, the iOS gods provide you an almost magical tool that will let you draw all of those things, and more: the Bézier path.

A Bézier path, named after the French engineer Pierre Bézier, can represent any combination of straight or curved lines, as shown in Figure 11-2. It can be as simple as a square, or as complex as the coastline of Canada. A Bézier path can be closed (circle, triangle, pie chart) or it can be open (a line, an arc, the letter "W").

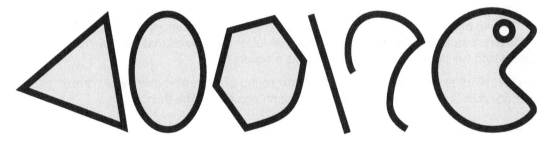

Figure 11-2. Bézier paths

You define a Bézier path by first creating a `UIBezierPath` object. You then construct the path by adding straight and curved line segments. When you're done, you can use the path object to draw into the graphics context by painting its interior (filling), drawing its outline (stroking), or both. You can reuse a path as often as you like.

> **Tip** For common shapes, like squares, rectangles, circles, ovals, rounded rectangles, and arcs, the `UIBezierPath` class provides class methods that will make a Bézier path with that shape in a single statement.

To show you how easy it is to create paths, you'll write an app that draws Bézier paths in a view. But before you get to that, let's briefly talk about the last major source of view content.

Images

An image is a picture, and doesn't need much explaining. You've been using image (`UIImage`) objects since the second chapter. Up until now, you've been assigning them to `UIImageView` objects (and other controls) that drew the image for you. But `UIImage` objects are easy to draw into the context of your own view too. The two most commonly used `UIImage` drawing methods are `-drawAtPoint:` and `-drawInRect:`. The first draws an image into your context, at its original size, with its origin (upper-left corner) at the given coordinate. The second method draws the image into the given rectangle, scaling and stretching the image as necessary.

When I say an image is "drawn" into your graphics context, I really mean it's copied. An image is a two-dimensional array of pixels, and the canvas of your graphics context is a two-dimensional array of pixels. So really, "drawing" a picture amounts to little more than overwriting a portion of your view's pixels with the pixels in the image. The exceptions to this are images that have transparent pixels or if you're using atypical blend modes, both of which I'll touch on later.

I'll explain a lot about creating, converting, and drawing images in your custom view later in this chapter by revisiting an app you already wrote. But before I get to that, let's draw some Bézier paths.

Shapely

You're going to create an app that uses Bézier paths to draw simple shapes in a custom view. Through a few iterations of the app, you'll expand it to include movement and resizing gestures, and learn about transforms and animation—along with a heap of `UIView` and Bézier path goodness. The design of the app is simple, as shown in Figure 11-3.

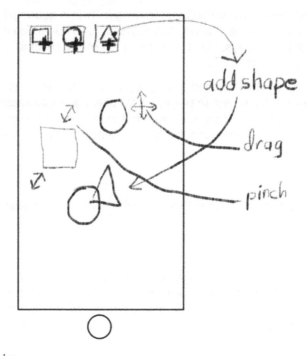

Figure 11-3. Shapely app design

The app will have a row of buttons that create a new shape. Shapes appear in the middle area where they can be moved around, resized, and reordered. Get started by creating a new project. In Xcode:

- Create a new project based on the single view app template.
- Name the project Shapely.
- Use a class prefix of SY.
- Set the devices to `Universal`.

The next thing to do is to create your custom view class. You've done this several times already. Select the Shapely group in your project navigator and choose **New File**... (from the **File** menu or by right/control+clicking on the group) and then:

- From the iOS group, choose the Objective-C class template.
- Name the class SYShapeView.
- Make is a subclass of UIView.
- Add it to your project.

Creating Views Programmatically

In this app, you'll be creating your view objects programmatically, instead of using Interface Builder. In fact, you'll be creating just about everything programmatically. By the end of the chapter, you should be good at it.

When you create any object, you must begin by initializing it. This is accomplished by sending a new instance an "init" message. Some classes, like NSString, provide a variety of init methods so you can initialize them in different ways: -initWithString:, -initWithFormat:, -initWithData:, -initWithCharacters:length:, and so on.

The UIView class, however, has what is called a *designated initializer*. There is only one init message that you should send a new UIView object to prepare it for use, and that message is -initWithFrame:. If you initialize it using any other init message, it might not work property—so don't do that. Your subclass is free to define its own init methods, but it must send [super initWithFrame:] so the UIView class gets set up correctly.

> **Note** View objects defined in Interface Builder files use a different initializer message, which is described in Chapter 15.

Your init method is going to create a new SYShapeView object that will draw a specific shape (square, circle, and so on) with a predetermined frame size. So you'll need a custom init method that tells the new object what kind of shape to draw. Your view will draw its shape in a specific color, so you'll need a property for its color too. Start by editing the SYShapeView.h interface file. Change it so it looks like this (new code in bold):

```
typedef enum {
    kSquareShape = 1,
    kRectangleShape,
    kCircleShape,
    kOvalShape,
    kTriangleShape,
    kStarShape,
} ShapeSelector;
```

```
@interface SYShapeView : UIView

- (id)initWithShape:(ShapeSelector)theShape;
@property (strong,nonatomic) UIColor *color;

@end
```

The enum statement creates an enumeration. An *enumeration* is a sequence of constant integer values assigned to names. You list the names and the compiler assigns each a number. Normally the numbers start with zero, but for this app you want them to start at 1 (kSquareShape=1, kRectangleShape=2, kCircleShape=3, and so on). The view will use these values to know which shape to draw.

The -initWithShape: method will be this class's initializer. It will create the object and establish which shape it will draw. Finally, a UIColor object property will determine the color of the shape. That was painless. Move over to the SYShapeView.m implementation file and write the init method.

Start by deleting the -initWithFrame: method that's included in the file template. You're defining your own init method, and won't be using the default one. Immediately before the @implementation SYShapeView section, add this code:

```
#define kInitialDimension        100.0f
#define kInitialAlternateHeight (kInitialDimension/2)
#define kStrokeWidth             8.0f

@interface SYShapeView ()
{
    ShapeSelector   shape;
}
@property (readonly,nonatomic) UIBezierPath *path;
@end
```

The #define statements establish three constants: the initial dimensions (height and width) of most new shape views, an alternate height for shapes that don't fit in a square, and the thickness of the line used to draw the shape.

Next, you add a private interface section where you define a ShapeSelector instance variable. This variable will determine which shape this view draws. The readonly path property will return a Bézier path object containing that shape, ready to draw.

The first method to write is your init method. In the @implementation SYShapeView section, add this code:

```
- (id)initWithShape:(ShapeSelector)theShape
{
    CGRect initRect = CGRectMake(0,0,kInitialDimension,kInitialDimension);
    if (theShape==kRectangleShape || theShape==kOvalShape)
        initRect.size.height = kInitialAlternateHeight;
```

```
        self = [super initWithFrame:initRect];
        if (self!=nil)
            {
            shape = theShape;
            self.opaque = NO;
            self.backgroundColor = nil;
            self.clearsContextBeforeDrawing = YES;
            }
        return self;
}
```

The method begins by defining a default frame with an origin of (0,0) that is kInitialDimension wide and high. It then examines the theShape parameter. If the shape being created is a rectangle or oval, it changes the height of the frame to kInitialAlternateHeight. The only difference between a square and a rectangle is the aspect ratio of the view. For rectangles and ovals, this changes the aspect ratio so it is no longer 1:1.

Now your method has enough information to send the superclass -initWithFrame:. If the superclass was successfully initialized, then your object can now initialize itself. The first order of business is to remember what kind of shape this view draws. Next, it alters a few of the UIView's standard properties.

The most important is resetting the opaque property. If your view object will have transparent regions, you must declare that your view isn't opaque. I'll explain the clearsContextBeforeDrawing property shortly.

> **Caution** If your view leaves any portion of its image transparent, or even semi-transparent, you *must* set the view's opaque property to NO or it may not appear correctly on the screen.

The -drawRect: Method

I think it's time to write your -drawRect: method. This is the heart of any custom view class. Add this method to your SYShapeView.m implementation file (replacing any -drawRect: method supplied by the file template):

```
- (void)drawRect:(CGRect)rect
{
    UIBezierPath *path = self.path;
    [self.color setStroke];
    [path stroke];
}
```

Whoa! That's it? Yes, that's all the code your class needs to draw its shape. It gets the Bézier path object from its path property. The Bézier path defines the outline of the shape this view will draw. You then set the color you want to draw with, and stroke (draw the outline of) the shape. The details of how the line is drawn—its width, the shape of joints, and so on—are properties of the path object.

You'll also notice that you didn't have to first clear the context (as I explained back in the "Fill and Stroke" section). That's because you set the view's clearsContextBeforeDrawing property. Set this to YES and iOS will pre-fill your context with (black) transparent pixels before it sends the -drawRect: message. For views that need to start with a transparent "canvas"—as this one does—why not let iOS do that work for you? If your view always fills its context with an image or color, set clearsContextBeforeDrawing to NO; leaving it YES will pointlessly fill the context twice, slowing down your app and wasting CPU resources.

Creating the Bézier Path

Clearly, the heavy lifting is creating that Bézier path object. Do that now. Add this method to your @implementation:

```
- (UIBezierPath*)path
{
    CGRect bounds = self.bounds;
    CGRect rect = CGRectInset(bounds,kStrokeWidth/2+1,kStrokeWidth/2+1);

    UIBezierPath *path;
    switch (shape) {
        case kSquareShape:
        case kRectangleShape:
            path = [UIBezierPath bezierPathWithRect:rect];
            break;

        default:
            // TODO: add cases for remaining shapes
            break;
    }
    path.lineWidth = kStrokeWidth;
    path.lineJoinStyle = kCGLineJoinRound;
    return path;
}
```

This method implements the getter for your object's path property. Its job is to return a UIBezierPath object that describes the shape this view draws (square, rectangle, circle, and so on), exactly fitting its current size (bounds).

The first two lines of code create a CGRect variable that describes the outer dimensions of the shape. The reason it is kStrokeWidth/2+1 pixels smaller than the bounds is explained in the "Avoiding Pixelitis" sidebar.

AVOIDING PIXELITIS: COORDINATES VERSUS PIXELS

All coordinates in Core Graphics are mathematical points in space; they do not address individual pixels. This is an important concept to understand. Think of coordinates as infinitely thin lines between the pixels of your display or image. This has three ramifications:

- Points or coordinates *are not* pixels.
- Drawing occurs on and inside lines, not on or inside pixels.
- One point may not mean one pixel.

When you fill a shape, you're filling the pixels inside the infinitely thin lines that define that shape. In the following figure, a rectangle `((2,1),(5,2))` is filled with a dark color. A lower-resolution display will have one physical pixel per coordinate space, as shown on the left. On the right is a "retina" display, with four physical pixels per coordinate space.

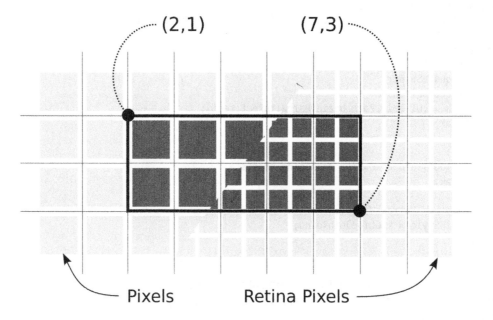

The rectangle defines a mathematically precise region, and the pixels that fall inside that region are filled with the color. This precision avoids a common programmer malady known as *pixelitis*: the anxiety of not knowing exactly what pixels will be affected by a particular drawing operation, common in many other graphic libraries.

This mathematical precision can have unanticipated side effects. One common artifact occurs when drawing a line with an odd width—"odd" meaning "not evenly divisible by 2." A line's stroke is centered over the mathematical line or curve. In the next figure, a horizontal line segment is drawn between two coordinates, with a stroke width of `1.0`. The upper line in the next figure does not draw a solid line on a lower-resolution display, because the stroke only covers ½ of the pixels on either side of the line. Core Graphics draws partial pixels using anti-aliasing, which means that the color of those pixels is adjusted using half the stroke's color value. On a retina display, this doesn't occur because each pixel is ½ of a coordinate value.

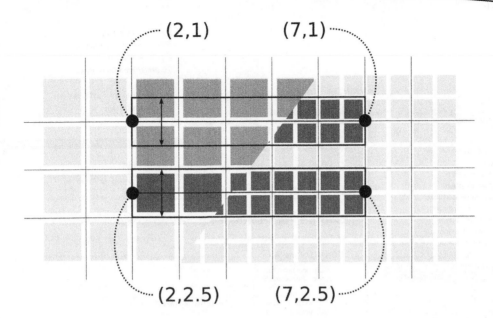

The lower line in the figure avoids the "half-pixel" problem by centering the line between two coordinates. Now the `1.0` width line exactly fills the space between coordinate boundaries, neatly filling the pixels, and appearing to the user as a clean, solid line.

If pixel-prefect alignment is important to your app, you may need to consult the `contentScaleFactor` property of `UIView`. It discloses the number of physical screen pixels between two whole coordinate values. As of this writing, it can be one of two values: `1.0` for lower resolution displays and `2.0` for retina displays.

The next block of code creates a `UIBezierPath` variable and then switches on the `shape` variable to build the desired shape. For right now, the case statement only makes the paths for square and rectangular shapes, as shown in Figure 11-4. You'll fill in the other cases later.

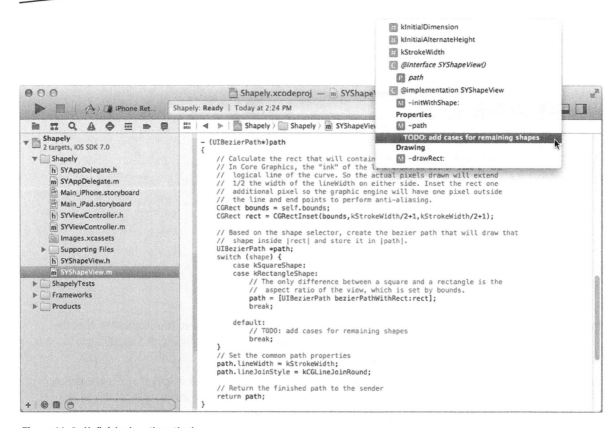

Figure 11-4. Unfinished -path method

> **Tip** If you start a // style comment with either TODO: or !!!:, that comment will automatically appear in the file navigation menu at the top of the editing area, as shown in Figure 11-4. This is a really handy way to make a note about something you need to address later, as it will appear prominently in your file's navigation menu until you remove it.

Sharp-eyed readers will notice that the code to create a square shape and a rectangular shape are the same. That's because the difference between these shapes is the aspect ratio of the view, and that was established in -initWithShape: when the object was created. If you go back and look at -initWithShape: you'll see these two lines of code:

```
if (theShape==kRectangleShape || theShape==kOvalShape)
    initRect.size.height = kInitialAlternateHeight;
```

When the view's frame was initialized, it was made half as high if the shape was a rectangle or oval. All other shape views begin life with a square frame.

Finally, the line width of the shape is set to `kStrokeWidth` and the joint style is set to `kCGLineJoinRound`. This last property determines how a joint (the point where one line segment ends and the next begins) is drawn. Setting it to `kCGLineJoinRound` draws shapes with rounded "elbows."

Testing Squares

That's enough code to draw a square-shaped view, so let's hook this up to something and try it out. The Shapely app creates new shapes when the user taps a button, so define a button to test it. The buttons get custom images, so start by adding those image resources to your project. Select the Images.xcassets asset catalog item in the navigator. Find the `Learn iOS Development Projects` ➤ `Ch 11` ➤ `Shapely (Resources)` folder and drag all 12 of the image files (addcircle.png, addcircle@2x.png, addoval.png, addoval@2x.png, addrect.png, addrect@2x.png, addsquare.png, addsquare@2x.png, addstar.png, addstar@2x.png, addtriangle.png, and addtriangle@2x.png) into the asset catalog, as shown in Figure 11-5. There are also some app icons in the `Shapely (Icons)` folder, which you're free to drop into the `AppIcon` group.

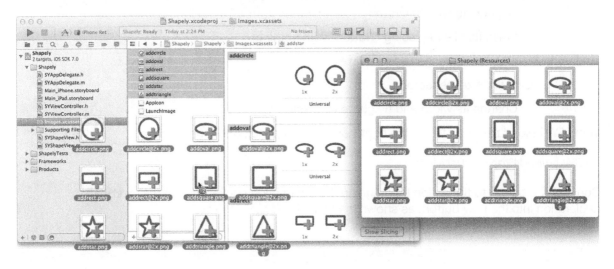

Figure 11-5. Adding button image resources

I'm going to start with the iPad interface this time and copy the finished work into the iPhone interface later. If you have an iPhone/iPod and want to play with this app on your device as you develop it, go ahead and start with the iPhone interface instead—the steps are the same.

Select the `Main_iPad.storyboard` (or `_iPhone.xib`) file. Switch to the assistant view (**View ➤ Assistant Editor ➤ Show Assistant Editor**). The interface for the interface View Controller (`SYViewController.h`) will appear in the right-hand pane. If it doesn't, select the `SYViewController.h` file from the navigation ribbon immediately above the right-hand editor pane. Bring up the object library (**View ➤ Utilities ➤ Show Object Library**) and drag a new `Button` object into your interface, as shown in Figure 11-6.

Figure 11-6. Adding the first button

Switch to the attributes inspector, select the root view object, and change its background property to `Black Color`. Select the new button again and make the following changes:

- In the attributes inspector
    - Change its type to `Custom`
    - Erase its title (replacing "Button" with nothing)
    - Change its image to `addsquare`
- Using the size inspector
    - Change its width and height to 44 pixels

In the `SYViewController.h` file (in the right-hand editing pane), add a new action:

- (IBAction)addShape:(id)sender;

Connect the button to the action by dragging the connection socket next to the `-addShape:` declaration into the new button, as shown in Figure 11-7.

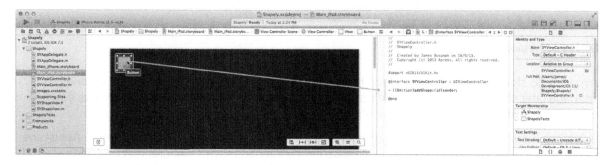

Figure 11-7. Connecting the first button

Switch to the SYViewController.m implementation file and add the action method. Begin by adding an import statement immediately after the others, so this module knows about the SYShapeView class:

```
#import "SYShapeView.h"
```

Towards the end of the @implementation section, add the new action method:

```
- (IBAction)addShape:(id)sender
{
    SYShapeView *shapeView = [[SYShapeView alloc] initWithShape:kSquareShape];
    shapeView.color = [UIColor whiteColor];
    [self.view addSubview:shapeView];

    CGRect shapeFrame = shapeView.frame;
    CGRect safeRect = CGRectInset(self.view.bounds,
                                  shapeFrame.size.width,
                                  shapeFrame.size.height);
    CGPoint newLoc = CGPointMake(safeRect.origin.x
                                 +arc4random_uniform(safeRect.size.width),
                                 safeRect.origin.y
                                 +arc4random_uniform(safeRect.size.height));
    shapeView.center = newLoc;
}
```

Your shape view is now ready to try out. The -addShape: action creates a new SYShapeView object that draws a square. It assigns it a color of white, and adds it as a new subview in the root view.

Up until this point in this book, you've been creating and adding view objects using Interface Builder. This code demonstrates how you do it programmatically. Anything you add to a view using Interface Builder can be created and added programmatically, and you can create things in code that you can't create in Interface Builder.

> **Note** The -addSubview: method makes a view the receiver's subview. The view will appear at the coordinates of its frame, in the receiver's (superview's) local coordinate system. You can only add a view to one superview at a time; a view can't appear in two superviews simultaneously. To remove the view, you send the view a -removeFromSuperview message.

The rest of the code in -addShape: just picks a random location for the new view, making sure it isn't too close to the edge of the display. Remember that SYShapeView's -initWithShape: method set the frame for the view, but its origin was left at (0,0). Unless you change that, all new shape views would appear in the upper-left corner of the view.

Fire up the iPad simulator and give your app a run, as shown in Figure 11-8. Tap the button a few times to create some shape view objects, as shown on the right in Figure 11-8.

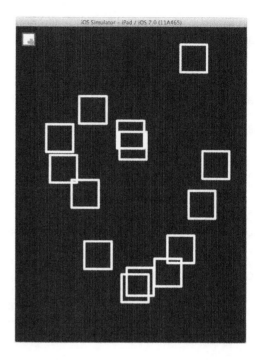

Figure 11-8. Working square shape views

So far, you've designed a custom `UIView` object that draw a shape using a Bézier path. You've created an action that creates new view objects and adds them to a view, programmatically. This is a great start, but you still want to draw different shapes, in different colors, so expand the app to do that.

More Shapes, More Colors

Back in Xcode, stop the app and switch to the `Main_iPad.storyboard` (or `_iPhone.xib`) file again. Your app will draw six different shapes, so create five more buttons. I did this by holding down the option key and dragging out copies of the first `UIButton` object, as shown in Figure 11-9. You could, alternatively, copy and paste the first button. If you're a masochist, you could drag in new button objects from the library and individually change them to match the first one. I'll leave those decisions to you.

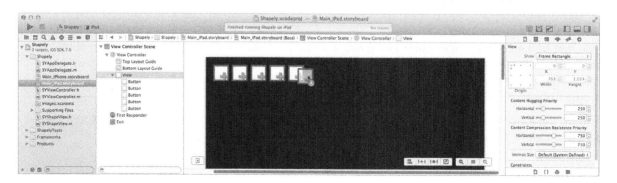

Figure 11-9. Duplicating the first button

Just as you did in DrumDub, you'll use the `tag` property of the button to identify the shape it will create. Since you duplicated the first button, all of the buttons are connected to the same -addShape: action in SYViewController. (If not, connect them now.) Working from left to right, use the attributes inspector to set the `tag` and `image` property of the buttons using Table 11-3.

Table 11-3. New shape button properties

Tag	Image
1	addsquare
2	addrect
3	addcircle
4	addoval
5	addtriangle
6	addstar

> **Note** Did you notice that you didn't add any constraints? That's because this interface doesn't need any. The buttons are never resized and they never need to be repositioned in relationship to other elements (like a navigation bar) or for different screen sizes.

You'll notice that the tag values, cleverly, match up with the enum constants you defined in SYShapeView.h. For each button to create its shape, change the first line of -addShape: (in SYViewController.m) to use the button's tag value instead of the kSquareShape constant:

```
SYShapeView *shapeView = [[SYShapeView alloc] initWithShape:[sender tag]];
```

Of course, the `path` property in SYShapeView still only knows how to create shapes for squares and rectangles, so you're not done yet. But before you leave SYViewController.m, let's make things a little more colorful. In the private @interface SYViewController () section, add an array instance variable and a readonly colors property:

```
@interface SYViewController ()
{
    NSArray *colors;
}
@property (readonly,nonatomic) NSArray *colors;
@end
```

In the `@implementation` section, add a (lazy) property getter for the `colors` array:

```
- (NSArray*)colors
{
    if (colors==nil)
        {
        colors = @[ UIColor.redColor,UIColor.greenColor,
                    UIColor.blueColor,UIColor.yellowColor,
                    UIColor.purpleColor,UIColor.orangeColor,
                    UIColor.grayColor,UIColor.whiteColor ];
        }
    return colors;
}
```

This method creates an array of UIColor objects that will be used to assign different colors to the shapes. It only creates the array once—the first time it's received. Now change -addShape: again so it assigns a random color to each new shape view:

```
- (IBAction)addShape:(id)sender
{
    SYShapeView *shapeView = [[SYShapeView alloc] initWithShape:[sender tag]];
    shapeView.color = [self.colors objectAtIndex:arc4random_uniform(self.colors.count)];
```

To draw those shapes, your SYShapeView object still needs some work. Switch to the SYShapeView.m file, find the -path property getter method, and finish it out with the code shown in bold in Listing 11-1. Oh, and you might as well remove the `default:` case from the unfinished version; you don't need that anymore.

Listing 11-1. Finished path property getter method

```
- (UIBezierPath*)path
{
    CGRect bounds = self.bounds;
    CGRect rect = CGRectInset(bounds,kStrokeWidth/2+1,kStrokeWidth/2+1);

    UIBezierPath *path;
    switch (shape) {
        case kSquareShape:
        case kRectangleShape:
            path = [UIBezierPath bezierPathWithRect:rect];
            break;

        case kCircleShape:
        case kOvalShape:
            path = [UIBezierPath bezierPathWithOvalInRect:rect];
            break;

        case kTriangleShape:
            path = [UIBezierPath bezierPath];
            CGPoint point = CGPointMake(CGRectGetMidX(rect),CGRectGetMinY(rect));
            [path moveToPoint:point];
```

```objc
            point = CGPointMake(CGRectGetMaxX(rect),CGRectGetMaxY(rect));
            [path addLineToPoint:point];
            point = CGPointMake(CGRectGetMinX(rect),CGRectGetMaxY(rect));
            [path addLineToPoint:point];
            [path closePath];
            break;

        case kStarShape:
            path = [UIBezierPath bezierPath];
            point = CGPointMake(CGRectGetMidX(rect),CGRectGetMinY(rect));
            float angle = M_PI*2/5;
            float distance = rect.size.width*0.38f;
            [path moveToPoint:point];
            for ( NSUInteger arm=0; arm<5; arm++ )
            {
                point.x += cosf(angle)*distance;
                point.y += sinf(angle)*distance;
                [path addLineToPoint:point];
                angle -= M_PI*2/5;
                point.x += cosf(angle)*distance;
                point.y += sinf(angle)*distance;
                [path addLineToPoint:point];
                angle += M_PI*4/5;
            }
            [path closePath];
            break;
    }
    path.lineWidth = kStrokeWidth;
    path.lineJoinStyle = kCGLineJoinRound;
    return path;
}
```

The kCircleShape and kOvalShape cases use another UIBezierPath convenience method to create a finished path object that traces an ellipse that fits exactly inside the given rectangle.

The kTriangleShape case is where things get interesting. It shows a Bézier path being created, one line segment at a time. You begin a Bézier path by sending it a -moveToPoint: message to establish the first point in the shape. After that, you add line segments by sending a series of -addLineToPoint: messages. Each message adds one edge to the shape, just like playing "connect the dots." The last edge is created using the -closePath: message, which does two things: it connects the last point to the first point, and makes this a closed path—one that describes a solid shape.

> **Note** This app only creates Bézier paths using straight lines, but you can mix in the messages -addArcWithCenter:radius:startAngle:endAngle:clockwise:, -addCurveToPoint:control Point1:controlPoint2:, and -addQuadCurveToPoint:controlPoint:, in any combination, to add curved segments to the path too.

The kStarCase creates an even more complex shape. If you're curious about the details, read the comments in the finished Shapely project code that you'll find in the Learn iOS Development Projects ➤ Ch 11 ➤ Shapely folder. In brief, the code creates a path that starts at the top-center of the view (the top point of the star), adds a line that angles down to the interior point of the star, and then another (horizontal) line back out to the right-hand point of the star. It then rotates 72° and repeats these steps, four more times, to create a five-pointed star.

> **Tip** Trigonometric math functions perform their calculations in *radians*. If your trig skills are a little rusty, angles in radians are expressed as fractions of the constant π, which is equal to 180°. The iOS math library includes constants for π (M_PI or 180°), π/2 (M_PI_2 or 90°), and π/4 (M_PI_4 or 45°), as well as other commonly used constants (*e*, the square root of 2, and so on).

Run your app again (see Figure 11-10) and make a bunch of shapes!

Figure 11-10. Multicolor shapes

Transforms

Next up on your app's feature list is dragging and resizing shapes. To implement that, you're going to revisit gesture recognizers, and learn something completely new. Start with the gesture recognizer.

Like view objects, you can create, configure, and connect gesture recognizers programmatically. The concrete gesture recognizer classes supplied by iOS (tap, pinch, rotate, swipe, pan, and long-press) have all the logic needed to recognize these common gestures. All you have to do is instantiate one, do a little configuration, and hook them up.

Return to the -addShape: action method in SYViewController.m. At the end of the -addShape: method, add this code:

```
UIPanGestureRecognizer *panRecognizer;
panRecognizer = [[UIPanGestureRecognizer alloc] initWithTarget:self
                                                action:@selector(moveShape:)];
panRecognizer.maximumNumberOfTouches = 1;
[shapeView addGestureRecognizer:panRecognizer];
```

The first three statements create a new pan (drag) gesture recognizer object. This recognizer will send its action message (-moveShape:) to your SYViewController object (self). The maximumNumberOfTouches property is set to 1. This configures the object to only recognize single finger drag gestures; it will ignore any two or three finger drags that it witnesses. Finally, the recognizer object is attached to the shape view that was just created and added to the superview.

> **Note** This code is equivalent to going into an Interface Builder file, dragging a new Pan Gesture Recognizer into a SYShapeView object, selecting it, and changing its Maximum Touches property to 1, and then connecting the recognizer to the -moveShape: action of the controller. And when I say "equivalent," I mean "identical to."

Now all you need is a -moveShape: action. At the beginning of the SYViewController.m file, locate the private @interface SYViewController () section and add this method declaration:

```
- (IBAction)moveShape:(UIPanGestureRecognizer *)gesture
```

Scroll down to the end of the @implementation section and add the method:

```
- (IBAction)moveShape:(UIPanGestureRecognizer *)gesture
{
    SYShapeView *shapeView = (SYShapeView*)gesture.view;
    CGPoint dragDelta = [gesture translationInView:shapeView.superview];
    CGAffineTransform move;
    
    switch (gesture.state) {
        case UIGestureRecognizerStateBegan:
        case UIGestureRecognizerStateChanged:
            move = CGAffineTransformMakeTranslation(dragDelta.x,dragDelta.y);
            shapeView.transform = move;
            break;
```

```
            case UIGestureRecognizerStateEnded:
                shapeView.transform = CGAffineTransformIdentity;
                shapeView.frame = CGRectOffset(shapeView.frame,dragDelta.x,dragDelta.y);
                break;

            default:
                shapeView.transform = CGAffineTransformIdentity;
                break;
        }
}
```

Gesture recognizers analyze and absorb the low-level touch events sent to the view object and turn those into high-level gesture events. Like many high-level events, they have a *phase*. The phase of continuous gestures, like dragging, progress through a predictable order: *possible*, *began*, *changed*, and finally *ended* or *canceled*.

Your -moveShape: method starts by getting the view that caused the gesture action; this will be the view the user touched and the one you're going to move. It then gets some information about how far the user dragged and the gesture's state. As long as the gesture is in the "began" or "changed" state, it means the user touched the view and is dragging their finger around the screen. When they release it, the state will change to "ended." In rare circumstances, it may change to "cancel" or "failed," in which case you ignore the gesture.

While the user is dragging their finger around, you want to adjust the origin of the shape view by the same distance on the screen, which gives the illusion that the user is physically dragging the view around the screen. (I hope you didn't think you could actually move things inside your iPhone by touching it.) The way you're going to do that uses a remarkable feature of the UIView class: the transform property.

Applying a Translate Transform

iOS uses affine transforms in a number of different ways. An *affine transform* is a 3x3 matrix that describes a coordinate system transformation. In English, it's a (seemingly) magical array of numbers that can describe a variety of complex coordinate conversions. It can move, resize, skew, flip, and rotate any set of points. And since just about everything (view objects, images, and Bézier paths) is a "set of points," affine transforms can be used to move, flip, zoom, shrink, and spin any of those things. Even more amazing, a single affine transform can perform all of those transformations in a single operation.

AFFINE TRANSFORMS

iOS provides functions to create and combine the three common transforms: translate (shift), scale, and rotate. These are illustrated in the following figure. The grey shape represents the original shape and the dark figure its transformation:

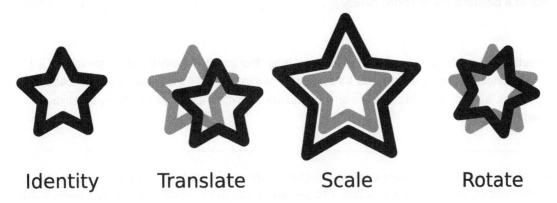

You create a basic transform using the function CGAffineTransformMakeTranslation, CGAffineTransformMakeScale, or CGAffineTransformMakeRotation. If you're a hotshot math whiz, you can create any arbitrary transform using CGAffineTransformMake.

The special identity transform (CGAffineTransformIdentity) performs no translation at all. This is the default value for the transform property, and the constant you use if you don't want any transformation performed.

Transforms can be combined. The effect of this is illustrated in the following figure:

To add transforms together, use the functions CGAffineTransformTranslate, CGAffineTransformScale, CGAffineTransformRotate, and CGAffineTransformConcat. These functions take one transform (which might already be the sum of other transforms), apply an additional transform, and return the combined transform. You would then use this combined transform value to perform all of the individual transforms, in a single operation.

The gesture cases for the "began" and "changed" states (in -moveShape:) take the distance the user dragged their finger and uses that to create a translate transform. Try to say "translate transform," three times fast. The transform property is set to this value and you're done. But what, exactly, does this magic property do?

When you set the `transform` property of a view, all of the coordinates that the view occupies in its superview are transformed before they appear on the screen. The view's content and location (its frame) doesn't change. What changes is where the view's image appears in the superview. I like to think of the `UIView transform` as a lens that "projects" the view so it appears elsewhere, or in a different way. If you apply a translate transform, as you just did in `-moveShape:`, then the view will appear at a different set of coordinates.

> **Caution** If you set the `transform` property to anything other than the identity transform, the value of the `frame` property becomes meaningless. It's not entirely meaningless, but it's unusable for most practical purposes. Just remember this: after you set a `transform` to anything other than the identity transform, don't use `frame`.

If you set the `transform` property back to the identity transform (`CGAffineTransformIdentity`), the view will reappear at its original location. Programmers call the `transform` property a *non-destructive translation*, because setting it doesn't alter any of the object's other properties. Set it back, and everything returns to where it was. In the `default:` case, this is exactly what happens. The `default:` case handles the "canceled" and "failed" states by setting the `transform` property back to the identity transform.

The gesture "ended" case is where the work happens. First, the view's transform property is reset back to the identity transform. Then the view's frame origin is updated, based on the total distance the user dragged the view. The updated `frame` permanently relocates the view object to its new location.

> **Note** The `transform` property of the view is set to the identity transform *before* the `frame` property is used to change its location.

Run your project and try it out. I didn't supply a figure, because (as my publisher explained it to me) the illustration in the book wouldn't move. Create a few shapes and drag them around. It's a lot of fun. When you're done playing, get ready to add zooming and pinching to the mix.

But before you get to that, let me share a few nuggets about affine transforms. Transforms can be used in a variety of places, not just to distort the frame of a view. They can be used to transform the coordinate system of the current graphics context while you draw your view. In essence, this use applies a transform to the bounds of your view, changing the effect of what you draw in your view, rather than translating the final results of your view. For example, you might have a complex drawing that you want to shift up or down in your view, or maybe draw something upside down. Rather than recalculate all of the coordinates you want to draw, use the `CGContextTranslateCTM`, `CGContextRotateCTM`, or `CGContextScaleCM` functions to shift, rotate, or resize all of the drawing operations. You'll use these functions in Chapter 16.

> **Tip** You can also shift the drawing coordinates of your view by changing the origin of the bounds property.

Transforms can also be used to change the points in a Bézier path. Create the desired transform and then send the path an -applyTransform: message. All of the points in the path will be altered using that transform. This is a *destructive* translation; the original points in the curve are lost.

Applying a Scale Transform

If one gesture recognizer is fun, then two must make a party. This time, you're going to add a pinch/zoom gesture that will resize your shape view. As before, start by creating and attaching a second gesture recognizer object at the end of the -addShape: method (CYViewController.m):

```
UIPinchGestureRecognizer *pinchGesture;
pinchGesture = [[UIPinchGestureRecognizer alloc] initWithTarget:self
                                        action:@selector(resizeShape:)];
[shapeView addGestureRecognizer:pinchGesture];
```

The pinch gesture recognizer object doesn't need any configuration because a pinch/zoom is always a two-finger gesture. At the top of the file add a prototype for the new action method in the private @interface SYViewController () section:

```
- (IBAction)resizeShape:(UIPinchGestureRecognizer*)gesture;
```

Finally, add the method to the @implementation section:

```
- (IBAction)resizeShape:(UIPinchGestureRecognizer*)gesture
{
        SYShapeView *shapeView = (SYShapeView*)gesture.view;
        CGFloat pinchScale = gesture.scale;
        CGAffineTransform zoom;

        switch (gesture.state) {
                case UIGestureRecognizerStateBegan:
                case UIGestureRecognizerStateChanged:
                        zoom = CGAffineTransformMakeScale(pinchScale,pinchScale);
                        shapeView.transform = zoom;
                        break;

                case UIGestureRecognizerStateEnded:
                        shapeView.transform = CGAffineTransformIdentity;
                        CGRect frame = shapeView.frame;
                        CGFloat xDelta = frame.size.width*pinchScale-frame.size.width;
                        CGFloat yDelta = frame.size.height*pinchScale-frame.size.height;
                        frame.size.width += xDelta;
                        frame.size.height += yDelta;
                        frame.origin.x -= xDelta/2;
```

```
                frame.origin.y -= yDelta/2;
                shapeView.frame = frame;
                [shapeView setNeedsDisplay];
                break;

        default:
                shapeView.transform = CGAffineTransformIdentity;
                break;
    }
}
```

This method follows the same pattern as -moveShape:. The only significant difference is in the code to adjust the view's final size and position, which requires a little more math than the drag method.

Run the project and try it out. Create a shape and then use two fingers to resize it, as shown on the left in Figure 11-11.

Figure 11-11. Resizing using a transform

> **Tip** If you're using the simulator, hold down the option key to simulate a two-finger pinch gesture. You'll have to first position a shape in the middle of the view, because the second "finger" in the simulator is always mirrored across the center-point of the display, and you have to have both "fingers" inside the view to be recognized as a pinch gesture.

You'll notice that when you zoom the shape out a lot, its image gets the "jaggies:" aliasing artifacts caused by magnifying the smaller image. The reason is because you're not resizing the view during the pinch gesture. You're just applying a transform to the original view's image. Bézier paths are resolution independent, and draw smoothly at any size. But a transform only has the pixels of the view's current image to work with. At the end of the pinch gesture, the shape view's size is adjusted and redrawn. This creates a new Bézier path, at the new size, and all is smooth again, as shown on the right in Figure 11-11.

Your app is looking pretty lively, but I think it could stand to be jazzed up a bit. What do you think about adding some animation?

Animation: It's Not Just for Manga

Animation has become an integral, and expected, feature of modern apps. Without it, your app looks dull and uninteresting; even if it's doing everything you intended it to. Fortunately for you, the designers of iOS know this and they've done a staggering amount of work, all so you can easily add animation to your app. There are four ways to add movement to your app:

- The built-in stuff
- DIY
- Core Animation
- OpenGL

The "built-in stuff" are those places in the iOS API where animation will be done for you. Countless methods, from view controllers to table views, include a Boolean animated parameter. If you want your view controller to slide over, your page to peel up, your toolbar buttons to resize smoothly, your table view rows to spritely leap to their new positions, or your progress indicator to drift gently to its new value, all you have to do is pass YES for the animated parameter and the iOS classes will do all of the work. So keep an eye out for those animated parameters, and use them.

> **Tip** Some view properties have two setters: one that's never animated and one that can be animated. For example, the UIProgressView class has a -setProgress: method (never animated) and a -setProgress:animated: method (optionally animated). If you're using the non-animated property setter, check the documentation to see if there's an animated alternative.

In the do-it-yourself (DIY) animation solution, your code performs the frame-by-frame changes needed to animate your interface. This usually involves steps like this:

1. Create a timer that fires 30 times/second.
2. When the timer fires, update the position/look/size/content of a view.
3. Mark the view as needing to be redrawn.
4. Repeat steps 2 and 3 until the animation ends.

The DIY solution is, ironically, the method most often abused by amateurs. It might work OK in a handful of situations, but most often it suffers from a number of unavoidable performance pitfalls. The biggest problem is timing. It's really difficult to balance the speed of an animation so it looks smooth, but doesn't run so fast that it wastes CPU resources, battery life, and drags the rest of your app and the iOS system down with it.

Using Core Animation

Smart iOS developers—that's you, since you're reading this book—use Core Animation. Core Animation has solved all of the thorny performance, load-balancing, background-threading, and efficiency problems for you. All you have to do is tell it what you want animated and let it work its magic.

Animated content is drawn in a *layer* (CALayer) object. A layer object is just like a UIView; it's a canvas that you draw into using Core Graphics. Once drawn, the layer can be animated using Core Animation. In a nutshell, you tell Core Animation how you want the layer changed (moved, shrunk, spun, curled, flipped, and so on), over what time period, and how fast. You then forget about it and let Core Animation do all of the work. Core Animation doesn't even bother your app's event loop; it works quietly in the background, balancing the animation work with available CPU resources so it doesn't interfere with whatever else your app needs to do. It's really a remarkable system.

Keep in mind that Core Animation doesn't change the contents of the layer object. It temporarily animates a copy of the layer, which disappears when the animation is over. I like to think of Core Animation as "live" transforms; it temporarily projects a distorted, animated, version of your layer, but never changes the layer.

Oh, did I say "a layer object is just like a UIView?" I should have said, "a layer object, *like the one* in UIView" because UIView is based on Core Animation layers. When you're drawing your view in -drawRect:, you're drawing into a CALayer object. You can get your UIView's layer object through the layer property, should you ever need to work with the layer object directly. The take-away lesson is this: *all* UIView objects can be animated using Core Animation. Now you're cooking with gas!

Adding Animation to Shapely

There are three ways to get Core Animation working for you. I already described the first: all of those "built-in" animated parameters are based on Core Animation—no surprise. The second, traditional, Core Animation technique is to create an animation (CAAnimation) object. An animation object controls an animation sequence. It determines when it starts, stops, the speed of the animation (called the *animation curve*), what the animation does, if it repeats, how many times, and so on. There are subclasses of CAAnimation that will animate a particular property of a view or animate a transition (the adding, removal, or exchange of view objects). There's even an animation class (CAAnimationGroup) that synchronizes multiple animation objects.

Honestly, creating CAAnimation objects isn't easy. Because it can be so convoluted, there are a ton of convenience constructors and methods that try to make it as painless as possible—but it's still a hard row to hoe. You have to define the beginning and ending property values of what's being animated. You have to define timing and animation curves, then you have to start the animation and change the actual property values at the appropriate time. Remember that animation doesn't change the original view, so if you want a view to slide from the left to right, you have to create an animation that starts on the left and ends on the right, and then you have to set the position of the original view to the right, or the view will reappear on the left when the animation is over. It's tedious.

Fortunately, the iOS gods have felt your pain and created a really simple way of creating basic animations called the *block-based animation methods*. These `UIView` methods let you write a few lines of code to tell Core Animation how you want the properties of your view changed. Core Animation then handles the work of creating, configuring, and starting the `CAAnimation` object(s). It even updates your view's properties so, when the animation is over, your properties will be at the end value of the animation—which is exactly what you want.

So how simple are these block-based animation methods to use? You be the judge. Find your `-addShape:` method in `SYViewController.m` file. At the end of the method and add this code:

```
shapeFrame = shapeView.frame;
CGRect buttonFrame = ((UIView*)sender).frame;
shapeView.frame = buttonFrame;
[UIView animateWithDuration:0.5
                      delay:0
                    options:UIViewAnimationOptionCurveEaseOut
                 animations:^{ shapeView.frame = shapeFrame; }
                 completion:nil];
```

The new code starts by getting the updated `frame` of the new shape view. Remember that its `frame` was adjusted when its `center` property was placed at a random position on the screen. This is the location you want the view to end up at.

The second line of code gets the frame of the button that's creating the new shape and the third line repositions your new shape view (again) so it is right on top of, and the same size as, the button. If you stopped here, your shape view would appear right on top of the button you tapped, covering it.

The last statement is the magic. It starts an animation that will last ½ second (`duration:0.5`), it starts immediately (`delay:0`), and uses an "ease out" animation curve (`options:UIViewAnimationOptionCurveEaseOut`). There are four canned curves to choose from: ease out (think of a plane landing), ease in (plane taking off), ease in-out (take off and landing), and linear (plane in flight at constant speed).

The method has two code block parameters. The first is the block that describes what you want animated, and by "describe" I mean you just write the code to set the properties that you want to change smoothly. `UIView` will automatically animate any of these seven properties:

- `frame`
- `bounds`
- `center`
- `transform`
- `alpha`
- `backgroundColor`
- `contentStretch`

If you want a view to move or change size, animate its center or frame. Want it to fade away? Animate its alpha property from 1.0 to 0.0. Want it to smoothly turn to the right? Animate its transform from the identity transform to a rotated transform. You can do any of these, or even multiple ones (changing the alpha and center) at the same time. It's that easy.

> **Note** Objective-C *blocks* are values that contain a snippet of executable code. You write a code block between ^{ and } as if it were a value (like a number). The block can be saved in a variable or passed as a parameter. Later, the receiver can execute that block of code just as if it were part of its method. Blocks are super-powerful. You can read all about them in *A Short Practical Guide to Blocks*, which you can find in Xcode's Documentation and API Reference.

The completion parameter is another code block that is executed when the animation ends. In Shapely, there's nothing else to do, since your only goal was to move the view from buttonFrame to shapeFrame. If there was, just pass a code block that does any post-animation chores. You can even start another animation!

Run your app again and create a few shapes. Pretty cool, huh? (Again, no figure.) As you tap each add shape button, the new shape flies into your view, right from underneath your finger, like some crazy arcade game. If you're fast, you can get several going at the same time. And all it cost you was four lines of code.

What if you want to animate something other than these seven properties, create animations that run in loop, move in an arc, or run backwards? For that, you'll need to dig into Core Animation and create your own animation objects; I'll show you how in Chapter 14. You can read about it in the *Core Animation Programming Guide* you'll find in Xcode's Documentation and API Reference.

OpenGL

Oops, I almost forgot about the last animation technology: OpenGL. *OpenGL* is short for Open Graphics Library. It's a cross-language, multi-platform, API for 2D and 3D animation. The flavor of OpenGL included in iOS is *OpenGL ES* (OpenGL for Embedded Systems). It's a trimmed down version of OpenGL suitable for running on very small computer systems, like iOS devices.

To be blunt, OpenGL is another world. An OpenGL view is programmed using a special C-like computer language called GLSL (the OpenGL Shading Language). To use it, you write *vertex* and *fragment* shader programs. These tiny little programs run in your device's GPU (Graphics Processing Unit), as opposed to the kind of code you have been writing, which runs in your CPU (Central Processing Unit). A GPU is a massively paralleled processer that might be running a hundred copies of your shader program simultaneously, each one calculating the value of a different pixel.

The results can be nothing less than stunning. If you've ever run a 3D flight simulator, shoot-em-up, or adventure game, you were probably looking at an OpenGL view. Even 2D games with swirling clouds, stars, or any number of special effects are written using OpenGL.

If you want to tap the full power of your device's graphic processing unit, OpenGL is the way to go—but you've got a lot to learn. You'll need a good book on OpenGL. Yes, there are whole books, thicker than this one, just on OpenGL. Your content appears in a special Core Animation layer (CAEAGLLayer) object, specifically designed to display an OpenGL context. To add this to your app, create a GLKView (OpenGL Kit View) object in your interface. GLKView is a subclass of UIView that hosts a CAEAGLLayer object. If you need one, there's also a handy GLKViewController class.

Needless to say, I won't be showing you any OpenGL examples in this book. (There's an OpenGL Game Xcode project template if you're dying to take a peek.) If that's the kind of power you want to harness for your app, at least you know what direction to go in. Start with the *OpenGL ES Programming Guide for iOS* that you'll find in Xcode's Documentation and API Reference. But be warned, you'd need to learn a lot of OpenGL fundamentals before much of that document will make any sense.

The Order of Things

While you still have the Shapely project open, I want you to play around with view object order a little bit. Subviews have a specific order, called their *Z-order*. It determines how overlapping views are drawn. It's not rocket science. The back view draws first, and subsequent views draw on top of it (if they overlap). If the overlapping view is opaque, it obscures the view(s) behind it. If portions of it are transparent, the views behind it "peek" through holes.

This is easier to see than explain, so add two more gesture recognizers to Shapely. Once again, go back to the -addShape: action method in SYViewController.m. Immediately after the code that attaches the other two gesture recognizers (before the animation code you just added), insert this:

```
UITapGestureRecognizer *dblTapGesture;
dblTapGesture = [[UITapGestureRecognizer alloc] initWithTarget:self
                                             action:@selector(changeColor:)];
dblTapGesture.numberOfTapsRequired = 2;
[shapeView addGestureRecognizer:dblTapGesture];

UITapGestureRecognizer *trplTapGesture;
trplTapGesture = [[UITapGestureRecognizer alloc] initWithTarget:self
                                             action:@selector(sendShapeToBack:)];
trplTapGesture.numberOfTapsRequired = 3;
[shapeView addGestureRecognizer:trplTapGesture];
```

This code adds double-tap and triple-tap gesture recognizers, which send a -changeColor: and -sendShapeToBack: message, respectively. Scroll up to the @interface SYViewController () private interface section and declare the new methods:

```
- (IBAction)changeColor:(UITapGestureRecognizer*)gesture;
- (IBAction)sendShapeToBack:(UITapGestureRecognizer*)gesture;
```

Now add the two new methods to the @implementation section:

```
- (IBAction)changeColor:(UITapGestureRecognizer*)gesture
{
    SYShapeView *shapeView = (SYShapeView*)gesture.view;
    UIColor *color = shapeView.color;
    NSUInteger colorIndex = [self.colors indexOfObject:color];
```

```
        NSUInteger newIndex;
        do {
            newIndex = arc4random_uniform(self.colors.count);
        } while (colorIndex==newIndex);
        shapeView.color = [self.colors objectAtIndex:newIndex];
}

- (IBAction)sendShapeToBack:(UITapGestureRecognizer*)gesture
{
    UIView *shapeView = gesture.view;
    [self.view sendSubviewToBack:shapeView];
}
```

The -changeColor: method is mostly for fun. It determines which color the shape is and picks a new color for it at random.

The -sendShapeToBack: action illustrates how views overlap. When you add a subview to a view (using UIView's -addSubview: message) the new view goes on top. But that's not your only choice. If view order is important, there are a number of methods that will insert a subview at a specific index, or immediately below or above another (known) view. You can also adjust the order of existing views using the -bringSubviewToFront: and -sendSubviewToBack:, which you'll use here. Your triple-tap gesture will "push" that subview to the back, behind all of the other shapes.

To make this effect more obvious, make a minor alteration to your -drawRect: method in SYShapeView.m, by inserting the two lines of code in bold:

```
- (void)drawRect:(CGRect)rect
{
    UIBezierPath *path = self.path;
    [[[UIColor blackColor] colorWithAlphaComponent:0.3] setFill];
    [path fill];
    [self.color setStroke];
    [path stroke];
}
```

The new code fills the shape with black that's 30% opaque (70% transparent). It will appear that your shapes have a "smoky" middle that darkens any shapes that are drawn behind it. This will make it easy to see how shapes are overlapping.

Run your app, create a few shapes, resize them, and then move them so they overlap, as shown in Figure 11-12.

Figure 11-12. Overlapping shapes with semi-transparent fill

The shapes you added last are "on top" of the shapes you added first. Now try double-tapping a shape to change its color. I'll wait.

I'm still waiting.

Is something wrong? Double-tapping doesn't seem to be changing the color of a shape? There are two probable reasons: the -changeColor: method isn't being received (you could test that by setting a breakpoint in Xcode), or it is being received and the color change isn't showing up (which you can test by resizing the shape). If you double-tap a shape and then resize it, you'll see the color change. OK, it's the latter. Take a moment to fix this.

The problem is that the SYShapeView object doesn't know that it should redraw itself whenever its color property changes. You could add a [shapeView setNeedsDisplay] statement to -changeColor:, but that's a bit of a hack. I'm a strong believer that view objects should trigger their own redrawing when any properties that change their appearance are altered. That way, client code doesn't have to worry about whether to send -setNeedsDisplay or not; the view will take care of that automatically.

Return to SYShapeView.m and add the following method:

```
- (void)setColor:(UIColor *)color
{
    _color = color;
    [self setNeedsDisplay];
}
```

This method replaces the default setter method created by the `color` property. The new method updates the `_color` instance variable (which is all the old setter method did), but also sends itself a `-setNeedsDisplay` message. Now whenever you change the view's color, it will immediately redraw itself.

Run the app and try the double-tap again. That's much better!

Finally, you get to the part of the demonstration that rearranges the view. Overlap some views and then triple-tap one of the top views. Do you see the difference when the view is pushed to the back?

What is that, you say? The color changed when you triple-tapped it?

Oh, for Pete's sake, don't any of these gesture recognizer things works? Well, actually they do, but you've created an impossible situation. You've attached both a double-tap and a triple-tap gesture recognizer to the same view. The problem is that there's no coordination between the two. What's happening is that the double-tap recognizer fires as soon as you tap the second time, before the triple-tap recognizers gets a chance to see the third tap.

There are a number of ways to fix this bug, but the most common recognizer conflicts can be fixed with one line of code. Return to the SYViewController.m file, find the `-addShape:` method, and locate the code that adds the double- and triple-tap recognizers. Immediately after that, add this line:

```
[dblTapGesture requireGestureRecognizerToFail:trplTapGesture];
```

This message creates a dependency between the two recognizers. Now, the double-tap recognizer won't fire unless the triple-tap recognizer fails. When you tap twice, the triple-tap recognizer will fail (it sees two taps, but never gets a third). This creates all of the conditions needed for the double-tap recognizer to fire. If you triple-tap, however, the triple-tap recognizer is successful, which prevents the double-tap from firing. Simple.

Now run your app for the last time. Resize and overlap some shapes. Triple-tap on a top shape to push it to the back and marvel at the results, shown in Figure 11-13.

Figure 11-13. Working Shapely app

> **Note** Hit testing knows nothing about the transparent portions of your view. So even if you can see a portion of one view in the middle, or near the edge, of the view on top of it, you won't be able to interact with it, because the touch events are going to the view on top. It would be possible to change that by overriding the `-hitTest:withEvent:` and `-pointInside:withEvent:` methods of your view, but that's more work than I want to demonstrate.

By now you should have a firm grasp of how view objects get drawn, when, and why. You understand the graphics context, Bézier paths, the coordinate system, color, a little about transparency, 2D transforms, and even how to create simple animations. That's a lot.

One thing you haven't explored much are images. Let's get to that by going back in time.

Images and Bitmaps

When you're drawing into a graphics context, one of the things you don't have access to are the individual pixels of your own creation. So you can fill the view with a color, but you can't ask the context what color a particular pixel was set to. The reason for this is encapsulation—there's that word again. Your code can't assume how, or even when, things actually get drawn. In all likelihood, your view is being drawn by a GPU into display memory your program doesn't even have access to.

This can be awkward when you want to work with the individual pixels of an image. If you need to do that, you'll have to allocate memory for those pixels. You can then manipulate those pixels directly, or use the graphics drawing function to "paint" into your pixel array.

Creating Images from Bitmaps

You already used the first method in the ColorModel app you wrote back in Chapter 8. In it, the CMColorView class was eventually rewritten to display a hue/saturation color field. It did that by constructing an image object using a formula for the colors of each individual pixel. I've extracted the topical portion of that code, which you'll find in Listing 11-2.

Listing 11-2. Image creation code from ColorModel

```
@interface CMColorView ()
{
    CGImageRef hsImageRef;
    float brightness;
}
@end

...

- (void)drawRect:(CGRect)rect
{
    CGRect bounds = self.bounds;
    CGContextRef context = UIGraphicsGetCurrentContext();

    if (hsImageRef!=NULL &&
        ( brightness!=_colorModel.brightness ||
          bounds.size.width!=CGImageGetWidth(hsImageRef) ||
          bounds.size.height!=CGImageGetHeight(hsImageRef) ) )
        {
        CGImageRelease(hsImageRef);
        hsImageRef = NULL;
        }

    if (hsImageRef==NULL)
        {
        brightness = _colorModel.brightness;
        NSUInteger width = bounds.size.width;
        NSUInteger height = bounds.size.height;
        typedef struct {
            uint8_t red;
            uint8_t green;
            uint8_t blue;
            uint8_t alpha;
        } Pixel;
        NSMutableData *bitmapData = [NSMutableData dataWithLength:sizeof(Pixel)
                                                      *width*height];
```

```
        for ( NSUInteger y=0; y<height; y++ )
        {
            for ( NSUInteger x=0; x<width; x++ )
            {
                UIColor *color = [UIColor colorWithHue:(float)x/(float)width
                                            saturation:1.0f-(float)y/(float)height
                                            brightness:brightness
                                                alpha:1];
                float red,green,blue,alpha;
                [color getRed:&red green:&green blue:&blue alpha:&alpha];
                Pixel *pixel = ((Pixel*)bitmapData.bytes)+x+y*width;
                pixel->red = red*255;
                pixel->green = green*255;
                pixel->blue = blue*255;
                pixel->alpha = 255;
            }
        }

        CGColorSpaceRef colorSpace = CGColorSpaceCreateDeviceRGB();
        CGDataProviderRef provider = CGDataProviderCreateWithCFData(
                                        (__bridge CFDataRef)bitmapData);
        hsImageRef = CGImageCreate(width,height,
                                   8,32,width*4,colorSpace,
                                   kCGBitmapByteOrderDefault,provider,NULL,
                                   false,kCGRenderingIntentDefault);
        CGColorSpaceRelease(colorSpace);
        CGDataProviderRelease(provider);
    }

    CGContextDrawImage(context,bounds,hsImageRef);

    ...
}
```

The CMColorView object keeps the finished image in its hsImageRef variable (a Core Graphics image reference, equivalent to an image object reference in Objective-C). It uses this image to draw the background of the view using CGContextDrawImage, the last statement in Listing 11-2. This is done because creating the image requires a lot of work. To avoid doing that work unnecessarily, the finished image is stored in the object and reused whenever possible. This technique is called *caching*.

The only time the image can't be used is (a) the very first time the view is drawn and (b) if anything about the view changes so that the saved image can't be used. This is what the first block of code is all about. It determines if the view has an image already, and if that image is still correct. If either isn't true, then it makes a new one.

The real work begins with the if (hsImageRef==NULL) statement. This block of code creates a new image from a bunch of individual pixel values. To do this, you must arrange the pixels in memory in a fashion that Core Graphics can understand. There are a number of formats that Core Graphics supports, but the most common is the red-green-blue-alpha (RGBA) format.

An RGBA image is a two-dimensional array of pixel values. Each pixel is represented by four (8-bit) bytes. Each byte is in unsigned integer value between 0 and 255. The first byte is the red value (or component) of the pixel, the next the green value, then the blue value, and finally the alpha (opacity) value. The first three combine to define the color of the pixel and the last determines its transparency, 0 being transparent and 255 being completely opaque.

An image that's 100 pixels high by 100 pixels wide will require a 40,000 (100•100•4) byte array. That's what the code leading up the creation of the NSMutableData object (`bitmapData`) is doing. It's calculating the number of pixels the image occupies, and then it allocates four bytes for each one (`sizeof(Pixel)*width*height`).

The next block of code spins in a loop, calculating the value for each pixel. When all of the pixels in the array have been set, it's time to turn this gigantic array of numbers into an image. That is a three-step process:

1. Obtain a color model.
2. Create an image data provider.
3. Create an image from the data provider using the color model.

The reason this is so convoluted is that there are lots of sources for image data (memory, resource files, network connections, and so on), and iOS needs to know what the color model is (RGB, HSL, CMYK, and so on). For your app, use the default RGB color model. The source of the image data is the bytes in the array you just filled in.

The function that does the work is `CGImageCreate`. The parameters describe the number of pixels in the image, the number of pixels in each row of the array (which might not be the same), the number of bytes that represent each pixel (4), the data provider, the color model, and a hint about how you want the image rendered. If you don't have any particular opinion on that matter, pass `kCGRenderingIntentDefault`.

That's it! Now you have a `CGImageRef` that's the image (object) created from the pile of pixel values in the array.

> **Tip** If you want to turn that `CGImageRef` into a `UIImage` object, use `[UIImage imageWithCGImage:myImageRef]`.

Creating Bitmaps From Drawings

You can also go the other direction—turning an image or drawing into a bunch of pixels—and there are two techniques, depending on what you want to do with the results.

The simplest, and recommended, technique is to call the `UIGraphicsBeginImageContext` function to create a graphics context using a block of memory (which it conveniently allocates for you). You only need to tell it how big of a drawing area you want.

You then immediately start drawing into the context, just as if you were responding to a -drawRect: message. All of the drawing functions work, and their results are written into the temporary memory buffer. When you're finished drawing, call UIGraphicsGetImageFromCurrentImageContext and iOS will return a new UIImage object containing the results of what you just drew. You'll use this technique in Chapter 13.

> **Note** This technique is called *off-screen drawing* because you're drawing in a graphics context that won't appear on the display, or in response to a -drawRect: message. You can initiate off-screen drawing at any time to render anything you want, and then save it in a UIImage object. You can even perform the drawing in a background thread.

When you're done, call UIGraphicsEndImageContext to dismantle the context and discard the temporary buffer.

While this technique is useful for turning any drawing into an image, it still doesn't give you access to the individual pixels of what was drawn; you can't get that from the context or the UIImage object. If you're on a pixel hunt, you'll need to use an even lower level function, CGBitmapContextCreate.

CGBitmapContextCreate creates a drawing context (just like UIGraphicsBeginImageContext), but the buffer is an array of bytes you supply, exactly as you did earlier in CMColorView. When the context is created, any drawing you perform is poured straight into that array. When you're done drawing, you can do anything with the resulting pixels that you want: count the number of black pixels, find the darkest and lightest pixel, you name it.

All of these techniques, and the extensive list of pixel formats supported, are described in the *Quartz 2D Programming Guide* you'll find in Xcode's Documentation and API Reference.

Advanced Graphics

Oh, there's more. Before your head explodes from all of this graphics talk, let me briefly mention a few more techniques that could come in handy.

Text

You can also draw text directly into your custom view. The basic technique is:

1. Create a UIFont object that describes the font, style, and size of the text.
2. Set the drawing color.
3. Send an NSString object any of its -drawAtPoint:... or -drawInRect:... messages.

You can also get the size that a string would draw (so you can calculate how much room it will take up) using the various -sizeWithFont:... methods.

You'll find examples of this in the Touchy app you wrote in Chapter 4 and later in the Wonderland app in Chapter 12. The -drawAtPoint:... and -drawInRect:... methods are just wrappers for the low-level text drawing functions, which are described in the "Text" chapter of the *Quartz 2D Programming Guide*. If you need precise control over text, read the *Core Text Programming Guide*.

Shadows, Gradients, and Patterns

You've learned to draw solid shapes and solid lines. Core Graphics is capable of a lot more. It can paint with patterns and gradients, and it can automatically draw "shadows" behind the shapes you draw.

You accomplish this by creating various pattern, gradient, and shadow objects, and then setting them in your current graphics context, just as you would set the color. Copious examples and sample code can be found in the *Quartz 2D Programming Guide*.

Blend Modes

Another property of your graphics context, and many drawing functions, is the blend mode. A blend mode determines how the pixels of what's being drawn affect the pixels of what's already in the context. Normally, the blend mode is `kCGBlendModeNormal`. This mode paints opaque pixels, ignores transparent ones, and blends the colors of partially transparent ones.

There are some two dozen other blend modes. You can perform "multiplies" and "adds," paint only over the opaque portions of the existing image, paint only in the transparent portion the existing image, paint using "hard" or "soft" light, affect just the luminosity or saturation—the list goes on and on. You set the current blend mode using the `CGContextSetBlendMode` function. Some drawing methods take a blend mode parameter.

The available blend modes are documented, with examples, in two places, both in the *Quartz 2D Programming Guide*. For drawing operations (shapes and fills), refer to the "Setting Blend Modes" section of the "Paths" chapter. For examples of blending images, find the "Using Blend Modes with Images" section of the "Bitmap Images and Image Masks" chapter.

The Context Stack

All of these settings can start to make your graphics context hard to work with. Let's say you need to draw a complex shape, with a gradient, drop shadow, rotated, and with a special blend mode. After you've set up all of those properties and drawn the shape, now you just want to draw a simple line. Yikes! Do you now have to reset every one of those settings (drop shadow, transform, blend mode, and so on)?

Don't panic, this is a common situation and there's a simple mechanism for dealing with it. Before you make a bunch of changes, call the `CGContextSaveGState` function to save almost everything about the current graphics context. It takes a snapshot of your current context settings and pushes them onto a stack. You can then change whatever drawing properties you need (clipping region, line width, stroke color, and so on) and draw whatever you want.

When you're done, call `CGContextRestoreGState` and all of the context's setting will be immediately restored to what they were when you called `CGContextSaveGState`. You can nest these calls as deeply as you need: save, change, draw, save, change, draw, restore, draw, restore, draw. It's not uncommon, in complex drawing methods, to begin with a call to `CGContextSaveGState`, so that later portions of the method can retrieve an unadulterated graphics context.

Summary

I think it's time for a little celebration. What you've learned in this chapter is more than just some drawing mechanics. Creating your own views, drawing your own graphics, and making your own animations, is like trading in your erector set for a lathe. You've just graduated from building apps using pieces that other people have made, to creating anything you can imagine.

I just hope the next chapter isn't too boring after all of this freewheeling graphics talk. It doesn't matter how cool your custom views are, users still need to get around your app. The next chapter is all about navigation.

EXERCISE

If there's a big flaw in Shapely's interface, it's that it allows the user to make shapes that are so big they cover the entire interface, and allow them to move shapes off the edge of the screen, or cover the button views. Wouldn't it be nice if Shapely would gently slide, or shrink, shapes the user has dragged so this doesn't happen? I think so too.

Here's your challenge: add code to Shapely so that shapes can't be moved off the edge of the screen or cover the add shape buttons. There are a variety of ways to approach this problem. You could simply prevent the user from moving or resizing the shape too much during the drag or pinch gesture. Another solution would be to let them move it wherever they want, and then gently "correct" it afterwards. Whatever solution you choose, make it clear to the user what's happening, so the user doesn't just think your app is broken.

You'll find my solution in the Learn iOS Development Projects ➤ Ch 11 ➤ Shapely E1 folder. (Hint: I added a -corralShape: method to SYViewController.m.)

Chapter 12

There and Back Again

Unless your app fits entirely on one screen, your users will need ways of getting around, not unlike the way people navigate cities and towns. We get around via roads, sidewalks, paths, and tracks. You'll need to lay down the "roads" between the screens of your app, so your users can easily get around too. This chapter will explore the tools and techniques for adding navigation to your app. In it, you will learn to:

- Use container view controllers
- Present and dismiss modal view controllers
- Set up a tab view controller
- Create navigation and table view controllers using storyboards
- Use a page view controller
- Learn about split view controllers

Urban planners have a proven set of solutions (expressways, one-way streets, roundabouts, intersections, overpasses) that they use to provide the best transportation solution for their populace. As an iOS app designer, you also have a rich set of navigation tools, which iOS users are already familiar with. The first step to adding elegant navigation to your app is to take stock of those tools and understand how they work together.

Measure Twice, Cut Once

Like those urban planners, you need a plan. iOS navigation, just like city streets, is difficult to tear up and replace, once built. So begin your design by carefully considering how you want your users to navigate your app. You'll need to live with your decision, or be willing to expend a fair amount of effort to change it in the future.

iOS navigation can also get complicated. Which is ironic, because the principal player (`UIViewController`) is a pretty straightforward class. The complication is not in the classes themselves, but in how they combine to form larger solutions. I think of them like the elements.

It's not difficult to explain the periodic table—each element has an atomic weight, a number of electrons, and so on. But it's quite a different matter to consider all of the ways those elements can combine into molecules and interact with one another. In this respect, iOS navigation is kind of like chemistry.

So sharpen your No. 2 pencil and get ready to take notes, because you're about to learn all about navigation: what it means, how it's done, the classes involved, and the roles they perform.

What is Navigation?

Every screen in your app is defined, and controlled by, a view controller. If your app has three screens, then it has (at least) three view controllers. The base class for all view controllers is UIViewController.

In its simplest terms, *navigation* is the transition from one view controller to another. Navigation is an activity that view controllers participate in, and view controllers are its currency. Now this is where things begin to get interesting. Navigation is not a class, per se, but there are classes that provide specific styles of navigation. While view controllers are the subjects of navigation, some view controllers *also* provide navigation, some *only* provide navigation, and some non-view controller classes provide navigation. Are you confused yet? Let's break it down.

View Controller Roles

View controllers come in two basic varieties. View controllers that just contain view objects are called *content view controllers*. This is the basic form of view controllers, and what you've mostly dealt with in this book so far. The entire purpose of navigation is to get a content view controller to appear on the screen so the user can see and interact with it.

The other kind is a container view controller. A *container view controller* presents other view controllers. It may, or may not, have content of its own. Its primary job is to present, and navigate between, a set of view controllers.

The intriguing part is that both content view controllers and container view controllers are both subclasses of UIViewController and are, therefore, all "view controllers." While a content view controller only displays views, a container view controller can present a parade of content view controllers and container view controllers, the latter of which may present other content view controllers or container view controllers, and so on, down the rabbit hole.

You won't get confused if you clearly understand the differences, and relationship, between container view controllers and content view controllers. So, let's review. Content view controllers display *only* tangible view objects. Examples of content view controllers are:

- UITableViewController
- UICollectionViewController
- UIViewController
- Every custom subclass of UIViewController you've created in this book

Note that `UIViewController` is on that list. The `UIViewController` base class is a content view controller. It has all of the basic properties and features needed to display a view, and that does not (implicitly) present any views owned by other view controllers.

Container view controllers present, and provide navigation between, the views in one or more other view controllers. Examples of container view controllers are:

- `UINavigationController`
- `UITabBarController`
- `UIPageViewController`

These view controllers present other view controllers, provide some mechanism for navigating between them, and may decorate the screen with additional view objects that enable that navigation.

So it's possible to have a tab bar (container view) controller that contains three other view controllers: a custom (content) view controller, a navigation (container view) controller, and a page (container) view controller. The navigation controller could contain a table (content) view controller. The page view controller could contain a series of custom (content) view controllers, one for each "page." Does that sound horribly complex? It's not. In fact, it's typical of a medium-sized app design, and it's exactly the organization of the app you're about to write. By the end of this chapter, this will seem like child's play.

Designing Wonderland

The app you're going to write is based on Lewis Carroll's famous book, *Alice's Adventures in Wonderland*. This seems appropriate, given the (sometimes) confounding and convoluted nature of navigation. Here's a summary of the screens in your app:

- A title page
- The full text of the book
- Some supplementary information about the author
- A list of characters
- Detailed information about each character

The key is to organize the app's navigation in a way that makes sense, is obvious, is visually appealing, and is easy to use. Think about how you would organize the content of your app while I review the basic styles of navigation available.

Weighing Your Navigation Options

To design your app, you need to know what styles of navigation are available, and then what classes and methods provide what you need. Table 12-1 lists the major styles of navigation and the principal class involved.

Table 12-1. Navigation Styles

Style	Class	Description
Modal	UIViewController	One view controller presents a second view controller. When the second view controller is finished, it disappears and the first view controller reappears.
Stack or Tree	UINavigationController	View controllers operate in a stack. View controllers modally present sub-view controllers, adding to the stack, and navigating deeper into the "tree" of scenes. A navigation bar at the top takes the user back to the previous view controller, removing the view controller from the stack, and navigation up the "tree" towards the root.
Random	UITabBarController	A tab bar appears at the bottom of the screen. The user can jump immediately to any view controller by tapping one of the buttons in the tab bar.
Sequential	UIPageViewController	The user navigates through a linear sequence of view controllers, moving one view controller at a time, forwards or backwards.
Concurrent	UISplitViewController	Presents two view controllers simultaneously, eliminating the need to navigate between them (iPad only).
Custom	UIViewController subclass	You decide.

Modal navigation is the simplest, and the one you've used the most in this book. When DrumDub presented the MPMediaPicker controller, or MyStuff presented the UIImagePickerController, these view controllers were presented modally. The new view controller took over the interface of the device until its task was complete. When it was done, it communicated its results to your controller (via a delegate message), which dismissed the modal controller, and resumed control of the interface. The presented view controller is responsible for implementing an interface that signals when it's done.

- Use modal navigation when you need to "step out" of the current interface to present relevant details, controls, or perform some task and then immediately return the user to where they were.

> **Note** On the iPad, modally presented view controllers can appear as pop-ups or overlays.

The second style of navigation is the stack or tree style, managed by a UINavigationController object. You see this style all over iOS. The Settings app is a particularly obvious example. The signature of the navigation controller is its *navigation bar* that appears at the top of the screen. It shows the user where they are, and has a button to return to where they were. When a content view controller (modally) presents a new view controller, the navigation controller adds it to the stack of view controllers the user can step back through. When used in the context of a navigation controller, a view doesn't have to provide a method for returning to the presenting view controller, because the back button in the navigation bar provides that action.

You can (within strict limits) customize the navigation bar, adding your own titles, buttons, or even controls. The navigation controller can also add a toolbar at the bottom of the display, which you can populate with buttons and indicators. Both of these elements are owned and managed by the navigation controller.

- Use a navigation controller when there are several layers of modal views, to keep the user informed about where they are, where they came from, and provide a consistent method of returning.

The `UITabBarController` manages a set of view controllers the user can maneuver through arbitrarily. Each view controller is represented by a button in a *tab bar* at the bottom of the screen. Tap a button and that view controller appears. The iOS Clock app is a perfect example.

- Use a tab bar to allow quick and direct access to functionally different areas of your app.

The `UIPageViewController` is equally easy to understand. It presents a sequence of view controllers, one at a time. The user navigates to the next, or previous, view controller in the sequence by tapping or swiping on the screen, as if leafing through the pages of a book. Apple's Weather app is the iconic example of a page view controller in action.

- Use a page view controller, as an alternative to `UIScrollView`, when you have more information than can be presented on a single screen or an unbounded set of functionally similar screens that differ only in content.

The `UISplitViewController` is a navigation controller that eliminates the need for navigation. This special container view controller simultaneously presents two view controllers, side-by-side, on an iPad. With the iPad's additional screen space, an interface that had a list in one screen and the details of an item on a second can be presented as a unified interface, creating a much simpler and fluid experience. A split view controller is part of your MyStuff app.

- Use a split view controller on the iPad to present more content on a single screen, reducing the need for navigation.

Finally, it's possible to create your own style of navigation. You can subclass `UIViewController` and create a container view controller with whatever new kind of navigation you invent. I would, however, caution you about doing this. The existing navigation styles are successful largely because they are familiar to users. If you start designing spiral sidewalks, or streets that go backwards on Tuesdays, you might be creating a navigation nightmare, rather than navigation nirvana.

Wonderland Navigation

Considering all of the available options, the design for the Wonderland app is shown in Figure 12-1. The main screen—called the initial view controller—will be a tab view with three tabs. The first tab contains a content view with the book's title and an info button that (modally) presents some details about the author.

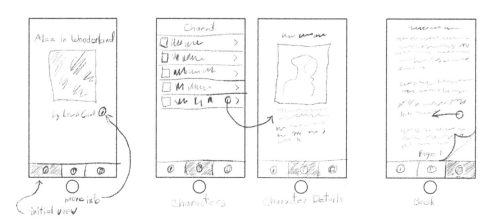

Figure 12-1. Wonderland app design

The middle tab lists characters in the book in a table view. Tapping a row transitions to a detail view with more information. This interface is under the control of a navigation controller, so a navigation bar provides a way back to the list.

The book appears in the last tab, a page view controller, where users can swipe and tap their way through the text.

Creating Wonderland

Launch Xcode and create a new project. (I'm sure you saw that one coming.) This time, create the project based on the `Tabbed Application` template. Name the app `Wonderland`, use a class prefix of `WL`, and make it `Universal`, as shown in Figure 12-2.

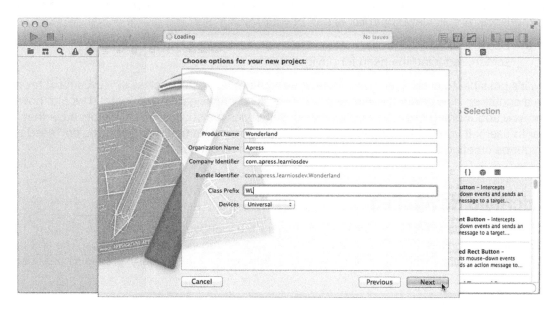

Figure 12-2. Project options for Wonderland

The initial view controller presented by your app will be a tab bar controller; the Tabbed Application template creates a project whose initial view controller is a tab bar controller. By cleverly choosing the Tabbed Application template, your first step is already done. You've created a UITabBarController object and installed it as the app's initial view controller.

> **Tip** The *initial view controller* is the view controller presented when your app starts. You can create it programmatically in the startup code of your application delegate object or you can let iOS present it for you. For the latter to happen, you need to set its Is Initial View Controller property (see Figure 12-3). You can set this in Interface Builder by checking the Is Initial View Controller option using the attributes inspector, or by dragging around the initial view controller arrow (shown on the left side of the tab bar controller object in Figure 12-3) and attaching it to the view controller of your choice.

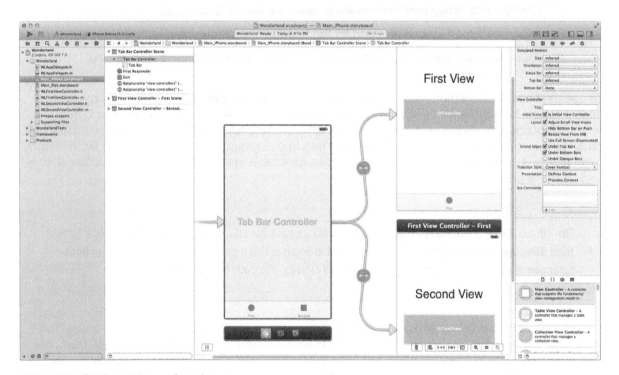

Figure 12-3. Starting tab bar configuration

Remember that a tab bar controller is a container view controller. It doesn't display (much) content of its own. Select the Main_iPhone.storyboard Interface Builder file, as shown in Figure 12-3. The big blank area in the middle of the tab view controller is going to be filled in with the contents of some other view controller. It shows that your tab bar controller comes pre-configured with two content view controllers, WLFirstViewController and WLSecondViewController.

To use a tab bar, you must provide a pair of objects for each tab: a view controller to display and a tab bar item (UITabBarItem) that configures that tab's button at the bottom of the screen. Each tab bar item defines a title and an icon. Icons smell suspiciously like resource files, so start there.

Adding Wonderland's Resources

I'm going to have you cheat (a little bit) and add all of the resources for this project at once. This will save you (me) from repeating these steps over again for each interface you're going to develop in this chapter. Just add them all now; I'll explain them later as you need them.

In earlier projects, I had you add individual resource files to the main top-level group (the folder icon) in your project navigator or to the Images.xcasset assest catalog. There are a sufficient number of resource files in this project that I'm going to have you create sub-groups so they don't become unwieldy. There are three ways you can organize source files in your project:

- Create a sub-group and then create or add new files to that group
- Import folders of source files and let the Xcode create groups for each folder
- Wait until you have too many files cluttering up your navigator and then decide to organize them

To use the first or last method, create a new sub-group using the **File ➤ New Group** command (also available by right/control+clicking in the project navigator). Name the new group and then import resource files, create new source files, or drag existing files into it. Developers tend to either organize their groups by file type (all of the data files in one group, class source files in another) or by functional unit (all of the source and resources files for a table in a single group). It's a matter of style and personal preference.

> **Tip** If you decide to use the last method, which is my personal favorite, make use of the **File ➤ New Group from Selection** command. Select the files you want to organize into a group and choose **New Group from Selection**. It creates a new sub-group and moves all of those items into it, in one step.

The middle method is handy when you're importing a large number of resource files at once. Find the Learn iOS Development Projects ➤ Ch 12 ➤ Wonderland (Resources) folder. These resource files have been organized into subfolders: Data Resources, Character Images, Info Images, and Tab Images. Instead of dragging the individual files into the project navigator, you'll drag the folders into your project, importing all of the resource files at once. Begin with the data (non-image) files in the Data Resources folder. Drag that folder and drop it into the Wonderland group, as shown in Figure 12-4.

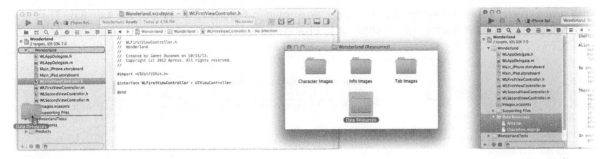

Figure 12-4. Adding a folder of resource files

When the import dialog appears, make sure the Create groups for any added folders option is selected. This will turn each folder's worth of resource files into group, as shown on the right in Figure 12-4.

To do something similar for your images, choose the Images.xcassets asset catalog item and drag all three folders of images (Character Images, Info Images, and Tab Images) into the catalog's group column, as shown in Figure 12-5. This will automatically create three groups of images, as shown on the right of Figure 12-5.

Figure 12-5. Importing groups of image files

In the interests of neatness, let's discard some detritus you don't need. Select the first and second image sets in the asset catalog. While holding down the command key, press the delete key (or choose **Edit ➤ Delete**) to remove these items from your project.

> **Note** You'll also find some app icons in the Wonderland (Icons) folder. Drop those into the AppIcon image set, if you like.

Configuring a Tab Bar Item

Now that you have all of your resources, configure the tab bar for the first tab. Each tab button in the tab bar is configured via a UITabBarItem object associated with its view controller. You'll find this object in the scene that defines that view controller. Select the Main_iPad.storyboard (or _iPhone) file.

Find and expand the first view controller group, as shown in Figure 12-6. Select the `Tab Bar Item - First` object and use the attributes inspector to change its title to "Welcome" and set its image to `tab-info`.

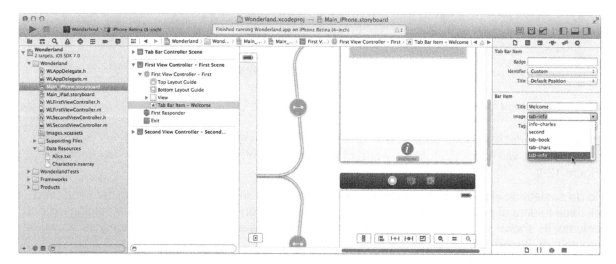

Figure 12-6. *Configuring a tab bar item*

> **Note** The image for the tab bar button is not displayed "as is." The image you supply is used like a stencil, creating a silhouette from the opaque pixels of the image. So don't bother designing your tab bar button images with pretty colors, only the transparency matters.

You'll repeat these steps for each content view you add to the tab bar. Now move on to the content for this first tab.

The First Content View Controller

The first tab presents a simple content view controller, based on `UIViewController`. The Xcode template has already created a custom view controller (`WLFirstViewController`) and attached it as the contents of the first tab. This is almost exactly what you want, so gut it and make it your own.

Select the `Main_iPad.storyboard` (or `_iPhone`) file. Double-click on the first view controller (upper-right) in the canvas to make it the focus. The view already contains some label and text view objects. Select these and delete them.

> **Note** You'll start out by editing the iPad version of the interface, mostly so I can demonstrate a few iPad-only features. Later I'll switch to the iPhone version, because it's easier to see. The steps for developing both interfaces are the same. So except for the few iPad-specific bits, follow the steps using either the iPad or iPhone interface. To develop the other one, come back and do the same steps again.

Using the object library, add two labels and one image view object. Using the attributes and size inspectors, set their properties as follows:

1. First label
   a. Text: `Alice's Adventures in Wonderland`
   b. Font: `System 30.0` (iPad), `System 16.0` (iPhone)
2. Second Label
   a. Text: `by Lewis Carroll`
   b. Font: `System 20.0` (iPad), `System 13.0` (iPhone)
3. Image View
   a. Image: `info-alice`
   b. Mode: `Aspect Fit`
   c. Size: 480x480 (iPad), 320x320 (iPhone)

> **Tip** After changing the text, font, or image of an object, if its content no longer exactly fits its dimensions, select it and use the **Editor ➤ Size to Fit Contents** command. It will resize the object so it's exactly the same size as the image or text it contains.

Arrange the views so they look something like those in Figure 12-7. You're going to add an "info" button and have that present a modal view controller. Start by adding the button. Drag a `Button` object into your interface. Use the attributes inspector to change the type to `Info Dark`, and position it just to the right of the "by Lewis Carroll" label, also shown in Figure 12-7.

378   CHAPTER 12: There and Back Again

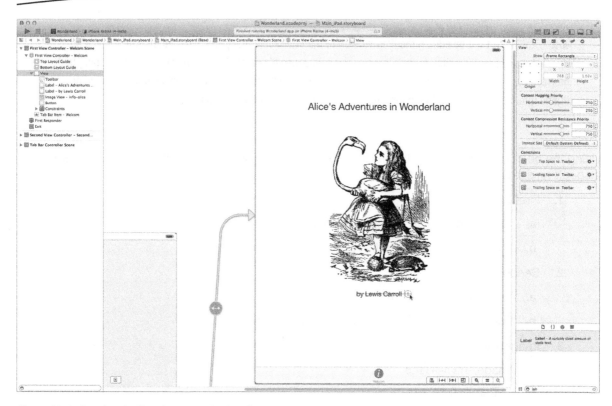

Figure 12-7. Creating the first view controller interface

Presenting a Modal View Controller

To present a view controller, you need a view controller to present. From the object library, drag in a plain-vanilla view controller object, positioning it to the right of the first view controller.

Create a modal transition by right/control-clicking on the dark gray info button and dragging it to the view controller you just added, as shown in Figure 12-8. When you release the mouse, choose `modal` from the list of styles.

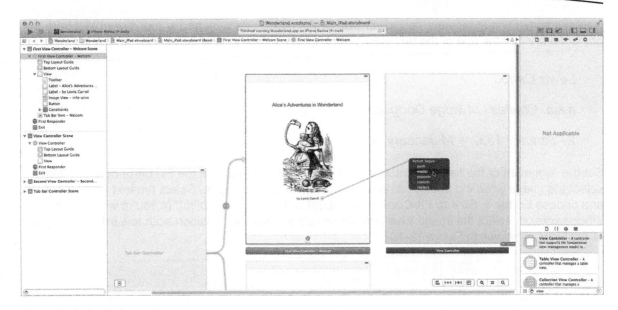

***Figure 12-8.** Creating a modal segue*

What just happened is this. Interface Builder has connected the button to a storyboard segue, which it created for this purpose. The segue is configured to perform a modal transition. If you were doing this programmatically, you would connect the button to your own action method which would send the first view controller a -presentViewController:animated:completed: message. Using a storyboard segue saves you from having to create an action and write that code.

Select the storyboard segue by clicking on the segue line, or the circle in the middle of the segue line, as shown in Figure 12-9. Using the attributes inspector, change the presentation to Form Sheet and the transition to Flip Horizontal.

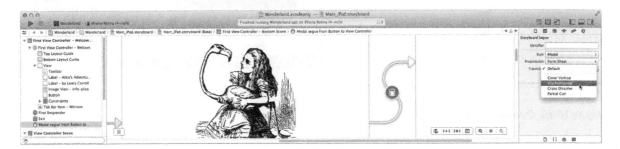

***Figure 12-9.** Editing a segue*

Now put something in the new view controller. Drag in an image view and a text view object from the object library. Set the text of the text view (using option+return to insert carriage returns) to:

Lewis Carroll

a.k.a. Charles Lutwidge Dodgson

27 January 1832 – 14 January 1898

Set the alignment of the field to centered (middle button) and uncheck the `Editable` behavior. Now select the image view and change its image property to `info-charles`. Select the text field object and choose **Editor ➤ Size to Fit Contents**. Repeat with the image object. (If you're working on the iPhone version, select the image view and set its size to `164x244`.) Position both towards the bottom of the view, as shown in Figure 12-10.

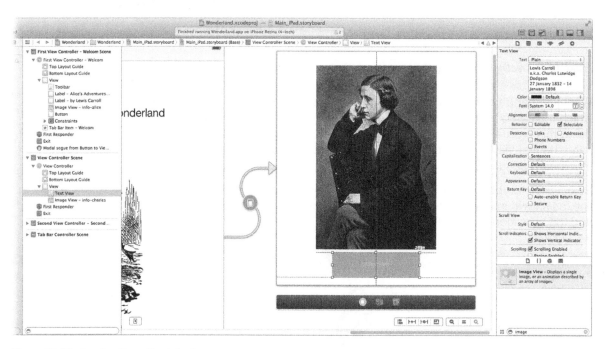

Figure 12-10. Creating the author info view

Set the project's scheme to use an iPad Simulator and run the project. The first view controller appears in the first tab of your app. Tapping the gray info button triggers a transition to the view controller you just created, making it appear in a "form sheet" floating above the screen. Isn't that cool?

It would be even cooler if the app wasn't stuck now. When presenting a view controller modally, you're responsible for providing the interface that will return the user to the previous view controller. Add that now.

Dismissing a View Controller

The controller that presents a view controller is normally responsible for dismissing it. You've already done this in your DrumDub and MyStuff apps. You presented a modal picker view controller that allowed the user to pick an image or song. When it was done, it sent your view controller a delegate message with the choice. That method retrieved the image/song and then sent itself a `-dismissViewControllerAnimated:completion:` message, causing the picker interface to retract.

If your modal view controller did something similar (let the user pick a planet to invade, or a pattern for their bowling ball), you'd create a delegate protocol—I explain how in Chapter 20—and send a completion message when your modal view controller was done. The presenting view controller would then dismiss it.

That, however, sounds like a lot of work and I'm quite fond of not doing too much work. In this situation, there's no information that needs to be sent back to the presenting controller. You just want the modal view controller to go away. For that, there's a simple solution.

In your project navigator, create a new Objective-C source file (**File ➤ New File**...). Base it on the Objective-C class template. Name it `WLAuthorInfoViewController`. Make it a subclass of `UIViewController`. Make sure the `With XIB for user interface` option is *not* checked. Create the new file.

> **Note** You don't need the XIB (Interface Builder) file for your new class because you've already created one for it in the storyboard file.

Select the `WLAuthorInfoViewController.h` interface file. In the `@interface` section, add an action method declaration:

```
- (IBAction)done:(id)sender;
```

In the `WLAuthorInfoViewController.m` implementation file, add the method to the `@implementation` section:

```
- (IBAction)done:(id)sender
{
    [self.presentingViewController dismissViewControllerAnimated:YES
                                                      completion:nil];
}
```

Return to the `Main_iPad.storyboard` file. Select the view controller in the view controller scene you just created (by clicking on the view controller object in the outline or the dock at the bottom of the scene) and use the identity inspector to change its class from `UIViewController` to `WLAuthorInfoViewController`. Add a button to the interface and change its title to "Done". (For the iPhone interface, you may want to rearrange the views a little.) Right/control-drag from the button to the view controller's placeholder object, as shown in Figure 12-11. Connect the button to the `-done:` action. When using storyboards, the key view controller objects for each scene are conveniently located below that scene, as well as in the outline.

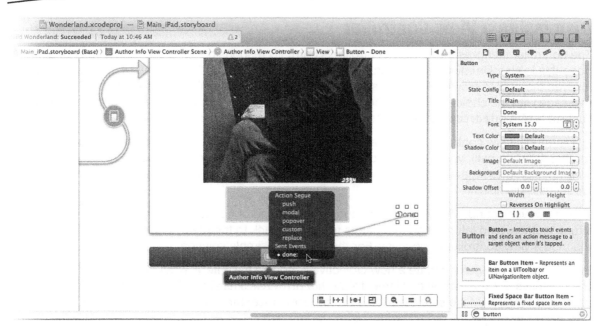

Figure 12-11. Connecting the "Done" button

Run the project again. Tap the info button and the modal view controller appears. Tap the "done" button, and it disappears again. How does it work? It's simple.

When one view controller presents another view controller, a relationship is formed. The initial view controller's presentedViewController property is set to the view controller it just presented. The presented view controller's presentingViewController property is, reflexively, set to the view controller that presented it. The -done: method simply gets the view controller that presented it from its presentingViewController property, and sends that object a -dismissViewControllerAnimated: completed: message on its behalf.

The "form sheet" presentation style is only applicable to the iPad. The iPhone version of the segue doesn't even have a presentation property. Since this is an app about a book, and you want both versions (iPhone and iPad) to work similarly, choose a modal presentation style that works on both devices and is a little more thematic.

Return to the Main_iPad.storyboard file and select the storyboard segue between the info button and the author info view controller. Use the attributes inspector and change the presentation to Default and the transition to Partial Curl. If you're in the iPhone interface, just set the transition to Partial Curl.

> **Note** When you change the presentation style of the segue, Interface Builder will resize the view controller layout size to match its best guess of the interface's size when presented. You may need to rearrange the view objects so they are still nestled at the bottom of the view. Use the **Editor ➤ Pin ➤ Height/Width** commands to fix the size of the image view and **Editor ➤ Pin ➤ Height** to fix the height of the text view. With those constraints added, choose **Editor ➤ Resolve Auto Layout Issues ➤ Add Missing Constraints in Author Info View Controller** to establish the rest of your layout.

Run the app again. Now tap the info button and see what happens, shown in Figure 12-12. That's pretty slick! This effect works for both the iPad and the iPhone, as shown on the right in Figure 12-12.

Figure 12-12. Partial Curl transition for iPad and iPhone

Congratulations! The first third of your Wonderland app is finished. You've created a custom view controller that presents a second view controller modally, and wrote the necessary code to dismiss that view controller when it's done. There are lots of different transition styles to choose from, but the basic formula for modally presenting and dismissing a view controller remains the same. Now you're ready to move on to the second tab.

Creating a Navigable Table View

The second tab of your Wonderland app presents a list of characters in a table view. Tapping a row navigates to a screen with some character details. Does this sound familiar? It should. You already built this app in Chapter 5. Well, you get to build it again. But this time, the focus is going to be on navigation.

You know from Chapter 5 that you're going to need:

- A navigation view controller
- A custom subclass of `UITableViewController` (for the table view)
- A data model
- A table view delegate object
- A data source object
- A table view cell object
- A custom subclass of `UIViewController` (for the detail view)
- View objects to display the detail view

Start with the navigation view controller. A navigation view controller is a container view controller. The view it initially displays is its *root view controller*. This view is its home base; the view that all navigation starts from, and eventually returns back to. To have the second tab of the Wonderland app present a navigable table view, you need to install a navigation controller as the second view controller in the tab bar, and then install a table view controller as the root view controller of the navigation controller. This is easier than it sounds.

Start by clearing some room. Select the `Main_iPhone.storyboard` (or `_iPad`) file. A `WLSecondViewController` already occupies the second tab. You don't need it. Select the second view controller scene in the Interface Builder canvas and delete it. Then select the `WLSecondViewController.h` and `WLSecondViewController.m` files and delete them too.

> **Note** This is the point where I'm switching to the iPhone interface, so that the illustrations are easier to see. If you want to continue developing the iPad interface, that's fine. Or, you can repeat the iPad interface changes in the iPhone storyboard and continue with that. It's your choice.

From the object library, drag in a navigation controller and place it underneath the first view controller, as shown in Figure 12-13. A new navigation controller comes pre-installed with a table view controller, which is exactly what you want. (See, I told you this wouldn't be too hard.) You'll also need a detail view, so drop in another view controller object next to the table view.

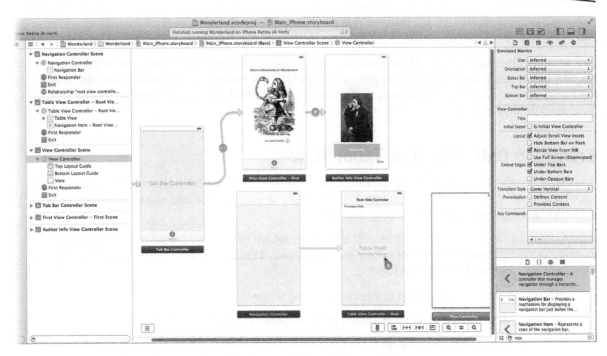

Figure 12-13. Adding a navigation controller, table view controller, and view controller

To add the navigation controller to the tab bar, right/control-drag from the tab bar controller to the navigation controller, as shown in Figure 12-14. When the pop-up appears, find the Relationship Segue category and choose view controllers. This special connection adds the view controller to the collection of controllers that the container view controller manages. A second tab appears in the tab view, and a companion tab bar item object is added to the navigation controller's scene.

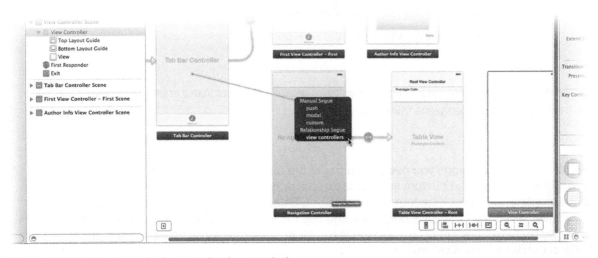

Figure 12-14. Making the navigation controller the second tab

Expand the `Navigation Controller` group in the navigation controller's outline and select the tab bar item. Use the attributes inspector to set the title to "Characters" and the image to `tab-chars`.

You've now added a navigable table view to your tab bar (container view) controller. It's the second tab. It has a title and icon. Tapping it will present the table (content) view controller inside the navigation (container view) controller. It sounds complicated, but the storyboard makes the organization easy to follow.

Breathing Data Into Your Table View

You can run your app right now, tap on the `Characters` tab, and marvel at the raging emptiness of your table view. You know, from Chapter 5, that without a data source and some data your table view has nothing to display. Let's tackle that now.

You're going to need a custom subclass of `UITableViewController`, so create one. You also know that you're going to need a custom subclass of `UIViewController` for your detail view. While you're here, you might as well create that too:

1. In the Wonderland group of the project, add a new file
    a. Use the **iOS ➤ Cocoa Touch ➤ Objective-C** class template
    b. Name the class `WLCharacterTableViewController`
    c. Make it a subclass of `UITableViewController`
    d. Do not create an XIB file for the new controller
2. Add a second new file:
    a. Use the Objective-C class template
    b. Name the class `WLCharacterDetailViewController`
    c. Make it a subclass of `UIViewController`
    d. Do not create an XIB file for the new controller

> **Note** A view controller can load its interface from a separate XIB file or from a scene in a storyboard file, but not both. For this project you're using a storyboard file.

Reviewing the list of things you need to do to get the table view working, you now have a navigation controller and custom subclasses of the table and view controllers. But the objects in the interface aren't your custom subclasses yet. Select the `Main_iPhone.storyboard` (or `_iPad`) file, select the table view controller, and use the identity inspector to change its class to `WLCharacterTableViewController`. Do the same for the detail view controller, making its class `WLCharacterDetailViewController`.

Creating the Detail View

Since you're already in the character detail view controller, go ahead and create its interface. Use the object library to add a label, an image view, and a text view to the character detail view controller, as follows:

1. Label
    a. Make its width 420 (iPad) or 280 (iPhone)
    b. Set alignment to centered (the middle button)
    c. Pin the height (**Editor ➤ Pin ➤ Height**)
2. Image View
    a. Make its size 420x420 (iPad) or 280x280 (iPhone)
    b. Set mode to Aspect Fit
    c. Pin the height (**Editor ➤ Pin ➤ Height**)
3. Text View
    a. Make its size 420x100 (iPad) or 280x100 (iPhone)
4. Constraints (Universal)
    a. Position the three views so they are centered in the view and stacked vertically, approximately like those shown in Figure 12-15.
    b. Select all three view objects (label, image view, and text view) using the shift key or by dragging out a selection rectangle
    c. **Choose Editor ➤ Pin ➤ Width**
    d. Select all three view objects
    e. Choose **Editor ➤ Align ➤ Horizontal Center in Container** (not **Horizontal Center**!)

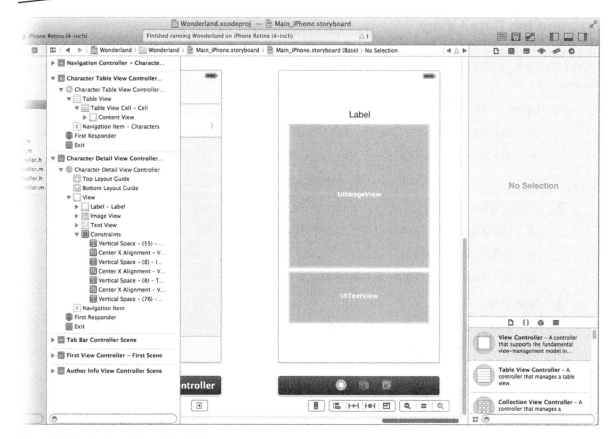

Figure 12-15. Rough position of detail views

5. Constraints (iPhone)

    a. Select just the label and the text view

    b. Choose **Editor ➤ Pin ➤ Height**

    c. Control/right-drag from the label to the image view and choose **Vertical Spacing**

    d. Control/right-drag from the image view to the text view and choose **Vertical Spacing**

    e. Control/right-drag from the label to the Top Layout Guide, as shown in Figure 12-16, and choose **Vertical Spacing**

    f. Control/right-drag from the text view to the Bottom Layout Guide and choose **Vertical Spacing**

    g. Select the vertical constraint above the label and use the attribute inspector to check the Standard option

    h. Select the vertical constraint below the text view and use the attribute inspector to check the Standard option.

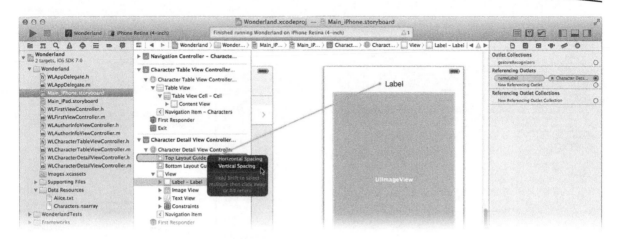

Figure 12-16. Adding a constraint to the top layout guide

6. Constraints (iPad)

   a. Select all three views

   b. Choose **Editor ➤ Pin ➤ Height**

   c. Select the image view

   d. Choose **Editor ➤ Align ➤ Vertically Center in Container**

   e. Control/right-drag from the top label to the image view and add a **Vertical Spacing** constraint

   f. Control/right-drag from the bottom label to the image view and add a **Vertical Spacing** constraint

On the iPhone, the label will be at the top of the container, the text view at the bottom, and the image view will resize to fill the space between. On an iPad, the three views will be grouped together, centered in the root view.

This seems like a lot of constraints, but it precisely describes how the views should adapt when their container view changes size. There are two things that will affect that size: the dimensions of different devices and the navigation bar and tab bar you're about to introduce (in the next section).

You'll need outlets for these view objects. Switch to the assistant editor; the WLCharacterDetailViewController.h interface file will appear on the right. (If it doesn't choose, **Automatic ➤ WLCharacterDetailViewController.h** from the navigation ribbon.)

Add the following outlet declarations to the @interface section:

```
@property (weak,nonatomic) IBOutlet UILabel *nameLabel;
@property (weak,nonatomic) IBOutlet UIImageView *imageView;
@property (weak,nonatomic) IBOutlet UITextView *descriptionView;
```

Use the outlet connectors, which now appear next to the property declarations, to connect them to their respective objects in the interface, as shown in Figure 12-17.

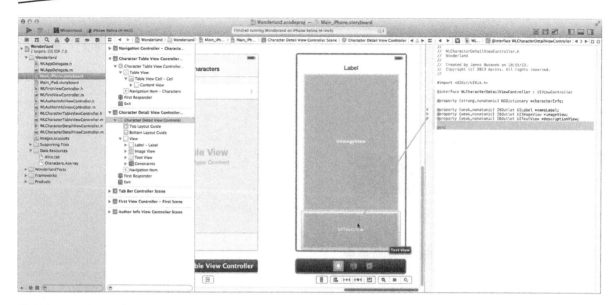

Figure 12-17. *Connecting character detail view outlets*

Adding the Data Model

What's left? You still have to create a data model and provide the table view with a data source and table view cell object. Start with the data model.

I have a surprise for you. I created a data model for you. Isn't that nice of me? The character detail info is stored in an object array (NSArray). Each element of the array contains a dictionary (NSDictionary). Each dictionary has the name of the character, the filename of its image, and a brief description. All of this information is stored in the Characters.nsarray file, one of the resource files you added earlier in this chapter.

> **Note** The Characters.nsarray file is a serialized property list XML file. You can open it in almost any plain text editor if you want to look at it. I created the file by writing an OS X command-line program that creates all of the dictionaries, assembles them into an array, and writes (serializes) the array to a file. The project that does this is in the Learn iOS Development Projects ➤ Ch 12 ➤ WLCharacterMaker folder. Property lists and serialization are explained in Chapter 18.

Add the data model to your table view controller by creating a property to store the array in your WLCharacterTableViewController.h interface file:

```
@property (strong,nonatomic) NSArray *tableData;
```

Switch to WLCharacterTableViewController.m and add this code to -viewDidLoad:

```
NSURL *dataURL = [[NSBundle mainBundle] URLForResource:@"Characters"
                                         withExtension:@"nsarray"];
self.tableData = [NSArray arrayWithContentsOfURL:dataURL];
```

This code locates the Characters.nsdata file in your apps resources, reads it in as an NSArray object, and stores it in your tableData property. You now have a data model!

Implementing Your Data Source

Now you need to feed the table view this information, via its data source object. The table view controller file template includes dummy implementations for all the key data source and delegate methods, they just need a little adjustment.

While still in the WLCharacterTableViewController.m file, find the -numberOfSectionsInTableView: method and delete it. You don't need it. Your table has one section, and that's the default.

Find the -tableView:numberOfRowsInSection: method and replace its code with this (shown in bold):

```
- (NSInteger)tableView:(UITableView*)table numberOfRowsInSection:(NSInteger)sec
{
    return self.tableData.count;
}
```

This method provides the table view with the number of rows in the list, which is the number of objects in the array.

> **Note** You might have noticed that you haven't connected the table view's delegate or dataSource outlets to your table view controller. That's because your controller is a subclass of UITableViewController, which is specifically designed to manage a table view. If you *do not* connect the delegate or dataSource outlets yourself, the controller makes itself both the delegate and the data source for the table, automatically. Isn't that convenient?

Defining a Table View Cell Object

The last piece of the puzzle is to supply the table view a table cell object for each row—the table view's rubber stamp. Find the -tableView:cellForRowAtIndexPath: method and edit it so it looks like this (new code in bold):

```
- (UITableViewCell *)tableView:(UITableView *)tableView
         cellForRowAtIndexPath:(NSIndexPath *)indexPath
{
    static NSString *CellId = @"Cell";
    UITableViewCell *cell = [tableView dequeueReusableCellWithIdentifier:CellId
                                                            forIndexPath:indexPath];
```

```
    NSDictionary *characterInfo = _tableData[indexPath.row];
    cell.textLabel.text = characterInfo[kNameKey];
    return cell;
}
```

This code should look very familiar—unless you skipped Chapter 5. The cell's appearance is defined by the cell prototype in the storyboard. Switch back to the Main_iPhone.storyboard (or _iPad) file and locate the table view controller.

At the top of the table view you'll see an area labeled Prototype Cells, as shown in Figure 12-18. Select the first, blank, cell and use the attributes inspector to change the style to Basic, set its identifier to Cell, and change its accessory to Disclosure Indicator (see Figure 12-18).

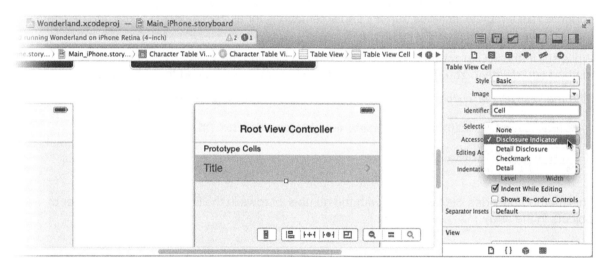

Figure 12-18. Defining a table cell

Now when your -tableView:cellForRowAtIndexPath: method asks for the "Cell" table cell object, it's already there. Your code just configures the text of the cell and it's done.

The code in -tableView:cellForRowAtIndexPath: is still showing an error because you haven't defined the keys used to retrieve the values from the dictionaries. Do that in WLCharacterTableView Controller.h, by adding this code immediately after the #import statements:

```
#define kImageKey        @"image"
#define kNameKey         @"name"
#define kDescriptionKey  @"description"
```

Your table view is now finished. Run the app in the simulator, tap the second tab, and this time your table is populated with the names from the data model, as shown in Figure 12-19.

CHAPTER 12: There and Back Again   393

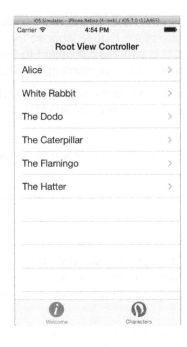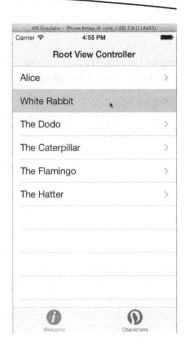

Figure 12-19. Working table view

Pushing the Detail View Controller

Tapping a row in the table, however, doesn't do much (on the right in Figure 12-19). That's because you haven't defined the action that presents the detail view. Also, the table's title is `Root View Controller`, which is a bit "on the nose." Fix the second one by selecting the `Main_iPhone.storyboard` (or `_iPad`) file, locating the character table view controller, double-clicking the title in the navigation bar, and changing it to "Characters," as shown in Figure 12-20.

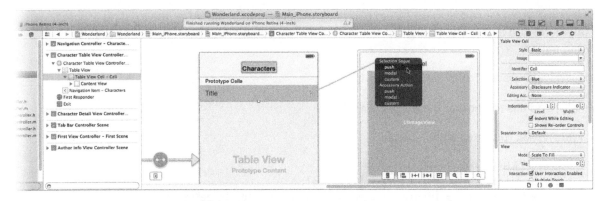

Figure 12-20. Creating a segue for the table cell

Right/control-drag from the prototype cell object over to the character detail view controller (also shown in Figure 12-20). When you release the mouse, choose the push option from the Selection Segue group. This configures all rows that use this cell object to "push" the character details view controller onto the navigation controller's stack, presenting it as the active view controller.

Just as you did in Chapter 5, you need some code to prepare the detail view based on the row the user tapped. Return to the WLCharacterTableViewController.m file. Add this method to your @implementation:

```
- (void)prepareForSegue:(UIStoryboardSegue *)segue sender:(id)sender
{
    WLCharacterDetailViewController *detailsController = segue.destinationViewController;
    detailsController.characterInfo = _tableData[self.tableView.indexPathForSelectedRow.row];
}
```

The segue object contains information about the view controllers involved (both coming and going). Use it to get the details view controller object the storyboard just created and loaded. You then use the tableView object to get the row number of the currently selected row—the one the user is tapping—and use that to get the character details from the data model and configure the new view controller (by setting characterInfo).

There are still a few loose ends. The list view controller doesn't know anything about WLCharacterDetailViewController, and that controller doesn't have a characterInfo property yet. These are pretty trivial tasks. Start by adding this #import statement immediately after the other #import statement:

```
#import "WLCharacterDetailViewController.h"
```

Switch to your WLCharacterDetailViewController.h interface file and add a property declaration to hold the details of one character:

```
@property (strong,nonatomic) NSDictionary *characterInfo;
```

Select the WLCharacterDetailViewController.m implementation file. After the existing #import statement, add a new one to pick up the dictionary key constants (kNameKey and so on) you wrote earlier:

```
#import "WLCharacterTableViewController.h"
```

Finally, add this method to the @implementation:

```
- (void)viewWillAppear:(BOOL)animated
{
    [super viewWillAppear:animated];
    self.nameLabel.text = _characterInfo[kNameKey];
    self.imageView.image = [UIImage imageNamed:_characterInfo[kImageKey]];
    self.descriptionView.text = _characterInfo[kDescriptionKey];
}
```

When the view controller is about to appear on the screen, this code will populate the view objects with details in characterInfo. Run the app in the simulator and try it out, as shown in Figure 12-21.

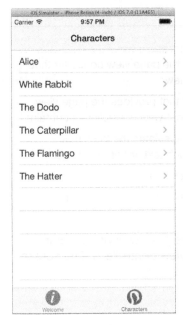  

Figure 12-21. Finished character table

Your app is now two-thirds finished. In this section, you created a navigable table view by nesting a table (content) view controller inside a navigation (container view) controller. You used a storyboard to configure the table's cell object and created its segue to the detail view controller.

By now you should be getting pretty comfortable with content and container view controllers, connecting them together, and creating segues to define your app's navigation. The final section of this chapter is going to show you how to use a page view controller.

Creating a Page View Controller

You have arrived at the third, and final, tab of your Wonderland app. This tab will display the text of the book, one page at a time. This tab uses a page view controller (UIPageViewController) object. It's a container view controller that manages a (potentially huge) collection of content view controllers. Each "page" consists of one or two content view controllers. The page view controller provides gesture recognizers that perform, and animate, the navigation between pages in the collection.

Adding a page view controller to your design is simple enough. Getting it to work is another matter. Page view controllers are typically code intensive, and this app is no exception. To make the situation even more exciting, you have to get the bulk of your code working before the page view will do anything at all. So settle in, this is going to be a long trip.

You're going to need a number of new classes, so create them all now. Use the **New File...** command to create new Objective-C class files in your project's Wonderland group. Table 12-2 lists the new classes you need to create, the superclass of each, and what its role will be. When creating new view controller classes, do not create an XIB file.

Table 12-2. Page View Classes

Class	Superclass	Description
WLBookViewController	UIPageViewController	Your custom version of the page view controller that will manage the page view
WLBookDataSource	NSObject	The data source object that provides the page view controller with the content view controllers it contains
WLPaginator	NSObject	A utility object that encapsulates the logic that determines out how much text will fit on a page
WLOnePageViewController	UIViewController	The content view controller(s)
WLOnePageView	UIView	A custom view object used to display the text

Just as table and picker views need a data source object, so does the page view controller. But instead of providing a value on a wheel or one row of a table, the page view controller's data source provides it with the view controllers it wants to display, on demand.

Adding the Page View Controllers

It's not all code. Use Interface Builder to create the two view controllers. Select the Main_Phone.storyboard (or _iPad) file. Drag a new Page View Controller from the object library and add it to your design. Also add a new View Controller object, as shown in Figure 12-22. Arrange them below the other scenes.

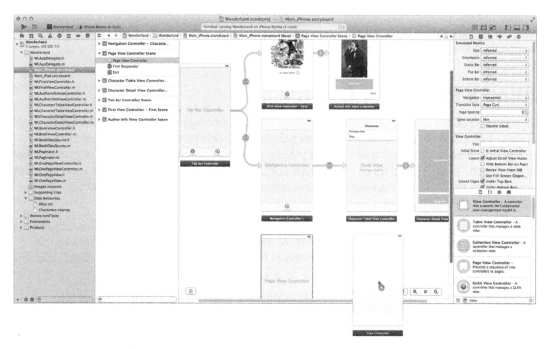

Figure 12-22. Adding the page view controller and single page view controller

Add the page view controller to the tab bar by right/control-dragging from the tab bar controller to the new page view controller, as shown in Figure 12-23. Select the `view controllers` relationship.

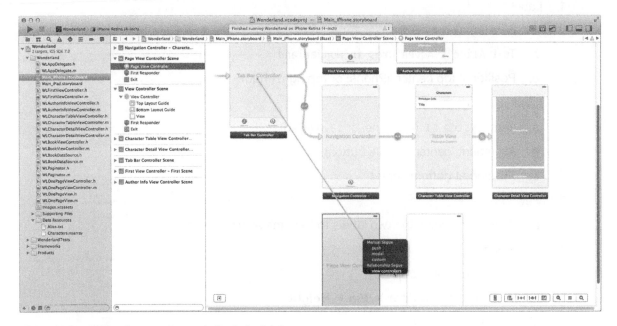

Figure 12-23. Adding the page view controller to the tab bar

As you did with the other tabs, select the tab bar item in the page view controller's scene. Use the attributes inspector to set its title to "Book" and its tab icon to `tab-book`.

Now configure the page view controller itself. Select the page view controller object and use the identity inspector to change its class to `WLBookViewController`. Switch to the attributes inspector and double-check that the following properties are set:

- Navigation: `Horizontal`
- Transition Style: `Page Curl`
- Spine Location: `Min`

These settings define a "book-like" interface where the user moves horizontally through a collection of view controllers, one per page. (If you set the Spine location to the `Mid`, you'd get two view controllers per page.) A transition between controllers emulates the turning of a paper page.

Designing a Prototype Page

Now move over to the plain view controller you just added. Use the identity inspector to change its class to `WLOnePageViewController`. Also change its `Storyboard ID` to "OnePage". This last step is important. This controller won't be connected in Interface Builder; you're going to create instances of it programmatically. To do that, you need a way to refer to it, and you'll use its storyboard ID to do that. (It's equivalent to `UIView`'s tag property.)

With the preliminaries out of the way, create the interface for the one page view controller. From the object library, add three view objects as follows:

1. Label
    a. Font: `System 15.0`
    b. Text: `Alice's Adventures in Wonderland`
    c. Position it top center (iPhone) or top right (iPad)
2. Label
    a. Font: `System 11.0` (iPhone) or `13.0` (iPad)
    b. Alignment: center (middle button)
    c. Position at bottom center
3. View
    a. Position between the two labels to fill in the available space
4. Constraints
    a. Select both label objects
    b. Fix their height (**Editor ➤ Pin ➤ Height**)
    c. Select both label objects
    d. Center them (**Editor ➤ Align ➤ Horizontal Center** in Container)
    e. Add a constraint from the top label to the top layout guide (refer to Figure 12-16)
    f. Select the newly created constraint and use the attributes inspector to check the `Standard` option
    g. Add a constraint from the bottom label to the bottom layout guide
    h. Select the newly added constraint (see Figure 12-24) and set its `Constant` to 60 (allowing for the tab bar at the bottom of the screen)
    i. Fill in the remaining constraints (**Editor ➤ Resolve Auto Layout Issues ➤ Add Missing Constraints in One Page View Controller**)

Select the `UIView` object and use the identity inspector to change its class to `WLOnePageView`. The finished interface should look like the one in Figure 12-24.

CHAPTER 12: There and Back Again   399

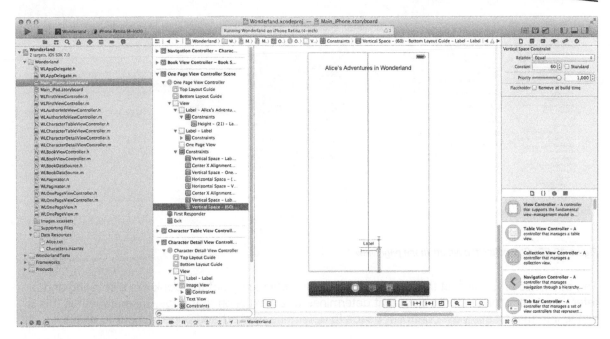

Figure 12-24. One page view controller interface

Switch to the assistant editor and, with the WLOnePageViewController.h file in the right pane, add two #import statements:

#import "WLOnePageView.h"
#import "WLPaginator.h"

And then add four properties to the @interface:

@property (nonatomic) NSUInteger pageNumber;
@property (strong,nonatomic) WLPaginator *paginator;
@property (weak,nonatomic) IBOutlet WLOnePageView *textView;
@property (weak,nonatomic) IBOutlet UILabel *pageLabel;

Connect the outlet sockets of the last two properties to the WLOnePageView object in the middle of the screen and the small label object at the bottom, as shown in Figure 12-25. The latter will display the page number.

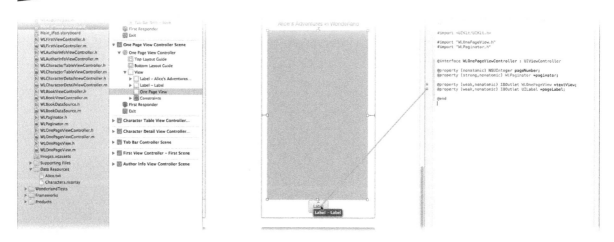

Figure 12-25. Connecting the outlets in the page view

The other two properties let this view controller know which page of the book it is displaying and a reference to the "paginator" object that determines what text is on that page. Taken together, this is all the information this view controller needs to determine the text and page number to display.

Coding the One Page View

You've now done just about all you can do in Interface Builder. It's time to roll up your sleeves and start coding. This time, start from the "tail" end of this design and work back up to the page view controller, filling in the details as you go. The last object in the chain is WLOnePageView, the custom view that display the text of a page. Select the WLOnePageView.h file. Add two properties to the @interface:

```
@property (strong,nonatomic) NSString *text;
@property (strong,nonatomic) NSDictionary *fontAttrs;
```

Switch to the WLOnePageView.m implementation file and write its -drawRect: method:

```
- (void)drawRect:(CGRect)rect
{
    [super drawRect:rect];
    [_text drawInRect:self.bounds withAttributes:_fontAttrs];
}
```

You should be able to decipher this, having read Chapter 11. When it's time to draw itself, it fills the view with the background color ([super drawRect:rect] does that for you), and then draws its text using the attributes stored in its fontAttrs property.

You're done with this class. Let's move on to the view controller. You've already defined the interface for the WLOnePageViewController class (in WLOnePageViewController.h). Select its implementation file (WLOnePageViewController.m) and fill in the missing code.

At the top of the file, find the private `@interface WLOnePageViewController ()` section and add a prototype for the `-loadPageContent` method (new code in bold):

```
@interface WLOnePageViewController ()
- (void)loadPageContent;
@end
```

The `-loadPageContent` method prepares the `WLOnePageView` object to display the text for this controller's page. Add that method now:

```
- (void)loadPageContent
{
    _paginator.viewSize = _textView.bounds.size;
    if (![_paginator availablePage:_pageNumber])
        _pageNumber = _paginator.lastKnownPage;
    _textView.fontAttrs = _paginator.fontAttrs;
    _textView.text = [_paginator textForPage:_pageNumber];
    [_textView setNeedsDisplay];
    _pageLabel.text = [NSString stringWithFormat:@"Page %u",
                                                 (unsigned int)_pageNumber];
}
```

This method loads the content of the view. It configures the paginator object with the size of its text view object. It configures the text view to use the same font attributes the paginator is using, and then asks the paginator for the text that appears on this page. It also updates the page number label at the bottom of the view.

There's also a little logic to handle the case where the page to display doesn't exist anymore. This can happen if you rotate the device; the dimensions of the view change, altering the text in each page, and changing the number of pages in the book. In this situation, the view changes to the last page available and displays that.

So when does `-loadPageContent` get sent? Under most circumstances, this kind of first-time-view-setup code would be invoked from your `-viewDidLoad` method. But `-loadPageContent` needs to be sent whenever the size of text view changes, and that can happen at any time, most notably when the user changes the display orientation. Solve that by adding a `-viewDidLayoutSubviews` method and sending `-loadPageContent` whenever the controller's view layout is adjusted:

```
- (void)viewDidLayoutSubviews
{
    [super viewDidLayoutSubviews];
    [self loadPageContent];
}
```

You're seeing a number of compiler errors because you haven't implemented the paginator object yet. Do that now.

The Paginator

The code for WLPaginator.h is in Listing 12-1 and the code for WLPaginator.m is in Listing 12-2. If you want to copy and paste the solution, you'll find the source files for the finished code in the Learn iOS Development Projects ➤ Ch 12 ➤ Wonderland project folder.

Listing 12-1. WLPaginator.h

```objc
#import <Foundation/Foundation.h>

@interface WLPaginator : NSObject

@property (strong,nonatomic) NSString *bookText;
@property (strong,nonatomic) UIFont *font;
@property (readonly,nonatomic) NSDictionary *fontAttrs;
@property (nonatomic) CGSize viewSize;
@property (readonly,nonatomic) NSUInteger lastKnownPage;

- (BOOL)availablePage:(NSUInteger)page;
- (NSString*)textForPage:(NSUInteger)page;

@end
```

Listing 12-2. WLPaginator.m

```objc
#import "WLPaginator.h"

@interface WLPaginator ()
{
    NSMutableArray  *ranges;
    NSUInteger      lastPageWithContent;
    NSDictionary    *fontAttrs;
}
- (NSRange)rangeOfTextForPage:(NSUInteger)page;
@end

@implementation WLPaginator

- (void)resetPageData
{
    ranges = [NSMutableArray array];
    lastPageWithContent = 1;
}

- (void)setBookText:(NSString *)bookData
{
    _bookText = bookData;
    [self resetPageData];
}
```

```objc
- (void)setFont:(UIFont *)font
{
    if ([_font isEqual:font])
        return;
    _font = font;
    _fontAttrs = nil;
    [self resetPageData];
}

- (NSDictionary*)fontAttrs
{
    if (fontAttrs==nil)
        {
        NSMutableParagraphStyle *style = [NSMutableParagraphStyle new];
        style.lineBreakMode = NSLineBreakByWordWrapping;
        fontAttrs = @{
                    NSFontAttributeName: self.font,
                    NSParagraphStyleAttributeName: style
                    };
        }
    return fontAttrs;
}

- (void)setViewSize:(CGSize)viewSize
{
    if (CGSizeEqualToSize(_viewSize,viewSize))
        return;
    _viewSize = viewSize;
    [self resetPageData];
}

- (NSUInteger)lastKnownPage
{
    return lastPageWithContent;
}

#define SpanRange(LOCATION,LENGTH) \
        ({ NSUInteger loc_=(LOCATION); NSMakeRange(loc_,(LENGTH)-loc_); })

- (NSRange)rangeOfTextForPage:(NSUInteger)page
{
    if (ranges.count>=page)
        return [ranges[page-1] rangeValue];

    CGSize constraintSize = _viewSize;
    CGFloat targetHeight = constraintSize.height;
    constraintSize.height = 32000;

    NSRange textRange = NSMakeRange(0,0);
    if (page!=1)
        textRange.location = NSMaxRange([self rangeOfTextForPage:page-1]);
    NSCharacterSet *wordBreakCharSet = [NSCharacterSet whitespaceAndNewlineCharacterSet];
```

```objc
        while (textRange.location<_bookText.length &&
            [wordBreakCharSet characterIsMember:[_bookText characterAtIndex:textRange.location]])
            {
            textRange.location += 1;
            }
        
        CGSize textSize = CGSizeMake(0,0);
        CGRect textBounds;
        NSCharacterSet *paraCharSet = [NSCharacterSet characterSetWithCharactersInString:@"\r"];
        while (textSize.height<targetHeight)
            {
            NSRange paraRange = [_bookText rangeOfCharacterFromSet:paraCharSet
                                    options:NSLiteralSearch
                                        range:SpanRange(NSMaxRange(textRange),_bookText.length)];
            if (paraRange.location==NSNotFound)
                break;
            
            textRange.length = NSMaxRange(paraRange)-textRange.location;
            NSString *testText = [_bookText substringWithRange:textRange];
            textBounds = [testText boundingRectWithSize:constraintSize
                                options:NSStringDrawingUsesLineFragmentOrigin
                                attributes:self.fontAttrs
                                context:[NSStringDrawingContext new]];
            textSize = textBounds.size;
            }
        
        while (textSize.height>targetHeight)
            {
            NSRange wordRange = [_bookText rangeOfCharacterFromSet:wordBreakCharSet
                                                    options:NSBackwardsSearch
                                                        range:textRange];
            if (wordRange.location==NSNotFound)
                break;
            textRange.length = wordRange.location-textRange.location;
            NSString *testText = [_bookText substringWithRange:textRange];
            textBounds = [testText boundingRectWithSize:constraintSize
                                options:NSStringDrawingUsesLineFragmentOrigin
                                attributes:self.fontAttrs
                                context:[NSStringDrawingContext new]];
            textSize = textBounds.size;
            }
        
        if (textRange.length!=0)
            lastPageWithContent = page;
        
        [ranges addObject:[NSValue valueWithRange:textRange]];
        return textRange;
}
```

```objc
- (BOOL)availablePage:(NSUInteger)page
{
    if (page==1)
        return YES;
    NSRange textRange = [self rangeOfTextForPage:page];
    return (textRange.length!=0);
}

- (NSString*)textForPage:(NSUInteger)page
{
    return [_bookText substringWithRange:[self rangeOfTextForPage:page]];
}

@end
```

The details of how `WLPaginator` works isn't important to this chapter, but if you're curious read the comments in the finished project. Conceptually, it's straightforward. The paginator object is configured with three pieces of information: the complete text of the book, the font it will be drawn in, and the size of the text view that displays a page. The object then splits up the text of the book into ranges, each range filling one page. Any view controller object can then ask the paginator for the text that fits on its page.

> **Note** This is hardly the most sophisticated way of implementing the paginator, but it's sufficient for this app.

Coding the Page View Data Source

You finally get to the heart of the page view controller: the page view data source. A page view controller data source must conform to the `UIPageViewControllerDataSource` protocol and implement these two required methods:

- `pageViewController:viewControllerBeforeViewController:`
- `pageViewController:viewControllerAfterViewController:`

The page view starts out with an initial view controller to display. When the user "flips" the page to the right or left, the page view controller sends the data source object one of these messages, depending on the direction of the page turn. The data source, using the current view controller as a reference, retrieves or creates the view controller that will display the next (or previous) page. If there is no page, it returns nil.

Your data source must implement these methods. It also needs a `readonly` property that returns the single paginator object used by all of the individual view controllers and a method to create the view controller for an arbitrary page. Your `WLBookDataSource.h` file, therefore, looks like this:

```objc
#import "WLPaginator.h"
#import "WLOnePageViewController.h"

@interface WLBookDataSource : NSObject <UIPageViewControllerDataSource>
```

```objc
@property (readonly,nonatomic) WLPaginator *paginator;

- (WLOnePageViewController*)pageViewController:pageViewController
                               loadPage:(NSUInteger)page;

@end
```

Now switch to the WLBookDataSource.m implementation file. You need an instance variable to store the single paginator object, so add this before the @implementation section:

```objc
@interface WLBookDataSource ()
{
    WLPaginator *paginator;
}
@end
```

In the @implementation section, write a getter method for the paginator property that lazily creates the object:

```objc
- (WLPaginator*)paginator
{
    if (paginator==nil)
        {
        paginator = [WLPaginator new];
        paginator.font = [UIFont fontWithName:@"Times New Roman" size:18];
        }
    return paginator;
}
```

The -pageViewController:loadPage: method is the workhorse of this data source. Add it now:

```objc
- (WLOnePageViewController*)pageViewController:(UIPageViewController*)pageViewController
                               loadPage:(NSUInteger)page
{
    if (page<1 || ![paginator availablePage:page])
        return nil;

    WLOnePageViewController *controller;
    controller = [pageViewController.storyboard
                        instantiateViewControllerWithIdentifier:@"OnePage"];
    controller.paginator = self.paginator;
    controller.pageNumber = page;
    return controller;
}
```

This method returns a configured WLOnePageViewController for any page in the book. It works by checking to see if the requested page number is in the book. If not, it returns nil.

It then asks the storyboard object to create the controller and views contained in the scene with the identifier "OnePage." This is done because segues and actions aren't used to navigate between view controllers in a page view. It's up to the data source to create them when requested.

> **Note** Remember, earlier, you assigned the view controller scene in the storyboard an identifier of "OnePage." This is why. If you need to programmatically load a view controller and its view objects from a storyboard scene, the -instantiateViewControllerWithIdentifier: message is your ticket.

Once it has a new one page view controller object, it connects it to the paginator and sets the page number it should display.

All that's left to do is to implement the two required data source protocol methods. These also go in your WLBookDataSource.m file:

```
- (UIViewController *)pageViewController:(UIPageViewController *)pageViewController
      viewControllerAfterViewController:(UIViewController *)viewController
{
    NSUInteger currentPageNumber = ((WLOnePageViewController*)viewController).pageNumber;
    return [self pageViewController:pageViewController loadPage:currentPageNumber+1];
}

- (UIViewController *)pageViewController:(UIPageViewController *)pageViewController
      viewControllerBeforeViewController:(UIViewController *)viewController
{
    NSUInteger currentPageNumber = ((WLOnePageViewController*)viewController).pageNumber;
    return [self pageViewController:pageViewController loadPage:currentPageNumber-1];
}
```

Since each one page view controller stores the page number it displays, all these two methods have to do is request the page after, or before, the current one.

Initializing a Page View Controller

Your book implementation is almost complete. The only thing left to do is perform some initial setup of the page view controller and data model when the page view controller is created. Switch to the WLBookViewController.m implementation file. Begin by creating an instance variable to store the data source object, by adding this #import statement and instance variable to the private @interface WLBookViewController () section at the beginning of the file (new code in bold):

```
#import "WLBookDataSource.h"

@interface WLBookViewController ()
{
    WLBookDataSource *bookSource;
}
@end
```

> **Note** Why it's necessary to create a bookSource instance variable has to do with a quirk of the automatic reference counting (ARC) memory management system. Read the comments in the finished project, and Chapter 21, for an explanation.

Find the -viewDidLoad method, and add the rest of the code in this section, starting with:

```objc
self.dataSource = bookSource = [WLBookDataSource new];
```

This creates, and retains, the data source object and makes it the data source for this page view controller.

```objc
NSURL *bookURL = [[NSBundle mainBundle] URLForResource:@"Alice"
                                         withExtension:@"txt"];
NSString *text = [NSString stringWithContentsOfURL:bookURL
                                          encoding:NSUTF8StringEncoding
                                             error:NULL];
bookSource.paginator.bookText = text;
```

This next block of code reads in the text of the book, stored in the Alice.txt file that was one of the resource files you added at the beginning. The file is a UTF-8 encoded text file with each line separated by a single carriage return (U+000d) character. This format is what the paginator expects. The entire text is read into a single string and stored in the paginator, which will use it to assign text to individual pages.

```objc
[self setViewControllers:@[[bookSource pageViewController:self loadPage:1]]
               direction:UIPageViewControllerNavigationDirectionForward
                animated:NO
              completion:nil];
```

This last statement is probably the most important. It creates the initial view controller that the page view controller will present. This must be done, programmatically, before the page view controller appears.

> **Caution** The initial view controllers for a page view controller is an array. The number of view controllers must exactly match the number of view controllers the page view controller presents at one time. If you configure the page view controller with a spine location of Mid, you must provide two initial view controllers: one for the left page and a second one for the right page.

That was a lot of code, but you're done! Run your app and test out the third tab, as shown in Figure 12-26.

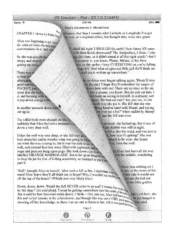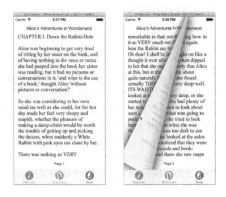

Figure 12-26. Working page view interface

You've created a truly complex app. You were aided, in part, by storyboards that allowed you to map out and define much of your app's navigation in a single file. But you also learned how to load storyboard scenes programmatically when you need to.

I encourage you to take a moment and review the scenes in your storyboard file and the classes you created to support them. Once you're comfortable that you understand the organization of your view controllers, how they work together, and the roles of the individual classes you created, you can consider yourself an iOS navigation engineer, first class.

Using Pop-Over Controllers

There's one oddball navigation class, the pop-over controller (UIPopoverController). The pop-over controller is not a view controller. It's a utility class that presents a view controller in a floating window, on top of an existing view controller. The first view controller never goes away, but is disabled while the pop-over's view controller is active. In this sense, it's work like any other modal view controller.

Coding a pop-over isn't difficult. You already did it in Chapter 7. Now that you know a lot more about view controllers, you might want to skip back and review the code you added to present the media picker interface on the iPad.

You can also create pop-over transitions using storyboard segues. When you create a modal segue in an iPad storyboard, you get the added option of popover. Just choose this segue type and the storyboard will wrap your view controller in a pop-over controller to present it.

Advanced Navigation

You have dived deep into the sea of iOS navigation, but you haven't covered everything. To go further, I suggest starting with two key documents: *View Controller Programming Guide for iOS* and the *View Controller Catalog for iOS* in the Xcode Documentation and API Reference. The first explains the nitty-gritty details about view controllers and navigation in general. The second describes each of the individual view controller subclasses, and how to use them.

Summary

You've traveled far in your quest to master iOS app development. In all but the simplest apps, navigation is an important part of your design, every bit as important as what your app does.

In this chapter you gained experience using all of the major view controller classes: UIViewController, UITableViewController, UINavigationController, UITabBarController, and UIPageViewController. More importantly, you learned the difference between content and container view controllers, and how to assemble and connect them using storyboards. You also learned the fundamentals of presenting modal view controllers. You added some new tricks to your table view skills; you learned how to create a table view using a storyboard, configure its cell object, create a row selection segue, and use the storyboard methods for preparing the details view controller. You created view controllers stored in a storyboard file programmatically, and used that to create a page view controller data source.

This is a huge accomplishment. It's so exciting that you should share it with your friends. The next chapter will show you how to do just that.

Chapter 13

Networking, the Social Kind

Social networking has exploded in recent years and mobile apps have played a huge part in that revolution. Not too long ago, it was quite difficult to add social networking features to your app. Today, recent additions to iOS have made it so easy that—given what you know about view controllers—the process can be accurately described as "trivial." In this, rather short, chapter you will learn how to:

- Share content via Facebook, Twitter, Sina Weibo, Tencent Weibo, Flickr, Vimeo, e-mail, SMS, and more
- Customize content for different services
- Draw images off-screen
- Refactor code in Xcode

Choosing which app to modify was probably the most difficult decision in this chapter. Would people you know want to learn interesting facts about the Surrealists in Chapter 2? Of course you'd want to share a shortened URL from Chapter 3. Do your friends want to know what your Magic Eight Ball prediction was in Chapter 4? You took pictures of your cool stuff in Chapter 7; what if someone wants to see them? It would be easy to add sharing features to all of these apps. In the end, I choose to expand on the ColorModel app from Chapter 8. You've spent a lot of time and effort picking just the right color, and I'm sure your friends will appreciate you sharing it with them.

Color My (Social) World

Start with the final ColorModel app from Chapter 8. You will add a button that shares the chosen color with the world. iOS includes a standard "Activity" toolbar item, just for this purpose, so use that. In the `Main.storyboard` interface file, add a toolbar to the bottom of the view controller's interface, as shown in Figure 13-1. The toolbar comes with one bar button item pre-installed. Select the new toolbar and choose Editor ➤ Resolve Auto Layout Issues ➤ Add Missing Constraints.

CHAPTER 13: Networking, the Social Kind

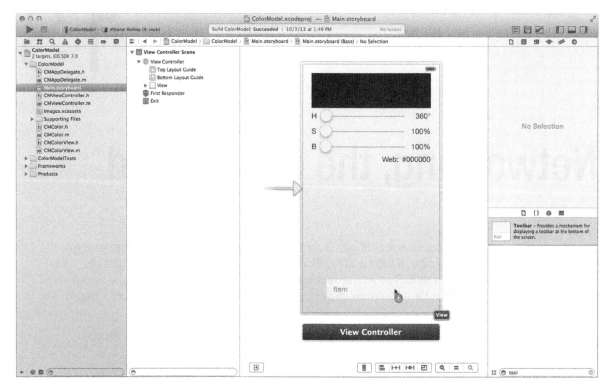

Figure 13-1. Adding a toolbar and toolbar button item

Select the included bar button item and change its identifier property to Action.

Switch to the assistant editor view (View ➤ Assistant Editor ➤ Show Assistant Editor). Switch to the CMViewController.h file (in the right pane) and add a new action:

- (IBAction)share:(id)sender;

Connect the action to the button by dragging the action connection to the button. I won't include a figure for that, because if you don't know what that looks like by now you've clearly skipped most of the earlier chapters.

Having Something to Share

Start out by sharing the red-green-blue code for the color. Currently, the code that generates the HTML value for the color is in the -observeValueForKeyPath:ofObject:change:context: method (CMViewController.m). You now have a second method that needs that conversion; consider reorganizing the code so this conversion is more readily accessible. Translating the current color into its equivalent HTML value feels as if it lies in the domain of the data model, so add this method declaration to `CMColor.h`:

```
- (NSString*)rgbCodeWithPrefix:(NSString*)prefix;
```

Switch to the `CMColor.m` implementation file, and add the new method to the `@implementation` section:

```
- (NSString*)rgbCodeWithPrefix:(NSString*)prefix
{
    if (prefix==nil)
        prefix = @"";
    CGFloat red, green, blue, alpha;
    [self.color getRed:&red green:&green blue:&blue alpha:&alpha];
    return [NSString stringWithFormat:@"%@%02lx%02lx%02lx",
            prefix,
            lroundf(red*255),
            lroundf(green*255),
            lroundf(blue*255)];
}
```

Now that your data model object will return the color's HTML code, replace the code in `CMViewController.m` to use the new method. Edit the end of `-observeValueForKeyPath:ofObject:change:context:` so it looks like this (replacement code in bold):

```
    else if ([keyPath isEqualToString:@"color"])
        {
        [self.colorView setNeedsDisplay];
        self.webLabel.text = [self.colorModel rgbCodeWithPrefix:@"#"];
        }
}
```

> **Note** I've mentioned it once already, but it bears repeating. If you're repeating yourself (writing the same code in multiple places), stop and think about how you could consolidate that logic.

Presenting the Activity View Controller

While still in the `CMViewController.m` implementation file, add the new action method:

```
- (IBAction)share:(id)sender
{
    NSString *shareMessage = [NSString stringWithFormat:
                              @"I wrote an iOS app to share a color!"
                              @" RGB=%@",
                              [self.colorModel rgbCodeWithPrefix:nil]];
    NSArray *itemsToShare = @[shareMessage];
```

```
        UIActivityViewController *activityViewController;
        activityViewController = [[UIActivityViewController alloc] initWithActivityItems:itemsToShare
                                                               applicationActivities:nil];
        [self presentViewController:activityViewController
                           animated:YES
                         completion:nil];
}
```

The method starts out by collecting the items to share. Items can be a message (string), an image, a video, a document, a URL, and so on. Basically, you can include any message, link, media object, or attachment that would make sense to share. These are collected together into a single NSArray.

The next section is just as straightforward. You create a UIActivityViewController, initializing it with the items you want to share. You then modally present the view controller.

That's all there is to it! Run the project and tap on the share button, as shown in Figure 13-2.

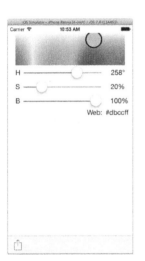
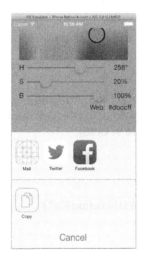

Figure 13-2. Sharing a message

> **Note** What sharing options appear for you will depend on what services you subscribe to, what services are supported in your region, and what activities Apple has added this month.

Tapping the share button presents a picker that lets the user decide how they want to share this message. While your goal is to add sharing to your app, the motivation behind the UIActivityViewController is to allow the user to do any number of things with the data items you passed in, all external to your application. This includes actions like copying the message to the clipboard, which is why it's named UIActivityViewController and not UIPokeMyFriendsViewController.

> **Tip** It's possible to invent and add your own activities to the list that appears. Create a concrete subclass of `UIActivity` and pass your activity object (or objects, if you've created more than one) in the `applicationActivities:` parameter.

Tapping the Twitter activity presents a tweet sheet. Tapping Mail composes a new mail message. Each activity has its own interface and options. Some, like the copy to clipboard action, have no user interface at all; they just do their thing and dismiss the controller.

> **Note** This is one of those rare cases where the modal controller dismisses itself. `UIActivityViewController` does not use a delegate to report what it did, and you are not responsible for dismissing it when it's done. In fact, the only way to find out if it performed an activity is to assign a code block to its `completionHandler` property before presenting it. The code block receives two values: an `activityType` string describing which activity was chosen (such as `UIActivityTypePostToFacebook`) and a Boolean `completed` parameter that is YES if it was successful.

UIACTIVITYVIEWCONTROLLER AND THE IPAD

Like the photo image picker you used in Chapter 7, you must present a `UIActivityViewController` in a popover on the iPad. This isn't an issue for this app, because ColorModel only runs on an iPhone. For a universal application—one designed to run on both the iPhone and iPad—you would check the idiom of the device to determine how to present the view controller. You'd replace the last statement in `-share:` with something like this:

```
if (UIDevice.currentDevice.userInterfaceIdiom==UIUserInterfaceIdiomPad)
    {
    UIPopoverController *popover;
    popover = [[UIPopoverController alloc]
                initWithContentViewController:activityViewController];
    [popover presentPopoverFromBarButtonItem:sender
                    permittedArrowDirections:UIPopoverArrowDirectionAny
                                    animated:YES];
    }
else
    {
    [self presentViewController:activityViewController
                       animated:YES
                     completion:nil];
    }
```

When presenting a popover that was initiated by touching an item in the toolbar, use the `-presentPopoverFromBarButton:permittedArrowDirection:animated:` method. This code assumes that view object that sent the `-share:` message (sender) is the bar button item. This is a safe assumption for this app, but if `-share:` was sent by other kinds of view objects, you'd have to case that out and decide which `UIPopoverController` method to send.

Sharing More

I admit, sharing a hexadecimal color code probably isn't going to get you a lot of "likes" on Facebook. It's pretty boring. When you share a color, what you want to share is a *color*. You can improve the user experience by preparing as much content as you can for the activity view controller. Include not just plain text messages, but images, video, URLs, and so on. The more the merrier.

It's a shame you can't attach the image displayed in the `CMColorView`. You went to a lot of work to create a beautiful hue/saturation chart, with the selected color spotlighted. But all that `-drawRect:` code draws into a Core Graphics context; it's not a `UIImage` object you can pass to `UIActivityViewController`.

Or could you?

If you remember the section "Creating Bitmaps From Drawings" in Chapter 11, it's possible to create a `UIImage` object by first creating an off-screen graphics context, drawing into it, and then saving the results as an image object. That would let you turn your drawing into a sharable UIImage object! So what are you waiting for?

Extracting Code

What you need now is a method that does the work of drawing the hue/saturation image in a graphics context. Let's call it `-drawColorInRect:context:`. You then need to change the `-drawRect:` method so it calls `-drawColorInRect:context:` to draw the UIView. Then you need a second method that creates an off-screen graphics context, calls `-drawColorInRect:context:` to draw the h/s chart into that, and saves the result as a UIImage.

So, how do you get from the `-drawRect:` method you have now to the three you need? Xcode is here to help! When you encounter refactoring problems like this, look to Xcode's Refactor command. There's an *extract* tool just for this situation. It takes a selected section of code in a method and extracts that into a separate method (or function). The result is a second method with the same logic, which the first method then calls. Once the code is extracted, you can then write other methods to call it.

> **Note** *Code refactoring* is the art of restructuring your code without changing what it does (see `http://refactoring.com/`). You refactor to better organize your classes, simplify their interfaces, reduce complexity, or—as in this example—consolidate and reuse code.

Start by finding the -drawRect: method in CMColorView.m. In the editor, select the code that starts with the statement if (hsImageRef!=NULL && and ends with the last statement in the method, but not the terminating } of the method, as shown in Figure 13-3. It's important that the first two lines of code are *not* selected—you'll see why in a moment. In the figure, a couple of if blocks have been collapsed so you can see the entire range of the selected code.

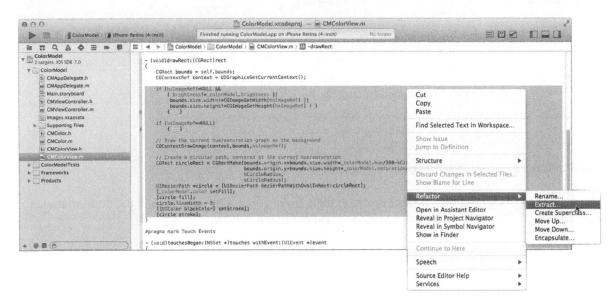

Figure 13-3. Selecting the code to extract

Choose the Refactor ➤ Extract... command from either the Edit menu or by right/control+clicking on the selected text, as shown in Figure 13-3. The extract tool analyzes the selected code, determines what local variables the code depends on, and converts those local variables into parameters. It then asks you to name the new method, as shown in Figure 13-4.

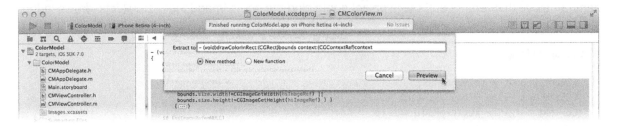

Figure 13-4. Extracting code into a new method

Edit the method's declaration so it is - (void)drawColorInRect:(CGRect)bounds context:(CGContextRef)context, make sure the New method option is selected, and click the Preview button. The refactoring tool will let you preview the changes it's about to make, as shown in Figure 13-5. Review all of the changes carefully to make sure this is what you want, and then click the Save button.

Figure 13-5. Previewing refactoring changes

The extract tool has created a new -drawColorInRect:context: method with just the code that was selected in -drawRect:. It has also rewritten -drawRect: so it is now:

```
- (void)drawRect:(CGRect)rect
{
    CGRect bounds = self.bounds;
    CGContextRef context = UIGraphicsGetCurrentContext();
    [self drawColorInRect:bounds context:context];
}
```

The important fact, from a refactoring standpoint, is that -drawRect: still does *exactly* what it did before the change. The only difference is that a portion of its code has been relocated to a new method that can be reused by other methods.

And that's exactly what you want to do next. Add a new property getter method (to CMColorView.m) named -image that returns a UIImage object containing the same image that -drawRect: draws in the interface:

```
- (UIImage*)image
{
    CGRect bounds = self.bounds;
    CGSize imageSize = bounds.size;
    CGFloat margin = kCircleRadius/2+2;
    imageSize.width += margin*2;
    imageSize.height += margin*2;
    bounds = CGRectOffset(bounds,margin,margin);

    UIGraphicsBeginImageContext(imageSize);
    CGContextRef context = UIGraphicsGetCurrentContext();
    [[UIColor clearColor] set];
    CGContextFillRect(context,CGRectMake(0,0,imageSize.width,imageSize.height));
    [self drawColorInRect:bounds context:context];
```

```
    UIImage *image = UIGraphicsGetImageFromCurrentImageContext();
    UIGraphicsEndImageContext();

    return image;
}
```

The new method starts out by getting the existing dimensions of the view object. It then creates a rectangle that is kCircleRadius/2+2 larger on every side. It does this so that when the color "spot" is drawn into the image, it won't get clipped if it's close to the edge of the h/s graph. (All UIView drawing is clipped to the bounds of the view.) A bounds rectangle is then offset so it is centered in the image.

The next step is to create an off-screen drawing context, the size of the final image. You then fill the context with transparent pixels ([UIColor clearColor]). This is done so that any pixels that aren't drawn end up as transparent pixels in the image. You then reuse the -drawColorInRect:context: method you just extracted to draw the h/s chart and selected color.

The final step is to extract what's been drawn into the graphics context as a UIImage. The context can then be discarded, and you return the finished UIImage object to the sender.

Switch to the CMColorView.h interface file, and add a readonly property declaration for the new image getter:

```
@property (readonly,nonatomic) UIImage *image;
```

Providing More Items to Share

Now if you want to get what the CMColorView object draws on the screen as an image, you simply fetch its image property. Use this in the -share: method. Select the CMColorViewController.m file and change the first few statements with the following code (changes in bold):

```
- (IBAction)share:(id)sender
{
    NSString *shareMessage = [NSString stringWithFormat:
                              @"I wrote an iOS app to share a color!"
                              @" RGB=%@"
                              @" @LearniOSAppDev",
                              [self.colorModel rgbCodeWithPrefix:nil]];
    UIImage *shareImage = self.colorView.image;
    NSURL *shareURL = [NSURL URLWithString:@"http://www.learniosappdev.com/"];
    NSArray *itemsToShare = @[shareMessage,shareImage,shareURL];
```

Run the app again. This time, you're passing three items (a string, an image, and a URL) to the UIActivityViewController. Notice how this changes the interface, as shown in Figure 13-6.

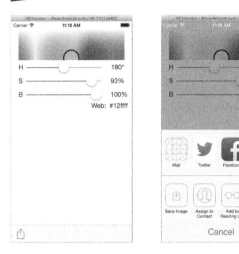  

Figure 13-6. Activities with more sharable items

Each activity responds to different kinds of data. Now that you include an image object, activities like Save Image and Assign to Contact appear. Each activity is also free to do what it thinks makes sense for the types of data you provide. The Mail activity will attach images and documents to a message, Facebook will upload images to the user's photo album, while Twitter may upload the picture to a photo-sharing service, and then include the link to that image in the tweet. It's completely automatic.

> **Tip** If you're curious about what activities work with what kinds of data, refer to the UIActivity class documentation. Its "Constants" section lists all of the built-in activities, and the classes of objects each responds to.

Excluding Activities

iOS's built-in activities are smart, but they aren't prescient; they don't know what the intent of your data is. Activities know when they can do something with a particular type of data, but not if they should. If there are activities that you, as a developer, don't think are appropriate for your particular blend of data, you can explicitly exclude them.

You've decided that printing a color example or assigning it to a contact don't make any sense. (You assume the user has no contacts for Little Red Riding Hood, The Scarlet Pimpernel, The Green Hornet, or other colorful characters.) Return to the -share: method in CMColorViewController.m. Immediately after the statement that creates the activityViewController, add this statement:

```
activityViewController.excludedActivityTypes = @[UIActivityTypeAssignToContact,
                                                 UIActivityTypePrint];
```

Setting this property excludes the listed built-in activities from the choices. Run the app again. This time, the excluded activities are, well, excluded (see Figure 13-7).

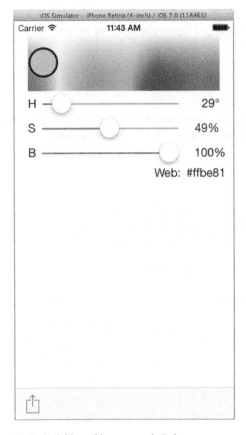 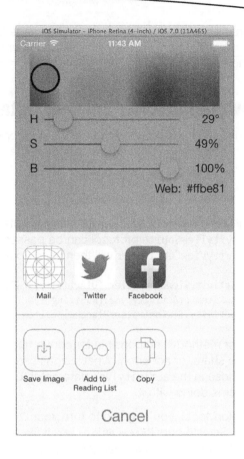

Figure 13-7. Activities with some excluded

The Curse of the Lowest Common Denominator

The activity view controller is a fantastic iOS feature, and it's likely to get better with time. About the only negative thing you can say about it is that it's too easy to use. Its biggest problem is that there's no obvious way of customizing that data items based on what the user wants to do with it.

Case in point: When I was developing the app for the chapter, I initially added a simple -rgbCode method to the CMColor class that returned the HTML code for the color (#f16c14). The problem with this is Twitter. On Twitter, so-called "hash tags" start with a pound/hash sign and are used to signal keywords in tweets. My color (#f16c14) would be interpreted as an "f16c14" tag, which doesn't make any sense. To avoid this, I rewrote the method so I could obtain the RGB value with, or without, the hash and purposely left it out from the message passed to UIActivityViewController. That way, if the user decided to share with Twitter, it wouldn't tweet a confusing message.

> **Note** Sina Weibo also uses hash tags, but the pound/hash signs bracket the tag (#Tag#). Thus, #f16c14 would not be a hash tag on Weibo.

But that's just the tip of the iceberg. Message length for mail and Facebook can be considerably longer than those on Twitter. Why should your text message or Facebook post be limited to 140 characters?

Providing Activity Specific Data

As it happens, the iOS engineers did not ignore this problem. There are several ways of customizing your content based on the type of activity the user chooses. The two tools iOS provides are:

- UIActivityItemSource
- UIActivityItemProvider

The first is a protocol, which your class adopts. Any object that conforms to the UIActivityItemSource protocol can be passed in the array of data items to share. The UIActivityViewController will then send your object these two (required) messages:

```
- (id)activityViewController:(UIActivityViewController *)activityViewController
          itemForActivityType:(NSString *)activityType
- (id)activityViewControllerPlaceholderItem:(UIActivityViewController *)activityViewController
```

The first method is responsible for converting the content of your object into the actual data you want to share, or act upon. What's significant about this message is that it includes the activity the user chose in the activityType parameter. Use this parameter to alter your content based on what the user is doing with it.

For ColorModel, you're going to turn your CMViewController object into a sharing message proxy object. Select your CMViewController.h file. Adopt the UIActivityItemSource protocol in your CMViewController class (changes in bold):

```
@interface CMViewController : UIViewController <UIActivityItemSource>
```

> **Tip** If you had a more complex conversion, or multiple conversions, I'd recommend creating new classes (possibly subclasses of UIActivityItemProvider) that did nothing but perform the transformation. This would make it easy to develop as many different kinds of conversions as you needed.

Switch to CMViewController.m. Add the first of UIActivityItemSource's two required methods:

```
- (id)activityViewController:(UIActivityViewController *)activityViewController
          itemForActivityType:(NSString *)activityType
{
    CMColor *color = self.colorModel;
    NSString *message = nil;
    if ([activityType isEqualToString:UIActivityTypePostToTwitter] ||
        [activityType isEqualToString:UIActivityTypePostToWeibo])
        {
        message = [NSString stringWithFormat:
                   @"Today's color is RGB=%@."
```

```
                    @"I wrote an iOS app to do this!"
                    @"@LearniOSAppDev",
                    [color rgbCodeWithPrefix:nil]];
    }
    else if ([activityType isEqualToString:UIActivityTypeMail])
    {
        message = [NSString stringWithFormat:
                    @"Hello,\n\n"
                    @"I wrote an awesome iOS app that lets me share"
                    @"a color with my friends.\n\n"
                    @"Here's my color (see attachment): hue=%.0f\u00b0,"
                    @"saturation=%.0f%%, "
                    @"brightness=%.0f%%.\n\n"
                    @"If you like it, use the code %@ in your design.\n\n"
                    @"Enjoy,\n\n",
                    color.hue,
                    color.saturation,
                    color.brightness,
                    [color rgbCodeWithPrefix:@"#"]];
    }
    else
    {
        message = [NSString stringWithFormat:
                    @"I wrote a great iOS app to share this color: %@",
                    [color rgbCodeWithPrefix:@"#"]];
    }

    return message;
}
```

This method performs the conversion from your object to the actual data object that the activity view controller is going to share or use. For this app, your controller will provide the message (`NSString` object) to post.

Your method examines the `activityType` parameter and compares it against one of the known activities. (If you provided your own custom activity, the value would be the name you gave your activity.) For Twitter and Weibo, it prepares a short announcement, avoiding inadvertently creating any hash tags, and including a Twitter-style mention. If the user chooses to send an e-mail, you prepare a rather lengthy message, without a mention. For Facebook, SMS, and any other activity, you create a medium-length message that doesn't worry about hash tags.

Find the `-share:` method and change the beginning of it so it looks like this (removing `shareMessage` and adding the new code in bold):

```
- (IBAction)share:(id)sender
{
    UIImage *shareImage = self.colorView.image;
    NSURL *shareURL = [NSURL URLWithString:@"http://www.learniosappdev.com/"];
    NSArray *itemsToShare = @[self,shareImage,shareURL];
```

Instead of preparing a message before the activity view controller is presented, you now pass your `CMViewController` object with a promise to provide the message. Once the user has decided what they want to do (print, Tweet, Message, and so on), your view controller will receive a -activityView Controller:itemForActivityType: message and produces the data.

Promises, Promises

You may have noticed the "chicken and egg" problem here. What activities are available is determined by the kinds of data you pass to the activity view controller. But with UIActivityItemSource, the data isn't produced until the user chooses an activity. So how does the activity view controller know what kind of activities to offer if it doesn't yet know what kind of data your method plans to produce?

The answer is the second required UIActivityItemSource method, and you need to add that now:

```
- (id)activityViewControllerPlaceholderItem:(UIActivityViewController *)activityViewController
{
    return @"My color message goes here.";
}
```

This method returns a placeholder object. While it could be the actual data you plan to share, it doesn't have to be. Its only requirement is that it be the same class of the object that -activityView Controller:itemForActivityType: will return in the future. Since your -activityViewController:item ForActivityType: returns an NSString, all this method has to do is return any NSString object.

> **Caution** The object that -activityViewController:itemForActivityType: returns should be "functionally equivalent" to the final data object, even if it's not the same data. For example, if you are supplying an NSURL object, the scheme (http:, mailto:, file:, sms:, and so on) of the placeholder URL should be the same.

Run the app again and try out different activities, as shown in Figure 13-8.

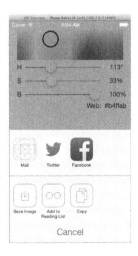   

Figure 13-8. Activity customized content

Big Data

The alternative technique for providing activity data is to create a custom subclass of UIActivityItemProvider. This class, which already conforms to the UIActivityItemSource protocol, produces your app's data object in the background. When the activity view controller wants your app's data, it sets the activityType property of your provider object and then requests its item property. Your subclass must override the -item method to provide the desired data, referring to activityType as needed.

UIActivityItemProvider is intended for large or complex data that's time-consuming to create, such as a video or a PDF document. It receives the -item message on a secondary execution thread—not on your app's main thread, which is the thread all of your code in this book has executed on so far. This allows your provider object to work in the background, preparing the data, while your app continues to run. It also requires an understanding of multi-tasking and thread-safe operations, topics that I visit in Chapter 24.

In short, if the data you need to share isn't particularly large, complicated, or time consuming to construct, or you're just not comfortable with multi-tasking yet, stick with adopting UIActivityItemSource.

Sharing with Specific Services

I'd like to round off this topic with some notes on other sharing services in iOS, and which ones to use.

The UIActivityViewController class is relatively new, and largely replaces several older APIs. If you search the iOS documentation for classes that will send e-mail, text messages (SMS), or Tweets, you're likely to find MFMailComposeViewController, MFMessageComposeViewController, and TWTweetComposeViewController. Each of these view controllers presents an interface that lets the user compose and send an e-mail message, a short text message, or a Tweet, respectively. The latter two don't offer any significant advantages over UIActivityViewController or SLComposeViewController (which I'll explain in a moment), and their use in new apps is not recommended.

The MFMailComposeViewController still has a trick or two to offer. Its biggest talent is its ability to create an HTML formatted mail message and/or pre-address the message by filling in the To, CC, and BCC fields. This allows you to create pre-addressed, richly formatted e-mail, with embedded CSS styling, animation, links, and other HTML goodies.

If you want to present your user with an interface to post to a specific social service—rather than asking them to choose—use the SLComposeViewController class. You create an SLComposeViewController object for a specific service (Twitter, Facebook, or Sina Weibo) using the +composeViewControllerForServiceType: message. You then configure that view controller with the data you want to share, as you did with UIActivityViewController, and present the view controller to the user. The user edits their message and away it goes.

> **Note** To use SLComposeViewController, add #import <Social/Social.h> to your implementation file.

Other Social Network Interactions

In ColorModel, we've only explored the sharing side of social networking. If you want your app to get information from your user's social networks, that's another matter altogether. Other types of interactions, like getting contact information about a user's Facebook friends, are handled by the SLRequest class.

An SLRequest works very similarly to the way an NSURLRequest works. You used NSURLRequest objects in Chapter 3 to send a request to the X.co URL shortening service. To use a social networking system, you prepare an SLRequest object in much the same manner, providing the URL of the service, the method (POST or GET), and any required parameters. You send the request, providing a code block that will process the response.

The biggest difference between SLRequest and NSURLRequest is the account property. This property stores an ACAccount object that describes a user's account on a specific social networking service. This property allows SLRequest to handle all of the authentication and encryption required to communicate your request to the servers. If you've ever written any OAuth handling code, you'll appreciate how much work SLRequest is doing for you.

To use other social networking features you must, therefore, prepare the following:

- Service Type
- Service URL
- Request method (POST, GET, DELETE)
- Request parameters dictionary
- The user's ACAccount object

The service type is one of SLServiceTypeFacebook, SLServiceTypeSinaWeibo, SLServiceTencentWeibo, or SLServiceTypeTwitter. The URL, method, and parameters dictionary are dictated by whatever kind of request you're making. For those details, consult the developer documentation for the specific service. Some places to start reading are listed in Table 13-1.

Table 13-1. Social Services Developer Documentation

Social Service	URL
Facebook	https://developers.facebook.com/docs/
Sina Weibo	http://open.weibo.com/wiki/
Tencent Weibo	http://dev.t.qq.com/
Twitter	https://dev.twitter.com/docs

Finally, you'll need the ACAccount object for the user's account. Account and login information is maintained by iOS for your app, so your app only needs to request it. Whether the user wants to authorize your app to use their account, or they need to sign in, it's all handled for you.

The basic steps to obtaining an account object are:

1. Create an instance of the `ACAccountStore` object.

2. Send the account store an `-accountTypeWithAccountTypeIdentifier:` message to get an `ACAccountType` object for the service you're interested in. An `ACAccountType` object is your key to the user's accounts on a specific service.

3. Finally, you send the account store a `-requestAccessToAccountsWithType:` message. If successful (and allowed) your app will receive an array of `ACAccount` objects for that user.

Services like Facebook allow an iOS user to be logged into only one account at a time. Twitter, on the other hand, permits a user to be connected to multiple accounts simultaneously. Your app will have to decide if it wants to use all of the account objects, selected ones, or just one. Once you have an `ACAccount` object, use it to set the `account` property of the `SLRequest`, and you're ready to get social!

Summary

You've learned how to add yet another nifty feature to your app, allowing your users to connect and share content with friends and family around the world—and it only took a smattering of code to get it working. You learned how to tailor that content for specific services, or exclude services. If you want more control over which services your app provides, you learned how to use the `SLComposeViewController` to create a specific sharing interface, along with the `SLRequest` class that provides a conduit for unlimited social networking integration.

During your journey, you also gained some practical experience in drawing into an off-screen graphics context, and using Xcode's refactoring tool. The refactoring command contains a powerful set of code maintenance tools. If you plan to rename or relocate a method or property, you should make friends with the refactoring tools and other global editing commands. To read more about them, search for "Make Projectwide Changes" in Xcode's Documentation and API Reference window.

Sharing posts with your friends and colleagues isn't the only way iOS apps communicate. In Chapter 3 you wrote an app that uses an Internet URL shortening service. In the next chapter, you're going to write an app that talks to another iOS device directly, via Wi-Fi or Bluetooth.

Chapter 14

Networking, The Nerdy Kind

You might use (social) networking to crowd-source the perfect color for your bookshelves or find a great place to stay on your next trip, but "networking" means something altogether different to computer engineers. A *data network* allows computer systems and devices to directly exchange information, and is largely what makes portable devices useful. (How sad would your iPhone be if it couldn't place telephone calls, get text messages, surf the web, send e-mail, or download apps?)

The goal of this chapter is to introduce you to some simple peer-to-peer networking. "Simple" and "peer-to-peer networking" are words you don't often see together. Networking is tricky. Peer-to-peer networking is downright thorny. So if you want to write an app that directly exchanges data with another device, what are your choices?

> **Note** Peer-to-peer means that two coequal computer systems are communicating directly with one another, exchanging data, without going through an intermediate computer system, such as a message or web server.

Your choices are to spend a lot of time learning about network communications—or use GameKit. The GameKit designers realized that it would be a lot of fun if two or more iOS users could sit down and all play the same game. The individual iOS apps would get together to form an ad-hoc network. They could then send live updates to each other, so everyone can participate. Knowing how incredibly difficult it is to construct a network (Wi-Fi, Bluetooth, and so on), coordinate the discovery of other players, maintain the connections between them, and distribute messages to all parties, they did you a huge favor: they wrote it for you. GameKit does all of that work automatically. All your app has to do is prepare the data.

As an added bonus, you get to learn GameKit and create a Game Center–aware app. That alone is worth reading this chapter. A Game Center–aware app can network with other players, post scores to a worldwide leaderboard, participate in challenges, and more. In this chapter you will:

- Develop a single-player and two-player game
- Assign your app an ID and register it with iTunes Connect

- Create leaderboards for your app in Game Center
- Record player scores
- Use GameKit to establish a peer-to-peer data connection with another iOS device
- Exchange real-time data between two iOS apps
- Learn some new things about loading view controllers, creating animations, and establishing the orientations a view controller supports

The chapter takes a departure from previous ones. Most of the code for your app isn't listed in this chapter. The bulk of the code for the game—which is actually secondary to this chapter's objective—is in the Learn iOS Development Projects ➤ Ch 14 folder. Your app will progress through several iterations, each of which is in a subfolder. I'll describe the important elements and milestones of the app's development, but not all steps in detail.

> **Note** To test GameKit, you must be a registered iOS developer. To test peer-to-peer communications, you must have two, provisioned, iOS devices. GameKit peer-to-peer networking does not work in the iOS simulator.

SunTouch

The app for this chapter is a game named SunTouch. Play begins with a star field. Touch a point in the field to blast a hole in space, as shown in Figure 14-1. Any suns hiding in that area are captured. The game ends when you've captured all of the suns. It's sort of asteroids meets minesweeper.

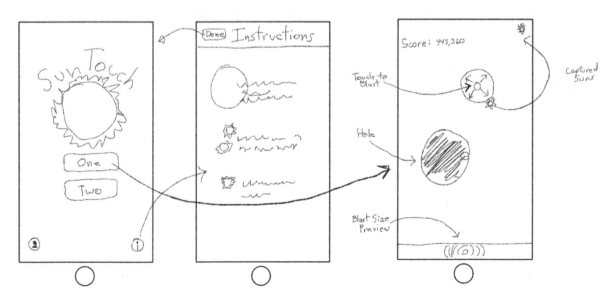

Figure 14-1. SunTouch design

There are two additional strategic elements. The size of the blast increases the longer you wait between blasts. An indicator at the bottom of the screen gives the user an idea of how big the blast radius will be. So waiting gives you a bigger blast and a better chance of capturing a sun. Countering that, the score for capturing a sun goes down over time. So the longer you wait to capture a sun, the lower your score. Does that all make sense? Let's get started.

Creating SunTouch

The first iteration of SunTouch is in the `Learn iOS Development Projects` ➤ `Ch 14` ➤ `SunTouch-1` folder. Your game will need an opening screen, a screen of instructions, and a screen to play the game. The app was based on the `Utility` app project template. This template has an initial view controller and an alternate view controller that appears when the user taps the small "info" button. On the iPad, this appears in a popover.

The project was created with a company identifier of `com.apress.learniosdev` and a class prefix of ST. Up to this point, the company identifier hasn't been that important. Now it is. To test an app that uses Game Center, you must register your app with Apple. To register, you must assign your app a unique app ID. If you, or your organization, own an Internet domain name, you can use that as a unique prefix for all of the apps you develop.

You don't have to worry about it just yet. You can change your app's identifier, after its project has been created, in the project settings. Just start thinking about the identifier you want to use; I'll show you how to change it when the time comes.

Designing the Initial Screens

In the first iteration, I've just done the window dressing. I added a backdrop graphic and two buttons to the initial view controller (`STMainViewController`), one to start a single player game and a second to start a two-player game, as shown in Figure 14-2. In the flipside view controller, I added image view and text view objects to provide some basic game-play instructions, also shown in Figure 14-2.

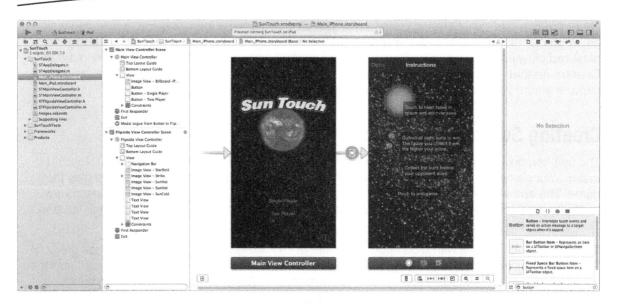

Figure 14-2. Initial and flipside interface design

If you were developing this project yourself, you would:

1. Create a new project based on the `Utility iOS app` template

   a. Set the class prefix to `ST`

   b. Make sure `Use Core Data` is not checked

2. Add the image resources in the `SunTouch (Resources)` folder to your `Images.xcassets` image catalog. Drop the icon resources in the `SunTouch (Icons)` folder into the catalog's `AppIcon` group.

3. In the `Main_iPhone.xib` (or `_iPad`) file, find the flipside view and follow these steps:

   a. If you're developing the iPad version, the flipside view is presented in a popover. Begin by selecting the Flipside View Controller and, using the attributes inspector, set its simulated metrics size to `Freeform`. Select the root view and, using the size inspector, set its height to 500.

   b. Add image view and text view objects as shown in Figure 14-2. The image resource files used are `Strike.png`, `SunHot.png`, and `SunCold.png`. The text is `white`, with a `black` background that's 50% transparent.

c. Add one more image view object, set its image to `Starfield.png`, its mode to `Aspect Fill`, and resize it to fill the view. With the image view selected, choose **Edit ➤ Arrange ➤ Send to Back**. This will put the star image behind the other view objects.

d. Pin the height and the width of the image view with the `Strike` image. For the background image view, add constraints so its top, bottom, left, and right edges are flush (0 pixels from) with the Top Layout Guide, Bottom Layout Guide, leading container, and trailing container, respectively. If you arrange the other views so they're clearly visible on a 3.5" iPhone, you don't need any other constraints.

4. In the main view controller:

    a. Add two button objects, labeled `Single Player` and `Two Player`. Set their shadow color to `White Color`. (This makes the button text easier to read on the dark background.)

    b. Add a **Vertical Spacing** constraint from the lower button to the `Bottom Layout Guide`, another from the upper button to the lower one, and then horizontally center both buttons in the container view.

    c. Add an image view object, set its image to `Billboard-iPhone.png`, and resize it to fill the view. Arrange it behind the other views. Use the **Editor ➤ Pin** submenu to pin its top, bottom, leading, and trailing space to its superview.

    d. Select the `Main View Controller` (iPhone version only) and use the attributes inspector to set its status bar option to None. This will hide the status bar information (battery, Wi-Fi indicator, and so one) that's normally at the top of the display.

    e. In the iPad version, change the title of the "Info" navigation bar button to "Instructions."

> **Tip** If you have a large view object in your interface, create and position it last. If you try to add it first, it will be very difficult—if not impossible—to add the views that go in front of it because Interface Builder will assume that the foreground objects should be subviews of the background object, instead of overlapping peers.

Run the project and test the flipside view, as shown in Figure 14-3. The code that accomplishes this is supplied by the template, and can be found in the `STMainViewController` and `STFlipsideViewController` classes.

Figure 14-3. Testing the game instructions

So far, the game is looking pretty snazzy. It's a shame there's no actual game yet. The next step is to create the single-player version of the game. This will become the foundation for integrating with Game Center and adding networking.

Creating the Single Player Version

The code for the single player game is in the Learn iOS Development Projects ➤ Ch 14 ➤ SunTouch-2 folder. This version of the project adds 12 files:

STGameDefs.h
STGameViewController.h, STGameViewController.m, STGameViewController.xib
STGameView.h, STGameView.m
STStrike.h, STStrike.m
STSun.h, STSun.m
STGame.h, STGame.m

The STGameDefs.h is a header file containing constants, macros, and in-line functions used by most of the other files. In larger projects, it's common to collect all of the globally relevant definitions into a single file that can be imported by whatever modules need them.

The game starts when the user taps the "single player" button in the main storyboard. A new view controller was added to the storyboard and its class changed to STGameViewController, as shown in Figure 14-4. A modal segue was added from the single player button to the new view controller. The segue was given the identifier singlePlayer. The game starts when the STGameViewController is presented.

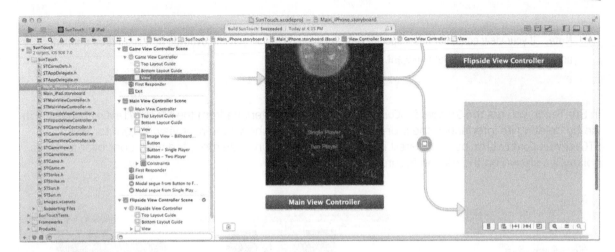

Figure 14-4. View controllers in storyboard

Loading STGameViewController

This project has an unusual Interface Builder file organization. So far, you've developed projects where the interfaces were all designed in a single storyboard file. This project defines the interfaces for the initial view and the flipside view in the storyboard file. The view objects for the STGameViewController, however, are defined in a separate STGameViewController.xib file. A view controller can obtain its view objects from a scene in a storyboard, its own .xib file, or can create them programmatically. Here's how it works:

1. When a view controller is loaded from a storyboard, it and its view objects are (normally) created at the same time. The view controller's view objects already exist when it's time to present the interface, so there's nothing more to do. This is the typical arrangement when using storyboards.

2. If the view controller is asked to present its interface and it doesn't have any view objects, it sends itself a -loadView message. The -loadView method first looks for the Interface Builder resource file the controller was initialized with. This applies when you programmatically create a view controller using the -initWithNibName:bundle: method. When creating view controller this way, it's recommended that you explicitly tell the view controller the name of the file that contains its interface.

3. If the view controller doesn't have an explicit .xib filename, it tries to load the interface file with the same name as its class, which in this case is STGameViewController.xib. This is how STGameViewController loads its interface in SunTouch.

4. Finally, if there were no views in the storyboard file, and no .xib file can be loaded, the -loadView method creates an empty UIView object as its view.

> **Note** If your view controller has a special view loading procedure, you can override its `-loadView` method and create its views however you want.

In SunTouch you get the `STGameViewController` to load its interface from the `STGameViewController.xib` file by deleting its interface in the storyboard. Figure 14-5 shows the root view object for the `STGameViewController` being deleted in Interface Builder. Once deleted, the view controller appears hollow, as shown on the right in Figure 14-5.

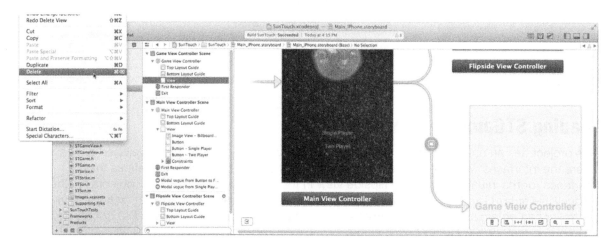

Figure 14-5. Deleting STGameViewController's view objects

So why did I do this? When using storyboards for a universal app, you must lay out your interface twice: once for the iPhone and again for the iPad. For interfaces like the game instructions, this is great, since the iPhone and iPad version are substantially different. The interface for `STGameViewController`, however, works equally well on the iPhone and iPad. By deleting the interface in the storyboard files, and supplying an `STGameViewController.xib` file, both the iPhone and iPad version load the same Interface Builder file. Now you have a single `STGameViewController.xib` file to maintain. You'll see where this reduces the work you have to do when you get to the two-player version of the game.

How SunTouch Works

I'm not going to explain everything in detail, but here's an overview of how the game works. The `-viewDidAppear:` method in `STGameViewController` starts everything when it sends itself the `-startGame` message. `-startGame` creates an `STGame` object (the game engine), connects it to the `STGameView` object, and then starts the game engine and the strike preview animation.

Gameplay works through messages sent to the `STGame` object. When the user touches the screen, a `-touchInGame:event:` action is sent to the game view controller. The controller determines where the user touched and sends a `-strike:radius:inView:` message to the game engine.

The game engine maintains the list of hidden suns. It uses the strike coordinates and radius to determine if a strike will capture a sun. These strike and capture events are communicated to the game view via notifications (kGameStrikeNotification and kGameSunCaptureNotification). The game view observes these notifications and creates the animations that you see on the screen.

The game engine also posts a kGameScoreDidChangeNotification notification whenever the score changes, and a kGameDidEndNotification notification when it's all over. The game and main view controllers observe these notifications to update the score view and dismiss the game view controller at the end. The game view controller also keeps two other animations going: the score weight is periodically updated using a timer (NSTimer) and the strike preview animation is restarted after each strike.

There are two interesting aspects of the game's design. First, there's the game space coordinate system. The location of the hidden suns, the coordinates of strikes, the size of the strike radius, and so on are stored and calculated using a logical coordinate system with values and distances between 0.0 and 1.0. "Why" you ask? Because the two-player game must translate between the coordinates of two iOS devices. The two players could be using different size devices, possibly in different orientations. By performing all game-play calculations in a unit coordinate system, these differences can be ignored. A sun at unit coordinates (0.25,0.25) is in the upper-left quadrant of the screen, regardless if that screen is an iPod Touch in landscape orientation or an iPad in portrait orientation. Methods in STGameView (-pointFromUnitPoint:, and so on) translate between game unit and view coordinates.

Customizing Core Animations

The other features you may want to look at are the animations. SunTouch uses several Core Animation sequences. Many animations use the block-based methods you learned in Chapter 11, but sometimes you need an animation that doesn't run in a straight line or uses one of the simple animation curves (ease in, ease out, ease in-out, or linear). In these situations, you need to create a CAAnimation object yourself.

Look at the code in -startStrikeGrowAnimation that you'll find in STGameViewController.m. This code creates an animation that changes the size of the strike preview image view object over time:

```
NSMutableArray *times = [NSMutableArray new];
NSMutableArray *values = [NSMutableArray new];
CGRect rect;
for ( float time=0.0f; time<=1.0f; time+=0.1f )
    {
    CGFloat r = STFloor((maxRadius-kStrikePreviewMinRadius)
                    *STSquareRoot(time)
                    +kStrikePreviewMinRadius);
```

```
        rect = CGRectMake(0,0,r*2,r*2);
        [times addObject:@(time)];
        [values addObject:[NSValue valueWithCGRect:rect]];
    }
CAKeyframeAnimation* animation;
animation = [CAKeyframeAnimation animationWithKeyPath:@"bounds"];
animation.duration = kStrikePreviewGrowDuration;
animation.beginTime = 0;
animation.calculationMode = kCAAnimationCubic;
animation.keyTimes = times;
animation.values = values;
[previewView.layer addAnimation:animation forKey:@"grow"];
```

This code creates a keyframe animation (CAKeyframeAnimation) object. CAKeyframeAnimation is a subclass of CAAnimation, used to manage an animation sequence. A keyframe animation defines several reference values at specific times during the animation. The animation object can then calculate a continuous curve of values by interpolating between keyframe values. A CAKeyframeAnimation object can animate almost any property of the view object: its frame, center, background color, rotation, scaling, transparency, drop shadow, a Core Image color filter, and so on. By creating a sequence of keyframe values, you can create any animation curve you want. You can make the view bounce, wink in and out, loop in a circle, pulse, or swing like a pendulum.

In this app, the keyframe defines a logarithmic size change. The code calculates 11 keyframe values at equidistant times (0.0 to 1.0, in 0.1 increments). The value of each keyframe is the view's bounds, which is scaled based on the elapsed time, squared. Intermediate values are calculated using cubic interpolation, which will closely approximate to the actual logarithmic curve; it's not perfect, but it's good enough.

Once the animation object is configured with the list of keyframe values and times, it is attached to the layer property of the view object. Remember (from Chapter 11) that UIView objects are built from CALayer objects. It's the CALayer object that actually appears in the interface, and is the object that can be animated.

Playing the Game

Run the app and give it a try, as shown in Figure 14-6. The single-player game will run in the simulator or on any provisioned device.

Figure 14-6. Single player game

> **Note** While using Core Animation to fling `UIImageView` objects around the screen is good enough for this project, I doubt anyone has created any killer iOS games using similar techniques. If you're interested in creating games, you should look into technologies like Sprite Kit (new in iOS 7), OpenGL, or one of the many game engines that have been developed for iOS. Game engines are third-party (read "not written by Apple") frameworks that make it much easier to write spectacular games. Apress publishes a diverse selection of books on iOS game development.

I recommend that you spend a little time exploring this project. Start by observing how the interface elements work: the strike animation, the hole left behind afterwards, the sun capture animation, the updating score and weight labels, and the strike size preview. Then trace the messages that make those things happen until you're comfortable with how the whole app works. Understanding how strikes are sent to the game (`STGame`) and how the game sends sun capture messages will be important when you get to the two-player version.

The next step is to add the GameKit to your app and integrate it with the Game Center.

Plugging into Game Center

Game Center is a service, provided by Apple, to enhance your game with social networking. Apps that work with Game Center are said to be *Game Center–aware*. The most visible part of the Game Center is its *leaderboard*, a public scoreboard displaying the highest scoring players from around the world. Game milestones, called *achievements*, that you've accomplished are also announced here.

Multi-player games can use Game Center to invite, and connect, with other players. This process is called *matchmaking*. Matchmaking can happen over the Internet at large, for slow games that can be played over arbitrary distances. Alternatively, your app can pair with iOS devices in your immediate vicinity (technically, on the same Wi-Fi subnet or within Bluetooth range), creating direct data connections for playing real-time action games.

It's your choice what Game Center features you support in your game. You can add all of these features, or just one. For SunTouch, you're going to add two: leaderboard scores and local matchmaking. For this to work, you must enable your app to use Game Center and configure Game Center for your game.

Configuring a Game Center–aware app

Enabling Game Center in your app is a multi-step process that involves configuring your app's project, configuring the iTunes Store, and adding specific code to your app. Specifically, you must:

- Assign your app a unique ID
- Register your unique ID with Apple
- Register your app with Apple and assign it that unique ID
- Configure the Game Center with the leaderboards and achievements your app will use
- Add the necessary digital certificates required for your app to use the Game Center servers
- Link your app to the GameKit framework
- Add "gamekit" as a capability of your app
- Add code to log the current player in
- Add a button so the user can access the Game Center leaderboards from within your app
- Request matchmaking when starting a multi-player game
- Send scores and achievements to Game Center
- Create a test player account and test your game in the sandbox

That sounds like a lot of steps, but none of them are particularly difficult and Xcode will do a lot of them for you.

Start with your app's project. Select the project in the navigator and switch to `General` tab and find the `Identity` group, as shown in Figure 14-7. It should be right at the top.

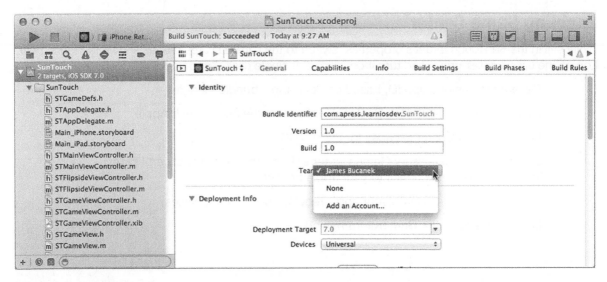

Figure 14-7. Editing the app ID

The bundle identifier uniquely identifies your app, in the universe of all iOS apps. The identifier can be any (RFC1034 compliant) name. If you (or your company) own an Internet domain, it's recommended that you base your app identifiers on that domain name, reducing the chance that someone else might try to use the same identifier. You can also add sub-domains to help you organize your apps into groups.

> **Note** RFC1034 is the document that describes exactly how domain names are written. RFC (Request For Comment) documents are managed by the Network Working Group. An RFC document starts as a proposal (thus, the name). Once it has been approved and accepted, it becomes the "law" of the Internet.

Whatever base identifier you choose, Xcode appends the app's product identifier to form the complete ID. So if you named your project SunTouch, and entered a base bundle identifier of com.mycompany.games, your app's ID will be com.mycompany.games.SunTouch.

Change your project's bundle identifier now so your app has a unique ID. You won't be able to register your app until you've done so.

You'll also need to choose a Team from the pop-up menu, also shown in Figure 14-7. Your app's identifier will belong to the iOS Developer account associated with the team you select and it designates the team members allowed to install and test your app. If you have not yet connected Xcode to your iOS Developer account, choose the **Add an Account…** command and Xcode will take you to the accounts pane of the preferences, where you can do so.

Enabling Game Center

While still in the SunTouch target's properties, switch to the Capabilities tab, as shown in Figure 14-8. Locate the Game Center group and turn it on. With that single click, Xcode does the following for you:

- Generates a unique app ID, based on your app's bundle identifier
- Connects with the iOS Dev Center and registers the new ID with Apple
- Enables Game Center services for the new ID
- Downloads the necessary Game Center entitlements and digital certificates, installing those resources into your app's project
- Adds the "gamekit" key to your app's required device capabilities
- Links your app to the GameKit framework

 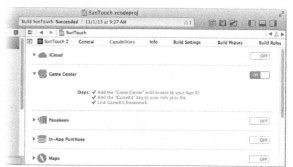

Figure 14-8. Enabling Game Center

> **Note** All of these steps can be performed manually, either in the project settings or through the iOS Dev Center.

See, I told you a lot of the steps were easy. If you want to see what Xcode did in the Dev Center, log into http://developer.apple.com/devcenter/ios, click on the Certificates, Identifiers & Profiles section, and click on Identifiers. The developer portal will list all of the identifiers registered to your account. Click on the identifier generated by Xcode, as shown in Figure 14-9.

Figure 14-9. Registered App ID

Your app's full ID consists of the unique Prefix (generated by Apple) and its app ID, concatenated together. Notice that Game Center services have already been enabled for use with this app ID. The name of your ID (Xcode iOS App ID com apress learniosapps SunTouch) that was generated by Xcode is awkward, but you can change that at any time by clicking the **Edit** button. The name of an identifier is solely for managing IDs in the iOS Dev Center; it doesn't appear anywhere in your app or to the user. In the edit ID page, you can also manually disable or enable services associated with this ID.

The next step is to configure Game Center with the leaderboards you want. A leaderboard is where game scores are posted. But before you can get to that, you must create an app in the iTunes App Store.

Creating an App in the iTunes Store

The next step is to register your app with the iTunes Store. If you thought you just did that, you didn't. What you've done is register an ID. Now you need to assign that ID to an app.

Log into your iOS Dev Center account (http://developer.apple.com/devcenter/ios) page and locate the iTunes Connect link. iTunes Connect is the portal you use to work with the iTunes Store. It's also the place where you setup and configure other online support services, such as Game Center, In-App Purchases, advertising, and subscription apps (magazines).

After signing into iTunes Connect, locate and click on the Manage Your Apps link. This will list all of the apps you have registered with the App Store. Apps go through a process of registration, configuration, submission, and approval before they appear in the App Store. To test an app with Game Center, you must register and configure your app. Click on the **Add New App** button and fill in the details, as shown in Figure 14-10.

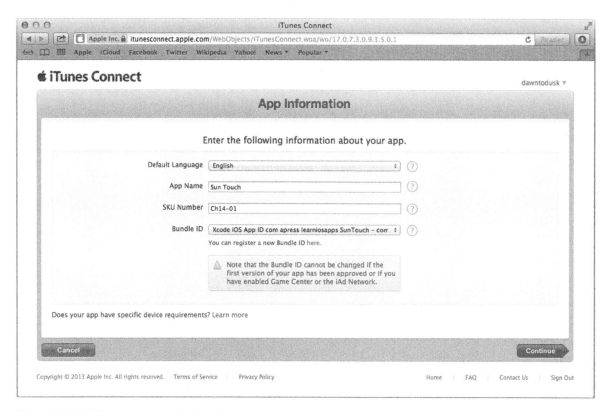

Figure 14-10. Adding a new app to the App Store

> **Note** If you've never used iTunes Connect before, it may ask additional questions about your company name and how you want that to appear in the App Store. Basically, if the portal asks for additional information I don't mention in this section, provide it and keep moving.

Select the default language and give your app a name ("Sun Touch"). This is the name of your app, as it will appear in the store. You must assign your app an SKU number, although it can be any identifier you choose. It only has to be unique among the apps that you develop, and Apple doesn't use it for anything except reporting.

Finally, choose the bundle ID you created in the previous section from the pop-up menu. If you forgot to create a unique ID, there's a convenient link that will take you back to the Certificates, Identifiers & Profiles page where you can correct that oversight.

You'll then be led through a series of screens that let you set the date your app will be available for sale, its price, its category, any content warnings, the required App Store icons and screen shots, a description of your app, and so on. Unless you actually plan to publish a version of SunTouch on the App Store, you don't need to be too concerned with the answers. Files for the required uploads (icons and screen shots) can be found in the `Learn iOS Development Projects` ➤ `Ch 14` ➤ `SunTouch (iTunes Connect)` folder.

> **Caution** These are the exact steps you'll take to prepare any app for distribution through Apple's App Store. After creating an app record, you have (as of this writing) approximately 180 days to submit your app for approval. If you wait too long, Apple may—at its discretion—delete your app from iTunes Connect and forbid you from using that app name in the future.

When you're finished, your app will appear in iTunes Connect. Locate your new app and click on its icon to manage it, as shown in Figure 14-11.

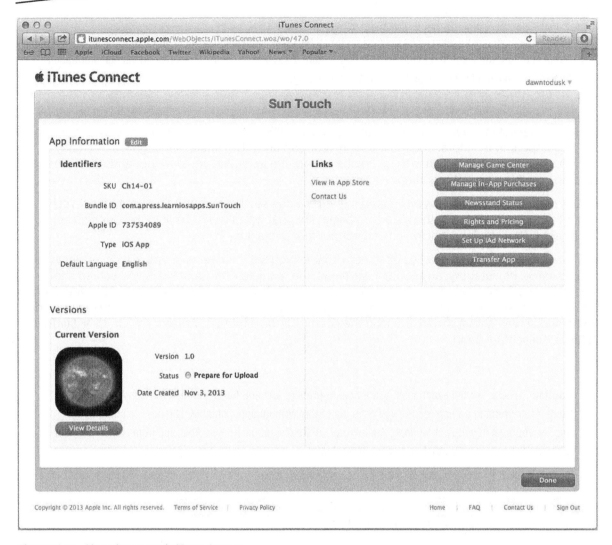

Figure 14-11. Managing an app in iTunes Connect

Configuring Game Center

Once you've created your app in iTunes Connect, click on the **Manage Game Center** button (see Figure 14-11). The Game Center management page is where you enable Game Center features for your app. Your app is already enabled for use with Game Center, as shown in Figure 14-12. If it wasn't, just turn it on now.

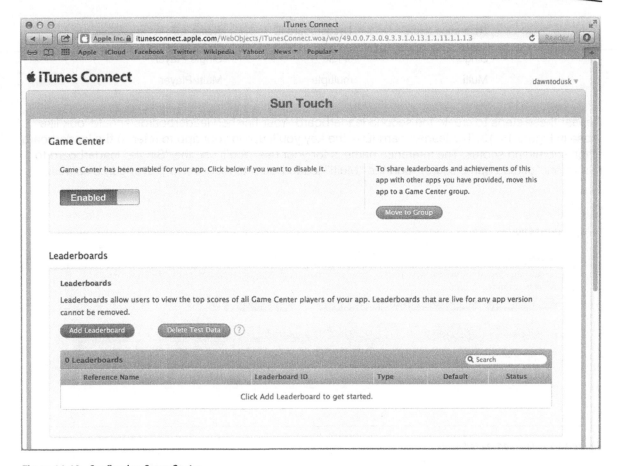

Figure 14-12. Configuring Game Center

To use the leaderboards feature in your app, you must create one or more leaderboards in the Game Center. You can create single scoreboards that are independent of one another, or combined scoreboards that aggregate other scoreboards. For SunTouch, create two independent (single) scoreboards by clicking the **Add Leaderboard** button, shown in Figure 14-12. Configure the boards as follows:

1. Choose to create a Single leaderboard
2. Fill in the leaderboard reference name and leaderboard ID (see table)
3. Score format type: Integer
4. Score Submission Type: Best Score
5. Sort Order: High to Low
6. Leave Score Range empty
7. Add at least one language to the Leaderboard Localization list
   a. Give the leaderboard a name in the choosen language (see table)
   b. Select the appropriate score formatting options (US English uses comma separators in integer numbers, for example)

Reference Name	Leaderboard ID	Name
Single	single	Single Player
Multi	multiple	Multi-Player

Repeat these steps to create the second leaderboard. Your finished leaderboards should look like those in Figure 14-13. The leaderboard ID is the key you'll use in your app to refer to the leaderboard when submitting scores. The reference name is for your use. You'll use the "Single" leaderboard to record one-person game scores, and the "Multi" leaderboard to record two-player game scores.

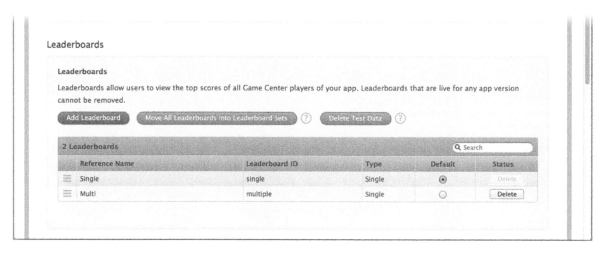

Figure 14-13. Finished leaderboards

Save your work by clicking the **Save** button and sign out of iTunes Connect. Your work there is done. Now you can add GameKit support to your app and create a test user.

Adding GameKit to Your App

The Game Center–aware version of SunTouch can be found in the `Learn iOS Development Projects` ➤ `Ch 14` ➤ `SunTouch-3` folder. You can open that, or follow these steps to add Game Center support to the single-player version of the game.

Now you need to add the code to your app to activate and interact with Game Center. At a minimum, you must:

- Obtain the local player as soon as possible
- If the local player is not logged in, present the login view controller
- Disable your game if the local player cannot, or refuses to, log in
- Add a button to your interface to allow the user to interact with Game Center

For games that record scores to a leaderboard, you must:

- Report each score to the appropriate leaderboard

Let's get started.

Obtaining the Local Player

The very first thing your app should do after launching is to obtain the local player (GKLocalPlayer) object. Add this code to `STMainViewController.m`:

```
- (void)viewDidAppear:(BOOL)animated
{
    [super viewDidAppear:animated];

    __weak GKLocalPlayer *localPlayer = [GKLocalPlayer localPlayer];
    localPlayer.authenticateHandler = 
                    ^(UIViewController *viewController, NSError *error) {
        if (viewController!= nil)
            [self showAuthenticationView:viewController];
        else if (localPlayer.authenticated)
            [self authenticatePlayer:localPlayer];
        else
            [self disableGameCenter];
    };
}
```

The local player object represents the user's identity in Game Center. Normally, a user will already be logged into Game Center and there's nothing to do. If they have not logged in, you should immediately present the Game Center authentication view, which allows the user to log into their Game Center account. If they can't, or won't, you should disable your game or run it in a mode that doesn't interact with Game Center.

All of those cases are handled in the code block you set for the `authenticateHandler` property. Unlike most objects, the process of logging into Game Center isn't one you explicitly initiate. It's an ongoing endeavor, as the player can log out or switch accounts at any time (using the Game Center app on their iOS device). The code block you set in `authenticateHandler` is executed whenever there's a change in the player's Game Center status.

In SunTouch, there are three conditions that require action. If the `viewController` is not `nil`, Game Center is telling your app that it wants it to present that view controller to the user. Typically, this is because the player is not logged in; that view controller presents a login screen so the player can authenticate with Game Center.

The second condition is that the player is now, or was already, authenticated and is ready to play your game. At this point your game should prepare itself for play. In SunTouch, the `-authenticatePlayer:` method readies itself by displaying the two "start game" buttons.

Finally, Game Center will signal your app that the local player is not, or is no longer, authorized. In other words, they logged out or weren't logged in. SunTouch sends a `-disableGameCenter` message that hides the two "start game" buttons. The user won't be able to play the game until they log in.

To finish this code, you need to add those three methods to the STMainViewController.m file:

```
- (void)showAuthenticationView:(UIViewController*)viewController
{
    [self presentViewController:viewController animated:YES completion:NULL];
}

- (void)authenticatePlayer:(GKLocalPlayer*)player
{
    self.singlePlayButton.hidden = NO;
    self.multiPlayButton.hidden = NO;
}

- (void)disableGameCenter
{
    self.singlePlayButton.hidden = YES;
    self.multiPlayButton.hidden = YES;
}
```

Adding a Game Center Button

You've already handled the first three requirements (obtaining the local player, logging the player in, and disabling the game when they aren't). All Game Center–aware apps should also provide a button so the user can access the Game Center interface from within the app. This is where the user can see their leaderboards, scores, and achievements.

In SunTouch, add a small (22x22 pixel) custom button to the main view controller in the Main_iPhone. storyboard (or _iPad) file. Use the GameCenter.png image, as shown in Figure 14-14. Fix its height and width, and add constraints to the Bottom Layout Guide and the closest container view edge.

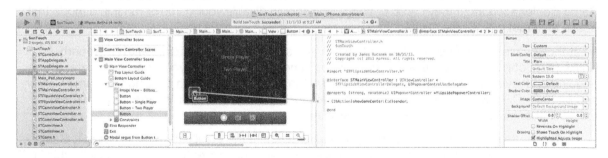

Figure 14-14. Adding a Game Center button

Switch to the assistant editor, so that STMainViewController.h appears in the right pane. Add an action method declaration:

- (IBAction)showGameCenter;

Connect the game center button to this action (see Figure 14-14). While you're in STMainViewController.h, there are some loose ends that need to be taken care of. The earlier code uses two button outlets. Declare those and connect them to the Single Player and Two Player buttons:

```
@property (weak,nonatomic) IBOutlet UIButton *singlePlayButton;
@property (weak,nonatomic) IBOutlet UIButton *multiPlayButton;
```

Select the two buttons in the storyboard and use the attributes inspector to hide them (by checking the hidden attribute). This way, the buttons won't appear when the app starts. If the player is logged into Game Center, the -authenticatePlayer: method will immediately reveal (unhide) them. The player probably won't even notice. This precaution does, however, prevent a nimble-fingered user from starting a game before the status of the local player can be determined.

If you're building both versions of the app, make the same changes (add the Game Center button, connect it to the -showGameCenter action, connect the two outlets to the buttons, and hide the buttons) in the other storyboard (_iPhone or _iPad).

For reasons I'll explain in a moment, your STMainViewController will need to adopt the GKGameCenterControllerDelegate, so add that now (new code in bold):

```
@interface STMainViewController : UIViewController
                                 <STFlipsideViewControllerDelegate,
                                  UIPopoverControllerDelegate,
                                  GKGameCenterControllerDelegate>
```

Finally (or firstly) import the GameKit.h header:

```
#import <GameKit/GameKit.h>
```

Now switch to STMainViewController.m and add the -showGameCenter action method and the GKGameCenterControllerDelegate handler method:

```
- (IBAction)showGameCenter
{
    GKGameCenterViewController *gameCenterController;
    gameCenterController = [GKGameCenterViewController new];

    if (gameCenterController!=nil)
        {
        gameCenterController.gameCenterDelegate = self;
        [self presentViewController:gameCenterController
                       animated:YES
                     completion:nil];
        }
}

- (void)gameCenterViewControllerDidFinish:(GKGameCenterViewController*)controller
{
    [self dismissViewControllerAnimated:YES completion:nil];
}
```

You've seen this kind of code before. The -showGameCenter method creates a GKGameCenterViewController, sets itself as the delegate, and modally presents the view controller to the user. When the view controller is done, your delegate receives a -gameCenterViewControllerDidFinish: message (which is why your controller had to adopt GKGameCenterControllerDelegate) that dismisses the game center view controller.

You've now satisfied the minimum requirements for a Game Center–aware app. But SunTouch uses leaderboards, so in the next section you'll add code to record the player's score.

Recording Leaderboard Scores

Recording the player's score to the leaderboard is probably the simplest part of your app. You only need two pieces of information: the leaderboard identifier and the final score. Select the STGameViewController.m file and locate the -finishGame method. At the end of the if block, change the code so it looks like this (new code in bold):

```
self.strikePreview.hidden = YES;
GKScore *scoreReport;
scoreReport = [[GKScore alloc] initWithLeaderboardIdentifier: ←
                                            kSinglePlayerLeaderboardID];
scoreReport.value = score;
[GKScore reportScores:@[scoreReport] withCompletionHandler:^(NSError *error) {
    }];
}
```

The -initWithLeaderboardIdentifier: initializer method creates a GKScore object for the leaderboard you want to post the score to. You then set the score property you want to report and send it to the Game Center servers (+reportScores:withCompletionHandler:). The completion handler block is executed when the score has been, or fails to be, delivered. You can examine the error parameter to see if it was successful and take whatever action you feel is appropriate. SunTouch isn't overly concerned if the player's score couldn't be posted.

> **Tip** When the score is successfully reported, and the completion handler executes, several properties of the GKScore object have been updated to reflect the results. The most interesting is the rank property. It is set to the player's new rank on the leaderboard (1 being the highest scoring player, 2 being the second highest, and so on). Your app can retrieve that value in the completion block and tell the player the good news.

Leaderboards are addressed using their ID. Switch to the STGameDefs.h file and add these two constants:

```
#define kSinglePlayerLeaderboardID   @"single"
#define kTwoPlayerLeaderboardID      @"multiple"
```

Now the -initWithLeaderboardIdentifier: method will create a leaderboard for the "single" leaderboard you defined in iTunes Connect.

> **Caution** Leaderboard identifiers are case sensitive. The identifier you pass to -initWithLeaderboardIdentifier: must *exactly* match the identifier you entered in iTunes Connect, or your scores won't post to the leaderboard.

Creating a Test Player

The only thing left to do is test your app. To do that, you must have a player account in Game Center. But it can't be just any player; it must be a *sandbox player*. Until your app is submitted and approved for distribution on the App Store, your app will use the Game Center sandbox. The *Game Center sandbox* is a set of servers that work identically to the way the public Game Center servers do, but the information, players, and scores are all private and are only used for development and testing.

When you run your pre-approved app, Apple automatically places it in the sandbox. You create a sandbox player by creating a new player account from within your (sandboxed) app. This can be done via iOS simulator or a provisioned device. The steps are simple:

1. If you already have a Game Center player account, launch the Settings app, go to the Game Center settings, and log out (tap your account name, choose Sign Out). See Figure 14-15.

Figure 14-15. Creating a sandbox player

2. Launch your app.
3. Since no player is logged in, your app will immediately present the player sign-in view controller (see Figure 14-15).
4. Create a new player account.

Creating an account in a sandboxed app creates a sandbox player account. You must provide an e-mail address for your account that is *not* associated with any regular Apple ID, so you may need to create a new e-mail account for testing.

> **Note** A sandbox player account can *only* be used with games running in the sandbox. If you're logged into your sandbox account on your iOS device, you'll have to log out and log into your regular account to play any games you've downloaded from the App Store. You can tell the difference by looking for the sandbox badge over your player icon, as shown on the right in Figure 14-15.

Play a few games. You'll see your scores appear on the leaderboard, which you can access via the Game Center button you added to your app, as shown in Figure 14-16.

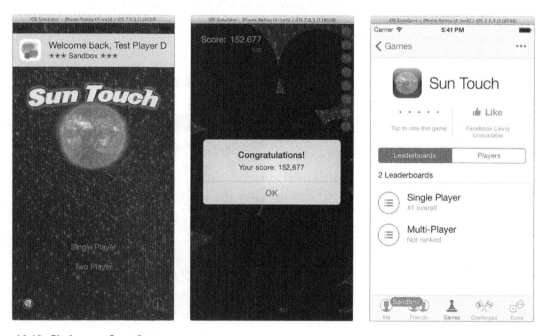

Figure 14-16. Playing your Game Center-aware app

Congratulations! You've created a Game Center–aware app, configured the Game Center servers, created a sandbox player account, and posted scores to your leaderboard. Which finally brings you to the point where you can add networking to your app.

Peer-To-Peer Networking

The moment you've been waiting for has arrived: adding peer-to-peer networking to your app. Broadly speaking, this will necessitate making three changes to SunTouch:

- Turning the single-player game into a two-player game
- Discovering and connecting with another iOS device
- Sending and receiving game data

Start with the first. In the two-player game, two players (one local and one remote) will be simultaneously blasting holes in space, trying to capture suns before the other player can, in a battle royale to become master of the universe—or something like that. The interface needs change to:

- Show the strike animation of the opposing player
- Show the areas of space blasted by the opposing player
- Animate and display suns captured by the opposing player

You already have code to animate strikes and show the areas of space that have already been blasted. You also have code that animates a sun being captured. Can you reuse this code to do the same for the opposing player? I think you can.

Turning SunTouch Into a Two-Player Game

You're going to make a minor change to STGameView so it "draws" transparent circles in the blasted holes, instead of filling them with black. You'll then create a subclass of STGameView, called STOpponentGameView, and position an instance of that view directly behind the STGameView object in the interface. The opponent game view will animate strikes and draw the blasted holes for the opponent. These animations and struck areas will only be visible through the transparent holes drawn in the foreground (local) game view. The effect will be like looking at a slice of Swiss cheese through a second slice of Swiss cheese.

> **Note** You'll find the finished two-player game in the `Learn iOS Development Projects` ➤ Ch 14 ➤ SunTouch-4 folder.

For the sun capture animations, you want the local player to see the suns being captured by their opponent. This adds to the strategy of the game; by observing where the opponent is capturing suns, the local player can infer what areas of space their opponent has already blasted. To be visible in the interface, the sun capture animation must occur in a view above the local player view. This is solved by having the local game view perform all sun capture animations. The only thing that changes is the color of the suns, indicating which player captured them.

That's the bulk of the two-player changes. Beyond that, there's a bunch of small details to attend to, which I'll get to shortly. Start by making those small changes in STGameView. Select the STGameView.h file and add an opponent property:

```
@property (readonly,nonatomic) BOOL opponent;
```

Now switch to the STGameView.m implementation file and add the getter method for this property:

```
- (BOOL)opponent
{
    return NO;
}
```

The opponent property will indicate if the view is displaying the game for the local or remote player. STGameView always returns NO, because it only displays the view for the local player. STOpponentGameView will return YES, because it always displays the view for the remote player.

The game view displays and animates the strikes initiated by the player, now players. It does this by observing kGameStrikeNotification notifications. In the two-player game, there are now two sources for these notifications: strikes by the local player and strikes from the remote player. The code that sends these notifications will change to indicate the source of the strike. Change the -strikeNotification: method so it starts like this (new code in bold):

```
- (void)strikeNotification:(NSNotification*)notification
{
    NSDictionary *info = notification.userInfo;
    STStrike *strike = info[kGameInfoStrike];
    BOOL opponent = [info[kGameInfoOpponent] boolValue];
    if (opponent!=self.opponent)
        return;
```

The new code gets the kGameInfoOpponent value from the notification. This value will be YES if the strike notification is coming from the remote player. It compares that value against this view's opponent property. If the values disagree, the notification is ignored. The end result? The local game view only animates strikes from the local player and the opponent game view only animates strikes from the remote player.

This leaves the sun capture animation to fix. The sun capture animations for both players are handled by the local (foreground) view. The only thing that changes is the image used for the suns. A SunCold.png image indicates a sun that was captured by the opponent. Find the -captureNotification: method and change the last statement to this (modified code in bold):

```
sunView.image = [UIImage imageNamed:(sun.localPlayer?@"SunHot":@"SunCold")];
```

This alteration uses a different sun image if the sun was captured by the opponent. (You haven't created the localPlayer property for STSun yet, but you'll get to that soon enough.)

Finally, modify the -setStrikeDrawColor method to this (new code in bold):

```
- (void)setStrikeDrawColor
{
    if (self.opaque)
        {
        [[UIColor blackColor] set];
        }
    else
        {
        [[UIColor clearColor] set];
        CGContextSetBlendMode(UIGraphicsGetCurrentContext(),kCGBlendModeCopy);
        }
}
```

The -setStrikeDrawColor method does exactly what it says. It's sent by the -drawRect: method when it wants to set the graphics context color used to draw a hole in space. In the single-player game, the local game view is opaque and strikes draw as black circles. In the two-player game, the local game view can be partially transparent (!opaque), and the holes are really holes; the context is set to "draw" with invisible pixels, making whatever portion of the view being filled transparent. Normally, the blend mode does not draw transparent pixels, which is why the blend mode is changed to kCGBlendModeCopy. The kCGBlendModeCopy mode performs no blending at all, replacing pixels in the context with the current color.

Subclassing STGameView

The remaining differences between the local and opponent's game view are supplied by the STOpponentGameView class. Create that class now. Select the STGameView.m file in the navigator and choose the **New File...** command. Use the Objective-C file template. Name the new class STOpponentGameView and make it a subclass of STGameView.

STOpponentGameView doesn't define any new properties or methods. It does all of its magic by overriding methods defined in STGameView. Here is all of the code to make STOpponentGameView work.

```objc
@implementation STOpponentGameView

- (void)observeNotificationsFromGame:(STGame*)game
{
    [super observeNotificationsFromGame:game];
    if (game!=nil)
        [[NSNotificationCenter defaultCenter] removeObserver:self
                                        name:kGameSunCaptureNotification
                                      object:game];
}

- (BOOL)opponent
{
    return YES;
}

- (UIImage*)strikeImage
{
    return [UIImage imageNamed:kOpponentStrikeImageName];
}

- (void)setStrikeDrawColor
{
    [[UIColor blackColor] set];
}

- (void)drawBackground
{
    [[UIColor darkGrayColor] set];
    CGContextFillRect(UIGraphicsGetCurrentContext(),self.bounds);
}

@end
```

The `-observeNotificationsFromGame:` method is sent when the game begins. The game view becomes the observer of key game engine notifications. This consists of observing the "strike" and "sun captured" notifications, so the view can draw and animate those events. In the case of a two-player game, however, all of the "sun captured" events are animated by the local (foreground) view. None of them are animated by the opponent (background) view. Rather than adding code to `-captureNotification:` to ignore them (the way you did in `-strikeNotification:`), the opponent view simply un-registers itself again from the notification center. It will still receive the "strike" notifications, but won't receive any "sun captured" notifications.

The remaining methods override methods in `STGameView`. When the `-drawRect:` method in `STGameView` sends itself the `-setStrikeDrawColor` and `-drawBackground` messages, the opponent game view will execute this code instead.

> **Tip** Defining overridable behaviors is an important pattern in object-oriented programming. I knew, when writing STGameView, that the strike image, hole color, and background would need to be different for the opponent game view. I planned ahead and wrote these aspects as individual methods. If you didn't plan ahead, use the extract refactoring tool to move a specific behavior into its own method, which your subclass can then override.

The finished `STOpponentGameView` class draws its strike animation using the `kOpponentStrikeImageName` image, draws its strike holes in black, and fills the rest of its view with dark grey. It draws and animates only strike events from the remote player, and it doesn't animate any sun capture events.

Now you just need to add an `STOpponentGameView` object to your interface.

Adding the Opponent Game View

Select the `STGameViewController.xib` Interface Builder file. From the object library, drag a new `View` object into the outline. Carefully insert the new view so it's a subview of the root view, and is ordered before (behind) the existing game view object. Do this by dropping the new view into the outline, as shown in Figure 14-17. You can't drop the new view object into the canvas, as you normally would, because it would become a subview of some other view, which is not what you want.

CHAPTER 14: Networking, The Nerdy Kind 459

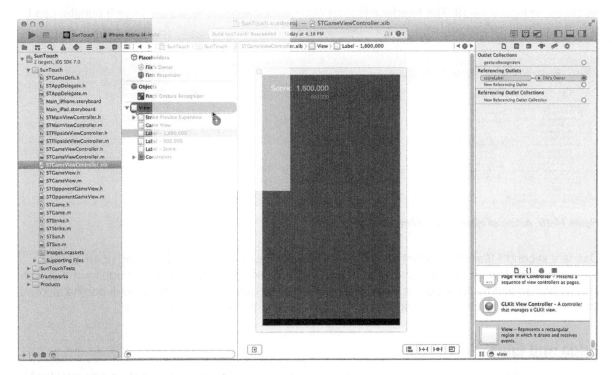

Figure 14-17. *Inserting the opponent game view*

Resize the view, using the resize handles or the size inspector, so it has the same frame as the game view. Add the exact same set of constraints you did for the game view; align the top, leading, and trailing edge to the superview, and add a vertical spacing constraint from the bottom to the top of the strike preview view. Using the identity inspector, change its class to STOpponentGameView, as shown in Figure 14-18.

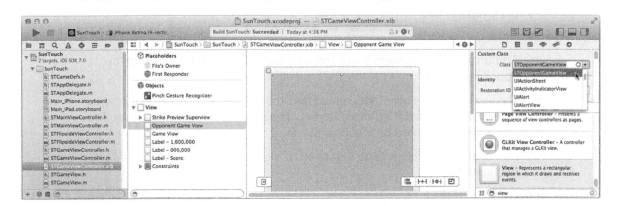

Figure 14-18. *The finished opponent game view*

Switch to the assistant editor. The STGameViewController.h file should appear in the right pane. Use the navigation ribbon above the pane to switch to the STGameViewController.m implementation file, as shown in Figure 14-19. The Interface Builder outlets for the game views are private outlets, used only by STGameViewController.

Figure 14-19. *Adding an opponentGameView outlet*

Define a second STGameView outlet named opponentGameView (see Figure 14-19) and connect it to the new game view object, also shown in Figure 14-19. Make the connection by dragging the outline connection socket to the Opponent Game View object in the outline. (Since this view is behind all of the other views, it's difficult to make the connection in the Interface Builder canvas.)

Odds and Ends

There are a smattering of additional code changes, some obvious and some not so obvious, that will finish turning your app into a two-player game. I'll summarize the changes here. If you're modifying the single-player version of SunTouch as you work through this section, use this as a guide to locate and copy the updated code from the source files in the Learn iOS Development Projects ➤ Ch 14 ➤ SunTouch-4 folder.

- STSun.h
    - Add a Boolean localPlayer property. This property establishes which player captured the sun.
- STGame.h
    - Add a readonly opponentScore property that calculates the score of the opposing player.
    - The -willCaptureSunAtIndex:gameTime: method is renamed to -willCaptureSunAtIndex:gameTime:localPlayer:. The new parameter is YES when the sun is being captured by the local player.
    - Define a kGameInfoOpponent key, used to identify the source of strike notifications.
- STGame.m
    - Add a synthetic, readonly, Boolean property named twoPlayer. This property is YES if this is a two-player game.
    - In -weightAtTime:, double the value of the weight if twoPlayer is YES. Scores for capturing a sun in a two-player game are doubled.

- Implement the -opponentScore getter method. The -score and -opponentScore methods both use the new -scoreForLocalPlayer: method, which calculates the score for either player.
- Add a new -startMultiPlayerWithMatch:started: method. This method is sent, instead of -startSinglePlayer, to start a two-player game.
- Change -strike:radius:inView: so it passes YES for the localPlayer parameter when sending -willCaptureSunAtIndex:gameTime:localPlayer:.
- -willCaptureSunAtIndex:gameTime:localPlayer: sets the localPlayer property of the sun that will be captured. This determines the image for the captured sun and which player gets credit.
- STGameViewController.h
  - Add a Boolean twoPlayer property. This property is set to YES when the user starts a two-player game.
- STGameViewController.m
  - In -viewDidLoad, twoPlayer is used to configure the views for a one- or two-player game. For a one-player game, the opponentGameView is removed (deleted), since it's not used, and the local game view's opaque property is set to YES. For a two-player game, both game views are used and the local game view's opaque property is set to NO, allowing it to have transparent regions that will show the opponent game view behind it.
  - In -finishGame, the twoPlayer property selects the end-of-game alert message. The two-player alert tells the local player if they won (or lost), and what both scores were. Two-player game scores are posted to the kTwoPlayerLeaderboardID leaderboard.
- STMainViewController.m
  - In the -prepareForSegue:sender: method, the game view controller's twoPlayer property is set to YES or NO before it is presented, based on the segue's identifier ("singlePlayer" or "twoPlayer"). Setting this property to YES begins the cascade of events that creates and runs a two-player game.
- Main_iPhone.storyboard/Main_iPad.storyboard
  - Create a modal segue from the "two player" button to the game view controller. Set the segue's identifier property to twoPlayer.

This completes the front-end of your two-player game. Now comes the network communications portion that will connect the game with another user playing on a second iOS device.

Matchmaking

Real-time, peer-to-peer, game communications can be roughly divided into two phases: matchmaking and live communications. Matchmaking is, by far, the most complicated, which is why it's so great that GameKit is going to do it for you.

Matchmaking is the process of discovering and connecting with a second instance of your app running on another iOS device. The biggest impact it will have on your app's design is that it radically changes how the game starts. In the single player version, `STGameViewController` created an `STGame` object and sends it a `-startSinglePlayer` message. This immediately starts the game.

Starting the two-player version is a multi-step process:

1. `STGameViewController` creates a `GKMatchRequest` object.

2. The match request is used to create and present a `GKMatchmakerViewController`.

3. The app waits for the `CKMatchmakerViewController` to locate and connect with a second player.

4. If successful, the `-matchmakerViewController:didFindMatch:` delegate method creates an `STGame` object and sends it a `-startMultiplayerWithMatch:` message.

5. The `STGame` object sends the remote app "game start" data. When it receives the corresponding "game start" data from the remote app, the game begins.

The next few sections will add this code to your app. Once that matching code is in place, you'll move on to the actual communications code.

Requesting a Match

Your game begins by requesting a match (connection) with one or more other users running the same app. It does this through a `GKMatchRequest` object. There are three types of matches you can request: peer-to-peer, hosted, and turn-based.

- Peer-to-peer sets up a direct communications link with all of the other devices. All of the participants are "peers" that communicate freely with one another. SunTouch will use peer-to-peer communications.

- A hosted match requires that your app provide its own network connection and communications. It's intended for games that use a centralized server (like an MMORPG) or one for which you've already written custom communications.

- Turn-based games do not require a direct connection with the other players. Infrequent communications are relayed—via the Game Center servers—to the other players, allowing for casual game play over distances limited only by the reach of the Internet. That means you could play a turn-based game with someone on the International Space Station, since they have Internet now.

Begin the process by requesting a match when the game starts. Select the `STGameViewController.m` file, find the `-startGame` method, and add the new code in bold:

```
- (void)startGame
{
    if (self.game==nil)
        {
        STGame *game = [STGame new];
        self.game = game;
```

```objc
    [self.gameView reset];
    [self.opponentGameView reset];
    if (self.twoPlayer)
    {
        GKMatchRequest *request = [GKMatchRequest new];
        request.minPlayers = 2;
        request.maxPlayers = 2;
        request.defaultNumberOfPlayers = 2;
        
        GKMatchmakerViewController *mmvc;
        mmvc = [[GKMatchmakerViewController alloc] initWithMatchRequest:request];
        mmvc.matchmakerDelegate = self;
        [self presentViewController:mmvc animated:YES completion:nil];
    }
    else
    {
        [self.gameView observeNotificationsFromGame:game];
        [game startSinglePlayer];
        [self startStrikeGrowAnimation];
    }
    }
}
```

The modified -startGame method starts the single-player game immediately. When twoPlayer is YES, it begins the matchmaking process. The match request is configured to limit the minimum, maximum, and default number of participants. Since SunTouch is strictly a one-on-one game, the only choice is 2 players.

A peer-to-peer match is established using the GKMatchmakerViewController. The code for this is simple: you create the view controller, make your object its delegate, and present it to the user.

> **Note** You didn't specify the type of match (peer-to-peer, hosted, or turn-based). That's because it's implied by which matchmaker view controller you use. GKMatchmakerViewController creates a peer-to-peer match. Use GKTurnBasedMatchmakerViewController to create a turn-based match. For hosted games—or to provide your own custom interface—use the GKMatchmaker or GKTurnBasedMatch class.

For this to work, your matchmaker delegate object must conform to the GKMatchmakerViewControllerDelegate protocol, so hop over to STGameViewController.h and add that (new code in bold):

```objc
@interface STGameViewController : UIViewController <UIAlertViewDelegate,
                            GKMatchmakerViewControllerDelegate>
```

Completing the Match

Your app handles the success, or failure, of the match by implementing the GKMatchmakerViewControllerDelegate methods. Start by adding the success method to STGameViewController.m:

```
- (void)matchmakerViewController:(GKMatchmakerViewController *)viewController
                    didFindMatch:(GKMatch *)match
{
    [self dismissViewControllerAnimated:YES completion:nil];
    if (match.expectedPlayerCount==0)
        {
        [self.game startMultiPlayerWithMatch:match started:^{
            [self.gameView observeNotificationsFromGame:self.game];
            [self.opponentGameView observeNotificationsFromGame:self.game];
            [self startStrikeGrowAnimation];
            }];
        }
}
```

When a match is established, the matchmaker view controller creates a GKMatch object and your delegate receives a -matchmakerViewController:didFindMatch: message. The match object is the one you'll use to communicate with the remote players.

It may take awhile for all of the players to connect, and you may receive this message multiple times. You should examine the expectedPlayerCount property of the match object. It reports the number of players you're still waiting (expecting) to connect with. Once it is 0, all of the players have connected. This is the point where SunTouch starts the game engine.

But the game still hasn't started yet! Before a SunTouch bout can begin, the game engine must first communicate with the other player to establish the parameters of the game (where the suns are hidden). You'll get to that later. For now, just know that -startMultiplayerWithMatch: begins the process of exchanging variables with the remote app and synchronizing the start of gameplay. This is called a *handshake*. When the handshake is finished, the game starts and the code block you passed in the started: parameter is executed, allowing the STGameViewController to perform its start-of-game housekeeping at the same time.

Finally, add the two failure delegate methods:

```
- (void)matchmakerViewControllerWasCancelled:(GKMatchmakerViewController *)controller
{
    [[NSNotificationCenter defaultCenter] postNotificationName:kGameDidEndNotifcation
                                                        object:self];
}

- (void)matchmakerViewController:(GKMatchmakerViewController *)controller
                didFailWithError:(NSError *)error
{
    [self matchmakerViewControllerWasCancelled:controller];
}
```

A `-matchmakerViewControllerWasCancelled:` message is received if the player decides they don't want to connect with another player. A `-matchmakerViewController:didFailWithError:` message is received if something went wrong. Both end the game, dismissing the game view controller, and returning to the initial screen.

Exchanging Data with Another Device

This is where the rubber meets the road, so to speak. The `GKMatch` object returned by the matchmaker is your conduit for communicating with the other iOS devices. At its core, it's ridiculously simple to use. It has a delegate property and some `-sendData...` methods. The `-sendData...` methods send data to the other devices. Your delegate object receives a `-match:didReceiveData:fromPlayer:` message when those other devices send data to your app. That sounds simple, doesn't it? The devil is in the details.

As the app designer, you must decide what information to send, how it's formatted, how the receiver will interpret it, which players you're going to send the data to, when to send the data, and how important it is that said data is received.

When designing your communications, there are a variety of ways you can organize it. There are methods to send data to all of the other participants, or to just one. This lets you choose to send updates to all of the other players, or specific updates to individual players. Your game might require that one device be designated as the host or master (for games structured like Dungeons and Dragons). The `GKMatch` class has a `-chooseBestHostPlayerWithCompletionHandler:` method for assisting the devices in choosing a ringleader.

In this respect, SunTouch is simple. There's never more than one other player, so communication topology isn't an issue. The only tricky part is deciding which app will pick the random locations for the suns. Both players must be using the same set of sun locations, or the game won't make any sense—or at least less sense than it already does. (How do you make a hole in space, and why would you want to?)

Remember that you have two identical versions of the program running, simultaneously, on two separate devices. There's no "leader" unless you pick one. For SunTouch, the solution is for both apps to pick a set of random sun locations. They then toss a coin—or the electronic equivalent—and choose a winner. Both apps will use the winner's set of suns. After that, your app sends data to the remote app describing strikes and captured suns. The remote app is, simultaneously, sending your app the opposing player's strikes and captured suns. SunTouch's communications can be summarized as follows:

- Send "game start" data to the remote app containing a list of random sun locations along with a random number (the "coin").

- When "game start" data is received, compare the remote app's random number to ours. This determines who wins the coin toss and which set of sun locations will be used.

- When the user initiates a strike, send "strike" data to the remote app containing the location and radius of the strike.

- When "strike" data is received from the remote app, animate a strike in the opponent's game view.

- When the local player captures a sun, send "sun captured" data to the remote app, including the time the sun will be captured.
- When "sun captured" data is received from the remote app, animate the captured sun and credit the opposing player. If both players uncover the same sun, the earliest capture wins.

All of the communications code is going into STGame. It's the two game engine objects that talk to each other. Your controller objects are only concerned with interaction with the local player, and the view objects just respond to notifications. You'll start to implement this by fleshing out the -startMultiPlayerWithMatch:started: method and then construct the individual send/receive data methods.

Starting the Game

Click on the STGame.h interface file. You're going to add some variables and a multi-player start method. Start with the variables. Edit the instance variable section of the @interface so it looks like this (new code in bold):

```
@interface STGame : NSObject
{
    NSArray*          suns;
    NSTimeInterval    startTime;
    GKMatch           *multiPlayerMatch;
    void              (^multiPlayStarted)(void);
    uint32_t          coinToss;
}
```

The multiPlayerMatch variable keeps a reference to the GKMatch object you need to communicate with the other apps. The funny-looking declaration after that defines the multiPlayerStarted variable. It's a code block variable; it holds a reference to a block of code that STGame can later execute. This is one of the parameters of the -startMultiPlayerWithMatch:started: method. Speaking of which, add a method declaration for it after -startSinglePlayer:

```
- (void)startSinglePlayer;
- (void)startMultiPlayerWithMatch:(GKMatch*)match
                  started:(void(^)(void))started;
```

Switch to STGame.m and write the new method:

```
- (void)startMultiPlayerWithMatch:(GKMatch*)match started:(void(^)(void))started
{
    multiPlayerMatch = match;
    multiPlayStarted = started;
    suns = [STGame randomSuns];
    coinToss = arc4random();
    match.delegate = self;
    [self sendGameStart];
}
```

The GKMatch object you're going to use to communicate with the other apps is saved, along with the reference to the code block to execute when the game actually gets underway. Next, a set of random sun locations is generated along with a random number that will act as the coin toss. The app that picks the highest random number is the one that determines the sun locations.

The STGame object is made the delegate for the GKMatch object. Data received by the match object will now be sent to STGame. Finally "game start" data is sent to the remote app. Presumably, the remote app is executing the exact same code, at nearly the same time, choosing a set of suns, a random number, and sending this app its "game start" data.

> **Note** You may have noticed that STGame does not conform to the GKMatchDelegate protocol. That's handled in a category, coming up next.

Creating a Data Messaging Category

You're going to consolidate all of your remote communications logic in a category of STGame named STDataMessaging. Select the STGame.m file in the project navigator and choose the **New File...** command, either from the **File** menu or by right+clicking on the STGame.m file.

> **Note** A category adds additional methods to the class. The methods are declared and implemented in a separate module, but are otherwise indistinguishable from the other methods of the class. I'll explain categories more in Chapter 20.

Choose the Objective-C category template. Name the category STDataMessaging and make it a category of STGame, as shown in Figure 14-20.

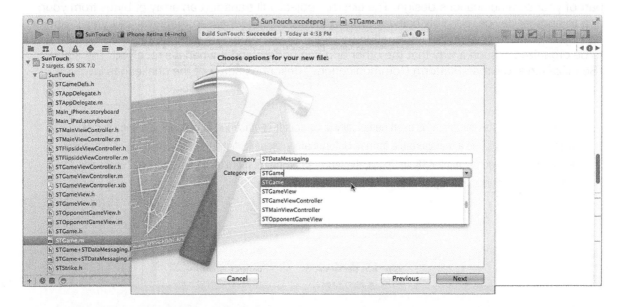

Figure 14-20. Creating the STDataMessaging category

The category is going to implement three methods that send game information to the other player: -sendGameStart, -sendStrike:, and -sendCaptureForSunIndex:. The category also implements the CGMatchDelegate methods to receive data from the other player. In the new STGame+STDataMessaging.h interface file, edit the category declaration so it looks like this (new code in bold):

```
@interface STGame (STDataMessaging) <GKMatchDelegate>
- (void)sendGameStart;
- (void)sendStrike:(STStrike*)strike;
- (void)sendCaptureForSunIndex:(NSUInteger)index;;
@end
```

The category declaration will need a definition of the STStrike class and few constants, so add this to the beginning of the file:

```
#import "STGameDefs.h"
@class STStrike;
```

> **Note** A @class directive declares a class without telling the compiler anything about that class. In other words, it informs the compiler that such a class exists, but that's all. It's used primarily in interface files where a declaration refers to a class name (-(void)sendStrike:(**STStrike***)strike;) but doesn't need, or want, to include the entire definition of the class (#import "STStrike.h").

Defining the Data Format

One of the design tasks I outlined earlier was deciding "how your data is formatted." This is a critical part of your communications design. The GKMatch object will transport an array of bytes from your app to another device, possibly halfway around the world, but what's in that array of bytes is entirely up to you. It has to contain the information you want to communicate with the other app, and it has to be organized in such a way that the other app can understand it when it's received. The sidebar "Serialization and Cross-Platform Communications" describes some of the challenges involved.

> **Note** The term "serialization" is used generically in computer engineering to describe the encoding of objects and values into a transportable format. Unfortunately, "serialization" means something very specific in Cocoa, described in Chapter 18. In Cocoa, the term "archiving" is more akin to the generic "serializing." Archiving is explained in Chapter 19.

SERIALIZATION AND CROSS-PLATFORM COMMUNICATIONS

Converting information (numbers, objects, properties, and so on) into a format that's transportable is generically referred to as *serialization*, *marshaling*, or *deflating*. You must do this whenever you exchange information with another computer system or process, which includes storing information in a file. Cocoa and Objective-C provide a number of tools to help serialize your data, and then turn that serialized data back into the objects and properties your app can use—a process called *deserialization*, *unmarshaling*, or *inflating*.

There are three aspects about the information in your app that can present a barrier to exchanging it with another app or device: memory addresses, word size, and byte order.

The biggest problem is memory addresses. An object in Objective-C is a small region of dynamic RAM that stores the properties of that instance. In your app, you refer to that object using its address. The memory address of an object is *utterly meaningless* to another process or computer system. Another device can't access the memory of your app—at least I hope it can't. Giving the address of an object to another process is akin to giving someone your telephone number ... in a parallel universe; they have no way to use it.

The solution is to convert the properties of your object(s) into a sequence of bytes that can be used to assemble equivalent objects by the recipient. Let's say you had a Person object that had name (string) and age (integer) properties. You can't pass the address of the Person, or string, object to another process. Instead, you serialize the object by creating an array of bytes and filling those bytes with the characters of the person's name and the binary value of their age. The computer receiving these bytes can use that data to construct a new string object and a new Person object with the same properties.

When it comes to exchanging that person's age, there are two additional issues to contend with. Different computer systems, and even different compilers, use different word sizes. A "word" in computer architecture is a sequence of bytes used to store a single number, such as an int. An int may be 16 bits (2 bytes) long on one computer system and 64 bits (8 bytes) long on another. So you can't simply write code that copies an int into an array of bytes and then extracts it again on the other system, because on one computer that means 2 bytes and on the other that means 8 bytes.

Mismatched word sizes are typically solved by using the fixed-size variable types in C and Objective-C. For example, int32_t is a variable type (just like int and char) that defines an integer that's always 32 bits (4 bytes) long. It doesn't matter on what kind of computer system you compile this on, or what kind of CPU it's running, an int32_t variable will always be 32 bits long.

The final problem is byte order. Different CPU architectures choose to store the bytes of a single integer in different orders. CPUs that store the least significant bits of the integer in the first (lowest) byte of memory are called *little-endian* machines. If the first byte contains the most significant bits of the integer, it's a *big-endian* machine. If you transmit the value of an integer, least significant byte first, to a system that expects the first byte to be the most significant, the integer value will arrive scrambled.

Byte order isn't a problem (yet) for SunTouch. As of this writing, all iOS devices are built with similar CPU architectures that all use the same (little-endian) byte order. Be aware that this could change in the future.

Word size, however, is not the same on all iOS devices. With the introduction of the A7 processor, some iOS devices have a 32-bit CPU while others have a 64-bit CPU. This means an NSInteger variable occupies 4 bytes (32 bits) when running on an iPhone 4S, but occupies 8 bytes (64 bits) when running on an iPhone 5S. (This statement presumes that you've compiled your app for both 32 and 64 bit architectures, which is the default Xcode build setting.) The length of all pointer and CGFloat variables will also be different. Any integer or floating point values you exchange between iOS devices will have to agree on a consistent word size.

If your app wanted to communicate with a different kind of computer system, running a different operating system, you'd need to concern yourself with both word size and byte order differences.

Chapters 18 and 19 explain the built-in Objective-C tools for serializing objects. These tools take care of all of the word size, byte order, and object inflating for you.

CHAPTER 14: Networking, The Nerdy Kind

When the SunTouch app receives data, it must be able to determine what kind of information the data block contains. The simplest approach, when doing this yourself, is to start every data block with an integer that described what kind of information the rest of the data block contains. In STGame+STDataMessaging.h, add this declaration:

```
typedef uint32_t STMessage;
enum {
    kSTStartGameMessage,
    kSTStrikeMessage,
    kSTCaptureMessage
};
```

This code defines a new integer variable type (STMessage) that is guaranteed to be 32 bits long regardless of what computer system it's compiled for. It then defines three constants, one for each type of data message SunTouch sends.

The rest of the declarations in STGame+STDataMessaging.h define the structures uses to exchange data between games:

```
typedef float STFloat;
typedef struct {
    STFloat x;
    STFloat y;
} __attribute__((aligned(4), packed)) STMessagePoint;

struct STStartGameMessage {
    STMessage       message;
    uint32_t        coinToss;
    STMessagePoint  sun[kSunCount];
} __attribute__((aligned(4), packed));

struct STStrikeMessage {
    STMessage       message;
    STMessagePoint  location;
    STFloat         radius;
} __attribute__((aligned(4), packed));

struct STCaptureMessage {
    STMessage       message;
    uint32_t        sunIndex;
    STFloat         gameTime;
} __attribute__((aligned(4), packed));
```

The first two declarations create two new variable types, STFloat and STMessagePoint. STFloat defines a single coordinate or distance variable and STMessagePoint defines a pair of STFloat values used to describe a coordinate.

> **Note** Why didn't you just use `CGFloat` and `CGPoint`? Because the length of `CGFloat` is different between 32- and 64-bit CPU architectures and the default alignment of the `CGPoint` structure could change someday. By defining your own, transportable, variable types you guarantee that variables in these structures will have the same size, order, and position on any iOS device SunTouch could run on.

The next three structures (`STStartGameMessage`, `STStrikeMessage`, and `STCaptureMessage`) define the organization of the data blocks that will be exchanged. Notice that every structure starts with an `STMessage` integer field. This will contain the appropriate message type constant. When your app receives a data block from another player, you know that the first 32 bits of the message will contain a number. You'll examine that number to determine what the data contains.

The rest of the fields should be obvious. The `__attribute__((aligned(4),packed))` gibberish is a special directive that tells the compiler exactly how to align and pack the fields within the structure. Just as word size and byte order change from one computer to another, so does the byte alignment of fields within a structure. By being explicit, SunTouch makes sure that—should the compiler's structure alignment rules change in the future—all versions of SunTouch will still be able to communicate with each other.

That's all the declarations you need. Now you can write the methods that send and receive data from the remote app.

Sending Data to a Player

Switch to the `STGame+STDataMessaging.m` implementation file. Start by `#import`ing the definitions of the `STStrike` and `STSun` classes; you're going to need them.

```
#import "STStrike.h"
#import "STSun.h"
```

Implement the `-sendGameStart` method:

```
- (void)sendGameStart
{
    struct STStartGameMessage message;
    message.message = kSTStartGameMessage;
    message.coinToss = coinToss;
    for ( NSUInteger i=0; i<kSunCount; i++ )
        {
        STSun *sun = suns[i];
        message.sun[i].x = sun.location.x;
        message.sun[i].y = sun.location.y;
        }
    
    NSData *data = [NSData dataWithBytes:&message length:sizeof(message)];
    [multiPlayerMatch sendDataToAllPlayers:data
                            withDataMode:GKMatchSendDataReliable
                                   error:NULL];
}
```

All of your methods to send data to the other players will follow this same pattern. Your method starts by allocating the appropriate data structure (STStartGameMessage, in this case). It sets the message field to the constant (kSTStartGameMessage) that identifies what kind of data it contains. It then fills in the remaining values of the structure.

> **Note** It's traditional to transmit all integer values in big-endian order over a network. Since all iOS devices (as of this writing) use little-endian integers, I'm skipping that step. If you need to flip the byte order of integers, use the Core Foundation byte swapping functions. Search for "byte swapping" in the Xcode documentation.

The last step is to transmit the finished structure to the other player. The NSData class converts the bytes of the structure into an NSData object—which is nothing more than an object that contains an array of bytes. You then send the -sendDataToAllPlayers:withDataMode:error: message to the GKMatch object. This method transmits those bytes to all other participating players. Since SunTouch is only a two-player game, the sole recipient is the opposing player's app.

The GKMatchSendDataReliable mode tells GKMatch that it's important that this data arrive. This might seem a silly thing to request—wouldn't you want all data to arrive? But not all game data is important enough to worry about whether it arrives safely or not.

Wireless communications can be spotty and unreliable. Data can get lost due to interference. If it's not critical that the message arrives, pass GKMatchSendDataUnreliable. This sends the data quickly, but makes no guarantees. This would be appropriate for status updates that occur continuously. It won't hurt (too much) if a few of them got lost; the next one will catch the game up. Messages that communicate vital information—such as a chess move—should be sent using GKMatchSendDataReliable. If there's a problem sending the message, GKMatch will try again until successful. This adds overhead, and it may take a while before it's delivered, but the message will get there.

You've implemented the code to send "game start" data to the other player. Now write the code to receive "game start" data from the other player.

Receiving Data from a Player

When a block of data is received from the remote player, your STGame object receives a -match:didReceiveData:fromPlayer: message. This will be the central location where you handle all received data:

```
- (void) match:(GKMatch*)match
didReceiveData:(NSData*)data
    fromPlayer:(NSString*)playerID
{
    STMessage message = *((STMessage*)data.bytes);
    switch (message) {
        case kSTStartGameMessage: {
            const struct STStartGameMessage *message = data.bytes;
```

```objc
            if (message->coinToss>coinToss)
            {
                STSun *otherSuns[kSunCount];
                for ( NSUInteger i=0; i<kSunCount; i++ )
                    otherSuns[i] = [STSun sunAt:message->sun[i].x
                                              :message->sun[i].y];
                suns = [NSArray arrayWithObjects:otherSuns count:kSunCount];
            }
            else if (message->coinToss==coinToss)
            {
                coinToss = arc4random();
                [self sendGameStart];
                return;
            }
            startTime = [NSDate timeIntervalSinceReferenceDate];
            multiPlayStarted();
        }
        break;
    }
}
```

The first step is to examine the 32-bit integer value that occupies the first four bytes of the received data block. The C syntax *((STMessage*) treats the first four bytes of the received data as an STMessage integer, and then gets that value and stores it in the message variable. Now the method knows what kind of data it just received. The rest is just a matter of handling each type.

The kSTStartGameMessage case treats (casts) the data bytes received as if it were an STStartGameMessages structure—which it is.

When your game receives "game start" data, it compares the coinToss value chosen by the other player with the one your game engine picked in -startMultiplayerWithMatch:started:. If the opponent's coinToss is bigger, the opponent won the coin toss. Discard the sun locations we picked and replace them with the ones the opponent picked. Now both games have the same sun locations.

In the case where your game picked the higher coinToss number, there's nothing to do, as you already have the sun locations. There is, however, a one-in-a-billion chance that both apps picked the same value for coinToss. If that happens, both apps pick a new random number and try again.

Once the coin toss is over and both games are using the same sun locations, the game is started.

If you're looking for a function named multiPlayStarted, you can stop. It isn't a function. It's the name of the code block variable that STGameViewController passed to STGame when it originally sent the -startMultiplayerWithMatch:started: message. It looks like a C function call, but what it's doing is executing the code block saved in the multiPlayStarted instance variable.

Executing the "game did start" code block is the last step in starting the game. The game is now running and both players are using the same list of hidden sun locations. The next thing that will happen is that one, probably both, of the players will touch their interface and cause a strike to occur.

Sending Strike Data

When a player touches the game view, a strike is initiated. But that same information must be communicated to the other player, so it can animate its opponent game view. Add the send strike data method to the STGame+STDataMessaging.m implementation file:

```
- (void)sendStrike:(STStrike*)strike
{
    if (multiPlayerMatch==nil)
        return;
    struct STStrikeMessage message;
    message.message = kSTStrikeMessage;
    message.location.x = strike.location.x;
    message.location.y = strike.location.y;
    message.radius = strike.radius;

    NSData *data = [NSData dataWithBytes:&message length:sizeof(message)];
    [multiPlayerMatch sendDataToAllPlayers:data
                              withDataMode:GKMatchSendDataReliable
                                     error:NULL];
}
```

The first statement does nothing if the multiPlayerMatch property is nil, inferring that this is a single-player game and there is no remote player to send data to. The rest of the method looks just like -sendGameStart, except the data consists of the location of the strike and its radius.

This method must be invoked every time the local user strikes. Switch to the STGame.m implementation file, find the -strike:radius:inView: method and change the beginning so it looks like this (new code in bold):

```
- (void)strike:(CGPoint)viewLocation
        radius:(CGFloat)viewRadius
        inView:(STGameView*)gameView
{
    STStrike* strike = [STStrike new];
    strike.location = [gameView unitPointFromPoint:viewLocation];
    strike.radius = [gameView unitRadiusFromRadius:viewRadius];
    [self sendStrike:strike];
```

Now every time the game engine receives a -strike:radius:inView: message, it will report that strike to the opposing player (assuming it's a two-player game). The -sendStrike: method is part of the STDataMessaging category. Add this #import towards the beginning of the file so STGame.m will recognize the new method:

```
#import "STGame+STDataMessaging.h"
```

Anything you send to the other player, you have to expect to receive.

Receiving Strike Data

Return to STGame+STDataMessaging.m, locate the -match:didReceiveData:fromPlayer: method, and add a new case to the switch statement:

```
case kSTStrikeMessage: {
    const struct STStrikeMessage *message = data.bytes;
    STStrike *strike = [STStrike new];
    strike.location = CGPointMake(message->location.x,message->location.y);
    strike.radius = message->radius;
    NSDictionary *strikeInfo = @{ kGameInfoStrike: strike,
                                  kGameInfoOpponent: @YES };
    [[NSNotificationCenter defaultCenter] postNotificationName:kGameStrikeNotification
                                                        object:self
                                                      userInfo:strikeInfo];
}
break;
```

When a block of data identifying itself with the kSTStrikeMessage value is received, an STStrike object is constructed from the location and radius information in the data. This is then posted as a strike notification, with the kGameInfoOpponent property set to YES. The game views observe this notification, causing the opponent game view to animate a strike in the background view.

The game engine isn't interested in opponent strikes; suns captured by the opponent will be communicated separately. And there's no time like the present to write that code.

Sending Sun Capture Data

This is starting to get monotonous, but you're almost done. Still in STGame+STDataMessaging.m, add the -sendCaptureForSunIndex: method:

```
- (void)sendCaptureForSunIndex:(NSUInteger)index
{
    if (multiPlayerMatch==nil)
        return;
    struct STCaptureMessage message;
    STSun *sun = suns[index];
    message.message = kSTCaptureMessage;
    message.sunIndex = (uint32_t)index;
    message.gameTime = sun.time;
    NSData *data = [NSData dataWithBytes:&message length:sizeof(message)];
    [multiPlayerMatch sendDataToAllPlayers:data
                              withDataMode:GKMatchSendDataReliable
                                     error:NULL];
}
```

You've got this: check multiPlayerMatch, fill an STCaptureMessage structure, convert it to NSData, and send that data to the other players. Done.

When does this happen? When the -strike:radius:inView: method determines that a strike will capture a sun. Switch to STGame.m, find -strike:radius:inView:, find the if block that determines when a sun is captured, and change it so it now reads (new code in bold):

```
if (sunDistance<=viewRadius)
    {
    NSTimeInterval strikeTime = self.gameTime+kStrikeAnimationDuration/2
                                            *(sunDistance/viewRadius);
    [self willCaptureSunAtIndex:i gameTime:strikeTime localPlayer:YES];
    [self sendCaptureForSunIndex:i];
    }
```

Receiving Sun Capture Data

Back in the STGame+STDataMessaging.m file, add one last case to the switch statement in the -match:didReceiveData:fromPlayer: method:

```
case kSTCaptureMessage: {
    const struct STCaptureMessage *message = data.bytes;
    [self willCaptureSunAtIndex:message->sunIndex
                    gameTime:message->gameTime
                  localPlayer:NO];
    }
    break;
```

This is the simplest one yet. The captured sun information from the opponent is passed to the game engine. Remember that you added an additional parameter to -willCaptureSunAtIndex:gameTime:localPlayer: so the method can distinguish between suns captured by the local player and sun captured by the opponent. When sun captured data is received from the remote game, you send the same message, but this time pass NO for the localPlayer.

> **Note** Network communication takes time. Not a long time, but long enough that it's possible for both players to think they've captured the same sun before they receive the capture data from the other player. This is called a *race condition*, and it's a notorious problem in real-time programming. Review the logic and the comments in the -willCaptureSunAtIndex:gameTime:localPlayer: and STGameView's -captureNotification: methods to see how SunTouch handles it.

Handling Match Disruption

All of your communications logic is finished, but there are a few additional GKMatchDelegate methods you should implement. Add them to your STGame+STDataMessaging.m file:

```
- (void) match:(GKMatch*)match
        player:(NSString*)playerID
didChangeState:(GKPlayerConnectionState)state
{
}
```

```
- (void)match:(GKMatch*)match didFailWithError:(NSError*)error
{
    [[NSNotificationCenter defaultCenter] postNotificationName:kGameDidEndNotifcation
                                                        object:self];
}
- (BOOL)match:(GKMatch *)match shouldReinvitePlayer:(NSString*)playerID
{
    return YES;
}
```

As mentioned earlier, wireless communication is subject to a variable quality of service. (The technical term is "flaky.") When iOS loses, or reestablishes, a connection with one of the other players, your delegate method will receive a -match:player:didChangeState: message. What you do depends on the type of game. SunTouch doesn't do anything. (It's sad that the other player can't capture your suns, but that's about it.) If this was a two-player battling robot game, it might make sense to pause the game until the connection can be reestablished.

The more dire -match:didFailWithError: message is received when a serious networking problem prevents the game from keeping, or reestablishing, a connection with one or more players. In this situation, the link to the other players is probably broken. SunTouch responds by ending the game.

Finally, the -match:shouldReinvitePlayer: method is received whenever a two-player game looses connection with the other player. If this method returns YES, the GKMatch object will automatically attempt to reestablish a connection with the other player. If you return NO, or there are more than two players, it's up to you to reconnect the disconnected players in your -match:player:didChangeState: method.

Testing a Two-Player Game

Please don't throw this book across the room if I tell you there's one more step before you can test the two-player version of SunTouch, but there's one more step before you can test the two-player version of SunTouch.

> **Note** Remember that you must have two, provisioned, iOS devices to test a two-player Game Center-aware app that uses peer-to-peer networking. The iOS simulator will not connect to a real iOS device, and vice versa.

You'll first need to get SunTouch running in two iOS devices. Plug both of your iOS devices into your Mac. In Xcode, set the scheme's target to the first device and click the Run button, as you've done countless times in this book so far. While the first app is still running, change the target of the scheme to the second iOS device, and click the Run button again. Now Xcode is running the same app in two iOS devices simultaneously.

> **Tip** Some games are awkward to play with the device plugged into a USB port. If you're not using Xcode to debug one or both apps, you can run the project to copy the app to the device, stop the app, unplug the device, and launch the app again from the springboard.

The last step is to create a second sandbox player. To play a two-player game, you must have two Game Center player accounts, and since both apps are using the sandbox servers, both players must be sandbox players. On your second iOS device, follow the same steps in the "Creating a Test Player" section that you did for the single version. Once you have two sandbox player accounts, you can start a two-player game.

With both apps running, tap the "two player" button on both. Both devices will present the matchmaker view controller, as shown in Figure 14-21. Tap the **Play Now** button on both. This uses Game Center's "auto-match" feature, which connects to the first local player it can locate.

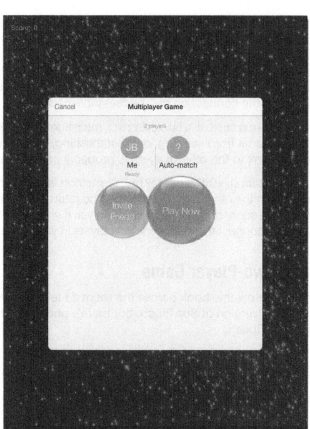

Figure 14-21. Connecting with a second SunTouch player

As soon as both devices have connected, SunTouch is off and running, as shown in Figure 14-22.

Figure 14-22. Two-player SunTouch communicating over local Wi-Fi

When you're done playing, you can stop the apps in Xcode. If you like, unplug the devices and re-launch SunTouch from the springboard.

> **Tip** When Xcode is running more than one instance of your app, the **Stop** button turns into a drop-down menu. Click it and choose which app to stop.

Advanced Networking

GameKit is a fantastic resource for peer-to-peer networking, but it's not the only network communications solution available—just the easiest to use.

If you want to create a more general networking solution, possibly connecting and communicating with a custom application running on almost any kind of computer, there are lots of resources and possible solutions. The best place to begin is the *Network Overview* document that you'll find in

Xcode's Documentation and API Reference window. The three areas of network communication that you most likely want to explore are:

- The high-level HTTP/URL services for communicating with Internet servers, like those you used in Shorty. These include the NSURLRequest and NSURLConnection classes.

- The low-level TCP/IP socket APIs for direct connection with almost any networked device or service. Start with the *Using Sockets and Socket Streams* document.

- The Bonjour service for advertising and discovering local services. If you wanted to perform your own matchmaking, so your users could effortlessly connect to another local computer, Bonjour is the tool of choice. (GameKit uses Bonjour.) On iOS, the Bonjour service also supports Bluetooth, for wireless peer-to-peer Bluetooth discovery. Start with the *Bonjour Overview* document.

One Last Detail

There's one aspect (no pun intended) that bothers me about SunTouch. The project settings allow SunTouch to run in portrait or landscape mode on both iPhones and iPads. While there are numerous cosmetic issues that I'd want to address before declaring this app ready to release, there's one rather glaring problem: If the player starts to play the game in one orientation, and then turns to another, the games gets sort of wonky. This is a side effect of the unit-space coordinate system the game engine uses. It results in peculiar behavior, like hidden suns now in areas of the screen that have already been blasted.

The project settings determine the allowed orientations for your entire app. Individual view controllers can also stipulate which orientations they support, and they can do so dynamically. You're going to exploit this last feature to put a stop to users flipping their devices mid-game.

The set of orientations a view controller is willing to work in is declared in the bits returned by its -supportedIntefaceOrientations method. iOS queries this when presenting a view controller. If the view controller doesn't support the current orientation, the orientation of the interface is changed to one that does. Your STFlipsideViewController could benefit from this feature. The game instructions are laid out vertically, and are unsightly when presented in landscape orientation.

Change STFlipsideViewController so that the view only appears in portrait orientation. Find the STFlipsideViewController.m implementation file and add this method (or review the finished project in the Learn iOS Development Projects ➤ Ch 14 ➤ SunTouch-5 folder):

```
- (NSUInteger)supportedInterfaceOrientations
{
    return UIInterfaceOrientationMaskPortrait;
}
```

This overrides the inherited -supportedInterfaceOrientations, which returns UIInterfaceOrientationMaskAll on the iPad and UIInterfaceOrientationMaskAllButUpsideDown on the iPhone. If you run the app, rotate the device, and present the flipside view controller, it still appears in portrait orientation, as shown in Figure 14-23, because that's the only orientation it supports now.

Figure 14-23. Limiting a view controller to portrait orientation

If your view controller supports a combination of orientations, either return one of the combination constants (UIInterfaceOrientationMaskAll) or construct a set of orientations by ORing individual ones together (UIInterfaceOrientationMaskPortrait|UIInterfaceOrientationMaskPortraitUpsideDown).

> **Note** Many container view controllers aggregate the supported orientations of their constituent view controllers. For example, the tab bar controller will rotate from portrait to landscape orientation only if all of its sub-view controllers support landscape orientation.

For the STGameViewController, the problem is a little different. You want to allow landscape, or even upside down, orientations but you don't want the orientation to change once the game begins. The solution is to create a "smart" -supportedInterfaceOrientations method that only supports the orientation it started out with.

In the STGameViewController.h interface file, add a lockedOrientation property to the class:

```
@property (nonatomic) UIInterfaceOrientation lockedOrientation;
```

Switch to the STMainViewController.m implementation file and find the -prepareForSegue:sender: method. In the if block that segues to the STGameViewController, add a line that captures the current orientation of the device (new code in bold):

```
gameViewController.twoPlayer = [segue.identifier isEqualToString:@"twoPlayer"];
gameViewController.lockedOrientation = self.interfaceOrientation;
}
```

Finally, switch to the STGameViewController.m file and override the -supportedInterfaceOrientation method:

```
- (NSUInteger)supportedInterfaceOrientations
{
    switch (self.lockedOrientation)
        {
        case UIInterfaceOrientationPortrait:
            return UIInterfaceOrientationMaskPortrait;
        case UIInterfaceOrientationPortraitUpsideDown:
            return UIInterfaceOrientationMaskPortraitUpsideDown;
        case UIInterfaceOrientationLandscapeLeft:
            return UIInterfaceOrientationMaskLandscapeLeft;
        case UIInterfaceOrientationLandscapeRight:
            return UIInterfaceOrientationMaskLandscapeRight;
        }
    return UIInterfaceOrientationMaskAll;
}
```

The new method allows only the orientation that matches the one set in lockedOrientation. Now you can start a SunTouch game in any orientation, but once started it won't respond to changes to the device's orientation until the game ends. Wasn't that simple?

Summary

In this chapter you covered a lot of diverse ground. You created a Game Center–aware application, assigned it a unique app ID, registered that ID and your app with Apple, used iTunes Connect to enable and configure Game Center for your app, implemented the various GameKit requirements, created a sandbox player, got the local player in your app, and reported scores to the worldwide leaderboard.

And all of that was just the prelude to adding real-time network communications to your app! You used the matchmaking feature of Game Center to connect with a second iOS device, sent live status updates to the other player, and processed remote messages received from the other player—all in real-time. You also learned some basics about serializing information, and constructing and interpreting inter-process data.

This is cause for some celebration and well-deserved congratulations. This was, by far, the most complex and difficult project in the book, and you made it through with flying colors. With the momentum you've built up, you can, honestly, coast through the rest of this book. Later chapters are going to introduce you to even more iOS services, like maps, and there's a lot of practical information about Objective-C and multi-tasking, but all of that is going to seem simple compared to what you've accomplished so far.

Speaking of practical information, the next chapter is going to focus on Interface Builder. Not so much how to use it, as how it works; something that's important to understand if you want to be an iOS master developer.

> **EXERCISE**

How complicated would it be, do you think, to turn SunTouch into a game that could be played by three, or even four, players at a time? Surprisingly, it's not that much work. Or, maybe the fact that it isn't difficult means SunTouch is a well-designed piece of software.

Your exercise for this chapter, if you're willing to borrow another iOS device from a friend or family member, is to get SunTouch to play up to four players simultaneously.

The parts of your app that will have to change probably aren't the ones that leap immediately to mind. If you treat all strikes and captured suns from any of the remote players as "the opponent," the logic to send strikes and handle captured suns from remote players requires only minor tweaks. The view classes don't need to change at all—how well designed is that?

The complicated problems are at the beginning and end of the game. You now have to arbitrate between up to four sets of sun locations, with all players getting the same set. But even that can be solved with a few lines of code. The really complicated problem is that there is now more than one opponent score, so the single -opponentScore method is meaningless.

I thought of several different ways of evolving SunTouch into a multi-player game. The solution I finally wrote can be found in the `Learn iOS Development Projects` ➤ `Ch 14` ➤ `SunTouch E1` folder. It adds a new `playerID` property to the `STSun` object. This property records the player that captured the sun. A new `-scoreForPlayer:` method calculates the score for any individual player. If you wanted to make the game even more colorful, you could modify `STGameView` to assign different colored suns to each player. Search the project for the string `*Multi-Player*` to find these, and other, changes.

Picking a leader to start the game and agreeing on a set of suns sounds like it would be tricky with so many players, but it only required a few minor code changes. The highest coin toss still determines the set of suns to use, the only difference is each app waits until its received a "start game" message from every other player. An alternative approach would be to use `GKMatch`'s `-chooseBestHostPlayerWithCompletionHandler:` method to let GameKit select one of the devices as the host. Once chosen, the host device would then pick a set of sun locations and communicate that to all of the other players, in a single message, starting the game and eliminating the need for the coin toss. (The only problem with `-chooseBestHostPlayerWithCompletionHandler:` is that it's not guaranteed to pick a host, so you must still provide a fallback mechanism.)

I went through several different solutions to this exercise, including one that added a new "score" message, broadcast whenever the local score changed. Can you think of another solution? While there are often lots of poor solutions, there's no single, correct, way to write software.

Chapter 15

If You Build It ...

Interface Builder is Xcode's "secret sauce." It makes the creation of complex interfaces effortless: drag interface elements into a canvas, connect them together, press a button, and they become working objects in your app. It's like magic.

> *Any sufficiently advanced technology is indistinguishable from magic.*
>
> —Arthur C. Clarke

"Magic" is often used to describe what we don't understand. Interface Builder can sometimes meet this criteria; it works, you just don't know how. Well, step behind the curtain and prepare to learn those secrets. In this chapter you will:

- Learn what Interface Builder files are (exactly)
- Find out how objects in an Interface Builder file become objects in your app
- Discover programmatic equivalents to what Interface Builder does
- Understand how placeholder objects work
- Programmatically load your own Interface Builder files
- Provide your own placeholder objects

Normally, Interface Builder files are loaded by your view controller objects, which hide a lot of the details. That's fine. In fact, it's great. If you're using a view controller object you *should* let it handle the details—that's what it's there for. But sometimes you'll find yourself in a situation where you can't use Interface Builder, but you need to accomplish something similar in code. Or what if you want to load an Interface Builder file that isn't managed by a view controller? These are easy to accomplish, if you first understand how Interface Builder works.

How Interface Builder Files Work

An Interface Builder file contains a serialized graph of objects. In Chapter 14, you learned a little of what serialization means and some of the challenges involved. In Chapters 18 and 19, you'll learn how to serialize objects and how to create objects that can be serialized (archived). But for now, all you need to know is that "serializing an object" means converting its properties into a transportable array of bytes, and eventually reversing the process to get them back again.

> **Note** I'm still using the term "serialize" in the generic, computer engineering, sense. In the language of Cocoa Touch, Interface Builder files are an *archive* of objects. Loading an Interface Builder file consists of *un-archiving* those objects.

So what's an object graph? An *object graph* is a set formed by an object, all of the objects that object refers to, all of the objects those objects refer to, and so on. The object—or small number of objects—that begins the graph is referred to as the *root* or *top-level* object(s).

Serialization starts at the root object. That object converts its properties into a serialized byte array. If any of its properties refer to other objects, those objects are asked to serialize their property values into the same byte array, and so on, until all of the objects and property values for the entire graph are converted. The finished array of bytes describe the entire set of objects, their properties, and their relationships.

Compiling Interface Builder Files

You use an Interface Builder file by creating one and adding it to your project. You then edit it and build your app.

But the .xib or .storyboard file that you edit in Xcode is not what ends up in your app's bundle. Like your source (.m and .h) files, your Interface Builder files are compiled. The nib compiler converts the design in your .storyboard or .xib file into serialized data that, when un-archived, will create the objects with the properties and connections you described. This compiled nib file is then added to your app's bundle as a resource file.

> **Note** Some interface editors take your design and turn it into source code, equivalent to what you drew, which you then compile as part of your app. These tools are called *code-generators*. Interface Builder is not a code-generator. Interface Builder is an *object compiler*.

Loading a Scene

When your apps needs the objects stored in an Interface Builder file, it *loads* the interface. Figure 15-1 shows the Detail View scene of the Main_iPhone.storyboard file (from MyStuff in Chapter 7). Figure 15-2 shows the (simplified) graph of objects contained in that scene.

CHAPTER 15: If You Build It …   487

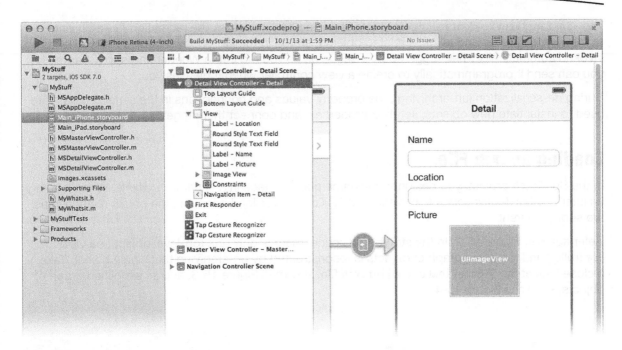

Figure 15-1. Detail View in Interface Builder

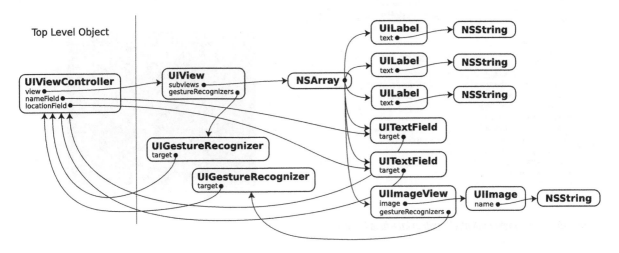

Figure 15-2. Graph of objects in the Detail View scene

A storyboard scene consists of at least one top-level object, the view controller. The view controller's view property refers to its single root view object (UIView). This, in turn, contains a collection of subviews (managed by an NSArray). Some of those view objects refer to additional objects, such as NSString, UIImage, and UIGestureRecognizer objects.

The `-instantiateViewControllerWithIdentifer:` method instigates the recreation (un-archiving) of the view controller, and all of its related objects, stored in the storyboard scene. This method is invoked automatically when triggered by a segue or, as you did in the Wonderland app (Chapter 12), you can send it programmatically to create a view controller when it pleases you.

During de-serialization (un-archiving), the property values and connections in the serialized data are used to instantiate new objects, set their properties, and connect them together.

Loading an .xib File

In the SunTouch project, you designed the game play interface in a separate `.xib` file. When loading an interface builder file yourself, or letting `UIViewController` load it for you, the object relationships are subtly different.

Refer again to Figure 15-2. In the storyboard scene, there is only one top-level object (the view controller) and the entire graph of objects is reconstructed by un-archiving that single object. Take a close look at the `STGameViewController.xib` file, shown in Figure 15-3, and its simplified graph of objects, shown in Figure 15-4.

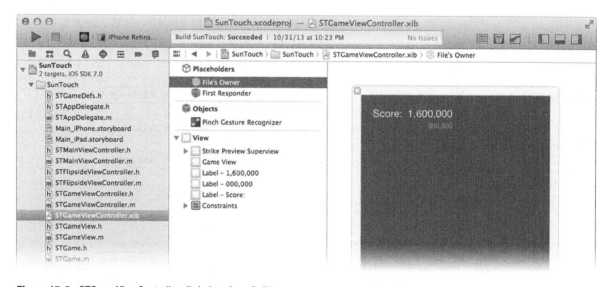

Figure 15-3. STGameViewController.xib in Interface Builder

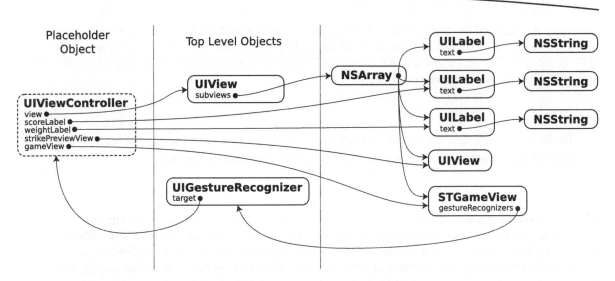

Figure 15-4. Graph of objects in STGameViewController.xib

The difference is the placeholder object. *Placeholder* objects—the most important being the file's owner—are objects that already exist when the Interface Builder file is loaded. During the un-archiving process, existing objects are substituted for the placeholders. The existing objects become part of the object graph, but are not created by, the Interface Builder file. Outlets in a placeholder can be set to objects created during the loading process, and objects in the graph can be connected to a placeholder. In Figure 15-4, the scoreLabel and weightLabel properties in the file's owner (the view controller) are set to the two new UILabel objects.

So far in this book, your use of Interface Builder files has been largely transparent. You either created interfaces in a storyboard scene or standalone .xib file, loaded automatically by its view controller. Now you'll learn how to load them yourself and how to designate placeholder objects.

Placeholder Objects and the File's Owner

When an Interface Builder file is loaded, the sender supplies the existing objects that will replace the placeholders in the file. The most common scenario is to use one placeholder object, referred to as the *file's owner*. This is typically the object loading the file; when a view controller loads its Interface Builder file, it declares itself as the file's owner. You can provide any object you choose or none at all, in which case there are zero placeholder objects. Optionally, you can supply as many additional placeholder objects as you wish. (Later in this chapter you'll load an Interface Builder file with multiple placeholders.) Think of the file's owner as the "designated placeholder," provided to make the common task of loading an Interface Builder file with one placeholder object as easy as possible.

The important rule to remember is that the class of the file's owner in the Interface Builder file *must* agree with the class of the owner object when the file is loaded. You set the class of the file's owner using the identity inspector in Interface Builder. When you set this, you're making a promise that the actual object will be of that class (or a subclass) when the file is loaded.

Changing the class of the file's owner from `UIViewController` to `UIApplication` won't magically give your Interface Builder file access to your app's `UIApplication` object. It just means that the `UIViewController` object (the file's real owner) will be treated as if it were a `UIApplication` object, probably with unpleasant consequences.

> **Caution** When changing the class of any placeholder object in Interface Builder, ensure that you set it to the class, or a superclass, of the actual object that will be supplied when the file is loaded.

The principle use of the file's owner is to gain access to the objects created in the Interface Builder file. To access any of those objects, you must obtain a reference to them. While it's possible to obtain references to the top-level objects, all other objects must be accessed indirectly, either via properties in the top-level objects or through connections set in the file's owner object. In the example shown in Figure 15-4, the `STGameView` object becomes accessible through the owner object's `gameView` property. Without a placeholder object, it would be awkward (sometimes impossible) to access the objects you just created.

When an Interface Builder file loads, only those outlets in the placeholder objects that are connected in the file are set. All other properties and outlets remain the same.

Objects within the Interface Builder file can only establish connections to other objects in the graph or to the placeholder objects. For example, an object being loaded by a view controller cannot be directly connected to the application delegate object. That object isn't in the graph. The exception is the first responder. The first responder is an implied object that could be any object in the responder chain. As you learned in Chapter 4, the responder chain goes all the way to the `UIApplication` object.

Now that you have a feel for how objects in an Interface Builder file get created, it's time to dig into the details of how objects are defined and connected to one another, and what that means to your app.

Creating Objects

Adding an object to an Interface Builder file is equivalent to creating that object programmatically. This is a really important concept to grasp. There is nothing "special" about objects created from Interface Builder files. You can always write code that accomplishes the exact same results; it's just excruciatingly tedious, which is why Interface Builder was invented in the first place.

In Figure 15-5, an object is being added to an Interface Builder file. This is borrowed from the `ColorModel` project in Chapter 8.

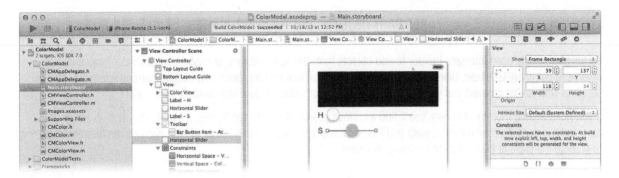

Figure 15-5. *Adding an object to an Interface Builder file*

The object being added is a `UISlider` object. It's being created with a frame of `((39,137),(118,34))` and it's a subview of the root `UIView`. The equivalent code (in the view controller) would be:

```
UISlider *newSlider = [[UISlider alloc] initWithFrame:CGRectMake(39,137,118,34)];
[self.view addSubview:newSlider];
```

This code creates a new `UISlider` object with the desired dimensions and adds it to the view controller's root view object. In both methods (Interface Builder and programmatically) the end result is the same.

> **Note** Interface Builder understands a few special object relationships, and creates those relationships for you. For example, when you add a view object as a subview, it's equivalent to sending an `-addSubview:` message to the superview. If you add Bar Button Items to a toolbar, the equivalent message would be `-setItems:animated:`. Dropping a new gesture recognizer into a view is the same as sending it an `-addGestureRecognizer:` message. Adding constraints is equivalent to sending `-addConstraint:` or `-addConstraints:`, and so on.

There's only one, technical, difference between how the `UISlider` object gets created in the Interface Builder file and how you create one programmatically. When you write code to create a view object, you use the `-initWithFrame:` initializer message. When an object is un-archived—which is how objects in an Interface Builder file get created—the object is created with an `-initWithCoder:` message. The coder parameter contains an object that has all of the properties the new object needs, including its frame. You'll learn all about `-initwithCoder:` in Chapter 19.

ARBITRARY OBJECTS AND THEIR ATTRIBUTES

So far, you've only used Interface Builder to add objects from the object library, or custom subclasses of those library objects (most often, `UIView`). Using the identity inspector, you can edit the class of an object, turning it into any custom subclass that you've created. But you can't change the object's class to just any class. Or can you?

If you poke around the object library, you'll find a curious object: `Object` (see figure). It's an `NSObject` object. By itself, it's nearly useless. But since every object you'll ever create is a subclass of `NSObject`, you can use the identity inspector to change the class of that object to anything you want.

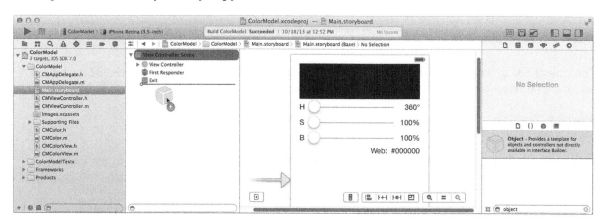

In addition, the identity inspector has a limited ability to set the properties of your custom object. In ColorModel app, you programmatically created the `CMColor` object that was the app's data model object and then set its initial property values. You could have created that object in Interface Builder. In your `CMViewController.h` interface, change the `colorModel` property so it's an Interface Builder outlet, like this (new code in bold):

@property (strong,nonatomic) **IBOutlet** CMColor *colorModel;

To create the actual `CMColor` object, drag an `Object` object into the top-level of the object outline (as shown above). Use the identity inspector to change its class to `CMColor`, and then connect the `colorModel` outlet to the new object, as shown in the next figure. (Make the `colorModel` property of the `CMColorView` class an outlet and connect it too.)

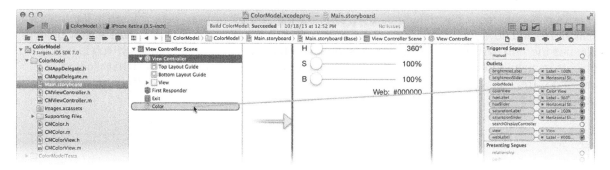

To edit the properties of your custom object, add them to the `User Defined Runtime Attributes` section, as shown in the next figure. You can set any object property that's one of these types: BOOL, any kind of number (integer or floating point), `NSString`, `CGPoint`, `CGSize`, `CGRect`, `NSRange`, or `UIColor`. Just click the + button and describe the name of the property, its type, and the value you want it set to (see next figure).

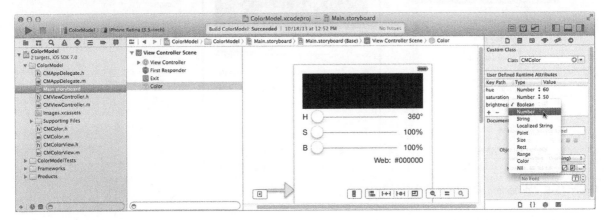

The project in the `Learn iOS Development Projects` ➤ `Ch 15` ➤ `ColorModel` folder has been modified to create, configure, and connect the `CMColor` object entirely in Interface Builder, as described here. Take a look at the code this displayed in `-viewDidLoad:`.

You can combine this technique with custom subclasses of other standard library objects. If you create a subclass `UIView`, you can set all of the standard `UIView` properties in the attributes inspector, and then use the identity inspector to set any additional properties that your class defines.

Editing Attributes

But the frame isn't the only property of the `UISlider` object. When you created your slider object in ColorModel, you used the attributes inspector to change several of its properties. You changed its maximum range to 360 and checked the `Update Events: Continuous` option. That was equivalent to writing this code:

```
newSlider.maximumValue = 360;
newSlider.continuous = YES;
```

Again, the resulting object is indistinguishable from the object created by the Interface Builder file, despite subtle differences in how those property values are set.

Connections

You've seen how objects, and their properties, in an Interface Builder file get created, but what about connections? Figure 15-6 shows the `hueSlider` outlet being connected to a slider object.

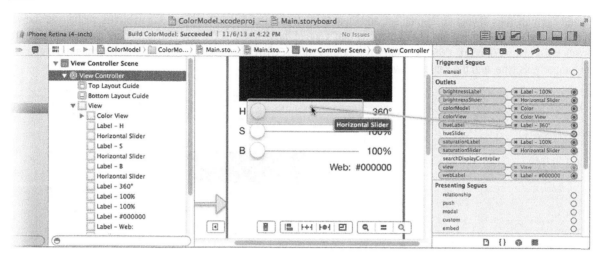

Figure 15-6. Connecting an outlet in Interface Builder

Here's the equivalent code:

```
self.hueSlider = newSlider;
```

And this time, when I say "equivalent" I mean "identical." Objects in an Interface Builder file are created in stages. During the first stage, all of the objects are created and have their attributes set. In the next stage, all of the connections are made. Those connections are made using the same methods you'd use to set an outlet property programmatically.

Action connections are a little more complicated. An action connection consists of two, and possibly three, pieces of information.

Objects that send a single action (UIGestureRecognizer, UIBarButtonItem, and so on) are connected by setting two properties: the target and the action. The target property is the object (usually a controller) that will receive the message. The action is the selector (-play:, -pause:, -someoneMashedAButton:) that determines which message the target receives. Some objects (such as UIGestureRecognizer) can be configured to send messages to multiple targets. You'd connect those objects, programmatically, like this:

```
[gestureRecognizer addTarget:viewController action:@selector(changeColor:)];
```

> **Note** In Shapely, you programmatically created gesture recognizer objects, but you set the target and action when you created the object. That works too.

To connect additional actions, send more -addTarget:action: messages with those additional actions. Disconnect actions using -removeTarget:action:.

Other single-event objects (such as `UIBarButtonItem`) have only a single target property. These objects can only send a single message to a single target. You can programmatically make an action connection by setting the `target` and `action` properties individually, like this:

```
barButtonItem.target = viewController;
barButtonItem.action = @selector(refresh:);
```

More complex control objects have a multitude of events, any of which can be configured to send action messages when they occur. A `UISlider` object can send action messages when: the user touches the control (`UIControlEventTouchDown`), they drag outside its frame (`UIControlEventTouchDragOutside`), release their finger outside its frame (`UIControlEventTouchUpOutside`), release their finger inside its frame (`UIControlEventTouchUpInside`), or the value of the slider changes (`UIControlEventValueChanged`). Each of these is identified by an event constant (see `UIControlEvents`). Any event can be configured to send action messages to multiple targets. In Figure 15-7, the Value Changed event is being configured to send a -changeHue: message to the view controller.

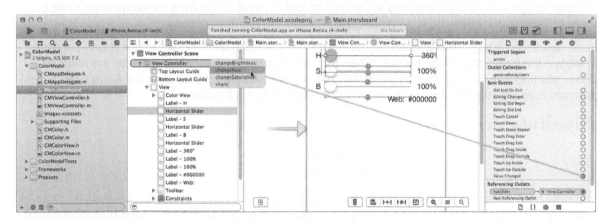

Figure 15-7. Creating an action connection for the Value Changed event

The code to create that same connection looks like this:

```
[newSlider addTarget:viewController
            action:@selector(changeHue:)
   forControlEvents:UIControlEventValueChanged];
```

> **Tip** `UIControlEvents` is a set of bits. Combine (OR) multiple constants together to attach an action message to multiple events at once.

Sending Action Messages

At this point, you shouldn't be surprised to learn that action messages can also be sent programmatically. If you want to send an action message, all you have to do is send a `-sendAction:to:from:forEvent:` message to your application object (`[UIApplication sharedApplication]`).

Subclasses of `UIControl` send events by sending themselves a `-sendAction:to:forEvent:` message. This, incidentally, just turns around and sends `-sendAction:to:from:forEvent:` to your application object, passing itself in the `from:` parameter.

> **Tip** If you're sending an action event in response to an iOS event (Chapter 4), it's polite to include the UIEvent object in the `forEvent:` parameter. Otherwise, pass `nil`.

You can programmatically cause any `UIControl` object to send the actions associated with one or more of its events by sending it a `-sendActionsForControlEvents:` message.

In all cases—both when sending action messages programmatically and when configuring control objects—the target object can be `nil`. When it is, the action message will be sent to the responder chain, starting with the first responder, instead of any specific object (see Chapter 4). To send an arbitrary message up the responder chain, use code that looks like this:

```
[[UIApplication sharedApplication] sendAction:@selector(orderIceCream:)
                                          to:nil /* responder chain */
                                        from:self
                                    forEvent:nil];
```

You now have a good grasp of how Interface Builder works and how objects get created, configured, and connected. You've also learned most of the equivalent code for what Interface Builder does, so you could programmatically create, configure, and connect objects, as you did in the Shapely app.

Forget all of that. Well, don't forget it—you might need it someday—but set it aside for the moment. It's great to know how Interface Builder files work, and the code you would write to do that same work. But the point of having Interface Builder is so you don't have to do that work! Instead of writing code to replace Interface Builder, it's time to put Interface Builder to work for you.

Taking Control of Interface Builder Files

Now that you understand what Interface Builder files are and how they work, you can easily add new ones to your app and load them when you want. This is the middle ground between the completely automatic use of Interface Builder files by view controllers and creating your view objects entirely with code. In this section you're going to learn to:

- Add an independent Interface Builder file to your project
- Programmatically load an Interface Builder file
- Designate multiple placeholder objects that Interface Builder objects can connect to

Back in Chapter 11 you wrote the Shapely app. Every time a button was tapped you created a new shape (SYShapeView) object, configured it, and attached a slew of gesture recognizers, using nothing but Objective-C. How much of that code could you accomplish using Interface Builder? Let's find out.

Declaring Placeholders

Starting with the finished Shapely project from Chapter 11, add a new Objective-C class file, name it SYShapeFactory, and make it a subclass of NSObject. Add another file, but this time choose the View file template from the iOS ➤ User Interface group, as shown in Figure 15-8. If Xcode asks for a device family, pick any one; it won't matter. Name the file SquareShape. This will add a standalone Interface Builder (SquareShape.xib) file that creates a single UIView object to your project.

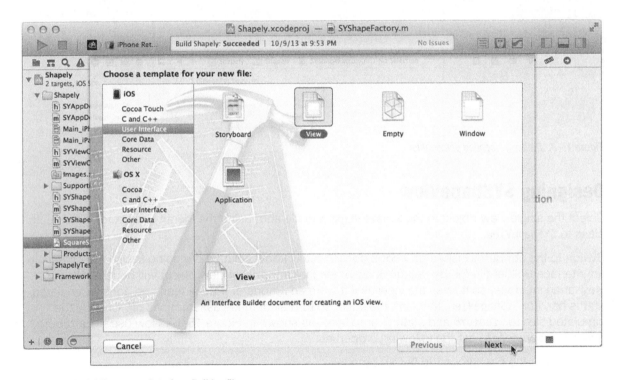

Figure 15-8. Adding a new Interface Builder file

The SYShapeFactory class will be this file's owner. This is your first placeholder object. To use the owner object, select the new SquareShape.xib file in the navigator, select the File's Owner in the placeholder group, and use the identity inspector to change its class to SYShapeFactory. You can now connect objects to the SYShapeFactory object that you'll provide later.

You also need to connect objects—specifically, the gesture recognizers—to your view controller. To accomplish that, you'll need a second placeholder object. From the object library, locate the External Object object and drag it into the outline, as shown on the left in Figure 15-9. Select it and change its class to `SYViewController`. With the placeholder object still selected, use the attributes inspector to assign it an identifier of `viewController`, as shown on the right in Figure 15-9. The objects in your new Interface Builder file can now connect to either the `SYShapeFactory` or your `SYViewController` object. Now it's time to design your objects.

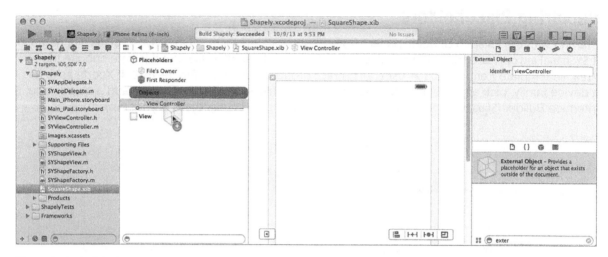

Figure 15-9. Defining a second placeholder

Designing SYShapeView

Select the single view object in the `SquareShape.xib` file and, using the identity inspector, change its class to `SYShapeView`.

Switch to the attributes inspector. Xcode doesn't really know what you're going to use the objects in an Interface Builder file for. By default, it assumes that a top-level view object will become the root view of an interface, so it sizes the view as if it were an iPhone or iPad screen and adds a simulated status bar. For `SYShapeView`, that isn't the case, so turn all of these assumptions off. Change the simulated size to `Freeform` and status bar to `None`, as shown in Figure 15-10. Now use the attribute and size inspectors to set the following properties:

- Set the background to `Default` (none)
- Uncheck the `Opaque` property
- Make sure `Clears Graphics Context` is checked
- Set its size to 100 by 100

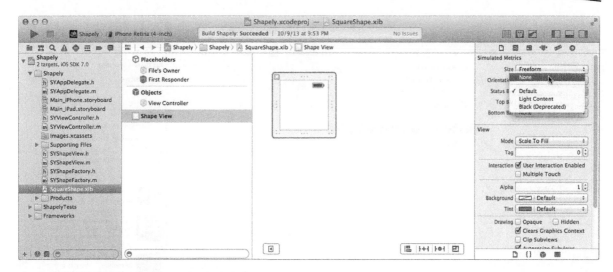

Figure 15-10. Designing the top-level view object

You've now replicated the size and properties of a new SYShapeView object produced with the -initWithShape: method—except for the shape property, which you'll address in a moment.

Select the SYShapeView.h file, remove the -initWithShape: method prototype, and replace it with a new property:

@property (nonatomic) ShapeSelector shape;

This makes the shape property settable. We'll need that later, because we can no longer use -initWithShape: to create the object (Interface Builder will create the object using -initWithCoder: instead).

Switch to the SYShapeView.m file and make the following changes:

- Discard the definitions for kInitialDimension and kInitialAlternateHeight
- Remove the shape instance variable from the private @interface SYShapeView () directive
- Delete the entire -initWithShape: method
- Replace the one reference to the shape variable with _shape (in the -path method, just follow the compiler warnings).

See how much code you've already eliminated? The entire purpose of the -initWithShape: constructor method was to create and configure a new SYShapeView object. Most of that work is now being done in your new Interface Builder file.

Connecting the Gesture Recognizers

Back in the SquareShape.xib file, it's time to add the gesture recognizers. From the object library, drag out a Pan Gesture Recognizer and drop it into the SYShapeView object. Select the recognizer object and use the attributes inspector to set its minimum and maximum touches to 1, as shown in Figure 15-11.

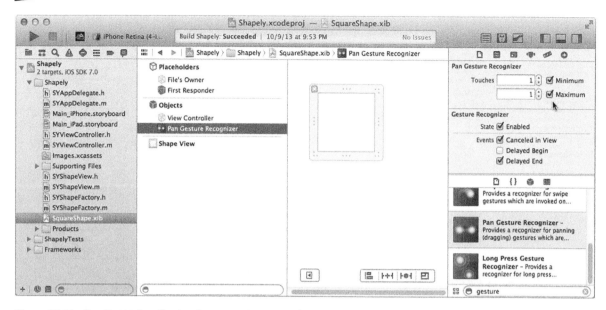

Figure 15-11. *Creating and configuring the pan gesture recognizer*

Switch to the connections inspector and connect its sent action to the -moveShape: method in the view controller placeholder, as shown in Figure 15-12.

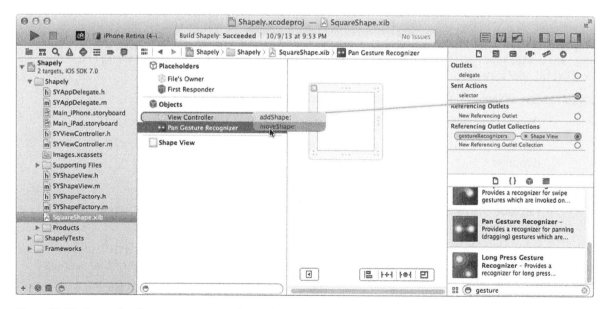

Figure 15-12. *Connecting the pan gesture recognizer action*

You've now created a pan gesture recognizer that recognizes only single-finger drag gestures. It's attached to the shape view object and it sends a -moveShape: message to the view controller, when triggered. The resulting gesture recognizer object is identical to the one you created, configured, and connected in the -addShape: method of SYViewController.

Add the other three gesture recognizers:

1. Drop a `Pinch Gesture Recognizer` into the shape view.

    a. Connect its sent action to the view controller's -resizeShape: method.

2. Drop a `Tap Gesture Recognizer` into the shape view.

    a. Set its Taps to 2

    b. Set its Touches to 1

    c. Connect its sent action to the -changeColor: method.

3. Drop a `Tap Gesture Recognizer` into the shape view.

    a. Set its Taps to 3

    b. Set its Touches to 1

    c. Connect its sent action to the -sendShapeToBack: method.

Much of the code you wrote in the -addShape: method has now been replicated using Interface Builder. There are two steps that can't be accomplished in Interface Builder; you'll address those in code shortly.

Build Your Shape Factory

Select the SYShapeFactory.h file. Add the following #include, @property, and method prototypes (new code in bold):

```
#import "SYShapeView.h"
#import "SYViewController.h"

@interface SYShapeFactory : NSObject

@property (strong,nonatomic) IBOutlet SYShapeView              *shapeView;
@property (strong,nonatomic) IBOutlet UITapGestureRecognizer *dblTapGesture;
@property (strong,nonatomic) IBOutlet UITapGestureRecognizer *trplTapGesture;

- (SYShapeView*)loadShape:(ShapeSelector)shape
         forViewController:(SYViewController*)controller;

@end
```

Your shape factory object defines outlets that will be connected to the shape view and selected gesture recognizers. You've also declared a -loadShape:forViewController: method that will do all of the work.

This is enough code to complete the necessary connections. Select the SquareShape.xib file, select the File's Owner, and use the connections inspector to connect the shapeView, dblTapGesture, and trplTapGesture outlets to their respective objects, as shown in Figure 15-13. Save the file. (Seriously, save the file by choosing **File ➤ Save**; it's important.)

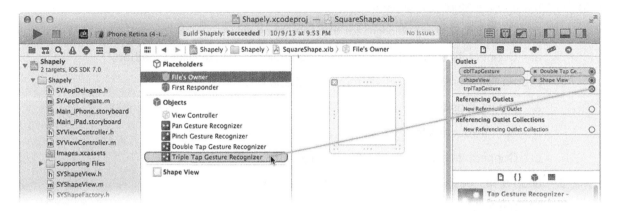

Figure 15-13. Connecting the factory outlets

> **Tip** Make sure you connect the right gesture recognizer outlet to the correct object, as both objects appear as Tap Gesture Recognizer in the outline. If you have Interface Builder objects that might be easily confused, use the identity inspector to change the object's label to something more descriptive. In Figure 15-13, I changed their labels to "Double Tap ..." and "Triple Tap ..." so I can tell which one is which. The label is cosmetic and doesn't alter the functionality of your Interface Builder design in any way.

The one aspect—sorry for the bad pun—that has not been addressed is the difference between the square, rectangle, circle, and oval shapes. If you remember, -initWithShape: would produce a 100 by 50 pixel view for rectangle and oval shapes and a 100 by 100 pixel view for everything else. In this version, you're going to replicate that logic using two Interface Builder files. SYShapeFactory will choose which one to load.

Start by creating the second Interface Builder file. Select the SquareShape.xib file and choose the **Edit ➤ Duplicate…** command, as shown in Figure 15-14.

CHAPTER 15: If You Build It ...   503

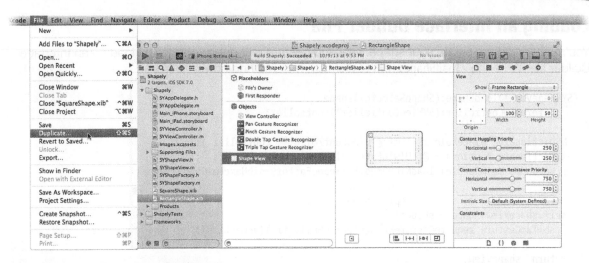

Figure 15-14. Creating the RectangleShape.xib file

Name the file RectangleShape. Select the new file, select the shape view object, and use the size inspector to change the height of the shape view to 50, as shown in Figure 15-14. Now you have two Interface Builder files, one that produces a 100 by 100 view and a second one that creates a 100 by 50 view.

Now switch to the SYShapeFactory.m file. Add a class method that will choose which Interface Builder file (SquareShape or RectangleShape) to load for given shape (new code in bold):

```
#import "SYShapeFactory.h"

@interface SYShapeFactory ()
+ (NSString*)nibNameForShape:(ShapeSelector)shape;
@end

@implementation SYShapeFactory

+ (NSString*)nibNameForShape:(ShapeSelector)shape
{
    switch (shape) {
        case kRectangleShape:
        case kOvalShape:
            return @"RectangleShape";

        default:
            return @"SquareShape";
    }
}
```

Loading an Interface Builder File

You're now ready to create your shape view and gesture recognizer objects by loading an Interface Builder file. Write the -loadShape:forViewController: method now:

```
- (SYShapeView*)loadShape:(ShapeSelector)shape
         forViewController:(SYViewController*)controller;
{
    NSDictionary *placeholders = @{ @"viewController": controller };
    NSDictionary *options = @{ UINibExternalObjects: placeholders };
    [[NSBundle mainBundle] loadNibNamed:[SYShapeFactory nibNameForShape:shape]
                                  owner:self
                                options:options];
    self.shapeView.shape = shape;
    [_dblTapGesture requireGestureRecognizerToFail:_trplTapGesture];

    return _shapeView;
}
```

The first two statements prepare the view controller to be a placeholder object when the Interface Builder file is loaded. You may pass as many placeholder objects as you like, just make sure their classes and identifiers agree with the external objects you defined in the Interface Builder file.

The third statement is where the magic happens. The -loadNibNamed:owner:options: method searches your app's bundle for an Interface Builder file with that name. The name (SquareShape or RectangleShape) is determined by the +nibNameForShape: method you added earlier. The owner parameter becomes the file's owner placeholder object. The options parameter is a dictionary of special options. In this case, the only special option is additional placeholder objects (UINibExternalObjects).

When -loadNibNamed:owner:options: is sent, the owner and any additional placeholder objects take the place of the File's Owner and the corresponding external objects defined in the Interface Builder file. The objects in the file are created, the properties of the objects are set according to the attributes you edited, and finally all of the outlet and action connections are established.

> **Tip** If you have code that needs to execute when your objects are created by an Interface Builder file, override your object's -awakeFromNib method. When an Interface Builder file or scene is loaded, every object it creates receives an -awakeFromNib message. This occurs after all properties and connections have been set.

The message returns an NSArray containing all of the top-level objects created in the file. You can access the objects created by the file either through this array or via outlets that you connected to the placeholders. In this app, you've used the latter technique.

> **Note** The main reason you created the SYShapeFactory class was to provide an owner object with outlets that conveniently provide references to the shape view and recognizer objects. Another solution would be to make the view controller the file's owner and dig through the returned NSArray of top-level objects to find the shape view and recognizer objects.

The last two statements take care of the two steps that can't be accomplished in Interface Builder. The shape property of the view is set and the double-tap/triple-tap dependency is established.

Replacing Code

Switch to the SYViewController.m file. Add an #import "SYShapeFactory.h" statement after the other #import statements. Now find the -addShape: method and replace the code that programmatically created a new SYShapeView object with the following (modified code in bold):

```
- (IBAction)addShape:(id)sender
{
    SYShapeView *shapeView = [[SYShapeFactory new] loadShape:[sender tag]
                                              forViewController:self];
```

Now, for the fun part: find the code in -addShape: that creates, configures, and connects the four gesture recognizers and delete it all. You don't need any of that now. All four of the gesture recognizers were created, configured, and connected by the Interface Builder file.

Run the finished app and observe the results. You shouldn't be able to tell any difference between this version of Shapely and the one from Chapter 11, which is the point. This exercise underscores the major advantages and disadvantages of creating your objects in Interface Builder:

- Objects are easy to create, configure, and connect in Interface Builder. This reduces the amount of code you have to write, saving time, and potentially reducing bugs. (Advantage)

- There are some properties and object relationships—like the double-tap/triple-tap dependency—that cannot be set in Interface Builder, and must be performed programmatically. (Disadvantage)

- You can easily choose between multiple Interface Builder files. Instead of writing huge if/else or switch statements, you can create a completely different set of objects simply by selecting a different Interface Builder file. (Advantage)

- You're limited to the configuration and initialization methods supported by Interface Builder. In Shapely, you had to prove a settable shape property in order to "fix" the object after it was created, since you could no longer use the -initWithShape: method. (Disadvantage)

- Interface Builder makes it easy to create complex sets of objects, especially ones like gesture recognizers and layout constraints. It requires pages and pages of dense, difficult to read, code to reproduce the layout constraints required for many interfaces. (Big Advantage)

- It can sometimes take considerable effort to obtain references to the objects created in an Interface Builder file. You might have to create special placeholder objects, or tediously dig through the top-level objects returned by `-loadNibNamed:owner:options:`. In this section you created a class (`SYShapeFactory`) for the sole purpose of providing outlets for the references to the shape view and gesture recognizers. (Disadvantage)

Interface Builder files aren't the best solution for every interface; sometimes a few lines of well-written code are all you need. But in the majority of cases, Interface Builder can save you from writing, maintaining, and debugging (literally) thousands of lines of code. It's an amazingly flexible and efficient tool that can free you from hours of work and improve the quality of your apps. You just needed to know how it works and how to use it.

Summary

Interface Builder is one of the cornerstones of Xcode, and it's what makes iOS app development so smooth. Understanding how it works gives you an edge. Understand what it can do and how, and you can push it to its limits or take over with your own code; it's your choice.

Loading Interface Builder files directly is where the real flexibility of Interface Builder becomes evident. You now know how to define practically any interface, a fragment of an interface, or just some arbitrary objects in an Interface Builder file and load them when, and where, you want. You know how to create any kind of objects you like, set its custom properties, and connect those with existing objects in your app. That's an incredibly useful tool to have at your fingertips.

Chapter 16

Apps with Attitude

In a feat of miniaturization that would make Wayne Szalinski[1] proud, most iOS devices are equipped with an array of sensors that detect acceleration, rotation, and magnetic orientation—which is a lot of "ations." The combined output of these sensors, along with a little math, will tell your app the attitude the device is being held in, whether it's being moved or rotated (and how fast), the direction of gravity, and the direction of magnetic north, with surprising accuracy. You can incorporate this into your app to give it an uncanny sense of immediacy. You can present information based on the direction the user is holding their device, control games through physical gestures, tell them if the picture they're about to take is level, and so much more.

In Chapter 4, you used the high-level "device shake" and "orientation change" events to trigger animations in the EightBall app. In this chapter, you're going to plug directly into the low-level accelerometer information and react to instantaneous changes in the device's position. In this chapter you will learn to:

- Collect accelerometer and other device motion data
- Use timers

You'll also get some more practice using affine transformations in custom view objects and use some of the fancy new animation features added in iOS 7. Let's get started.

> **Note** You will need a provisioned iOS device to test the code in this chapter. The iOS simulator does not emulate accelerometer data.

---

[1]Wayne Szalinski was the hapless inventor in the movie *Honey, I Shrunk the Kids*.

Leveler

The app you're going to create is a simple, digital, level called Leveler.[2] It's a one-screen app that displays a dial indicating the inclination (angle from an imaginary vertical plumb line) of the device, as shown in Figure 16-1.

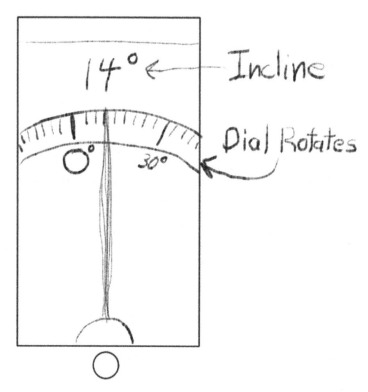

Figure 16-1. Leveler design

Creating Leveler

Create a new Xcode project, as follows:

- Use the Single View Application template
- Product Name: Leveler
- Class Prefix: LR
- Devices: Universal
- After creating the project, edit the supported interface orientations to support all device orientations

---

[2] Look up the word "leveler" for an interesting factoid on English history.

Leveler is going to need some image and source code resources. You'll find the image files in the Learn iOS Development Projects ➤ Ch 16 ➤ Leveler (Resources) folder. Add the hand.png and hand@2x.png files to the Images.xcassets image catalog. In the finished Leveler-1 project folder, locate the LRDialView.h and LRDialView.m files. Add them to your project too, alongside your other source files. Remember to check the Copy items into destination group's folder option in the import dialog. You'll also find a set of app icons in the Leveler (Icons) folder that you can drop into the AppIcon group of the image catalog.

You'll first lay out and connect the views that will display the inclination before getting to the code that gathers the accelerometer data.

Pondering LRDialView

The source files you just added contain the code for a custom UIView object that draws a circular "dial." After reading Chapter 11, you shouldn't have any problem figuring out how it works. The most interesting aspect is the use of affine transforms in the graphics context. In Chapter 11, you applied affine transforms to a view object, so it appeared either offset or scaled from its actual frame. In LRDialView, an affine transform is applied to the graphics context before drawing into it. Anything drawn afterwards is translated using that transform.

In LRDialView, this technique is used to draw the tick marks and angle labels around the inside of the "dial." If you're interested, find the -drawRect: method in LRDialView.m. The significant bits of code are in bold, and irrelevant code has been replaced with ellipses:

```
#define kCircleDegrees      360
#define kMinorTickDegrees   3

...

- (void)drawRect:(CGRect)rect
{
    CGContextRef context = UIGraphicsGetCurrentContext();
    CGRect bounds = self.bounds;
    CGFloat radius = bounds.size.height/2;
    ...
    CGContextTranslateCTM(context,radius,radius);
    for ( NSUInteger angle=0; angle<kCircleDegrees; angle+=kMinorTickDegrees )
        {
        ... draw one vertical tick and horizontal label ...
        CGContextConcatCTM(context, ↵
                CGAffineTransformMakeRotation(kMinorTickDegrees*M_PI/180));
        }
}
```

The -drawRect: method first applies a translate transform to the context. This offsets the drawing coordinates, effectively changing the origin of the view's local coordinate system to the center of the view. (The view is always square, as you'll see later.) After applying this transform, if you drew a shape at (0,0), it will now draw at the center of the view, rather than the upper-left corner.

The loop draws one vertical tick mark and an optional text label below it. At the end of the loop, the drawing coordinates of the context are rotated 3°. The second time through the loop the tick mark and label will be rotated 3°. The third time through the loop all drawing will be rotated 6°, and so on, until the entire dial has been drawn. Context transforms accumulate.

The key concept to grasp is that transformations applied to the drawing context affect the coordinate system of what's being drawn into the view, as shown in Figure 16-2. Context transforms don't change its frame, bounds, or where it appears in its superview.

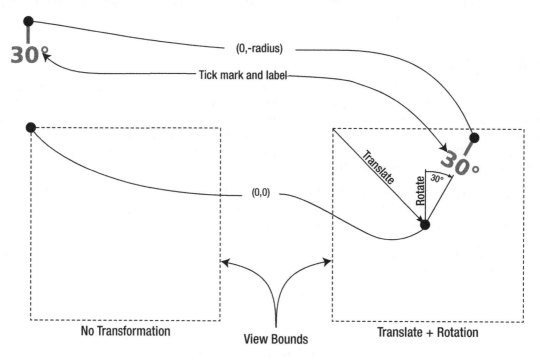

Figure 16-2. Graphics context transformation

To change how the view appears in its superview, you set the transform property of the view, as you did in the Shapely app. And that's exactly what the view controller will do (later) to rotate the dial on the screen. This underscores the difference between using affine transforms while drawing and using a transform to alter how the finished view appears.

Also note that the view only draws itself once. All of this complicated code in -drawRect: executes only when the view is first drawn or resized. Once the view is drawn, the cached image of the dial appears in the display and gets rotated by the view's transform property. This second use of a transform simply transcribes the pixels in the cached image; it doesn't cause the view to redraw itself at the new angle. In this respect, the drawing is very efficient. This is important, because later on you're going to animate it.

Creating the Views

You're going to add a label object to the Interface Builder file, and then write code in `LRViewController` to programmatically create the `LRDialView` and the image view that displays the "needle" behind the dial. Start with the `Main_iPhone.storyboard` (or `_iPad`) file.

Drag a label object into the interface. Using the attributes inspector, change the following:

> Text: 360° (press Option+Shift+8 to type the degree symbol)
>
> Color: `White Color`
>
> Font: `System 60.0` (iPhone) or `System 90.0` (iPad)
>
> Alignment: middle

Select the label object and choose Editor ➤ Size to Fit Content. Position the object so it is centered at the top of the interface. Select the root view object and change its background color to `Black Color`.

Select the label and add the following constraints:

1. Fix its width (Editor ➤ Pin ➤ Width)
2. Fix its height (Editor ➤ Pin ➤ Height)
3. Center it (Editor ➤ Align ➤ Horizontal Center in Container)
4. Control/right-drag to the `Top Layout Guide` and create a Vertical Spacing constraint
5. Using the attributes inspector, select the constraint and check its `Standard` option

The finished interface should look like the one in Figure 16-3.

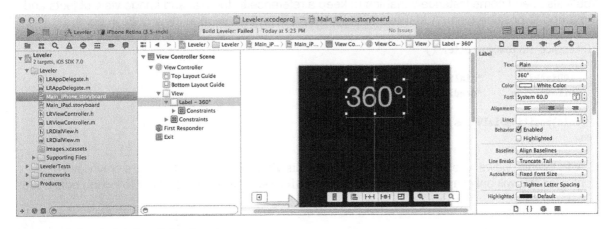

Figure 16-3. Leveler Interface Builder layout

Switch to the assistant view. With the LRViewController.h file in the right-hand pane, add this outlet property:

```
@property (weak,nonatomic) IBOutlet UILabel *angleLabel;
```

Connect the outlet to the label view in the interface, as shown in Figure 16-4.

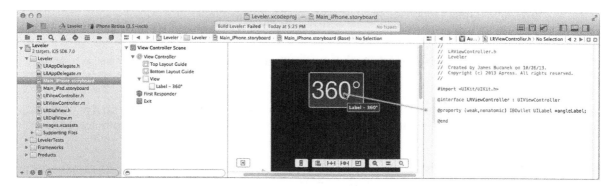

Figure 16-4. Connecting angle label outlet

You'll create and position the other two views programmatically. Switch back to the standard editor and select the LRViewController.m file. You'll need the definition of the LRDialView class and the name of the image resource file, so add the following #import and #define declarations immediately after the existing #import directives:

```
#import "LRDialView.h"

#define kHandImageName      @"hand"
```

You'll also need some instance variables to keep a reference to the dial and image view objects and a method to position them. Add those to the private @interface section (new code in bold):

```
@interface LRViewController ()
{
    LRDialView      *dialView;
    UIImageView     *needleView;
}
- (void)positionDialViews;
@end
```

Create the two views when the view controller loads its view. Since this is the app's only view controller, this will only happen once. Find the -viewDidLoad method and add the following bold code:

```
- (void)viewDidLoad
{
    [super viewDidLoad];
    
    dialView = [[LRDialView alloc] initWithFrame:CGRectMake(0,0,100,100)];
    [self.view addSubview:dialView];
```

```objc
    needleView = [[UIImageView alloc]
                    initWithImage:[UIImage imageNamed:kHandImageName]];
    needleView.contentMode = UIViewContentModeScaleAspectFit;
    [self.view insertSubview:needleView belowSubview:dialView];
}
```

When the view is loaded, the additional code creates new LRDialView and UIImageView objects, adding both to the view. Notice that the needleView is deliberately placed behind dialView. The dial view is partially transparent, allowing the needleView to show through it.

No attempt is made to size or position these views. That happens when the view is displayed or rotated. Catch those events by adding these two methods:

```objc
- (void)viewWillAppear:(BOOL)animated
{
    [self positionDialViews];
}

- (void)didRotateFromInterfaceOrientation:(UIInterfaceOrientation)fromOrientation
{
    [self positionDialViews];
}
```

Just before the view appears for the first time, and whenever the view is rotated to a new orientation, reposition the dialView and needleView objects. You'll also need to add this method for the iPhone version:

```objc
- (NSUInteger)supportedInterfaceOrientations
{
    return UIInterfaceOrientationMaskAll;
}
```

While you edited the supported orientations for the app, remember (from Chapter 14) that each view controller dictates which orientations it supports. By default, the iPhone's UIViewController does not support upside-down orientation. This code overrides that to allow all orientations.

Finally, you'll need the code for -positionDialView:

```objc
- (void)positionDialViews
{
    CGRect viewBounds = self.view.bounds;
    CGRect labelFrame = self.angleLabel.frame;
    CGFloat topEdge = CGRectGetMaxY(labelFrame)+labelFrame.size.height/3;
    CGFloat dialHeight = ceilf((CGRectGetMaxY(viewBounds)-topEdge)*2);
    dialView.transform = CGAffineTransformIdentity;
    dialView.frame = CGRectMake(0, 0, dialHeight, dialHeight);
    dialView.center = CGPointMake(CGRectGetMidX(viewBounds),
                                  CGRectGetMaxY(viewBounds));
    [dialView setNeedsDisplay];
    
    CGSize needleSize = needleView.image.size;
    CGFloat needleScale = (dialHeight/2)/needleSize.height;
```

```
        CGRect needleFrame = CGRectMake(0,0,
                                    needleSize.width*needleScale,
                                    needleSize.height*needleScale);
    needleFrame.origin.x = CGRectGetMidX(viewBounds)-needleFrame.size.width/2;
    needleFrame.origin.y = CGRectGetMaxY(viewBounds)-needleFrame.size.height;
    needleView.frame = CGRectIntegral(needleFrame);
}
```

This looks like a lot of code, but all it's doing is sizing the `dialView` so it is square, positioning its center at the bottom center of the view, and sizing it so its top edge is just under the bottom edge of the label view. The `needleView` is then positioned so it's centered and anchored to the bottom edge, and scaled so its height equals the visible height of the dial. This is a lot harder to describe than it is to see, so just run the app and see what I mean in Figure 16-5.

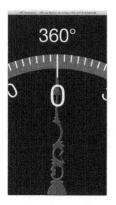

Figure 16-5. Dial and needle view positioning

That pretty much completes all of the view design and layout. Now you need to get the accelerometer information and make your app do something.

Getting Motion Data

All iOS devices (as of this writing) have accelerometer hardware. The accelerometer senses the force of acceleration along three axes: X, Y, and Z. If you face the screen of your iPhone or iPad in portrait orientation, the X-axis is horizontal, the Y-axis is vertical, and the Z-axis is the line that goes from you, through the middle of the device, perpendicular to the screen's surface.

You can use accelerometer information to determine when the device changes speed and in what direction. Assuming it's not accelerating (much), you can also use this information to infer the direction of gravity, since gravity exerts a constant force on a stationary body. This is the information iOS uses to determine when you've flipped your iPad on its side or when you're shaking your iPhone.

In addition to the accelerometer, recent iOS devices also include a gyroscope and a magnetometer. The former detects changes in rotation around the three axes (pitch, roll, yaw) and the magnetometer detects the orientation of a magnetic field. Barring magnetic interference, this will tell you the device's attitude relative to magnetic North. (Which is a fancy way of saying it has a compass.)

Your app gets to all of this information through a single gatekeeper class: CMMotionManager. The CMMotionManager class collects, interprets, and delivers movement and attitude information to your app. You tell it what kind(s) of information you want (accelerometer, gyroscope, compass), how often you want to receive updates, and how those updates are delivered to your app. Your Leveler app will only use accelerometer information, but the general pattern is the same for all types of motion data:

1. Create an instance of CMMotionManager
2. Set the frequency of updates
3. Choose what information you want and how your app will get it (pull or push)
4. When you're ready, start the delivery of information
5. Process motion data as it occurs
6. When you're done, stop the delivery of information

There's no better place to start than step 1.

Creating CMMotionManager

Before all of the other #import statements in LRViewController.m, pull in the CoreMotion framework definitions:

```
#import <CoreMotion/CoreMotion.h>
```

You'll need to specify how fast you want motion data updates. For neatness, define this as a constant, just after the #import statements:

```
#define kAccelerometerPollingInterval   (1.0/15.0)
```

You will need an instance variable to store the CMMotionManager object reference and methods to process the motion data and rotate the dial. Add those to your private interface (new code in bold):

```
@interface LRViewController ()
{
    CMMotionManager *motionManager;
    LRDialView      *dialView;
    UIImageView     *needleView;
}
- (void)positionDialViews;
- (void)updateAccelerometerTime:(NSTimer*)timer;
- (void)rotateDialView:(double)rotation;
@end
```

Locate the -viewDidLoad: method and add this code to the end of the method:

```
motionManager = [CMMotionManager new];
motionManager.accelerometerUpdateInterval = kAccelerometerPollingInterval;
```

You've completed the first two steps in using motion data. The first statement creates a new `CMMotionManager` object and saves it in your `motionManager` instance variable.

> **Caution** Do not create multiple instances of `CMMotionManager`. If your app has two or more controllers that need motion data, they share a single instance of `CMMotionManager`. I suggest creating a `readonly` property in your application delegate class that returns a singleton `CMMotionManager` object. Any code can retrieve it via `[UIApplication.sharedApplication.delegate motionManager]`.

The next statement tells the manager how long to wait between measurements. This property is expressed in seconds. For most apps, 10 to 30 times a second is adequate, but extreme apps might need updates as often as 100 times a second. For this app, you'll start with 15 updates per second by setting the `accelerometerUpdateInterval` property to 1/15th of a second.

Starting and Stopping Updates

To perform the third and fourth steps in getting motion data, locate the `-viewWillAppear:` method and add this statement (new code in bold):

```
- (void)viewWillAppear:(BOOL)animated
{
    [self positionDialViews];
    [motionManager startAccelerometerUpdates];
}
```

Just before the view appears, you request that the motion manager begin collecting accelerometer data. The accelerometer information reported by `CMMotionManager` won't be accurate—or even change—until you begin its update process. Once started, the motion manager code works tirelessly in the background to monitor any changes in acceleration and report those to your app.

> **Tip** To conserve battery life, your app should request updates from the motion manager *only* while your app needs them. For this app, motion events are used for the lifetime of the app, so there's no code to stop them. If you added a second view controller, however, that didn't use the accelerometer, you'd want to add code to `-viewWillDisappear:` to send `-stopAccelerometerUpdates`.

Push Me, Pull You

It might not look you like you've performed the third step in getting motion data, but you did. It was implied when you sent the `-startAccelerometerUpdates` message. This method starts gathering motion data, but it's up to your app to periodically ask what those values are. This is called the *pull* approach; the `CMMotionManager` object keeps the motion data current and your app pulls the data from it as needed.

The alternative is the *push* approach. To use this approach, send the -startAccelerometerUpdates ToQueue:withHandler: message instead. You pass it an operation queue (that I'll explain in Chapter 24) and a code block that gets executed the moment motion data is updated. This is much more complicated to implement because the code block is executed on a separate thread, so all of your motion data handling code must be thread-safe. You really only need this approach if your app must, absolutely, positively, process motion data the *instant* it becomes available. There are very few apps that fall into this category.

Timing is Everything

Now you're probably wondering how your app "periodically" pulls the motion data it's interested in. The motion manager doesn't post any notifications or send your object any delegate messages. What you need is an object that will remind your app to do something at regular intervals. It's called a timer, and iOS provides just that. At the end of the -viewWillAppear: method, add this statement:

```
[NSTimer scheduledTimerWithTimeInterval:kAccelerometerPollingInterval
                                 target:self
                               selector:@selector(updateAccelerometerTime:)
                               userInfo:nil
                                repeats:YES];
```

An NSTimer object provides a timer for your app. It is one of the sources of events that I mentioned in Chapter 4, but never got around to talking about.

> **Note** Making a functioning timer is a two-step process; you must create the timer object and then add it to the run loop. The -scheduledTimerWithTimeInterval:target:selector:userInfo:repeats: method does both for you. If you create a timer using a different method, you'll have to send the run loop object an -addTimer:forMode: message before the timer will do anything.

Timers come in two flavors: single-shot or repeating. A timer has a timeInterval property and a message it will send to an object. After the amount of time in the timeInterval property has passed, the timer *fires*. At the next opportunity, the event loop will send the target object the timer's message. If it's a one-shot timer, that's it; the timer becomes invalid and stops. If it's a repeating timer, it continues running, waiting until another timeInterval amount of time has passed before firing again. A repeating timer continues to send messages until you send it an -invalidate message.

> **Caution** Don't use timers to poll for events—such as waiting for a web page to load—that you could have determined using event messages, delegate methods, notifications, or code blocks. Timers should only be used for time-related events and periodic updates.

The code you added to -viewWillAppear: creates and schedules a timer that sends your view controller object an -updateAccelerometerTime: message approximately 15 times a second. This is the same rate that the motion manager is updating its accelerometer information. There's no point in checking for updates any faster, or slower, than the CMMotionManager object is gathering them.

Everything is in place, except the -updateAccelerometerTime: and -rotateDialView: methods. While still in LRViewController.m, add the first method:

```
- (void)updateAccelerometerTime:(NSTimer *)timer
{
    CMAcceleration acceleration = motionManager.accelerometerData.acceleration;
    double rotation = atan2(-acceleration.x,-acceleration.y);
    [self rotateDialView:rotation];
}
```

The first statement retrieves the accelerometerData property of the motion manager. Since you only started the gathering of accelerometer information, this is the only motion data property that's valid. This property is a CMAccelerometerData object, and that object only has one property: acceleration. The acceleration property—which is a structure, not an object—contains three numbers: x, y, and z. Each value is the instantaneous force being exerted along that axis, measured in G's.[3] Assuming the device isn't being moved around, the measurements can be combined to determine the *gravitational vector*; in other words, you can figure out which way is down.

Your app doesn't need all three. You only need to determine which direction is up in the X-Y plane, because that's where the dial lives. Ignoring the force along the Z-axis, the arctangent function calculates the angle of the gravitational vector in the X-Y plane. The result is used to rotate the dialView by that same angle. Simple, isn't it?

> **Note** You might have questioned why the arctangent function was given the negative values of x and y. That's because the dial points up, not down. Flipping the direction of the force values calculates the angle *away* from gravity.

Complete the app by writing the -rotateDialView: method:

```
- (void)rotateDialView:(double)rotation
{
    dialView.transform = CGAffineTransformMakeRotation(rotation);

    NSInteger degrees = round(-rotation*180.0/M_PI);
    if (degrees<0)
        degrees+=360;
    _angleLabel.text = [NSString stringWithFormat:@"%u\u00b0",(unsigned)degrees];
}
```

---

[3] G is the force of gravity, equal to an acceleration of approximately 9.81 meters per second every second.

This method turns the rotation parameter into an affine transform that rotates `dialView`. The last block of code converts the `rotation` value from radians into degrees, makes sure it's not negative, and uses that to update the label view.

It's time to plug in your provisioned iOS device, run your app, and play with the results, as shown in Figure 16-6. Notice how the app switches orientation as you rotate it. If you lock the device's orientation, it won't do that, but the dial still works.

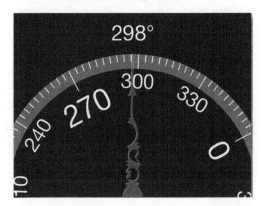

Figure 16-6. Working Leveler app

Herky-Jerky

Your app works, and it was pretty easy to write, but boy is it hard to look at. If it works anything like the way is does on my devices, the dial jitters constantly. Unless the device is perfectly still, it's almost impossible to read.

It would be really nice if the dial moved more smoothly—a lot more smoothly. That sounds like a job for animation. What you want is an animation that makes the dial appear to have mass, gently drifting towards the instantaneous inclination reported by the hardware.

So what are your choices? In the past, you've used Core Animation to smoothly move views around. But Core Animation is like a homing pigeon; you take it to where you want it to start, tell it where you want it end up, and let it go. Once started, it's not designed to make in-flight course corrections should the end point change. And that's exactly what will happen when new accelerometer information is received.

You could try to smooth out the updates yourself by clamping the rate at which the view is rotated. To make it look really nice, you might even go so far as to create a simple physics engine that gives the dial simulated mass, acceleration, drag, and so on. But as I mentioned in chapter 11, the do-it-yourself approach to animation is fraught with complications, is usually a lot of work, and often results to sub-standard performance.

Lucky for you, iOS 7 introduced view dynamics. *View dynamics* is a new animation service that endows your views with a simulated physicality that mimics mass, gravity, acceleration, drag, collisions, and so on. View dynamics takes a substantially different approach to animation. Instead of describing what you want the animation to do—move this many pixels, rotate that many degrees, and so on—you describe the "forces" acting on a view and let the dynamic animator create an animation that simulates the view's reaction to those forces.

Using Dynamic Animation

Dynamic animation involves three players:

- The dynamic animator object
- One or more behavior objects
- One or more view objects

The *dynamic animator* is the object that performs the animation. It contains a complex physic engine that's remarkably intelligent. You'll need to create a single instance of the dynamic animator.

Animation occurs when you create behavior objects and add those to the dynamic animator. A *behavior* describes a single impetus or attribute of a view. iOS includes predefined behaviors for gravity, acceleration, friction, collisions, connections, and more, and you're free to invent your own. A behavior is associated with one or more view (UIView) objects, imparting that particular behavior to all of its views. The dynamic animator does the work of combining multiple behaviors for a single view—acceleration plus gravity plus friction, for example—to construct the animation for that view.

So the basic formula for dynamic animation is:

1. Create an instance of UIDynamicAnimator
2. Create one or more UIDynamicBehavior objects, attached to UIView objects
3. Add the UIDynamicBehavior objects to the UIDynamicAnimator
4. Sit back and enjoy the show

You're now ready to add view dynamics to Leveler.

Creating the Dynamic Animator

You'll need to create a dynamic animator object, and for that you'll need an instance variable to save it in. Find the private @interface LRViewController () declaration in LRViewController.m. Add an instance variable for your animator (new code in bold). While you're here, add some constants and a variable to contain an attachment behavior, all of which will be explained shortly:

```
#define kSpringAnchorDistance    4.0
#define kSpringDamping           0.7
#define kSpringFrequency         0.5

@interface LRViewController ()
{
    CMMotionManager         *motionManager;
    LRDialView              *dialView;
    UIImageView             *needleView;
    UIDynamicAnimator       *animator;
    UIAttachmentBehavior    *springBehavior;
}
```

You'll need to create the dynamic animator, create the behavior objects you want, and connect those to your views. The perfect place to do all three is in the -positionDialViews method. Find the -positionDialViews method and add this code to the very beginning (new code in bold):

```
- (void)positionDialViews
{
    if (animator!=nil)
        [animator removeAllBehaviors];
    else
        animator = [[UIDynamicAnimator alloc] initWithReferenceView:self.view];
```

This code simply determines if a UIDynamicAnimator objects has already been created or not. If it has, it resets it by removing any active behaviors. If it hasn't, it creates a new dynamic animator.

When you create a dynamic animator, you must specify a view that will be used to establish the coordinate system the dynamic animator will use. The dynamic animator uses its own coordinate system, called the *reference coordinate system*, so that view objects in different view hierarchies (each with their own coordinate system) can interact with one another in a unified coordinate space. Using the reference coordinate system you could, for example, have a view in your content view controller collide with a button in the toolbar, even though it resides in an unrelated superview.

For your app, make the reference coordinate system that of your view controller's root view. This makes all dynamic animator coordinates the same as your local view coordinates. Won't that be convenient? (Yes, it will.)

Defining Behaviors

So what behavior(s) do you think the dial view should have? If you look through the behaviors supplied by iOS, you won't find a "rotation" behavior. But the dynamic animator will rotate a view, if the forces acting on that view would cause it to rotate. Rotating the dial view, therefore, isn't any more difficult that rotating a record platter, a merry-go-round, a lazy susan, or anything similar: anchor the center of the object and apply an oblique force to one edge.

You'll accomplish this using two attachment behaviors. An *attachment behavior* connects a point in your view with either a similar point in another view or a fixed point in space, called an *anchor*. The length of the attachment can be inflexible, creating a "towbar" relationship that keeps the attachment point at a fixed distance, or it can be flexible, creating a "spring" relationship that tugs on the view when the other end of the attachment moves. To rotate the dial view, you'll use one of each, as shown in Figure 16-7.

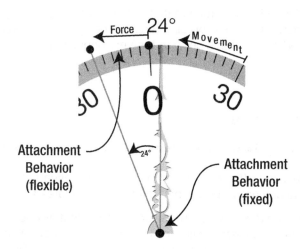

Figure 16-7. dialView attachment behaviors

Create the first behavior by adding this code to the end of the -positionDialViews method:

```
CGPoint dialCenter = dialView.center;
UIAttachmentBehavior *pinBehavior;
pinBehavior = [[UIAttachmentBehavior alloc] initWithItem:dialView
                                attachedToAnchor:dialCenter];
[animator addBehavior:pinBehavior];
```

The attachment behavior defines a rigid attachment from the center of the dial view to a fixed anchor point, at the exact same location. When you create an attachment behavior, the distance between the two attachment points defines its initial length, which in this case is 0. Since the attachment is inflexible and its length is 0, the net effect is to pin the center of the view at that coordinate. The view's center can't move from that spot.

> **Note** Most dynamic behaviors can be associated with any number of view objects. Gravity, for example, can be applied to a multitude of view objects equally. The attachment behavior, however, creates a relationship between two attachment points, and therefore only associates with one or two view objects.

All that remains is to add that behavior to the dynamic animator. All by itself, this doesn't accomplish much, except to prevent the view from being moved to a new location. Things get interesting when you add a second attachment behavior, using the following code:

```
CGRect dialRect = dialView.frame;
CGPoint topCenter = CGPointMake(CGRectGetMidX(dialRect),
                                CGRectGetMinY(dialRect));
springBehavior = [[UIAttachmentBehavior alloc]
                        initWithItem:dialView
                   offsetFromCenter:UIOffsetMake(0,topCenter.y-dialCenter.y)
```

```
                      attachedToAnchor:topCenter];
springBehavior.damping = kSpringDamping;
springBehavior.frequency = kSpringFrequency;
[animator addBehavior:springBehavior];
```

The first two statements calculate the point at the top center of the view. A second attachment behavior is created. This time the attachment point is not in the center of the view, but at its top-center (expressed as an offset from its center).

Again, the anchor point is the same location as the attachment point, creating a zero-length attachment. What's different is that the `damping` and `frequency` properties are then set to something other than their default values. This creates a "springy" connection between the anchor point and the attachment point. But since the anchor and the attachment point are currently the same, no force is applied (yet).

Animating the Dial

The stage is set and all of the players are in place. You've defined a behavior that pins the center of the dial to a specific position, and a second that will "tug" the top-center point towards a second anchor point. The action begins when you move that second anchor point, as shown in Figure 16-7.

Locate the `-rotateDialView:` method and delete the first statement, the one that created an affine transform and applied it to the view. Replace that code with the following (new code in bold):

```
- (void)rotateDialView:(double)rotation
{
    CGPoint center = dialView.center;
    CGFloat radius = dialView.frame.size.height/2 + kSpringAnchorDistance;
    CGPoint springPoint = CGPointMake(center.x+sin(rotation)*radius,
                                      center.y-cos(rotation)*radius);
    springBehavior.anchorPoint = springPoint;
```

Instead of the traditional approach of telling the graphics system what kind of change you want to see (rotate the view by a certain angle), you describe a change to the physical environment and let the dynamic animator simulate the consequences. In this app, you moved the anchor point attached to the top-center point of the view. Moving the anchor point creates an attraction between the new anchor point and the attachment point in the view. Since the center of the view is pinned by the first behavior, the only way the top point of the view can get closer to the new anchor point is to rotate the view, and that's exactly what happens.

Run the app and see the effect. The dial acts much more like a "real" dial. There's acceleration, deceleration, and even oscillation. These effects are all courtesy of the physics engine in the dynamic animator.

Try altering the values of `kSpringAnchorDistance`, `kSpringDamping`, and `kSpringFrequency` and observe how this affects the dial. For extra credit, add a third behavior that adds some "drag" to the dial. Create a `UIDynamicItemBehavior` object, associate it with the dial view, and set its `angularResistance` property to something other than 0; I suggest starting with a value of 2.0. Don't forget to add the finished behavior to the dynamic animator.

You now have a nifty inclinometer that's silky smooth and fun to watch. Now that you know how easy it is to add motion data to your app, and simulate motion using view dynamics, let's take a look at some of the other sources of motion data.

Getting Other Kinds of Motion Data

As of this writing, there are three other kinds of motion data your app can use. You can collect and use the other kinds of data instead of, or in addition to, the accelerometer data. Here are the kinds of motion data iOS provides:

- Gyroscope: measures the rate at which the device is being rotated around its three axes
- Magnetometer: measures the orientation of the surrounding magnetic field
- Device Motion: combines information from the accelerometer, magnetometer, and gyroscope to produce useful values about the device's motion and position in space

Using the other kinds of motion data is identical to what you've done with the accelerometer data, with one exception. Not all iOS devices have a gyroscope or a magnetometer. You will have to decide if your app must have these capabilities, or can function in their absence. That decision will dictate how you configure your app's project and write your code. Let's start with the gyroscope.

Gyroscope Data

If you're interested in the instantaneous rate at which the device is being rotated—logically equivalent to the accelerometer data, but for angular force—gather gyroscope data. You collect gyroscope data almost exactly as you do accelerometer data. Begin by setting the gyroUpdateInterval property of the motion manager object, and then send it either a -startGyroUpdates or -startGyroUpdatesToQueue:withHandler: message.

The gyroData property returns a CMGyroData object, which has a single rotationRate property value. This property is a struct (just like CMAcceleration) with three values: x, y, and z. Each value is the rate of rotation around that axis, in radians per second.

You must consider the possibility that the user's device doesn't have a gyroscope. There are two approaches:

- If your app requires gyroscopic hardware to function, add the gyroscope value to the Required Device Capabilities collection of your app's property list.
- If you app can run with, or without, a gyroscope, test the gyroAvailable property of the motion manager object.

The first approach makes the gyroscope hardware a requirement for your app to run. If added to your app's property list, iOS won't allow the app to be installed on a device that lacks a gyroscope. The App Store may hide the app from users that lack a gyroscope, or warn them that your app may not run on their device.

If your app can make use of gyroscope data, but could live without it, test for the presence of a gyroscope by reading the gyroAvailable property of the motion manager object. If it's YES, feel free to start and use the gyroscope data. If it's NO, make other arrangements.

Magnetometer Data

The magnitude and direction of the magnetic field surrounding your device is available via the magnetometer data. By now, this is going to sound like a broken record:

- Set the frequency of magnetometer updates using the magnetometerUpdateInterval property.
- Start magnetometer measurements using the -startMagnetometerUpdates or -startMagnetometerUpdatesToQueue:withHandler: messages.
- The magnetometerData property returns a CMMagnetometerData object with the current readings.
- The CMMagnetometerData object's sole property is the magneticField property, a structure with three values: x, y, and z. Each is the direction and strength of the field along that axis, in mT (microteslas).
- Either add the magnetometer value to your app's Required Device Capabilities property or check the magnetometerAvailable property to determine if the device has one.

Like the accelerometer and gyroscope data, the magnetometerDate property returns the raw, unfiltered, magnetic field information. This will be a combination of the Earth's magnetic field, the device's own magnetic bias, any ambient magnetic fields, magnetic interference, and so on.

Teasing out magnetic North from this data is a little tricky. What looks like North might be a microwave oven. Similarly, the accelerometer data can change because the device was tilted, or because it's in a moving car, or both. You can unravel some of these conflicting indicators by collecting and correlating data from multiple instruments. For example, you can tell the difference between a tilt and a horizontal movement by examining the changes to both the accelerometer and gyroscope; a tilt will change both, but a horizontal movement will only register on the accelerometer.

If you're getting the sinking feeling that you should have been paying more attention in your physics and math classes, you can relax; iOS has you covered.

Device Motion and Attitude

The CMMotionManager also provides a unified view of the device's physical position and movements through its device motion interface. The device motion properties and methods combine the information from the accelerometer, gyroscope, and sometimes the magnetometer. It assimilates all of this data and produces a filtered, unified, calibrated picture of the device's motion and position in space.

You use device motion in much the way you used the preceding three instruments:

- Set the frequency of device motion updates using the `deviceMotionUpdateInterval` property.
- Start device motion update by sending a `-startDeviceUpdates`, `-startDeviceMotionUpdatesToQueue:withHandler:`, `-startDeviceMotionUpdatesUsingReferenceFrame:`, or `-startDeviceMotionUpdatesUsingReferenceFrame:toQueue:withHandler:` message.
- The `deviceMotion` property returns a `CMDeviceMotion` object with the current motion and attitude information.
- Determine if device motion data is available using the `deviceMotionAvailable` property.

There are two big differences between the device motion and previous interfaces. When starting updates, you can optionally provide a `CMAttitudeReferenceFrame` constant that selects a *frame of reference* for the device. There are four choices:

- Direction of the device is arbitrary
- Direction is arbitrary, but use the magnetometer to eliminate "yaw drift"
- Direction is calibrated to magnetic North
- Direction is calibrated to true North (requires location services)

The neutral reference position of your device can be imaged by placing your iPhone or iPad flat on a table in front of you, with the screen up, and the home button towards you. The line from the home button to the top of the device is the Y-axis. The X-axis runs horizontally from the left side to the right. The Z-axis runs through the device, straight up and down.

Spinning your device, while still flat on the table, changes its *direction*. It's this direction that the reference frame is concerned with. If the direction doesn't matter, you can use either of the arbitrary reference frames. If you need to know the direction in relationship to true or magnetic North, use one of the calibrated reference frames.

> **Note** Not all attitude reference frames are available on every device. Use the `+availableAttitudeReferenceFrames` method to determine which ones the device supports.

The second big difference is the `CMDeviceMotion` object. Unlike the other motion data objects, this one has several properties, listed in Table 16-1.

Table 16-1. Key CMDeviceMotion properties

Property	Description
attitude	A CMAttitude object that describes the actual attitude (position in space) of the device described as a triplet of property values (pitch, roll, and yaw). Additional properties describe the same information in mathematically equivalent forms, both as a rotation matrix and a quaternion.
rotationRate	A structure with three values (x, y, and z) describing the rate of rotation around those axes.
userAcceleration	A CMAcceleration structure (x, y, and z) describing the motion of the device.
magneticField	A CMCalibratedMagneticField structure (x, y, z, and accuracy) that describes the direction of the Earth's magnetic field.

At first glance, all of this information would appear to be the same as the data from the accelerometer, gyroscope, and magnetometer—just repackaged. It's not. The CMDeviceMotion object combines the information from multiple instruments to divine a more holistic picture of what the device is doing. Specifically:

- The attitude property combines information from the gyroscope to measure changes in angle, the accelerometer to determine the direction of gravity, and it may also use the magnetometer to calibrate direction (rotation around the Z-axis) and prevent drift.
- The userAcceleration property correlates accelerometer and gyroscope data, excluding the force of gravity and changes in attitude, to provide an accurate measurement of acceleration.
- The magneticField property adjusts for the device bias and attempts to compensate for magnetic interference.

In all, the device motion interface is much more informed and intelligent. If there's a downside, it's that it requires more processing power, which steals app performance and battery life. If all your app needs is a general idea of motion or rotation, then the raw data from the accelerometer or gyroscope is all you need. But if you really want to know the device's position, direction, or orientation, then the device motion interface has it figured out for you.

> **Note** A device may need to be moved in a figure-8 pattern to help calibrate the magnetometer. iOS will automatically present a display that prompts the user to do this if you set the showsDeviceMovementDisplay property of CMMotionManager to YES.

Measuring Change

If your app needs to know the rate of change of any of the motion measurements, it needs time information. For example, to measure the change in angular rotation you'd subtract the current rate from the previous rate, and divide that by the time delta between the two samples.

But where can you find out when these measurements were taken? In earlier sections I wrote, "CMAccelerometerData's only property is acceleration," along with similar statements about CMGyroData and CMMagnetometerData. That's not strictly true.

The CMAccelerometerData, CMGyroData, CMMagnetometerData, and CMDeviceMotion classes are all subclasses of CMLogItem. The CMLogItem class defines a timestamp property, which all of the aforementioned classes inherit.

The timestamp property records the exact time the measurement was taken, allowing your app to accurately compare samples and calculate their rate of change, record them for posterity, or for any other purpose you might imagine.

> **Tip** If you need to calculate the change in attitude (subtracting the values of two CMAttitude objects), the -multiplyByInverseOfAttitude: method will do the math for you.

Summary

In this chapter you've tapped into the unfiltered data of the device's accelerometer, gyroscope, and magnetometer. You know how to configure the data you want to collect, interpret it, and learned how to use timers to collect it. You've also learned how to exploit the device motion data for a more informed view of the device's position in space. There's almost no motion or movement that your app can't detect and react to.

Well, almost. Despite the incredibly detailed information about the direction of the device and how it's being moved around, there's still one piece of information missing: where the device is located. You'll solve that remaining mystery in the next chapter.

Chapter 17

Where Are You?

If you think the accelerometer, gyroscope, and magnetometer are cool, you're going to love this chapter. In addition to those instruments, many iOS devices contain radio receivers allowing them to triangulate their position by timing radio signals they receive from a network of satellites—either the Global Positioning System or the Russian Global Navigation Satellite System. This technology is generically referred to as *GPS*.

What does that mean to you? As a user, it means your iOS device knows where it is on the planet. As a developer, it means your app can get information about the device's location and use that to show your user where they are, what's around them, where they've come from, or how to get to where they want to go. In this chapter you will:

- Collect location information
- Display a map showing the user's current location
- Add custom annotations to a map
- Monitor the user's movement and offer direction
- Create an interface for changing map options

This chapter will use two iOS technologies: Core Location and Map Kit. Core Location provides the interface to the GPS satellite receivers and provides your app with data about where the device is located, in a variety of forms. Map Kit supplies the view objects and tools to display, annotate, and animate maps. The two can be used separately or together.

Creating Pigeon

The app for this chapter is called Pigeon. It's a utility that lets you remember your current location on a map. Later it will show you where you are and where the marked location is, so you can fly back to it. The design for Pigeon is shown in Figure 17-1.

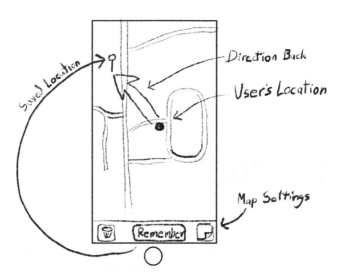

Figure 17-1. Pigeon design

The app has a map and three buttons. The middle button remembers your current location and drops a pin into the map to mark it. When you move away from that location, the map displays where you are, the saved location, and an arrow showing the direction back. A trash button forgets the saved location, and an info button lets the user change map display options. Let's get started.

Start by creating the project and laying out the interface. In Xcode, create a new project as follows:

1. Use the Single View Application template
2. Name the project Pigeon
3. Use a class prefix of HP
4. Set devices to Universal

Select the Main_iPhone.storyboard file. (You can choose to develop the iPhone interface, the iPad interface, or both; the steps are the same.) Add a toolbar to the bottom of the interface. Add and configure toolbar button items as follows (from left to right):

1. Bar Button Item: set its identifier to Trash
2. Flexible Space Bar Button Item
3. Bar Button Item: set its title to Remember Location
4. Flexible Space Bar Button Item
5. Button (not a Bar Button Item): set its type to Info Light

From the object library, add a Map View object to fill the rest of the interface. Set the following attributes for the map view object:

    Check Shows User Location

    Check Allows Zooming

Uncheck Allows Scrolling

Uncheck 3D Perspective

Complete the layout by choosing the **Add Missing Constraints to View Controller** command, either from the **Editor ➤ Resolve Auto Layout Issues** submenu or the Resolve Auto Layout Issues button at the bottom of the editor pane. The finished interface should look like Figure 17-2.

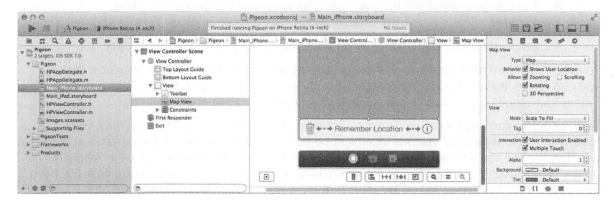

Figure 17-2. Pigeon interface

You'll need to wire these views up to your controller, so do that next. Switch to the assistant editor and make sure HPViewController.h appears in the right-hand pane. Immediately after the #import <UIKit/UIKit.h> statement, add an #import statement to pull in the Map Kit declarations:

#import <MapKit/MapKit.h>

Add the following connections to the @interface section:

```
@property (weak,nonatomic) IBOutlet MKMapView *mapView;
- (IBAction)dropPin:(id)sender;
- (IBAction)clearPin:(id)sender;
```

Connect the mapView outlet to the map view object. Connect the actions of the left and center toolbar buttons to the -clearPin: and -dropPin: actions, respectively. Now you're ready to begin coding the actions.

Collecting Location Data

Getting location data follows the same pattern you used to get gyroscope and magnetometer data in Chapter 16, with only minor modifications. The basic steps are:

- Create an instance of CLLocationManager.
- If precise (GPS) location information is a requirement for your app, add the gps value to the app's Required Device Capabilities property.

- Check to see if location services are available using the +locationServicesAvailable or +authorizationStatus methods.
- Designate an object to be the CLLocationManager's delegate. Adopt the CLLocationManagerDelegate protocol and make that object the delegate.
- Send -startUpdatingLocation to begin collecting location data.
- The delegate object will receive messages whenever the device's location changes.
- Send -stopUpdatingLocation when your app no longer needs location data.

The only significant difference between using CLLocationManager and CMMotionManager is that you can create multiple CLLocationManager objects and data is delivered to its delegate object (rather than requiring your app to pull the data or pushing it to an operation queue).

Another difference is that location data may not be available, even on devices that have GPS hardware. There are a lot of reasons this might be true. The user may have location services turned off. They may be somewhere they can't receive satellite signals. The device may be in "airplane mode," which doesn't permit the GPS receivers to be energized. Or your app may specifically have been denied access to location information. It doesn't really matter why. You need to check for the availability of location data and deal with the possibility that you can't get it.

Finally, there are a number of different methods of getting location data depending on the precision of the data and how quickly it's delivered. Knowing that the user moved 20 feet to the left is a different problem from knowing when they've arrived at work. I'll describe the different kinds of location monitoring towards the end of the chapter.

Pigeon needs precise location information that only GPS hardware can deliver. Select the Pigeon project in the project navigator, select the Pigeon target (pop-up menu in upper-left corner, as shown in Figure 17-3), switch to the Info tab, and locate the Required device capabilities in the Custom iOS Target Properties group. Click the + button and add a gps requirement, as shown in Figure 17-3.

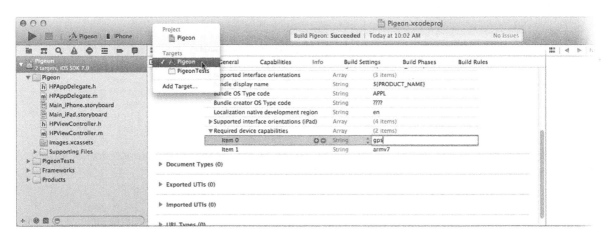

Figure 17-3. Adding gps device requirement

You're now probably thinking that I'm going to have you add some code to:

- Make the `HPViewController` adopt the `CLLocationManagerDelegate` protocol
- Implement the `-locationManager:didUpdateLocations:` delegate method to process the location updates
- Create an instance of `CLLocationManager`
- Make the `HPViewController` the location manager's delegate
- Send `-startUpdatingLocation` to begin collecting location data

But you're not going to do any of that.

Now I'm sure you wondering why not, so let me explain. Pigeon uses both location services *and* the Map Kit. The Map Kit includes the `MKMapView` object, which displays maps. Among its many talents, it has the ability to monitor the device's current location and display that on the map. It will even notify its delegate when the user's location changes.

For this particular app, `MKMapView` is already doing all of the work for you. When you ask it to display the user's location, it creates its own instance of `CLLocationManager` and begins monitoring location changes, updating the map and its delegate. The end result is that `MKMapView` has all of the information that Pigeon needs to work.

> **Note** Pigeon is a little bit of an anomaly; you'll configure the map view so it always tracks the user's location and the map view is always active. If this wasn't the case, then relying on the map view to locate the user wouldn't be a solution and you'd have to resort to using `CLLocationManager` in the usual way.

This is a good thing. All of that `CLLocationManager` code would look so much like the code you wrote in Chapter 16 that it would make this app a little boring, and I certainly don't want you to get bored. Or maybe you haven't read Chapter 16 yet, in which case you have something to look forward to.

Regardless, all you need to do is setup `MKMapView` correctly. Let's do that now.

Using a Map View

Your map view object has already been added to the interface and connected to the `mapView` outlet. You've also used the attributes inspector to configure the map view so it shows (and tracks) the user's location and you disallowed user scrolling. There's one more setting that you need to make, and you can't set it from the attributes inspector.

Select the `HPViewController.m` file and location the `-viewDidLoad` method. At the end, add this statement:

```
[_mapView setUserTrackingMode:MKUserTrackingModeFollow];
```

This sets the map's tracking mode to "follow the user." There are three tracking modes—which I'm sure you've see in places like Apple's Maps app—listed in Table 17-1.

Table 17-1. *User tracking modes*

Tracking Mode	Description
MKUserTrackingModeNone	The map does not follow the user's location.
MKUserTrackingModeFollow	The map is centered at the user's current location and it moves when the user moves.
MKUserTrackingModeFollowWithHeading	The map tracks the user's current location and the orientation of the map is rotated to indicate the user's direction of travel.

The code you added to -viewDidLoad: sets the tracking mode to follow the user. The combination of the showsUserLocation property and the tracking mode force the map view to begin gathering location data, which is what you want.

If you've played with the Maps app, you also know that you can "break" the tracking mode by manually panning the map. You disabled panning for the map view, but there are still circumstances where the tracking mode will revert to MKUserTrackingModeNone. To address that you need to add code to catch the situation where the tracking mode changes and "correct" it, if necessary.

That information is provided to the map view's delegate. Wouldn't it be great if your MPViewController object were the delegate for the map view? I thought so too.

Switch to HPViewController.h and adopt the MKMapViewDelegate protocol (new code in bold):

@interface HPViewController : UIViewController **<MKMapViewDelegate>**

Return to HPViewController.m and add this map view delegate method to the @implementation:

```
- (void)           mapView:(MKMapView *)mapView
   didChangeUserTrackingMode:(MKUserTrackingMode)mode
                    animated:(BOOL)animated
{
    if (mode==MKUserTrackingModeNone)
        [mapView setUserTrackingMode:MKUserTrackingModeFollow];
}
```

This message is received whenever the tracking mode for the map changes. It simply sees if the mode has changed to "none" and sets it back to tracking the user.

Of course, this message is only received if your HPViewController object is the delegate object for the map view. Select the Main_iPhone.storyboard (or _iPad) file. Select the map view object and use the connections inspector to connect the map view's delegate outlet to the view controller, as shown in Figure 17-4.

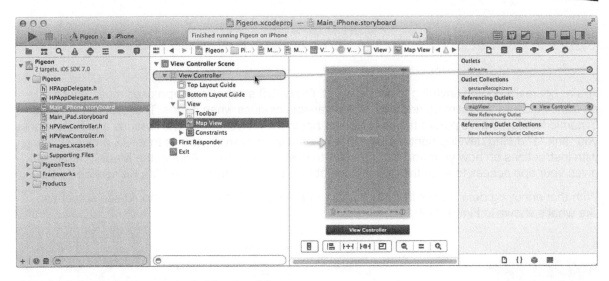

Figure 17-4. Connecting the map view's delegate outlet

You've done everything you need to see the map view in action, so fire it up. Run your app in the simulator, or on a provisioned device. You may see build warnings that you haven't implemented the `-dropPin:` and `-clearPin:` methods; ignore them, for now.

Having problems? Maybe your app isn't ready to run. If your app crashes with a blank screen and a nasty message in the console pane, it's because your app isn't linked to the MapKit framework. In most cases, Xcode will automatically link your app to the frameworks it needs, but in some situations you need to do that explicitly. Don't worry, this is really easy to fix.

Select the `Pigeon` project, make sure the `Pigeon` target is selected, and switch to the `General` tab. Locate the `Linked Frameworks and Libraries` section, as shown on the left in Figure 17-5. Click on the + button and choose a new library or framework to link against, as shown on the right in Figure 17-5.

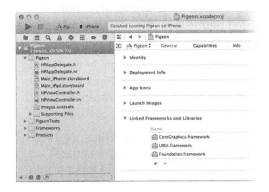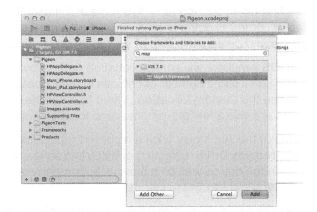

Figure 17-5. Adding a framework to the project

> **Tip** Use the search field in the "add library" dialog to quickly find the library or framework you're looking for.

You're not really adding anything to your project. Every iOS symbol your app uses must, eventually, be translated into the memory address of that variable or class when it runs. This process is called *dynamic linking*, and it's part of the mechanism that launches your app. The libraries and frameworks you "link to" during development are little more than a list of symbol names that iOS provides, along with instructions on how your app can connect to them when it runs. Adding the MapKit framework gives your app access to all of the classes, variables, and constants in the Map Kit service.

With that annoying detail out of the way, run your app again. This time, you should see something like what's shown in Figure 17-6.

Figure 17-6. Testing map view

The first time your app runs, iOS will ask the user if it's OK for your app to collect location data. Tap OK, or this is going to be a really short test. Once it's granted permission, the map locates your device and centers the map at your location (second screen shot in Figure 17-6).

The iOS simulator will emulate location data, allowing you to test location-aware apps. In the **Debug** menu you'll find a number of choices in the **Location** submenu (third screen shot in Figure 17-6). Choose the Custom **Location…** item to enter the longitude and latitude of your simulated location. There are also a few pre-programmed locations, such as the **Apple** item, also shown in Figure 17-6.

Some of the items play back a recorded trip. Currently the choices are **City Bicycle Ride**, **City Run**, and **Freeway Drive**. Selecting one starts a series of location changes, which the map will track, as though the device was on a bicycle, accompanying a jogger, or in a car. Go ahead and try one; you know you want to.

The map can also be zoomed in and out by pinching or double tapping, as shown on the right in Figure 17-6. You can't scroll the map, as you disabled that option in Interface Builder.

While the freeway drive is playing back, add the code to mark your location on the map.

Decorating Your Map

There are three ways of adding visual elements to a map: annotations, overlays, and subviews.

An *annotation* identifies a single point on the map. It can appear anyway you like, but iOS provides classes that mark the location with a recognizable "map pin" image. Annotations can optionally display a *callout* that consists of a title, subtitle, and accessory views. The callout appears above the pin when selected (tapped).

An *overlay* identifies a path or region on the map. You won't use overlays in Pigeon, but that's how lines (like driving directions) are drawn and arbitrary areas (like a city park) are highlighted.

A *subview* is like any other subview. MKMapView is a subclass of UIView, and you are free to add custom UIView objects to it. Use subviews to add additional controls or indicators to the map.

Annotation and overlay are attached to the map. They are described using map coordinates (which I'll talk about later) and they move when the map moves. Subviews are positioned in the local graphics coordinate system of the MKMapView object. They do not move with the map.

Your Pigeon app will create an annotation—that is, "put a pin"—at the user's current location when they tap the "remember location" button. The trash button will discard the pin. That sounds like a couple of action methods to me.

Adding an Annotation

When the user taps the "remember location" button, you'll capture their current location and add an annotation to the map. I thought it would be nice if the user could choose a label for the location, to make it easier to remember what they're trying to remember. To accomplish all that, you'll need an instance variable to store the annotation object and your HPViewController will need to be an alert view delegate. Add both of those to the private @interface section in HPViewController.m (new code in bold):

```
@interface HPViewController () <UIAlertViewDelegate>
{
    MKPointAnnotation    *savedAnnotation;
}
@end
```

The next step is to write the -dropPin: method. It begins by presenting an alert view configured so the user can type in a label. Add this to the @implementation section:

```
- (IBAction)dropPin:(id)sender
{
    UIAlertView *alert = [[UIAlertView alloc]
                          initWithTitle:@"What's here?"
                                message:@"Type a label for this location."
                               delegate:self
                      cancelButtonTitle:@"Cancel"
                      otherButtonTitles:@"Remember", nil];
    alert.alertViewStyle = UIAlertViewStylePlainTextInput;
    alert.delegate = self;
    [alert show];
}
```

This method creates an alert and sets its style to UIAlertViewStylePlainTextInput. This presents an alert view with a regular text field the user can type something into. The functional part of the -dropPin: action occurs when the user finishes typing in their label and taps the "Remember" button. Add that after the -dropPin: method:

```
- (void)    alertView:(UIAlertView *)alertView
 clickedButtonAtIndex:(NSInteger)buttonIndex
{
    CLLocation *location = _mapView.userLocation.location;
    if (location==nil)
        return;

    NSString *name = [[alertView textFieldAtIndex:0] text];
    name = [name stringByTrimmingCharactersInSet:
                        [NSCharacterSet whitespaceAndNewlineCharacterSet]];
    if (name.length==0)
        name = @"Over Here!";

    [self clearPin:self];
    savedAnnotation = [MKPointAnnotation new];
    savedAnnotation.title = name;
    savedAnnotation.coordinate = location.coordinate;
    [_mapView addAnnotation:savedAnnotation];
    [_mapView selectAnnotation:savedAnnotation animated:YES];
}
```

The first step is to get the user's current location. Remember that the map view has been tracking their location since the app was started, so it should have a pretty good idea of where they are by now. You must, however, consider the possibility that the map view doesn't know (location==nil). The user may have disabled location services, is running in "airplane mode," or is spelunking. Regardless, if there's no location there's nothing to do.

The next bit of code cleans up what the user typed. It strips off any leading or trailing whitespace characters (a.k.a. spaces) and supplies a readable label if the user neglected to.

Now the method gets down to work. It clears any existing pin; Pigeon remembers only one location at a time. It creates a new annotation object, sets its title and coordinates, adds the annotation to the map, and selects it. Since you haven't done anything special (yet), the map view will use the standard red map pin annotation view to indicate the location on the map. Programmatically selecting the new annotation causes its callout to pop-up, as if the user tapped the pin.

While you're still in HPViewController.m, toss in the -clearPin: method, which doesn't need much explanation:

```
- (IBAction)clearPin:(id)sender
{
    if (savedAnnotation!=nil)
        {
        [_mapView removeAnnotation:savedAnnotation];
        savedAnnotation = nil;
        }
}
```

Run the app and give it a try. Tap the "remember location" button, enter a label, and a pin appears at your current location, as shown in Figure 17-7.

Figure 17-7. Testing the annotation

Map Coordinates

The coordinates of the annotation object were set to the coordinates of the user's location (provided by the map view). But what are these "coordinates?" Map Kit uses three coordinate systems, listed in Table 17-2.

Table 17-2. Map coordinate systems

Coordinate System	Description
Latitude and Longitude	The latitude, longitude, and sometimes altitude, of a position on the planet. These are called *map coordinates*.
Mercator	The position (x,y) on the Mercator map of the planet. A Mercator map is a cylindrical projection of the planet's surface onto a flat map. The Mercator map is what you see in the map view. Positions on the Mercator map are called *map points*.
Graphics	The graphics coordinates in the interface, used by `UIView`. These are referred to simply as *points*.

Map coordinates (longitude and latitude) are the principle values used to identify locations on the map, stored in a `CLLocationCoordinate2D` structure. They are not XY coordinates, so calculating distance and heading between two coordinates is a non-trivial exercise that's best left to location services and Map Kit. Annotations are positioned at map coordinates.

Map points are XY positions in the Mercator map projection. Being XY coordinates on a flat plane, calculating angles and distances is much simpler. Map points are used when drawing overlays. This simplifies drawing and reduces the math involved.

> **Note** The Mercator projection is particularly convenient for navigation because a straight line between any two points on a Mercator map describes a heading the user can follow to get from one to the other. The disadvantage is that east-west distances and north-south distances are not to the same scale—except at the equator.

Map points are eventually translated into graphic coordinates, so they can appear somewhere on the screen. There are methods to translate map coordinates into graphic coordinates. Additional methods translate the other way. You'll use these, along with some utility methods to calculate the distance between coordinates, later in this project.

Adding a Little Bounce

Your map pin appears on the map, and it moves around with the map. You can tap on it to show, or hide, its callout. Which is pretty impressive, considering you only needed a few lines of code to create it. We do, however, love animation and I'm sure you've seen map pins that "drop" into place. Your pin doesn't drop; it just appears. So how do you get your map pin to animate, or change its color, or customize it in any other way? The answer is to use a custom annotation view.

An annotation in a map is actually a pair of objects: an annotation object and an annotation view object. An *annotation object* associates information with a coordinate on the map—the data model. An *annotation view object* is responsible for how that annotation looks—the view. If you want to customize how an annotation appears you must supply your own annotation view object.

You do this by implementing the `-mapView:viewForAnnotation:` delegate method. When the map view wants to display an annotation, it sends its delegate this message with the annotation object. The method's job is to return an annotation view object that represents that annotation. If you don't implement this method, or decide to return `nil` for an annotation, the map view uses its default annotation view, which is a plain map pin.

Add this method to `HPViewController.m`:

```
- (MKAnnotationView *)mapView:(MKMapView *)mapView
           viewForAnnotation:(id<MKAnnotation>)annotation
{
    if (annotation==self.mapView.userLocation)
        return nil;
```

```
        NSString *pinID = @"Save";
        MKPinAnnotationView *view = (MKPinAnnotationView*) ↵
                    [self.mapView dequeueReusableAnnotationViewWithIdentifier:pinID];
        if (view==nil)
            {
            view = [[MKPinAnnotationView alloc] initWithAnnotation:annotation
                                                   reuseIdentifier:pinID];
            view.canShowCallout = YES;
            view.animatesDrop = YES;
            }
        return view;
}
```

The first statement compares the annotation to the map view's user annotation object. The user annotation object, like any other annotation object, represents the user's position in the map. The map view automatically added it when you asked it to display the user's location. This automatic annotation is available via the map view's `userLocation` property. If you return `nil` for this annotation, the map view uses its default user annotation view—the pulsing blue dot that we're all familiar with. If you want to represent the user's location some other way, this is where you'd provide that view.

The rest of the code works exactly like the table view cell code from Chapter 4. The map view maintains a cache of reusable `MKAnnotationView` objects that you recycle using an identifier. Your map only uses one kind of annotation view: a standard map pin view provided by the `MKPinAnnotationView` class. The pin is configured to display callouts and animate itself ("drop in") when added to the map.

> **Tip** If you want to give the user the ability to move the pin they just dropped, all you have to do is set the `draggable` property of the annotation view object to YES.

Run the app again. Now when you save the location, the pin animates its insertion into the map, which is a lot more appealing.

Your `-mapView:viewForAnnotation:` delegate method can return a customized version of a built-in annotation view class, as you've done here. `MKPinAnnotationView` can display pins of different colors, can allow or disallow callouts, have custom accessory views in its callout, and so on. Alternatively, you can subclass `MKAnnotationView` and create your own annotation view, with whatever custom graphics and animations you want. You could represent the user's location as a waddling duck. Let your imagination run wild.

> **Note** Overlay objects and overlay view objects work almost identically to annotations. The big difference is that an overlay occupies a region of the map, not just a point.

Pointing the Way

The other technique for augmenting your map view is to add your own subviews. These can impart additional information (direction of travel, elapsed trip time, and so on) or you can add control objects (switches, music playback buttons, and the like).

Pigeon is going to add an image view that displays an arrow. The arrow will point from the user's current location back to the location they marked on the map. Here's how it will work:

> The map view delegate receives a message when the user's location changes.
>
> This method will calculate the coordinate (on the screen) of the user's location and the remembered location, and the real-world distance between them.
>
> If the distance is more than 50 meters away, position the image view (the arrow) over the user's screen location and rotated so it points towards the remembered location.
>
> Otherwise, hide the arrow.

To make this happen, you're going to need an arrow image, an instance variable for the image view, a method that hides the arrow, and a method to display the arrow and point it in the correct direction. Start by adding the arrow.png resource file, which you'll find in the Learn iOS Development Projects ➤ Ch 17 ➤ Pigeon (Resources) folder, to your Images.xcassets image catalog. While you're adding images, there's a set of app icons in the Pigeon (Icons) folder you can drop into the AppIcons group.

In the HPViewController.m file, locate the private @interface section. Define the threshold distance constant, add an instance variable, and declare a couple of methods, as follows (new code in bold):

```
#define kArrowDisplayDistanceMin    50.0
@interface HPViewController () <UIAlertViewDelegate>
{
    MKPointAnnotation   *savedAnnotation;
    UIImageView         *arrowView;
}
- (void)hideReturnArrow;
- (void)showReturnArrowAtPoint:(CGPoint)userPoint towards:(CGPoint)returnPoint;
@end
```

The next step is to catch when the user's location changes. When the user moves, the distance between the user and the remembered location changes, the map moves, and it alters the angle between the two. Your HPViewController is already the map view's delegate. All you have to do is implement this method:

```
- (void)        mapView:(MKMapView *)mapView
   didUpdateUserLocation:(MKUserLocation *)userLocation
{
    if (savedAnnotation!=nil)
        {
        CLLocationCoordinate2D coord = savedAnnotation.coordinate;
        CLLocation *toLoc = [[CLLocation alloc] initWithLatitude:coord.latitude
                                            longitude:coord.longitude];
```

```
        CLLocationDistance distance =
                        [userLocation.location distanceFromLocation:toLoc];
        if (distance>=kArrowDisplayDistanceMin)
            {
            CGPoint userPoint = [mapView convertCoordinate:userLocation.coordinate
                                        toPointToView:self.mapView];
            CGPoint savePoint = [mapView convertCoordinate:coord
                                        toPointToView:self.mapView];
            [self showReturnArrowAtPoint:userPoint towards:savePoint];
            return;
            }
        }
    [self hideReturnArrow];
}
```

The arrow is only displayed when there's a saved location and the real-world distance between it and the user is more than 50 meters. The first two conditions test those prerequisites. The -distanceFromLocation: method is particularly handy, as it handles the math involved in determining the distance between two map coordinates.

To position the arrow, you need to know that position on the screen and the position of the remembered location. The -convertCoordinate:toPointToView: method performs that conversion. You pass the method the map coordinate and it returns the view coordinate of that point on the map. Those coordinates are passed to your -showReturnArrowAtPoint:towards: method. In all other cases, the arrow view is hidden.

The last step is to implement the -hideReturnArrow and -showReturnArrowAtPoint:towards: methods:

```
- (void)hideReturnArrow
{
    arrowView.hidden = YES;
}

- (void)showReturnArrowAtPoint:(CGPoint)userPoint towards:(CGPoint)returnPoint
{
    if (arrowView==nil)
        {
        UIImage *arrowImage = [UIImage imageNamed:@"arrow"];
        arrowView = [[UIImageView alloc] initWithImage:arrowImage];
        arrowView.opaque = NO;
        arrowView.alpha = 0.6;
        [self.mapView addSubview:arrowView];
        arrowView.hidden = YES;
        }

    CGFloat angle = atan2f(returnPoint.x-userPoint.x,userPoint.y-returnPoint.y);
    CGAffineTransform rotation = CGAffineTransformMakeRotation(angle);

    void (^updateArrow)(void) = ^{
        arrowView.center = userPoint;
        arrowView.transform = rotation;
        };
```

```
        if (arrowView.hidden)
            {
            updateArrow();
            arrowView.hidden = NO;
            }
        else
            {
            [UIView animateWithDuration:0.5 animations:updateArrow];
            }
}
```

What the -hideReturnArrow method does should be obvious.

The -showReturnArrowAtPoint:towards: method begins by lazily creating the image view object, if this is the first time it's being displayed. The next couple of statements calculates the angle between the user's point and the remembered point and creates a transform to rotate the arrow so it points from one to the other.

The rest of the code gets a little fancy—but in a good way. If the arrow was previously hidden, you want it to appear immediately, at its correct position, with no animation. If it's currently being displayed, you want it to animate smoothly to its new position. The solution here captures the code that positions and rotates the arrow view in a code block variable (updateArrow). The following if statement either executes the code block immediately (no animation) and shows the view, or it passes the code block to UIView for animation. See, that wasn't too hard.

Run the app and test it out. Tap the "remember location" button to drop a pin in the map and then use the iOS simulator's debug menu to move the simulated location. If you're using a real device, then just move 50 meters in any direction, as shown in Figure 17-8.

CHAPTER 17: Where Are You?   545

Figure 17-8. *Testing the direction arrow*

> **Note** This technique works largely because the user location is constantly being updated, incrementally refining the position and angle of the arrow view. This was more of an exercise in adding subviews to the map view and translating map coordinate into graphics coordinates, than it was a recommendation on how to provide in-map directions. If I were writing this app "for real," I'd use an overlay and custom overlay view to draw the route from the user back to the saved location.

Are you still wondering what the info button in the toolbar is for? I saved that for the exercise at the end of the chapter. Before you get to that, let's take a brief tour of some location services and map features you haven't explored yet.

Location Monitoring

Pigeon is the kind of app that uses immediate, precise (as possible), and continuous monitoring of the user's location. Because of this, it requires an iOS device with GPS capabilities and gathers location data continuously. This isn't true for all apps. Many apps don't need precise location information, continuous monitoring, or to be immediately notified of movement.

For apps with less demanding location requirements, the Core Location framework offers a variety of information and delivery methods. Each method involves a different amount of hardware and CPU involvement, which means that each will impact the battery life and performance of the iOS device in varying ways.

As a rule, you want to gather the *least* amount of location information your app needs to function. Let's say you're writing a travel app that needs to know when the user has left one city and arrived at the next. Do not fire up the GPS hardware (the way Pigeon does) and start monitoring their every movement. Why? Because your app will never get the notification that they've arrived in their destination city, because *the user's battery will have been completely drained*! And the first thing the user is going to do, after recharging, is to delete your app. Take a look at some other ways of getting location information that don't require as much juice.

Approximate Location and Non-GPS Devices

Location information is also available on iOS devices that don't have GPS hardware. These devices use location information that they gather from Wi-Fi base stations, cell phone towers, and other sources. The accuracy can be crude—sometimes kilometers, instead of meters—but it's enough to place the user in a town. This is more than enough information to suggest restaurants or movies that are playing in their vicinity.

So even if you left out the "gps" hardware requirement for your app, you can still request location information and you might get it. Consult the horizontalAccuracy property of the CLLocation object for the uncertainty (in meters) of the location's reported position. If that value is large, then the device probably isn't using GPS or it's in a situation where GPS is not accurate.

> **Note** iOS devices with GPS also use this alternative location information to improve the speed of GPS triangulation—which, by itself, is rather slow—and to reduce power consumption. This system is called *Assisted GPS*.

If your app only needs approximate location information, gather your location data by sending CLLocationManager the -startMonitoringSignificantLocationChanges message instead of the -startUpdatingLocation message. This method only gets a rough estimate of the user's location and only notifies your app when that location changes in a big way, saving a great deal of processing power and battery life.

Monitoring Regions

Getting back to that travel app, some iOS devices are capable of monitoring significant changes in location, even when the device is idle. This is accomplished using *region monitoring*. Region monitoring lets you define an area on the map and be notified when the user enters or exits that region. This is an extremely efficient (low-power) method of determining when the user has moved.

You could, for example, create two region (CLRegion) objects: one around the city the user is in and a second encompassing the city they are traveling to next. You would send the location manager object a -startMonitoringForRegion: message for each one, up to 20. Then all your app has to do is sit back and wait until the delegate object receives a -locationManager:didEnterRegion: or -locationManager:DidExitRegion: message.

Use region monitoring to be notified when the user arrives at work or at their family reunion. To learn more about region monitoring, find the "Monitoring Shape-Based Regions" section of the *Location Awareness Programming Guide* that you'll find in Xcode's Documentation and API Reference window. The *Location Awareness Programming Guide* also describes how to receive location data in the background—when your app isn't the active app, something I haven't discussed in this book.

Reducing Location Change Messages

Another way to stretch battery life is to reduce the amount of location information your app receives. I already talked about receiving only significant changes or monitoring regions, but there's a middle ground between that extreme and getting second-by-second updates on the user's location.

The first method is to set the location manager's distanceFilter and desiredAccuracy properties. The distanceFilter reduces the number of location updates your app receives. It waits until the device has moved by the set distance before updating your app again. The desiredAccuracy property tells iOS how much effort it should expend trying to determine the user's exact location. Relaxing that property means the location hardware doesn't have to work as hard.

Another hint you can provide is the activityType property. This tells the manager that your app is used for automotive navigation, as opposed to being a personal fitness app. The location manager will use this hint to optimize its use of hardware. An automobile navigation app might, for example, temporarily power down the GPS receivers if the user hasn't moved for an extended period of time.

Movement and Heading

Your app might not be interested so much in where the user is, as what direction they're going in and how fast. If heading is your game, consult the speed and course properties of the CLLocation object that you obtain from the location property of the CLLocationManager.

If all you want to know is the user's direction, you can gather just that by sending the location manager the -startUpdatingHeading message (instead of -startUpdatingLocation). The user's heading can be determined somewhat more efficiently than their exact location.

To learn more about direction information, read the "Getting Direction-Related Events" chapter of the *Location Awareness Programming Guide*.

Geocoding

What if your app is interested in places on the map? It might want to know where a business is located. Or maybe it has a map coordinate and wants to know what's there.

The process of converting information about locations (business name, address, city, zip code) into map coordinates, and vice versa, is called *geocoding*. Geocoding is a network service, provided by Apple, that will convert a dictionary of place information (say, an address) into a longitude and latitude, and back again, as best as it can. Turning place information into a map coordinate is called *forward geocoding*. Turning a map coordinate into a description of what's there is called *reverse geocoding*.

Geocoding is performed through the `CLGeocoder` object. `CLGeocoder` will turn either a dictionary of descriptive information or a map coordinate into a `CLPlacemark` object. A placemark object is a combination of a map coordinate and a description of what's at that coordinate. This information will include what country, region, and city the coordinate is in, a street address, and a postal code (if appropriate), even whether it's a body of water.

Getting Directions

Another resource your app has at its disposal is the Maps app. Yes, the standard Maps app that comes with iOS. There are methods that let your app launch the Maps app to assist your user. This is a simple way of providing maps, locations, directions, and navigation services to your user without adding any of that to your app.

You use the Maps app via the `MKMapItem` object. You create one or more `MKMapItem` objects either from the current location (`+mapItemForCurrentLocation`) or from a geocoded placemark object (`-initWithPlacemark:`).

Once created, send the map item object an `-openInMapsWithLaunchOptions:` message (for one map item) or pass an array of map items to `+openMapItems:launchOptions:`. The launch options are a dictionary that can optionally tell the Maps app what region of the globe to display, a region on the map to highlight, whether you want it provide driving or walking directions to a given location, what mode to use (map, satellite, hybrid), whether to display traffic information, and so on.

Code examples using `MKMapItem` are shown in the "Providing Directions" chapter of the *Location Awareness Programming Guide*.

Summary

You've traveled far in your journey towards mastering iOS app development. You've passed many milestones, and learning to use location services is a big one. You now know how to get the user's location, for a variety of purposes, and display that on a map.

Speaking of which, you also learned a lot about maps. You now know how to present a map in your app, annotate it with points of interest, and customize how those annotations look. You learned how to track and display the user's location on the map and add your own view controls to the interface.

But you know what? Pigeon still has the same problem that MyStuff has. What good is an app that's supposed to remember stuff, if it forgets everything when you quit the app? There should be some way of storing its data somewhere, so when you come back to the app it hasn't lost everything. Not surprisingly, there's a bunch of technologies for saving data, and the next two chapters are devoted to just that.

EXERCISE

MKMapView can display graphic maps, satellite images, or a combination of both. It can orient the map to true north or rotate the map based on the orientation of the device. It's rude not to let your user choose which of these options they want to use. Pigeon locked the map view's orientation and display mode. Your exercise is to fix that.

These two aspects of the map display are controlled by two properties: mapType and userTrackingMode. The map type can be set to display graphics (MKMapTypeStandard), satellite imagery (MKMapTypeStellite), or a combination of the two (MKMapTypeHybrid). The user's tracking mode can be either follow the user (MKUserTrackingModeFollow), or follow them with heading (MKUserTrackingModeFollowWithHeading).

The controls you add to the interface are up to you. Some apps add a button right to the map interface that toggles between different map types and tracking modes. For Pigeon, I decided to place the settings on a separate view controller and use a page curl transition to reveal them.

You'll find the finished project in the Learn iOS Development Projects ➤ Ch 17 ➤ Pigeon E1 folder. Basically, here's what I did:

1. Created a subclass of UIViewController named HPMapOptionsViewController.
2. Added a view controller object to the storyboard and changed the class of the object to HPMapOptionsViewController.
3. In HPMapOptionsViewController, I created a mapView property and two UISegmentControl outlets: mapStyleControl and headingControl.
4. I defined three action methods: -changeMapStyle:, -changeHeading:, and -done:.
5. In the new view controller, I created one segment control with three options (Map, Satellite, and Hybrid), connecting it to the mapStyleControl outlet and its Value Changed action to -changeMapStyle:.
6. I created a second segment control, below the first, with two options (North and Heading), connecting it to the headingControl outlet and its Value Changed action to -changeHeading:.
7. I constrained the lower segment control to the Bottom Layout Guide (Standard), constrained the upper segment control to the lower one, and then centered both in the container view.
8. In HPMapOptionViewController's implementation, I used the mapView property to get the current map type and tracking mode and set the two segment controls in -viewWillAppear:.
9. The -changeMapStyle: action changes the map's type.
10. The -changeHeading: action changes the map's tracking mode.
11. The –done: method dismisses the view controller.
12. In HPViewController, I added a -prepareForSeque: method that sets the mapView property of the HPMapOptionsViewController when the segue is "mapOptions".
13. In the storyboard, I created a modal segue from the info button in the toolbar to the new view controller, setting its transition to "partial curl" and assigning it an identifier of "mapOptions".

550 CHAPTER 17: Where Are You?

> **Note** When creating the segue, make sure you have the button (UIButton) object imbedded *inside* the bar button item selected; it's this imbedded control that sends the action message, not the bar button item.

14. Finally, I added a tap gesture recognizer to the root view object of HPMapOptionsViewController and connect it to the -done: action and set the background color of the view to a very light (90%) grey.

This is all stuff you learned in Chapters 10 and 12. Here's the finished interface in action:

Chapter 18

Remember Me?

One of the marvelous qualities of iOS devices, which make them such an indispensable part of our lives, is their ability to remember so much stuff: pictures, phone numbers, addresses, appointments, to-do lists, lesson notes, project ideas, keynote presentations, playlists, articles you want to read—the list seems endless. But so far, none of the apps you've developed in this book remember anything. MyStuff starts with an empty list every time you launch it. Wonderland doesn't even remember what page you were reading. And consider Pigeon, poor Pigeon. Its only task is to memorize one location and it can't even do that. You're going to fix all of that, and more.

As you might imagine, there are lots of different ways of storing information in iOS. The next two chapters will explore the basic ones. You're going to begin with user defaults (sometimes called "preferences"). This is the technology most often used to remember small bits of information like your settings, what tab you were viewing, what page number you were last looking at, your list of favorite URLs, and so on. In this chapter you will:

- Learn about property lists
- Add and retrieve values from the user defaults
- Create a settings bundle for your app
- Store and synchronize property list data in the cloud
- Preserve and restore views and view controllers

The mechanics of property lists and how to use them are simple; it will only take a page or two to explain the whole thing. How best to use them is another matter. Much of this chapter will be focused on the strategies of using property lists, so put on your thinking cap and let's get started.

Property Lists

A property list is a graph of objects, where every object is one the following classes:

- NSDictionary
- NSArray

- `NSString`
- `NSNumber` (any integer, floating point, or Boolean value)
- `NSDate`
- `NSData`

While a property list can be a single string, it is most often a dictionary that contain strings, numbers, dates, or other arrays and dictionaries. Instances of these classes are called *property list objects*.

Seriously, that's it.

Serializing Property Lists

Property lists are used throughout iOS because they are flexible, universal, and easily serialized. In this case, "serialize" (the Cocoa term) means "serialize" (the computer science term). Cocoa uses the term *serialization* to mean converting a property list into a transportable stream of bytes. You don't often serialize property lists yourself, but they are regularly serialized behind the scenes.

> **Note** A property list can be serialized into two different formats: binary and XML. The binary format is unique to Cocoa. It can be read and understood only by another Cocoa (OS X) or Cocoa Touch (iOS) app. The XML format is universal and can be exchanged with practically any computer system in the world. The advantage of the binary format is efficiency (both size and speed). The advantage of the XML format is portability.

A serialized property list written to a file is called a *property list file*, often a *.plist file*. Xcode includes a property list editor so you can directly create and modify the contents of a property list file. You'll use the property list editor later in this chapter.

For the Wonderland app, I wrote a Mac (OS X) utility application that generated the `Characters.nsarray` resource file. That was a property list (an array of dictionaries containing strings), serialized in the XML format, and written to a property list file. Later, you added that as a resource file, which your app turned back into an `NSArray` object by *deserializing* the file.

> **Tip** If you want to serialize a property list yourself, use the `NSPropertyListSerialization` class, or one of the `-writeTo...` methods in `NSArray` and `NSDictionary`.

User Defaults

One of the premier uses of property list objects is in the user defaults. The *user defaults* is a dictionary of property list objects you can use to store small amounts of persistent information, such as preferences and display state. You can store any property list value you want into the user defaults (`NSUserDefaults`) object, and later retrieve it. The values you store there are serialized and preserved between runs of your app.

A user defaults (`NSUserDefaults`) object is created when your app starts. Any values you stored there the last time are deserialized and become immediately available. If you make any changes to the user defaults, they are automatically serialized and saved so they'll be available the next time your app runs.

> **Note** The user default values are local to your app. In other words, your app can't get or change the values stored by other iOS apps.

Using `NSUserDefaults` is really simple. You obtain your app's singleton user defaults object using [`NSUserDefaults standardUserDefaults`]. You send it "set" messages to store values (`-setInteger:forKey:`, `-setObject:forKey:`, `-setBool:forKey:`, and so on). You retrieve values using the "get" messages (`-integerForKey:`, `-objectForKey:`, `-boolForKey:`, and so on).

Making Pigeon Remember

You're going to use user defaults to give Pigeon some long-term memory. When you add user defaults to an app you need to consider:

- What values to store
- What property list objects and keys you will use
- When to store the values
- When to retrieve the values

Each decision affects subsequent ones, so start at the top. For Pigeon, you want it to remember:

> The remembered map location (duh)
>
> The map type (plain, satellite, or hybrid)
>
> The tracking mode (none or follow heading)

The next step is to decide what property list objects you're going to use to represent these properties. The map type and tracking mode are easy; they're both integer properties, and you can store any integer value directly in the user defaults.

The `MKPointAnnotation` object that encapsulates the map location, however, isn't a property list object and can't be stored directly in the user defaults. Instead, its significant properties need to be converted into property list objects, which can be stored. The typical technique is to turn your information into either a string or a dictionary of property list objects, both of which are compatible with user defaults. For Pigeon, you're going to convert the annotation into a dictionary containing three values: its latitude, its longitude, and its title. This is enough information to reconstruct the annotation when the app runs again.

You also have to pick keys to identify each value stored. At the top-level, you want to choose keys that won't be confused with any keys iOS might be using. A number of iOS frameworks also use your app's user defaults to preserve information. The simplest technique is to use the same class prefix that your project uses. For example, it's unlikely the keys "HPMapType" and "HPFollowHeading" would conflict with any reserved keys. Keys used for values in sub-dictionaries can be anything you want.

Minimizing Updates and Code

With the first part out of the way, you can now turn your attention to the much subtler problem of deciding when and where to preserve your values in the user defaults, and when to get them back out again.

Tackle the storage problem first. As a rule, you want to make updates to the user defaults as infrequently as possible, while still keeping your code simple. The common solutions are:

- Capture the value when it changes
- Capture the value at some dependable exit point

The first solution is perfect for Pigeon. It only saves three values, and none of those change that often. The user might change map type and heading from time to time, but they're unlikely to fiddle with those settings a dozen times a minute. Likewise, the user will save a location when they arrive somewhere, but won't save another location until they've traveled someplace else.

The reason you want to limit user default updates is that every change triggers a chain of events that results in a fair amount of work occurring in the background. It's something to avoid, as long as it doesn't overly complicate your design. A good design will minimize updates with a minimal amount of code. When you start working with cloud-based storage (later in this chapter) it's even more important to avoid gratuitous changes.

On the other hand, some values you want to preserve might change all the time or in many different places. For example, remembering the playback location of an audio book is something that changes constantly. It would be ludicrous to capture the playback position every second the audio was playing. Instead, it makes a lot more sense to simply note the user's current playback position when they exit the app. You'll explore that technique later in this chapter.

You're going to start by preserving the map type and tracking mode, because these are the simplest. Then you'll tackle preserving and restoring the map location.

Defining Your Keys

This tutorial starts with the version of Pigeon in the exercise for Chapter 17. You'll find that version in the Learn iOS Development Projects ➤ Ch 17 ➤ Pigeon E1 folder. If you came up with your own solution to the exercise, you should have no problem adapting this code to your app.

Begin by defining the keys used to identify values in your user defaults. Select the HPViewController.h file and add these three constants:

```
#define kPreferenceMapType          @"HPMapType"
#define kPreferenceHeading          @"HPFollowHeading"
#define kPreferenceSavedLocation    @"HPLocation"
```

Writing Values to User Defaults

Locate the code where the map type and tracking mode get changed. If you're working with the version of Pigeon I wrote for Chapter 17, that code is in HPMapOptionsViewController.m. Add this #import statement so the code can use the key constants you just defined:

```
#import "HPViewController.h"
```

Now find the code where each setting gets changed. In HPMapOptionsViewController that happens in the -changeMapStyle: and -changeHeading: methods. Change the code so it looks like this (new code in bold):

```
- (IBAction)changeMapStyle:(id)sender
{
    MKMapType mapType = self.mapStyleControl.selectedSegmentIndex;
    self.mapView.mapType = mapType;
    [[NSUserDefaults standardUserDefaults] setInteger:mapType
                                               forKey:kPreferenceMapType];
}

- (IBAction)changeHeading:(id)sender
{
    MKUserTrackingMode tracking = self.headingControl.selectedSegmentIndex+1;
    self.mapView.userTrackingMode = tracking;
    [[NSUserDefaults standardUserDefaults] setInteger:tracking
                                               forKey:kPreferenceHeading];
}
```

The change is straightforward, and you should have no problem adapting the same idea to your own app. When a setting is changed, the new value is also stored in the user defaults. That's all you have to do. NSUserDefaults takes care of everything else: converting the simple integer value into the appropriate property list (NSNumber) object, serializing the values, and storing them so they'll be available the next time your app runs.

That's the first half. Now you need to add the code to retrieve these saved values and restore the map options when your app starts.

Getting Values from User Defaults

Select the HPViewController.m file and locate the -viewDidLoad method. Replace the [_mapView setUserTrackingMode:MKUserTrackingModeFollow] statement with this code:

```
    NSUserDefaults *userDefaults = [NSUserDefaults standardUserDefaults];
    _mapView.mapType = [userDefaults integerForKey:kPreferenceMapType];
    NSUInteger trackingMode;
    if ([userDefaults objectForKey:kPreferenceHeading]!=nil)
        trackingMode = [userDefaults integerForKey:kPreferenceHeading];
    else
        trackingMode = MKUserTrackingModeFollow;
    _mapView.userTrackingMode = trackingMode;
```

This new code retrieves the integer values for the map type and tracking mode from the user defaults and uses them to restore those properties before the map is displayed. The result is that when the user runs the app and changes the map type, every time they launch the app after that the map type will be the same.

But there's a hitch. The very first time the app is run—or if the user never changes the map type or tracking mode—there are no values at all for those keys in the user defaults. If you request the property list object for a non-existent key, user defaults will return `nil`. If you request a scalar value (Boolean, integer, or floating-point) user defaults will return NO, 0, or 0.0. Here are three ways of dealing with this situation:

- Choose your values so that `nil`, NO, 0, or 0.0 is the default
- Test to see if user defaults contains a value for that key
- Register a default value for that key

The map type property adopts the first solution. Conveniently, the initial map type in Pigeon is `MKMapTypeStandard`, whose integer value is 0. So if there is no value in user defaults for the `kPreferenceMapType` key, it returns a 0 and sets the map type to standard—which is perfect.

The tracking mode isn't so lucky. The initial tracking mode Pigeon uses is `MKUserTrackingModeFollow`, whose integer value is 1. If there's no value for the `kPreferenceHeading` key, you don't want to set `trackingMode` to `MKUserTrackingModeNone` (0) by mistake.

Instead, the code uses the second solution. It first gets the property list (NSNumber) object for that key. If there's no value for that key, user defaults returns `nil` and you know that a tracking value has never been set. You use this knowledge to either restore the user-selected mode or set the correct default.

> **Note** The code uses the method `-objectForKey:` to test for the presence of any value. A property list *object* ultimately represents every value in a property list. The methods `-boolForKey:`, `-integerForKey:`, and so on, convert the simple integer, floating-point, or Boolean values to, and from, an NSNumber object for you.

That's everything you need to preserve and restore these map settings. It's time to test it out, but that will require a little finesse.

Testing User Defaults

Using either a provisioned device or the simulator, run your updated Pigeon app. Tap the settings button and change the map type and tracking mode, as show in Figure 18-1. This will update the user defaults with the new values, but those values may, or may not, be saved in persistent storage yet. That's because the user defaults tries to be as efficient as possible and may wait for additional changes before beginning the serialization and storage process.

Figure 18-1. Testing the map settings

One way to get its attention is to push your app into the background. Do this by tapping the home button or use the **Hardware ➤ Home** command in the simulator, shown in the third image in Figure 18-1. When your app enters the background, it doesn't immediately stop running, but it prepares itself for that eventuality. One of those steps is to serialize and preserve all of your user defaults.

With your user defaults safely stored, you can now stop your app and start it running again. Switch back to Xcode and click the stop button. Once the app stops, click the run button. The app starts up again. This time, it loads the map type and tracking mode from the saved user defaults and restores those properties. When the view controller loads, the map is exactly as the user left it last time.

Congratulations, you've learned the basics of preserving and restoring values in the user defaults. In the next few sections you're going to refine your technique a little, and deal with the (slightly) more complex problem of preserving and restoring the user's saved map location.

Registering Default Values

The code to restore the tracking mode is awfully ugly. Well, maybe not "awfully ugly," but it's a little ugly. If you had a dozen of these settings to restore, you'd have a lot of repetitive code to write. Fortunately, there's a more elegant solution.

Your app can register a set of default values for specific keys in user defaults—yes, they're default defaults. When your code requests a value ([userDefaults integerForKey:kPreferenceHeading]), the user defaults checks to see if a value for that key has been previously set. If not, it returns a default value. For integers that value is 0—unless you've specified something else. You do that using the -registerDefaults: method.

Select the HPAppDelegate.m implementation file. This is your app's delegate object. It receives a lot of messages about the state of your app. One of those is the -application:willFinishLaunching WithOptions: method. This is the first message your app object receives, and is normally the first opportunity for code that you've written to run.

Add this #import towards the top of the file, so your new code can use your key constants:

#import "HPViewController.h"

In the @implementation section, add this method (or update it if it already exists):

```
- (BOOL)              application:(UIApplication *)application
 willFinishLaunchingWithOptions:(NSDictionary *)launchOptions
{
    [[NSUserDefaults standardUserDefaults] registerDefaults:@{
        kPreferenceHeading: @(MKUserTrackingModeFollow)
    }];
    return YES;
}
```

The -registerDefaults: message establishes a backup dictionary for the user default's primary dictionary. The user defaults object actually manages several dictionaries, arranged into domains. When you ask it to retrieve a value, it searches each domain until it finds a value and returns it. The -registerDefaults: method sets up a domain behind all of the others, so if none of the other domains contain a value for kPreferenceHeading, this dictionary provides one.

> **Note** Each domain in the user defaults has its own purpose and properties. The domain into which you store values is persistent; it will be serialized and preserved between app runs. The registration domain is not persistent. The values you pass to -registerDefaults: disappear when your app quits. You can read about domains in "The Organization of Preferences" chapter of the *Preferences and Settings Programming Guide*.

Now you can clean up the code in -viewDidLoad. Return to HPViewController.m and replace the code you previously added with this (updated code in bold):

```
NSUserDefaults *userDefaults = [NSUserDefaults standardUserDefaults];
_mapView.mapType = [userDefaults integerForKey:kPreferenceMapType];
_mapView.userTrackingMode = [userDefaults integerForKey:kPreferenceHeading];
```

Isn't that a lot simpler? Because you've registered a defaults dictionary, your code doesn't have to worry about the situation where there is no value for kPreferenceHeading, because now there will always be one.

Now that your map settings are persistent, it's time to do something about that saved map location.

Turning Objects into Property List Objects

The big limitation of property lists is that they can only contain property list objects (NSNumber, NSString, NSDictionary, and so on). Anything you want to store in user defaults (or any property list) *must* be converted into one of those objects. Here are three most common techniques for storing other kinds of values:

- Convert the value(s) into a string
- Convert the values into a property list dictionary
- Serialize the object(s) into an NSData object

The first technique is simple enough, especially since there are a number of Cocoa Touch functions that will do this for you. For example, let's say you need to store a CGRect value in your user defaults. CGRect isn't a property list object—it's not even an object. You could store each of its four floating-point fields as separate values, like this:

```
CGRect saveRect = self.someView.frame;
[userDefaults setFloat:saveRect.origin.x forKey:@"HPFrame.x"];
[userDefaults setFloat:saveRect.origin.y forKey:@"HPFrame.y"];
[userDefaults setFloat:saveRect.size.height forKey:@"HPFrame.height"];
[userDefaults setFloat:saveRect.size.width forKey:@"HPFrame.width"];
```

And you'd have to reverse the process to restore the rectangle. That seems like a lot of work. Fortunately, there are two functions—NSStringFromCGRect and CGRectFromString—that will convert a rectangle into a string object and back again. Now the code to save your rectangle can look something like this:

```
[userDefaults setObject:NSStringFromCGRect(self.someView.frame)
           forKey:@"HPFrame"];
```

So if you can find functions that will convert your value to and from a property list object, use them.

The second technique is what you're going to use for the map location. You're going to write a pair of methods. The first will return the salient properties of your MKPointAnnotation object as a dictionary of NSString and NSNumber objects. A second method will take that dictionary and set them again.

Start by adding a new category to your project. Select a file, like HPViewController.m, in your project navigator and choose the New ➤ File . . . command (**File** menu or right/control+click). From the Cocoa Touch group, choose the Objective-C category template. Name the category HPPreservation and make it a category on MKPointAnnotation.

> **Note** A category adds additional methods to an existing class. In Chapter 14 you used a category to add methods to your own class, but they can just as easily add new methods to classes you didn't write. I explain the ins and outs of categories in Chapter 20.

In the `@interface` of `MKPointAnnotation+HPPreservation.h`, add two method declarations:

```
- (NSDictionary*)preserveState;
- (void)restoreState:(NSDictionary*)state;
```

In `MKPointAnnotation+HPPreservation.m`, define three constants for the dictionary keys, immediately after the `#import` statements:

```
#define kInfoLocationLatitude    @"lat"
#define kInfoLocationLongitude   @"long"
#define kInfoLocationTitle       @"title"
```

In the `@implementation` section, write the two methods:

```
- (NSDictionary*)preserveState
{
    CLLocationCoordinate2D coord = self.coordinate;
    return @{ kInfoLocationLatitude:   @(coord.latitude),
              kInfoLocationLongitude:  @(coord.longitude),
              kInfoLocationTitle:      self.title };
}

- (void)restoreState:(NSDictionary*)state
{
    CLLocationCoordinate2D coord;
    coord.latitude = [state[kInfoLocationLatitude] doubleValue];
    coord.longitude = [state[kInfoLocationLongitude] doubleValue];
    self.coordinate = coord;
    self.title = state[kInfoLocationTitle];
}
```

The first method returns a new dictionary (`NSDictionary`) object with three values: the latitude, the longitude, and the title of the annotation. The values in the dictionary are `NSNumber` and `NSString` objects, all perfectly suited to being stored in a property list. Which is exactly what you're going to do.

The second method reverses the process, setting the coordinates and the title of the annotation using the values in the dictionary. Now let's go use these to save and restore the map location.

Preserving and Restoring savedLocation

Return to `HPViewController.m`. You're going to use the same technique you used to preserve and restore the map settings for the remembered map location. You're going to save the location information (dictionary) when it's established, and restore it when the app starts again. The `savedLocation` object isn't, however, a simple integer, so the code is a little more involved. Furthermore, you're now establishing a new location from two places in the code: when the user sets it and when the app starts again. As you know by now, I'm not fond of repeating code, so I'm going to have you consolidate the code that sets the location. This will come in handy later, when you add a third avenue for setting the location.

To summarize, here's what you're going to change:

- Add a -setLocation: method to set or clear the saved location
- Write -preserveAnnotation and -restoreAnnotation methods to store, and retrieve, the map location from the user defaults
- Add code to -dropPin: and -clearPin: to preserve the map location
- Restore any remembered location when your app launches

Begin by importing the category you just created, immediately after the other #import statements:

```
#import "MKPointAnnotation+HPPreservation.h"
```

Add the new method declarations to the private @interface HPViewController () section:

```
- (void)setAnnotation:(MKPointAnnotation*)annotation;
- (void)preserveAnnotation;
- (void)restoreAnnotation;
```

Add the new -setAnnotation: method to the @implementation section:

```
- (void)setAnnotation:(MKPointAnnotation*)annotation
{
    if ([savedAnnotation isEqual:annotation])
        return;
    if (savedAnnotation!=nil)
        [_mapView removeAnnotation:savedAnnotation];
    savedAnnotation = annotation;
    if (annotation!=nil)
        {
        [_mapView addAnnotation:annotation];
        [_mapView selectAnnotation:annotation animated:YES];
        }
}
```

This method will be used throughout MKViewController to set, or clear, the annotation object. It follows a common setter method pattern that handles the cases where the savedAnnotation variable is nil, the annotation parameter is nil, both are nil, or neither are nil. It also deliberately takes no action if the same annotation object is set again.

Find the -alertView:clickedButtonAtIndex: method. Locate the [self clearPin:self] statement. Delete it, along with all of the statements in the method that follow it, and replace them with the following code:

```
    MKPointAnnotation *newAnnotation = [MKPointAnnotation new];
    newAnnotation.title = name;
    newAnnotation.coordinate = location.coordinate;
    [self setAnnotation:newAnnotation];

    [self preserveAnnotation];
}
```

The new code makes two changes. First, it uses the new -setAnnotation: method to add the annotation to the map. Second, it sends the -preserveAnnotation message to store the new map location in the user defaults. Now make a similar change to the -clearPin: method (modified code in bold):

```
- (IBAction)clearPin:(id)sender
{
    if (savedAnnotation!=nil)
        {
        [self setAnnotation:nil];
        [self preserveAnnotation];
        }
}
```

Add the new -preserveAnnotation and -restoreAnnotation methods:

```
- (void)preserveAnnotation
{
    NSUserDefaults *userDefaults = [NSUserDefaults standardUserDefaults];
    if (savedAnnotation!=nil)
        {
        NSDictionary *annotationInfo = [savedAnnotation preserveState];
        [userDefaults setObject:annotationInfo
                        forKey:kPreferenceSavedLocation];
        }
    else
        {
        [userDefaults removeObjectForKey:kPreferenceSavedLocation];
        }
}

- (void)restoreAnnotation
{
    NSUserDefaults *userDefaults = [NSUserDefaults standardUserDefaults];
    NSDictionary *restoreInfo = 
                [userDefaults dictionaryForKey:kPreferenceSavedLocation];
    if (restoreInfo!=nil)
        {
        MKPointAnnotation *restoreAnnotation = [MKPointAnnotation new];
        [restoreAnnotation restoreState:restoreInfo];
        [self setAnnotation:restoreAnnotation];
        }
}
```

-preserveAnnotation converts the savedAnnotation object into a dictionary, suitable for storing in the user defaults. If there is no map location, it intentionally deletes any saved value for that key from the user defaults. You can't store nil as a value in user defaults. To store nothing, delete the value by sending the -removeObjectForKey: message.

The -restoreAnnotation method reverses the process, retrieving the dictionary of map location information from user defaults and turning it back into an MKPointAnnotation object with the same information. There's only one thing left to do. In -viewDidLoad, add this statement to the end of the method:

`[self restoreAnnotation];`

Pigeon now has the memory of an elephant! Reuse the test procedure you employed earlier to test the map settings:

1. Run Pigeon
2. Remember a location on the map
3. Press the home button to put the app in the background
4. Stop the app in Xcode
5. Run the app again

When the app is restarted, the saved location is still there. Success!

This project demonstrates several common techniques for putting user defaults to work in your app. Remembering user preferences, settings, and working data (like the saved map location) are all perfect uses for the user defaults.

Another common use is to save your app's display state. When the user selects the Artists tab in the Music app, taps down into an album, and ultimately a song, they aren't surprised when they start Music the next day and find themselves at the same track, of the same album, of the same artist, in the Artists tab. That's because the Music app went to some effort to remember exactly what view controller the user left off at, and reconstructed it the next time it was launched.

From what you know so far, you might think that you'd have to write code to capture the state of tab view and navigation view controllers, convert those into property list objects, store them in user defaults, and unroll the whole thing again when the app restarts. That's basically what happens, but you'll be happy to know that you don't have to do (much) of that yourself. iOS has a specific mechanism for saving and restoring the state of your view controllers.

Persistent Views

In the section "Minimizing Updates and Code" I said the primary techniques for capturing user defaults was (a) when the value changes or (b) at a dependable exit point. You used technique (a) in Pigeon because it was a perfect fit. The values you were saving were only changed in a handful of places, and they change infrequently. But that isn't always the case.

Some changes occur constantly (like which view controller the user is in) and some changes occur in a myriad of different ways, making it very difficult to catch them all. In these situations, the second approach is the best. You don't worry about trying to monitor, or even care about, what changes are being made. Just arrange to capture that value before the user quits the app, dismisses the view controller, or exits whatever interface they're using. There are two exit points that make good places to capture changes:

- Dismissing a view controller
- The app entering the background

For view controllers, you can capture your values in the code that dismisses the view controller. You might have to do a little extra work in circumstances like a popover view controller, as tapping outside the popover can dismiss it implicitly. You'd want to catch that message (`-popoverControllerDidDismissPopover:`) too, so you don't miss that exit route. But for the most part, it's usually pretty easy to catch all of the ways a view controller can be dismissed.

Fading Into the Background

The other great place to capture changes, and particularly the view state, is when the app switches to the background. To appreciate this technique, you need to understand the states an iOS app progresses through. Your iOS app is always in one of these states:

- Not running
- Foreground
- Background
- Suspended

Your app is in the "not running" state before it's launched, or after it's ultimately terminated. Very little happens when it's not running.

The foreground state is the one you have the most experience with. This is when your app appears in the device's display and your user is interacting with it. Foreground has two sub-states, active and inactive, that it jumps between. Active means your app is running. Inactive occurs when something interrupts it (like a phone call or an alert), but it's still being displayed. Your app's code does not run when it's inactive. The inactive state usually doesn't last long.

Your app moves to the background state when you press the home button, switch to another app, or the screen locks. Your app continues to run for a short period of time, but will quickly move to the suspended state.

Your app does not execute any code once suspended. If iOS later decides that it needs the memory your app is occupying, or the user shuts down their device, your suspended app will terminate (without warning) and return to the not running state.

But your app might not be terminated. If the user re-launches your app, and it's still in the background state, your app isn't restarted; it's simply activated again. It moves directly to the foreground state and instantly resumes execution. Your app may enter, and exit, the background state repeatedly over its lifetime.

> **Note** You can make special arrangements that allow your app to continue to run in the background. For example, you can request to play music or receive user location changes, even while your app is not the foreground app. See the section "Background Execution and Multitasking" in the *iOS App Programming Guide* for further details.

Apps take advantage of this small window of background processing to prepare themselves for termination. This is when the user defaults serializes its property values and saves them to persistent storage. It's also the perfect time to capture the state of your interface.

Your app can discover when it has entered the background state in two ways. Your app delegate object receives an `-applicationDidEnterBackground:` message. Around the same time, a `UIApplicationDidEnterBackgroundNotification` notification is posted. Override that method, or have any object observe that notification, and save whatever state information you need.

> **Caution** iOS allots your app approximately 5 seconds of background processing time to save its state and finish up any work in progress. Your app must wrap up within that time, or take explicit steps to enable background processing.

iOS also provides a mechanism to capture, and later restore, the state of your view controllers. This is automatically invoked when your app enters the background state.

Preserving View Controllers

As an example, take the Wonderland app. (I mean that, literally. Go find the finished Wonderland app from Chapter 12. You're going to modify it.) The user can spend all day jumping between tabs, browsing characters in the table view, and flipping through the page view. You want to catch the point when the app switches to the background and remember what tab they had active and what page of the book they were looking at. You'll use this to restore those views the next time the app is launched.

When an iOS app enters the background, iOS examines the active view controller. If properly configured, it will automatically preserve its state in the user defaults. This is a combination of what iOS already knows about the view controller and additional information that your code supplies. Specifically, iOS will remember what tab view was being displayed, the scroll position in a table view, and so on. To that, you can add custom information that only your app understands. For Wonderland, you're going to remember the page number the user was reading. (Remember that a page view controller has no concept of a page number; that's something you invented for your page view controller data source.)

The first thing to address is the "properly configured" prerequisite. To put iOS to work for you, preserving and restoring your view controllers, you must do two things:

1. Implement the `-application:shouldSaveApplicationState:` and `-application:shouldRestoreApplicationState:` app delegate methods
2. Assign restoration identifiers to your view controllers, starting with the root view controller

The first step tells iOS that you want its help in preserving and restoring your app's view state. These methods must be implemented, and they must return YES, or iOS will just pass your app by. They also serve a secondary function. If you have any custom, app-wide, state information that you want to preserve, these are the methods to do that in. Wonderland doesn't have any, so it only needs to return YES.

Open the Wonderland project from Chapter 12 and select the `WLAppDelegate.m` file. Add the following two methods to the `@implementation` section:

```
- (BOOL)              application:(UIApplication *)application
   shouldSaveApplicationState:(NSCoder *)coder
{
    return YES;
}

- (BOOL)              application:(UIApplication *)application
   shouldRestoreApplicationState:(NSCoder *)coder
{
    return YES;
}
```

Assigning Restoration Identifiers

Once iOS is given the green light to save your view state, its starts with the root view controller being displayed and checks for a restoration ID. A restoration ID is a string property (`restorationIdentifier`) used to tag the state information for that view controller. It also acts as a flag, inviting iOS to preserve, and ultimately restore, that view controller's state. If the `restorationIdentifer` property is `nil`, iOS ignores the view controller; nothing gets persevered, and nothing will be restored.

iOS then looks for any view (`UIView`) objects that have a `restorationIdentifier` set, and preserves them. If the root view controller is a container view controller, the entire process repeats with each sub-view controller, capturing the state of each view controller with a restoration ID and ignoring those without.

> **Note** The search for restorable view controllers skips any view controller that lacks a restoration ID. Thus, to save the state of a table view controller inside a navigation view controller inside a tab view controller, every one of those controllers must have a restoration ID, or else the state of the table view controller won't be captured.

You can set restoration IDs programmatically, but if your view controller is defined in an Interface Builder file it's simplest to set them there. Select the `Main_iPhone.storyboard` (or `_iPad`) file. Select the root tab bar view controller and switch to the identity inspector, as shown in Figure 18-2. Locate the `Restoration ID` property and set it to `TabViewController`.

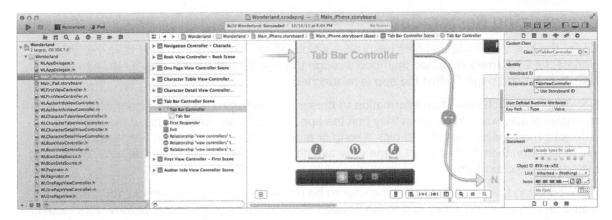

Figure 18-2. Setting restoration ID property

You've now done everything required to get iOS to save, and restore, that state of your tab view controller. This, unfortunately, won't do you much good. What you want is the sub-view controller that was visible when the user quit Wonderland to reappear when they launch it again. For that to happen, each of the sub-view controllers must be restored too. Using the identity inspector, select each of the sub-view controllers and assign them restoration IDs too, using Table 18-1 as a guide.

Table 18-1. Wonderland view controller restoration IDs

View Controller	Restoration ID
Root Tab View Controller	TabViewController
WLFirstViewController	CoverViewController
UINavigationController	CharacterNavController
WLBookViewController	BookViewController

This is enough to remember, and later restore, the top-level tab the user was viewing when they quit the app. Give it a try:

1. Run the Wonderland app
2. Choose the character or book tab
3. Press the home button to push the app into the background
4. Stop the app in Xcode
5. Run the app again

The restoration ID strings can be anything you want; they just have to be unique within the scope of the other view controllers.

Customizing Restoration

So far, the only view state that gets restored is which tab the user was in. If they were viewing a character's information, or had thumbed through to page 87 of the book, they'll return to the character list and page 1 when the app is relaunched.

Deciding how much view state information to preserve is up to you. As a rule, users expect to return to whatever they were doing when they quit the app. But there are limits to this. If the user had entered a modal view controller to pick a song or enter a password, it wouldn't necessarily make sense to return them to that exact same view two days later. You'll have to decide how "deep" your restoration logic extends.

For Wonderland, you definitely want the user to be on the same page of the book. Your users would be very annoyed if they had to flip through 86 pages to get back to where they were reading yesterday. The page view controller, however, knows nothing about the organization of your book data. That's something you created when you wrote the `WLBookDataSource` class. If you want to preserve and restore the page they were on, you'll have to write some code to do that.

Each view and view controller object with a restoration ID receives an `-encodeRestorableStateWithCoder:` message when the app moves to the background. During application startup, it receives a `-decodeRestorableStateWithCoder:` message to restore itself. If you want to preserve custom state information, override these methods.

Select the `WLBookViewController.m` implementation file. Add these two methods to the `@implementation` section:

```
- (void)encodeRestorableStateWithCoder:(NSCoder *)coder
{
    [super encodeRestorableStateWithCoder:coder];
    WLOnePageViewController *currentView = self.viewControllers[0];
    [coder encodeInteger:currentView.pageNumber forKey:@"page"];
}

- (void)decodeRestorableStateWithCoder:(NSCoder *)coder
{
    [super decodeRestorableStateWithCoder:coder];
    NSUInteger page = [coder decodeIntegerForKey:@"page"];
    if (page!=0)
        {
        WLOnePageViewController *currentView = self.viewControllers[0];
        currentView.pageNumber = page;
        }
}
```

The first method obtains the current view controller being displayed in the page view controller. The `WLOnePageViewController` knows which page number it's displaying. This number is saved in the `NSCoder` object.

> **Note** `NSCoder` is the workhorse of iOS's archiving framework. You use it by storing values and properties, which are converted into serialized data. You'll learn all about `NSCoder` in the next chapter.

When your app is relaunched, the page view controller receives a `-decodeRestorableStateWithCoder:` message. It looks inside the `NSCoder` object to see if it contains a saved page number. If it does, it restores the page number before the view appears, returning the user to where they were when they quit. That wasn't too hard, was it?

Test out your new code. Launch Wonderland, flip through a few pages of the book, then quit the app and stop it in Xcode. Launch it again, and the last page you were looking at will reappear, as if you'd never left.

Deeper Restoration

Exactly how much view state information you decide to preserve is up to you. Here are some tips to developing a restoration strategy:

- `UIView` objects can be preserved too. Assign them a restoration ID and, if necessary, implement `-encodeRestorableStateWithCoder:` and `-decodeRestorableStateWithCoder:` methods.
- If you want to restore the state of a data model for a table or collection view, your data source object should adopt the `UIDataSourceModelAssociation` protocol. You then implement two methods (`-indexPathForElementWithModelIdentifier:inView:` and `-modelIdentifierForElementAtIndexPath:inView:`) that remember, and restore, the user's position in the table.
- You can encode and restore anything you want in your app delegate's `-application:shouldSaveApplicationState:` and `-application:shouldRestoreApplicationState:` methods. You can use these methods to perform your own view controller restoration, or use a combination of the automatic restoration and a custom solution.

The gory details are all explained in the "State Preservation and Restoration" chapter of the *iOS App Programming Guide*, which you can find in Xcode's Documentation and API Reference window.

Pigeons in the Cloud

Cloud storage and synchronization are hot new technologies that make iOS devices even more useful. Set an appointment on one, and it automatically appears on all of your other devices. The technology behind this bit of magic is complex, but iOS makes it easy for your app to take advantage of it.

There are a number of cloud storage and synchronization features in iOS, but the easiest to use, by far, is the `NSUbiquitousKeyValueStore` object. It works almost identically to user defaults. The difference is that anything you store there is automatically synchronized with all of your other iOS devices. Wow!

There are both practical limits and policy restrictions on what information you should, or can, synchronize between devices. Your first task is to decide what it makes sense to share. Typically, user settings and view states are only preserved locally. It would be weird to change the map type on your iPhone, and then suddenly have your iPad's map view change too. On the other hand, if your user was reading *Alice's Adventures in Wonderland* on their iPad, wouldn't it be magic if they could reach for their iPhone and open it up at the same page?

Another reason to carefully choose what you synchronize is that the iCloud service strictly limits how much information you can share through NSUbiquitousKeyValueStore. The limits are:

- No more than 1MB of data, in total
- No more than 1,000 objects
- A "reasonable" number of updates

Apple doesn't spell out exactly what "reasonable" is, but it's a good idea to keep the number of changes you make to NSUbiquitousKeyValueStore to a minimum.

> **Caution** If you abuse these limits, the iCloud servers may delay your updates or possibly stop synchronizing your data entirely.

Storing Values in the Cloud

Let your Pigeon app spread its wings by adding cloud synchronization. The only piece of information you'll synchronize is the remembered map location—the map type and tracking mode aren't good candidates for syncing. You use NSUbiquitousKeyValueStore almost exactly the way you use NSUserDefaults. In fact, they are so similar that you'll be reusing many of the same strategies and methods you wrote at the beginning of this chapter.

You get a reference to the singleton NSUbiquitousKeyValueStore object via [NSUbiquitousKeyValueStore defaultStore]. Any values you set are automatically serialized and synchronized with the iCloud servers.

Select HPViewController.m and add an instance variable to the private @interface HPViewController (). This will retain the cloud store object (new code in bold):

```
@interface HPViewController () <UIAlertViewDelegate>
{
    MKPointAnnotation       *savedAnnotation;
    UIImageView             *arrowView;
    NSUbiquitousKeyValueStore *cloudStore;
}
```

Initialize the new variable by adding these statements to the end of the -viewDidLoad method:

```
cloudStore = [NSUbiquitousKeyValueStore defaultStore];
[cloudStore synchronize];
```

This code retrieves and saves a reference to the singleton cloud store object, and then requests an immediate synchronization. This prompts iOS to update any values in the store that might have been changed by other iOS devices, and vice versa. It will happen eventually, but this hurries the process along when the app first starts, and is the only time you'll need to send -synchronize.

> **Note** There's a reason I have you create and store a reference to the NSUbiquitousKeyValueStore object, rather than just use [NSUbiquitousKeyValueStore defaultStore] when you need it. It will all make sense by the end of the chapter.

Now update the -preserveAnnotation method so it stores the annotation information in both the user defaults and the cloud (new code in bold):

```
- (void)preserveAnnotation
{
    NSUserDefaults *userDefaults = [NSUserDefaults standardUserDefaults];
    if (savedAnnotation!=nil)
        {
        NSDictionary *annotationInfo = [savedAnnotation preserveState];
        [userDefaults setObject:annotationInfo
                         forKey:kPreferenceSavedLocation];
        [cloudStore setDictionary:annotationInfo
                           forKey:kPreferenceSavedLocation];
        }
    else
        {
        [userDefaults removeObjectForKey:kPreferenceSavedLocation];
        [cloudStore removeObjectForKey:kPreferenceSavedLocation];
        }
}
```

Cloud Watching

Unlike user defaults, the values in the cloud can change at any time. So it's insufficient to simply read them when your app starts. Your app has to be prepared to react to changes, whenever they occur. In addition, your iOS device doesn't always have access to the cloud. It may be in "airplane" mode, experiencing spotty cell reception, or maybe you're using your device inside a Faraday cage—for a little privacy. No matter what, your app should continue to work in an intelligent manner under all of these conditions.

The preferred solution is to mirror your cloud settings in your local user defaults. This is what -preserveAnnotation does. Whenever the location changes, both the user defaults *and* the cloud are updated with the same value. If the cloud can't be updated just now, that won't interfere with the app. Likewise, if a value in the cloud changes, you should update your user defaults to match.

Which brings you to the task of observing changes in the cloud. So how do you find out when something in the cloud changes? At this point in the book, you should be chanting "notification, notification, notification," because that's exactly how you observe these changes. Your view controller observes the NSUbiquitousKeyValueStoreDidChangeExternallyNotification notification (which is also the runner up for being the longest notification name in iOS). You'll create a new method to process those changes, so begin by adding that to the private @interface HPViewController () section in HPViewController.m:

```
- (void)cloudStoreChanged:(NSNotification*)notification;
```

Find the -viewDidLoad method and augment the code that sets up the cloud store (new code in bold):

```
cloudStore = [NSUbiquitousKeyValueStore defaultStore];
NSNotificationCenter *center = [NSNotificationCenter defaultCenter];
[center addObserver:self
           selector:@selector(cloudStoreChanged:)
               name:NSUbiquitousKeyValueStoreDidChangeExternallyNotification
             object:cloudStore];
[cloudStore synchronize];
```

> **Caution** You must register to observe change notifications *before* sending -synchronize, or your app may miss pre-existing changes in the cloud.

The -cloudStoreChanged: message will now be received whenever something in the cloud changes. The last step is to write that method:

```
- (void)cloudStoreChanged:(NSNotification*)notification
{
    NSDictionary *cloudInfo = [cloudStore dictionaryForKey: ↵
                                         kPreferenceSavedLocation];
    NSUserDefaults *localStore = [NSUserDefaults standardUserDefaults];
    [localStore setObject:cloudInfo forKey:kPreferenceSavedLocation];
    [self restoreAnnotation];
}
```

Whenever the cloud values change—and there's only one value, so you don't even need to worry about which one changed—it retrieves the new value and copies it into the local user defaults. It then sends -restoreAnnotation to restore the map location from the user defaults, which is now the same as the value in the cloud.

Between -preserveAnnotation and -cloudStoreChanged:, the user defaults always has the latest (known) location. Should something interfere with cloud synchronization, the app still has a working location and continues to function normally.

Finally, consider the -restoreAnnotation method you wrote earlier. It never considered the possibility that there was an existing map annotation. That's because the only place it was sent was when your app started. Now, it can be received at any time, to either set or clear the saved map location. Add an else clause to the end of the method to take care of that possibility (new code in bold):

```
if (restoreInfo!=nil)
    {
    MKPointAnnotation *restoreAnnotation = [MKPointAnnotation new];
    [restoreAnnotation restoreState:restoreInfo];
    [self setAnnotation:restoreAnnotation];
    }
else
    {
    [self setAnnotation:nil];
    }
```

Enabling iCloud

All of your iCloud code is ready to run, but there's just one problem: none of it will work. Before an app can use the iCloud servers, you must add an iCloud entitlement to your app. This, in turn, requires that you register your app's bundle identifier with Apple and obtain an entitlement certificate. These aren't complicated steps, but they are required.

Select the Pigeon project in the navigator. Make sure the Pigeon target is selected (either from the sidebar or the pop-up menu) and switch to the Capabilities tab. Locate the iCloud section and turn it on, as shown in Figure 18-3.

Figure 18-3. Enabling iCloud services

Choose the developer team that will be testing this app and click Choose. Xcode will register your app's unique ID with the iOS Dev Center and enable that ID for use with the iCloud service. It will then download and install the necessary entitlement certificates that permit your app to use the iCloud servers. You should now enable use of the key-value store, as shown in Figure 18-4. This is the iCloud service that the `NSUbiquitousKeyValueStore` class depends on.

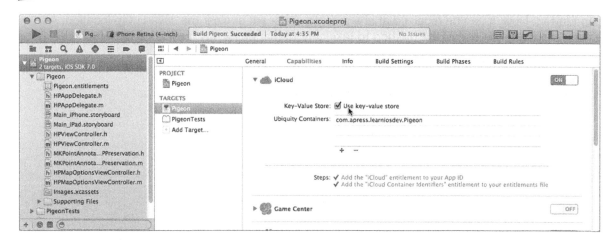

Figure 18-4. *Enabling iCloud's key-value store*

When you enabled the key-value store, Xcode generates one ubiquity container identifier. This identifier is used to collate and synchronize all of the values you put in NSUbiquitousKeyValueStore. Normally, you use the bundle identifier of your app—which is the default. This keeps your app's iCloud values separate from the iCloud values stored by any of the user's other apps.

> **Tip** You're allowed to enter a key-value store identifier used by another app (that you wrote and registered). This allows your app to share a key-value store with another app. You might do this, for example, if you've created a "light" and a "professional" version of the same app. Both apps can use the same key-value store to share and synchronize their settings.

Testing the Cloud

To test the cloud version of Pigeon, you'll need two, provisioned, iOS devices. Both devices will need active Internet connections, be logged into the same iCloud account, and have iCloud Documents & Data turned on.

Start the Pigeon app running on both devices. Tap the "remember location" button on one device, give it a name, and wait. If everything was set up properly, an identical pin should appear on the other device, typically within a minute. Try remembering a location on the second device. Try clearing the location.

> **Tip** Even if you only have one iOS device, you can still tell if NSUbiquitousKeyValueStore is working by checking the value returned by -synchronize. If -synchronize returns YES, then cloud values were successfully synchronized and everything is working. If it returns NO, then there's a problem. It could be network related. It could also mean your app's identifier, entitlements, or provisioning profiles are not correctly configured.

You don't need to have both apps running simultaneously—that's just the coolest way to experience iCloud syncing. Launch Pigeon on one device, remember a location, and quit it. Count to twenty. Launch Pigeon on a second device, and you'll instantly see the updated location. That's because the ubiquitous key-value store works constantly in the background, whenever it has an Internet connection, to keep all of your values in sync.

Not everyone will want their map locations shared with all of their other devices. Some users would be perfectly happy with the first, non-cloud, version of Pigeon. Why not make all of your users happy and give them the option?

Add a configuration setting so they can opt-in to cloud synchronization, or leave it off. The question now is where do you put that setting? Do you add it to the map options view controller? Do you create another settings button that takes the user to a second settings view? Maybe you'd add a tiny button with a little cloud icon to the map view? That would be pretty cute.

There are lots of possibilities, but I want you to think outside the box. Or, more precisely, I want you to think outside your app. Your task is to create an interface to let the user turn cloud synchronization on or off, but don't put it in your app. Confused? Don't be; it's easier than you think.

Bundle Up Your Settings

A *settings bundle* is a property list file describing one or more user default values that your users can set. See, yet another use for property lists. Users set them, not in your app, but in the Settings app that comes with every iOS system. Using a settings bundle is quite simple:

> You create a list of value descriptions.
>
> iOS turns that list into an interface that appears in the Settings app.
>
> The user launches the Settings app and makes changes to their settings.
>
> The updated values appear in your app's user defaults.

Settings bundles are particularly useful for settings the user isn't likely to change often and you don't want cluttering up your app's interface. For Pigeon, you're going to create a trivially simple settings bundle with one option: synchronize using iCloud. The possible values will be on or off (YES or NO). Let's get started.

Creating a Settings Bundle

In the Pigeon project, choose the **New ➤ File...** command (via the File menu or by right/control-clicking in the project navigator). In the iOS section, locate the Resource group and select the Settings Bundle template, as shown in Figure 18-5.

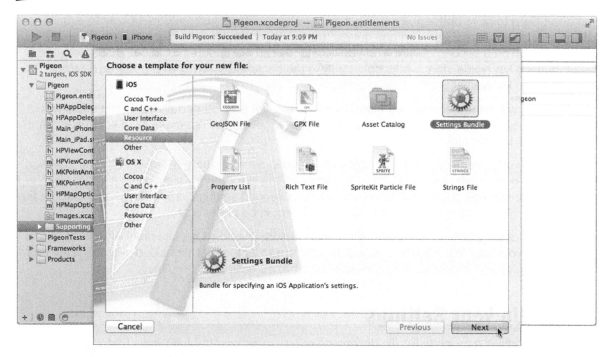

Figure 18-5. *Creating a settings bundle resource*

Make sure the Pigeon target is selected, and add the new Settings resource to your project.

> **Caution** Do not change the name of the new file. Your settings bundle *must* be named Settings.bundle, or iOS will ignore it.

A settings bundle contains one property list file named Root.plist. This file contains a dictionary. You can see this in Figure 18-6. The Root.plist file describes the settings that appear (first) when the user selects your app in the Settings app.

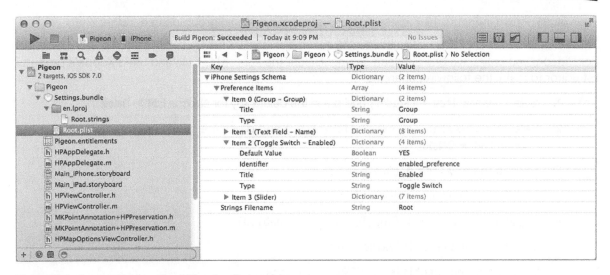

Figure 18-6. Property list from the settings bundle template

The dictionary contains an array value for the key Preference Items. That array contains a list of dictionaries. Each dictionary describes one setting or organization item. The kinds of setting you can include are listed in Table 18-2 and the organizational items are in Table 18-3. The details for each type are described in the "Implementing an iOS Settings Bundle" chapter of the *Preferences and Settings Programming Guide* that you can find in Xcode's Documentation and API Reference window.

Table 18-2. Settings bundle value types

Settings Type	Key	Interface	Value
Text Field	PSTextFieldSpecifier	Text field	A string
Toggle Switch	PSToggleSwitchSpecifier	Toggle switch	Any two values, but YES and NO are the norm
Slider	PSSliderSpecifier	Slider	Any number within a range
Multi-value	PSMultiValueSpecifier	Table	One value in a list of values
Radio Group	PSRadioGroupSpecifier	Picker	One value in a list of values
Title	PSTitleValueSpecifier	Label	Display only (value can't be changed)

Table 18-3. Settings bundle organization types

Settings Type	Key	Description
Group	PSGroupSpecifier	Organizes the settings that follow into a group.
Child Table	PSChildPaneSpecifier	Presents a table item that, when tapped, presents another set of settings, creating a hierarchy of settings.

Your settings bundle can invite the user to type in a string (like a nickname), let them turn settings on and off, pick from a list of values ("map," "satellite," "hybrid"), or choose a number with a slider. If your app has a lot of settings, you can organize them into groups or even link to another set with even more settings.

The values shown in Figure 18-6 present three settings in a single group named, rather unimaginatively, `Group`. Those settings consist of a text field, a toggle switch, and a slider.

For Pigeon, you only have one Boolean setting. Select the `Root.plist` file and used Xcode's property list editor to make the following changes:

1. Select the row `Item 3 (Slider)` and press the delete key (or choose **Edit ➤ Delete**).
2. Select the row `Item 1 (Text Field - Name)` and press the delete key (or choose **Edit ➤ Delete**).
3. Expand the row `Item 0 (Group - Group)`.
   a. Change the value of its `Title` to `iCloud`
4. Expand the row `Item 1 (Toggle Switch - Enabled)`
   a. Change the `Default Value` to `NO`
   b. Change the `Identifier` to `HPSyncLocations`
   c. Change the `Title` to `Sync Locations`

Your finished settings bundle should look like the one in Figure 18-7.

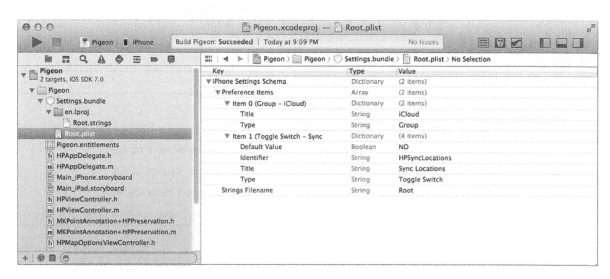

Figure 18-7. Pigeon settings bundle

Using Your Settings Bundle Values

Your settings bundle is complete. All that's left is to put the values you just defined to work in your app. Select the `HPViewController.h` file and add this constant:

```
#define kPreferenceLocationsInCloud @"HPSyncLocations"
```

Switch to your HPViewController.m file, locate the -viewDidLoad method, and add the following conditional to your cloud store setup code (new code in bold):

```
if ([userDefaults boolForKey:kPreferenceLocationsInCloud])
    {
    cloudStore = [NSUbiquitousKeyValueStore defaultStore];
    NSNotificationCenter *center = [NSNotificationCenter defaultCenter];
    [center addObserver:self
        selector:@selector(cloudStoreChanged:)
            name:NSUbiquitousKeyValueStoreDidChangeExternallyNotification
        object:cloudStore];
    [cloudStore synchronize];
    }
```

That's it! If you're saying "but what about all of those places in the code that store values into cloudStore," you don't have to worry about those. Your existing code takes advantage of an Objective-C feature that ignores messages sent to nil objects. If the kPreferencesLocationsInCloud value is NO, cloudStore never gets set and remains nil. Messages sent to nil, like [cloudStore removeObjectForKey:kPreferenceSavedLocation], do nothing. The net effect is that, with cloudStore set to nil, Pigeon doesn't make any changes to iCloud's ubiquitous key-value store, and it won't receive any notifications of changes. For a complete explanation, see the "nil is Your Friend" section in Chapter 20.

Testing Your Settings Bundle

Run Pigeon, as shown in Figure 18-8. If you still have two iOS devices connected, you can verify that your app is no longer saving the map location to the cloud. Each app is functioning independently of the other.

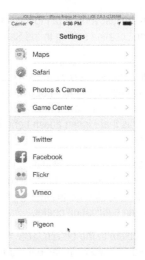

Figure 18-8. Testing the settings bundle

In Xcode, stop your app(s). This will return you to the springboard (second screen shot in Figure 18-8). Locate your Settings app and launch it. Scroll down until you find the Pigeon app (third screen shot in Figure 18-8). Tap it, and you'll see the settings you defined (on the right in Figure 18-8).

Change your `Sync Locations` setting to on—do this in both devices—and run your apps again. This time, Pigeon uses iCloud synchronization to share the map location.

Summary

Pigeon can no longer be accused of being a bird-brained app! Not only will it remember the location the user saved, but also the map style and tracking mode they last set. In doing this, you learned how to store property list values into the user defaults, how to convert non-property list objects into ones suitable to store, and how to get them back out again. More importantly, you understand the best times to store and retrieve those values.

You learned how to handle the situation where a user defaults value is missing, and how to create and register a set of default values. You also used user defaults to preserve the view controller states, which gives your app a sense of persistence. You did this by leveraging the powerful view controller restoration facility, built into iOS.

You also took flight into the clouds, sharing and synchronizing changes using the iCloud storage service. iCloud integration adds a compelling dimension to your app that anyone with more than one iOS device will appreciate. And if that wasn't enough, you defined settings the user can access outside of your app.

You've taken another important step in creating apps that act the way users expect. But it was a tiny step. User defaults, and particularly the ubiquitous key-value store, are only suitable for small amounts of information. To learn how to store "big data," step into the next chapter.

EXERCISE

You may have noticed a flaw in the last version of Pigeon—which I cleverly sidestepped by having you stop your app in Xcode before changing the Sync Location setting in the Settings app. Knowing what you now know about app states, the problem should be obvious.

Pigeon only examines the value of the `kPreferencesLocationsInCloud` value when it first starts. If a Pigeon user switches to the Settings app, changes the `Sync Location` setting, and then immediately returns to Pigeon, Pigeon is probably still running. It would have been moved the background state and suspended for a bit, but would be reactivated when the user returned. The bug is that Pigeon doesn't check the value of `kPreferencesLocationsInCloud` again, and won't know that it's changed.

There are a couple of ways of solving this. One would be to add code to the `-applicationWillEnterForeground:` app delegate method. The solution I picked was to observe the `NSUserDefaultsDidChangeNotification`, posted by `NSUserDefaults`. Remember that the values in a settings bundle make changes to your app's user defaults, and you can observe those changes via the notification center.

You'll find my solution to this problem in the `Learn iOS Development Projects` ➤ `Ch 18` ➤ `Pigeon E1` folder. See if you can think of a third—very similar, but more targeted—solution. (Hint, read the documentation for the `-applicationWillEnterForeground:` method.)

Chapter 19

Doc, You Meant Storage

If you want your iOS app to store more than a few tidbits of information, you need documents. iOS provides a powerful document framework that brings data storage into the 21st century. The iOS document (UIDocument) class takes care of, or lets you easily implement, modern features like auto-saving, versioning, and cloud storage. In the process, you'll finally learn how to archive objects. In this chapter you will:

- Create a custom document object
- Use a document object as your app's data model
- Learn how to archive and unarchive your data model objects
- Design a document that can be loaded or saved incrementally
- Handle asynchronous document loading
- Manage document changes and auto-saving

You'll find numerous "how-to" guides for using UIDocument because, quite frankly, it's a complicated class to use. There are a lot moving parts and more than a few details you must pay attention to. This has led many developers to ignore UIDocument and "roll their own" document storage solution. Don't do that. Conquering UIDocument isn't *that* hard, and the rewards are substantial.

UIDocument can seem overwhelming—until you understand *why* UIDocument works the way it does. Once you understand some of the reasoning behind its architecture, and what it's accomplishing for you, the code you need to write will all make sense. So in this chapter, you'll concentrate not on just the how, but the why. By the end, you'll be using UIDocument like a pro.

Document Overview

The word "document" has many meanings, but in this context a *document* is a data file (or package) containing user-generated content that your app opens, modifies, and ultimately saves to persistent storage. We're all used to documents on desktop computer systems. In mobile devices, the concept of a document takes a backseat, but it's still there, and in much the same form. In a few apps, like the Pages word processing app, the familiar document metaphor appears front and center; you launch the app, see a collection of your named documents, choose one to work on, the document opens, and you being typing. In other apps, it's not as clear that you're using individual documents, and some apps hide the mechanics of documents entirely. You can choose any of these approaches for your app. iOS provides the tools needed for whatever interface you want, but it doesn't dictate one.

This flexibility lets you add document storage and management to your app completely behind the scenes, loosely coupled to your user interface, or echoing the legacy document metaphor of desktop computer systems. Whatever you decide to do with your interface, the place to start is the UIDocument class. Here are the basic steps to using UIDocument in your app:

- Create a custom subclass of UIDocument
- Design an interface for choosing, naming, and sharing documents (optional)
- Convert your app's data model to, and from, data that's suitable for permanent storage
- Handle asynchronous reading of documents
- Move documents into the cloud (optional)
- Observe change notifications from shared documents and handle conflicts (optional)
- Implement undo/redo capabilities, or at least track changes to a document

You're going to revisit the MyStuff app and modify it so it stores all of those cool items, their descriptions, and even their pictures, in a document. There are no interface changes to MyStuff this time. The only thing your users will notice is that their stuff is still there when they relaunch your app!

Where, Oh Where, Do My Documents Go?

So where do you store documents in iOS? Here's the short answer: Store your documents in your app's private Documents folder, and optionally in the cloud.

The long answer is that you can store your documents anywhere your app has access to, but the only place that makes much sense is your app's private Documents folder. Each iOS app has access to a cluster of private folders called its *sandbox*. The Documents folder is one of these and is reserved, by iOS, for your app's documents. The contents of this folder are automatically backed up by iTunes. If you also want to exchange documents through iTunes, your documents must be stored in the Documents folder.

This is somewhat different than what you're used to on most desktop computer systems, where apps will let you load and save documents to any location and your Documents folder is freely shared by all of your apps. In iOS, an app only has access to the files in its sandbox and these directories are inaccessible to the user—unless you deliberately expose the Documents folder to iTunes—or other apps.

> **Note** If you're interested in what the other folders in the sandbox are, and what they're used for, read the section "About the iOS File System" in the *File System Programming Guide*, which you can find in Xcode's Documentation and API Reference window.

For MyStuff, you're going to store a single document in the Documents folder. You won't, however, provide any user interface for this document. The document will be automatically opened when the app starts, and any changes made by the user will be automatically saved there. Even though you'll be using the standard document classes, and storing your data in the Documents folder, the entire process will be invisible to the user.

That's not to say that you can't, or shouldn't, provide an interface that lets your users see what documents are in their Documents folder. A typical interface would display the document names, possibly a preview, and allow the user to open, rename, and delete them. You could do that in a table view, a collection view, or even using a page view controller. If document manipulation makes sense for your app, create the interface that presents your documents in their best light.

Where you'll save your document seems like a great place to start. You'll begin by creating a custom subclass of UIDocument and defining where and how your document gets stored.

MyStuff on Documents

Pick up with the version of MyStuff at the end of Chapter 7, where you added an image for each item. In the project navigator, choose **New ➤ File…**, from either the **File** menu or by right/control-clicking in the navigator. Use the Objective-C class template, name the new class MSThingsDocument, and make is a subclass of UIDocument. Add it to the project.

Declare two class methods in MSThingsDocument.h interface file (new code in bold):

```
@interface MSThingsDocument : UIDocument
+ (NSURL*)documentURL;
+ (MSThingsDocument*)documentAtURL:(NSURL*)url;
@end
```

Switch to the MSThingsDocument.m implementation file. Add these constant definition after the #import statements:

```
#define kThingsDocumentType     @"mystuff"
#define kThingsDocumentName     (@"Things I Own." kThingsDocumentType)
```

Add the first method to the @implementation section:

```
+ (NSURL*)documentURL
{
    static NSURL *docURL = nil;
    if (docURL==nil)
        {
        NSFileManager *fileManager = [NSFileManager defaultManager];
        docURL = [fileManager URLForDirectory:NSDocumentDirectory
```

```
                                inDomain:NSUserDomainMask
                       appropriateForURL:nil
                                  create:YES
                                   error:NULL];
        docURL = [docURL URLByAppendingPathComponent:kThingsDocumentName];
        }
    return docURL;
}
```

The +documentURL method returns an NSURL object with the filesystem location of the one and only document used by your MyStuff app. There's a little code in there so the location is only constructed once, because it never changes.

The important method here is the -URLForDirectory:inDomain:appropriateForURL:create:error: method. This is one of a handful of methods used to locate key iOS directories, like the Documents directory in your app's sandbox. The NSDocumentDirectory constant tells which one—of the half-dozen or so designated directories—you're interested in. To locate directories in your app's sandbox, specify the NSUserDomainMask. The create flag tells the file manager to create the directory if it doesn't already exist. This was gratuitous, because the Documents directory is created when your app is installed and should always exist.

> **Caution**   Do not "hard code" paths to standard iOS directories, using constants like @"~/Documents/". Use methods like -URLsForDirectory:inDomain: to determine the path of well-known directories. The standard directory locations change from time to time; don't make assumptions about their names or paths.

Once you have the URL of your Documents folder, append the document's name, creating a complete path to where your document is, or will be, stored.

Now write a method to open your document. MyStuff isn't going to present a document interface. When it starts, it either creates an empty document or re-opened the existing document. Consolidate that logic into a method, immediately after the +documentURL method:

```
+ (MSThingsDocument*)documentAtURL:(NSURL *)url
{
    MSThingsDocument *document;
    document = [[MSThingsDocument alloc] initWithFileURL:url];

    NSFileManager *fileManager = [NSFileManager defaultManager];
    if ([fileManager fileExistsAtPath:url.path])
        {
        [document openWithCompletionHandler:nil];
        }
```

```
    else
        {
        [document saveToURL:url
            forSaveOperation:UIDocumentSaveForCreating
          completionHandler:nil];
        }

    return document;
}
```

This method creates a new instance of your `MSThingsDocument` object at the given (file) URL. It then uses the file manager to determine if a document at that location already exists (`-fileExistsAtPath:`). If it does, it sends the document object an `-openWithCompletionHandler:` message to open the document and read the data it contains. If it doesn't exist, one is created by sending the `-saveToURL:forSaveOperation:completionHandler:` message. The opened document object is then returned to the sender.

> **Tip** The name of MyStuff's document is irrelevant, because no one (except its developer) will ever see it. If, however, you do want your users to have access to the documents your app's `Documents` folder, all you have to do is add the `UIFileSharingEnabled` key (with a value of YES) to your app's `info.plist`. This flag tells iTunes to expose the documents stored in the `Documents` folder to the user. Through iTunes, the user can browse, download, upload, and delete documents in that folder. See the "App-Related Resources" chapter of the *iOS App Programming Guide*. Also check out *Technical Q&A #1699* (QA1699). It describes how to selectively share some documents through iTunes, while keeping other documents hidden.

Supplying Your Document's Data

In your subclass of `UIDocument`, you are required to override two methods: `-contentsForType:error:` and `-loadFromContents:ofType:error:`. These two methods translate your app's data model objects into a form that `UIDocument` can save, and later converts that saved data back into the data model objects your app needs.

This is also where implementing `UIDocument` gets interesting. The key is to understand what `UIDocument` is doing for you, and what `UIDocument` expects from `-contentsForType:error:` and `-loadFromContents:ofType:error:`. There's a strict division of responsibilities:

- `UIDocument` implements the actual storage and retrieval of your document's data
- `-contentsForType:error:` and `-loadFromContents:ofType:error:` provide the translation between your data model objects and a serialized version of that same information

`UIDocument` might be storing your document on a filesystem. It might be storing your document in the cloud. It might be transferring your document over a USB connection. Someday it might store your document on a wireless electronic wallet you carry around on a key fob. I don't know, and you shouldn't care. Let `UIDocument` worry about where and how your document's data gets stored.

When `UIDocument` wants to save your document, it sends the `-contentsForType:error:` message. Your implementation should convert your data model objects into data suitable for storage. `UIDocument` takes the returned data and stores it on the filesystem, in the cloud, or wherever.

When it's time to read the document, `UIDocument` reverses the process. It first reacquires the data (from wherever it was saved) and passes that to `-loadFromContents:ofType:error:`, which has the job of turning it back into the data model objects of your app.

The $64,000 question is "how do you convert your data model objects into bytes that `UIDocument` can store?" That is a fantastic question, and the answer will range from stunningly simple to treacherously complex. Broadly, you have four options:

- Serialize everything into a single `NSData` object
- Describe a multi-part document using file wrapper objects
- Back your document with Core Data
- Implement your own storage solution

The first solution is the simplest, and suitable for the majority of document types. Using string encoding, property list serialization, or object archiving (which you'll learn shortly) convert your data model object(s) into a single array of bytes. Your `-contentsForType:error:` method then returns those bytes as an `NSData` object that `UIDocument` stores somewhere. Later, `UIDocument` retrieves that data and passes it to your `-loadFromContents:ofType:error:` method, which unarchives/deserializes/decodes it back into the original object(s). If this describes your app's needs, then congratulations—you're pretty much done with this part of your `UIDocument` implementation!

Your MyStuff app is a little more complicated. It's cumbersome to convert all of the app's data—descriptions and images—into a single stream of bytes. Images are big and time consuming to encode. Not only will it take a long time to save the document, the entire document will have to be read into memory and converted back into image objects before the user can use the app. No one wants to wait tens of seconds, and certainly not minutes, to open an app!

> **Note** The situation is more dire than just annoying your users. If you tried to encode and compress several dozen images when the document was saved, it would probably take so long that iOS would assume your app had "locked up" and will forcibly terminate it. Your app will have appeared to crash and the document would never get saved.

The solution MyStuff will employ is to archive the descriptions of the items (much like the first solution) into a single `NSData` object, but store the images in individual files inside a package. A *package* is a directory containing multiple files that appears, and acts, like a single file to the user. All iOS and OS X apps are packages, for example.

Wrapping Up Your Data

You might be seeing the glimmer of a conundrum. Or, maybe you don't. Don't worry if you missed it, because it's a really subtle problem. The concept behind -contentsForType:error: is that it returns the raw data that represents your document—just the data. The code in -contentsForType:error: can't know how that data gets stored, nor does it do the storing. Creating a design that states "images will be stored in individual files" is a non-starter, because -contentsForType:error: doesn't deal with files. The document might end up being stored in something that doesn't even resemble a file. It might get put into the records of a database, or become a tag in an XML file.

So how does -contentsForType:error: return an object that describes not one, but a collection of, individual data blobs,[1] one of which contains the archived objects and others that contain individual image data? Well it just so happens that iOS provides a tool for this very purpose. It's called a file wrapper, and it brings us to the second method for providing document data.

A *file wrapper* (NSFileWrapper) object is an abstraction of the data stored in one or more files. There are three types of file wrappers: regular, directory, and link. Conceptually, these are equivalent to a single data file, a filesystem directory, and a filesystem symbolic link, respectively. File wrappers allow your app to describe a collection of named data blobs, organized within a hierarchy of named directories. If this sounds just like files and folders, it should. And when your UIDocument is stored in a file URL, that's exactly what these file wrappers will become. But by maintaining this abstraction, UIDocument can just as easily transfer this data collection over a network or convert the wrappers into the records of a database.

Using Wrappers

Using file wrappers isn't terribly difficult. A *regular file wrapper* represents an array of bytes, like NSData. A *directory file wrapper* (or just *directory wrapper*) contains any number of other file wrappers. One significant difference between wrappers and files/folders is that a wrapper has a preferred name and a key. Its *key* is the string that uniquely identifies the wrapper, just as a filename uniquely identifies a file. Its *preferred name* is the string it would like to be identified as. If the preferred name of a wrapper is unique, its key and preferred name will be the same. If, however, you add two or more wrappers with identical preferred names to a directory wrapper, the directory wrapper will generate unique keys for the duplicates. In other words, it's valid to add multiple wrappers with the same name to the same directory wrapper. One side effect is that adding a wrapper with the same name as an existing wrapper doesn't replace, or overwrite, an existing wrapper, as it would on a filesystem.

Your -contentsForType:error: method will create a single directory wrapper that contains all of the other regular file wrappers. There will be one regular file wrapper with the archived version of your data model objects. Each item that has a picture will store its image as another file wrapper. You'll modify MyWhatsit to store the image in the document when the user adds a picture, and get the image from the document when it needs it again.

---

[1]Blob is actually a database term meaning Binary Large Object, sometimes written BLOb.

Incremental Document Updates

Organizing your document into wrappers confers a notable feature to your app: incremental document loading and updates. If your user has added 100 items to your MyStuff app, your document package (when saved to a filesystem) will consist of folding containing 101 files: one archive file and 100 image files. If the user replaces the picture of their astrolabe with a better one, only a single file wrapper will be updated. UIDocument understands this. When it's time to save the document again, UIDocument will only re-write that single file in the package. This makes for terribly fast, and efficient, updates to large documents. These are good qualities for your app.

Similarly, file wrapper data isn't read until it's requested. When you open a UIDocument constructed from file wrappers, the data for each individual wrapper stays where it is until your app wants it. For your images, that means your app doesn't have to read all 100 images files when it starts. It can lazily retrieve just the images it needs at that moment. Again, this means your app can get started quickly and does the minimum work required to display your interface.

Constructing Your Wrappers

Select the MSThingsDocument.m implementation file. Just before the @implementation section, define two more constants and add a private @interface section that declares two instance variables:

```
#define kThingsPreferredName    @"things.data"
#define kImagePreferredName     @"image.png"

@interface MSThingsDocument ()
{
    NSFileWrapper   *docWrapper;
    NSMutableArray  *things;
}
@end
```

The two constants define the preferred wrapper names for the archived MyWhatsit objects and any image added to the directory wrapper. The docWrapper instance variable is the single directory wrapper that will contain all of your other wrappers. For all intents and purposes, docWrapper is your document's data. The things variable is the array of MyWhatsit objects that constitute your data model.

> **Note** Later on, you'll replace the things array in MSMasterViewController with your new MSThingsDocument. The document object will become the data model for your view controller.

Now add the -contentsForType:error: method to the @implementation section:

```
- (id)contentsForType:(NSString *)typeName
            error:(NSError *__autoreleasing *)outError
{
    if (docWrapper==nil)
        docWrapper = [[NSFileWrapper alloc] initDirectoryWithFileWrappers:nil];
```

```
    if (things==nil)
        things = [NSMutableArray array];

    NSFileWrapper *wrapper = docWrapper.fileWrappers[kThingsPreferredName];
    if (wrapper!=nil)
        [docWrapper removeFileWrapper:wrapper];

    NSData *thingsData = [NSKeyedArchiver archivedDataWithRootObject:things];
    [docWrapper addRegularFileWithContents:thingsData
                         preferredFilename:kThingsPreferredName];

    return docWrapper;
}
```

This message is received when UIDocument wants to create or save the document. If the document doesn't exist yet, docWrapper and things will be nil. In this circumstance, the code creates an empty directory wrapper and stores it in docWrapper. It also creates a new, empty, things array, which will become the data model for the app.

The rest of the method assembles all of the data UIDocument will need to store the document. It checks to see if the docWrapper already contains a wrapper named things.data. This is the wrapper that contains the archived version of your data model objects. There should only be one of these, so if it already exists, it's first removed from the directory wrapper. Remember that adding another wrapper with the same name won't replace an existing wrapper.

The last step is to archive (serialize) all of the MyWhatsit objects into a portable NSData object. I'll explain how that happens in the next section. The data is passed to the -addRegularFileWithContents:preferredFilename: method. This is a convenience method that creates a new regular file wrapper, containing the bytes in thingsData, and adds it to the directory wrapper with the preferred name. This method saves you from explicitly coding those steps.

You return the directory wrapper, containing all of the data in your document, to UIDocument. Now you might be asking, "But what about all of the image data? Where does that get created?" That's a really good question. Image data is represented by other regular file wrappers in the same directory wrapper. When the document is first created, there are no images, so the directory wrapper only contains things.data. As the user adds pictures to the data model, each image will add a new wrapper to docWrapper. When your document is saved again, the file wrappers containing the images are already in docWrapper! Each regular file wrapper knows if it has been altered or updated, and UIDocument is smart enough to figure out which files need to be written and which ones are already current.

Interpreting Your Wrappers

The reverse of the previous process occurs when your document is opened. UIDocument obtains that data saved in the document, and then sends the -loadFromContents:ofType:error: message. This method's job is to turn the document data back into your data model. Add this method immediately after your -contentsForType:error: method:

```
- (BOOL)loadFromContents:(id)contents
                  ofType:(NSString *)typeName
                   error:(NSError * __autoreleasing *)outError
```

```
{
    docWrapper = contents;
    NSFileWrapper *wrapper = docWrapper.fileWrappers[kThingsPreferredName];
    NSData *data = wrapper.regularFileContents;
    if (data!=nil)
        things = [NSKeyedUnarchiver unarchiveObjectWithData:data];
    return (things!=nil);
}
```

The contents parameter is the object that encapsulates your document's data. It's always going to be the same (class of) object you returned from -contentsForType:error:. If you adopted the first method and returned a single NSData object, the contents parameter will contain an NSData object—with the same data. Since MyStuff elected to use the file wrapper technique, contents is an equivalent directory wrapper object to the one you returned earlier.

The first step is to save contents in docWrapper; you'll need it, both to read image wrappers and to later save the document again. The rest of the method finds the things.data wrapper that contains the archived MyWhatsit object array. It immediately retrieves the data stored in that wrapper and unarchives it, recreating the data model objects.

The -loadFromContents:ofType:error: method must return YES if it was successful, and NO if there were problems interpreting the document data. If the wrapper contained a things.data wrapper, and the data in that wrapper was successfully converted back into an array of MyWhatsit objects, the method assumes the document is valid and returns YES.

This, almost, concludes the work needed to save, and later open, your new document. There's one glaring hole: the array of MyWhatsit objects can't be archived! Let's fix that now.

OTHER STORAGE ALTERNATIVES

The last two document storage solutions available to you are Core Data and DIY (Do It Yourself). DIY is one I rarely find appealing. It should be your last resort, because you'll be forced to deal with all of the tasks, both mundane and exceptional, that UIDocument normally handles for you. My advice is work very hard to make one of the first three solutions work. If that fails, you can perform your own document storage handling. Consult the "Advanced Overrides" section of UIDocument's documentation.

One of the most interesting document solutions is Core Data. iOS includes a fast and efficient relational database engine (SQLite) with language-level support. Core Data is far beyond the scope of this book, but it's an incredibly powerful tool if your app's data fits better into a database than a text file. (It's a shame I don't have enough pages, because MyStuff would have made a perfect Core Data app.)

One of the huge advantages of using Core Data is that document management is essentially done for you. You don't have to do much beyond using the UIManagedDocument class (a subclass of UIDocument). Many of the features in this chapter that you will write code to support—incremental document updating, lazy document loading, archiving and unarchiving of your data model objects, background document loading and saving, cloud synchronization, and so on—are all provided "for free" by UIManagedDocument.

The prerequisite, of course, is that you must first base your app on Core Data. Your data model objects must be NSManagedObjects, you must design a schema for your database, and you have to understand the ins and outs of Object-Oriented Database (OODB) technology. But beyond that (!), it's child's play.

Archiving Objects

In Chapter 18 you learned all about serialization. Serialization turns a graph of property list objects into a stream of bytes (either in XML or binary format) that can be stored in files, exchanged with other processes, transmitted to other computer systems, and so on. On the receiving end, those bytes are turned back into an equivalent set of property list objects, ready to be used.

Archiving is serialization's big sister. *Archiving* serializes (the computer science term) a graph of objects that all adopt the NSCoding protocol. This is a much larger set of objects than the property-list objects.[2] More importantly, you can adopt the NSCoding protocol in classes you develop. Your custom objects can then be archived right along with other objects. This is exactly what needs to happen to your MyWhatsit class.

Adopting NSCoding

The first step to archiving a graph of objects is to make sure that every object adopts the NSCoding protocol. If one doesn't, you either need to eliminate it from the graph or change it so it does. In MyWhatsit.h, change the @interface declaration so it adopts NSCoding (new code in bold):

```
@interface MyWhatsit : NSObject <NSCoding>
```

The NSCoding protocol requires a class to implement two methods: -initWithCoder: and -encodeWithCoder:. The first "init" method reconstructs an object from data that was previously archived. The second creates the archive data from the existing object. Both of these processes work through an NSCoder object. The NSCoder object does the work of serializing (encoding), and later deserializing (decoding), your object's properties.

The coder identifies each property value of your object using a key. Define those keys now by adding these declarations before the @implementation section in your MyWhatsit.m file:

```
#define kNameCoderKey       @"name"
#define kLocationCoderKey   @"location"
```

Now you can add the two required methods to the @implementation section:

```
- (id)initWithCoder:(NSCoder *)decoder
{
    self = [super init];
    if (self!=nil)
        {
        _name =     [decoder decodeObjectForKey:kNameCoderKey];
        _location = [decoder decodeObjectForKey:kLocationCoderKey];
        }
    return self;
}
```

---

[2]All property list objects adopt NSCoding. Property list objects are, therefore, a subset of the archivable objects.

The -initWithCoder: method follows the typical pattern for an "init" method. But instead of initializing the new object's properties with default values, or from parameters, it retrieves the previously archived values from the coder object. In this case, both of the values are (NSString) objects. Coder objects can also directly encode integer, floating-point, Boolean, and other C primitive types. UIKit adds categories to NSCoder to encode point, rectangle, size, affine transforms, and similar data structures.

```
- (void)encodeWithCoder:(NSCoder *)coder
{
    [coder encodeObject:_name       forKey:kNameCoderKey];
    [coder encodeObject:_location   forKey:kLocationCoderKey];
}
```

Translation in the other direction is provided by your -encodeWithCoder: method. This method preserves the current values of its persistent properties in the coder object. Your MyWhatsit objects are now ready to participate in the archiving process.

SUBCLASSING AN <NSCODING> CLASS

When you subclass a class that already adopts NSCoding, you do things a little differently. Your -initWithCoder: method will look like this:

```
- (id)initWithCoder:(NSCoder *)decoder
{
    self = [super initWithCoder:decoder];
    if (self!=nil)
        {
        ... perform subclass decoding here ...
        }
    return self;
}
```

And your -encodeWithCoder: method should look like this:

```
- (void)encodeWithCoder:(NSCoder *)coder
{
    [super encodeWithCoder:coder];
    ... perform subclass encoding here ...
}
```

Your super class already encodes and decodes its properties. Your subclass must allow the superclass to do that, and then encode and decode any additional properties defined in the subclass.

Archiving and Unarchiving Objects

When you want to flatten your objects into bytes, use code like this:

```
NSData *data = [NSKeyedArchiver archivedDataWithRootObject:things];
```

The NSKeyedArchiver class is the archiving engine. It creates an NSCoder object and then proceeds to send the root object (things) an -encodeWithCoder: message. That object is responsible for preserving its content in the coder object. Most likely, it will send the coder object -encodeObject:forKey: messages for the objects it refers to. Those objects receive an -encodeWithCoder: message, and the process repeats until all of the objects have been encoded. The only limitation is that every object must adopt NSCoding.

When you want your objects back again, you use the NSKeyedUnarchiver class, like this:

```
things = [NSKeyedUnarchiver unarchiveObjectWithData:data];
```

During the encoding process, the coder recorded the class of each object. The decoder then uses that information to create new objects and sends each one an -initWithCoder: message. The resulting object is the same class, and has the same property values, as the originally encoded object.

> **Note** The predecessor to keyed archiving was *sequential archiving*. You may occasionally see references to sequential archiving, but it is not used in iOS.

The Archiving Serialization Smackdown

Now that you've added both serialization (property lists) and archiving (NSCoding objects) to your repertoire, I'd like to take a moment to compare and contrast the two. Table 19-1 summarizes their major features.

Table 19-1. Serialization vs. Archiving

Feature	Serialization	Archiving
Object Graph	Property list objects only	Objects that adopt NSCoding
XML?	Yes	No
Portability	Cocoa or Cocoa Touch apps, or any system that can parse the XML version	Only another process that includes all of the original classes
Editors?	Yes	No

Property lists are much more limited in what you can store in them, but make up for that in the number of ways you can store, share, and edit them. Use property lists when your values need to be understood by other processes, particularly processes that don't include your custom classes. An example is the settings bundle you created in Chapter 18. The Settings app will never include any of your custom Objective-C classes, yet you were able to define, exchange, and incorporated those settings into your app using property lists. Property lists are the "universal" language of values.

Archiving, by contrast, can encode a vast number of classes and you can add your own classes to that roster by adopting the `NSCoding` protocol. Everything you create in Interface Builder is encoded using keyed archiving. When you load an Interface Builder file in your application, `NSKeyedUnarchiver` is busy translating that file back into the objects you defined. Archiving is extremely flexible, and has long reach, which is why it's the technology of choice for storing your data model objects in a document.

So why don't we use archiving for everything? When unarchiving, every class recorded in the archive must exist. So forget about trying to read your `MyStuff` document using another app or program that doesn't include your `MyWhatsit` code—you can't do it. Archives are, for the most part, opaque. There are no general purposes editors for archives, like there are for property lists. There is no facility for turning archive data into XML documents. Interface Builder is the closest thing to an archive editor there is, but it's a one-way trip; you edit your interface and compile it into an archive, but you can't open a compiled archive file and edit it.

Serialization, Meet Archiving

Now that you have a feel for the benefits and limitations of archiving and serialization, I'm going to show you a really handy trick for combining the two. (You may have already figured this out, but you could at least pretend to be surprised.) `NSData` is a property list object. The result of archiving a graph of `NSCoding` objects is an `NSData` object. Do you see where this is going?

By first archiving your objects into an `NSData` object, you can store non-property list objects in a property list, like user defaults! Your code would look like this:

```
NSUserDefaults *userDefaults = [NSUserDefaults standardUserDefaults]
NSData *data = [NSKeyedArchiver archivedDataWithRootObject:dataModel];
[userDefaults setObject:data forKey:@"data_model"];
```

What you've done is archive your data model objects into an `NSData` object, which can be stored in a property list. To retrieve them again, reverse the process:

```
NSData *modelData = [userDefaults objectForKey:@"data_model"];
dataModel = [NSKeyedUnarchiver unarchiveObjectWithData:modelData];
```

The disadvantages of this technique are the same ones that apply to archiving in general. The process retrieving the objects must to be able to unarchive them. Also, any editors or other programs that examine your property values will just see a blob of data. Contrast this to the technique you used in Pigeon to convert the `MKAnnotation` object into a dictionary. Those property list values (the location's name, longitude, and latitude) are easily interpreted, and could even be edited, by another program.

> **Caution** Don't go crazy with this technique. Services like `NSUserDefaults` and `NSUbiquitousKeyValueStore` are designed to store *small* morsels of information. Don't abuse them by storing multi-megabyte sized `NSData` objects that you've created using the archiver.

I think that's enough about archiving and property lists. It's time to get back to the business of getting MyStuff documentified.

Document, Your Data Model

Where were we? Oh, that's right, you created a `UIDocument` class and wrote all of the code needed to translate your data model objects into document data and back again. The next step is to make your `MSThingsDocument` object the data model for `MSMasterViewController`.

> **Note** In a "big" app, you'd probably create a custom data model class that was separate from your `UIDocument` class. In MVC-speak, you'd have a *data model* and a *data model controller* (the document object). Both the document and the view controller would connect to the data model object. For MyStuff, I'm having you combine the data model and document into a single class. It simplifies the design and reduces the amount of code you have to write. It won't hurt the design, but you should know where your MVC lines are drawn.

Your current `MSMasterViewController` is using an `NSArray` as its data model object. The array object provides a number of methods that the view controller is using. This includes counting the number of objects in the array, along with adding, removing, and locating objects in the array. `UIDocument` doesn't have any of these methods—because it's not a data model. Turn it into a data model by replicating the functions the view controller needs. Select `MSThingsDocument.h` and add these methods to its `@interface` section (new code in bold):

```
@class MyWhatsit;

@interface MSThingsDocument : UIDocument

+ (NSURL*)documentURL;
+ (MSThingsDocument*)documentAtURL:(NSURL*)url;

@property (readonly) NSUInteger whatsitCount;
- (MyWhatsit*)whatsitAtIndex:(NSUInteger)index;
- (NSUInteger)indexOfWhatsit:(MyWhatsit*)object;
- (void)removeWhatsitAtIndex:(NSUInteger)index;
- (MyWhatsit*)anotherWhatsit;

@end
```

Switch to the `MSThingsDocument.m` implementation file. Add another `#import` directive to get the `MyWhatsit` class definition:

```
#import "MyWhatsit.h"
```

Now add the code for the data model methods to the `@implementation` section:

```
- (NSUInteger)whatsitCount
{
    return things.count;
}

- (MyWhatsit*)whatsitAtIndex:(NSUInteger)index
{
    return things[index];
}

- (NSUInteger)indexOfWhatsit:(MyWhatsit*)object
{
    return [things indexOfObject:object];
}

- (void)removeWhatsitAtIndex:(NSUInteger)index
{
    [things removeObjectAtIndex:index];
}

- (MyWhatsit*)anotherWhatsit
{
    MyWhatsit *newItem = [MyWhatsit new];
    newItem.name = [NSString stringWithFormat:@"My Item %u",self.whatsitCount+1];
    [things addObject:newItem];
    return newItem;
}
```

The purpose of these methods should be obvious. The view controller will now send these messages to your document object to count the number of items, get the item at a specific index, discover the index of an existing item, remove an item, or create a new item. The next step is to make these changes in the view controller. Select your `MSMasterViewController.h` file and add this `#import` statement:

```
#import "MSThingsDocument.h"
```

Select your `MSMasterViewController.m` file in the project navigator. Find the private `@interface` section and replace the old things array with your document object (new code in bold):

```
@interface MSMasterViewController () {
    MSThingsDocument *document;
}
```

Your document object is now your data model. Now you need to go through your view controller code and replace every reference to the old `things` array with equivalent code for your document.

> **Tip** Your file is now awash with compiler errors. Isn't that great? I use this technique all the time. When I need to redefine, or repurpose, a property value, I deliberately change the name of the property/variable—if only temporarily. The compiler will immediately flag all references to the old name as an error. This becomes my roadmap to where I need to make my changes. If I liked the original property name, I'll use the refactor tool to rename it back, once everything is working.

You'll also be removing the code that created the fake items for testing and replacing that with code to load your data model from the document. Start in the `-awakeFromNib` method. Delete the code that filled the `things` array with items. You don't need that anymore, because MyStuff will fill the data model from the contents of the document. Find the `-viewDidLoad` method and add this statement to the end of the method:

```
document = [MSThingsDocument documentAtURL:[MSThingsDocument documentURL]];
```

You should remember these methods from the beginning of the chapter. This statement requests a new `MSThingsDocument` object with the contents of the document at `[MSThingsDocument documentURL]`, which is the fixed document in your app's Documents folder. That's it. Your document object is created, and loaded, in a single statement.

The rest of the work is mostly replacing code that used `things` with code that will use `document`. Find the `-insertNewObject:` method and change it so it reads (modified code in bold):

```
- (void)insertNewObject:(id)sender
{
    MyWhatsit *newItem = [document anotherWhatsit];
    NSUInteger newIndex = [document indexOfWhatsit:newItem];
    NSIndexPath *indexPath = [NSIndexPath indexPathForRow:newIndex
                                                inSection:0];
    [self.tableView insertRowsAtIndexPaths:@[indexPath]
                          withRowAnimation:UITableViewRowAnimationAutomatic];
}
```

This is the biggest change. The document object now takes care of creating a new `MyWhatsit` object—you'll understand why when you work on the code for `MyWhatsit` images. The code is also modified to ask `document` where in the array it added the new item, rather than assuming that it inserted at the beginning of the array. This is a smart change, because the `-anotherWhatsit` method actually inserts new items at the end of the array. And if you ever altered that again, this code would still work.

The rest of the changes are so mundane that I've summarized them below. (Hint: follow the trail of compiler errors and replace the `things` statements with equivalent `document` statements.)

- In -tableView:numberOfRowsInSection:

  things.count becomes document.whatsitCount

- In -tableView:cellForRowAtIndexPath:, -tableView:didSelectRowAtIndexPath:, and -prepareForSeque:

  things[indexPath.row] becomes [document whatsitAtIndex:indexPath.row]

- In -tableView:commitEditingStyle:forRowAtIndexPath:

  [things removeObjectAtIndex:indexPath.row] becomes [document removeWhatsitAtIndex:indexPath.row]

- In -whatsitDidChangeNotification:

  [things indexOfObject:notification.object] becomes [document indexOfWhatsit:notification.object]

Your MSThingsDocument object is now your app's data model. This is an important step. It's not important that you combined the document and data model into a single object, but it is important that you've encapsulated all of the changes to the data model—counting, getting, removing, and creating items—behind your own methods, rather than simply using NSArray methods. You'll see why shortly.

You might think that you've written enough code that your app would be able to store its MyWhatsit objects (at least the name and location bits) in your document and retrieve them again. But there are still a few small pieces missing.

Tracking Changes

One thing you haven't written is any code to save your document. You've written code to convert your data model objects into something that can be saved, but you've never asked the UIDocument object to use it.

And you won't.

At least, that's not the ideal technique. UIDocument embraces the *auto-save document model*, where the user's document is periodically saved to persistent storage while they work, and again automatically before your app quits. This is the preferred document-saving model for iOS apps.

For auto-saving to work, your code must notify the document that changes have been made. UIDocument then schedules and performs the saving of the new data in the background. There are two ways to communicate changes to your document: send it an -updateChangeCount: message or use the document's NSUndoManager object. As you register changes with the NSUndoManager, it will automatically notify its document object of those changes.

> **Note** The alternative to using an undo manager and auto-saving is to explicitly save the document by sending it a -saveToURL:forSaveOperation:completionHandler: message (or one of the closely related methods). This would imply an interface that works more like traditional desktop applications, where the user deliberately saves their document.

You're not going to embrace NSUndoManager for this app—although it's a great feature to consider, and not at all difficult to use. Consequently, you'll need to send your document object an -updateChangeCount: message whenever something changes. UIDocument will take it from there.

So when does your data model change? One obvious place is whenever items are added or removed. Select the MSThingsDocument.m implementation file. Locate the -removeWhatistAtIndex: and -anotherWhatsit methods. At the end of -removeWhatistAtIndex:, and again just before the return statement in -anotherWhatsit, add the following statement:

```
[self updateChangeCount:UIDocumentChangeDone];
```

This message tells the document object that its content was changed. There are other kinds of changes (changes due to an undo or redo action, for example), but unless you've created your own undo manager, this is the only constant you need to send.

The other place that the document changes is when the user edits an individual item. You already solved that problem way back in Chapter 4! Whenever a MyWhatsit object is edited, your object posts a MyWhatsitDidChange notification. All your document needs to do is observe that notification.

Back at the top of MSThingsDocument.m, declare a new method to the private @interface MSThingsDocument () section:

```
- (void)whatsitDidChange:(NSNotification*)notification;
```

In your +documentAtURL: method, observe this notification by adding this code immediately before the return statement:

```
NSNotificationCenter *center = [NSNotificationCenter defaultCenter];
[center addObserver:document
           selector:@selector(whatsitDidChange:)
               name:kWhatsitDidChangeNotification
             object:nil];
```

For objects, like UIDocument, that can be destroyed before the app quits, remember that you must remove the object from the notification center before it is destroyed. Do this by adding a -dealloc method to the class:

```
- (void)dealloc
{
    [[NSNotificationCenter defaultCenter] removeObserver:self];
}
```

Finally, add the new notification handler method:

```
- (void)whatsitDidChange:(NSNotification *)notification
{
    if ([self indexOfWhatsit:notification.object]!=NSNotFound)
        [self updateChangeCount:UIDocumentChangeDone];
}
```

Its only purpose is to notify the document that a `MyWhatsit` object in this document has changed, and that's what it does.

Testing Your Document

Surely, you've written enough code by now to see your document in action. Run your app, either in the simulator or in a provisioned device. It contains nothing when first launched, as shown in Figure 19-1. Enter the details for a couple of items.

Figure 19-1. Testing document storage

Now either wait about 20 seconds or press the home button to push the app into the background state. When you created a new item, the document was notified of the change. The auto-save feature of `UIDocument` periodically saves the document when the user isn't doing anything else, and will immediately save it when your app is moved to the background state.

With your data safely saved in the document, stop the app and run it again from Xcode. You should be rewarded for all of your hard work with the list of items you entered earlier.

What you see, however, is an empty screen, shown on the right in Figure 19-1.

So what went wrong? Maybe your document isn't being opened when your app starts? Maybe it didn't get saved in the first place? What you do know is that you've got a bug; it's time to turn to the debugger.

Setting Breakpoints

Switch back to Xcode and set a breakpoint in your `-contentsForType:error:` by clicking in the gutter to the left of the code, as shown in Figure 19-2. A breakpoint appears as a blue tab.

CHAPTER 19: Doc, You Meant Storage

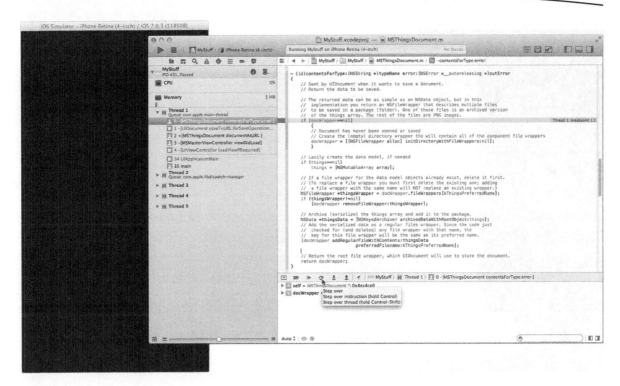

Figure 19-2. Setting a breakpoint in -contentsForType:error:

Uninstall your My Stuff app on your device or simulator. (Tap and hold the My Stuff app icon in the springboard until it starts to shake, tap the delete (x) button, agree to delete the app, and press the home button again.) This deletes your app and any data, including any documents, stored on the device. Run the app again. Xcode will reinstall the app and it will run with a fresh start.

Almost immediately, Xcode stops at the breakpoint in the -contentsForType:error: method, as shown in Figure 19-2. If you look at the stack trace on the left, you can see that the -contentsForType:error: message was sent from the +documentAtURL: method, which was sent from -viewDidLoad. Together, this tells you that -contentsForType:error: is being sent to create the initial, empty, document when no document exists.

Stepping Through Code and Examining Variables

Another way to verify this is to examine the value of the things array when the method executes. The things object is your data model. When the method is entered for the first time, you can see that the things variable is nil. You can examine its value either in the debugging pane (at the bottom of the window) or by hovering your cursor over a variable name, as shown in Figure 19-3.

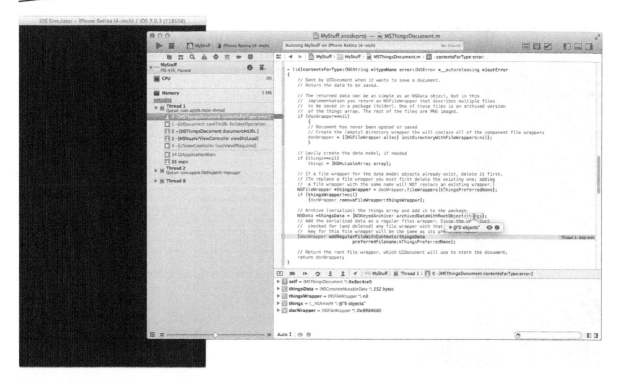

Figure 19-3. Stepping through -contentsForType:error:

Click on the Step Over button (See Figure 19-2) to execute one line of code. Continue stepping over lines, watching as the code compares the `things` variable to `nil` and then creates an empty array (replacing `nil` with `"0 objects"`), as shown in Figure 19-3.

> **Tip** **Step Over** executes a complete statement in your source code and stops when it finishes. **Step Into** executes one statement; if it's a function call or message in your app, it will move into that function or message and stop again. **Step Out** allows the remainder of a function or method to execute, stopping again when it returns to its sender.

To let your app run at full speed again, click the **Continue** button, just to the left of the **Step Over** button. Your app will resume full speed execution until it encounters another breakpoint. Back in your app, add an item or two and then pause. The auto-save mechanism will eventually kick in and send another -contentForType:error: message, and your app will again stop at the breakpoint. This time, the `things` array contains new `MyWhatsit` objects, as shown in Figure 19-4.

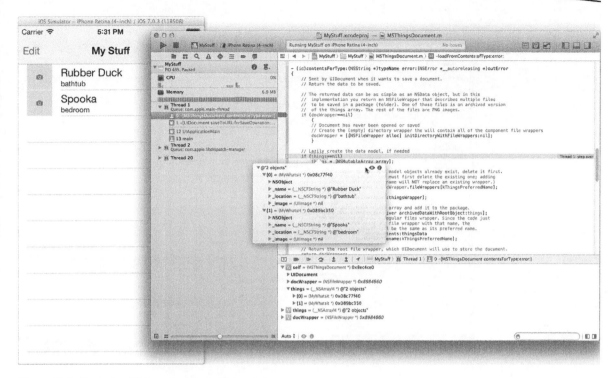

Figure 19-4. Contents of things array during second save

This confirms that your app is adding MyWhatsit objects to the things array, serializing it, and returning it to UIDocument for saving. The problem isn't that the document isn't being saved. So there must be a problem loading the document.

By the way, this is called the "divide and conquer" debugging technique. Decide what your code should be doing, set a breakpoint somewhere in the middle of that process, and see if that step is happening correctly. If not, the problem is either right there or earlier in your code. If it is happening correctly, the problem is after that point. Choose another breakpoint and repeat until you've found the bug.

> **Tip** Remove a breakpoint by dragging it out of the gutter. Relocate a breaking by dragging it to a new location. Disable or enable a breakpoint by clicking on it.

Run the app again, but first set a breakpoint in your -loadFromContents:ofType:error: method. When your app starts, you'll see that the -loadFromContents:ofType:error: method is received immediately, as shown in Figure 19-5.

CHAPTER 19: Doc, You Meant Storage

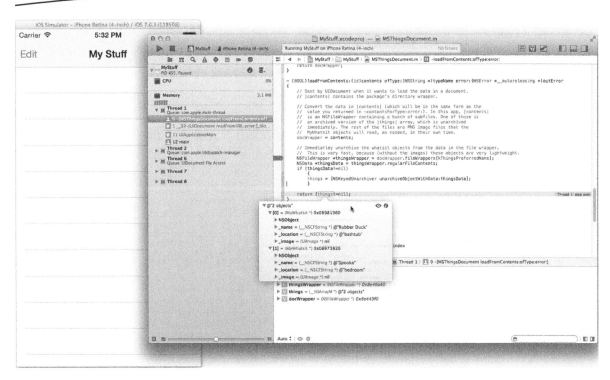

Figure 19-5. Checking to see that -loadFromContents:ofType:error: is received

Using the step over command, you can watch the code obtain the wrapper object, extract its data, and turn that data back into the things array. As you can see in Figure 19-5, all of your data has been restored.

So your document is being opened, its contents read, and yet the table view is still empty. What insanity is this? To make matters worse, if you try to add a new item, your app crashes. Why is this happening (to you)?

As it turns out, the problem isn't that mysterious. If you set a breakpoint in the +documentAtURL: method and also in MSMasterViewController's -tableView:numberOfRowsInSection: method (one of the first messages the table view data source receives), as shown in Figure 19-6, you'll discover two things. First, -tableView:numberOfRowsInSection: is received after +documentAtURL:, but *before* the -loadFromContents:ofType:error: message is received. Secondly, if you examine the document object (also shown in Figure 19-6), you'll see that the things array is still nil.

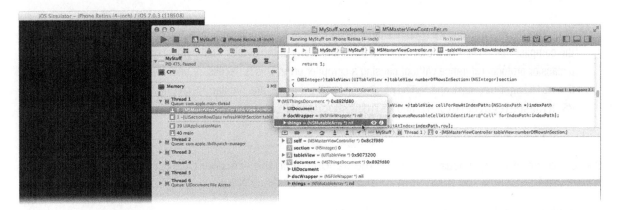

Figure 19-6. Examining the document object in the debugger

Have you figured it out yet? UIDocument's -openWithCompletionHandler: method (sent in +documentAtURL:) is *asynchronous*. It starts the process of retrieving your document's data in the background and returns immediately. Your app's code proceeds, displaying the table view, with a still empty data model.

Some time later, the data for the document finishes loading and is passed to -loadFromContents:ofType:error: to be converted into a data model. That's successful, but the table view doesn't know that and continues to display—what it thinks is—an empty list.

What your document needs to do is notify your view controller when the data model has been updated, so the table view can refresh itself. You could accomplish this using a notification or a code block property, but I think the most sensible solution is to use a delegate message. As a bonus, you'll get practice creating your own protocol.

Define a new delegate protocol. You could add a new header file to the project just for this protocol, but since it goes hand-in-hand with the MSThingsDocument class, I recommend adding it to the end of the MSThingsDocument.h interface file:

```
@protocol MSThingsDocumentDelegate <NSObject>
@optional
- (void)gotThings:(MSThingsDocument*)document;
@end
```

This defines a protocol with one, optional, method (-gotThings:), sent whenever your document object loads new things from the document. Back up to the beginning of the MSThingsDocument.h file, find the @class MyWhatsit statement, and add a forward declaration for the new protocol and a delegate property (new code in bold):

```
@class MyWhatsit
@protocol MSThingsDocumentDelegate;

@interface MSThingsDocument : UIDocument
+ (NSURL*)documentURL;
+ (MSThingsDocument*)documentAtURL:(NSURL*)url;
@property (weak) id<MSThingsDocumentDelegate> delegate;
```

> **Tip** Use the @class and @protocol directives to create forward declarations. A *forward declaration* tells the compiler that a class or protocol exists, but without any of the details. That symbol can then be used in a class or protocol reference without causing a compiler error. This is necessary because some definitions, like MSThingsDocument and MSThingsDocumentDelegate, are circular; MSThingsDocument refers to MSThingsDelegateProtocol, and MSThingsDocumentProtocol refers to MSThingsDocument.

Switch to the MSThingsDocument.m implementation file. In the +documentAtURL: method, change the statement that opens the document to this (modified code in bold):

```
[document openWithCompletionHandler:^(BOOL success){
    if (success)
        {
        if ([document.delegate respondsToSelector:@selector(gotThings:)])
            [document.delegate gotThings:document];
        }
}];
```

The modified code now performs an action after the document is finished loading, which includes the unarchiving of the data model objects. Now it sends its delegate a -gotThings: message, so the delegate (your view controller) knows that the data model has changed.

> **Tip** This is how you send an optional message to a delegate. Delegate objects are not required to implement optional methods, and you do not want to send a message the object doesn't implement; it will result in a nasty exception and your code will stop executing. The -respondsToSelector: method determines if an object implements ("responds to") a specific method.

Switch to the MSMasterViewController.h file and make your view controller a document delegate (new code in bold):

```
@interface MSMasterViewController 
                : UITableViewController <MSThingsDocumentDelegate>
```

Over in the MSMasterViewController.m implementation file, make two changes. Immediately after obtaining the new document object in -viewDidLoad, make the view controller the document's delegate object (new code in bold):

```
document = [MSThingsDocument documentAtURL:[MSThingsDocument documentURL]];
document.delegate = self;
```

Finally, add the optional `-gotThings:` method to the `@implementation` section:

```
- (void)gotThings:(MSThingsDocument *)document
{
    [self.tableView reloadData];
}
```

Run your app again, as shown in Figure 19-7, and voilà! The data in your document appears in the table view.

Figure 19-7. Working document

Make changes or add new items. Press the home button to give `UIDocument` a chance to save the document, stop the app, restart it, and your changes persist. The only content MyStuff doesn't save is any images you add. That's because images aren't part of the archived object data. You're going to add image data directly to the document's directory wrapper, so attack that problem next.

> **Tip** The **Debug ➤ Deactivate Breakpoints** command will disable all breakpoints in your project, allowing you to run and test your app without interruption.

Storing Image Files

Image data storage takes a different route than the other properties in your `MyWhatsit` objects. Here is how it's going to work:

- When a new, or updated, image (`UIImage`) object is added to a `MyWhatsit` object, the image is converted into the PNG (Portable Network Graphics) data format and stored in the document as a file wrapper. The `MyWhatsit` object remembers the key of the file wrapper.

- When the document is saved, `UIDocument` automatically includes the data from all the file wrappers in the document. The image file wrapper keys are archived by the `MyWhatsit` objects.

- When the document is opened again, the file wrapper objects for the image data are restored.

- When client code requests the image property of a `MyWhatsit` object, `MyWhatsit` uses its saved key to locate and load the data in the file wrapper, eventually converting it back into the original `UIImage` object.

The key to this design (no pun intended) is the relationship between the `MyWhatsit` objects and the document object. A `MyWhatsit` object will use the document object to store, and later retrieve, the data for an individual image. From a software design standpoint, however, you want to keep the code that actually stores and retrieves the image data out of the `MyWhatsit` object. The single responsibility principle encourages the `MyWhatsit` object to do what it does (represent the values in your data model) and the document object to do what it does (manage the storage and conversion of document data) without polluting one class with the responsibilities of the other.

The solution is to create an *abstraction layer*, or *abstract service*, in the `MSThingsDocument` class to store and retrieve images. `MyWhatsit` will still instigate image management, but the mechanics of how those images get turned into file wrappers stays inside `MSThingsDocument`. Let's get started.

Add two public methods to the `@interface` in `MSThingsDocument.h`:

```
- (NSString*)setImage:(UIImage*)image existingKey:(NSString*)key;
- (UIImage*)imageForKey:(NSString*)key;
```

The first method will store, or replace, an image in the document. The second will retrieve one. Now modify `MyWhatsit` to use these methods to save and restore its image property.

Select the `MyWhatsit.h` interface file. Add a forward reference to the `MSThingsDocument` class, a new document property, and a `readonly imageKey` property (new code in bold):

@class MSThingsDocument;

@interface MyWhatsit : NSObject <NSCoding>

@property (weak,nonatomic) MSThingsDocument *document;
@property (readonly,nonatomic) NSString *imageKey;

While you're here, delete the -initWithName:location: method you originally added to help with testing in Chapter 5. You're not using it anymore.

The document property contains a reference to the document where this object stores and retrieves its image. The imageKey property is the key of the file wrapper that contains this object's image data. Modify your image handling to use these new properties.

Select the MyWhatsit.m implementation file. Begin by importing the document object interface, just below the other #import directives:

```
#import "MSThingsDocument.h"
```

Before the @implementation section, add one more archiving key and a private interface section that defines two instance variables, one for the image and one for the image data key:

```
#define kImageKeyCoderKey    @"image.key"

@interface MyWhatsit ()
{
    UIImage *image;
    NSString *imageKey;
}
```

> **Note** Previously, an instance variable to store the image property (_image) was created automatically by the compiler. In this version, however, you're going to provide a custom setter method (-setImage:) for the image property. When you do that, it becomes your responsibility to define the storage for that property.

Delete the -initWithName:location: method you are no longer using.

In the -encodeWithCoder: method, add a statement to archive the value of the imageKey property:

```
[coder encodeObject:imageKey forKey:kImageKeyCoderKey];.
```

To the -initWithCoder: method, add a matching statement, immediately after the other -decodeObjectForKey: messages, to restore it when it's unarchived:

```
imageKey = [decoder decodeObjectForKey:kImageKeyCoderKey];
```

You don't add the actual image data to the archive, but your object does need to remember the key to where that data is stored in the document's directory wrapper.

> **Note** Your NSCoding methods do not encode, or decode, either the image or document property of the object. When the object is unarchived, these property values will be nil. This makes them *transient* properties. Properties preserved by archiving are called *persistent* properties.

Now you can define a custom getter and setting method for the image property. Start with the getter:

```
- (UIImage*)image
{
    if (image==nil && imageKey!=nil)
        image = [_document imageForKey:imageKey];
    return image;
}
```

The image property getter method now checks for the situation where it does not have an image object (image==nil), but it does have a key for an image stored in the document (imageKey!=nil). In that case, it retrieves the image object stored in the document. This is done lazily; that is, the first time the image property is requested. When the table view first appears, only those items visible in the list will load their images. The rest of the items in the document won't be loaded until the user scrolls the list to reveal them.

The image property setter method has to keep the document up to date. After the getter, add its companion setter method:

```
- (void)setImage:(UIImage *)newImage
{
    imageKey = [_document setImage:newImage existingKey:imageKey];
    image = newImage;
}
```

The setter method either adds, or replaces, the image in the document. The document's -setImage:existingKey: method stores the image data in a file wrapper and returns the key identifying that wrapper. The existingKey parameter passes in the key of the image data the object had previously stored. This is used by the document to delete any old image data before adding the new. Finally, the image object is retained.

Finally, a getter method for the imageKey property must be supplied:

```
- (NSString*)imageKey
{
    return imageKey;
}
```

That concludes all of the changes to the MyWhatsit class. Select the MSThingsDocument.m implementation file. Obviously, you need to supply the two image storage methods you defined in the interface. Start with the -setImage:existingKey: method:

```
- (NSString*)setImage:(UIImage *)image existingKey:(NSString *)key
{
    if (key!=nil)
        {
        NSFileWrapper *imageWrapper = docWrapper.fileWrappers[key];
        if (imageWrapper!=nil)
            [docWrapper removeFileWrapper:imageWrapper];
        }
```

```
    NSString *newKey = nil;
    if (image!=nil)
        {
        NSData *imageData = UIImagePNGRepresentation(image);
        newKey = [docWrapper addRegularFileWithContents:imageData
                                      preferredFilename:kImagePreferredName];
        }
    
    [self updateChangeCount:UIDocumentChangeDone];
    return newKey;
}
```

It works just as you would expect it to. If the sender included a key for an existing file wrapper, that file wrapper is first removed. If an image is being stored (image!=nil), the image is encoding into the PNG file format by the UIImagePNGRepresentation function. The compressed image data is then added to the directory package as a new file wrapper, and the key that identifies that wrapper is returned to the sender. Of course, you didn't forget to tell the document that its content has changed before returning.

That takes care of storing a new image in the document and replacing an existing image with a new one. Now add the code to retrieve images from the document:

```
- (UIImage*)imageForKey:(NSString *)key
{
    UIImage *image = nil;
    if (key!=nil)
        {
        NSFileWrapper *imageWrapper = docWrapper.fileWrappers[key];
        if (imageWrapper!=nil)
            image = [UIImage imageWithData:imageWrapper.regularFileContents];
        }
    return image;
}
```

This method performs the inverse of the -setImage:existingKey: method. It uses key to find the file wrapper in the document, sends the wrapper a -regularFileContents message to retrieve the data, and uses that PNG image data to reconstruct the original UIImage object, which is returned to the sender.

Note The data that a regular file wrapper represents isn't read into memory until you send it a -regularFileContents message. File wrappers are just lightweight placeholders for the data in persistent storage, until you request that data.

Sneakily, there's one more place where an image is removed from the document: when the user deletes a MyWhatsit object. Locate the -removeWhatsitAtIndex: method. Add code to the beginning of the method to remove the image file wrapper for that item, before removing that item (new code in bold):

```
- (void)removeWhatsitAtIndex:(NSUInteger)index
{
    MyWhatsit *thing = things[index];
    if (thing.imageKey!=nil)
        [self setImage:nil existingKey:thing.imageKey];
    [things removeObjectAtIndex:index];
    [self updateChangeCount:UIDocumentChangeDone];
}
```

> **Tip** Another way of handling this would be let the MyWhatsit object delete its own image before being removed. You'd do that by defining (something like) a -prepareToBeRemovedFromDocument: method that would remove any document resources belonging to that MyWhatsit. It all depends on which side of the data-model/data-model-controller fence you want to encapsulate the logic.

All of the mechanics for saving, retrieving, and deleting images from the document are in place. Sadly, none of it will work. The MyWhatsit must be connected to the working MSThingsDocument object through its document property for any of this new code to function. At this point, no one is setting that property.

So where should the document property be set, and what object should be responsible for setting it? The answer is the MSThingsDocument object. It should take responsibility for maintaining the connection between itself and its data model objects.

As it turns out, this is an incredibly easy problem to solve, because there are only two locations where MyWhatsit objects are created: when the document is unarchived and when the user creates a new item. Start with the -anotherWhatsit method and add a statement to set the new object's document property (new code in bold):

```
- (MyWhatsit*)anotherWhatsit
{
    MyWhatsit *newItem = [MyWhatsit new];
    newItem.document = self;
```

> **Note** Methods like -anotherWhatsit are called factory methods. A *factory method* creates new, correctly configured, objects for the client. The objects might be different classes or need to be initialized in a special way—like being added to a collection and having their document property set—before being returned. Write factory methods to create objects that need to be created in a way that the sender shouldn't be responsible for.

Locate the -loadFromContents:ofType:error: method. Immediately after the things array is unarchived, add this statement (new code in bold):

```
if (thingsData!=nil)
  {
  things = [NSKeyedUnarchiver unarchiveObjectWithData:thingsData];
  [things makeObjectsPerformSelector:@selector(setDocument:)
                          withObject:self];
  }
```

The -makeObjectsPerformSelector:withObject: message sends a message with one parameter to every object in the collection (equivalent to [things[0] setDocument:self], [things[1] setDocument:self], and so on). When it's done, every MyWhatsit object in the array will have its document property set with the document where its image is stored.

Your document implementation is finally finished! Give it a spin by running MyStuff. Add some items, attach some pictures, and quit the app, as shown in Figure 19-8. Stop the app in Xcode and start it again. All of the items, along with their pictures, are preserved in the document.

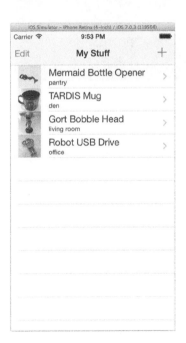  

Figure 19-8. Testing image storage

Well, almost. There are some performance problems and some irregularities in the image orientation. You'll fix the former in Chapter 24, and you can take a stab at the orientation problem in the exercise at the end of this chapter.

> **Note** In the rush to add image storage to your MyWhatsit object, I wanted to make sure you didn't miss a remarkable fact: you did not change the interface to your data model. None of the code that uses the MyWhatsit object, like the code in MSDetailViewController, required any modifications. That's because the meaning and use of the image property never changed. The only thing that changed was how that data gets stored. This is encapsulation at work.

If you're running MyStuff on a provisioned device, you can see your app's document file(s) in the Devices tab of the Organizer window (**Window ➤ Organizer**). Select the **Devices** tab, select the Applications installed on your device, and then select the MyStuff app. The organizer window will show you the files in your app's sandbox, as shown in Figure 19-9.

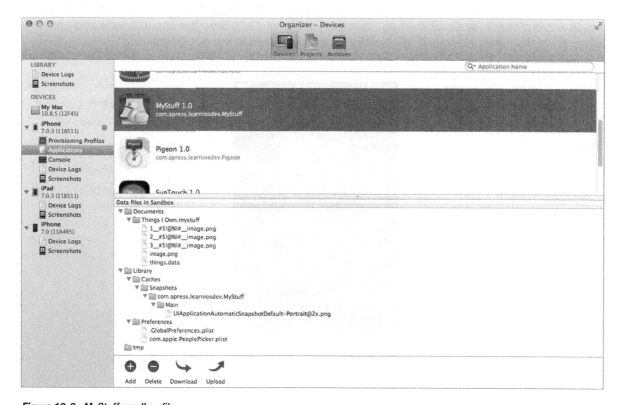

Figure 19-9. MyStuff sandbox files

You can clearly see your Things I Own.mystuff document package inside your app's Documents folder. The funny filenames (1_#$!@%!#_image.png) is how UIDocument handles two or more file wrappers with the same preferred name. It gives the files crazy names so they can all be stored in the same directory.

If you need to get these files, use the **Download** button at the bottom of the window. Xcode will copy the files from your iOS device and save them on your hard drive, where you can examine them.

Odds and Ends

What you've accomplished in MyStuff is a lot, but it really represents the bare minimum of support required for document integration. There are lots of features and issues that I skipped over. Let's review a couple of those now.

iCloud Storage

You can store your documents in the cloud, much as your stored property list values in the cloud in Chapter 18. Documents, naturally, are a little more complicated.

Apple's guidelines suggest that you provide a setting that allows the user to place all of their documents in the cloud or none of their documents in the cloud. A piecemeal approach is not recommended. When the user changes their mind, your app is responsible for moving (copying) the locally stored documents into the cloud or in the other direction. This isn't a trivial task. It involves multi-tasking, which I don't get to until Chapter 24.

Once in the cloud, you open, modify, and save documents much the way you do from your local sandbox. All of the code you wrote for -contentsForType:error: and -loadFromContents:ofType:error: won't need any modification (if you wrote them correctly), you'll just use different URLs. In reality, the data of your "cloud" documents are actually stored locally on the device. Any changes are synchronized with the iCloud storage servers in the background, but you always retain a local copy of the data, both for speed and in case the network connection with the cloud is interrupted.

There are some subtle, and not so subtle, differences between local and cloud-based documents. One of the big differences is change. Changes to your cloud documents can occur at any time. The user is free to edit the same document on another device, and network interruptions can delay those changes from reaching your app immediately.

In general, your app observes the UIDocumentStateChangedNotification notification. If the iCloud service detects conflicting versions (local vs. what's on the server), your document's state will change to UIDocumentStateInConflict. It's then up to your app to compare the two documents and decide what to keep and what to discard. You might query the user for guidance, or your app might do it automatically.

To learn more about iCloud documents, start with the *Document-Based App Programming Guide for iOS*, that you can find in Xcode's Documentation and API Reference window. It's a good read, and I strongly suggest you peruse it if you plan to do any more development involving UIDocument. The chapters "Managing the Life Cycle of a Document" and "Resolving Document Version Conflicts" directly address cloud storage.

Archive Versioning

When implementing NSCoding, you might need to consider what happens when your class changes. One of the consequences of archiving objects to persistent storage is that the data is—well—persistent. Users will expect your app to open documents created years ago. I'm trying to improve my software all of the time, and I assume you are too. I'm always adding new properties to classes, or changing the type and scope of properties. It often means creating new classes and periodically abandoning old ones. All such changes alter the way classes encode themselves and pose challenges when unarchiving data created by older, and sometimes newer, versions of your software.

There are a number of techniques for dealing with archive compatibility. Your newer code might encode its values using a different key. When decoding, your software can test for the presence of that key to determine if the archive data was created by modern or legacy software. You might encode a "version" value in your archive data and test that version when decoding. Newer software might encode a value in both its modern form and a legacy form, so that older software (that knows nothing of the newer form) can still interpret the document data.

There are even techniques for substituting one class for another during unarchiving. This can solve the problem of an encoded class that no longer exists. A thorough discussion of these issues, and some solutions, are discussed in the "Forward and Backward Compatibility for Keyed Archives" chapter of the *Archives and Serializations Programming Guide*.

Summary

Embracing `UIDocument` adds a level of modern data storage to your app that users both appreciate and have come to expect. You've learned how, and where, to store your app's documents. More importantly, you understand the different roles that objects and methods play that, together, orchestrate the transformation of model objects into raw data, and back again. You learned how to construct multi-file documents that can be incrementally saved and lazily loaded. Along the way, you learned how to archive objects and create objects that can be archived.

You've come a long way, and you should be feeling pretty confident in your iOS aptitude. Adding persistent storage to your apps was really the last major iOS competency you had to accomplish. The next couple of chapters dig into Objective-C, to hone your language knowledge and proficiency.

EXERCISE

If you used your iOS Device's built-in camera to take pictures of your stuff, you might notice an annoying problem. The picture appears fine when you first add it. But later, after they're saved to the document and reloaded, some of the images are on their side or upside down.

Try searching the iOS developer forums, or the Internet in general, for what the problem might be. You'll find my first "fix" for the problem in the `Learn iOS Development Projects` ➤ `Ch 19` ➤ `MyStuff E1` folder. Hint: I only changed two lines of code, both in `MSThingsDocuments.m`.

The "fix" in `MyStuff E1` doesn't really solve the problem; it just works around it. To really address the issue took a little more work. I changed how the cropped image is created in the `-imagePickerController:didFinishPicking MediaWithInfo:` method. You'll find that solution in the `Learn iOS Development Projects` ➤ `Ch 19` ➤ `MyStuff E2` folder. Using what you learned in Chapter 10, and the code you wrote in Chapter 13, you shouldn't have any trouble figuring out how it works. And maybe you can come up with a different solution.

Chapter 20

Being Objective

As promised, I didn't start out this book with a dry lesson on Objective-C. You dove right in and started creating apps—and I think that's fantastic. The fact that Xcode empowers even novice programmers to design and create quality iOS apps opens a world of possibilities. But you don't want to stay a novice forever. You don't get the good seats in the monastery's dining hall, and there's never any fan mail. I'm not saying that reading this one chapter will turn you into an Objective-C guru, but it should definitely up your game.

If you're struggling at all with Objective-C, or just relatively new to it, give this chapter a good read. It's basically a crash course that will put you on a firm footing. If you've already read a book on Objective-C, or have been programming in it for a while, the contents of this chapter may not surprise you. In that case, treat it as a handy reference to the "good bits" of Objective-C. In this chapter you will:

- Learn how Objective-C classes are declared and objects are created
- Understand the relationship between properties, instance variables, getters, and setters
- Use introspection to examine objects and classes
- Explore the differences between protocols and categories, and what they're good for
- Learn to love `nil`
- Get the skinny on collection objects
- Become familiar with some really useful shortcuts

There are no projects for this chapter, so you can give Xcode the day off. I'll start with the basics, which you're welcome to skim, and then I'll take you on a whirlwind tour of the classes and features that you'll regularly use, or just need to know about. Let's start at the foundation.

Objective-C is C

Objective-C is C. It's a deceptively simple statement, but it has far-reaching ramifications. C and BASIC were the first truly popular programming languages for computers. Almost a half-century after its invention, C is still the most popular programming language[1] in the world. Its concise syntax, and the efficiency with which it can be compiled into computer code, have made it the workhorse of the industry. When new languages were developed, it was natural that they adopted many of C's conventions, both because the syntax is really good and because so many programmers already knew C. We now live in a world awash with C-like languages: C++, C#, Perl, Java, JavaScript, and PHP, to name just a few.

A "C-like" language is one that kind of, sort of, looks like C, but isn't. The authors of the language liked the C syntax, but wanted to make changes to it, for whatever reason. If you already know C, it's easier to learn these languages. But it also means that you can't take standard C code and compile it using Java or C#, for example.

> **Note** C++ is, by far, the C-like language most closely related to C. C++ started out as a C preprocessor; your C++ code was first translated into plain C, which was then compiled by a C compiler. C++ has since diverged from C sufficiently that it is no longer a super-set of the C language, although you can still insert plain C into a C++ program using its special `extern "C" { /* Plain C code here */ }` syntax.

In contrast, Objective-C is a *strict superset* of the C language. It means that Objective-C adds object-oriented features to C, but doesn't change or take away any of its C-ness. For the most part, it does this by introducing a few keywords that begin with @ (like `@interface`, `@private`, `@selector`, and so on) and the square-bracket syntax for sending messages to objects (`[object message]`)[2]. Everything in between—and I mean *everything*—is standard (ISO/IEC 9899:2011) C.

For you, it means that any standard C code can be dropped into your project and used as is. You can sprinkle your Objective-C app with `struct` and `typedef` statements, use the preprocessor, and define your own C functions. And it means you have direct, unfiltered, access to any C function your app can link to.

That last bit is huge. More computer code has been written in C than any other language—several *billion* lines, at last estimate. iOS is built on top of the Core Foundation and BSD libraries, which contain thousands of useful C functions, all at your disposal. And if your app needs something exceptional—maybe you need to calculate elliptic cypher codes, or predict planetary orbits—I can guarantee you that someone has already written that code in C.

---

[1] Popularity as defined by various indices, like the Language Popularity Index (lang-index.sourceforge.net).
[2] Recent extensions to Objective-C are not as distinct. Modern features like fast enumeration and property accessors are harder to spot as being Objective-C additions to C.

> **Tip** There's also an Objective-C++ language. It adds the same additions to C++ that Objective-C adds to C. Objective-C++ is particularly useful for OpenGL programming, where a lot of the code is written in C++.

This is good for me too, because all I have to do is declare that "Objective-C is C" and I can move on to explaining what Objective-C adds to C. As I see it, you have three paths to Objective-C mastery:

- If you already know how to program in C, you're almost there. Read the rest of this chapter to find what Objective-C adds to C.
- If you're not familiar with C, or a little shaky, you have two routes:
  - Learn C and then read the rest of this chapter. There are numerous C tutorials and references on the Internet. Apress also publishes an exceptional book, Learn C on the Mac, 2nd Edition, by David Mark and yours truly—but now I'm just bragging.
  - Instead of reading this chapter, get a book on Objective-C. A thorough treatise on Objective-C will explain the entire language, which encompasses C.

If you're good with C, it's time to move on to Objective-C.

Objective-C Classes

You've seen this a hundred times so far, and I explained it in Chapter 6, but here is again, in its complete glory. A class in Objective-C is declared by an `@interface` directive, typically in a `.h` (header) file:

```
@interface ClassName : SuperClassName <ProtocolName>
{
    @public
    int instanceVariable;
}
@property (nonatomic) int property;
+ (void)classMethod;
- (void)instanceMethod:(int)param1 withTwoParameters:(int)param2;
@end
```

Here are the salient points:

- The `@interface` declaration informs the compiler of the existence of the class and describes it: what it inherits, what additional instance variables, properties, and methods it implements, and what protocols it adopts. It does not generate any code.
- Although technically optional, for all practical purposes you must specify a superclass. If you don't inherit from a specific class, inherit `NSObject`.
- Protocols are optional. Separate multiple protocols with commas. Omit the brackets if you don't adopt any.

- Instance variables are declared in the block between two curly brackets. If your class doesn't declare any instance variables, you can omit the block entirely. Only instance variables can be declared inside the block.

- You can optionally insert visibility directives (@public, @protected, or @private) between instance variable declarations. All variables that follow one are assigned that visibility. Variables declared before the first one are @protected.

- The @end directive marks the end of the @interface declaration and is required. You cannot nest another declaration (@interface, @category, @protocol, or @implementation) inside an @interface.

Most of this should all make sense to you by now. The only keywords not mentioned in this book so far are the visibility directives. The visibility of a variable determines what methods are allowed direct access to those variables. The choices are listed in Table 20-1.

Table 20-1. Visibility Directives

Directive	Meaning
@public	Any code with a reference to the object can directly manipulate the instance variable
@protected	Only methods of this class or one of its subclasses may directly manipulate the variable
@private	Only methods of this class may directly manipulate the variable

When I say "directly manipulate," I mean the code can use the instance variable in a C expression to get or change its value directly. (See the section on "Properties" later in this chapter for those details.) Visibility does not apply to methods or properties; those are always public. The most useful visibility directive is @private, but its use has largely been replaced by extensions, which are described in the section "Categories," later in this chapter.

Implementing Your Class

The code for a class appears in its @implementation section, typically in a .m (implementation) file:

```
@implementation ClassName

+ (void)classMethod
{
}

- (void)instanceMethod:(int)param1 withTwoParameters:(int)param2
{
}

@end
```

You're responsible for implementing every method (and possibly some properties) listed in your class's @interface directive. That includes any required methods of the protocols your class adopts.

> **Caution** Not implementing a method that you've declared may only result in compiler warning. This may not stop you from building and running your app, but if a message for one of those unimplemented methods is received, your application will throw an exception and fail. Pay attention to compiler warnings.

Creating and Destroying Objects

Creating an object is a two-step process:

1. Allocate the object
2. Initialize the object

You tell the class to allocate it, and then send the object an "init" message to initialize it, like this:

```
id myObject = [[MyClass alloc] init];
```

Classes may have alternative init methods, some with parameters, that initialize the object in different ways. Some classes are documented with *designated* init methods; these are the only init messages you should send those objects, even if it inherits other init methods from its superclass. All initializer methods traditionally begin with the letters "init."

> **Tip** The NSObject base class defines a +new class message that allocates a new object, sends it an -init message, and returns it to the sender. The statements [[AnyClass alloc] init] and [AnyClass new] are functionally identical. I'm mystified why programmers don't use the [MyClass new] shorthand more often.

If you define an init method for your class, it must follow this pattern:

```
- (id)init
{
    self = [super init];
    if (self)
        {
        instanceVariable = 1;
        }
    return self;
}
```

Your class must first send the appropriate init method to your object's superclass. Often this is -init, but it can be any init method the superclass implements.

You must then reassign the returned value to your self variable and check to see that it is not nil. If the superclass fails to initialize the object, it will destroy it and return nil. This indicates that there is no longer any object to initialize; your method should immediately return nil.

Your code then proceeds to initialize its instance variables and properties. All instance variables and properties are pre-initialized to 0, 0.0, NO, or nil when your object was allocated. You only need to set those values that shouldn't be zero.

Like the superclass, if something might go wrong during your initialization, you can destroy your object and return nil (self = nil), indicating that your initialization failed.

The next chapter describes how, and when, objects are destroyed.

Class Clusters

It's important that you update the self variable when sending the init method to the superclass (self = [super init]). Objective-C has a unique ability to substitute a different object for the one you initialize. That is, you allocate an object of one class, you send it an -init message, but the object you get back isn't the one you allocated. In fact, it might not even be the same class.

This technique is called a *class cluster*, and is a variant of the factory pattern. Writing your own class cluster isn't difficult. Your code would look like this:

```
- (id)initCluster:(int)param
{
    self = [super init];
    if (self)
        {
        if (param<0)
            {
            self = [[SpecialNegativeClass alloc] init];
            }
        }
    return self;
}
```

Class clusters are used in iOS to optimize memory and to simplify the class interface. For example, you'd think that the statement [[NSNumber alloc] initWithBool:YES] would create a new NSNumber object every time it's executed. But NSNumber objects are immutable (can't be changed), so any two NSNumber objects that represent YES are interchangeable. iOS takes advantage of this and pre-allocates two NSNumber objects, one for YES and a second one for NO. Executing [[NSNumber alloc] initWithBool:YES] will actually return one of those two objects, in place of the one you tried to create.

Referring to Objects

Objective-C uses C's pointer syntax to refer to objects. Here is a variable that points to an Objective-C object of a specific class:

```
SpecificClass *anObject;
```

A pointer to an Objective-C object is called an *object pointer*, *object reference*, or just *object*. Unlike some languages, you cannot declare a variable that contains the object (SpecificClass anObject). All objects in Objective-C are dynamically allocated, so you can only declare and manipulate pointers to objects.

When a variable is declared with a specific class, the Objective-C compiler knows what methods, properties, and instance variables are defined for that object. It will complain if you attempt to access a property or method it doesn't implement. This is great, at least most of the time. Try to send a message that your object doesn't understand, or access a variable it doesn't have, and you'll be rewarded with a compile error.

It's a problem when the object is actually a subclass of the class that it's declared to be. For example, in your DrumDub app, you retrieved a UIButton object using a tag, and then set its enabled property. You might have initially written code like this:

```
[[self.view viewWithTag:i+1] setEnabled:active];
```

That statement, sadly, won't compile. The problem is that the method -viewWithTag: returns a UIView*, not a UIButton*. You and I know that the object returned was a UIButton, but the compiler doesn't. The only thing the compiler is sure of is that the object is a UIView, and UIView has no -setEnabled: method; your program won't compile, and you'll never get to play your sound effects. In these cases, the C cast syntax comes to your rescue:

```
[(UIButton*)[self.view viewWithTag:i+1] setEnabled:active];
```

This code says, "I know that -viewWithTag: returns a UIView*, but I also know the object is a UIButton, so treat it that way." The only caution is that it had better be a UIButton or things will go very badly. In the section "Introspection," I talk about how to check to see that an object is, in fact, a UIButton—in case there's some doubt.

Can I See Your id?

You may occasionally see the type id used in Objective-C. This special type means "a pointer to any object." It is treated differently than just a pointer to an object. In the following bullet points, assume this code:

```
id anyObj;
SpecificClass *specificObj;
```

- You can send any message to an object of type id ([anyObj anyMessage]). The compiler will not complain. It has no idea what kind of object anyObj is, and assumes you do. Again, it's up to you to ensure that anyObj responds to -anyMessage.

- You cannot access instance variables (anyObj->instanceVariable), or refer to properties (anyObj.enabled=YES), through an id reference. You'll first have to cast the variable to a specific type (((SpecificClass*)anyObj)->instanceVariable), or use the equivalent getter or setter message ([anyObj setEnabled:YES]).

- An id reference can be assigned to any object pointer variable or parameter (specificObj=anyObj). The compiler will never complain about this, and you don't need a C cast operator. The assumption is that you know the class of the object. (So you better be sure.)

- Any object pointer can be assigned to an id variable or parameter (anyObj=specificObj). The compiler will never complain about this, and you don't need a C cast operator. An id variable refers to any object, and specificObj is an object, so what's the problem?

The id type is used in variables, methods, and parameters where (almost) any object would be acceptable. This simplifies your code, because the compiler relaxes the rules for dealing with that reference.

A good example is the collection classes (NSArray, NSDictionary, and so on). Every value in a collection is of type id, because it truly can be "any object." This makes it easy to store and retrieve objects from a collection, even objects of specific types:

```
SpecificClass *specificObj = [[SpecificClass alloc] init];
[array appendObject:specificObj];
specificObj = [array lastObject];
```

The compiler won't generate any warnings for this code, and you don't have to cast the object in the assignment statement. If -lastObject returned a type of NSObject*, instead of id, you'd have to write specificObj = (SpecificObject*)[array lastObject] every time—yuck.

> **Caution** The * in id is implied. You do not include the C pointer operator when using id. If you write id *, you've actually written "a pointer to a pointer to any object."

Method Names

Method names in Objective-C are traditionally verbose. It's one of Objective-C's charms, and substantially improves its readability. Consider this C function call:

```
CGBitmapContextCreate(pixes,768,1024,8,space,kCGImageAlphaPremultipliedLast);
```

Unless you're looking at the documentation, it's a challenge to tell exactly what each of those parameters means. Now contrast that with a similar Objective-C message:

```
[[CIImage alloc] initWithBitmapData:pixes
                    bytesPerRow:768*4
                        size:CGSizeMake(768,1024)
                      format:kCIFormatARGB8
                  colorSpace:space];
```

It's much easier to intuit what each of the parameters in the second statement is for. When Objective-C messages get too long to fit on a single line, the convention is to write each parameter on its own line, aligning the colons, as illustrated above. Xcode's source code editor will do this automatically.

Methods that begin with a minus sign (-) are instance methods. They execute in the context of the receiving object. Methods that being with a plus sign (+) are class methods. They execute in the context of the class.

Method Name Construction

Parameters in a method are separated by colons. The words and the colons, together, form the method's signature. A *method signature* uniquely identifies a method. Take this method as an example:

```
- (BOOL)getBytes:(void *)buffer maxLength:(NSUInteger)maxBufferCount usedLength:(NSUInteger *)
usedBufferCount encoding:(NSStringEncoding)encoding options:(NSStringEncodingConversionOptions)
options range:(NSRange)range remainingRange:(NSRangePointer)leftover;
```

(Yes, that's an action method.) The signature of that method is:

`getBytes:maxLength:usedLength:encoding:options:range:remainingRange:`

Use a signature in a `@selector()` directive to specify a particular method.

> **Tip** You'll sometimes see method names written as `-[ClassName method:name:]` in documentation, while debugging, or in conversations between programmers. This is shorthand that uniquely identifies the method of a class. It isn't Objective-C syntax, and you'll never use it in a program, but it is informative.

The types of each parameter, and the return value of the method, are expressed in parentheses immediately before the name of each parameter and method. The following method takes two parameters, a `CGPoint struct` and a pointer to a `UIEvent` object, and returns a `BOOL` value:

`- (BOOL)pointInside:(CGPoint)point withEvent:(UIEvent *)event;`

Technically, parameter and returns types are optional. If omitted, the type defaults to `id`. These two methods are identical:

```
- (id)objectforKey:(id)key;
- objectForKey:key;
```

I don't recommend omitting the type for parameters or return values. The convention is to explicitly declare the type of the return value and every parameter. It's not that much typing, and it avoids a lot of confusion.

One fallacy about Objective-C, that you might overhear, is that it uses named parameters. It does not. You can't alter the order of the parameters in an Objective-C message. The methods `-setLineDash:count:phase:` and `-setLineDash:phase:count:` are two, distinct, methods. Technically, the individual words of a message are called *tokens*. Sometimes—and I've done it in the book—programmers will refer to the token to identify a parameter, but it's not the "name" of the parameter.

It's also a little known fact that the tokens are optional. There's a method in the CAMediaTimingFunction that's defined as:

```
+ (id)functionWithControlPoints:(float)c1x :(float)c1y :(float)c2x :(float)c2y;
```

You send that message like this:

```
[CAMediaTimingFunction functionWithControlPoints:100.0:120.0:180.0:200.0];
```

And if you want to be perverse, the following is a perfectly valid Objective-C method:

```
- :i :j :k;
```

> **Note** Don't ever use such a method in your class. If you do, don't tell anyone where you learned this.

The +initialize Method

Every class inherits an +initialize method. The class receives this message when it is first initialized. The Objective-C runtime library initializes classes lazily, so the +initialize message is sent just before the class is first used, most likely just before the first object of that class is created.

The +initialize method is a handy place to write code that should be executed once, and before any code in the class gets a chance to run. Consider this +initialize method:

```
static NSNumberFormatter *Formatter;
+ (void)initialize
{
    if (Formatter==nil)
        {
        Formatter = [[NSNumberFormatter alloc] init];
        Formatter.roundingMode = NSNumberFormatterRoundHalfEven;
        }
}
```

Any method of this class would be safe in assuming that the Formatter variable contained an initialized NSFormatter object, because the +initialize message is guaranteed to be sent before any other class message is received, or any instance of this class is created. Use +initialize to create singleton objects, initialize global variables, create shared collections, pre-fetch user default values, and so on.

> **Caution** Your subclasses will inherit your +initialize method, which means it could be received again when a subclass is initialized. In the preceding code, the if (Formatter==nil) condition prevents this code from executing more than once.

Properties

Object properties are the public face of the values stored in an object. More often than not, they are implemented simply as an instance variable whose value can be queried or altered. But they can also be synthetic values—values derived from other information. Regardless, the interface the client sees is a value that can be obtained, and optionally changed, via a property name.

You add properties to your class in one of four ways:

1. Public instance variable (pre-properties)
2. Private instance variable combined with your own getter and setter methods
3. A `@property` declaration backed by a private instance variable and optional getting and setting methods
4. A modern `@property` declaration

These four techniques recapitulate the history of property values in Objective-C. Reprising the evolution of properties will help explain both what options you have, and why you have them. Let's begin in the dark ages.

Instance Variables

A long time ago (in the 1980s), Objective-C was born. In its original incarnation, it was a very (very) thin layer on top of C that added Smalltalk-like messaging to special `structs` called objects. The values of an object were stored in its instance variables and accessed exactly like the fields of a C struct. Here's an example:

```
@interface DarkAge : Object
{
    BOOL dawn;
}
@end
...
DarkAge *darkest = [[DarkAge alloc] new];
if (darkest->dawn==NO)
    ...
```

You can still do this today. Programmers, however, quickly discovered that there are a number of problems to this arrangement. The biggest problem is that it's counter to the philosophy of encapsulation. The client code has too much access, and too many responsibilities, when modifying the values of an object. This realization ushered in the second age object values.

Using Getters and Setters

The convention that spread through the industry was to declare a private instance variable, and then write methods that returned and set the value stored in that variable. Together, these are called the *accessor* methods. The method that retrieves the value is referred to as the *getter* method, and the method that sets the value is the *setter* method. The getter method would have the same name as the variable and the setter method would be the name of the variable prefixed with "set." (A value that couldn't be modified would omit the setter method.) Here's a class written this way:

```
@interface GoGetter : NSObject
{
    @private
    BOOL eager;
}
@end

@implementation GoGetter

- (BOOL)eager
{
    return eager;
}

- (void)setEager:(BOOL)newEager
{
    eager = newEager;
}

@end
```

This was a huge improvement—at least in terms of good software design, encapsulation, and flexibility. The client code now used the getter ([obj eager]) and setter ([obj setEager:YES]) methods to access the object's values. Any special cases, necessary memory management, notification of changes, and so on could all be handled—consistently and reliably—in the getter and setter methods. Technologies like Key-Value Observing (see Chapter 8) were now possible.

It also created two paths for affecting object values: direct manipulation of the instance variable and sending the accessor messages. Using directives like `@private` or `@protected`, you can limit direct access to the instance variables to just those methods defined by the class (or its subclasses). Direct access to variables is sometimes preferred. It's faster and may avoid unwanted side effects of the accessor methods. The canonical example is the accessor methods themselves, which must be able to affect the instance variables directly; they obviously can't use the getter and setter methods.

Life was looking pretty good, except for the poor programmer who had to write the same getter and setter methods, over and over again. Programmers cried out for a solution. Surely, there must be some way that Objective-C could rescue them from this tedium? The giant brains that oversee Objective-C heard their calls, and the age of properties began.

Declared Properties

Objective-C 2.0 introduced the `@property` directive. This formalized the conventions that programmers had been using, and added a property accessor syntax that greatly simplified their use. Property values could now be retrieved by writing `obj.value` and set it using `obj.value=nil`. A property declaration looks like this:

```
@property (nonatomic) id value;
```

Classes inherit the properties of their superclass. You cannot (with one exception) change the definition of an inherited property in your class, although you can override its accessor methods.

Initially, the @property declaration did little beyond legitimizing the relationship between the instance variable and the getter and setter methods. It didn't generate any code or define storage for the variable. The programmer was still responsible for all that. But it did sweeten the syntax.

Programmers could now take pre Objective-C 2.0 code, like the GoGetter class, add @property declarations to it, and use the property getter syntax (replacing [obj setEager:YES] with obj.eager=YES). It was definitely an improvement.

But Objective-C 2.0 had one more gift. If the getter and setter methods were generic—all they did was return or set the value of an instance variable—the programmer could use the new @synthesize directive and Objective-C would write that code for them. Now their classes looked like this:

```
@interface GoldenAge : NSObject
{
    @private
    BOOL joyful;
}
@property BOOL joyful;
@end

@implementation GoldenAge
@synthesize joyful;
@end

...

GoldenAge *age = [[GoldenAge alloc] init];
age.joyful = YES;
```

It had all the benefits of encapsulation, with none of the code. The accessor syntax was particularly welcome, as nested setters and getters in Objective-C can be quite difficult to read at times. Consider these two, equivalent, statements:

```
[layer setRasterizationScale:[layer rasterizationScale]*2];
layer.rasterizationScale *= 2;
```

You have to admit, the second statement is easier on the eyes. And this brings up an important point. The property accessor syntax added by Objective-C 2.0 did not, fundamentally, change how getter and setter methods are sent or how they work. It only changed the syntax used to send them. Computer language designers call this *syntactic sugar*; it "sweetens" the language, but doesn't change what it does.

The statements in Table 20-2 demonstrate the translation that occurs when using property accessor syntax. The last two rows in the table illustrate the difference between accessing an instance variable directly (from within an instance method) and invoking the object's own accessor method for that same property.

Table 20-2. Property Accessor Message Equivalency

Objective-C 2.0	Objective-C (any version)
v = obj.property;	v = [obj property];
obj.property = v;	[obj setProperty:v];
obj.property += v;	[obj setProperty:[obj property]+v];
property = v;	property = v;
self.property = v;	[self setProperty:v];

> **Tip** You don't have to use the @property directive to benefit from the accessor syntax. Objective-C will let you treat any method that takes no parameters and returns a value as if it were the getter for a property, and any method that returns nothing, starts with the word "set," and takes a single parameter as the setter method for a property. The NSPort class has never been updated with @property declarations; it only defines the methods -delegate and -setDelegate:. Yet, Objective-C will let you write port.delegate = nil, because those two methods conform to the accessor pattern for a delegate property.

Automatic Properties

Modern Objective-C compilers (LLVM) have finally "closed the loop" on properties. Today, if you declare a @property in your @interface and then you do *not* write either the required accessor methods or include a @synthesize directive, Objective-C will synthesize everything for you. It adds an instance variable to your object (beginning with an underscore character) and generates the getter and setter methods.

This is largely what you've been using in this book. The following class illustrates modern properties:

```
@interface Nirvana : NSObject
@property BOOL automatic;
@end

@implementation Nirvana
@end
```

This class has a private BOOL instance variable named _automatic, and implements two methods named -automatic and -setAutomatic:. The tedious work of allocating and implementing the property is now done for you. You are not, however, compelled to use the modern solution. If your class has special needs, you can back up and use any of the previous solutions. Table 20-3 summarizes the different combinations in which properties are declared and implemented.

Table 20-3. Property Implementation Choices

@interface	@implementation	Notes
`@property id prop;`	(nothing)	Creates an instance variable named _prop and generates the methods -(id)prop and -(void)setProp:(id)prop;
`@property (readonly)` ↪ `id prop;`	`-(id)prop;`	No instance variable is added and you must implement your own getter method
`@property id prop;`	`-(id)prop;` `-(void)setProp:(id)prop;`	If you supply your own setter method, no instance variable (_prop) will be added. You are reasonable for how the property value is stored.

`{`
`id prop;`
`}`
`@property id prop;`
	`@synthesize prop;`	Generates the methods -(id)prop and -(void)setProp:(id)prop that use the prop variable for storage

`{`
`id prop;`
`}`
`@property id prop;`
	(nothing)	Results in a compiler warning that you have declared your own variable (prop) which duplicates the _prop variable added by the compiler

The Anatomy of a Property

A property declaration consist of four parts:

- The @property keyword
- An optional list of property attributes, within parentheses
- The property type
- The property name

The @property keyword, type, and name don't need any explanation. The possible property attributes, on the other hand, afford you several options that affect how your property is implemented and treated.

Mutability

The readonly attribute declares a property that can be read, but not set. The expression `obj.property` is allowed, but the statement `obj.property=nil` is not. Here's a readonly property:

`@property (readonly) NSDate *created;`

As you saw in Table 20-3, specifying the `readonly` attribute means Objective-C won't allocate an instance variable for your property (what good is a variable for something that never changes?), and you must supply a getter method.

The `readwrite` attribute is the opposite of the `readonly` attribute. All properties are `readwrite` by default, so you normally don't declare them as such.

There is one use for the `readwrite` attribute. Objective-C allows you to declare a `readonly` property in a class, and then re-declare the same property as `readwrite` in a subclass. This is the *only* time that Objective-C will allow you to re-declare a property in a subclass, and all other aspects of the property must be identical. This feature supports the *immutable superclass, mutable subclass* design pattern.

Storage

The `copy` attribute applies to object properties. (Scalar and struct properties are always copied.) Without it, setting an object property retains a pointer to the object. The `copy` attribute changes the code in the setter method so that the object is duplicated—the mechanics of which are explained later in the "Copying Objects" section. The object keeps the reference to the duplicate object, not the one passed to the setter method. Here's an example:

`@property (copy) NSDictionary *collection;`

This can be important when the property is a mutable object. Take, for example, a dictionary property. If your property were set to a mutable dictionary object, both the object and the sender would be referring to the same dictionary. If the sender later modified the dictionary, the dictionary the property is pointing to would change too—because it's the same dictionary. Making a copy of the dictionary prevents this from happening.

The attributes `retain` and `assign` are alternatives to the `copy` attribute in a non-ARC (Automatic Reference Counting) environment. In this book, you've used ARC exclusively in your projects, so these attributes don't apply (although they're allowed, for compatibility with older software).

Lifetime Qualifiers

In an app that uses ARC, the attribute `strong` or `weak` determines how the property retains the object reference, and you've seen them throughout this book:

`@property (strong) NSString *title;`

The details of this are explained in Chapter 21. In short, a `strong` property will guarantee that the object exists as long as your property refers to it, and is the default. A `weak` property won't prevent the object from being destroyed, if no other objects have a strong reference to it.

> **Note** The attributes `assign`, `retain`, `strong`, `weak`, and `copy` are mutually exclusive; you can use only one.

If you're using legacy code in an ARC project, the retain attribute is equivalent to strong, and assign is broadly equivalent to weak.

Accessor Method Names

Use the attributes getter= and/or setter= when the property's getter or setter method names don't follow the usual pattern. One use for these attributes is when you are adding @property declarations to older code that already implements accessor methods with non-standard names.

A more contemporary use involves getter methods for Boolean values. Boolean properties often indicate state information. Their getter method has a history of being prefixed with the past or present form of the "to be" verb, such as -isEnabled or -hasConnection. To allow these getter methods to work as a property, override the getter name in the property declaration, like this:

@property (getter=hasConnection) BOOL connected;

Now the statements obj.connected and [obj hasConnection] are equivalent. Note that there will be no -connected method.

Atomic

As explained in Chapter 24, some properties must be accessed and set atomically. This ensures their integrity when being used from multiple threads of execution. If this is not a concern (which is most of the time), specify the nonatomic keyword. If it is a concern, and Chapter 24 will explain when it is, use the atomic keyword or nothing; atomic is the default. Here are two examples:

@property (nonatomic) NSString *name;
@property (atomic) NSPort *port;

It's somewhat unfortunate that atomic is the default. It certainly produces the safest code, but it also introduces thread synchronization code that executes every time the setter method is received. For the best performance, specify the nonatomic attribute for all of your object and struct properties that don't need to be atomic.

Keeping Your Promises

When you implement your own getter and setter methods, as opposed to letting Objective-C generate them, you are obligated to deliver the behavior specified by your property's attributes. Table 20-4 itemizes your responsibilities.

Table 20-4. Required Accessor Method Behavior

Attribute	Your Implementation
readonly	You must implement a getter method. You can still implement a setter method, often for your class's own consumption.
copy	Your setter method must copy the object being set, and retain the reference to the duplicate object. You can make an exception for immutable objects.
strong, weak, retain, assign	Retain the object value using the rules declared in the property. For example, do not strongly retain an object in a property declared as weak.
getter=, setter=	Name your getter and setter methods according to the property declaration.
atomic	Code your getter and setter method so that access, and changes to, the property value are atomic. This usually involves the use of mutual exclusion semaphores.

Introspection

Introspection is the ability to examine the metadata of an object. You can determine what class the object is, what methods it implements, what properties it declares, and so on. The extent to which you can plumb the details of an object or class is staggering, but there are really only three tests that are useful on a regular basis.

Class

Every object has a `class` property. This property is the class of the object. A class is, itself, an object (of type `Class`). The class object has properties and methods that describe the class.

> **Note** A `Class` object acts very much like any other object, but in some ways doesn't. For example, `Class` is a type, not a class. So even though it acts like an object, it isn't a subclass of `NSObject`. When you send a class message (+classMethod), the context is the `Class` object, so the `self` variable refers to that class. The `class` (property) of a `Class` (object) returns itself.

There are two methods useful for testing the class of an object: `-isKindOfClass:` and `-isMemberOfClass:`. The first determines if an object is a specific class, or any subclass of that class. You use it like this:

```
if ([view isKindOfClass:[UIControl class]]) ...
```

This expression is true if `view` is a `UIControl` object, or any subclass of `UIControl`. It would be false if `view` were a `UIView`, and it would be true if `view` were a `UIButton`. The expression `[UIControl class]` returns the `Class` object for `UIControl`. Remember that the `class` of a class is itself, so this statement is essentially a constant. You'd think you could write `[view isKindOfClass:UIControl]`, but obscure Objective-C syntax rules prohibit that.

The second method tests to see if an object is a specific class. You use it just like the
-isKindOfClass: message:

```
if ([view isMemberOfClass:[UIControl class]]) ...
```

The message returns YES if the receiver is that class, and NO in all other cases. This statement will be false if view were a UIView or if view were a UIButton. That's because neither is a UIControl. In fact, this statement would be unlikely to ever be true, since UIControl is an abstract class.

> **Caution** The method -isMemberOfClass: is preferred to the expression [view class]==[UIControl class]. The method correctly handles special objects—such as proxy objects that are placeholders for objects in another process—for which the equality test will fail.

You might be tempted to use this test to determine if a class implements a particular method or property (like buttonType, if it was a UIButton). That's not recommended, because there's another, much more relevant, test for methods.

Method

Probably the single most useful introspection test is the -respondsToSelector: message. It returns YES if the object responds to the message selector—implying that it implements that method. You typically use it like this:

```
if ([delegate respondsToSelector:@selector(saveTheUniverse)])
    [delegate saveTheUniverse];
```

The beauty of this code is that it's fast, specific, and it works correctly even when the receiver is nil. It's the only practical technique for determining which optional protocol methods an object has elected to implement.

It also avoids the problem of making assumptions. Novice programmers will often test the class of an object, and then *assume* that it implements a particular method based on that knowledge. Not only is this slower, but if the class implementation changes, that assumption could be wrong one day.

Objective-C encourages functional testing. If you want to know if an object has a tag property, test to see if it implements a -tag method; don't check its class and then guess.

Protocol

When dealing with delegate objects, it's sometimes useful to see if an object adopts a particular protocol. This is a little more specific than testing its class, and more efficient than testing for a bunch of different methods. It won't tell you if the object has implemented any of the optional protocol methods, but it implies that it's implemented all of the required ones.

One application for this test is to require that an object adopts a protocol. For example, the delegate setter for your class might check to see if the proposed object does, in fact, adopt the correct protocol, and abort the program if it doesn't:

```objc
if (![newDelegate conformsToProtocol:@protocol(MyClassDelegate)])
    @throw [NSException exceptionWithName:NSInvalidArgumentException
                                   reason:@"does not conform to protocol"
                                 userInfo:nil];
```

These three introspection techniques are your bread and butter, but they barely scratch the surface of what you can find out about objects and classes. Search Xcode's Documentation and API Reference window for "introspection" and you'll find a number of articles and guides similar to what I've written here. If you really want to dig deep, the definitive guide is the *Objective-C Runtime Reference*.

Protocols

A *protocol* defines a set of methods a class promises to implement. A protocol is defined using a @protocol directive. Here's a protocol declaration:

```objc
@protocol PromiseDelegate

- (void)pledge:(Promise*)promise;    // required method
@property BOOL crossHeart;           // required property

@optional
- (void)swear;                       // optional method
@property BOOL hopeToDie;            // optional property

@end
```

A protocol looks just very much like an @interface, except that it can't declare instance variables. A protocol can define properties, but those properties won't automatically allocate any instance variables or generate the getter or setter methods, the way they would in an @interface. You can also specify that methods/properties are optional using the @optional and @required directives; @required is the default.

A protocol is often in its own .h (header) file, named after the protocol. If a protocol goes hand-in-glove with a class, you may find both defined in the class's .h file.

Adopting Protocols

A class *adopts* one or more protocols by listing them after its @interface directive, like this:

```objc
@interface Agent : NSObject <PromiseDelegate>
```

A class is responsible for implementing the required protocol methods, and the getters and setters for any required properties. It's free to implement all, some, or none of the optional methods. An object of a class that adopts a protocol is said to *conform* to that protocol.

A category (next section) can also adopt protocols. A protocol can adopt protocols (superprotocols?), like this:

`@protocol PromiseDelegate <NSCoding>`

Adopting a protocol that adopts another protocol adopts both. Using this protocol declaration, the Agent class adopts both the PromiseDelegate and NSCoding protocols.

Referring to Conforming Objects

Any number of classes can adopt the same protocol. The protocol defines a behavior, independent of the class hierarchy, that any class can adopt. This allows disparate objects to share a common functionality and be treated homogenously, a central feature of *aspect programming*. Objective-C provides a special syntax for referring to any object that conforms to a protocol:

`id<PromiseDelegate> promisor;`

The type `id<PromiseDelegate>` can be used anywhere an object reference type (`id` or `Agent*`) would be acceptable. The `promisor` variable can be set to any object that adopts the `PromiseDelegate` protocol. The type can include multiple protocols, separated by commas.

The `NSCoding` protocol is an excellent example. Any class, no matter what its superclass, can elect to adopt the `NSCoding` protocol and participate in archiving and unarchiving. You can treat all such objects uniformly by referring to them as `id<NSCoding>` objects.

There is, however, a stumbling block with this scheme. When you declare a variable to be `id<PromiseDelegate>`, the Objective-C compiler assumes that the object implements *only* those methods and properties in the `PromiseDelegate` protocol. An `id<PromiseDelegate>` type is, therefore, more like a specific class reference (`UIButton*`) than a wildcard (`id`). Attempting to send the object any message *not* in the protocol results in a compiler error. This creates problems for a statement like this one:

```
if ([promisor respondsToSelector:@selector(swear)])    // * compiler error *
    [promisor swear];
```

The `PromiseDelegate` protocol only defines two methods and two properties. The method `-respondsToSelector:` is not among those. You're probably saying, "But promisor *must* implement `-respondsToSelector:`, because that's defined in NSObject, and every object inherits from NSObject!" And you're correct, promisor does inherit `-respondsToSelector:`—but the Objective-C compiler doesn't assume that, because the type of promisor is `id<PromiseDelegate>`.

> **Tip** A less elegant way around this problem is to cast the object variable as `id`, as in `[(id)promisor respondsToSelector:...]`. Objective-C will allow you send an `id` object any message without complaining.

The Cocoa Touch framework defines the special NSObject protocol to help you get around this inconvenience. The NSObject protocol declares almost all of the same methods that NSObject implements. By adopting NSObject in your protocol (@protocol PromiseDelegate <NSObject>), any use of the type id<PromiseDelegate> implies that the object adopts *both* the PromiseDelegate and NSObject protocols, which includes all of the commonly used methods in NSObject.

Categories

A *category* implements additional methods for an existing class, compiled independently of that class. If you're used to object-oriented languages like Java or C#, categories will seem strange, even bizarre. It's a unique feature, but it neatly solves a number of vexing programming problems.

A category declares, and implements, a set of methods. These methods are compiled and linked to your app in their own module. When your app runs, the category adds its methods to an existing class. It can be any class: one that you wrote or even one that's part of the operating system.

> **Caution** Do not attempt to override a method in a category. A category cannot (reliably) be used to replace an existing method. If you try this, only one of those methods will execute, and it's unpredictable which one it will be.

You declare a category as if you were defining a class. The class name is a class that's already been defined. Instead of a superclass, you follow the class with the category name in parentheses, like this:

```
@interface NSString (WordCount)
- (NSUInteger)wordCount;
@end
```

This defines a category of NSString named WordCount. It adds one new method, -wordCount, to the existing NSString class. You then implement those methods in a similarly named @implementation section:

```
@implementation NSString (WordCount)

- (NSUInteger)wordCount
{
    return /* count number of words in self here */;
}

@end
```

When your app loads, this category inserts its method into the NSString class. You can now send a -wordCount messages to *any* NSString object. The methods you implement execute in the context of the object, and are indistinguishable from methods defined by the original class.

Categories are typically written as a .h (interface) and .m (implementation) file, exactly as a regular class would be. When importing header files, remember that the compiler must see both the class interface and the category's interface, before it will recognize your category's methods and properties.

> **Tip** When choosing filenames for a category, the convention is to use the class name "plus" the category name, as in `NSString+WordCount.h` and `NSString+WordCount.m`. Xcode's Objective-C category file template will do this for you.

I mentioned that categories help solve peculiar programming problems. Let's talk about three of them.

Single Responsibility

The single responsibility principle encourages an object, and by extension a class, to do one thing well. But that can be limiting. Sometimes you need an object to do a variety of unrelated tasks.

Single responsibility means that string objects only do "string" things. This is great. This is how it should be. But when it comes time to do "non-string" things with strings, like drawing a string in graphics context, software designers have a problem. They'd like to be able to tell a string, "Draw yourself." But they don't want to "pollute" the string class with non-string related code. Programmers using other object-oriented languages end up organizing all of the drawing code in other classes, which result in methods like this:

```
[graphicsContext drawString:string at:point];
```

Categories give you the tools to simplify your design, without "polluting" the `NSString` class. Using a category, you can add drawing methods directly to the string class. All of the drawing code is maintained, and compiled, separately from the `NSString` class. Now your app can draw a string like this:

```
[string drawAt:point];
```

You code is actually more object oriented, simpler, and easier to code. And this example isn't hypothetical. All of the string drawing functions in iOS are defined in a category of `NSString` provided by the UIKit framework, specifically `NSString(UIStringDrawing)`.

Module Organization

Categories are also useful for organizing your methods. In particularly complex classes, it helps to group your methods into categories, pun intended.

In Chapter 14, the `STGame` object was responsible for all of the gameplay logic. Later, you also made it responsible for communicating with `STGame` objects on other iOS devices. Rather than just shoving new methods into `STGame`, you created a category, `STGame(STDataMessaging)`. All of the communications code was neatly organized in its own module.

This can be very helpful in large projects where multiple programmers are contributing to the same class. One programmer could be working on the game logic, while another one refines the communications code. Since the category is separate from the main class, they won't step on each other's toes.

Private Methods

Objective-C programmers soon discovered another use for categories: hiding methods. Let's say you've written a Star Gazer app. It has a `Star` class that represents a star. Your `Star` object is immutable; stars don't change. But then you create the Star Editor app that allows users to edit stars. You don't want to make the `Star` class in your Star Gazer app mutable. In that context, stars should still be immutable.

Categories solve this problem neatly. Both apps use the `Star` class and Star Editor adds a `Star(MutableStar)` category with the methods needed to alter it. These methods are "private" to the Star Editor app.

And the desire for private methods can be much more mundane. Objective-C methods have no visibility attribute; you can't declare a method to be `@private` or `@protected`, as you can with instance variables. So programmers quickly started to use categories to "hide" class methods that were intended only for internal consumption. Almost every class would define a category like this:

```
@interface MyClass (Private) // private methods
- (void)doSomethingSecret;
@end
```

This practice became so widespread, that it inspired a change to the Objective-C language.

Extensions

Objective-C 2.0 introduced the extension. An *extension* is an unnamed category of a class. I've been referring to these as "the private `@interface`" for your class throughout this book, but they are technically extensions. Here's an example of an extension:

```
@interface MyClass ()
- (void)doSomethingSecret;
@end
```

The rules for an extension differ slightly from a regular category:

- There can only be one extension per class, and it must be declared before the `@implementation` of the class.

- The methods and properties declared in an extension are implemented in the `@implementation` section of the class, right alongside the class's regular methods—not in a separate category `@implementation`.

- Extensions can declare additional instance variables and properties that create instance variables. These variables become part of the object, just as if they had been declared in the class's `@interface`.

nil is Your Friend

If you're an experienced programmer, but new to Objective-C, you probably have a healthy fear of NULL pointers. And you should. In most languages, NULL pointers and object references are ticking time bombs. Call a method on a NULL Java object, and your code will throw an uncaught exception. Dereference a NULL pointer in C, and your app just crashed. Terminated. Pushing up daisies. Dead. An ex-app.

The Unbearable Lightness of nil

Objective-C, in contrast, takes a decidedly different attitude towards nil. You can send a nil object any message. It's perfectly safe. It's even encouraged, and it will change the way you write your software. Let's take a look.

An Objective-C invocation involves a message and a receiver. The receiver is usually a variable, like this:

```
[obj doSomething];
```

If the object obj implements the -doSomething method, it executes. If it does not implement the -doSomething method, it throws an exception (that's bad). But if obj is nil (points to address 0), Objective-C does a curious thing: it quietly does nothing and goes on. In Chapter 18, the cloudService variable will be nil when the user isn't synchronizing their location with the cloud. When the user removed the saved map location, this code executes:

```
[cloudStore removeObjectForKey:kPreferenceSavedLocation];
```

If cloudStore referred to the ubiquitous value store, then the value with that key would be removed. If cloudStore was nil, the statement would do nothing and continue. It wasn't necessary to pepper the code with if (cloudStore!=nil) ... statements to prevent that line from executing.

Pay attention to those places in your code where you don't want something to happen when an object is missing or hasn't been set. Look back through the projects in this book for examples; there are probably more than you realize. Let the nil-ness of the variable implicitly skip whatever you would have done if there were an object. You might not start a timer, if there's no timer. You might not set a lock, if there's no lock, and so forth.

The Virtues of Being Positive

And it doesn't just return, it returns an empty value. If the message you sent a nil object returns an object, scalar, or pointer value, Objective-C *guarantees* the return value will 0, 0.0, NO, NULL, or nil. This makes it possible to write the following with impunity:

```
if ([delegate conformsToProtocol:@protocol(MyClassDelegate)])
    {
    // do something with delegate
    }
```

If `delegate` is `nil`, the message `-conformsToProtocol:` will return `NO`. This makes sense. A `nil` object doesn't implement your protocol. It doesn't implement anything.

This also means `nil` applies to property values. The expression `collection.count` will always be 0 if `collection` is `nil`, because `collection.count` gets translated into `[collection count]`. And there's a cascade effect. The statement `[viewController.button.superview.backgroundColor setFill]` will do nothing if `backgroundColor` is `nil`, `superview` is `nil`, `button` is `nil`, or `viewController` is `nil`.

You can exploit this in your own design by expressing return and property values in the positive sense. Define methods like `-hasContent` instead of `-isEmpty`. If an object reference is `nil`, the message `-hasContent` returns `NO`. This makes sense; a `nil` object doesn't have any content. But `-isEmpty` would also return `NO`, implying that it has content; believe me, it doesn't. In short, choose properties and return values so they still make sense when sent to `nil` objects.

When nil Is Bad

That's not to say `nil` is harmless all the time. If used as a C pointer, it has all the hazards associated with dereferencing a `NULL` pointer. Which is yet another reason to embrace properties; getter and setter methods are perfectly safe when used with a `nil` object. If `obj` is `nil`, the statement `obj.var=0` is safe and does nothing. In contrast, the statement `obj->var=0` will crash your app.

A `nil` parameter can also be a hazard. A lot of methods do not tolerate `nil` parameters. In the statement `[array removeObject:obj]`, array can be `nil`, but `obj` must not be. Most methods that allow `nil` parameters will say so in the documentation. If it doesn't, assume `nil` is not allowed.

Finally, a message sent to a `nil` object does nothing, but the parameters of that message are prepared first. This means that any side effects of assembling the parameters will occur. In the following code, the `-useConnection` message isn't sent if `downloader` is `nil`, but the `+createConnection` message still gets sent:

```
[downloader useConnection:[DownloadSource createConnection]];
```

If you wanted to prevent `+createConnection` from being sent, you'd need to first test to see that `downloader!=nil`.

Copying Objects

The Cocoa framework defines a protocol for copying (duplicating) objects. Not all objects can be copied. Those that can adopt the `NSCopying` protocol and implement a `-copyWithZone:` method. There are three ways to make your objects copyable:

- Adopt `NSCopying` and create a new object in your `-copyWithZone:` method
- Inherit `NSCopying` and send the superclass a `-copyWithZone:` message
- Take a shortcut

Adopting NSCopying

If your class is the one adopting NSCopying, its -copyWithZone: must create a new object and duplicate its properties, as appropriate. Here's an example:

```
@interface Recipe : NSObject <NSCopying>
@property NSString *title;
@property NSMutableArray *ingredients;
@end

@implementation Recipe

- (id)copyWithZone:(NSZone *)zone
{
    Recipe *copy = [[[self class] allocWithZone:zone] init];
    if (copy!=nil)
        {
        copy->_title = _title;
        copy->_ingredients = [_ingredients copy];
        }
    return copy;
}

@end
```

The Recipe class is the first to adopt NSCopying, so it must create a new object in its -copyWithZone: method. Notice how it creates the new object, with the statement [[[self class] allocWithZone:zone] init]. There are three steps to creating a duplicate object correctly:

1. Get the class of the original object. Subclasses of Recipe inherit this -copyWithZone: method, so it's possible that self could be a subclass of Recipe. The expression [self class] gets the class of the object, rather than assuming it's a Recipe object.

2. Send the -allocWithZone: message to allocate the object in the requested memory zone. In iOS the zone parameter is typically nil, but this satisfied the memory management contract for -copyWithZone:.

3. Finally, the newly created object receives its -init message and you test to see that it's not nil, in case the object couldn't be created.

> **Note** Memory zones are not used in iOS. But to maintain compatibility with Cocoa (OS X) classes, the -copyWithZone: message still includes a zone parameter.

After that, the individual property values of the original object (self) are copied to the new object (copy). What gets copied and how is up to you, but as a rule the copy should be functionally identical to the original, and autonomous. To that end, the title reference is simply copied. The title property is an NSString, and NSString objects are immutable, so both objects can safely refer to the same string object. This is called a *shallow* copy. The ingredients array, however, is duplicated so that the ingredients of the copy are not coupled to the ingredients of the original. This is called a *deep* copy.

Other properties might be treated differently. For example, an object with a UUID (Universally Unique Identifier) property might generate a new UUID when the object is copied, so that both objects have unique IDs. You'll make these kinds of decisions on a case-by-case basis.

Inheriting NSCopying

When your class inherits NSCopying, it's your responsibility to see that it upholds its copy contract. This is an easy thing to overlook. Your subclass should implement its -copyWithZone: method, like this:

```
@interface AssignedRecipe : Recipe
@property Chef *chef;
@end

@implementation AssignedRecipe

- (id)copyWithZone:(NSZone *)zone
{
    AssignedRecipe *copy = [super copyWithZone:zone];
    if (copy!=nil)
        {
        copy->_chef = _chef;
        }
    return copy;
}

@end
```

Recipe already adopts NSCopying and creates the copy of the object in its -copyWithZone: method. All the subclass has to do is let the superclass create the new copy and then duplicate any subclass-specific properties.

Copying Something Special

As an alternative, your -copyWithZone: implementation might do something completely different. For example, if your object is immutable, or a singleton, then its -copyWithZone: method could be this:

```
- (id)copyWithZone:(NSZone *)zone
{
    return self;
}
```

Any attempt to copy your object will return a reference to itself.

Copying an Object

When you want to copy an object, first make sure it adopts NSCopying. To make a copy, send it a -copy message. (NSObject's -copy method just executes [self copyWithZone:nil]). The returned value is the duplicate object. If you were writing a property setter that specified the copy attribute, your code would look like this:

```
@property (copy) NSDictionary *options;

...

- (void)setOptions:(NSDictionary*)options
{
    _options = [options copy];
}
```

Mutable Copies

A few classes, most notably the collection classes, adopt the special NSMutableCopying protocol and implement the -mutableCopyWithZone: method.

The base class collections (NSArray, NSDictionary, NSSet, and so on), along with NSString, are all immutable—they can't be changed. If you copy an immutable object, you'll just end up with another immutable object, possibly the same object.

If you need a mutable copy of a string, collection, or any immutable object that conforms to NSMutableCopying, send it a -mutableCopy message. If the array (for example) was already a mutable array, you'll receive a copy of the array, the same as sending -copy. But if it was an immutable array (NSArray), it will return a new mutable array (NSMutableArray) with the same contents.

Attributed Strings

You've seen, throughout this book, a number of UIView classes and drawing methods that use attributed strings, instead of regular strings. An *attributed string* associates a variable number of attribute values with a range of characters within the string. Attributes can express the font the characters are drawn in (font family, size, style), color, typographical adjustments (character spacing), alignment (right justified, superscript, subscript), text decorations (underline, strikethrough), and so on. Attributed strings are very flexible and can describe arbitrarily complex typography. In concept, they're not complicated, although they can be a little tedious in practice.

Attributes are expressed as a dictionary of values. The key identifies the kind of attribute. This dictionary is then associated with a range of characters. The following example shows how attributed strings are constructed:

```
NSMutableAttributedString *fancyString;
fancyString = [[NSMutableAttributedString alloc] initWithString:@"iOS "];
NSDictionary *iOSAttrs = @{
    NSFontAttributeName: [UIFont italicSystemFontOfSize:30],
```

```
    NSForegroundColorAttributeName: [UIColor redColor],
    NSKernAttributeName: @4, };
[fancyString setAttributes:iOSAttrs range:NSMakeRange(0,3)];

NSDictionary *appAttrs = @{
    NSFontAttributeName: [UIFont boldSystemFontOfSize:28],
    NSUnderlineStyleAttributeName: @(NSUnderlineStyleSingle) };
NSAttributedString *secondString;
secondString = [[NSAttributedString alloc] initWithString:@"App!"
                                            attributes:appAttrs];
[fancyString appendAttributedString:secondString];

self.label.attributedText = fancyString;
```

The first block of code creates a mutable attributed string from a plain string. It then creates a dictionary, defining three attributes: the italic system font at 30pts, the color red, and a kerning (inter-character spacing) of 4pts. Those attributes are applied to the first three characters of the string. Note that the space character (4th character in the string) has no attributes.

The second technique is to create an attributed string directly from a string and a dictionary of attributes. The appAttrs dictionary describes the system bold font at 28pts and the underline style. When you create an attributed string this way, the attributes apply to all of the characters.

Finally, the second attributed string is appended to the first. The appended string retains all of its attributes. The fancyString object now has 8 characters, with one set of attributes for the first three, a different set for the last four, and still no attributes for the space. All attributes have default values and a character will use the default values for any attributes it's missing.

When the attributed string is assigned to a UILabel, as shown in Figure 20-1, its attributes determine how it is drawn.

Figure 20-1. An attributed string in a label

Here are some tips for using attributed strings:

- An attributed string is not a subclass of NSString. It has an NSString (its string property), but it isn't an NSString.
- If the attributes apply to the entire string, you can create a single, immutable, attributed string using NSAttributedString.
- If you want to create an attributed string with a mixture of different attributes, you must create an NSMutableAttributedString and construct it piecemeal.
- Using a mutable attributed string, you can set the attributes for a range of characters (-setAttributes:range:), which replace any previous attributes for that range. You can also add (-addAttributes:range:) or remove (-removeAttributes:range:) attributes. These methods combine with, or selectively remove from, the existing attributes.

Caution Never change an attribute by altering the value object in an attribute dictionary that's already been assigned to a range. You must always replace the attributes to change them.

Find the *NSAttributedString UIKit Additions Reference* in Xcode's Documentation and API Reference window. The "Constants" section lists all of the attribute keys supported by iOS, and what kind of value object to supply for each.

Collections

You've probably learned almost everything you need to know about collections through osmosis. The array (NSArray) and dictionary (NSDictionary) collections are used extensively throughout iOS. You just saw how dictionaries describe attributes in a string.

There are, however, a few collection objects that you might not have heard of, and some fine points you should be aware of. And it's always nice to know how to work with the objects in a collection. Let's start with what's on the menu.

Collection Classes

Table 20-5 lists the major collection classes in iOS.

Table 20-5. Collection classes

Immutable Class	Mutable Class	Description
NSArray	NSMutableArray	An ordered collection of objects. Objects are identified by their position (index) in the collection.
	NSPointerArray	Like an NSMutableArray, but can be tailored to store things other than objects (integer values, pointers, NULL).
NSDictionary	NSMutableDictionary	An unordered collection of objects. A unique key object addresses each value object.
	NSMapTable	Like an NSMutableDictionary, but can be tailored to store things other than objects (integer values, pointers, NULL).
NSSet	NSMutableSet	An unordered collection of unique objects. Objects are either in the set or they are not. Individual objects cannot be addressed.
	NSHashTable	Like NSMutableSet, but can be tailored to store things other than objects (integer values, pointers, NULL).
NSIndexSet	NSMutableIndexSet	A set of integer values.

The traditional collection classes, NSArray, NSDictionary, NSSet, and NSIndexSet, all come in two flavors: an immutable base class and a mutable subclass. NSArray, NSDictionary, and NSSet can only store object values, and that does *not* include nil. NSIndexSet is a special collection that efficiently keeps track of a set of integer values.

The newer NSPointerArray, NSMapTable, and NSHashTable are essentially professional versions of NSArray, NSDictionary, and NSSet. They can be configured to store things other than objects, use different memory management rules, and they can store nil/NULL values. Unless you have a burning need to store a nil value in an array, or you are storing a bazillion small value objects, you're better off using the `NSArray`, `NSDictionary`, and `NSSet` classes. If you want to step up to `NSPointerArray`, `NSMapTable`, or `NSHashTable`, read the appropriate chapter in the *Collections Programming Topics* document that you'll find in Xcode's Documentation and API Reference window.

Here are a few details about collections that you should know:

- Object and key equality in arrays, dictionaries, and sets is determined by the `-isEqual:` method of the objects. Every object inherits an `-isEqual:` method from `NSObject`. It's used to determine if two objects are equivalent. If you add custom objects to a collection, and test for their presence (using methods like `-containsObject:`), or do anything with sets, those objects *must* implement their `-isEqual:` and `-hash` methods correctly. See the documentation for `-hash`.

- Objects used for the keys in dictionaries are copied when added to the collection. For typical keys (`NSNumber` and `NSString`), this doesn't matter because they are both immutable and already conform to `NSCopying`. If you use unusual objects for your dictionary keys, they must implement `NSCopying`, and be aware that they'll be copied when added.

- You can sort arrays in one of four ways: supply a comparison message the objects respond to, supply an array of comparison descriptors, supply a C function that compares the objects, or pass a code block that compares the objects. Immutable arrays can create a new, sorted, array. Mutable arrays can be sorted in place. See the "Arrays: Ordered Collections" section of the *Collections Programming Topics* document.

- All of the collections have methods for adding, subtracting, and combining collections. If you need to make wholesale changes to a collection, such as combining two arrays (-addObjectsFromArray:), determining the intersection of two sets (-intersectSet:), or removing multiple keys from a dictionary (-removeObjectsForKeys:), look for methods that already do that work for you.

Enumeration

A lot of times you'll want to do something with all of the objects in a collection. The Objective-C language provides a `for` loop syntax just for collections, and the collection objects themselves have a variety of enumeration methods. Let's start with Objective-C.

Fast Object Enumeration

Objects in a collection can be processed, one at a time, using a special form of C's `for` loop syntax:

```
for ( id obj in collection ) { ... }
```

The loop's code block is executed once for every object in the collection. The `obj` variable will refer to a different object during each iteration. For arrays, the order is always the order of the objects in the array. For dictionaries and sets, the order is unpredictable.

> **Caution** You cannot modify a collection during the execution of the `for` loop. Modifying the collection will throw an exception. Either loop through a duplicate of the collection (that won't change), or just avoid making changes until the loop is finished.

When using the `for` loop on a dictionary, `obj` will be the keys in the dictionary, not the values. To work with the values, you can use the key to get the value at the beginning of the code block (`id v = collection[obj]`), or you can loop through the values using code like `for ( id v in dictionary.allValues )`. The `allValues` property returns an array of just the value objects in the dictionary.

> **Note** Technically, the `collection` term of the `for` loop can be any object that conforms to `NSFastEnumeration`. If you create a custom class that adopts `NSFastEnumeration`, you can pass your object as the `collection` term of a `for` loop. Your object is responsible for supplying the individual object values.

Collection Enumeration

The alternative technique is to use one of the many enumeration methods in the collection classes. Broadly, these come in two flavors:

- Send a simple message to every object in the collection. An example is `-makeObjectsPerformSelector:`.
- Execute a code block with every object in the collection. Examples are `-enumerateObjectsUsingBlock:` and `-enumerateKeysAndObjectsUsingBlock:`.

The latter method is the most flexible, and in many ways very similar to using the `for` loop technique. Most of the block-based enumeration methods include a `stop` parameter. This parameter points to a BOOL value. If, while processing the objects, your code wants the enumeration to stop, set the BOOL value to YES, like this:

```
*stop = YES;
```

Shortcuts

Who doesn't love shortcuts? It means less typing, and your code is often easier to read. You've already seen how accessor syntax simplifies your code. The latest version of Objective-C adds a fresh batch of shortcuts, which I've summarized in Table 20-6.

Table 20-6. Objective-C shortcuts

Task	Shortcut	Equivalent Code

Create NSNumber	`@3`
	`@3.14159267`
	`@YES`
	`@((int)expression)`
		`[NSNumber numberWithInteger:3]`
		`[NSNumber numberWithDouble:3.14159267]`
		`[NSNumber numberWithBool:YES]`
		`[NSNumber numberWithInteger:expression]`

Create NSArray	`@[a,b,c]`	`[NSArray arrayWithObjects:a,b,c,nil]`
Create NSDictionary	`@{ @"key": v }`	`[NSDictionary dictionaryWithObject:v` `                  forKey:@"key"]`

Create NSDictionary	`@{ @"key1": v1,`
	`   @"key2": v2 }`
		`[NSDictionary dictionaryWithObjectsAndKeys:`
		`     v1, @"key1",`
		`     v2, @"key2",`
		`     nil]`

Object in an NSArray	`array[1]`	`[array objectAtIndex:1]`
Replace object in an NSMutableArray	`array[1] = obj`	`[array replaceObjectAtIndex:1 withObject:obj]`
Object in an NSDictionary	`dictionary[@"key"]`	`[dictionary objectForKey:@"key"]`
Set object in an NSMutableDictionary	`dictionary[@"key"] = obj`	`[dictionary setObject:obj forKey:@"key"]`

Summary

There's more to Objective-C; I didn't cover everything. But you've learned a lot. And I mean, a *lot*—enough to write professional-level iOS apps. Some of the topics I didn't cover are Key-Value Coding, code blocks, exceptions, programmatic method invocation, and the toll-free bridge, to name a few. Don't panic; there are technology guides for all of those included in the Xcode documentation. If you need something I missed, hit the docs. It's all there.

I also don't expect you to memorize everything in this chapter the first time around. Most Objective-C developers, myself included, learned these lessons over the course of years. Use this chapter as a reference, or just come back when things feel fuzzy.

It's confession time. In the preceding chapters, I deliberately sidestepped one of the most onerous programming tasks there is: memory management. You're now ready to tackle that topic.

Chapter 21

The Elephant in the Room

So far, I've been ignoring a huge part of app development, memory management. It can be a difficult and painful topic, and has been the bane of many a programmer. I, personally, have spent days tracking down memory leaks and over-release bugs. If you have any programming experience, you've probably dedicated a significant portion of your brain to dealing with memory management rules.

So how did I pull this off—ignoring such an important topic—for most of this book? The answer is Automatic Reference Counting (ARC). Apple, in collaboration with the Objective-C language developers, has baked efficient—and nearly foolproof—memory management right into Objective-C and iOS. This is a huge boon for modern iOS developers, like you.

It's delightful that you haven't been burdened with memory management in this book. But that's not to say that ignorance is bliss. To be a proficient iOS developer, it helps to know when objects get destroyed, how ARC replaces traditional memory management, and what those strong and weak property attributes mean. In this chapter you will learn:

- The principles of memory management
- How garbage collection works
- How reference counting works
- How ARC implements reference counting for you
- What lifetime qualifiers mean
- What ARC doesn't do

In Chapter 18 you created the page view controller's data source programmatically. You also had to store a reference to it in *both* the controller's data source outlet and an instance variable—a variable you never used. This seems like Voodoo, unless you understand the retention rules for object references. If you didn't, you would have gone insane trying to figure out why the data source of your view controller kept disappearing. I want to save you from that fate, so let's set sail for the mysterious land of memory management.

Memory Management

What is memory management? Memory management is how an app manages its dynamically allocated memory. At a fundamental level, memory management is a simple concept:

1. Your app's process is allotted a range of memory locations (bytes), called its *logical address space*.
2. The bulk of those locations are placed into a vast pool of available memory called *the heap*.
3. Whenever your app needs a block of memory to store something (like an object) it requests a block of bytes from the heap.
4. A block of free bytes is found (allocated) and can now by utilized by your app. The pointer to this block of bytes becomes the object's reference.
5. Your app uses the block/object to store values and do wonderful things.
6. When your app is done with the block/object, it passes the address back to the heap. That range of locations is returned to the pool of free bytes, ready to be used for some other purpose.

It's kindergarten rules: you take something off the shelf, play with it, and put it back when you're done. As simple as it sounds, the operating system is already doing an incredible amount of work for you, keeping track of what memory is in use and efficiently recycling it.

Determining when your app needs a block of memory is easy. Figuring out when it should be returned to the heap keeps programmers up through the night. Giving blocks back in a timely fashion is important, which brings us to the first three pitfalls of memory management:

- Running out of memory
- Neglecting to return enough memory to the heap, and running out of memory
- Forgetting to return blocks you're no longer using, and running out of memory

You'll encounter the first problem when your app's memory needs exceed that of the device. This is a real possibility on iOS devices. Handheld computer systems have a *tiny fraction* of the memory available to typical desktop computers, and they don't employ technology (like virtual memory stores) to extend that. So while it's practically impossible for modern desktop applications to run out of addressable memory, it's a daily occurrence for even the best iOS apps. If your app deals with large amounts of data, it's something you'll have to contend with.

The second problem is just poor app design. Failing to return memory that you don't need will mean your app uses more memory than it should. This reduces the performance of your app, other apps, and the iOS device in general. In Chapter 23, you're going to analyze your app's memory usage and take steps to release objects you don't really need.

The last problem is called a *memory leak*, and that's a bug. If you allocate a block of memory, forget to return it, and forget its address, that block of memory is lost—it stays allocated, and it can never (ever!) be used again. Repeat this a few thousand times, and your app will begin to suffer, eventually running out of free memory, and dying.

Your Grandfather's Memory Management

Simple memory management follows the steps outlined at the beginning of "Memory Management;" your code allocates a block of memory when it wants one, and frees it again when it's finished with it. You can do this directly, should you need to. Pass the number of bytes you want to allocate to the `alloc` function. It will return a pointer to an allocated block of memory. When you have finished using that memory, pass the same pointer to the `free` function, returning it to the pool of available memory.

When you allocate a new Objective-C object (`[[MyClass alloc] init]`), that +alloc class method eventually ends up calling `alloc` (the C function) to carve out a little chunk of the heap for your new object. When the object gets destroyed, `free` is called to recycle it.

That sounds simple. So why isn't this chapter ending already? When code allocates an object, some other code has to take responsibility for destroying it when it's no longer needed. Specifically, you have to answer the general question "what code is responsible for destroying the object when your app is done with it?" Answering that question can be a little tricky.

We've already talked about how objects form graphs. Objects refer to other objects, which refer to even more objects. Several objects can refer to the same object. An object can refer to an object that refers back to the original object, creating a loop. In these situations, answering the question "who's responsible for this object" isn't easy, or even meaningful.

Here's a simple example. In the last chapter, you saw how to use an attributed string to display styled text in a `UIView`. Figure 21-1 shows a similar graph of objects. It has two buttons, with different titles, but both titles use the same font.

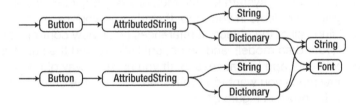

Figure 21-1. Attributed string object graph

Now pretend the attributed string of a button is replaced with a different one. The graph of objects now looks like the one in Figure 21-2.

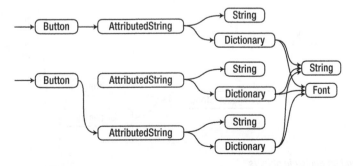

Figure 21-2. Object graph with leaked objects

There's no longer a reference to the original attributed string. Unless the attributed string, string, and dictionary objects are destroyed, they'll "leak," wasting precious memory. It won't take long before thousands (millions!) of leaked objects choke your app to death.

You might suggest that the button take responsibility for destroying the attributed string object. That's an excellent suggestion. You could make a general rule that the object with the reference destroys the original object when it's done with it.

But which object should destroy the font object? Several objects reference it. No one object is "responsible" for the font object. So when the dictionary that refers to it is destroyed, does it, or does it not, need to destroy the font object?

And this is the central problem with object reclamation in an undirected graph of objects—determining which objects are still useful and which ones aren't. Computer scientists and engineers have spent decades trying to solve this problem, and they've come up with two solutions: garbage collection and reference counting.

Garbage Collection

iOS doesn't use garbage collection (although it made a brief appearance in OS X's Cocoa). The poster children for garbage collection are currently Java and C#. Understanding how garbage collection works is useful, mostly, as a conceptual basis for what automatic memory management does for you. You can then appreciate the logic behind reference counting when we get to that. To that end, here's the Cliff Notes version of garbage collection.

In garbage collection, the operating system keeps track of every object your app creates. It periodically traces the graph of objects in your app. It starts with your permanent objects (like your application object), and finds all of the objects it references (your view controllers), all of the objects those objects reference (your data model), and so on, until it's created the set of *reachable objects*. These are all of the objects your app has access to. (If you have no way of referring to an object, you can't use it, no matter how much you want to.) What's left over are the *unreachable objects*; in other words, the garbage. This is shown in Figure 21-3.

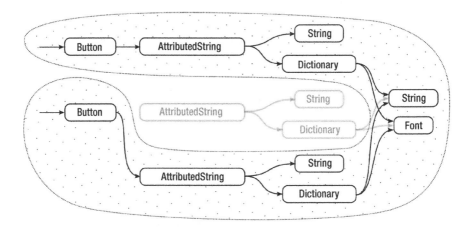

Figure 21-3. Reachable and unreachable objects

The attributed string, and the dictionary and string objects it refers to, have become unreachable. These objects are destroyed and their memory recycled.

The beauty of garbage collection is that it takes almost no effort on the part of the programmer. You simply set, or forget, object references as needed. The operating system will eventually come around to figure out which objects you're using and which ones you're not.

That sounds fantastic, doesn't it? So why doesn't iOS use garbage collection? There are a couple of reasons. Garbage collection shifts all of the work onto the operating system. Periodically sifting through tens of thousands of objects to determine who references what is not a trivial task. This requires a significant amount of CPU time, which translates into battery drain and intermittent unresponsiveness.

Secondly, research has concluded that garbage collection is only truly efficient when there is substantially more memory available than the application uses.[1] When memory is tight, the performance of garbage collection plummets, further reducing your app's performance.

Garbage collection works great, therefore, when there's lots of CPU capacity, no reason to conserve that capacity, and a surfeit of memory. What does that sound like? I hope you said "desktop computers" or "servers," because that's not the description of tiny handheld computing platforms, like iOS devices.

What you want is a solution like garbage collection—that can automatically determine what objects are in use and which ones need to be destroyed—without so much overhead. That solution is called reference counting.

Reference Counting

Reference counting counts the references to an object to determine if it's still in use. It's a cooperative system, whereby each object remembers the number of references to it—called its *reference count*. Objects that use an object inform it when they establish a reference to it, and again later when they no longer need it. An object is destroyed when the last referring object breaks its connection. Here's the scheme, in brief:

- When an object wants to maintain a reference to another object, it sends that object a `-retain` message. The `-retain` message increases the receiver's reference count by one.

- When an object stops referring to an object, it first sends the object a `-release` message. The `-release` message decrements the receiver's reference count by one.

- When an object's reference count becomes 0, it destroys itself.

In essence, it shifts the responsibility for determining when an object is no longer being used from the operating system to the object and the objects that refer to that object.

---

[1]Recent studies conclude that garbage collection matches the efficiency of reference counting only when the total heap memory is at least 4 to 5 times that of the application's memory footprint: *Quantifying the Performance of Garbage Collection vs. Explicit Memory Management* by Matthew Hertz and Emery D. Berger, Dept. of Computer Science, University of Massachusetts Amherst, Amherst, MA.

Returning to the attributed string example, each object reference in the graph is accompanied by a -retain message. Each message increments the object's reference count by one, and it knows that one more object is using it. Shared objects, like the Font object, have a reference count of two or more, as they're being used by more than one object, as shown in Figure 21-4.

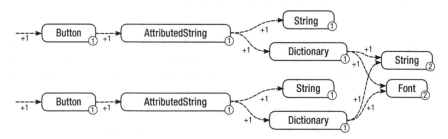

Figure 21-4. Reference counted objects

The sending of retain and release messages is typically encapsulated in the property setter method. The setter method sends a retain message to the object reference being set, and a release message to the reference being displaced. When you set a different attributed string object for the button object, the first thing that happens is a new retain message is sent to the new attributed string object, as shown in Figure 21-5. The attributed string object has, already, sent -retain messages to the string and dictionary it refers to, and the dictionary has already sent -retain messages to the string and font objects in its collection.

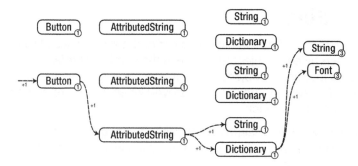

Figure 21-5. Retaining a new property

Before the button's setter method returns, it sends a -release message to the object it was previously referencing. That object had a reference count of 1. The -release message drops the object's reference count to 0 and it immediately destroys itself. As part of its destruction, it sends -release messages to all of the objects it still has references to. This begins a cascade of -release messages that systematically seek out and destroy all objects that no longer have an active reference, as shown in Figure 21-6.

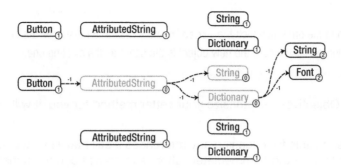

Figure 21-6. Releasing old objects

Reference counting gives you most of the benefits of garbage collection, with less than one-third of the calories. All iOS apps use reference counting. When you start a new project you'll be using Automatic Reference Counting (ARC). Existing projects may use ARC or manual reference counting (also called *managed memory*, or just *reference counting*). The decision changes how your write your code. Let's start with old-fashioned reference counting.

Manual Reference Counting

When writing iOS apps using traditional reference counting, your code is responsible for retaining and releasing your object references as you change them. If you're looking at non-ARC Objective-C code, it will be peppered with -retain, -release, and -autorelease messages. (I'll explain -autorelease shortly.) But it isn't as hard as it sounds. Here are the basics:

- Send a -retain message to an object you want to continue referencing it.
- For an object you retained, send a -release message to it immediately before discarding the reference.
- Every new (just created) object has a reference count of 1. If you create an object (with [[SomeClass alloc] init] or -copy), you've already retained it and must release it when you're finished with it.
- When an object is destroyed, it receives a -dealloc message. The -dealloc method must release all of the objects it still references.

You typically send your retain and release messages in your property setting methods—yet another good reason to use setter methods for changing property values. Now can you appreciate what the retain attribute is for? The setter method for a retain property promises to retain the new object and release the old one. A typical property and setter pair look like this:

```
@property (retain) UIFont *font;

...

- (void)setFont:(UIFont*)font
{
    [font retain];
    [_font release];
    _font = font;
}
```

> **Note** Pay attention to the order in which the `-retain` and `-release` messages are sent in the setter method. Now consider the case where the new object is the same as the existing one.

Even better, if you let Objective-C synthesize your setter method for you, it will send all of the correct messages.

Your object is also responsible for releasing any references it still has when it's destroyed. Every object receives a `-dealloc` method, immediately after its reference count reaches 0 and just before its memory is returned to the heap. Here's a typical `-dealloc` method:

```
- (void)dealloc
{
    [_font release];
    [super dealloc];
}
```

That wasn't too complicated, and it works pretty well—except for two gigantic flaws. Well, one gigantic flaw and a serious problem. Let's look at the gigantic flaw first.

Jumping into the Pool

This reference counting thing works great for about five minutes, until you need to create and return an object from a method. Think about it. If the code that creates an object is responsible for releasing it when it's done, that means it's impossible to create an object *and* return it to the sender. You end up with code like this:

```
- (NSArray*)allThatJazz
{
    NSMutableArray *jazz = [[NSMutableArray alloc] init];
    [jazz addObject:hands];
    [jazz release];
    return jazz;         // oops, jazz no longer exists!
}
```

You might be tempted to suggest that `-allThatJazz` return a retained object, and make the sender responsible for releasing it, but that creates a royal mess. Now every sender has to know which messages return objects they have to release and which ones don't. And forget about changing your mind and later deciding that `-allThatJazz` should now return an object that doesn't need to be released, because then you'd have to change all the code that uses it. No, there's a better way.

The solution is a clever construct called the autorelease pool. The *autorelease pool* defers sending `-release` messages to objects. After your code is finished, the autorelease pool is *drained* (yes, that's the actual term). It sends `-release` messages to all of the objects in the pool. Objects that no longer have any references are destroyed.

Use the autorelease pool to schedule a -release message to be sent to an object "at some point in the future." You do this by sending the object an -autorelease message instead of a -release message. If a -release message means "I'm completely done with this object," then the -autorelease message means "I will be done with this object, after this code is finished."

> **Caution** Signal your disinterest in an object by sending either a -release or an -autorelease message, but never both. The meaning of the two ("I'm done with this object") is exactly the same, and balances one -retain message. The only difference is the timing (now instead of later).

Using the autorelease pool, the -allThatJazz method now looks like this:

```
- (NSArray*)allThatJazz
{
    NSMutableArray *jazz = [[[NSMutableArray alloc] init] autorelease];
    [jazz addObject:hands];
    return jazz;
}
```

The jazz object is called an *autoreleased object*. The object has a non-zero reference count and is guaranteed to exist until the autorelease pool is drained. Even better, the object that sent the message doesn't have to worry about it either:

```
- (void)fosse
{
    NSArray *jazz = [self allThatJazz];
    if (jazz.count<3)
        [self yell:@"More!"];
}
```

Notice that this code doesn't retain or release the object, although it's clearly "using" it. That's because of this very important rule: *Every Objective-C method returns an object that's retained by another object*. The object will be retained either by the object you requested it from or the autorelease pool.

> **Caution** The exception to this rule is methods that return newly created objects. Those method names will begin with the words "init," "copy," or "new." When using those methods, follow the rule for new objects.

What that means is that you don't have to retain an object to use it immediately. In fact, you don't have to retain an object unless you want to continue using that object *after* your method returns. So as long as the -fosse method doesn't need to use jazz after it returns, it doesn't have to retain or release it.

And what if it did need to use it later? Then it would send the object a `-retain` message and store it in a more permanent variable. That's usually a property, whose setter method will send the `-retain` message automatically:

```
- (void)fosse
{
    NSArray *jazz = [self allThatJazz];
    self.modernJazz = jazz;
}
```

Are you still wondering when the autorelease pool is drained? Autorelease pools are created, and drained, by your app's event loop. Back in Chapter 4, I explained how your app is "event driven." Before each event is dispatched to your code, an autorelease pool is created. Every object that receives an `-autorelease` message is added to that pool. When all of your code finishes executing, and control returns to the event loop, the autorelease pool is drained, destroying all the temporary objects. Before the next event is dispatched, a new autorelease pool is created, and the process repeats.

> **Note** It's possible to create your own autorelease pools using the `@autoreleasepool { ... }` directive. It creates a new pool, executes the code in the block, and immediately drains the pool. The use of `@autoreleasepool` is rare.

Autorelease pools solve the huge flaw in reference counting, and generally means that most of your code doesn't have to send any `-retain` or `-release` messages. I'll get to the other big problem shortly, but first let's review what you've learned so far.

Quick Summary

That's 99% of manual memory management. Here's a simplified summary of how to use it:

- After creating an object (`[[Class alloc] init]` or `-copy`), either:
    - Use it and then send it a `-release` message
    - Send it an `-autorelease` message
- An object returned by a message can be safely used for the duration of the method.
- If you store an object reference anywhere where it could be used after the method returns, it should be retained (normally handled by a property setter method).
- If your code sent an object a `-retain` message, you must send it a matching `-release` or `-autorelease` message before discarding the reference to it (normally handled by a property setter method or by `-dealloc`).

With these basic rules, and some help from your setter methods, object destruction and memory management is something that happens, more or less, in the background. You get most of the benefits of garbage collection with almost none of the costs. There is, however, one situation where garbage collection still beats reference counting. Let's take a look at that problem next.

OBSCURE REFERENCE COUNTING PITFALLS

There are a few, oddball, situations where following these simplified rules can still get you into trouble. Consider this code:

```
id obj = [array objectAtIndex:0];
[array removeObjectAtIndex:0];
[obj doSomething]; // ! crash !
```

So what's wrong? The problem is that the code is relying on the -objectAtIndex: message to return either a retained (by array) or autoreleased object. It does that. The object is, in fact, retained by array. But the next line removes the object from the array. The array is no longer retaining the object. If this was the object's only reference, it destroys itself. The next line of code blows up your app, because obj now points to garbage. (Note: Automatic Reference Counting is not fooled by this kind of code.)

You'll sometimes see the addition of reference counting messages to work around problems like this:

```
id obj = [[[array objectAtIndex:0] retain] autorelease];
[array removeObjectAtIndex:0];
[obj doSomething]; // safe as houses
```

A complete set of memory management rules can be found in the *Advanced Memory Management Programming Guide*, which you can find in Xcode's Documentation and API Reference window.

Breaking the Cycle

Now let's talk about "the other problem" with reference counting. An object can, indirectly, refer to itself. This causes its reference count to be artificially high, preventing it from being released. Take the simple example of a classroom data model, shown in Figure 21-7.

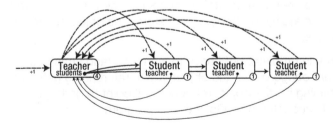

Figure 21-7. Circular retains

A Class object creates a Teacher object and adds Student objects to it. The Teacher maintains a reference to each student, which necessitates sending each a -retain message. Each Student needs a connection to its Teacher. That connection is a property that references and retains the Teacher object.

When class is over, the Teacher object is released. What happens next is, well, nothing. As you see in Figure 21-8, the Teacher's reference count drops from 4 to 3, and it just sits there, thinking that it has three other objects that are still using it. And there are, but those three objects are the three Student objects it's retaining.

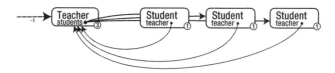

Figure 21-8. Releasing an over-retained Teacher

This is called the *circular retain problem*, and reference counting can't fix it. The objects in the circle are leaked and can never be destroyed.

The solution is to *not* retain all of the object references. In Figure 21-9, the Student objects have been modified so they do not send -retain messages to the Teacher object. Now when the Teacher is released, its reference count will drop to 0. It will destroy itself *and* its three Student objects.

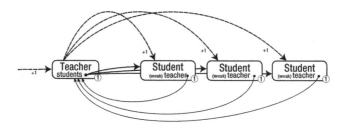

Figure 21-9. Unretained object references

The Student objects are using *unretained references*. Unretained references are used in parent-child relationships (like the Teacher-Student example), delegates, and sometimes target objects to avoid creating circular retains. To create an unretained property, use the assign attribute (@property (assign) id delegate). An assign property simply stores the object reference; it doesn't send any retain or release messages.

This fixes the circular retain problem, but I have to warn you (and I can't stress this enough), *unretained references are dangerous*. If the object you're referencing gets destroyed—and it can, because you're not retaining it—the object reference will point to garbage memory. This is one of the most vexing bugs you'll encounter in an Objective-C program.

> **Note** Unretained references are sometimes called *weak references*. I'm avoiding this term for now because ARC defines a weak reference that means something different.

The key is to write your code in a way that ensures an unretained reference won't ever end up pointing to a destroyed object. The Teacher object, for example, could set the teacher property of each Student to nil before releasing them in its -dealloc method. If some other object was still retaining a Student object, it won't have a teacher property pointing to garbage memory.

This is also why, throughout this book, I've repeatedly warned you to remove your object from the notification center before your object is destroyed. In several places, you've seen this code:

```
- (void)dealloc
{
    [[NSNotificationCenter defaultCenter] removeObserver:self];
}
```

The reason is because the notification center uses unretained references. (Don't ask why; it's a convoluted reason with a long history.) If you allow your object to be destroyed, but leave it registered with the notification center, the next notification message will be sent to garbage. And trust me, that's a hard bug to diagnose.

Scared Straight

Let's wrap up this discussion with all of the ways reference counting and memory management can go horribly wrong. Oh, come on, it'll be fun!

- Creating or retaining an object and then forgetting to send it a -release or -autorelease message. This will create a memory leak. It's called an *over-retain* bug.
- Erroneously sending an object a -release or -autorelease message. This causes the object to be prematurely destroyed while there are still references to it. The next message sent to the reference will behave badly. This is called an *over-release* bug.
- Creating circular retains. This eventually results in leaked objects.
- Failing to clear an unretained object reference once the object is destroyed. This is called a *dangling pointer bug*.

There are a hundred different scenarios that can lead to one of these bugs, but all of them fall into those four categories.

Are you now too scared to write another line of Objective-C? Take a deep breath and relax, because Automatic Reference Counting is here to save you. ARC prevents three of these four tragedies, and gives you the tools to easily avoid the fourth. Let's now return to the safe confines of ARC.

Automatic Reference Counting

Automatic Reference Counting is a feature of the Objective-C compiler. It analyses your source code to determine exactly when you stop using an object reference, and automatically inserts code to send the correct -retain and -release messages. This consistency means your code is immune from half of the reference counting bugs: over-retain and over-release. They simply don't happen.

The two remaining problems, avoiding circular retains and dangling pointers, is aided by a new weak qualifier. Any variable or property can be declared to be weak. It doesn't retain the object it refers to (just like an unretained reference), but it's also safe. The Objective-C runtime automatically sets the variable to nil if the object it's pointing to should be destroyed. So you can solve those annoying circular retention problems without worrying about dangling references that could crash your app.

ARC comes at a (slight) cost. There are certain programming practices that ARC doesn't allow. But I'm sure that, after reviewing them, you'll agree the benefits of ARC far outweigh the few obscure features you have to give up:

- Your code can't send -retain, -release, or -autorelease messages. That's the compiler's job now.
- Your -dealloc method no longer sends [super dealloc] at the end. The compiler does that for you.
- You cannot put object pointers in a C struct (struct { int number; id obj }).
- You cannot convert object pointers into C type pointers (void *cPtr = obj), or vice versa.
- All automatic object pointer variables are initialized to nil.

There are some other, far more obscure, limitations, but those are the big ones. If you think about it, it's not much to give up. Most of what you have to abandon (sending your own -retain and -release messages), is what you want ARC to save you from in the first place.

Enabling ARC

You enable ARC in your project settings. It will be turned on for all new projects. If you want to change it in an existing project, visit the project's build settings. Find the Apple LLVM - Language - Objective-C section, and change the Objective-C Automatic Reference Counting setting, as shown in Figure 21-10.

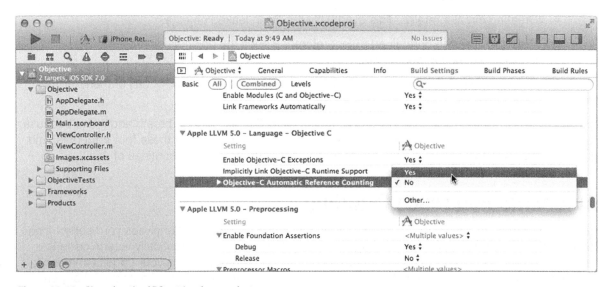

Figure 21-10. Changing the ARC setting for a project

> **Note** It's possible to enable ARC on a file-by-file basis. ARC is completely compatible with non-ARC code, so you can mix and match. You do this by adding either the `-fobjc-arc` or `-fno-objc-arc` compiler flag to specific files in your project's build phase. For a "how to," find the *Controlling How an Individual File is Compiled* guide in Xcode's Documentation and API Reference window.

Strong and Weak References

ARC introduces two new object reference qualifiers: `strong` and `weak`. Under ARC, all object reference variables are `strong` by default. And this doesn't apply to just properties; *all* object references—property values, instance variables, automatic variables, parameter variables, and static variables—act like a `retain` property under ARC.

For `@property` declarations, the new `strong` attribute makes this explicit, and replaces the `retain` attribute. If you feel the need to explicitly declare that an instance or automatic variable is strong, use the new `__strong` (that's two underscore characters) type qualifier, like this:

```
- (void)doSomething
{
    id __strong value;
    ...
```

To address circular retains, and similar problems, ARC provides the `weak` attribute. Use `weak` in place of `assign` in `@property` declarations to create a reference that does not retain the object. With variables, the `__weak` type qualifier will do the same.

As you've seen, circular retains are a perfect use for the `weak` qualifier. Another situation where `weak` is useful is in view controller outlets that refer to view objects. Throughout this book, you've written Interface Builder outlets that look like this:

```
@interface DDViewController : UIViewController

@property (weak,nonatomic) IBOutlet UIBarButtonItem *playButton;
@property (weak,nonatomic) IBOutlet UIBarButtonItem *pauseButton;
@property (weak,nonatomic) IBOutlet UIImageView *albumView;
@property (weak,nonatomic) IBOutlet UILabel *songLabel;
@property (weak,nonatomic) IBOutlet UILabel *albumLabel;
@property (weak,nonatomic) IBOutlet UILabel *artistLabel;
```

Why were all of those properties weak? A weak reference allows those view objects to be automatically released. As you'll learn in Chapter 23, iOS may send your app warning messages when it's starting to run out of memory. View controllers—that are not being displayed—react by releasing their view objects. (A view controller can always reload its view objects from its Interface Builder file.) If these properties were `strong`, those view objects wouldn't be released because the individual properties would still retain them. By making them weak, once the view controller releases its view objects, these properties are set to `nil`.

There are, unfortunately, pitfalls to using the `weak` qualifier too. The problem is that a weak reference does not retain its object. If all of the references to an object are weak, the object gets destroyed. This was the problem you ran into in the Wonderland app.

The page view controller's data source property is weak (`assign`), to avoid circular retains. Your natural inclination is to create your data source object and assign it to the property, like this:

```
self.dataSource = [WLBookDataSource new];
```

If you run the app, you'll find the `WLBookDataSource` object is immediately destroyed again. That's because the `dataSource` property is weak, and there are no other strong references to the object.

The solution was to create a second, strong, reference to the object in `WLBookViewController`, like this:

```
@interface WLBookViewController ()
{
    WLBookDataSource *bookSource;    // strong reference to dataSource
}
@end
```

When the data source object is created, it's assigned to *both* the property and the instance variable:

```
self.dataSource = bookSource = [WLBookDataSource new];
```

The mystery is finally explained. The second, strong, reference retains the data source object and keeps it alive for the lifetime of the `WLBookViewController` object.

What ARC Doesn't Do

ARC is a fantastic technology, and probably the best compromise in balancing the needs of the developer with the demands of running on a mobile device. Its reach, however, stops right at the border of Objective-C. Core Foundation (the C functions at iOS's core) also uses reference counting, but ARC takes a decidedly "hands off" approach.

You encountered this already in your ColorModel app. In the code that created the hue/saturation field image, you used some Core Graphics functions. These were C functions that returned pointers to object-like structures called types. Core Foundation types use reference counting too:

```
CGColorSpaceRef colorSpace = CGColorSpaceCreateDeviceRGB();
CGDataProviderRef provider = CGDataProviderCreateWithCFData(
                                  (__bridge CFDataRef)bitmapData);
hsImageRef = CGImageCreate(...);
CGColorSpaceRelease(colorSpace);
CGDataProviderRelease(provider);
```

There are two things of interest in this code. First, you're responsible for the memory management of these types, even though this is an ARC app. The values returned by `CGColorSpaceCreateDeviceRGB` and `CGDataProviderCreateWithCFData` are new (retained) type references. It's your responsibility to release them, using the appropriate Core Foundation release functions, `CGColorSpaceRelease` and `CGDataProviderRelease`.

Secondly, there's that pesky rule that you can't convert an Objective-C object pointer into a C pointer. But that's exactly what happens in the parameter of `CGDataProviderCreateWithCFData`. The parameter is a `CFDataRef` (a C pointer), but `bitmapData` is an `NSData` object. CFData and NSData are functionally interchangeable, members of the toll-free bridge. A select number of classes in Objective-C have Core Foundation counterparts, either of which can substitute for the other. The special __bridge qualifier relaxes ARC's normal rules to allow the Objective-C object reference to be passed as a C type reference.

And the border between Objective-C and Core Foundation isn't completely closed. ARC has an emigration policy, of sorts. A Core Foundation function that returns a toll-free bridge type is often cast and stored in an Objective-C object reference, so it can be treated as an object. In pre-ARC code, it would look like this:

```
NSString *strObj = (NSString*)CFUUIDCreateString(0,uuid);
```

This particular function creates a new string from a UUID structure and stores it in a string object reference. But again, ARC doesn't allow this because `CFUUIDCreateString` returns a `CFStringRef` pointer, not an object. This is fixed by adding the `__bridge_transfer` qualifier:

```
NSString *strObj = (__bridge_transfer NSString*)CFUUIDCreateString(0,uuid);
```

Two wonderful things happen. The compiler stops complaining, allowing the C type pointer to be converted into an Objective-C object pointer. But even more significant, ARC takes responsibility for releasing strObj. The `__bridge_transfer` qualifier says "This C pointer represents an Objective-C compatible object with a retain count of 1. Store it in an object reference and treat it like any newly created object." ARC takes it from there.

If you need to go the other direction—taking an ARC-managed object and converting it into a Core Foundation reference—use the `__bridge_retained` qualifier, like this:

```
NSString *objString = @"Hello!";
CFStringRef coreString = (__bridge_retained CFStringRef)objString;
// do C function things with coreString
CFRelease(coreString);
```

ARC transfers ownership *and* memory management of the Objective-C object to you, as if it was a newly created `CFStringRef`. From there, you treat it like any `CFStringRef`, which includes releasing it (`CFRelease`) when you're done.

Those are the highlights of using the Core Foundation and the toll-free bridge. These, and additional issues, are discussed in the *Transitioning to ARC Release Notes* that can be found in Xcode's Documentation and API Reference window.

Summary

Memory management is a critical part of successful iOS app development. With the help of technologies like ARC, you shouldn't spend too much of your day worrying about it. With your newfound knowledge of ARC and circular retains, you can make intelligent decisions about what kind of reference to define (strong or weak), and how to solve the occasional mystery of disappearing (weakly retained) objects. More importantly, you understand when and why objects get destroyed, which will be important for reducing your app's memory use. In a later chapter, you'll get to see just how much memory your app is using.

But before you get to that, we're going to take a little trip and visit a part of iOS development that's often overlooked. A place where you can ask the question "¿Qué pasa, Alicia?"

Chapter 22

Êtes-vous Polyglotte?

Dumella rah!

Maybe you prefer kia ora, guten tag, bom dia, hallo, saluton, bonjour, ¡hola, 你好, or ciao? I bet at least one of your users does. If you're developing apps for world-wide distribution, here's something to think about: most of your potential users don't speak your language.

Apple has a long history of embracing technologies that allow software to be translated and localized, so people around the world can enjoy them, in their native tongue. Xcode and iOS work together to help you adapt your app to different languages and regions. In this chapter you will:

- Internationalize your project and code
- Add localizations to your app
- Localize app resources
- Localize string constants
- Use localized system objects

Pigeon is a great little app, and one that I'm sure people from all over the world would love to use. But that's going to be hard if they can't understand it. Let's localize Pigeon so that people who speak Spanish can enjoy it too. In the process, you'll learn how to localize your app for practically any user, wherever they live.

The Localization Process

Preparing an app for international distribution is often described as "translating" an app. Natural language translation is a part of it, but omits other important elements. The correct term is *localizing*, and it encompasses not just language differences, but cultural and regional ones too.

Localizing your app is usually one of the last phases of app development. After you've designed all of the interfaces, written all of the code, and everything works the way it should, you then begin the process of localizing it for other languages. There are two big steps:

1. Internationalize your project and code
2. Localize your resources and strings

The first step is purely technical, and prepares your app for step 2. Internationalization consists of project and code changes that *allow* your app to be localized. There usually isn't a lot to do, but it lays the groundwork for what comes next.

The second step is localization. An internationalized app can be localized for different languages, *without modifying the code*. Once your app is internationalized, localizations can be added at will. Your app may have been born speaking English, but by adding localizations, it can effortlessly switch to French, Arabic, German, Chinese, Russian, Hebrew, Korean, or Portuguese. Popular apps often come with dozens of localizations. And you don't have to do a thing; your app will automatically use the best localization based on the user's profile, region, and preferences.

The localization process is also designed to be cooperative. If you're like me (who has enough trouble with my native language, let alone 20), you'll need professional help translating your app. iOS app localization is deliberately organized around a set of resource files. You identify the resource files that need to be localized and give copies to your translator or translation service. They will translate them into another language, returning localized versions of those same files. You simply add those translated files to your project, and your app is suddenly muy versado!

Language Bundles

iOS organizes all of the language-specific resources of your app into *localization bundles*. Each bundle is a subdirectory in your app named after a language: `en.lproj` contains all of the English resources, `fr.lproj` the French resources, `es.lproj` the Spanish resources, and so on. When your app is launched, the user's preferred language selects the localization bundle to use. Whenever your code requests a resource file, the bundle manager looks first in the preferred language bundle for a localized version of that file. If there isn't one, it uses the one from the default language, or the universal version.

> **Note** Language identifiers (`en`, `fr`, `de`, `ja`, and so on) are defined by the ISO 639-1 and ISO 639-2 standards. See http://www.loc.gov/standards/iso639-2/php/English_list.php. iOS uses ISO 639-2 for those languages not defined in ISO 639-1. You'll be glad to know that Klingon (`tlh`) was recently added to the ISO 639-2 standard. MajQa'!

Here's an example. Let's pretend that you've localized the Wonderland app for English and French. It will contain two language bundles: `en.lproj` and `fr.lproj`. When you created Wonderland, you added a resource file containing the text of the book, stored in a file named `Alice.txt`. If you did nothing else, your app would always show the English version of the book, because that's the only version of `Alice.txt` in your app.

If you had a French translation of the book, that would be stored in a file named Alice.txt too, but placed inside the fr.lproj folder. In the WLBookViewController.m file, you wrote code that loaded the text of the book into a string object:

```
NSURL *bookURL = [[NSBundle mainBundle] URLForResource:@"Alice"
                                         withExtension:@"txt"];
NSString *text = [NSString stringWithContentsOfURL:bookURL
                                    encoding:NSUTF8StringEncoding
                                       error:NULL];
```

If your app's user spoke French, the NSBundle object would first search the fr.lproj for a file named Alice.txt. If it found one, it would load the French version of the file instead of the original English one. Your code doesn't change and it doesn't make any language-specific decisions. It simply requests a resource, and the bundle manager delivers the localized version, if available and appropriate.

Since all view controllers get their view objects from Interface Builder files, all of your app's interfaces can be easily localized. The same goes for sound files (particularly important if the sounds include spoken words), icons, graphics, and so on. You don't have to localize everything, just those resources that need to be translated.

Xcode handles the creation and the maintenance of the localization bundles. You just tell Xcode what languages you want to support, and which resource files need to be localized. Xcode will create the localization bundles and organize the files.

Programmatic Localization

Localized resource files make it easy to localize the bulk of your app's language-specific interface. There are still a couple of sources of natural language content that aren't in resource files. These include the string constants in your program and formatted values.

iOS includes a mechanism for translating string constants and formatting values the way the user expects. Take the following code from the Shorty app, earlier in the book:

```
UIAlertView* alert = [[UIAlertView alloc]
        initWithTitle:@"Could not load URL"
              message:error.description
             delegate:nil
    cancelButtonTitle:@"That's Sad"
    otherButtonTitles:nil];
```

Internationalizing this code requires a couple of changes. First, the string constants need to be replaced with variables that will supply localized versions of each string. Secondly, objects that provide text the user will see should provide a localized version (when available). The internationalized code looks like this (changes in bold):

```
UIAlertView* alert = [[UIAlertView alloc]
        initWithTitle:NSLocalizedString(@"Could not load URL",nil)
              message:error.localizedDescription
             delegate:nil
    cancelButtonTitle:NSLocalizedString(@"That's Sad",nil)
    otherButtonTitles:nil];
```

The string literals are replaced with a special macro that substitutes a localized string when the user's language changes. The `error.description` property is replaced with the `error.localizedDesription` property. It's the same information, just translated into the user's native language.

Localize Now!

Normally, I'd suggest that you internationalize your app completely before beginning the localization process. I'm betting, however, you want to jump in and see how localization works right away. So let's do that; it won't cause any issues for this project. You'll get to internationalize your code shortly.

> **Caution** If this were a large project, I'd strongly urge you to internationalize first and localize second. Internationalizing your code can often result in resource file changes, which would require them to be re-localized.

Localizing your project is a three-step process:

1. Add the languages you want to support to your project
2. Choose which resource files need to be localized, and into what languages
3. Edit the localized version of the files

Begin with the finished Pigeon project from Chapter 18. Select the project in the project navigator, and then select the Pigeon project (not the target) in the editor pane, as shown in Figure 22-1. Choose the `Info` tab and scroll down until you find the `Localizations` section.

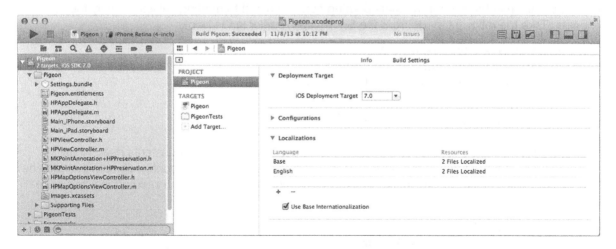

Figure 22-1. Project localizations

Your project has two localizations already: a Base localization and one for the development language. The *development language* is the language of the developer who created the project—that's you. The *base localization* is the localization used when no other localization is a good fit for the user.

Notice that Xcode says that some files have already been localized. You won't find any indication of this in project navigator (yet), but if you open the project folder in the Finder (choose the `Pigeon` folder in the project navigator, right/control+click, and choose **Reveal in Finder**), you'll see the structure of the localization bundle, as shown in Figure 22-2.

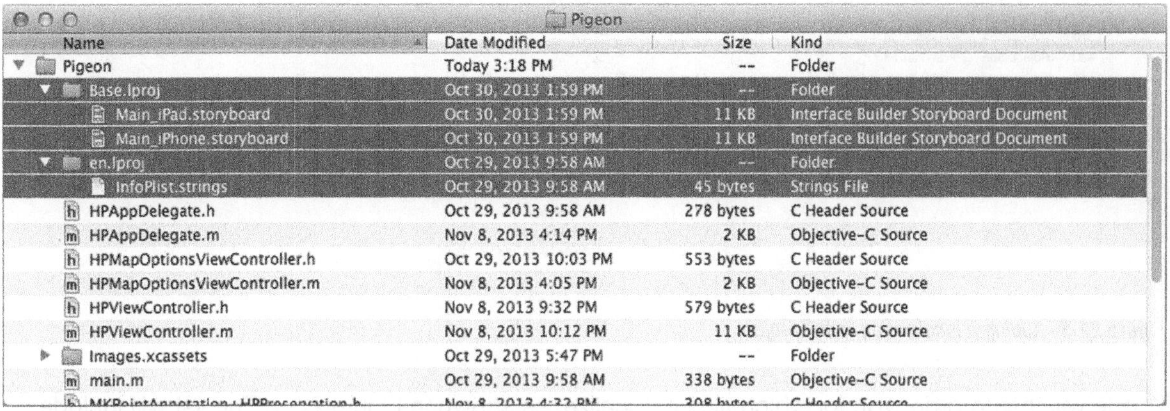

Figure 22-2. Default localization bundle structure

In Pigeon, the `InfoPlist.strings` and the two storyboard files are localized. A *localized file* is one that has been moved into one or more specific localization bundles. Files that have not been localized are stored outside the localization bundles and are used for every language.

> **Tip** To localize a resource file, select the file in the project navigator and click the **Localize...** button in the file inspector. This only applies to files that can be localized and haven't been.

Since there's still only one version of every file, the distinction between localized and non-localized resource files is largely meaningless. Let's change that. Back in Xcode, return to the Project Info tab, click the + button at the bottom of the `Localizations` group and choose to add a localization for **Spanish (es)**, as shown in Figure 22-3. Common languages are listed in the main menu. Many (many!) more languages can be found in the **Other** submenu at the bottom.

CHAPTER 22: Êtes-vous Polyglotte?

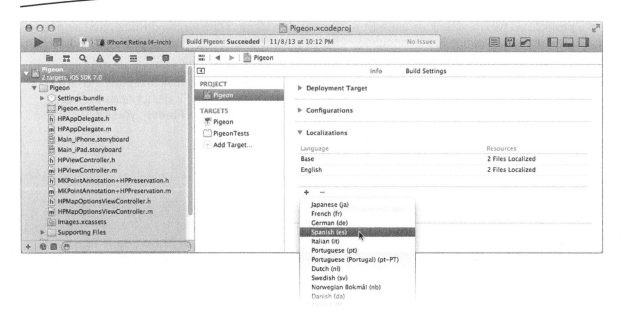

Figure 22-3. Adding a localization to the project

Xcode will then prompt you for which files to localize, as shown in Figure 22-4. The list will include all of the files that are currently localized. If a file doesn't need to be localized for this language, uncheck it. The Reference Language is the version of the file that will be copied to create this localization. If you've already localized for some languages, it might be easier to choose a language that's similar to the one that you're creating. If you were creating a localization for Icelandic, it's probably easier to start with the existing Norwegian translation, rather than English.

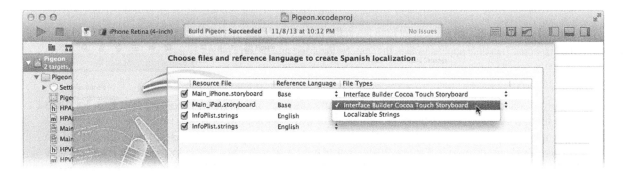

Figure 22-4. Choosing files to localize

In the File Types column, some files have a choice of how that file is localized. There are two ways to localize Interface Builder files: localizing the entire file or creating just a string translation file. If you choose the former, a copy of the entire Interface Builder file is placed in the localization bundle. This permits you to change anything in the interface for the new language. You can change the titles of buttons, choose different images, set different text alignments, specify different fonts, add different layout constraints, and so on. Localizing for languages like Hebrew, that read right-to-left, often require radical alterations to the layout of the interface. Views might need to be resized to accommodate longer (German) or shorter (Chinese) titles.

On the other hand, if the only changes required are the textual titles of buttons and other control objects, you can localize the interface with a `Localizable Strings` file. You'll learn about, and create, these files later in this chapter. For this demonstration, change the file type of both storyboard files to `Interface Builder Cocoa Touch Storyboard`, as shown in Figure 22-4. Click the Finish button.

> **Note** Pigeon could easily be localized for Spanish using Localizble Strings files for both storyboards. That, however, would have denied you the experience of localizing an Interface Builder file.

In the project navigator, the `InfoPlist.strings` and the two storyboard files now have expansion triangles next to them, as shown in Figure 22-5. Expand them and you'll see the localized version for each language.

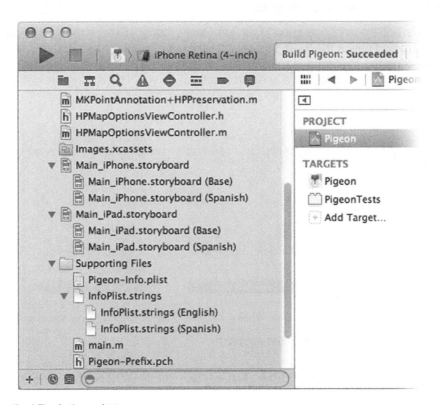

Figure 22-5. Localized files in the navigator

The files in your project folder have changed too. If you return to the Finder you'll see that Xcode has created an `es.lproj` bundle and copied the three resource files into it, as shown in Figure 22-6.

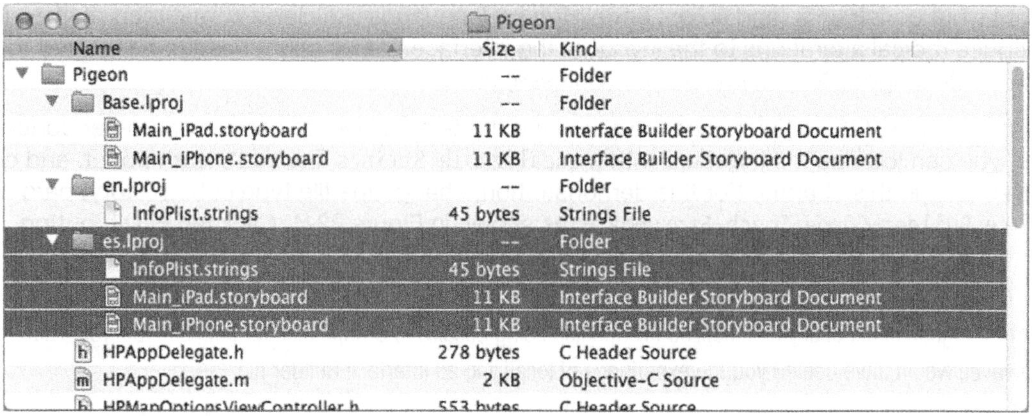

Figure 22-6. Project file structure with multiple localization bundles

Xcode, thankfully, hides the bundle structure from you in the project navigator. Instead, it presents the much more rational picture of your resource files, grouping together the specific localizations of that resource into a single, expandable, item.

To localize a file, just edit the language-specific version. Really, that's it. Expand the Main_iPhone.storyboard (or _iPad) file group and select the Main_iPhone.storyboard (Spanish) localization, as shown in Figure 22-7. Selecting the file group is the same as selecting the base or development language version. So if you don't choose to edit a specific localization, you'll be editing the default one.

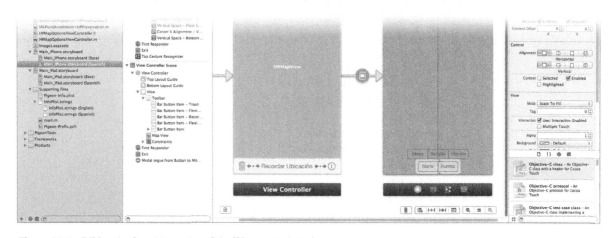

Figure 22-7. Editing the Spanish version of the iPhone storyboard

Edit the button titles in the two view controllers, resizing them as needed, using Table 22-1.

Table 22-1. Spanish button titles

English Title	Spanish Title
Remember Location	Recordar Ubicación
Map	Mapa
Satellite	Satélite
Hybrid	Híbrido
North	Norte
Heading	Rumbo

Run the app. You won't notice any difference, as shown on the left in Figure 22-8, because the preferred language is still English. Press the home button and open the Settings app.
In **General ➤ International ➤ Language**, change the language to **Español** and tap the **Done** button. The simulator, or device, will perform a "warm" restart. This will cause all running apps to stop. When they start again, they'll be using a different set of localized resources.

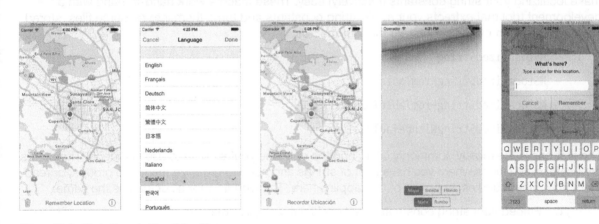

Figure 22-8. First attempt at localizing Pigeon

From Xcode, run the Pigeon app again. This time, it's in Spanish! The middle of Figure 22-8 shows localized labels for the buttons, and even some of the map labels have changed (courtesy of the Map Kit).

You're not done yet, though. Tap the Recordar **Ubicación button** and take a look at the alert (on the right in Figure 22-8). That doesn't look like Spanish to me. That's because you didn't internationalize your app first. It's time to circle back and do this right.

Internationalizing Your App

Internationalizing your app consists of making the code and project changes needed to support localization. This breaks down into four tasks:

- Adding language bundles to your app
- Translating string constants
- Getting localized properties
- Using iOS formatter objects

You've already done the first one in the previous section, adding an `es.lproj` localization bundle to your app. The problem in Pigeon is that it has string constants that are in English. These need to be replaced with localized versions.

Internationalizing String Constants

The Cocoa Touch framework has a set of macros—they look like C functions, but they're not—that make localizing your string constants (relatively) easy. These macros work hand-in-hand with a development tool that extracts your app's string constants and turns them into resource files, stored in your localization bundles. Here are the four macros:

NSLocalizedString

NSLocalizedStringFromTable

NSLocalizedStringFromTableInBundle

NSLocalizedStringWithDefaultValue

The first one is the mostly commonly used, and the only one you're going to use in Pigeon. The others are useful in situations where you have a lot of strings and need to organize them into groups, or read them from other bundles, but none of that applies here. The workflow for all of them is the same:

1. Embed your string constants in `NSLocalizedString...` macros
2. Run the `genstrings` tool to extract the strings in your code
3. Localize and edit your `.strings` resource files

I could explain how this all works, but it's so much easier to just show you. Select the `HPViewController.m` file and find all of the strings the user will see. In Pigeon, these are in just two sections of code. In the `-dropPin:` method, edit the alert object construction code so it looks like this (modified code in bold):

```
UIAlertView *alert = [[UIAlertView alloc]
      initWithTitle:NSLocalizedString(@"What's here?",@"Pin alert title")
            message:NSLocalizedString(@"Type a label for this location.",
                                      @"Pin alert message")
           delegate:self
  cancelButtonTitle:NSLocalizedString(@"Cancel",@"Pin alert cancel button")
  otherButtonTitles:NSLocalizedString(@"Remember",@"Pin alert save button"),
                    nil];
```

The string constants are rewritten as `NSLocalizedString` statements. The first argument is the original, untranslated, string literal. The second is a hint or a description of what the string means or how it's used in the program. This second argument doesn't become part of your program. It's used solely to aid the translator.

There's only one other English string constant in this program, and that's in the -alertView:clickedButtonAtIndex: method. Find and edit this statement (modified code in bold):

name = **NSLocalizedString(**@"Over Here!"**,@"Default location label");**

The strings in your app have now been internationalized. The next step is to turn them into resources.

> **Note** You only localize the strings the user will see. All other string constants—dictionary keys, encoding keys, user defaults, table cell identifiers, and so on—are never localized.

Using the genstrings Tool

When you installed Xcode, it installed a host of command-line tools. Included was the genstrings tool. genstrings scans code (C, Objective-C, C++, and others), finds the string constants in NSLocalizedString ... macros, and compiles them into .strings (with an 's') files. Using the genstrings tool is one of the few times you need to step outside the comfortable confines of Xcode.

Launch the Terminal application from the Finder, the Dock, LaunchPad, or your favorite app-launching utility. Terminal lets you use OS X's command shell. You're going to run the genstrings tool from the command line to scan all of the Objective-C source files in your project, compiling all NSLocalizedString ... statements into a .strings file. Follow these steps:

1. Select the Pigeon folder group (not the project) in the project navigator.

2. Show the file inspector (on the right in Figure 22-9) and click the arrow to the right of its Full Path. This will reveal the folder in the Finder.

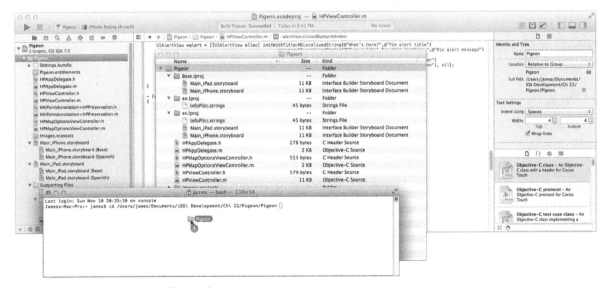

Figure 22-9. Setting up the genstrings tool

3. Open a Terminal window and type cd, and the space bar (at the bottom in Figure 22-9). 'cd' is the shell's *change directory* command.

4. In the Finder, drag the Pigeon folder, inside the Pigeon project folder, into the Terminal window and drop it.

5. Make sure the Terminal window is active again and press the Return key. This sets the shell's default directory to the Pigeon folder, which contains all of your source files and the es.lproj language bundle.

6. Type the command genstrings -o es.lproj *.m into the Terminal window and press the Return key.

When genstrings is finished scanning all of your source files and creating a .strings file—which should happen faster than you can blink—a new Localizable.strings file will appear in the es.lproj bundle, as shown in Figure 22-10. This file isn't a part of your project yet, so drag it into the Supporting Files group in the project navigator, also shown in Figure 22-10.

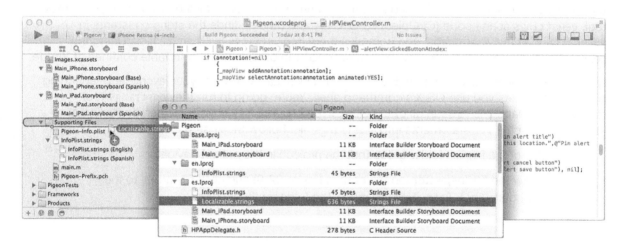

Figure 22-10. Adding the initial Localizable.strings file

> **Note** If you change your strings in the future, you can run the genstrings tool again to update the existing Localizable.strings file; you don't have to add it to the project again.

Make sure the Pigeon target is selected and add it to the project. Select the Localizable.strings file in the navigator and show the file inspector (**View ➤ Utilities ➤ Show File Inspector**), as shown in Figure 22-11.

Figure 22-11. Newly created Localizable.strings file

A `.strings` file is a resource file containing a list of string substitutions. The format is reminiscent of C source. On the left of each = statement is the original string (the key). On the right is its localized translation (the value). Above each replacement is the comment, as a C-style comment, from the original `NSLocalizedString ...` statement.

> **Note** You don't have to use your original string as the key, but that's the most convenient way to use `NSLocalizedString`. You could also write `NSLocalizedString(@"KEY1",nil)`, and then in the English `.strings` file translate that into something readable, like this: `"KEY1" = "Welcome to Pigeon!";`. This would require that you have an English `.strings` file as well.

Localizing Your Strings File

Select the `Localizable.strings` file. In the file inspector, find the `Localization` section. The Spanish localization, as shown in Figure 22-11, is the only language checked because there's only one version of `Localizable.strings`. In this project, you only need a `Localizable.strings` file for Spanish. All other languages will use the original, untranslated, strings in the source code. When you're ready to add a third language, simply check it in the `Localization` section of the file inspector and Xcode will duplicate the existing `Localizable.strings` file and copy it into the new language bundle. Then you'll have a group of `Localizable.strings` file, just like `Main_iPhone.storyboard`.

With the `Localizable.strings` file selected, edit the right (value) side of each string using Table 22-2.

Table 22-2. Spanish string constants

Comment	Spanish String
Pin alert cancel button	Cancelar
Pin alert save button	Recordar
Pin alert title	¿Lo que aquí?
Pin alert message	Crear una letrero para esta ubicación.
Default location label	¡Aquí está!

When you're finished, the edited .strings file should look something like the one in Figure 22-11.

Testing Your String Localization

Run Pigeon again. Assuming the user's language setting is still set to Español, the app will appear in Spanish, as shown in Figure 22-12.

Figure 22-12. Spanish version of Pigeon

Here's how it works. The NSLocalizedString... macros expand into code that sends a -localizedStringForKey:value:table: message to the app's NSBundle object, passing the literal string as the key. This method searches for a .strings file in the preferred localization bundle. If it finds a file, it searches that file for the key (original string) and returns its translation.

The default .strings file is Localizable.strings, but you can define others if you have a lot of strings to organize. Each strings file is referred to as a *table*, and you pass the name of the table in the -localizedStringForKey:value:table: message or NSLocalizedStringFromTable macro. Using those macros, genstrings will automatically create multiple .strings files, one for each table name.

If there is no .strings file for that language, or the key can't be found in the .strings file, no translation is performed and the macro or message returns the original string.

Localizing Interfaces Using Localizable Strings

Now that you understand `.strings` files, you can appreciate the use of `.strings` file to localize an Interface Builder file. When you localized `Main_iPhone.storyboard`, you localized the entire file by choosing the `Interface Builder Cocoa Touch Storyboard` option. You then proceeded to create a localized version of that storyboard.

If you had chosen the `Localizable Strings` option instead, Xcode would have created a localized strings file for that Interface Builder file, named `Main_iPhone.strings`. The file would have contained substitutions for various text properties (mostly control titles) of the view objects in that interface, like this one:

`"jkj-WQ-xYm.title" = "Remember Location";`

The key is an identifier that only Interface Builder and iOS understand; don't change it. In this instance, it identifiers the bar button item's title property. Edit the value for your localization, like this:

`"jkj-WQ-xYm.title" = "`**`Recordar Ubicación`**`";`

When iOS loads the interface file, it replaces the appropriate text properties with those in the `Main_iPhone.strings` file found in the localization bundle.

If the localized version of your interface can be accomplished by only altering the titles of control and text objects, then use a localizable strings file rather than duplicating the entire Interface Builder file. The advantage is that you can later alter the Interface Builder file, adding new views, adjusting constrains, and so on, without having to replicate those changes in all of the copies you've made for other languages.

Those are the highlights of internationalization and localization. In the next couple of sections, I'm going to describe some unusual localization problems and tips on writing code to keep your app international.

Localizing Settings.bundle

One of Pigeon's resources is the `Settings.bundle` that defines its settings in the Settings app. It's a bundle, like your app's bundle, and has its own localization bundles. If you expand it in the project navigator or Finder, you'll see that it contains a `Root.strings` file in its default localization bundle. Select the `Root.strings` file, as shown in Figure 22-13.

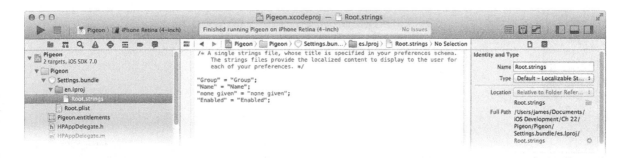

Figure 22-13. Default Root.strings file

This file is left over from the original Settings.bundle template. It's supposed to contain the translations for any visible strings in the Root.plist file. You edited the Root.plist file in Chapter 18, but never edited this file. Let's fix that now. Edit the English Root.strings file so it contains this:

```
"iCloud" = "iCloud";
"Sync Locations" = "Sync Locations";
```

> **Tip** Any string translation that results in the same string ("iCloud" = "iCloud";) is superfluous and can be omitted from the .strings file. When a translation isn't found, the original value is used, so a missing substitution means no substitution. The exception is when using NSLocalizedStringWithDefaultValue or -localizedStringForKey:value:table: with a default value; these return an alternate value when a substitution isn't found.

The keys are the visible text—the group name and toggle switch title—in the settings bundle. Save the file (**File ► Save**). Unfortunately, the current version of Xcode doesn't manage localized files inside other bundles, so you'll have to create the Spanish localization manually. It's pretty easy:

1. Open a Terminal window.

2. Type cd and the spacebar.

3. Drag the Settings.bundle directly from the project navigator in Xcode and drop it into the Terminal window.

4. Switch to the Terminal window and press Return.

5. Type the command cp -R en.lproj es.lproj and press Return, as shown in Figure 22-14.

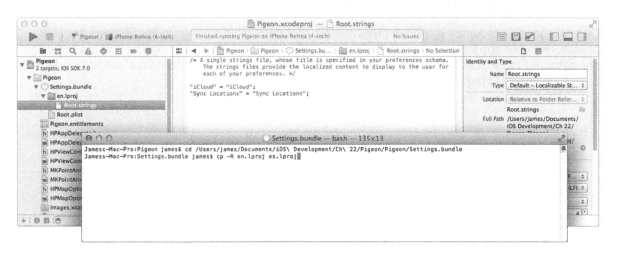

Figure 22-14. Creating an es.lproj from the en.lproj bundle in Settings.bundle

Returning to Xcode, you'll now see that the Settings.bundle contains a new es.lproj bundle, as shown in Figure 22-15.

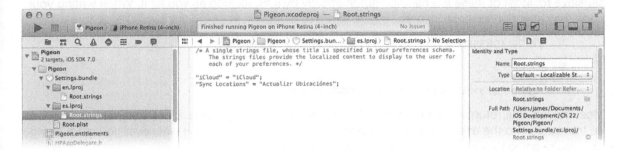

Figure 22-15. Localized Settings.bundle strings

Expand the new es.lproj folder in the navigator, select the Root.strings file, and edit it as follows (new text in bold):

"Sync Locations" = "**Actualizar Ubicaciónes**";

Run Pigeon. After it starts, press the home button and tap the Settings app—oops, I mean the Ajustes app. Find the settings for Pigeon and you'll see its localized settings, as shown in Figure 22-16.

 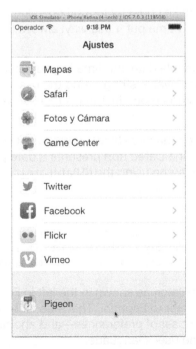 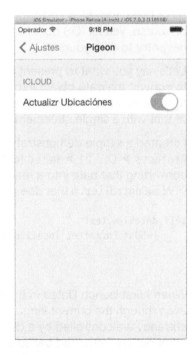

Figure 22-16. Localized Pigeon settings

Other Code Considerations

In addition to language differences, there are also regional preferences that your app should be sensitive to. Most of these are handled automatically by iOS, as long as you let it. When writing your code, pay attention to these issues:

- Visible messages
- Dates
- Numbers, including percentages and currency

Most objects that return a string intended for the user to see will provide a localized version. This will be translated into the user's language, whenever possible. Look for these whenever you get a string that you're going to show the user. Here are some examples:

```
-[NSError localizedDescription]
-[UIDocument localizedName]
-[UIDevice localizedModel]
-[PKPass localizedName]
```

Dates and numbers, including currency, are formatted for the user's region and personal preference. This cannot be inferred from their language; French speakers in France format currency differently than French speakers in Canada. In addition to the user's region, iOS may provide personal preferences (such as a 12- or 24-hour clock) that the user can customize.

All of these variables and choices make correctly formatting values extremely challenging. Unless, of course, you let iOS do it for you. Let me put it this way: *always* let iOS format dates and numbers; never try to do it yourself.

Let's say you want to present a readable date and time to your user. Use the `NSDateFormatter` class to convert the date object into a displayable string, using the user's desired language, calendar, and formatting style. This is such a common procedure that's there's even convenience method to do all of that with a single statement.

I created a simple demonstration app, named Dated, which you'll find in the `Learn iOS Development Projects` ➤ `Ch. 22` ➤ `Dated` folder. The Dated app presents a date picker and the results of converting that date into a readable string using the `NSDateFormatter` class. Here's the code in `DTViewController.m` that does all of the work:

```
self.dateView.text =
    [NSDateFormatter localizedStringFromDate:self.datePicker.date
                            dateStyle:NSDateFormatterFullStyle
                            timeStyle:NSDateFormatterLongStyle];
```

When I first launch Dated in the simulator, as shown in the left in Figure 22-17, the date is in English, even though the current language is set to Español. That's because dates, times, numbers, and currency are controlled by a different set of preferences—and another reason you can't assume how numbers are formatted based on the user's language.

Figure 22-17. Localizing dates using NSDateFormatter

In the Ajustes (Settings) app, I changed the Formato regional (Region Format) setting from Estados Unidos (United States) to España (Spain), as shown in the middle of Figure 22-17. Returning to the Dated app, both the app picker and the formatted date have been translated to Spanish, using the date style conventions common in Spain.

Use `NSNumberFormatter` to format numbers, percentages, and currency. Both of these classes handle all of the subtle details. For more information, refer to the *Data Formatting Guide* that you can find in Xcode's Documentation and API Reference window.

Localizing Your App's Name

Your app's `.strings` files are most often used to localize the string constants in your program, as you've already seen. They are, actually, general-purpose string translation files and are used for a variety of purposes, like translating the visible strings in the `Settings.bundle`.

One important `.strings` files is the `InfoPlist.strings` file, that's localized automatically for you. The substitutions in this `.strings` file are applied to your app's `Info.plist` file. This is the property list file that contains the information (metadata) about your app. You've edited this file earlier in the book, when you added device requirements like `gps`.

Expand the `InfoPlist.strings` group and select the `InfoPlist.strings (Spanish)` item. The `InfoPlist.strings` file contains substitutions for any user-visible property values contained in the `Info.plist` file. In iOS, this is pretty much limited to the name of your app. The keys of the `InfoPlist.strings` file are not, however, the original strings; they're the `Info.plist` property keys. To localize a specific property, add a property key and its localized value to your `InfoPlist.strings` file, like this:

```
"CFBundleDisplayName" = "Paloma";
```

For a Spanish-speaking user, the app's name becomes Paloma in the springboard, the Settings app, and elsewhere, as shown in Figure 22-18.

  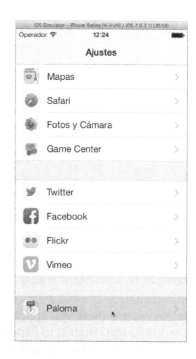

Figure 22-18. Localizing your app's name

Summary

Localization is one of the last things you do to your app, but it certainly isn't the least important. Localizing dramatically broadens your app's horizons. And as you've seen, it's not that much work. I'll go so far as saying that localizing your app is the single most significant step you can take to broaden its appeal.

While you've done all of the common steps, your app can support localization in more sophisticated, and non-standard, ways. It's possible to switch languages within your own app, provide your own localization logic, or even add unsupported languages like Hawaiian or Klingon. Start with the *Internationalization Programming Topics* document that you can find in Xcode's Documentation and API Reference window.

As localization is one of the last app development tasks you undertake, it's fitting that this is one of the last chapters in this book. But your iOS journey doesn't have to stop here. There's so much more to perfect your app and refine your app development skills. The next two chapters will improve your app's performance, taking it to even greater heights.

Chapter 23

Faster, Faster

I've spent a lot of this book explaining the "correct" way to do things in iOS: the correct way to use a delegate, the correct way to define a data model, the correct way to register for notifications, and so on. But there's more to creating great apps than ensuring that they're correct. Of course, you want your app to be bug free. You want its buttons to work, and you surely don't want it to crash, but there are other aspects too. The fit, finish, and performance of your app are just as important as its features. In this chapter you're going to focus on performance.

Xcode provides a suite of tools for profiling and performance testing, which you haven't even looked at, called Instruments. In this chapter you'll fire up Instrument and:

- Learn the fundamentals of code optimization
- Analyze method execution time
- Identify "hot spots" and reorganize your code to improve app responsiveness
- Trace object allocations to quantify memory usage
- Stress test your app
- Implement low memory handling

The notion of performance is often confined to measuring how fast code X accomplishes task Y. My definition is much broader. For me, the performance of an app is simply how well it performs for the user; it should be efficient, respond smartly, and (ideally) not grind to a crawl under a heavy load. You can apply metrics to some of these aspects—and we'll measure some in this chapter—but in the end, what's important is how your app feels. Does it feel lively or sluggish? Is it jerky or smooth? That's the litmus test.

As you piled on new features to MyStuff in Chapter 19, your app was starting to feel a little fatigued. Some actions were getting slow. It's losing its responsiveness. In this chapter, you'll put MyStuff on the test bench and see what's ailing it. But before you get to that, let's talk a little about the overall process.

Performance Optimization

Performance optimization is the art of getting the best performance from your code. There are hundreds of different ways to solve almost any software problem. Some of those ways are going to be more efficient—use less memory, require fewer resources, execute faster—than other solutions. In the simplest terms, performance optimization is the search for a solution with the best performance. Now we're going to go look at some code and try to figure out how to make it run faster, right?

Wrong.

The mistake practically every programmer makes is optimizing code that doesn't need optimizing. I've done it. It's hard not to. You see code that you *know* could be made faster, or more efficient, and you're just chomping at the bit to rewrite it. Don't. Take a deep breath, three if you have to, and carefully read the following.

Code optimization serves a purpose: making your app better. If your work isn't making your app better, you shouldn't be doing it. Just jumping in and rewriting code to make it faster is a fool's errand. First, you don't know what to optimize. Seriously, you don't. Even programmers with decades of experience can't accurately guess where an app's performance problems are.

Secondly, it's even harder to look at some code and tell if it's adversely impacting your app. You might know how to make it better, or use fewer objects, but that doesn't mean that's going to translate into a tangible difference for your app.

Finally, code optimizations—particularly code to improve execution performance—will often complicate your code and could introduce new bugs. That makes it harder to read, harder to debug, and harder to maintain. You'd better be getting some significant benefit for what it's costing you, or your development efforts are going backwards, not forwards.

Here's the way to achieve purposeful, rational, and effective performance optimization:

1. Establish a performance criterion
2. Measure the performance of your app and record a baseline
3. Optimize your code
4. Measure the performance of your modified app and compare it to the baseline
5. Repeat steps 3 and 4 until the goal in step 1 is achieved

Begin by writing your code simply and directly. Don't worry too much about optimization and performance at the outset. Concentrate on writing concise, straightforward, solutions that are robust, bug free, and easy to maintain. Now you can begin the process of performance analysis and optimization.

Step one is crucial. You *must* begin by deciding what your app's performance criteria are. It doesn't have to be fancy, or even specific. It can be as simple as "I want my app to be responsive." That's actually an exceptional performance criterion. As you test your app, if you find a place or two where it isn't as responsive as you'd like it to be, then that's the code you concentrate on. The rest of the code you ignore. It doesn't matter how much better you can make it, it isn't—by definition—impinging on your app's performance.

Once you've established that something needs to be improved, measure and analyze your app's current performance, using a tool like Instruments. This becomes your baseline. This is also a critical step. You cannot evaluate the effectiveness of your optimizations if you don't have something to measure your progress against.

Then, and only then, should you start changing your code. Because you've taken the first two steps, you know what you need to accomplish and you have the information (from the baseline measurements) needed to formulate a plan to achieve that goal.

You should then measure your app's performance again and compare it to the baseline. This will tell you, definitively, what progress you've made. If the change meets your original performance criterion, you're done. Get back to adding cool new features.

If not, then just try again. Optimization is as much art as science, and it's not uncommon to try two or three different solutions before you find one you're happy with. The point is, you'll know if you're making real progress or not, and how much.

OK, the sermon is over. Let's put this to the test, so to speak.

Fixing a Slow Tap

At the end of Chapter 19, you added document storage to MyStuff and fixed an image rotation problem. I've been playing with MyStuff on my iPhone, and it's starting to drag a little. When I choose a new image from my photo library, there's a definite hiccup—a pause of about a second—between when I tap the image and it returns me to the detail view controller. It's long enough that, every time I do it, I have a momentary sense that I didn't actually touch the image and I should try again. That's too long.

> **Note** You might not be experiencing these performance deficiencies. For this chapter, I deliberately tested MyStuff on an older iPhone 4. Newer, faster, devices are probably much more responsive, but I want *all* of my users to get a great app experience, not just the ones with the latest hardware.

The programmer voice inside my head is telling me what's wrong, "Dude, the did-pick-image method has to crop, rotate, and resize the image, and then it has to encode it into a compressed PNG format and store that in a file wrapper. Of course it's going to take a second or two!" I then have to remind my programmer voice, "Dude, that doesn't matter, the interface sucks."

If you're following my line of reasoning, you've already taken your first step in your performance optimization journey. You wrote the code in a simple, straightforward, manner that works. You then established a performance criterion for your app, specifically that touch responses shouldn't lag. A full second to respond to a tap is too slow.

> **Note** In most situations, if the visual feedback in response to a gesture happens within ¼ to ⅓ of a second, the interface will feel lively and responsive. Anything that happens in less than 1/10th of a second will appear to be instantaneous. A delay of ½ second or more, and the interface begins to feel sluggish.

The next step is to measure the performance of the app, gather information, and establish a baseline. For that, you'll use Instruments.

Launching Instruments

Instruments is the front-end for a suite of analysis, profiling, and faultfinding tools, much as Xcode is the front-end for your editors, compilers, and debuggers. You can use the Instruments app by itself, but Xcode makes it so easy to use directly from your project, I can't imagine why you'd want to.

For this chapter, start with the version of MyStuff after you added document support and fixed the image rotation problem (second exercise in Chapter 19). You'll find this project in the `Learn iOS Development Projects` ➤ `Ch 19` ➤ `MyStuff E2` folder.

Instruments is normally launched when you profile your app. This is determined by a set of schemes defined in your project. When you run your app (using the **Run** button or menu command), the Run scheme is used. When you profile your app, the Profile scheme is used. To see your project's schemes, choose **Edit Scheme...** from either the **Scheme** control in the toolbar or by choosing **Product** ➤ **Scheme** ➤ **Edit Schemes...** from the menu. This will present the scheme editor, as shown in Figure 23-1.

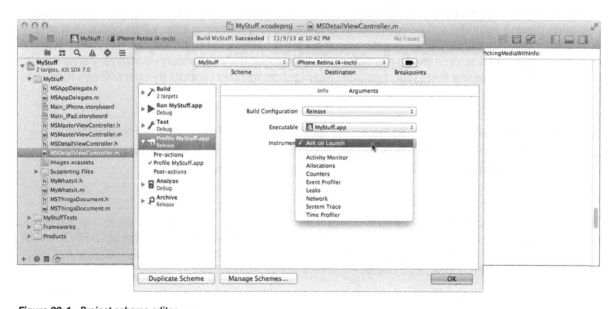

Figure 23-1. Project scheme editor

There's nothing here to change, I just wanted you to know where it was. The default configuration for the Profile scheme is to launch Instruments and prompt you (`Ask on Launch`) for the type of analysis to perform, which is perfect to get started. So what are you waiting for? Close the scheme editor and profile your app by choosing **Product** ➤ **Profile** (Command+I) from the menu or from the **Run** button's drop-down menu. Xcode will build your project and launch Instruments, as shown in Figure 23-2.

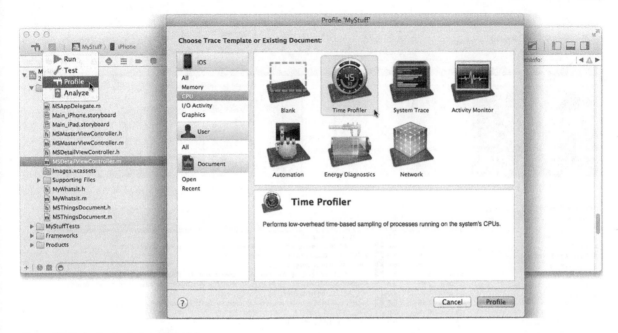

Figure 23-2. Instruments template picker

Each Instruments template describes a different kind of analysis. They're organized into groups for convenience. For your first foray into performance analysis, choose the iOS ➤ CPU group and select the `Time Profiler`. This is the most commonly used instrument for measuring code performance. It works by sampling your code as it executes, thousands of times a second. At each sample, it records the functions and methods that are executing at that instant. By aggregating hundreds of thousands of these samples, it can paint a remarkably accurate picture of where your app is spending its time. These are the methods that you want to make faster.

> **Note** While you can do performance analysis in the simulator, it's not that useful. Performance is highly dependent on the model of CPU, hardware components, memory speed, and other physical traits of the device. All performance tests should be done on real iOS devices.

Click the **Profile** button and your app begins executing, under the watchful eye of the Time Profiler instrument, as shown in Figure 23-3. You want to find out what's taking so long when a new image is added, so immediately started adding new items and selecting images for those items from your camera roll. Repeat this several times. You should notice a sizable spike in CPU activity as you tap on an image in the photo picker, creating a series of "humps" in the CPU usage graph.

CHAPTER 23: Faster, Faster

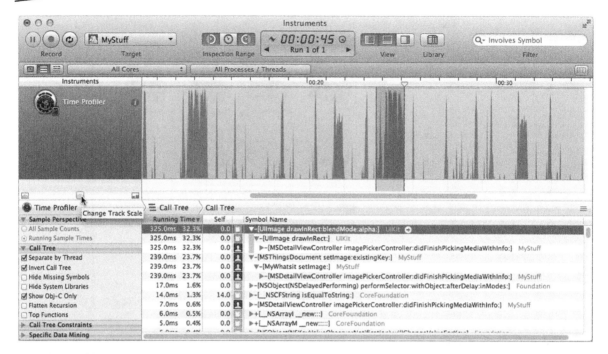

Figure 23-3. Initial sample of MyStuff

After adding a few new images, press the home button to push the app into the background, wait a few seconds, and click the Record button in the Instruments toolbar. This stops recording and terminates the app.

Congratulations, you have a baseline! You've captured the code activity associated with the performance problem you're trying to solve. Now it's time to mine this mountain of data for some answers.

Finding the Hot Spots

Begin by isolating just the performance information you're interested in studying. Using the mouse in the Instruments timeline (at the top of the window), drag the sample cursor (hollow triangle with dotted line) just to the left of one of those "humps" in the graph recorded just as you tapped an image in the photo library picker. To make this easier, drag the **Change Track Scale** control, shown at the middle-left of the window in Figure 23-3, to zoom in on the samples you're interested in. Click on the left mask button in the Inspection **Range control** in the toolbar. Drag the cursor just to the right of the hump and click on the right mask button. Now all of the data you're going to work with in the lower panes will contain only samples from the highlighted range (lower pane in Figure 23-3), because this is the code you're interested in profiling.

> **Note** Code performance numbers are going to vary wildly from one CPU to the next. That's why it's important to measure your app on actual hardware (not the simulator) and to repeat your tests on as many different configurations of hardware as you can get your hands on.

Now you want to find the *hot spots* in your code. This is optimization slang for the code that's eating up all of your CPU time. Less colorfully, it's the regions of code that accumulated the most samples. With the Time Profiler instrument selected in the trace document, locate the **Invert Call Tree** and **Show Obj-C Only** options in the Time Profiler sidebar. Check both of these, as shown in Figure 23-3.

The **Show Obj-C Only** option filters out all of the C functions from the analysis. I recommend this option for Objective-C programmers, particularly to get started.

The **Invert Call Tree** option inverts the Call Tree you see to the right. When *not* checked, the Call Tree summarizes the calling hierarchy of your entire app. Each line in the table shows a method or function and how much time your app spent in it. Expand a line and you see the methods it invoked, and the breakdown of time spent in each sub-method. Expand one of those, and you get the idea.

The Call Tree is normally sorted by "heaviest" method. That is, the first line of each group will be the method that used the most CPU time. To dig down into the pile and find the heaviest code path in the tree, keep expanding the first line of each group.

With the **Invert Call Tree** option checked, the Call Tree is turned inside out. Now, the method listed at the top is the heaviest leaf method in your app. Expand it, and it lists what methods called it—instead of what methods it called. In Figure 23-3, you see that 32.3% of your app's response time was spent in the `-drawInRect:blendMode:alpha:` method. Working backwards, by expanding the lines, and you find that it's the `-imagePickerController:didFinishPickingMediaWithInfo:` method that's using it (to resize and crop the chosen image).

> **Tip** Inverting the call tree is particularly useful for identifying heavy methods that are invoked from a variety of different places.

Looking a little further down the list, the next heaviest method is the `-setImage:existingKey:` method. This is the method you added to store the new image in the document. When the user taps on an image in the picker, 23.7% of the time is spent storing it in the new document. If you expand its caller you see that it, too, is being called from the `-imagePickerController:didFinishPickingMediaWithInfo:` method.

This corroborates your suspicion that the image conversion and document storage code you added in Chapter 19 are slowing down the interface when the user picks an image. Let's dig into the `-imagePickerController:didFinishPickingMediaWithInfo:` method and find out what's going on. Turn the **Invert Call Tree** option off again, and begin expanding the heaviest methods in the call tree until you uncover the `-imagePickerController:didFinishPickingMediaWithInfo:` method, as shown in Figure 23-4.

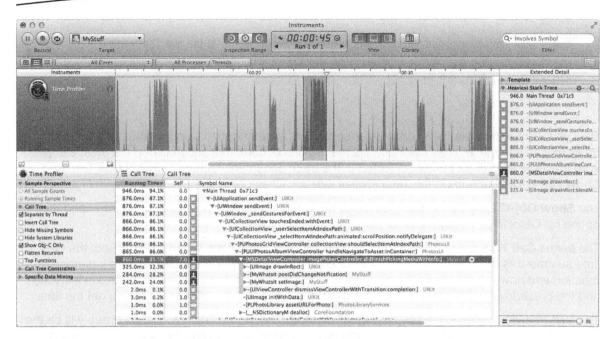

Figure 23-4. Details of -imagePickerController:didFinishPickingMediaWithInfo: execution time

In this set of samples, it shows that the image picker delegate method spent close to a second (860 milliseconds) responding to the tap. Expanding that line, you see the amount of time spent in each message the picker method sent. While this is accurate information, it's sometimes a little hard to translate into what your code is doing. Instruments will help you here too.

Double click the `-imagePickerController:didFinishPickingMediaWithInfo:` method line and Time Profiler will switch to its source view, as shown in Figure 23-5.

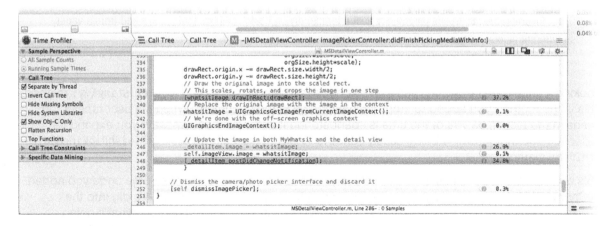

Figure 23-5. Time Profiler source view

Instruments overlays the time spent in each line of your source code, clearly identifying the hot spots in your code. This view is particularly good at identifying loops that are taking a long time to execute.

What have you learned from Figure 23-5? You've learned that when the user tapped on an image in the photo picker, 37.3% of the time was spent cropping image, 26.9% storing it in the document, and 0.3% dismissing the photo picker view controller. In a big surprise, 34.8% of the time was spent notifying any observers that the data model changed.

Huh?

The Hubris of Experience

Yes, it caught me off guard too. When I was originally planning the projects for these chapters, I *knew* that the image compression and document storage code in Chapter 19 would add a lot of overhead to the MyStuff app. I've worked with the LZ77 compression algorithm used by the PNG format, and I know how CPU intensive it can be. I planned to start this chapter by showing you how much time the image conversion and compression routines were taking up when the user chose an image, and what to do about it. But when I *actually* ran Instruments on MyStuff, what did I find? I find that almost a third of the delay is tangled up in the data model notification. Something that I guessed wouldn't have even showed up on the radar.

And this is why *you can't assume you know where your performance problems are*. Even with years of programming experience, you're going to guess wrong. I did. You must start by measuring your real-world performance. If you don't, you'll be tilting at windmills.

So what is going on? Digging into the `-postDidChangeNotification` method, shown in Figure 23-6, it turns out that the MyWhatsit change notification was observed by the view controller, and that triggered a redraw of the table view (`-reloadRowsAtIndexPaths:withRowAnimation:`). This, apparently, is a much more expensive operation than I thought.

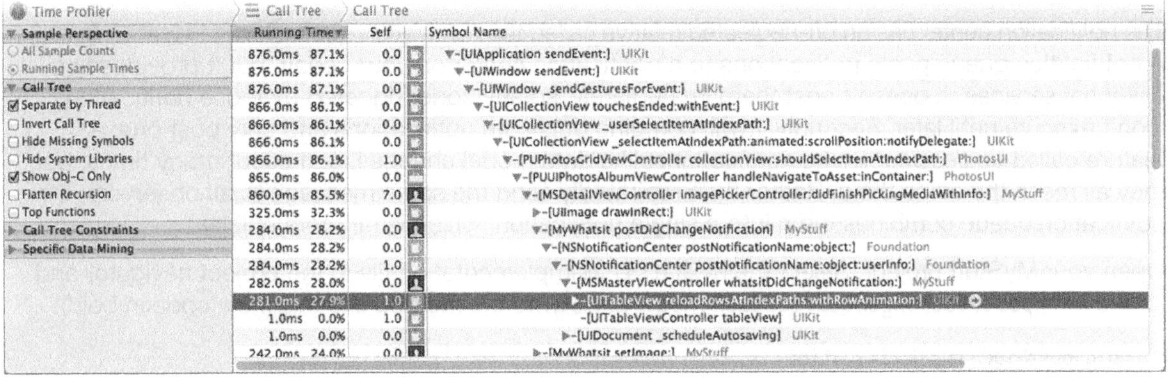

Figure 23-6. Time sample details of -postDidChangeNotification

Fine, I guessed wrong. Can we get back to improving MyStuff now?

Picking the Low Hanging Fruit

With all of this knowledge, you now need to formulate an optimization plan. You've identified three hot spots in your photo picker handling code:

- Data model notification
- Image conversion
- Image compression and document storage

The trick is to pick the "low hanging fruit." Find the code that is hurting performance the most and is the easiest to improve.

Graphics operations are data and CPU intensive, by their very nature, and the iOS graphics library is already heavily optimized. It's unlikely you're going to get much improvement by rewriting the code that crops the image.

That leaves the data model notification and document storage as candidates for improvement. And in a nice surprise, the heaviest is also the easiest to solve.

Deferring Notifications

In iOS, notifications are delivered immediately. When you post a notification, all of the observers are sent their notification messages, and control returns to your method only after they're all done. In this instance, the act of notifying everyone that the data model object changed triggered a series of expensive and time-consuming operations.

You can't avoid this work—the data model has to send its notifications, and the observers have to be notified—but you can procrastinate. It's not critical to the code that picks a new image that these notifications are delivered before that code is finished. You can take advantage of this to defer the notification. The notification will still happen, just not at the moment the user taps an image. This will, in turn, improve the response time to the tap event.

The notification center has an oft-neglected relative called the notification queue (NSNotificationQueue). A notification queue posts notifications to a notification center on your behalf, but it provides two essential services. It doesn't post them immediately, so any code triggered by those notifications won't execute until later. Secondly, it will combine duplicate notifications and only post one; a feature called *coalescing*. Some notifications, like data model changes, can occur many times, but they all mean the same thing. Rather than repeatedly send the same message to all observers, the notification queue combines them into a single notification, which is far more efficient.

Open your MyStuff project. Select the MyWhatsit.m implementation file in the project navigator and locate the -postDidChangeNotification method. Rewrite the method like this (new code in bold):

```
- (void)postDidChangeNotification
{
    NSNotification *noti;
    noti = [NSNotification notificationWithName:kWhatsitDidChangeNotification
                                         object:self];
    [[NSNotificationQueue defaultQueue] enqueueNotification:noti
                                          postingStyle:NSPostWhenIdle];
}
```

To use a notification queue, you must create a notification object. (When you use the notification center's -postNotification... messages, the NSNotification object is created for you.) Once you create the notification, push it onto the queue.

Each notification queue is attached to a notification center. iOS, conveniently, creates a notification queue attached to the default notification center for you. Anything you add to the default queue will (eventually) be posted to the default notification center.

When your modified MyWhatsit object receives a -postDidChangeNotification message, it doesn't notify its observers immediately. This method has become an asynchronous method. It merely queues the notification to be delivered in the future.

So when does it get delivered? You have are a few choices, controlled by the postingStyle parameter. The two most useful are NSPostWhenIdle and NSPostASAP.

- NSPostASAP will post the notification as soon as the current code finishes executing and control returns to the event loop. Use this to post notifications that must be sent before the next event is dispatched.
- NSPostWhenIdle saves notifications until the event loop is idle. It waits until all pending events (touch events, timers, deferred messages, user interface updates) have been dispatched. Before the event loop goes to sleep again, any queued notifications are sent. Use NSPostWhenIdle when you want notifications to be handled immediately *after* you've responded to all user and timer events.

Now the work of updating the data model, refreshing the table view, and notifying the document of changes is still handled, but it's handled after you've responded to the tap event, dismissed the view controller, and updated everything on the screen.

Once More into The Breach

Close and save your Instruments trace document, as shown in Figure 23-7. Give it a descriptive name, like Baseline Profile. Close the profile window.

Figure 23-7. Saving your baseline trace document

Return to Xcode and profile your app again. Perform the same steps you did before: choose the `Time Profiler` template, add images to your app, stop it, narrow the inspector range to the code that picks a new image, and review the call tree, as shown in Figure 23-8.

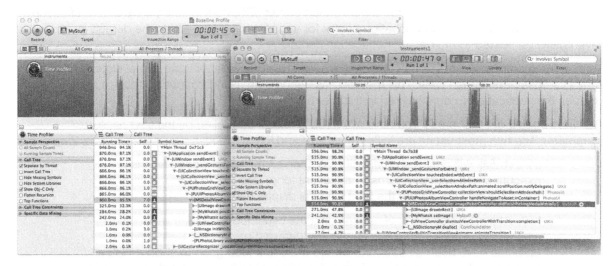

Figure 23-8. Profiling revised code

This time, it only took half a second (514 milliseconds) to execute the code in the `-imagePickerController: didFinishPickingMediaWithInfo:` method. That's an improvement of over 67%. Open the baseline trace document you saved and compare two, similar, execution sections. In the modified code, the `-postDidChangeNotification` method doesn't even show up in the sample, it happens so fast!

If you dig around the call tree, you'll eventually find where the data model notification is posted, and all of the busy work associated with it still gets done. But it's not happening when the user taps the interface, so they don't see it.

Your app should feel much more responsive now. The key to creating responsive apps is to keep your event loop running and ready to react immediately to the user or other events. That often means breaking up the work so it doesn't happen all at once. Notification queues are a great way to defer tasks that you don't want interfering with your interface, and can be safely performed later.

This is great progress, but it still hasn't gotten the response time below ½ second. The next "heavy" on the list is the code that adds the image to the document. You'll learn a different way of deferring that work in the next chapter.

Save your second trace document and close it. Now you're ready to look at a completely different aspect of your app's performance.

Precious Memory

The amount of RAM available to mobile apps is minuscule when compared to most computing environments. Yet, users expect mobile apps to accomplish many of the same tasks: surf the web, play videos, read books, and edit documents. An iOS app is under tremendous pressure to conserve, and make the best use of, its memory. Xcode has several tools to help you analyze and improve your app's memory use.

Quantifying memory use isn't as conclusive as measuring code performance. Poor use of memory degrades your apps, other apps, and the iOS device in general, in odd and subtle ways. Generally, you want your app to use as little memory as possible. But that can be counter to making your app faster, because caching data and objects is one of the ways of improving its performance.

In this section you're going to work through the bare minimum of responsible memory use by stress testing your app and responding to iOS's low memory warnings. When an app starts to use too much memory, iOS first gives it a chance to release memory it's not relying on. It does this by sending low memory warning notifications. If the app responds, it (and other apps) can all continue to run. If it doesn't, or can't recover enough memory, iOS will begin terminating apps, in order to keep the active app running.

If an app continues to ignore these warnings, it runs the risk of running out of memory. This usually has disastrous results. The app will crash, and the user will be left staring at the springboard. This situation should be avoided at all costs.

In this section you're going to use Instruments to trace the memory usage of your app and find its breaking point. You'll then modify your code and use Instruments again to verify that it behaves correctly. But first, you have to push it to its limit.

Breaking MyStuff

MyStuff is an unbounded app. You put no limits on the number of items the user can add. Now you might expect that number to be reasonable, and MyStuff's memory needs to be nominally modest. And most of the time, you'd be right. But if I have 20 model train cars, you know there's somebody with 300. What happens to MyStuff when the user wants to track 100, or 500, or 2,000 items? Is that crazy? Absolutely. Is it OK if MyStuff crashes after adding the 500th item? No, it is not.

When you develop any app, you need to stress test it. How you do that will depend on the nature of the app. For MyStuff, its Achilles' heel is the memory used by all of those item image objects. If the user keeps adding items and images, it's going to run out.

You've already written MyStuff to keep its image objects in memory, lazily loaded from the document's file wrapper objects. You also have to establish a performance criterion: MyStuff should use its memory efficiently and not crash if the user enters 1,000 items. That's a reasonable goal. The next step is to test it.

I don't know what you're doing this weekend, but I don't want to spend it entering 1,000 items (with pictures) into MyStuff. I suggest you do what any respectable programmer would do; you cheat. Add some code to MyStuff to generate hundreds of test items.

The first step is to make `MyWhatsit` copyable. Select the `MyWhatsit.h` interface file and adopt the `NSCopying` protocol (new code in bold):

```
@interface MyWhatsit : NSObject <NSCoding,NSCopying>
```

Switch to the `MyWhatsit.m` implementation file and add the necessary `-copyWithZone:` method (you learned how to do this in Chapter 20):

```
- (id)copyWithZone:(NSZone *)zone
{
    MyWhatsit *copy = [[[self class] alloc] init];
    if (copy!=nil)
        {
        copy->_name = _name;
        copy->_location = _location;
        copy->image = image;
        copy->imageKey = imageKey;
        }
    return copy;
}
```

Select the `MSThingsDocument.m` file, find the `-loadFromContents:ofType:error:` method, and locate the code that unarchives the `things` array. Immediately after that, add this test code (in bold):

```
    if (thingsData!=nil)
        {
        things = [NSKeyedUnarchiver unarchiveObjectWithData:thingsData];
#if 1 // STRESS TESTING: generate a thousand test items
        if (things.count>10)
            {
            NSUInteger cloneIndex = 0;
            while (things.count<1000)
                [things addObject:[things[cloneIndex++] copy]];
            }
#endif
        [things makeObjectsPerformSelector:@selector(setDocument:)
                                withObject:self];
        }
```

Run the modified MyStuff app. Add more than 10 items to the list, with images. Press the home button, to push the app to the background, and let it save its document. Run it again. This time, your list will have 1,000 items. Now it's time to see how well MyStuff handles that!

> **Note** When you're done testing, change the statement `#if 1` to `#if 0`. This will disable all of the code between the `#if 0` and the `#endif`.

Measuring Memory

Memory and CPU usage are such important performance metrics for apps that Xcode includes a set of "mini" instruments right in its debug navigator. Run your MyStuff app from within Xcode. Switch to the debug navigator (if it doesn't appear automatically), as shown in Figure 23-9.

CHAPTER 23: Faster, Faster

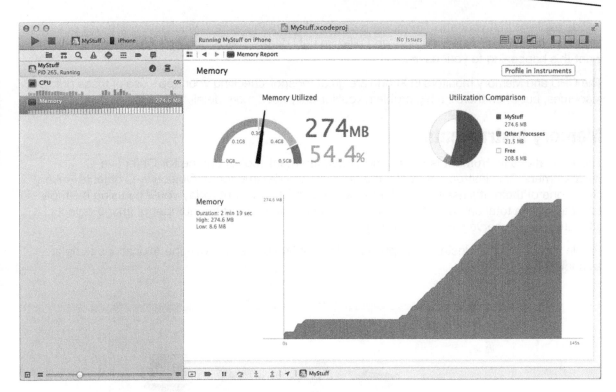

Figure 23-9. Xcode's CPU and memory monitors

The stress-test code you added will generate a 1,000 test items. Start scrolling through the list. As each table row reveals a new `MyWhatsit` item, it requests the item's image. This, in turn, loads a new `UIImage` object from the document and saves it in the `image` property of the object.

As you scroll, you'll notice the memory use of the app begins to climb, as shown in Figure 23-9. Keep scrolling and the app will eventually run out of memory. You'll be rewarded with a fatal app crash, accompanied by the message shown in Figure 23-10.

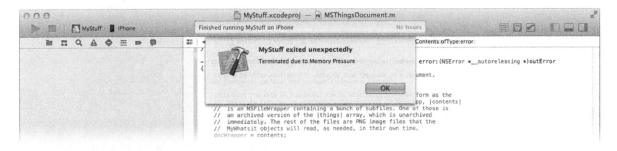

Figure 23-10. Memory pressure failure

Xcode explains that your app "Terminated due to Memory Pressure," which is a polite way of saying it used up all of its available memory and died an ugly death. This is horrible. You definitely don't want this happening to your users.

The CPU and Memory monitors in Xcode are great for spot-checking your app's use of these precious resources, but when there's a big problem you'll usually need more detail. Turn again to Instruments.

Memory Instruments

The Allocations instrument is the memory measurement tool of choice for Objective-C programmers. This instrument tracks the creation and destruction of Objective-C objects—every single one of them. It's useful in finding all kinds of problems, but today you'll be using it simply to measure the total amount of memory your app is using, count the number of image objects allocated, and observe memory warnings.

Profile your app. When Instruments presents its template picker, choose the Allocations template, as shown in Figure 23-11.

Figure 23-11. Allocations template

MyStuff starts running and the Allocations instrument begins collecting data. At the top, you'll see a graph of all memory allocations. (You can chart any set of allocations you like by checking different items in the categories.) Begin scrolling through the list of items in the MyStuff app. As you remember from Chapter 5, table cell view objects are prepared lazily. As you scroll, the images for each item that's about to be displayed is lazily loaded from the document. Each time this happens, another `UIImage` object is created. You can see the effect it has on the overall memory usage, shown in Figure 23-12.

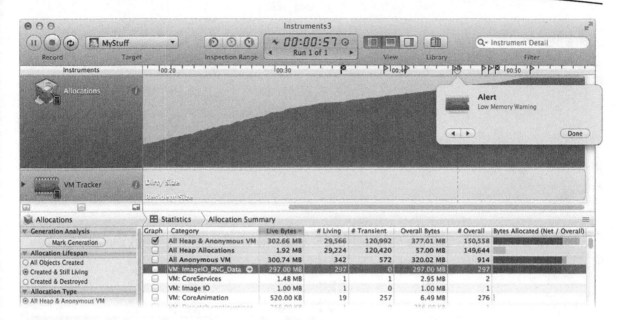

Figure 23-12. Baseline memory use in MyStuff with 1,000 items

If you keep scrolling the table, the memory use goes up and up and up and . . . boom! The app crashes.

> **Note** Your app might not crash after scrolling through 300 items, or even 600. Apple keeps making newer iOS devices with more memory, so by the time you read this the latest iOS gizmo might not run out of memory even after loading 1,000 images. This is one reason why you need to test your app on as many different configurations of hardware (CPU/memory combinations) as you can. An app that runs for days on the latest generation of hardware might not last 5 minutes on one that's a few years old.

You'll notice a set of flags in the timeline. Click on one, as shown in Figure 23-12, and it will show you that a Low Memory Warning was sent to your app—several, actually. iOS was trying to warn your app that it was running out of memory. Your app ignored those warnings and kept loading images, to its peril. You may also see black flags (with an X) in the timeline. These indicate where iOS terminated another running app in order to provide your app with more memory. This underscores how poor memory management impacts other apps, not just yours.

If you sort the list by the amount of memory each type of allocation is occupying, you'll see that the biggest consumer is VM: ImageIO_PNG_Data allocations, as shown in Figure 23-13. If you scroll down the list of object/allocation types, you'll also find the UIImage object listed. It's easier to find these objects if you filter the list; the keyword "image" has been used in Figure 23-13 to eliminate many uninteresting categories.

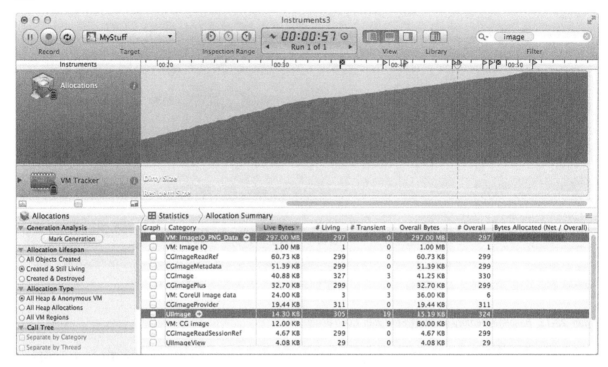

Figure 23-13. UIImage allocations in baseline stress test

In this sample, the app crashed after creating 324 UIImage objects, 305 of which still exist and are occupying memory. So we've learned that MyStuff, running on this particular flavor of iPhone, can load about 300 images into memory at once. But there are 1,000 images in the list! What can you do about that?

> **Note** You can't tell how much memory, in total, the UIImage objects are consuming by looking at this one line in the Allocations instrument. The memory size for a UIImage is just the memory occupied by that object; it doesn't include any memory occupied by other objects or memory allocations the UIImage refers to. The bulk of an image's data is allocated in separate ImageIO_PNG_Data allocations that will appear elsewhere in the list. This is also true of collection objects (like NSArray).

Heed the Warnings

It turns out, this problem is also easy to address. Your MyWhatsit object has two image references: the ID of the compressed image data in the document (NSString) and the working image object (UIImage) in memory. The image object can be easily recreated, at a moment's notice, from the data in the document.

If your app is running out of memory, the first thing it should do is discard all of the objects that can be easily reconstructed. Your view controller objects already do this. Every NSViewController object receives a -didReceiveMemoryWarning message when memory starts to run low. (The custom view controller class template includes stubs for these methods, so I know you've seen them around.) If the view controller has loaded its view objects, but isn't being displayed—it had been presented but has since been dismissed—it destroys all of its view objects.[1] Its view objects are easily recreated from its Interface Builder file, should it be presented again.

The solution for MyStuff is for every MyWhatsit object to observe these low memory warnings. When one is received, it can discard its UIImage object, knowing that it can reload it from the document using its imageKey property.

Select the MyWhatsit.h file. Add this new method prototype to the @interface section:

```
- (void)memoryWarning;
```

Switch to the MyWhatsit.m implementation file and add the new method:

```
- (void)memoryWarning
{
    if (imageKey!=nil && image!=nil)
        image = nil;
}
```

The method is simple. If the object has an image (image!=nil) and it has a key it can use to reload that image from the document (imageKey!=nil), then it discards its image object (image=nil). The next request for its image (-image) will create a new image from the document.

Now the question is: who is going to send the MyWhatsit objects this -memoryWarning message? That sounds like a job for the document object. Select the MSThingsDocument.m implementation file. In the private interface section, add a prototype for a new -memoryWarning: method (new code in bold):

```
@interface MSThingsDocument ()
{
    NSFileWrapper   *docWrapper;
    NSMutableArray  *things;
}
- (void)whatsitDidChange:(NSNotification*)notification;
- (void)memoryWarning:(NSNotification*)notification;
@end
```

Locate the +documentAtURL: class method and find the code that registers to observe the kWhatsitDidChangeNotification notification. Immediately after that, add another one:

```
[notificationCenter addObserver:document
                       selector:@selector(memoryWarning:)
                           name:UIApplicationDidReceiveMemoryWarningNotification
                         object:nil];
```

---

[1] This is why you don't want your view object outlets to be strong references.

Finally, add the new -memoryWarning: notification handler:

```
- (void)memoryWarning:(NSNotification*)notification
{
    [things makeObjectsPerformSelector:@selector(memoryWarning)];
}
```

The -memoryWarning: method observes the iOS notification that the app is running low on memory. It turns around and sends a -memoryWarning message to each of its MyWhatsit objects, giving each one a chance to release some memory.

> **Caution** In Objective-C method signatures, colons are significant. The signature -memoryWarning (without a colon) and -memoryWarning: (with a colon) are unique methods, but are easy to mix up.

Stress Test, Round #2

Profile MyStuff again. This time you didn't save and close the trace document from the last profile. When you work this way, Instruments reuses the open trace document and the data you gather from this run accumulates in the same document. You'll see a message like "Run 2 of 2" in the toolbar run status, as shown in Figure 23-14. This is the other technique for comparing multiple measurements of your app: collect multiple runs in a single trace document, and then flip back through them—using the arrows in the run status or through the **Run Browser** window in the **View** menu—to compare and contrast your progress.

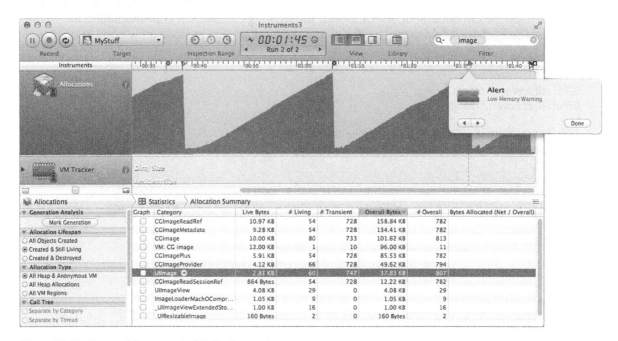

Figure 23-14. Successful stress test of MyStuff

You do the same thing you did last time; when MyStuff starts running, begin scrolling down through the list, forcing the table view to load each item's image. As you see in Figure 23-14, the memory consumption begins to rise, just as before.

Eventually your app starts to run out of memory and receives a low memory warning (flag in the timeline). This time, it responds to that warning by releasing all of its UIImage objects, dramatically reducing its memory use. As you continue to scroll, new rows are drawn, causing it to load new image objects, and the cycle repeats. What doesn't repeat is the crash. This time, you can successfully scroll all the way to the end of your 1,000 row table without incident.

If you look at the number of UIImage objects in Figure 23-11, it says that there have been a total of 807 objects created, 747 of those have since been destroyed, and 60 remain in memory. If you continued scrolling, the living count will climb again, until the next memory warning destroys them. MyStuff is now correctly responding to memory warnings.

THE ALLOCATIONS INSTRUMENT

The Allocations instrument is a hidden gem for Objective-C programmers. You used it in a rather rudimentary fashion in this chapter, but it can track down all kinds of memory management issues.

The Allocations instrument traces every object allocation and destruction, recording what routine created it and what routine was responsible for its destruction. In a non-ARC app, it will also record every -retain, -release, and -autorelease message sent to an object (and by whom), which can be invaluable in finding retain/release mismatches.

The Object Summary lists all of the objects, by class, that have ever been allocated. You can use the options on the left to filter this to just the objects that still exist, or only objects that have been destroyed.

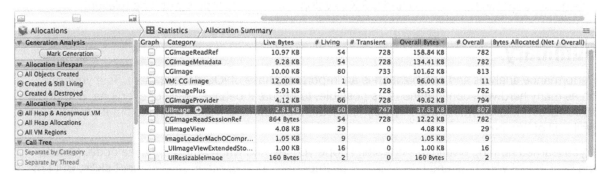

If you click the focus button (arrow) just to the right of a class, the list will expand to list every instance of that object in your app, present and past. Each line records the time the object was created and its address in memory. If your app is stopped in Xcode's debugger at the same time, you can use the address of an object to find its history in the Instruments, and vice versa.

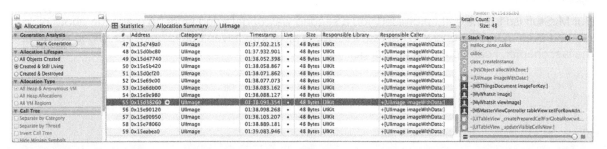

The extended detail pane on the right (**View ➤ Extended Detail**) shows the stack trace when the object was created. This is the code path in your app that created this object. The Live column indicates if the object still exists. This is how you find objects that are leaking—should have been destroyed, but weren't—possibly due to a circular retain.

Click on the focus button next to a specific instance, and the list shows the complete history of that object.

In an ARC application, this is going to be pretty boring, but can still be used to identify the code responsible for destroying the object. In a non-ARC app, this trace can include every place where a `-retain`, `-release`, and `-autorelease` message was sent. Working backwards, you can identify code that was supposed to send a `-retain` that didn't, or uncover code that wasn't supposed to send a `-release` that did.

You've addressed two significant performance problems in MyStuff. In the process, you've learned a little about Instruments and how to measure code performance and Objective-C memory usage. But this barely scratches the surface of what Instruments can do. I suggest you start by reading the *Instruments User Guide*, which you can find in Xcode's Documentation and API Reference window. This guide is written for both iOS and OS X developers, so some topics won't be relevant.

Summary

Performance analysis and optimization is an important phase of iOS development. Test your app on as many hardware configurations as possible, to ensure it behaves well for everyone, and under stressful conditions. This is the only way to ensure that your app not only works, but it works well—all of the time.

If you learned nothing else in this chapter, I hope you learned when *not* to optimize code. Making the best use of your time and talents is just as important as your other development skills. But I'm sure you did learn other things. You've learned how to launch Instruments to analyze your app's performance. You can find hot spots in your code, and trace its memory usage. These tools reveal behaviors in your app that you might not have realized and help you focus your coding efforts in the right direction.

But MyStuff isn't done yet! I promised you a second way of deferring work, to make the photo picker method even more responsive. That requires some skills you haven't developed yet. Since you're at the last chapter, I can't put it off any longer.

Chapter 24

Twice As Nice

This is the final chapter, and the last topic I wanted to cover in this book. Your apps are pretty much done. Localization and performance optimizations are typically the last details you address. The next step is to upload them to the App Store (see the "Submitting Your App to the App Store" sidebar) and start dreaming about your next project.

But I can't let you go just yet. There's a bug in one of your apps, you still have some performance issues, and they're all wrapped around the topic of concurrency. *Concurrency* is when two or more sequences of code (called threads) are executing at the same time. This allows your iOS device to, literally, do more than one thing at a time. It also severely complicates your job as a programmer. In this chapter, you're going to:

- Learn the basics of multitasking
- Execute code blocks on another thread
- Use mutual exclusion locks to synchronize multiple threads
- Explore thread safety
- Embrace the main thread

Concurrent programming, or multithreading, is reminiscent of the game of Go, often described as "a minute to learn, a lifetime to master." The basic principles are straightforward, but it adds a complexity to your app that's often difficult to grasp. Adding even small amounts of multitasking to your app can have broad ramifications for your design, introduce subtle bugs, make your code difficult to test, and could create conditions that will bring your app to a screeching halt.

So why do it? We use multitasking because it's impossible to write a modern app without it. It's what allows your app to stay "alive" while it's also loading web pages, updating the user's location, playing music, synchronizing documents, animating views, and so much more. iOS tries to insulate your app from the mechanics of multitasking, but sometimes you have to deal with it, and it would be a shame not to take advantage of its power.

> **SUBMITTING YOUR APP TO THE APP STORE**

In this book, you've experienced every major phase of iOS app development except one: publishing your finished app on Apple's App Store. With everything you've accomplished so far, the remaining steps for submitting your app are almost trivial:

1. Register your app's unique ID in the iOS Dev Center. You did this in chapter 14 for SunTouch and again in chapter 18 for Pigeon.

2. Log into iTunes Connect and create an app, as you did for SunTouch in chapter 14. You'll need to provide the artwork, screen shots, contact information, and other material that will appear on the App Store.

3. Still in iTunes Connect, click the Prepare for Upload button and answer any remaining questions. There's some legal stuff you'll have to agree to. You'll also want to make sure the services your app needs, like Game Center and iCloud, are enabled for your live app.

4. Back in Xcode, choose `iOS Device` (or any real iOS device) as your run target.

5. Choose **Product ▶ Archive** to build your app and package it into a distribution archive.

6. In the Organizer window, choose the archive you just created and click the **Validate...** button. This pre-flights your app and make sure it's ready for submission. Address any problems that are reported.

7. When you're ready, select the archive in the Organizer window and click the **Distribute...** button. Choose the `Submit to iOS App Store` option and follow the instructions.

Apple will review your app. If it's accepted, it will appear in the App Store! If you have any problems or questions, consult the iTunes Connect guides or contact Developer Services (using the **Contact Us** button in the iTunes Connect portal).

Concurrent Programming

A *thread* is a sequence of computer code that executes one statement at a time. It's what we usually think of as "a computer program" and exactly what you've written so far in this book. Most of the time, your design and coding are focused entirely on the main thread of your app. In fact, the term "your app" is nearly synonymous with the code executing on the main thread.

In a multithreaded environment, more than one thread can be executing concurrently. I've occasionally mentioned background threads and asynchronous methods throughout this book. Your app has even communicated with them through delegate methods. But for the most part, these were activities that occurred "behind the curtain." Which is, honestly, the way it should be. When properly designed, and correctly implemented, multitasking enhances the power of your app without complicating it.

Sometimes, however, those complications invade your code. On the benefits side, multitasking is a powerful tool and there's no reason you can't use it in your app. For that, you'll need to learn some basic concepts, and then prepare to expand your thinking into the fourth dimension.

Threads

A thread executes a single sequence of computer code. *Multitasking* or *multithreading* is a mechanism that executes two or more threads concurrently. Threads have a state. The truly interesting states are running and sleeping. When a thread is *running*, it's executing its code. When it's *sleeping*, it does nothing.

In small microprocessors, the central processing unit (CPU) can only perform one operation at a time. So to be very literal, only a single thread is ever executing. The CPU periodically (a few hundred times a second) stops executing the current thread, saves everything it knows about it, and starts to execute a different thread. This is called a *task switch*. It jumps from one thread to the other so quickly that it gives the illusion that all of them are running at the same time. Two threads can be described as running *concurrently*, but not simultaneously.

Many newer microprocessors have multiple cores. These devices contain the hardware for two (or more) complete CPUs on a single chip. In this environment, two threads literally execute *simultaneously*, each CPU running a different program. Both CPUs perform the same task-switching that single-core processors do, so all of the threads still appear to be running at once, but the CPU is accomplishing twice the work. As of this writing, multi-core CPUs are just beginning to appear in small, portable, computer systems like iOS devices. By the time you read this, multi-core CPUs could be the norm.

Synchronization

Having the CPU executing two, three, or even twenty different threads concurrently certainly sounds wonderful. Think about how much work your app can do! The problem is how to coordinate that work so it doesn't collide. If you were the only person in the world with a car, there would be no need for lanes, stoplights, or roundabouts. Add just one more driver to the road, and you better have some agreement about which one of you goes through the intersection first. And that's exactly the kind of mayhem that awaits your app. Take this simple fragment of code:

```
if (singleton==nil)
    singleton = [[MySingle alloc] init];
```

You've written code like this in a dozen places. As long as only one thread is executing this code at any one time, it works great. Now consider what would happen if two threads were executing this code simultaneously:

1. Thread A would test `singleton` and find that it is `nil`.
2. Thread B would test `singleton` and find that it is `nil`.
3. Thread A would allocate and initialize a new `MySingle` object.
4. Thread B would allocate and initialize a second `MySingle` object.
5. Thread A would store its `MySingle` object in `singleton`.
6. Thread B would overwrite the object Thread A just created with its instance of `MySingle`.

Two `MySingle` objects get created, the threads are using different objects, the reference to one object gets lost—it's a mess.

To tame this confusion, programmers coordinate threads using a variety of means. The principle one is the *mutual exclusion semaphore*, or *mutex* for short. It grants one thread the right to a resource, and forces all other threads to wait. Here's an example of how it's used:

```
@synchronized (self)
{
if (singleton==nil)
    singleton = [[MySingle alloc] init];
}
```

The Objective-C @synchronized directive protects a block of code with a mutex. The mutex is used to allow one, and only one, thread to execute the block at a time. Here's how it works:

1. Thread A locks the mutex. This is the first request, so thread A is successful.
2. Thread B tries to lock the mutex. The mutex is already locked, so thread B's request is denied. Thread B is put to sleep—it stops executing.
3. Thread A checks the singleton variable, sees it is nil, creates a new MySingle object, and stores it in singleton.
4. Thread A unlocks the mutex.
5. Unlocking the mutex wakes thread B, which (again) attempts to lock the mutex. It's the only one requesting it now, so the lock is successful.
6. Thread B tests singleton and sees an object has already been created.
7. Thread B unlocks the mutex.

A hundred different threads could all be trying to execute this code at the same time, but it will still behave exactly as you intended. The mutex prevents any other thread from running this code, until the thread that's currently executing it is done. This code is now said to be *atomic*. The word atomic comes from the Greek word atomos, meaning "indivisible." The action performed by that code block cannot be broken up or interrupted.

iOS includes an arsenal of objects and functions to help coordinate and synchronize thread activity. Effective concurrent programming revolves largely around how, when, and when not, to use these tools. Before I get to them, let's first talk about how you can run your code in multiple threads.

Running Multiple Threads

You've started code running in a separate thread, indirectly, throughout this book whenever you sent an asynchronous message. The UIWebView class's -loadRequest: method creates a second thread of execution that loads the web page's content in the background.

Arranging for code you've written to run in a different thread is pretty easy too. You identify the code you want executed and request Grand Central Dispatch (GCD) to run it. For Objective-C programmers, the interface to GCD is the operation queue. An *operation queue* (NSOperationQueue) object manages an array of *operation* (NSOperation) objects, each encapsulating one executable task to be performed. You can create your own custom subclasses of NSOperation, or you can use concrete subclasses that you configure to execute a specific method or a block of code.

> **Note** An `NSThread` object represents a single thread of execution, but you rarely deal with thread objects directly. Grand Central Dispatch automatically creates, schedules, and terminates the threads your operation objects will run in.

In the last chapter, I told you there was another way of deferring work to improve the responsiveness of the `-imagePickerController:didFinishPickingMediaWithInfo:` method. In this chapter you're going to arrange for the image compression (`UIImagePNGRepresentation`) to execute on a separate thread. This will defer the work of compressing the image and allow your main thread to respond to the user's touch event quicker.

Creating an Operation Queue

The first step is to create an operation queue. This queue needs to be accessible to all `MyWhatsit` objects, which will be using it to schedule work, so make it a property of the `MSThingsDocument` class. Start with the final version of MyStuff from Chapter 23. You can find that in the Learn iOS Development Projects ➤ Ch 23 ➤ MyStuff-2 folder. Select `MSThingsDocument.h` and add this property to the `@interface` section:

```
@property (readonly) NSOperationQueue* editOperations;
```

Now you need to implement this property. Switch to the `MSThingsDocument.m` implementation file and add an instance variable to the private `@interface` section (new code in bold):

```
@interface MSThingsDocument ()
{
    NSFileWrapper      *docWrapper;
    NSMutableArray     *things;
    NSOperationQueue   *editOpQueue;
}
```

Create a getter method for the property that lazily creates the queue by adding this method to the `@implementation` section:

```
- (NSOperationQueue*)editOperations
{
    if (editOpQueue==nil)
        editOpQueue = [[NSOperationQueue alloc] init];
    return editOpQueue;
}
```

Your document object now provides an operation queue for use by any code that wants to schedule changes (edits) to the document, to be run asynchronously.

Adding an Operation

The one place you want to use the new operation queue is in the MyWhatsit object. Select the MyWhatsit.m implementation file, find the -setImage: method, and edit it so it looks like this (new code in bold):

```
- (void)setImage:(UIImage *)newImage
{
    [_document.editOperations addOperationWithBlock:^{
        imageKey = [_document setImage:newImage existingKey:imageKey];
    }];
    image = newImage;
}
```

When the user chooses a new image for an item, the -imagePickerController:didFinishPickingMediaWithInfo: method will eventually send the MyWhatsit object a -setImage: message. Previously, this method would compress and store the image in the document object (using -setImage:existingKey:) before returning.

Now the code that stores the image data in the document is merely scheduled to execute at some later time. The -setImage: method has become an asynchronous method. It returns immediately and serious work happens in a background thread.

The -addOperationWithBlock: message is a convenience method that creates an NSBlockOperation object, an operation object that executes a code block, and adds it to the operation queue. To add some other kind of operation, you'd first create a custom subclass of NSOperation, or instantiate one of its concrete subclasses (NSBlockOperation or NSInvocationOperation), and add it to a queue. The documentation for the NSOperation class has extensive notes on how to subclass it.

There is very little about operation queues that you can configure. For the most part, you just add operation objects to a queue and forget it. GCD will manage all the details, including creating the thread the operation will execute in (sometimes called "spawning a thread"). It also manages the number of concurrently running operations so it's doing the most amount of work, but not so much that it bogs down your app's main thread, a technique called *load balancing*. You can also create dependencies between two or more operations. The operation queue ensures the operations that an operation depends on are executed first, before running that operation.

Measuring the Effects

Profile MyStuff again using the Time Profiler Instruments template. Just as before, add several new items, choosing images from your photo library. Each photo creates a CPU spike in the time profile graph, as shown in Figure 24-1. As before, stop recording and isolate one of those spikes.

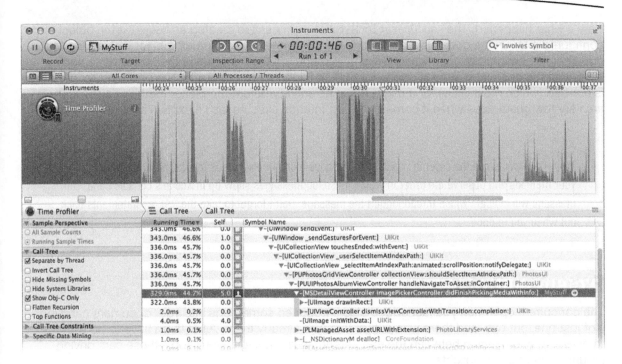

Figure 24-1. Time profile with multiple threads

Expand the call tree until you find the -imagePickerController:didFinishPickingMediaWithInfo: method, also shown in Figure 24-1. You can see that the total time spent in the -imagePickerController:didFinishPickingMediaWithInfo: method is only 329 milliseconds. That's less than a third of a second, which is a substantial improvement over the half-second it was taking in the last chapter. The response time to the user's photo-picker tap is now well within our performance goals for responsiveness, and almost three times faster than it was when you started.

If you look further down the call tree list, you'll see other threads, as shown in Figure 24-2. Digging into those, you'll find where the -[MSThingsDocument setImage:existingKey:] method executed (it took 254 milliseconds). It still takes time, and CPU resources, to execute this code, but since it's running in its own thread, it doesn't interfere with your app's event loop, which means your app stays responsive.

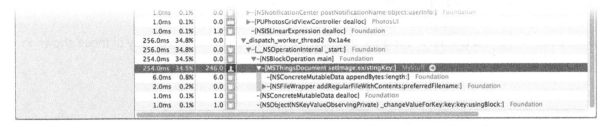

Figure 24-2. -setImage:existingKey: running in another thread

Here's what happened. The -addOperationWithBlock: message created an NSOperation object and configured it to run the code block passed in the parameter. The operation object was added to the document's operation queue. Grand Central Dispatch will then determine the best time to begin executing the operation. The scheduled operation might not run until after the photo picker method is finished (which most likely), or it might run in its entirety before the picker method finishes. There are very few guarantees when it comes to when threads execute, as I'll explain shortly.

> **Tip** One way to see the order in which asynchronous methods execute is to add NSLog statements to your methods and observe the order in which those log messages show up in Xcode's console pane. The message will indicate which thread logged the message. Don't forget to take the NSLog statements back out when you're done.

Execution Order

The concurrent operation you just added also introduced some bugs into your document handling. Not just one, but two, and there was a third that was already there. All of them have to do with the total lack of coordination between the concurrent tasks running in your app—those cars driving around without any stoplights.

When you run multiple threads concurrently, it ridiculously complicates the possible execution order of your code. Consider two blocks of code named A and B. Before multitasking, there was only one possible execution order, shown in Figure 24-3.

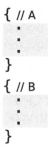

Figure 24-3. Execution order of a single thread

If the code in A and B are run in separate threads, the execution order can be any of those shown in Figure 24-4.

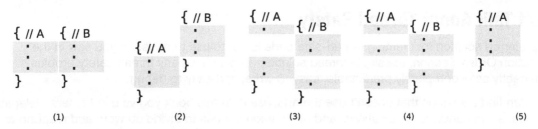

Figure 24-4. Possible execution order of two threads

The code could execute simultaneously (1). The B code could execute completely before the A code even starts (2), or vice versa. Portions of the A and B code could execute alternately (3). Portions of the A and B code could execute alternately, other sections could execute simultaneously, and at other times neither is executing (4). In extreme cases, the B code might not execute at all (5), or at least not start for a very long time.

> **Note** If the code in both A and B consisted of *only* three atomic statements, there are over 30 different orders in which the code could execute. Now consider that useful background tasks will have hundreds of nonatomic statements, and there could be a dozen or so other threads running concurrently alongside them. When I ponder all of the possible execution orders, the word "gazillion" comes to mind.

So how do you inject some order into this chaos? It's possible to write your code so that it behaves rationally and predictably, while still reaping the benefits of concurrent execution. It just takes some careful planning and a little practice.

Thread Safety

Thread-safe code behaves rationally, and predictably, when being executed from multiple threads concurrently. The first big bug you introduced into MyStuff is that its `-setImage:existingKey:` method isn't thread-safe. There's nothing stopping the user from choosing several images rapidly, which could add several operation objects to the operation queue. GCD may then elect to run two or more of those operations simultaneously, which means that multiple threads would be executing the `-setImage:existingKey:` method at the same time. That would be a disaster.

There are many techniques for creating thread-safe code. Here are the big four:

1. Don't use threads
2. Don't share data
3. Share only immutable objects
4. Make concurrent actions and mutations atomic

Don't Talk About Thread Safety

The preferred solution for creating thread-safe code is not to use threads. As you saw in the "Execution Order" section, the single thread solution doesn't have any thread safety problems. It's perfectly safe, completely predictable, easy to write, and easy to debug.

If you can find a solution that doesn't use threads, *use it*. In this book you've used timers, delegate methods, event handlers, notifications, and notification queues to divide up work and respond to events in a timely fashion—all on the main thread. Keep doing that. As long as all of your code is executing on the main thread, you have (by definition) no thread safety issues.

But not everything can be performed on the main thread. The biggest problem is code that takes a long time to execute. It will tie up the main thread, destroying its responsiveness, and may kill your app entirely if it takes too long. For those problems, threads are the only solution.

The remaining techniques all deal with the problem of sharing data, which is at the nexus of all thread safety problems.

Not Sharing Is Caring

The second way to skirt around thread safety issues is to not share the same data. Almost all concurrency problems are caused by multiple threads trying to change the same data or objects simultaneously. You've already seen a trivial example in the "Synchronization" section, earlier in this chapter. In short, any code that modifies something—sets variables, alters the contents of collections, changes properties, and so on—that is accessible to a second thread, isn't thread-safe.

So the second solution to writing thread-safe code is to *not* share any data. If the data in thread A is used and modified by thread A only, and the data in thread B is used and modified in thread B only, the code is implicitly thread-safe.

iOS apps are, themselves, an extreme example of this arrangement. Your iOS device is running several different apps right now (assuming it's turned on). Each is running in its own thread. But each is also in a separate process; a process is an island and has no access to any data or variables in any other process. There are no thread safety issues between apps, because they have no shared data.

Of course, that also means the threads can't communicate (they don't share any data), which isn't practical. One thread-safe solution is to hand off the data to the other thread, so that the threads are never using the same object *at the same time*. This is the technique used by the UIWebView object. Here's what happens:

1. The main thread prepares an NSURLRequest object.
2. The main thread passes the NSURLRequest object to the -loadRequest: method.
3. The -loadRequest: method makes a copy of the NSURLRequest object and starts a background thread.
4. The background thread uses its copy of the URL request to send the web page request and collects the response from the server in an NSData object.
5. The background thread terminates.
6. The NSData collected by the background thread is passed back to the main thread.

At no point did the main thread and the background thread use, or even have access to, the same objects. The background thread used a copy of the `NSURLRequest` object, made before the thread started. The main thread can do whatever it wants with its original copy; it doesn't affect the copy used by the background thread, and vice versa.

Similarly, the `NSData` object was accessible only to the background thread while it was being constructed. Once finished, the background thread handed the object to the foreground (main) thread at which point it didn't touch it again.

This simple, sequential hand-off technique means that neither the background thread nor the main thread has any thread safety issues to worry about.

Promise Me You'll Never Change

There's one class of objects that can be safely shared by multiple threads: immutable objects. The properties of immutable objects can never change, so they can be safely used and accessed by any number of threads concurrently.

This includes the immutable base classes for strings (`NSString`), numbers (`NSNumber`, `NSValue`), collections (`NSArray`, `NSDictionary`, `NSSet`), and bytes (`NSData`). For collection objects, it's important that not only the collection object is immutable, but that the objects in the collection are also immutable.

> **Tip** Technically, shared objects don't have to be immutable; they just can't change. Once an object is created, you can treat it as immutable and share it with another thread, as long as no subsequent code makes any alterations to it. That's a promise you have to be careful to keep.

The Atomic Age

OK, so your code can't execute on the main thread. Your solution is to create a second thread that must share objects and send messages that mutate data. In this situation, you need to make your code thread-safe. This largely consists of making your methods and properties atomic. *Atomic* code executes in its entirety before any other thread or process can interrupt it or execute it again.

You have a wide selection of tools to choose from, but most thread synchronization is accomplished using the mutual exclusion semaphore. It's so popular, there are nearly a dozen different kinds to choose from. For the Objective-C programmer, the simplest to use are the @synchronized directive and the various `NSLock` classes. Let's start by using @synchronized to make the `-setImage:existingKey:` method atomic.

Creating an Atomic Method

Select the `MSThingsDocument.m` file and locate the `-setImage:existingKey:` method. Rewrite it so it looks like this (new or modified code in bold):

```
- (NSString*)setImage:(UIImage *)image existingKey:(NSString *)key
{
    NSString *newKey = nil;
    @synchronized (docWrapper)
    {
    if (key!=nil)
        {
        NSFileWrapper *imageWrapper = docWrapper.fileWrappers[key];
        if (imageWrapper!=nil)
            [docWrapper removeFileWrapper:imageWrapper];
        }
    if (image!=nil)
        {
        NSData *imageData = UIImagePNGRepresentation(image);
        newKey = [docWrapper addRegularFileWithContents:imageData
                                 preferredFilename:kImagePreferredName];
        }
    }
    [self updateChangeCount:UIDocumentChangeDone];
    return newKey;
}
```

You added a mutex around the block of code that modifies the `docWrapper` object. This code is now atomic; only one thread can execute it at a time. Every atomic block of code that changes the object should leave it in a stable state, ready to receive the next message or change. In this specific case, all of the logic to either add, remove, or replace a data file wrapper in the document is completed without interruption. When it's finished, the next action that might need the `docWrapper` object can safely proceed.

The `@synchronized` directive is easy to use because it creates the mutex object for you. The object in parentheses is not the mutex; that object is used merely to identify the mutex, and is called the *token*. For a mutex to work, both threads must refer to the same mutex, so picking your token is important. The most commonly used token is `self`:

```
@synchronized (self)
{
    ...
}
```

This mutex prevents multiple threads from executing this code for the same object. It also prevents any other code, similarly protected, from executing at the same time, on the same object. It does *not* prevent two threads from executing this code for different objects.

It doesn't matter what object you choose for the token. What's important is that the token is related to the data being mutated; any two threads attempting to mutate the same data *must* refer to the same token. Because of this, I chose the `docWrapper` object, because that's the shared object being changed. You can't get more related than that. You could have used `self` in this situation—it would have been just as effective.

Creating an Atomic Property

I told you that scheduling even a tiny bit of code to execute in its own thread complicates your job. Return to the MyWhatsit.m file. The code block in -setImage: looks simple, but it's fraught with complications:

```
imageKey = [_document setImage:newImage existingKey:imageKey];
```

Sticking this code into an operation queue means that it could execute at any time. It also means that the relationship you previously assumed between the image and imageKey variables has evaporated, specifically:

- The imageKey variable could be set at any time (by the second thread). Code that refers to the imageKey variable more than once could read one value the first time and a different value the second time.
- The imageKey variable may, or may not, be set when -setImage: returns.
- At any given moment, the imageKey variable is no longer guaranteed to be the image tag of the image variable.

To fix MyWhatsit, the imageKey variable needs to be made atomic. It's being referred to, and modified by, multiple threads and must now be made thread-safe. Start in the MyWhatsit.h file and change the declaration for the imageKey property (modified code in bold):

```
@property (atomic) NSString *imageKey;
```

Switch to the MyWhatsit.m file. Locate the existing -imageKey getter method and add an atomic setter method:

```
- (void)setImageKey:(NSString *)key
{
    @synchronized (self)
    {
    imageKey = key;
    }
}
```

Now, any code that sets the imageKey property will do it in the thread-safe manner.

> **Note** It's not necessary to rewrite the getter method. A single load of a pointer variable is implicitly thread-safe. The CPU always transfers the entire word in a single, atomic, operation. Said another way, reading or setting a single scalar value cannot be interrupted by another thread.

The first method to rewrite is the -image method. Change the method so it looks like this (new code in bold):

```
- (UIImage*)image
{
    @synchronized (self)
    {
    if (image==nil && imageKey!=nil)
        image = [_document imageForKey:imageKey];
    }
    return image;
}
```

This code is now thread-safe because it obtains a lock on the object before evaluating the imageKey variable. Remember that imageKey could change at any time, so it's possible that the valueKey in the if statement will be different than the valueKey passed to the -imageForKey:. The mutex prevents that from happening. Any code that would try to set the imageKey property (using the setter you just wrote) between the if and the -imageForKey: message would stop and wait for this method to finish. Are you beginning to see how this all works together?

Lastly, the -setImage: code needs to change once more (new code in bold):

```
- (void)setImage:(UIImage *)newImage
{
    [_document.editOperations addOperationWithBlock:^{
        self.imageKey = [_document setImage:newImage existingKey:imageKey];
        }];
    image = newImage;
}
```

The only change is how the imageKey property is set. It now goes through the thread-safe setter method. When the background task ultimately gets around to setting the imageKey property, it coordinates that change with any other threads currently using that value.

> **Note** The -encodeWithCoder:, -copyWithZone:, and -memoryWarning methods don't need to change. They all fetch the value of imageKey once, and only once, which keeps them thread-safe. If the code were changed so that wasn't true, those methods would need to be made thread-safe too.

You only made the setting, and use of, the imageKey property atomic. You didn't change any of the other MyWhatsit properties. That's because the imageKey property is the only value that could be modified from another thread. If you later wrote code to set the name or location properties from another thread, you'd need to repeat this analysis and take steps to make those properties thread-safe too.

Making a Nonatomic Method, Atomic

That takes care of two bugs—making -setImage:existingKey: and the imageKey property atomic—but you still have one more bug, which you've had since you added document support to MyStuff. You'll only encounter it if you select an image at the same instant the document object is auto-saving itself. And this underscores just how subtle, and hard to find, concurrency bugs can be. You could have tested MyStuff for days, shipped it to customers, and never run into it. Here's how you'd find it.

Running MyStuff under the control of Xcode, repeatedly add items and select images for those items from your photo library. The more items you add quickly, the longer it will take UIDocument to update the files during its auto-save, and the more likely you are to encounter the bug. When it happens, it appears in the console pane of Xcode, like the incident shown in Figure 24-5.

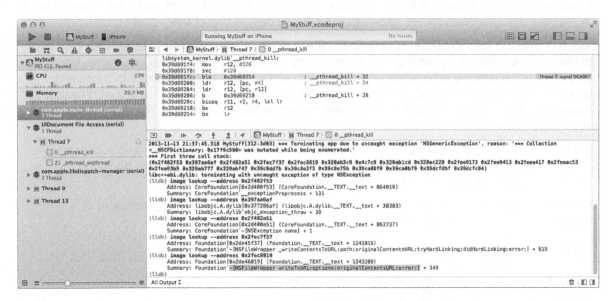

Figure 24-5. A concurrency bug

The message is an exception, a kind of software "abort" when something goes wrong. When you run your app under Xcode's control, exceptions are caught and logged to the console. Looking in the stack pane, you can see that the exception was caught in thread 7, which is labeled UIDocument File Access. This is a pretty good clue that the problem occurred while the document was trying to read or write from the filesystem.

The description of the exception ("Collection was mutated while being enumerated") tells you what happened, but not why. The code that threw the exception is no longer running, so you can't consult the stack view. Instead, you have to investigate the stack trace recorded by the exception. This, unfortunately, is just a string of numbers.

I'll save you from looking this up on the Internet (lldb.llvm.org). The exception message is followed by a list of the return code addresses that were on the stack when the exception occurred. If you know what code those addresses refer to, you'll have a pretty good idea of what was going on when it happened.

That (lldb) prompt in the console window is the debugger's command prompt. You can send commands directly to the debugger just by typing them in. In this situation, the `image lookup --address` command is extremely useful. It tries to identify the method/function name of any code address. If you plug in the addresses from the stack trace, you quickly get a picture of what the code was doing when the exception was thrown, as shown in Figure 24-5.

Working backwards up the stack, you quickly uncover the method responsible was `-writeContents: toURL:forSaveOperation:originalContentsURL:error:`. It writes the docWrapper (NSFileWrapper) object, which blows up because it was modified in the middle of being written. Now you know where it's choking, you have to figure out why. It's obvious that some other code is modifying the docWrapper while it's being written. Looking around that stack pane, you can't see any other code that is modifying docWrapper. It's likely that whatever modified it did so and has exited already, so there's no trace of it in the debugger. You'll have to look through your code and find all of the places that modify docWrapper and determine, empirically, if one of them could be the problem.

It doesn't take too long to zero in on a suspect; the `-setImage:existingKey:` method changes (mutates) the docWrapper by adding and removing regular file wrappers. At the same time, the UIDocument is periodically auto-saving the document, and it writes the docWrapper to persistent storage on a background thread. The problem is that a collection object (like docWrapper) cannot be changed while it's being enumerated. You might remember this obscure rule from the "Collections" section in Chapter 20.

With the detective work out of the way, your approach is obvious. You need to keep docWrapper from being modified while it's being written. That sounds like a mutex. But where do you put it? The method that's running on the background thread belongs to UIDocument.

The solution is to wrap the UIDocument method in a mutex. Select the MSThingsDocument.m implementation file, and add this method:

```
- (BOOL)writeContents:(id)contents
                toURL:(NSURL *)url
     forSaveOperation:(UIDocumentSaveOperation)saveOperation
  originalContentsURL:(NSURL *)originalContentsURL
                error:(NSError * __autoreleasing *)outError
{
    @synchronized (docWrapper)
    {
    return [super writeContents:contents
                    toURL:url
             forSaveOperation:saveOperation
          originalContentsURL:originalContentsURL
                    error:outError];
    }
}
```

This method overrides UIDocument's `-writeContents:toURL:forSaveOperation:originalContentURL:error:` method and prevents it from running if some other thread is currently modifying docWrapper (specifically, `-setImage:existingKey:`). Once it is running, it will block any other thread from modifying docWrapper until the `-writeContents:...` method is finished.

As you can see, writing thread-safe code isn't always obvious. It takes a fair degree of planning, testing, and analysis. Which is why the first rule is still the best; avoid it when you can.

I'll now wrap up with a brief tour of some other concurrency tools at your disposal.

Concurrency Roundup

Here's a loose collection of tips, concepts, and tools that will help you get started using multitasking, and hopefully keep you out of trouble.

The Thread-Safe Landscape

Making even a single property of an object (like MyWhatsit's image property) thread-safe is often a non-trivial task. Consequently, *most classes and properties are not thread safe*. Read that again. The classes, or specific methods, that are thread-safe are usually documented. If you want a list, look up the *Thread Safety Summary* in Xcode's Documentation and API Reference window. It lists all of the Cocoa classes that are thread-safe; it's not a very long list.

Of particular note, the UI classes are not thread-safe. Not only are they not thread-safe, the only thread that should use them is the main thread. In other words, you must not do anything with the user interface objects—not even telling a UIView object it needs to be redrawn—from any thread except your main thread. One of the very few exceptions is off-screen drawing. You can create an off-screen drawing context (UIGraphicsBeginImageContext) and draw in a background thread. The resulting UIImage object is not, ironically, thread-safe, and must be passed back to the main thread before it can be used.

> **Caution** Do *not* attempt to send any message to a UI class from any thread other than the main thread.

To use any object, message, or property that isn't thread-safe in a thread-safe manner requires that you provide your own thread synchronization and atomicity.

Sending Messages To Main

Earlier I described how UIWebView would "pass an object to the main thread." There are a handful of methods that will send a message, or perform a code block, on a specific thread. The thread in question must be running an event loop. This excludes any threads used by your operation objects, but it does include the main thread, and that's where this trick is the most useful.

So many thread safety issues disappear when code is run on the main thread. You can avoid a lot of problems if you can schedule a method or block of code to execute there. This works, not surprisingly, through the main thread's run loop. Messages are added to the event queue and are executed in their turn. The two most useful techniques are:

- Send the -performSelectorOnMainThread:withObject:waitUntilDone: message to any object. It will arrange for that object to receive the Objective-C message (with an optional object parameter). The message is dispatched to the object by the main thread's run loop. If waitUntilDone is YES, the sending thread will sleep until the main thread has executed the message.

- The +[NSOperationQueue mainQueue] object is a special operation queue that runs its operations on the main thread. If you need a code block, or anything more complicated than a single message, to run on the main thread, turn that into an operation object and add it to this queue.

You already know that you can't send any UI objects messages from another thread. So how does your waveform analysis thread tell its custom UIView object to redraw itself once it's finished with the calculations? Here's how:

```
[waveView performSelectorOnMainThread:@selector(setNeedsDisplay)
                           withObject:nil
                        waitUntilDone:NO];
```

Results of background tasks can, similarly, be delivered to your main thread through its run loop, avoiding numerous thread safety issues:

```
[[NSOperationQueue mainQueue] addOperationWithBlock:^{
    [xrayViewController addImage:image sequence:n forPatient:patientID];
    }];
```

Lock Objects

You've created mutex objects using the @synchronized directive, but it's sometimes more convenient, efficient, and flexible to create the mutex objects yourself. The workhorse mutex class is NSLock. Here's an example:

```
NSLock *lock = [[NSLock alloc] init];

...

[lock lock];
// do thread-safe stuff here
[lock unlock];
```

This is equivalent to the @synchronized blocks you used earlier, but just a tad faster because you're not asking Objective-C to dynamically create and keep track of the mutex objects for you.

Lock objects are also more flexible. The -tryLock and -lockBeforeDate: messages will attempt to acquire the lock and return NO if they were unsuccessful. Instead of being forced to go to sleep, your code can use this information to do something else if the lock is currently locked by another (possibly long-running) task.

> **Caution** Always unlock a mutex object on the same thread that locked it. You must *never* lock a mutex object on one thread and then unlock it on another. If you're trying to signal or join threads, use the NSCondition or NSConditionLock classes.

There are some subtle hazards that you need to avoid. If the code protected by your lock can throw an exception, or your method needs to return a value, steps have to be taken to ensure the lock is unlocked before returning. Here's an atomic method using the @synchronized directive:

```
- (BOOL)doItSafely
{
    @synchronized (self)
    {
    return [obj doSomething];
    }
}
```

Here's a functionally identical method, written using an NSLock object:

```
- (BOOL)doItSafely
{
    BOOL result;
    @try {
        [lock lock];
        result = [obj doSomething];
    }
    @finally {
        [lock unlock];
    }
    return result;
}
```

The @finally block intercepts any software exceptions that -doSomething might throw and ensures that the NSLock is unlocked before exiting the method. If lock wasn't unlocked, the next time -doItSafely is received the program will seize up, which brings you to the next hazard of using mutual exclusion semaphores.

Deadlocks

A deadlock occurs when code tries to lock a mutex that will never be unlocked. The code stops executing—forever. If this happens to your main thread, your app just died. This can occur in the same thread or between threads, where it's known by the more colorful term "deadly embrace."

When most programmers first start writing thread-safe code, the inclination is to "lock everything." This leads to code like this real-time order processing system:

```
NSLock *lock = [[NSLock alloc] init];

...

- (NSUInteger)availableProduct:(int)productID
{
    NSUInteger count = 0;
    [lock lock];
    for ( Item *item in inventory )
```

```objc
        if (item.productID==productID)
            count++;
    [lock unlock];
    return count;
}
- (void)orderProduct:(int)productID count:(NSUInteger)count
{
    [lock lock];
    // Customer can't order more than what's in stock
    if (count>[self availableProduct:productID])
        count = [self availableProduct:productID];
    if (count!=0)
        {
        // Create an item and add it to the order
        OrderItem *item = [[OrderItem alloc] init];
        item.productID = productID;
        item.count = count;
        item.taxExempt = NO;
        [order addObject:item];
        }
    [lock unlock];
}
```

The first receipt of -orderProduct:count: will cause the program to seize. It will never execute another line of code. Can you see why?

The -orderProduct:count: method acquires lock and sends itself an -availableProduct: message. That method tries to acquire lock. It can't, and the thread goes to sleep waiting for lock to be unlocked, which will never happen.

Recursive Locks

There are two ways to solve this kind of problem. The first is to use a *recursive lock*. Replace the NSLock with an NSRecursiveLock, like this:

NSRecursiveLock *lock;

A recursive lock allows a single thread to acquire the lock multiple times. Other threads treat the lock like any other mutex. Now -orderProduct:count: and -availableProduct: can both acquire the mutex (in the same thread), do their work, and return. You must still balance every -lock message with an -unlock message, or the mutex will remain locked (to other threads) for all eternity.

Multiple Locks

Another solution is to use two locks, like this:

```objc
NSLock *inventoryLock = [[NSLock alloc] init];
NSLock *orderLock = [[NSLock alloc] init];

...
```

```
- (NSUInteger)availableProduct:(int)productID
{
    NSUInteger count = 0;
    [inventoryLock lock];
    ...
    [inventoryLock unlock];
    return count;
}
- (void)orderProduct:(int)productID count:(NSUInteger)count
{
    [orderLock lock];
    if (count>[self availableProduct:productID])
        count = [self availableProduct:productID];
    ...
    [orderLock unlock];
}
```

Once again, -orderProduct:count: runs smoothly. This technique can, however, easily lead to a deadly embrace between two threads:

1. Thread A locks inventoryLock
2. Thread B locks orderLock
3. Thread A tries to lock orderLock, can't, and goes to sleep.
4. Thread B tries to lock inventoryLock, can't, and goes to sleep.

Now both threads are suspended and will never wake up. If you use multiple mutex objects to protect different data objects, try to always lock and unlock them in the same order.

Spin Locks

Mutex objects are great, but they're also slow (relatively speaking). If a mutex object gets locked and unlocked a few times, that's no big deal. But it you use a mutex object in code that gets executed hundreds of thousands of times, it can hurt your app's performance. When you run your Time Profile in Instruments, you'll see that a significant amount of your app's CPU time is spent locking and unlocking the mutex.

A spin lock is a high-performance mutex that doesn't put the losing thread to sleep. If the thread can't obtain the mutex (because another thread already locked it), the thread "spins" waiting for the mutex to be unlocked again. Spin locks are useful for protecting small sections of code that:

- Are called thousands and thousands of times
- Execute very quickly
- Have a very low probability of competing with a second thread

The process of "spinning" is a huge waste of CPU resources, but spin locks make up for that by being extremely fast when locking and unlocking a mutex that's not locked by any other thread. These are called *optimistic locks*.

Spin locks are opaque C variables and you use C functions to lock and unlock them. Other than that, you use them exactly the way you'd use an NSLock object:

```
static OSSpinLock spinner;

...

OSSpinLockLock(&spinner);
// do something really quick here
OSSpinLockUnlock(&spinner);
```

As an example, iOS's memory management functions (the ones that allocate and return memory blocks to the heap) use spin locks. Think about it; all memory functions have to be thread-safe, since any thread can create and destroy objects. They also have to be extremely fast, and the probability of two threads allocating an object at exactly the same moment is really small. For functions like this, spin locks are perfect.

Further Reading

When you're ready to wade into the deep end of concurrency and thread safety, here are two good places to start, both of which can be found in Xcode's Documentation and API Reference window:

- Start with the *Concurrency Programming Guide*. This is your roadmap to all things concurrent. It describes asynchronous app design, Grand Central Dispatch, and how to use operation queues.
- The *Thread Programming Guide* contains a thorough discussion of threads and thread synchronization. Here you'll find descriptions of all of the low-level tools—exclusion semaphores, locks, spin locks, signals, conditions, atomic functions, and memory barriers—to synchronize your threads and data.

Summary

Multithreading is definitely an advanced app development technique. Master it, and you can create apps that do an amazing amount of work, while staying responsive and smooth. I won't declare you a concurrency guru just yet, but you've got all of the basics and you know where to find out more.

You've learned a tremendous amount about iOS app development since Chapter 1. It's been an exciting journey, and one that's only just begun. With the foundation you have now, you can explore many of the technologies I didn't cover in this book, and go deeper into the ones I did.

I hope you've enjoyed reading this book as much as I enjoyed writing it. Use your imagination, apply what you've learned, and promise to write (james@learniosappdev.com) or tweet (@LearniOSAppDev) me when you've written something great. Good luck!

Index

A

Accessor methods, 627
Accessory view, 141
Ad-hoc distribution, 4
Animation
    add shapes
        block-based animation methods, 353
        core animation programming guide, 354
        curve, 352
        properties, 353
    built-in stuff, 351
    Core animation, 352
    DIY solution, 352
    OpenGL, 354–355
    steps, 351–352
    types, 351
Application music player, 262
Application Programming Interface (API), 3–4
Apps, 507
    CMMotionManager, 514
        dynamic animator (*see* Dynamic animator)
        framework definitions, 515
        gravitational vector, 518
        NSTimer object, 517
        pull and push approach, 516
        updateAccelerometerTime:method, 518
        update process, 516
        viewDidLoad:method, 515
    Leveler (*see* Leveler)
    motion data
        device motion and attitude, 525–526
        frame of reference, 526
        gyroscope data, 524
        magnetometer data, 525
        measurements, 527

Arbitrary objects, 492
Archiving serialization
    benefits and limitations, 594
    definition, 591
    encodeWithCoder: method, 592
    features, 593
    initWithCoder: method, 592
    @interface declaration, 591
    MyWhatsit.m file, 591
    NSCoding protocol, 591, 594
    NSKeyedUnarchiver, 594
    and unarchiving objects, 593
Atomic age
    concurrency bugs, 727
    docWrapper object, 724
    imageKey property, 725–726
    setImage:existingKey: method, 724, 728
    token, 724
    UIDocument method, 728
    writeContents:method, 728
Attributed strings
    constructs, 645
    points, 647–648
    UILabel, 646–647
Automatic properties, 630
Automatic Reference Counting (ARC), 653, 665
    Core fundation, 668
    enable, 666
    stpes, 666
    strong and weak, 667
    weak qualifier, 666
Auto-save document model, 598

B

Bonjour Overview document, 480

C

Class clusters, 622
CLLocationManager, 533
Cloud storage
    Cloud watching, 571
    features, 569
    HPViewController ( ), 570
    iCloud, 573
    NSUbiquitousKeyValueStore, 570
    and synchronization, 569
    testing, 574
Code refactoring, 416
Collection
    collection classes, 648
    collection enumeration methods, 650
    fast object enumeration, 649
Concurrency definition, 713
Concurrent programming. *See* Thread
Controllers, Interface builder, 496
    gesture recognizers
        moveShape: method, 500
        SYShapeView object, 499
        SYViewController, 501
    loadShape:forViewController: method, 504
    placeholders declared
        SYShapeFactory class, 497
        User Interface group, 497
        viewController, 498
    replace code, 505
    SYShapeFactory
        factory outlets, 502
        RectangleShape.xib file, 503
        SquareShape.xib file, 502
    SYShapeView
        initWithShape: method, 499
        properties, 498
Coordinates *vs.* pixels
    mathematical precision, 334
    pixelitis, 334
    pixel-prefect alignment, 335
    ramifications, 334
Coordinate system, 521
Custom view objects. *See* Animation;Draw simple shapes;Transforms
    drawn
        Bézier path, 328
        core graphics context, 326
        fill and stroke functions, 327
        fundamental painting tools, 327
        images, 328
    event-driven programs, 325
    exercise, 365
    graphics
        blend modes, 364
        context stack, 364
        shadows, gradients and patterns, 364
        text, 363
    images and bitmaps
        bitamps creation from drawing, 362–363
        image creation, 359–362
    view coordinate system, 321
        converts, 324–325
        coordinate value types, 323
        frame and bounds, 323–324
        graphics coordinate system, 322–323
        translation methods, 324
    Z-order, 355, 359
        overlapping shapes, 357
        working shapely app, 358

D

Dangling pointer bug, 665
Data network. *See* Networking
Deadlocks
    definition, 731
    multiple locks, 732–733
    real-time order processing system, 731
    recursive locks, 732
Delegate pattern, 186
Design patterns and principles, 184
Document
    UIDocument (*see* UIDocument)
Draw simple shapes
    -drawRect:method, 332–333
        Bézier path object, 333, 336
        unfinished-path method, 336
    shapely app design, 329
    shapes and colors
        duplication, 340
        getter method, 342–343
        multicolor shapes, 344
        properties, 341
        trigonometric math functions, 344

steps, 330
testing squares
    action method, 339
    add first button, 337–338
    connection, 338–339
    shape view, 339
testing squares:-addSubview:method, 339
view objects programmatically
    designated initializer, 330
    enumeration, 331
    init method, 331–332
    initWithFrame:method, 331
    SYShapeView, 330
Xcode, 329
Dynamic animator
    basic formula, 520
    behavior definition, 521
    creation, 520
    damping and frequency
        properties, 523
    players, 520
    rotateDialView:method, 523

E, F

Encapsulation, 184
Enumeration methods, 650
Events
    advanced event handling, 134
    delivery methods
        direct delivery, 100
        first responder, 102
        hit testing, 101
    event-driven applications, 97
    event handling, 103
    event queue, 98
    high *vs.* low-level events, 107
    Magic Eight Ball app, 107
        design, 108
        EBViewController object, 114
        first responder, 119
        handling shake events, 116
        image setting, 112
        import app icons, 120
        interface creation, 109
        on iOS device, 121
        project creation, 108
        responder chain, 119
        testing, 117
        UIApplication object, 120
    responder chain, 104, 123
    run loop, 98
    Touchy app, 124
        custom view, 126
        design, 125
        drawRect: message, 131
        handle touch events, 128
        interface builder, 132
        project creation, 125
        testing, 133
        UIEvent object, 129
        updateTouches: method, 130

G

Game Center–aware
    achievements, 440
    app ID, 441
    configuration, 440–441
    game center button, 450–452
    game center configuration
        boards, 447
        window, 446
    GameKit requirement, 448
    iTunes Store
        app Store, 444
        connection, 446
    local player, 449–450
    matchmaking, 440
    recording leaderboard scores, 452
    sandbox, 453
    test player creation
        playing screen, 454
        sandbox player, 453
Garbage collection, 656
Getter method, 627
Global positioning system (GPS)
    geocoding, 547
    getting directions, 548
    iOS technology, 529
    location data, 531
        CLLocationManager, 532
        device requirement, 532
        MKMapView objects, 533
    location monitoring, 545
        movement and heading, 547

Global positioning system (GPS) (cont.)
    non-GPS devices, 546
    reduce location, 547
    region monitoring, 546
  map decorations
    add little bounce, 540
    annotation, 537
    map coordinate systems, 539
    MKMapView object, 537
    overlay, 537
    sub view, 537
  pigeon creation, 529
    design, 530
    HPViewController, 531
    #import statement, 531
    interface, 531
    Main_iPhone.storyboard file, 530
    Map Kit declarations, 531
    Map View object, 530
    Resolve Auto Layout Issues, 531
    trash button, 530
  pointing, 542
  using map view object
    delegate outlet, 535
    dynamic linking, 536
    HPViewController object, 534
    MapKitframework, 535–536
    MPViewController object, 534
    showsUserLocation property, 534
    testing, 536
    tracking modes, 534
    viewDidLoad method, 533
Grand Central Dispatch (GCD), 716
Group footer, 139
Group header, 139

H

Hot spots
  Change Track Scale control, 696
  Inspection Range control, 696
  Invert Call Tree option, 697
  NSNotificationQueue
    coalescing, 700
    definition, 700
    NSPostASAP, 701
    NSPostWhenIdle, 701
    postDidChangeNotification method, 700

  photo picker handling code, 700
  postDidChangeNotification method, 699
  setImage:existingKey: method, 697
  Show Obj-C Only option, 697
  Time Profiler template, 698, 702
  trace document, 701–702

I, J

iCloud, 573, 615
Inheritance, 182
Inherits NSCopying, 644
+initialize method, 626
Instance methods, 180
Instance variables, 627
Instruments, 691
  hot spots (see Hot spots)
  memory (see Memory)
  performance optimization, 692
  slow tap fixing
    did-pick-image method, 693
    instruments, 694
    photo library, 693
    scheme editor, 694
    template picker instrument, 695
    Time Profiler instrument, 695
    view controller, 693
Integrated Development Environment (IDE), 3–4
Interface builder, 485
  controllers, 496
    gesture recognizers, 499
    loadShape:forViewController: method, 504
    placeholders declared, 497
    replace code, 505
    SYShapeFactory, 501
    SYShapeView, 498
  files work
    arbitrary objects, 492
    compilation, 486
    connections, 493
    editing attributes, 493
    file's owner, 489
    loading interface, 486
    object graph, 486
    objects creation, 490

placeholder objects, 489
root/top-level object, 486
sending action message, 496
.xib file, 488
Introspection
class, 634
method, 635
protocol, 635–636
iOS app, 57
iOS app development, Xcode
application category, 7
Bundle identifier, 8
new project options, 8
project template browser, 7
Single View Application template, 7
iOS developer
download project files, 5
join Apple's iOS developer program
paid registration, 5
payment details, 5
registered developer, 4
uses, 4
iOS devices, 551
persistent views (see Persistent views)
Pigeon
cloud storage (see Cloud storage)
getting values, user defaults, 555
HPMapType, 554
HPViewController.h file, 554
MKPointAnnotation object, 553
testing, user defaults, 556–557
update and code, 554
writing values, user defaults, 555
plist file, 552
property list object, 551
alertView:clickedButtonAtIndex:
method, 561
clearPin: method, 562
Cocoa Touch functions, 559
floating-point fields, 559
@interface HPViewController ( ), 561
MKPointAnnotation, 559–560
preserveAnnotation method, 562
restoreAnnotation method, 562
savedLocation object, 560
techniques, 559
testing, 563
view controllers, 563

registerDefaults: method, 557–558
serialization, 552
settings bundle
creation, 575
definition, 575
Root.plist file, Xcode, 576, 578
testing, 579
types, 577
viewDidLoad method, 579
user defaults, 552
iOS navigation, 367
iPod music library, 255
add sound effects, 271
audio session configuration, 273
AVAudioPlayer objects, 278
AVAudioSession class, 283
complications, 272
createAudioPlayers and
destroyAudioPlayers method, 278
DrumDub interface, 282
interruptions, 272
kNumberOfPlayers constant, 278
playing sounds, 275
route change, 272
UIButton object, 280
audio recording/signal processing, 288
interruptions
audio route change, 287
callbacks, 287
handler implementation, 285
iOS app design, 256
media metadata, 266–267
album artwork and song metadata, 271
album view position, 266
DDViewController.xib, 269
label object, 268
MPMediaItemArtwork object, 270
musicPlayer property getter method, 271
outlet properties, 269
model-view-controller design pattern, 266
music picker interface
audio content categories, 258
DDViewController.m file, 257
MPMediaPickerController class, 257
testing, 259
music player object
mediaItemCollection parameter, 261
playback queue, 261

iPod music library (*cont.*)
    private instance variable and
        readonly property, 260
    singleton and lazy initialization, 261
    playback control, 262
    playing item, 269
    receiving notifications, 264

K

Key Value Observing (KVO)
    change property, 244
    defective, 246
    dependencies, 246
    observeValueForKeyPath, 245

L

Learn iOS Development Projects, 5
Leveler
    angle label layout connection, 512
    dial and needleView positioning, 513–514
    interface builder layout, 512
    LRDialView
        context transformations, 510
        drawRect: method, 509
    viewDidLoad method, 512
    Xcode project creation, 508
Logical address space, 654

M

Manual reference counting
    autoreleased object, 661
    basics, 659
    breaking cycle
        circular retain problem, 664
        circular retains, 663
        over-retained teacher, 664
        unretained object references, 664
    pool, 660
    quick summary, 662
    reference counting pitfalls, 663
    scared straight, 665
Map decorations
    add little bounce
        mapView:viewForAnnotation:
            delegate method, 540–541
        MKPinAnnotationView, 541

annotations
    call out, 537
    clearPin: method, 538
    dropPin: method, 537–538
    HPViewController, 537
    testing, 539
map coordinate systems, 539
    CLLocationCoordinate2D structure, 540
    map points, 540
MKMapView object, 537
overlay, 537
pointing
    distanceFromLocation: method, 543
    hideReturnArrow method, 544
    HPViewController, 542
    showReturnArrowAtPoint:towards:
        method, 543–544
    testing, 545
subview, 537
Memory
    allocations template, 706
    black flags timeline, 707
    copyWithZone: method, 704
    heed warnings, 708
        +documentAtURL:class method, 709
        imageKey property, 709
        memoryWarning: method, 709
    ImageIO_PNG_Data allocations, 707
    measurement, 704
    MSThingsDocument.m file, 704
    MyStuff, 703
    NSCopying protocol, 703
    RAM, 702
    Stress Test, Round #2, 710
    UIImage object, 706
Memory leak, 654
Memory management. *See* Automatic
    reference counting (ARC)
    attributed string object graph, 655
    concept, 654
    garbage collection, 656
    heap, 654
    leaked objects, 655
    manual reference counting
        autoreleased object, 661
        basics, 659
        cycle, 663
        pool, 660

quick summary, 662
reference counting pitfalls, 663
scared straight, 665
memory leak, 654
overview, 653
pitfalls, 654
reachable and unreachable objects, 656–657
reference counting
counted objects, 658
releasing old objects, 659
retain messages, 658
scheme, 657
Memory Pressure, 706
Method names
construction, 625
function, 624
+initialize method, 626
Method signature, 625
Model-view-controller design pattern, 217, 251
agile development, 252
Color Model, 221
controller, 227
data model, 223
initial design, 222
interface, 228
project creation, 222
view objects, 224
complex view objects
CMColorView.m, 240–241, 243
replace with CMColorView object, 239
to CMColor data model, 240
updated ColorModel design, 239
consolidating updates, 235
controller objects, 219
data model objects, 218
KVO (see Key Value Observing (KVO))
multiple views, 231
HSB value labels, 232
label outlets, 233
placeholder values, 232
realign sliders, 233
multi-vector data model changes
binding the sliders, 250
-changeHSToPoint: method, 249
touch event handlers, 248
MVC communications, 220
over engineering, 252
view objects, 219

Multiple threads
load balancing, 718
measurement, 718
NSOperation class, 718
operation queue, 716–717
order execution, 720–721
setImage:existingKey method, 718
setImage: method, 718
Multitasking/multithreading, 76, 715
MyStuff app, 189
cell identifiers, 155
data model, 146
data source object
optional information, 149
Xcode refractoring system, 151
design
adding pictures, 190
camera techniques, 216
camera testing, 209
cropping and resizing, 206
C vs. Objective C programming, 207
getter method, 192
imageView object, 193
import image, 205
iPad interface, 210
MSDetailViewController.h, 197
MSMasterViewController, 196
popover controller, 212
presentImagePickerUsingCamera method, 203
setter method, 192
sticky keyboard, 213
synthetic property, 191
UIActionSheet delegate, 202
UIImagePickerController method, 201–202
viewImage property, 191
init methods, 148
iPad design, 144
iPhone design, 144
Master Detail template, 146
MyWhatsit
class creation, 147
implementation, 149
rubber stamp implementation, 152
table cell cache, 153
testing, 156
test objects, 156

N

Navigation
    view controllers
        container view
            controllers, 368–369
        content view controllers, 368
    view objects, 369
    wonderland design
        initial view controller, 371
        modal navigation, 370
        stack/tree style, 370
        styles and class, 369
        UIPageViewController, 371
        UISplitViewController, 371
        UITabBarController, 371
    wonderland design (*see also* Wonderland app design)
Networking. *See* Peer-to-peer networking
    communication, 480
    exercise, 483
    Game Center–aware
        achievements, 440
        configuration, 440–441
        game center button, 450–451
        game center configuration, 446–448
        iTunes Store, 444–445
        local player, 449
        matchmaking, 440
        recording leaderboard scores, 452
        test player creation, 453–454
    GameKit, 429
    overview, 479
    peer-to-peer, 429
    project details
        STFlipsideViewController, 480
        STGameViewController, 482
        view controller/portrait orientation, 480–481
    single player game
        core animations, 437–438
        simulator, 438
        STGameDefs.h, 434
        STGame ViewController, 435–436
        SunTouch, 436–437
        version, 434
        view controllers, 435

SunTouch
    creation, 431
    design, 430
    initial screens, 431–434
Next Interface Builder (NIB), 22
nil
    nil Is Bad, 642
    unbearable lightness, 641
    virtues, 641
NSCopying, 643
NSFileWrapper
    contentsForType:error: method, 587–588
    definition, 587
    directory file wrapper, 587
    docWrapper, 588
    instance variable declaration, 588
    Interpreting, 589
    loadFromContents:ofType:error: method, 587
    loading and updates, document, 588
    NSData object, 589
    regular file wrapper, 587
    things.data, 589
    types, 587
    unique keys, 587
NSNotificationQueue
    coalescing, 700
    definition, 700
    NSPostASAP, 701
    NSPostWhenIdle, 701
    postDidChangeNotification method, 700

O

Objective-C
    attributed strings
        constructs, 645
        points, 647–648
        UILabel, 646–647
    billion lines, 618
    categories
        declaration, 638
        extensions, 640
        module organization, 639
        NSString class, 638
        parentheses, 638
        private methods, 640
        single responsibility, 639

classes
  class cluster, 622
  creating and destroying objects, 621
  .h (header) file, 619
  @implementation section, 620
  points, 619–620
  reference, 622
  type id, 623
  visibility directives, 620
collection
  collection classes, 648
  collection enumeration methods, 650
  fast object enumeration, 649
copying (duplicating) objects, 642
  adopting NSCopying, 643
  copyWithZone, 644
  inherits NSCopying, 644
  mutable copies, 645
  object copying, 645
introspection
  class, 634
  method, 635
  protocol, 635
languages, 618
method names
  construction, 625
  function, 624
  +initialize method, 626
nil
  nil Is Bad, 642
  unbearable lightness, 641
  virtues, 641
overview, 617
paths, 619
properties
  accessor message equivalency, 630
  accessor method names, 633
  anatomy, 631
  atomic, 633
  automatic properties, 630
  declaration, 628
  instance variables, 627
  lifetime qualifiers, 632
  mutability, 632
  points, 627
  required accessor method, 634
  setter and getter method, 627
  storage, 632

protocols
  adopts, 636–637
  conforming objects, 637
  definition, 636
shortcuts, 650
strict superset, 618
struct and typedef statements, 618
Object-oriented languages, 179
Objects
  classes and cookies, 179
  class methods, 180
  data and codes, 177
  definition, 179
  design patterns and principles, 184
    decorator pattern, 187
    delegate pattern, 186
    encapsulation, 184
    factory pattern and class clusters, 187
    lazy initialization pattern, 187
    open closed principle, 185
    single responsibility principle, 185
    singleton pattern, 187
    stability, 185
  inheritance
    abstract and concrete classes, 183
    class hierarchy, 182
    overriding methods, 183
  instance methods, 180
  Objective-C programming terms, 181
  object-oriented languages, 179
  procedural languages, 179
  structures, 178
  subtype polymorphism, 178
Observer pattern, 244
Open closed principle, 185

P, Q

Peer-to-peer networking, 429
  data exchange (device)
    data format definition, 468, 470
    data message category, 467–468
    deserialization, unmarshaling/inflating, 469
    handling match disruption, 476
    little-endian machines, 469
    receiving data, 472–473
    sending data, 471–472
    serialization, marshaling/deflating, 469

Peer-to-peer networking (cont.)
  starting game, 466
  strike data (receive), 475
  strike data (sending), 474
  sun capture data (receive), 476
  sun capture data (send), 475–476
  SunTouch's communications, 465
  testing (two-player game), 477–478
  utterly meaningless, 469
 interface, 455
 matchmaking, 461
  completion, 464
  match connection, 462–463
  multi-step process, 462
 two-player game (SunTouch), 454
  kGameStrikeNotification, 456
  odds and ends, 460–461
  opponent game view, 458–460
  -setStrikeDrawColor method, 456
  STGameView, 455, 457–458
  STOpponentGameView, 455
Persistent views
 background state, 564–565
 capture changes, 563
 decodeRestorableStateWithCoder:
   message, 568
 encodeRestorableStateWithCoder:
   message, 568
 foreground state, 564
 not running state, 564
 NSCoder object, 569
 restorationIdentifer property, 566–567
 restoration strategy, 569
 suspended state, 564
 techniques, 563
 view controllers, 565
 WLBookDataSource class, 568
Pigeon creation, 529
 design, 530
 HPViewController, 531
 #import statement, 531
 interface, 531
 Main_iPhone.storyboard file, 530
 Map Kit declarations, 531
 Map View object, 530
 Resolve Auto Layout Issues, 531
 trash button, 530

Procedural languages, 179
Property list object
 alertView:clickedButtonAtIndex: method, 561
 clearPin: method, 562
 Cocoa Touch functions, 559
 floating-point fields, 559
 @interface HPViewController ( ), 561
 MKPointAnnotation, 559–560
 preserveAnnotation method, 562
 restoreAnnotation method, 562
 savedLocation object, 560
 techniques, 559
 testing, 563
 view controllers, 563
Protocols, 77
 adopts, 636–637
 conforming objects, 637
 definition, 636

R

Reference counting
 counted objects, 658
 releasing old objects, 659
 retain messages, 658
 scheme, 657
Request For Comment (RFC), 441

S

Segue, 35
 adding image view object, 36
 adding new view controller, 35
 adding text view, 38
 creation, 40
 customize background image view, 37
 navigation bar, 41
 pasting text in text field, 40
 semi-transparent background
   color setting, 39
Setter method, 627
Single player game
 core animations, 437
 simulator, 438
 STGameDefs.h, 434
 STGame ViewController
  delete, 436
   STGameViewController.xib file, 435

SunTouch, 436–437
version, 434
view controllers, 435
Single responsibility principle, 185
Social networking
   account object, 426
   activity view controller, 421
      UIActivityItemProvider, 425
      UIActivityItemSource, 422, 424
   Activity View Controller, 413
   code refactoring, 416
   ColorModel app, 411
   excluded activities, 420
   NSURLRequest, 426
   Request method, 426
   Service Type, 426
   Service URL and parameters dictionary, 426
   sharing, 413–414, 416, 419
      Mail activity, 420
      MFMailComposeViewController, 425
      SLComposeViewController, 425
      UIActivityViewController, 425
   SLRequest, 426
   UIActivityViewController, 415
Social working. *See* Networking
Software Development Kits (SDKs), 3–4
Speed optimization. *See* Instruments
Storyboards
   finished app, 43
   frictionless development, 34
   segue, 35
Strong and weak references, 667
SunTouch
   creation, 431
   design, 430
   initial screens
      flipside interface design, 431–432
      game instructions, 433–434
      steps, 432–433
Surrealist app
   attributes inspector, 30
   customize button objects, 30
   customize buttons, 33
   debugging, 45
      constraints, 46
      testing, 54
   deleting and connecting objects, 24
   design phase, 17

initial view controller, 25–26
Interface Builder, 21
   canvas, 23
   outline, 23
   object library, 23
   project creation, 18
      Class Prefix setting, 20
      iOS project templates, 19
      setting details, 19–20
   resources
      into a project, 31
      preview, 32
   root view controller, 24, 26
   storyboards
      finished app, 43
      frictionless development, 34
      segue, 35
   table view controller, 24–25
   target project settings, 20
   testing, 42
   view controller object, 27
Synchronization, 715

T

Table editing
   insert and remove items, 164
   interfaces, 164
   notification observer matching, 173
   objectives, 168
   observer pattern, 170
   observing notifications, 172
   posting notifications, 171
   tasks, 163
Tables
   Detail View
      configuration, 159
      —configureView message, 161
      creation, 157
      iPad, 162
      iPhone, 161
      MyStuff, 162
      —setDetailItem: method, 161
   editing
      insert and remove items, 164
      interfaces, 164
      modeless interface, 174
      model interface, 174

Tables (cont.)
    notification observer matching, 173
    objectives, 168
    observer pattern, 171
    observing notifications, 172
    posting notifications, 171
    tableView, 166
    tasks, 163
  editing, 163 (see Table editing)
  table view, 137
    cell accessory views, 141
    cell styles, 139
    custom cells, 142
    grouped table style, 138
    plain table style, 138
Table view
  cell accessory views, 142
  cell object and rubber stamps, 143
  cell styles, 139
    default, 140
    subtitle, 140
    value 1 and value 2, 141
  custom cells, 142
  description, 142
  grouped table style, 138
  plain table style, 138
  reusable cell object, 143
Task switch, 715
Testing
  asynchronous, 605
  Continue button, 602
  debugging pane, 601
  delegate property, 605
  document storage, 600
  gotThings: method, 607
  loadFromContents:ofType:error:
      method, 604
  MSThingsDocument.h interface file, 605
  respondsToSelector: method, 606
  sett up breakpoint, contentsForType:error:
      method, 601
  Step Over button, 602
  things array, 603
Thread
  deadlocks
    definition, 731
    multiple locks, 732–733
    real-time order processing
        system, 731
    recursive locks, 732
  definition, 714–715
  lock objects, 730
  multiple threads
    load balancing, 718
    measurement, 718
    NSOperation class, 718
    operation queue, 716–717
    order execution, 720–721
    setImage:existingKey method, 718
    setImage: method, 718
  multitasking/multithreading, 715
  optimistic locks, 733
  spin lock, 733
  synchronization, 715
  task switch, 715
  techniques, sending messages
      to main thread, 729
  Thread-Safe Landscape, 729
  Thread Safety
    atomic age (see Atomic age)
    immutable objects, 723
    techniques, 721
    UIWebView object, 722
    usage, 722
Transforms, 345
  -addShape:action method, 345
  method declaration, 345
  phase, 346
  scale transform
    @implementation section, 349
    resize, 350
  translate transform
    affine transform, 346–347
    destructive translation, 349
    non-destructive translation, 348
tryLock, 730

U

UIDocument
  archive version, 615
  archiving serialization
    benefits and limitations, 594
    definition, 591

encodeWithCoder: method, 592
features, 593
initWithCoder: method, 592
@interface declaration, 591
MyWhatsit.m file, 591
NSCoding protocol, 591, 594
NSKeyedUnarchiver, 594
and unarchiving objects, 593
contentsForType:error: method, 586
data model
  awakeFromNib method, 597
  document statements, 597
  insertNewObject: method, 597
  MSMasterViewController.m
    file, 595–596
  MyWhatsit class, 596
  things array, 597
  viewDidLoad method, 597
Documents folder, 582
+documentURL method, 584
file wrapper (see NSFileWrapper)
iCloud storage, 615
Image file storage
  abstraction layer, 608
  file wrapper, 608
  imageKey property, 609–610
  initWithName:location: method, 609
  MyStuff sandbox files, 614
  Portable Network Graphics, 608
  removeWhatsitAtIndex: method, 612
  setImage:existingKey:
    method, 610–611
  testing, 613
  things array, 613
loadFromContents:ofType:error:
  method, 586
MSThingsDocument.h
  interface file, 583
MyStuff's document, 583
NSDocumentDirectory, 584
overview, 581
package, 586
sandbox, 582
testing (see Testing)
track changes, 598
UIFileSharingEnabled key, 585

URL shortening app, 57
  Bar Button Item, 74
  clipboard testing, 90
  design, 58
  (IBAction) clipboardURL:(id)
    sender, 89
  interface cleanup, 90
  iPad Version
    iPhone interface, 93
    pasting objects, 94
    testing, 95
  project creation, Xcode, 58
  URL shortening, 73
    absoluteString property, 79
    asynchronous method, 77
    background thread, 77
    delegate, 77
    designing, 76
    escape sequence, 83
    finished interface, 75
    kGoDaddyAccountKey, 83
    multitasking, 76
    NSURLConnection delegate, 85
    optional delegate method, 77
    private variables, 85
    protocol, 77
    required delegate method, 77
    service request URL, 82
    shortURLData, 84
    shortURL: method, 81
    testing, 87–88
    toolbar, 74
    UIWebViewDelegate protocol, 78
    URL string encoding, 83
    X.co service, 82
  web browser
    action connection settings, 69
    coding, 63
    debugging, 72
    Navigation bar, 59
    properties, 62
    SUViewController, 64, 66
    testing, 71–72
    URL Field, 62
    web view, 61
    web view outlet, 66

V

View dynamics, 519
View objects, 291
　buttons
　　attributed string, 298
　　code, 300
　　control class, 296
　　control states, 299
　　event handling, 295
　　Gesture recognizers, 295
　　properties, 298
　　responder and view classes, 295
　　types, 297
　　UIButton class, 294
　grouped tables, 316
　image views, 315–316
　page control
　　properties, 303
　　weather app, 302
　pickers
　　anything picker, 314–315
　　date picker modes, 313–314
　　views, 312
　progress indicators, 305–306
　scroll view
　　bounds and frame, 318
　　conceptual arrangement, 317
　　keyboard, 319
　　scrolling app, 319
　　talents, 318
　segmented controls, 304–305
　steppers, 303–304
　switches and sliders
　　key visual customization
　　　properties, 301–302
　　properties, 301
　　setting apps, 300
　text views
　　labels, 307–308
　　text editing behavior, 310–311
　　text fields, 308–310
　Xcode's documentation
　　sample code, 292
　　UICatalog app, 294
　　UICatalog project, 292–293
　　walled garden, 293

W

Wonderland app design
　advanced navigation, 409
　content view controller, 376–378
　creation, 372
　detail view controller, 393–395
　dismiss view controller, 381
　modal view controller, 378
　navigation view controller, 383
　　root view controller, 384
　　to tab bar, 385
　page view controller
　　classes, 395
　　initialization, 407
　　One Page View code, 400
　　page view data source, 405
　　Paginator, 402
　　prototype page design, 397
　　to tab bar, 397
　pop-over controller, 409
　project options, 372
　resource files, 374
　tab bar configuration, 373
　tab bar item configuration, 375
　Tabbed Application template, 373
　UITableViewController, 386
　　data model, 390
　　data source object, 391
　　detail view controller, 387
　　table cell, 391
　　tableView:cellForRowAtIndexPath method, 392

X, Y, Z

Xcode
　API, 3–4
　App execution
　　developer mode, 15
　　iPhone simulator, 16
　　scheme and target selection, 15
　IDE, 3
　installation, 2
　iOS app development (see iOS app development, Xcode)
　iOS developer (see iOS developer)

SDKs, 3
setting up
   license agreement, 5
   startup window, 6
system requirements, 1
workspace window, 9
   debug area, 14
   editor area, 11
   navigator area, 10
   toolbar, 14
   utility area, 12
.xib file, 488
   graphical representation, 489
   placeholder objects, 489
   STGameViewController.xib file, 488

Get the eBook for only $10!

> Now you can take the weightless companion with you anywhere, anytime. Your purchase of this book entitles you to 3 electronic versions for only $10.

This Apress title will prove so indispensible that you'll want to carry it with you everywhere, which is why we are offering the eBook in 3 formats for only $10 if you have already purchased the print book.

Convenient and fully searchable, the PDF version enables you to easily find and copy code—or perform examples by quickly toggling between instructions and applications. The MOBI format is ideal for your Kindle, while the ePUB can be utilized on a variety of mobile devices.

Go to www.apress.com/promo/tendollars to purchase your companion eBook.

All Apress eBooks are subject to copyright. All rights are reserved by the Publisher, whether the whole or part of the material is concerned, specifically the rights of translation, reprinting, reuse of illustrations, recitation, broadcasting, reproduction on microfilms or in any other physical way, and transmission or information storage and retrieval, electronic adaptation, computer software, or by similar or dissimilar methodology now known or hereafter developed. Exempted from this legal reservation are brief excerpts in connection with reviews or scholarly analysis or material supplied specifically for the purpose of being entered and executed on a computer system, for exclusive use by the purchaser of the work. Duplication of this publication or parts thereof is permitted only under the provisions of the Copyright Law of the Publisher's location, in its current version, and permission for use must always be obtained from Springer. Permissions for use may be obtained through RightsLink at the Copyright Clearance Center. Violations are liable to prosecution under the respective Copyright Law.

CPSIA information can be obtained at www.ICGtesting.com
Printed in the USA
LVOW03s2201260214

375270LV00004B/3/P